ANNUAL REVIEW OF PSYCHOLOGY

EDITORIAL COMMITTEE (1969)

ANNUAL REVIEW OF PSYCHOLOGY

PAUL H. MUSSEN, *Editor*

University of California, Berkeley

MARK R. ROSENZWEIG, *Editor*

University of California, Berkeley

VOLUME 20

1969

ANNUAL REVIEWS, INC.
PALO ALTO, CALIFORNIA

ANNUAL REVIEWS, INC.
PALO ALTO, CALIFORNIA, U.S.A.

Standard Book Number 8243–0220–6

Library of Congress Catalog Card Number: 50–13143

FOREIGN AGENCY

Maruzen Company, Limited
6, Tori-Nichome Nihonbashi
Tokyo

PRINTED AND BOUND IN THE UNITED STATES OF AMERICA BY
GEORGE BANTA COMPANY, INC.

PREFACE

This is the first volume of the *Annual Review of Psychology* that the present editors have brought to press, although the authors of these chapters had been selected and recruited by the previous editors and editorial committees. For the past 13 years, Professor Paul R. Farnsworth of Stanford University has been the editor, guiding the policies and publication of the *Review*, and setting and maintaining the high standards that have made it an increasingly valuable source of reference and criticism. Professor Farnsworth's devotion to the *Review* has not ceased with his retirement from the editorship, and we wish to thank him for generously giving of his time, and for his thoughtful guidance and wise counsel which have greatly facilitated our assumption of the editorial duties.

The present editors will strive to maintain the standards set by Professor Farnsworth and previous editors, keeping the composition of the *Review* broadly representative of the whole field of psychology. At the same time, we intend to be flexible about modifying and revising the "master plan" of subject organization, responding to trends and developments in research and scholarly activity, adding chapters as needed, redefining and combining topics, and stressing areas that are developing rapidly. For the first time, the present volume contains entire chapters on such expanding research areas as instructional psychology, physiological basis of memory, and electrical stimulation of the brain.

Chapters originally scheduled on animal learning, attention, engineering psychology, mathematical models, and psychopharmacology have had to be deferred to Volume 21. Unfortunately, the announced chapters on psychotherapeutic processes and on sleep and dreams will not appear.

With the 1968 meeting of the Editorial Committee, Dr. Frank Geldard completed his five-year term of conscientious, valuable service to the *Review*. Professor William D. Neff has accepted the Board's invitation to fill this position for the next term.

We wish to acknowledge the cheerful and efficient collaboration of Miss Jean Heavener, who has completed her first full year as assistant editor. We also wish to thank Mrs. Dorothy Read, who accomplished the painstaking task of preparing the subject index.

P. H. M.

M. R. R.

A WORD ABOUT REPRINTS

The reader may be puzzled by the conspicuous number (129 to 143) aligned in the margin with the title of each review in this volume. The number is a key for use in the ordering of reprints. These are priced uniformly at $0.95 each, postpaid. Payment must accompany the order if the purchase totals less than $10.00. All payments are to be made to Annual Reviews, Inc., in U.S. dollars. California orders are subject to 5 per cent sales tax. Delivery in the U.S.A. will require approximately two to six weeks.

Reprints at $0.95 each are available from the *Annual Review of Biochemistry* as well as the *Annual Review of Psychology* (since 1961 for both Reviews) and from the *Annual Review of Microbiology* and the *Annual Review of Physiology* starting with the 1968 volumes.

The sale of reprints of articles published in the *Reviews* has been initiated in the belief that reprints as individual copies, as sets covering stated topics, and in quantity for classrooom use will have a special appeal to students and teachers.

CONTENTS

ERRATA

Volume 19

P. 264, line 4, beginning "He also noted . . . . . ." should read:

Korner (127a) noted that when newborns are picked up they open their eyes and appear to scan the field of view. She argues that an infant's earliest visual experiences may therefore tend to occur in conjunction with handling by the mother.

Reference 127a is as follows:

Korner, A. F., Grobstein, L. Visual alertness as related to soothing in neonates: implications for maternal stimulation and early deprivation. *Child Develpm.*, **37,** 867–76 (1966)

TOPICS AND AUTHORS

ANNUAL REVIEW OF PSYCHOLOGY

VOLUME 21 (1970)

DEVELOPMENTAL PSYCHOLOGY[1,2]   129

By John H. Flavell and John P. Hill

University of Minnesota, Minneapolis, Minnesota

The annual number of articles and books which might be judged as pertinent to developmental psychology easily runs to four figures these days. Each passing year brings new opportunities for publication in the area (new journals and augmented old ones, new hard cover outlets for research and research reviews), and these opportunities are invariably exploited to the full. The result is an unmanageable bibliography, far larger than could possibly be surveyed in a chapter of this size. The problem, then, is somehow to reduce the mass of information, and it becomes more and more difficult to find nonarbitrary ways to do this as the field continues to grow.

We have attempted to reduce it in three ways. First, we have taken advantage of precedent to omit certain topics, such as development in animals, mental retardation, gerontology, and much of the child-clinical literature. Second, within the topics covered we did not cite all the studies we found, nor even all of those that impressed us as being carefully designed and executed. The grounds for exclusion of the better articles were varied and doubtless not always consistently maintained from study to study; lack of apparent developmental import and failure to articulate clearly with existing theory and research were two frequent ones. For whomever it may console, it did in fact prove considerably more difficult to "publish" in this year's *Annual Review* chapter than in the best of the field's journals. And finally, for those articles included, "publication" most commonly meant allusion only, or the briefest possible summary of results or implications. Thus the reader should be able from this review to find out which of the year's publications he may want to read, but he will not learn much more than that unless he does read them.

INFANCY

Research on infant behavior has a special claim on the developmentalist's attention. Interpretations of ontogenetic changes in the structure of the "black box" must ultimately be founded on a knowledge of its initial design, and only infancy research can provide this knowledge. Accordingly, most infant studies need only be carefully done to show some promise of scientific significance; a verdict of "rigorous but trivial" ("wrongheaded," "irrele-

[1] The survey of the literature pertaining to this review was concluded in April 1968.

[2] Acronyms used in this chapter include: CR (conditioned response); CS (conditioned stimulus); STM (short-term memory).

1

vant") seldom seems as applicable in this area as in most others covered by this review. Several good reviews of recent infancy research can be found in Stevenson, Hess & Rheingold (280).

Vision.—Research on the infant's visual capacities and preferences continues to flourish, perhaps to the neglect of other sense modalities [Eisenberg (64)]. Initially launched by the methodological innovations of Fantz and others, it is rather ironic that this research area should currently be undergoing a methodological malaise. Wickelgren (301), for example, has discovered that the newborn's eyes often fail to converge on a common stimulus and suggests that we might better assess his visual abilities monocularly. Doris, Casper & Poresky (61) point out that neonatal attention is highly fatigable and subject to great variability as a function of organismic state; the fact that the young infant's eyes are directed at a stimulus is simply no guarantee that visual information is being registered and processed. Response systems such as visual fixation, sucking, smiling, vocalizing, and cardiac reaction have been used to index visual interest and attention, with several of these systems containing a number of distinct or partially distinct component measures (e.g., length of total fixation, number of fixations; total fixation, number of fixations; total sucking time, number of sucking bursts). However, the various measures continue to show uncertain correlations, both with one another and with stimulus change, and it is unclear as yet just what organismic process each one tracks [Fantz & Nevis (76); McCall & Kagan (179); Meyers & Cantor (189); Sameroff (258); Wickelgren (301)].

As to substantive findings, Doris, Casper & Poresky (61) provide evidence that brightness discrimination ability improves markedly during the first few months of life, presumably in consequence of the neurological maturation of the visual system which occurs during that period [Ellingson (72)].

Munsinger & Weir (201) presented all pairwise combinations of 5-, 10-, 20-, and 40-turn random shapes to children 9 to 41 months old. While previous research by Munsinger and his colleagues had suggested that visual preference is an inverted-U shaped function of this index of stimulus complexity, the positive relationship found in the present study proved to be linear at all age levels. McCall & Kagan (179) find that attention to random forms may be controlled by stimulus variables other than "complexity" as defined by number of turns; for their group of 4-month-old infants, number of fixations was positively related to mean contour length but unrelated to number of turns. In a similar vein, Fantz & Nevis (76) assert that infant looking preferences are determined not only by degree of patterning (complexity) but also by form of patterning (configurational aspects).

Kagan (136) is generally critical of stimulus-centered approaches to the study of attention and other psychological processes, arguing that attention is always a function of the nature of the input taken in relation to the attained cognitive structure of the perceiver. A derivative of this alternative, more relativistic approach is the "discrepancy hypothesis" described and tested by McCall & Kagan (180): stimuli which are moderately discrepant from a subject's schema will elicit more attention than those which are either very similar or very discrepant. An attempt was made to create a new visual schema by repeatedly exposing a specific stimulus pattern to a small group of infants during their fourth month of life. Stimulus patterns constituting graded discrepancies from the familiarized one did, as predicted, elicit increased visual interest when presented subsequent to this familiarization period. However, the relationship between interest and discrepancy proved to be linear rather than curvilinear, obtained for only one of the two attention measures used and held true only for the female infants. While the McCall-Kagan hypothesis continues to seem intuitively plausible to us, these results could hardly be taken as firm evidence in support of it.

There is another stimulus dimension which clearly and powerfully controls attentional distribution by the fourth month of life, although the origin and genesis of its effects remain obscure. Haaf & Bell (103) provide strong evidence that, with these two dimensions independently varied, the degree to which a visual array resembles a human face overrides its degree of formal complexity as a determinant of visual interest at this age level; similar results have also been obtained by McCall & Kagan (179).

Bower (23) continues his program of research documenting the innate basis of fundamental perceptual abilities: the present contribution appears to demonstrate that infants of one month of age ($N = 4$) are responsive to the Gestalt law of good continuation, although not to the law of proximity. Finally, Vurpillot (287) has written a review of the recent literature on infant visual perception; a briefer review in English can be found in Caron (38).

Intelligence.—Some four decades have elapsed since Piaget carried out a detailed, stage-by-stage analysis of the developmental course of sensory-motor intelligence. While his studies of older children have now been replicated to the point of tedium, the infancy work has for a long time lain fallow —a rather glaring omission given the fact that the data base for this work consisted of only three subjects (his own infants). However, there are now at least two large-scale replication projects in progress, one by Sybille Escalona (personal communication) and the other by Uzgiris & Hunt (285). The results so far obtained by both accord very closely with Piaget's. First, large samples of infants regularly show the very same sorts of sensory-motor responses that Piaget had observed in his sample of three. Second, the use of standardized testing procedures is quite feasible in this domain, and the behavioral reactions which they elicit show high interobserver and short-term test-retest reliability. Third, and most important from Piaget's point of view, the scalability of the test items varies from very high to perfect: infants almost never acquire responses characteristic of a later Piagetian stage without having first achieved those which define the earlier stages.

It could be argued that Piaget's account of the genesis of the object concept (object permanence) may have been his most important single scientific contribution. The implicit notion that objects with which one loses receptor contact may still maintain their existence or "objecthood' is an absolute cornerstone of all human—and doubtless much subhuman—epistemic processing; to discover the fact and detail of its ontogenesis is correspondingly significant. Moreover, the object concept has developmental pride of place within a whole network of achieved invariances—amid-transformations, the later-emerging Piagetian conservations being the most famous examples. Excepting the replication projects just mentioned, there appear to have been just two recent studies of the object concept, both exceedingly interesting. Charlesworth (42) did a combined cross-sectional and longitudinal study of behavior change across one particular stretch of this concept's evolution (Piaget's stage 4). His research method was most imaginative. The infant is seated in a highchair and sees a small but attention-eliciting object on the highchair tray. The experimenter then cups his hand over the object for a few seconds. On some trials the object has miraculously disappeared from view after uncupping (there is a foot-operated trap door in the tray), and the child's reaction to this state of affairs is film-recorded. Behavioral indications that the infant expected to see the object reappear (surprise reactions, searching activity, etc.) became increasingly frequent at about 7 to 8 months of age, consistent with Piaget's early findings. Based on a number of studies using a variety of assessment techniques, Bower (22) concludes that infants as young as 2 to 3 months have what might be described as a perceptual version of the notion of object permanence. If an object disappears in a manner that would suggest annihilation to the adult (e.g., appears to "implode" or to "dissolve"), the infant behaves as if it no longer existed for him. However, if the object disappears slowly and continuously (e.g., progressively obscured by a screen), he behaves for a time as if it were still present or would shortly reappear. Bower suggests that these perceptual-level categorizations of permanence-impermanence are later subordinated to higher level, conceptual ones (the object concept proper). Unlike the 3-month-old, the 1-year-old has through experience come to believe in the permanent existence of certain objects (e.g., his mother) and will continue to expect their reappearance even when the perceptual mechanism has given a verdict of out-of-existence rather than out-of-sight. One hopes that Bower's exciting findings will not remain as long unverified by others as were Piaget's original studies in this area.

Testing for sequential invariance of cognitive acquisitions is becoming a popular research enterprise. Kohen-Raz (153) finds that a large number of the items from the Bayley Infant Scale of Mental Development align themselves in a developmental order that is almost without exception and he offers the interesting hypothesis that the scalable items in infant tests might predict later intelligence better than the nonscalable ones.

The evidence continues to suggest that low birth weight [Drillien (62); Willerman & Churchill (302)] and perinatal complications [Werner et al. (298)] can have deleterious effects on later IQ. Willerman & Churchill's study is particularly convincing, since the Ss were twins of differing birth weight.

Learning.—Three of the past year's infant learning studies could as reasonably have been assigned to the previous section, since visual preferences and learning processes received equal billing. Caron (38) and Levison & Levison (165) find that head-turning responses in 3-month-old infants can be operantly conditioned with nothing but visual input as the reinforcement. Both studies also report interesting qualitative variations among infants in their cognitive and emotional reactions to extinction. Conditioning procedures may prove an unexpectedly good research vehicle for the study of early individual differences in temperament and personality, as well as providing information about perceptual-processing needs and the learning process. Lu (176) reports evidence that infants 3 to 7 months old can acquire a visual preference for an originally nonpreferred stimulus (the color red) if the stimulus is repeatedly paired with such reinforcement as a red light continually present during feedings. The evidence was not strong, however, nor was the possibility ruled out that repeated exposure to the light without food reinforcement would have had the same effect on preference.

Brackbill and her colleagues have obtained some very perplexing results concerning differences between infant and adult conditioning. Pupillary constriction and dilation can be classically conditioned in infants when the CS is as abstract as the time interval between illumination changes but not when it is as concrete as a sound (24, 79); sound can, however, serve this function when the CR is eyeblink (170). In contrast, about half of their adult subjects could establish conditioned constriction and dilation responses to the auditory CR but none to the temporal CR (24)! In their pupillary conditioning experiments, the infant's head was held in position by by one of the experimenters and his eye held open if he started to doze; it is therefore at least conceivable that a Rosenthal-type experimenter bias could have been partly responsible for the peculiar pattern of results.

Watson (292) has proposed and obtained some putative empirical support for an intriguing hypothesis about the interaction of cognitive abilities with learning in infancy. The hypothesis bears upon the temporal interval between an initial reinforced response and the next repetition of this response. If the interval is too short, there will not have been enough cognitive-processing time to establish the response-reward linkage; if too long, an established linkage will have faded as a consequence of the infant's inadequate memory capacities; with medium intervals, the previous reinforcement can have its customary effect on response strength. Infant memory is certain to figure prominently in future theorizing about early learning, object-concept development, and other phenomena; whether or not his hypothesis is correct, Watson's article is noteworthy for calling attention to this fact.

Social responsiveness.—The superfluity of the distinction between "nonsocial" and "social" behavior nowhere is more apparent than in the study of infancy. The genesis of such a "distinctively social" phenomenon as attachment, for example, cannot be conceptualized, let alone studied empirically, without considering the development of attentional processes and the capacity to conserve objects. However, conforming to a habit whose existence implies that the same soma harbors an object psyche and a social psyche, we report separately here on studies that feature human behavioral or appearance characteristics as stimuli or involve the modification of responses that frequently are labeled "social."

The beginnings of a much needed observational literature on mother-infant interaction emerged in 1967. Rubenstein's (252) findings constitute good evidence for the importance of stimulus change in early experience. She time-sampled maternal attentiveness to 5-month-old infants (frequency of looking at, touching, holding, or talking to the infant observed during home visits) and found that infants who received the most attention at 5 months were also most responsive to novel stimuli at 6 months and preferred novel to familiar stimuli. Moss (196) reports moderate stability over the first three months for maternal attentiveness and responsiveness variables, particularly looking at, talking to, smiling at, and imitating the infant. The frequency of these maternal behaviors increases significantly over this period while, as might be expected, behaviors involving physical contact decrease in frequency. On the whole, mothers of 3-week-olds are more responsive to boys than girls, but the differences are no longer present at 3 months. Indeed, when irritability and sleep time are controlled statistically, most of the early sex differences are not significant. Moss argues that obtained correlations between irritability (crying) and maternal contact are best interpreted in terms of infant-to-mother influence until, through the mother's responsiveness and provision of stimulus change, the infant becomes attached and the mother's reinforcement value increases. Other observational studies are reported by Levine, Fishman & Kagan (163) and Gewirtz & Gewirtz (89). Mahler & McDevitt (183) made extensive psychoanalytic interpretations on the basis of their observation of early infant behavior; the focus was on infant behaviors that are seen as precursors of later coping and defense mechanisms.

Robson (236) opts for the addition of eye-to-eye contact to the list of attachment-mediating responses. In support of his argument, Moss & Robson (197) report that the frequency of mother-infant eye contact observed in 3-month-olds under naturalistic conditions is related positively to total fixation time for social (faces) but not geometric (checkerboard) stimuli. The infants had longer fixation times to the social than to the geometric stimuli [see also Haaf & Bell (103), cited earlier]. Carpenter & Stechler (39) made weekly observations of 6 infants' scanning, fixating, peripheral viewing, head movement, mouth movement, vocalizing, and smiling behavior to the successive presentation of the mother's face, a store mannikin's head, and a nonsense form. Curves indicating change in differential responsiveness are presented for 6 infants over the first 8 weeks of life. Fixating and scanning increase over the 8-week period; as mouth and head movements decrease at 5 weeks, smiling and vocalizing begin to increase. For both perceptual and affective behavior, as each response observed is in its own ascendancy, the mother as stimulus evokes the greatest amount of it: should additional subjects behave in the same way, the study will provide some of the best available evidence about the timing and nature of early discrimination of social from nonsocial stimuli.

Infant responsiveness to adult behavioral characteristics was studied experimentally by Etzel & Gewirtz (75), who effected reduction of high rate crying in a 20-week-old infant by combining nonreinforcement of crying with reinforcement of smiling. The reinforcers employed consisted in a concatenation of verbal praise ("Good boy, William "), two head nods, and a two-second full smile. A variety of additional physical stimuli were first required to evoke full smiles from a 6-week-old infant so that they could be (socially?) reinforced and, at first, to reinforce smiles when they occurred. Reduction of this infant's crying was accomplished by the time he was 8 weeks old. If one were to adopt the criterion for the presence of social attachment suggested by Wahler (289)—that "the infant has become socially attached when it can be demonstrated that his behavior is subject to social reinforcement control" (289, p. 1080)—then the Etzel & Gewirtz data would qualify as a demonstration of attachment in an 8-week-old infant. Wahler's own findings indicate that the stimulus constellation of a verbal statement, "Hi [infant's first name]," a smile, and touching the infant's chest effected increases in 3-month-olds' smiling responses when emitted by the infants' mothers but not when emitted by strangers. These data are not consistent with the commonly encountered assumption that specific attachment develops in the third quarter of the first year. However, differential responsiveness to the mothers in terms of smiling, crying and vocalization also is reported for 14- to 26-week-old infants by Ainsworth (2) in her extensive field study of the first 15 months of the lives of 28 Ganda infants. Characteristic attachment-related behaviors of 27- to 39-week-old Ganda infants include following, approach, and greeting responses and use of the mother as a secure base for exploration. Clinging and stranger anxiety are additions to the baby's attachment repertoire during the last quarter of the first year. Ainsworth's other empirical observations on infancy in Ganda and her theoretical conjectures about infant attachment in general will be of interest to students of infant development.

Other studies.—Both careful experimentation and untold centuries of informal observation attest to the fact that nonnutritive sucking has an inborn quieting effect on young infants. Cohen (46) has recently shown, however, that practice does play some role in sharpening the functional connection: with increasing experience with the pacifier, the neonate quiets more quickly when it is inserted and resumes crying more promptly when it is withdrawn. Nonnutritive sucking also appears to render the neonate less responsive to tactual stimulation [Wolff & Simmons (312)]. Tickling a sleeping newborn ordinarily results in bursts of diffuse motility. With a pacifier in his mouth, however, tickling has little effect if he happens to be sucking on it when stimulated and usually leads to renewed sucking rather than motility if he does not. The authors suggest that there is a congenital, neurologically-determined hierarchy of dominant and subordinate motor functions: for instance, defecation inhibits visual attention, crying, and sucking; sucking inhibits diffuse motility and modifies respiration. It is becoming clear that the "black box" begins its postnatal developmental career with considerable internal organization on both the efferent and the afferent side. Kaye (143) offers a detailed survey of the research evidence on sucking behavior, particularly as a dependent variable in infant perception and learning experiments.

Individual differences in neonatal attention span, alertness, irritability, and social responsiveness show good interrater reliability and appear to be substantial [Cobb et al. (45)]. In contrast, Crowell (53) finds basic physiological reactions to be quite similar from newborn to newborn.

COGNITIVE PROCESSES

Perception.—Studies of spatial orientation and intermodal phenomena appear to be dominating the recent perceptual-development literature. These studies are interesting in their own right and also for the light they may shed eventually on one of society's most pressing applied-perceptual-research problems—the teaching of reading. More traditional topics have not been wholly neglected, however; there continues to be a steady production of papers on, for example, developmental aspects of perceptual illusions and constancies.

Previous research has indicated that discrimination learning involving mirror-image visual forms is very poor in 5 to 6-year-old children, in keeping with their well-known propensity for mirror-image letter reversals. Are children of this age literally incapable of perceptually registering the differences between such forms? Independent studies by Robinson & Higgins (235) and Over & Over (211, 212) both show that this clearly is not the case. It appears that if the child is required to create and store a representation of the stimulus (e.g., to draw it or, as in a discrimination-learning test, to re-identify or recognize it over trials), he is likely to experience considerable difficulty. On the other hand, if he must simply indicate by gesture the directional-orientational properties of each member of a mirror-image pair (235) or match one of them to a standard (211, 212), he performs much better. Whatever the basal difficulty level of any particular type of discrimination (and mirror-image discriminations are doubtless harder than most for young children), it makes sense to expect variations in test performance as a function of what the child is called upon to do with the information discriminated.

Huttenlocher (130, 131) has confirmed previous findings that objects are more difficult for young children to discriminate or copy when aligned in the horizontal (left-right) versus vertical (up-down) dimension. An even more powerful determinant of copying difficulty, apparently, is whether or not the figure must be reproduced around its axis of symmetry. For instance, it is harder for the child to copy ⌐or⌐ than ⌐or⌐ if the reproduction

is to be made alongside the original, while the reverse is true with reproductions in the vertical plane. The mirror-image problem is clearly at work
in determining differential difficulty here, but what accounts for the mirror-
image problem itself? Huttenlocher makes the interesting hypothesis that
young children may begin to compare sample and copy at the point where
they are closest to one another and then work outwards in both directions
from this midline; such an analysis would in fact render ⌐indistinguishable
from its mirror image⌐.

Strang (282) has reconfirmed Ghent's hypothesis that the location of the
focal point largely determines whether a meaningless figure is judged to be
right side up or upside down, although it is still unclear why focal point
should be used as a cue or with what other stimulus variables it may be correlated or confounded. For an excellent recent review of evidence on the
development of spatial orientation, see chapter 13 of Howard & Templeton (129).

Pick & Pick (225) have utilized the size-weight illusion as a vehicle for
studying developmental trends in intermodal (intersensory) integration. Information about object size was conveyed haptically to one group of subjects of varying ages, visually to a second, and both haptically and visually
to a third (the usual stimulus-presentation method for this illusion); information regarding object weight was transmitted haptically to all three
groups. The magnitude of the illusion increased with age in the first presentation condition, decreased in the second, and showed no significant age trends
in the third. The Picks hypothesize that sensitivity to haptic as opposed to
visual size is a relatively late acquisition, and also that the ability to discriminate between two dimensions such as size and weight may be achieved
earlier when each is conveyed through a separate modality (second group)
than when both are conveyed through the same modality (first group).

The ability to identify visually the duplicate of a form that one is perceiving only haptically (haptic-to-visual transfer) improves with age in both
middle- and lower-class children, but more slowly in the latter group (48).
On the basis of recent evidence by Denner & Cashdan (55), it appears that
haptic exploration of forms when accompanied by visual input may sometimes do little more than activate and focus visual attending. Nursery school
children inspected a hexagon incased in a clear plastic ball either visually,
visually and haptically, or visually and manually but not haptically. Delayed visual recognition of the form was equally good in the latter two
groups, with the first group's performance inferior to both.

Pick, Pick & Klein (226) review the literature on intermodal phenomena
and find great gaps in our current knowledge of how the various senses interact to produce knowledge about the world. Support for one important
generalization is beginning to emerge, however. Contrary to the view of
Berkeley and other philosophers, it is vision rather than touch that appears
to be the developmentally precocious and dominant source of perceptual information—a conclusion which is certainly in keeping with the recent evi-

dence on infant visual skills. Rock & Harris (237) have reached essentially the same conclusion: if anything, vision "teaches" touch, rather than the other way around.

Intermodal integration is discussed in recent papers dealing with the acquisition (and misacquisition) of reading skill. Rudnick, Sterritt & Flax (253) cite evidence that visual abilities decrease, and auditory or auditory-visual cross-modal abilities increase in importance as the child moves beyond the beginning reading level. Beery (14) finds that these later abilities do in fact correlate with reading skill in 8- to 13-year-olds; research by Reed (232) also lends some support to the hypothesis by Rudnick et al. It is reasonable to suppose that reading calls upon a whole assemblage of perceptual and intellectual processes, with different processes assuming functional prominence at different stages of reading mastery; reading is no more homogenous across development than readers are.

Differences in veridicality notwithstanding, perceptual illusions and perceptual constancies are much alike. Judgment is similarly discrepant from input to the receptors in both instances; moreover, the perceptual mechanisms which produce the discrepancy in the two instances may at least overlap. In a very comprehensive developmental study (427 subjects, 3 to 88 years of age), Leibowitz & Judisch (159) find that the Ponzo illusion increases sharply until about age 13, remains stable through middle age, and then declines. The authors speculate that this particular illusion—one of the intriguing minority which augments with development—may share some common mechanisms with size constancy; Leibowitz and his co-workers recently have confirmed previous evidence that the latter has a similar developmental course during childhood [Leibowitz, Pollard & Dickson (160)]. Leibowitz & Gwozdecki (158) have reconfirmed the fact that the Poggendorff illusion is among the decrease-with-age majority in this respect; so is the Muller-Lyer under normal visual presentation, but no age changes are found when it is presented tactually [Over (210)]. Pollack & Silvar (228) offer evidence that the magnitude of this famous illusion is partly dependent upon the amount of pigmentation in the Fundus oculi, and they raise the interesting possibility that some of the existing data on cultural differences in illusion size may be explained on a purely anatomical basis.

Unlike size constancy (160, 231), shape constancy may decrease rather than increase during middle childhood [Meneghini & Leibowitz (187)]. As these authors suggest and as Lichte & Borresen (168) have demonstrated, however, instructing the subject in a shape constancy experiment is a very delicate matter, and age differences in the interpretation of the task might have been responsible for Meneghini & Leibowitz's results.

Sheer amount of unreinforced exposure to a visual stimulus may not importantly determine the degree to which it is differentiated by the perceiver. Young children's ability to recognize a partially masked classmate's face was unrelated to how long they had known him but positively related to whether or not he was a good friend [Chance, Goldstein & Schicht (40)].

Attention.—The current emphasis on attention is by no means limited to infancy research; much of the year's literature on postinfantile behavior and development either implicitly or explicitly deals with attentional processes. Like Kagan (136), we believe that this current emphasis is not misplaced and wish to reinforce it by giving this essentially interdisciplinary topic its own by-line. Accordingly, the present section reviews some of the recent studies whose principal message concerns developmental changes in attention, regardless of the task setting used by the experimenter (e.g., learning, concept formation, memory, or perceptual). As a consequence, all of these studies logically could have been treated elsewhere in the chapter, and by the same token many of their close relatives could justifiably have been cited here.

Maccoby and her students have carried out several interesting developmental investigations of selective attention in the auditory mode [Maccoby (181); Maccoby & Konrad (182)]. There is improvement across the primary school years in the ability to give an accurate reproduction of one of two simultaneously presented messages; this improvement is especially marked for messages of high sequential probability, no doubt as a consequence of the older child's superior knowledge of the language. There are indications that the younger child may be less prone spontaneously to alert and set himself for the incoming messages, although quite able to maintain for a short time (2 sec) a set induced by the experimenter's preparatory signal; however, a study by Grim (100) suggests that he may also have problems with set maintenance over longer preparatory intervals.

Studies of visual attention are more numerous and cover a wider range of tasks. Younger children have more difficulty than their elders in identifying stimuli through visual as well as through auditory noise, with different properties of the noise (high versus low density and systematicity) having differential effects on the developmental curves [Munsinger & Gummerman (200)]; there also appears to be an increase with age in sensitivity to symmetry-asymmetry of form on visual search problems [Forsman (82)]. When 5- to 8-year-olds are asked to name the objects in a randomly-set arranged at random, the older ones are more likely to scan and name them in some systematic order [Elkind & Weiss (71)]. First-graders and poor-reading second-graders did the most left to right scanning, suggesting to the authors that children may be especially prone to practice spontaneously those skills which are currently being acquired (the young child who is observed to repeat recently discriminated phonological and morphological forms to himself would be a familiar example of the same thing).

There are two excellent studies which show that selective attention to, and subsequent retention of, central information increases with age during the elementary school years, whereas memory for task-irrelevant or incidental material remains essentially constant [Hagen (104); Hagen & Sabo (105)]. Crane & Ross (51) appear to have found essentially the same thing through the unlikely offices of a complex, irrelevant-redundant-relevant

(TRR) discrimination learning procedure—hardly the most direct and sensitive method for studying selective attention, one would think.

Developmental changes in attentional distribution undoubtedly contribute to age differences in performance on a variety of learning and cognitive tasks. For the latter, a study by Elkind, Van Doorninck & Schwarz (70) demonstrates that younger children find it harder to attain a concept if its defining attribute in a series of pictures is an activity or the physical setting rather than the central character (e.g., a picture of a dog, running, on a beach). Thus, while older children appear better able than younger children to stay focussed on the relevant versus irrelevant features in a display when the former are pre-identified by the experimenter (Hagen's studies), they also seem better able to avoid an attentional commitment to any particular, salient feature before this identification has been established (the present study). Wright & Smothergill (315) distinguish between "instrumental" and "consummatory" (e.g., motivated by stimulus deprivation) observing responses; the former but not the latter yield information which the subject may utilize for the task at hand (learning a discrimination, attaining a concept, solving a problem, etc.). Something akin to this distinction might apply to Kofsky's (151) findings: lower-class children who had been pretrained in labeling and discriminating relevant stimulus attributes paid more attention to these attributes than did control subjects in a subsequent concept attainment task, but did not identify the concept any better! Selective attending is surely a necessary condition for mastery of any task, but one would seldom expect it to be a sufficient condition.

Haptic discrimination tasks provide a good setting for the study of selective attention because much of the attentional processing can be directly observed. Cirillo, Wapner & Rand (43) show that adults are superior to 8- to 10-year-olds in "tuning" their haptic behavior to what the problem requires. On a matching-to-sample task, the adult's manual scanning patterns are found to change more radically than the child's when size replaces angle as the experimenter-defined basis for matching.

While evidence for the effects of stimulus novelty on attention deployment in infancy ranges from the positive to the ambiguous [Meyers & Cantor (189)], such effects can be clearly demonstrated in older subjects. Endsley (73) finds that preschool children select novel toys in preference to familiar ones in direct relation to the amount of prior exposure to the latter. The same positive relationship between amount of previous exposure and preference for the novel input is found even when the latter is a damaged toy [Harris (107)]. After exposure to a novel input, however, the previously familiarized one regains some of its initial allure [Lewis, Goldberg & Rausch (166)]. According to Sackett (255), children who are retarded by dint of gross brain injury differ from other retardates in showing a lack of this apparently very fundamental organismic preference for stimulus change. Livson (172) offers a brief but good review of the literature on curiosity and makes some interesting distinctions among its various forms.

Given the ubiquity of attention as a mediating component in cognitive processing, and given also the amount of research attention currently being paid to it, we were not surprised to find something like a program of mother-administered attention training for retardates reported in the year's literature [Santostefano & Stayton (260)].

Memory.—Memory becomes essentially continuous with perceptual-attentional processes on the input side and melds with a variety of other cognitive processes on the storage-and-output side. With respect to the former, Belmont (15) points out that the classical studies showing that short-term memory (STM) increases in span until adolescence or thereabouts confound original learning (what gets into storage) with STM proper (that fraction of what gets in that is subsequently retrievable). Using an experimental design intended to unconfound the two, he failed to find any developmental changes in STM between the ages of 8 and 20. As Belmont indicates, it is possible that STM for his relatively uncodable material (the subjects made delayed brightness comparisons) may develop prior to age 8, and also that STM for more codable (e.g., namable and rehearsable) content may continue to improve past this age. Much of the recent literature on children's recall which we shall be reviewing suggests that at least the second possibility is true. Inglis & Sykes (132) present evidence for what looks like a genuine improvement in STM for digits from age 5 to age 10. Reminiscent of the Grim (100) study referred to in the previous section, Bogartz (21) shows that 4- to 5-year-olds make more guessing choices on each trial of a single-alternation problem when the intertrial intervals are 15.7 sec versus 7.7 sec, suggesting that they have difficulty in holding an alternation rule in short-term storage over the more extended intervals. Consistent with the aforementioned distinction by Wright & Smothergill (315) between instrumental and consummatory attention, Bogartz's theoretical model of the young learner carefully distinguishes between mere attending and the cognitive encoding of what has been attended to.

One good way to amplify STM for an object sequence is to name the objects in order of their appearance during stimulus presentation and to try to keep objects and order "alive" in memory after stimulus offset by repeated rehearsal of the resulting ordered list. Flavell, Beach & Chinsky (81) had shown that the spontaneous (i.e., uninstructed) utilization of this mnemonic technique increases with age during the early school years. A subsequent study [Keeney, Cannizzo & Flavell (144)] indicates that: first-graders who do not spontaneously rehearse show poorer ordered recall than those who do; they can be induced easily by instruction to use a rehearsal mnemonic; this induced rehearsal mediates their recall just as effectively as spontaneous rehearsal mediates that of their age mates. In the same vein, Bernbach's (17) data suggest that the qualitative differences which previous investigators have observed between the short-term forgetting curves of nursery school and adult subjects are largely due to the children's failure spontaneously to name and rehearse the items.

Another way to augment STM is to group together for recall purposes items which are conceptually or associatively interrelated (clustering). Evidence is accumulating that children as young as 4 years of age show clustering effects in their verbal recall [Rossi & Wittrock (251)] and also that the tendency to cluster increases with age [Mandler & Stephens (184); Willner (304)]. On the basis of these and other recent studies [e.g., Munsinger (199)], it can be concluded that changes in the nature and complexity of the subject's coding-and-storage operations are in good part responsible for observed developmental increases in STM.

The most striking demonstrations of the developmental dependence of mnemonic operations on evolving cognitive ones are to be found in some recent Genevan research [briefly summarized in Piaget (222), with a book-length presentation soon forthcoming]. If a child is shown a series of sticks ordered by length, for example, what he will recall having seen when tested a week later largely depends upon his current grasp of seriation operations; that is, what is stored for later recall is a function of how the child intellectually assimilated or construed what was presented, rather than of what he saw in the literal sense. More interestingly, when retested 6 months later, the child's memory for the series may actually improve somewhat, in apparent congruence with the added understanding of seriation which these 6 months have produced. Piaget views memory as a coding and decoding system and hence entailing some code. This code, however, is dependent upon cognitive-operational level and therefore alters its character with age. As he puts it: "In a word, memory seems to be a special case of intelligent activity, applied to the reconstruction of the past rather than to knowledge of the present or anticipation of the future" [Piaget (222, p. 16)]. Whether or not Piaget's data prove reproducible by others and his interpretations of them plausible, one would hope that they represent the beginning of serious research on a neglected problem—the developmental study of long-term memory.

Language.—A distinction can be made between the basic developmental acquisition of a linguistic system—its phonology, morphology-syntax, and semantics—and the developmental acquisition of its various interspeaker (communicative, sociolinguistic) and intraspeaker (cognitive) functions. We shall take up these topics in the order given.

The research pickings on phonological development continue to be very slim. Olmstead (208) presents a theory of phonological development, but no test of it apparently has been completed as yet. According to Eisenberg (65), the newborn's auditory system is already a complex and specialized affair. It is probably no less preadapted for the jobs it will have to do than the visual system appears to be, and the most important of these jobs is speech perception. Curiously enough, the recent article of greatest potential significance for future research on phonological acquisition makes virtually no mention of development at all [Liberman et al. (167)]. Liberman and his colleagues have convincing research evidence that the relations between the physical-acoustic properties of speech sounds and the psychological units which are used by the speaker-hearer in phonological decoding (speech perception) and encoding (speech production) are unbelievably remote and complicated. As with Piaget's (222) analysis of memory, speech perception and production are conceived as operating by means of a very complex phonological code, a code which effects radical transformations of acoustic signals into phonemes and phoneme groups in the input side, and of verbal intentions into acoustic signals on the output side. Which aspects of the code are innately given and which aspects are acquired (and acquired through what experiences and learning mechanisms) now emerge as the important questions to ask about phonological development. It might be possible to use various physiological measures to track developmental changes on the decoding side, as is being done in studies of infant visual abilities.

There is considerably more recent evidence on morphological-syntactic development, although apparently little of significance on semantic acquisition. Roger Brown and his co-workers continue to derive important conclusions and hypotheses from observing the speech development of young Adam, Eve, and Sarah [Klima & Bellugi (148)]. The rules of negation in adult English grammar are very complex, and Klima & Bellugi find their developmental origin in a negative-operator-plus-sentence structure (e.g., "No play that"), a structure that may well prove to the the initial stage of negation acquisition in all human languages. Very soon thereafter, however, there emerges in the child's speech a profusion of intricate and English-specific surface structures which implicate the rapidly developing auxiliary verb system and which, unlike the initial one, apparently are generated by grammatical transformations. The same rapid development from simple to complicated, transformation-derived structures is found for interrogatives.

Other recent studies of grammatical development are cross-sectional rather than longitudinal, deal with older children, and are consequently somewhat less interesting. The relative difficulty level or age of mastery of linguistic imitation, comprehension, and production continues to attract research attention, particularly in the case of passive sentences. It has been reconfirmed that these three forms of language performance are of increasing difficulty level in the order given above [Hayhurst (113); Lovell & Dixon (175); Turner & Rommetveit (284)]. In an excellent article on the acquisition of pluralization rules, Anisfeld & Tucker (4) illustrate how comprehension and production tests may tap quite different aspects of the child's linguistic knowledge; they also remind us that children call upon much more than their implicit grasp of the grammatical rule under study when trying to cope with the psycholinguist's tasks. The length [Cowan et al. (50)] and grammatical maturity [Kaplan & Yonas (139)] of the child's linguistic productions in experimental situations are proving to be highly sensitive to all manner of stimulus and setting variables, suggesting that production indices of underlying linguistic competence are highly vulnerable to diagnostic error of the false-negative variety.

The ability to comprehend and especially to produce passive sentences is a relatively late achievement [Hayhurst (113); Lovell & Dixon (175); Turner & Rommetveit (284)]. A passive sentence is harder to manage if the interchanging of subject and object would still result in a meaningful sentence, if the subject is included rather than omitted (e.g., "The cake is being cut by X"), and if the sentence is negative rather than affirmative [Hayhurst (113); Turner & Rommetveit (284)]; that negation makes sentences harder for children to process has also been demonstrated by Zern (319). Why are passive constructions so difficult for young children to manage? It may in part have to do with a relative inability to see a sentence as consisting of discrete words whose positions are potentially reorderable— perhaps a lack of "operational mobility," in the Piagetian sense, with respect to sentences and their verbal constituents. It has been shown recently, for instance, that young children have difficulty both in recalling [Salzinger, Salzinger & Hobson (257)] and unscrambling [Braun-Lamesch (25)] scrambled sentences.

The developmental acquisition of the interspeaker functions of language —its social-communicative uses, rules, and conventions— is a subarea within the rapidly growing new field of sociolinguistics [Ervin-Tripp (74)]. Studies by Flavell (80) and Glucksberg & Krauss (94) have independently documented the intimate developmental relation between social-cognitive and verbal-communicative abilities. Young children fail to take account of the informational needs and other relevant attributes of their audience when communicating to them. It has been noted in both investigations, for example, that the young child may egocentrically engage in "verbal pointing" when addressing a listener who is blindfolded or behind a screen (e.g., "It goes like this," gesturing in the air, or "You pick this up and put it there").

There are a number of recent studies which in one way or another deal with the nature and development of intraspeaker, cognitive-mediational uses of language. Some have already been cited [e.g., Keeney, Cannizzo & Flavell (144)]; others will be mentioned in subsequent sections, especially those dealing with learning. For the present, we propose to examine briefly the topic in a broader context from the standpoint of the ancient question it raises: what is the relationship between language and thought? The question is obviously not whether covert verbal activity is a highly frequent concomitant of cognitive processes in linguistically endowed children and adults. Both introspective and physiological [Sokolov (277)] evidence suggests that it is. The question rather concerns the nature and importance of its functional role in the thinking process. One may variously ask whether verbalization and cognition are essentially synonomous; whether language is a necessary condition for thinking (developmentally prior to it and necessarily present in every contemporary act of thinking); whether it is only a sufficient condition for thought; or, while being neither synonomous, necessary, nor sufficient, whether it may yet serve one or more useful subsidiary functions within the total cognitive enterprise.

Our reading of the recent evidence suggests that the lattermost position comes closest to the truth [see also Lenneberg (161)]. Linguistic ability does not appear to be either synonomous with or a necessary precondition for cognitive processing of at least low to middling levels of developmental maturity (its status with respect to more advanced forms of thinking is uncertain). On the one hand, sensory-motor intelligence clearly evolves without it; on the other hand, linguistically-deficient deaf children manage to acquire concrete operations and other middle-childhood-level intellectual skills [Furth (87)]. Nor does language appear to be a sufficient condition. Despite the absence of any detectable language retardation, blind children show curious, very pronounced developmental lags on certain types of cognitive tasks [Hatwell (112)]; likewise, the cognitive inadequacies of retardates are hardly explicable by appeal to the absence of a supporting linguistic system. As for normal children, Sinclair's (274) studies suggest that mere knowledge of the relevant linguistic distinctions is not sufficient for the acquisition of concrete-operational structures.

Our own position on the matter [see also Furth (86); Inhelder et al. (134)] is that verbalization chiefly serves as an aid to perceptual-attentional and mnemonic processes, those processes whose function is to deliver up to the thinker the objects and occasions for his thinking. Symbols, particularly linguistic symbols, provide us with the coded raw materials for thinking, and as such serve a kind of intrapersonal communicative function in addition to the more familiar interpersonal one. Versatile creatures that we are, other symbolic means are apparently exploited when language is denied us, as with the young deaf. In this view, then, it would be inaccurate to assert that one thinks in words, but approximately correct to say that one often thinks about them and by means of them (in rather the same sense that one could be said to think by means of perceiving and remembering). We further believe that language does not play the active and essential role *vis-à-vis* young children's performance on simple motor and set-maintenance tasks that Luria and other Russian investigators have assigned to it [for a recent American study in this tradition, see Bem (16)], and also that current controversies about verbal-mediational versus attentional factors in discrimination learning [Wolff (311)] will likely prove to have been ill-conceptualized. It might finally be mentioned that verbalization, like any other intellectual subsidiary, can subvert as well as assist efficient and veridical cognitive activity. As a study by Rosenbaum (245) suggests, verbalization uses up precious cognitive time and resources which in some instances might be better employed otherwise. In his words: "The present study may be regarded as adding to the list of potentially interfering but frequently required responses, the necessity for active verbalization of covert responses" (245, p. 622).

Thought (Piagetian research).—The constraints imposed by fixed page allotments are nowhere more keenly felt than when trying to survey a year's worth of Piagetiana. The issues are varied and complex, the positions taken on them no less so, and the annual research output unmanageably abundant.

While an adequate review is thus impossible, one can at least choose his own brand of poor coverage. Ours will be to highlight very cursorily what strikes us as new, innovative, or otherwise—that vague word again—"interesting" on the current Piagetian scene.

The preoperational period of cognitive growth is generally thought of in negative terms: the preschooler is said to be a nonconserver, is said to fail to grasp the class-inclusion relation, etc. A more positive specification of what might be acquired during this important period would be desirable on several grounds, not the least of which would be the possibility it would afford for showing some added developmental continuity and transition between sensory-motor and concrete-operational intelligence. Several recent studies may point the way. For instance, the object concept of late infancy and the conservations of middle childhood both involve the belief that something stays the same while other things change. In the former case, however, what stays the same is a qualitative, essentially nonmetric property of a single object (its "existence"), whereas in the latter case it is an equivalence relation between two objects with respect to some quantitative and precisely measurable attribute such as length or weight [Elkind (69); Piaget (222)]. It is beginning to look as if the preoperational period may be replete with acquired invariances of the former, "qualitative identity" variety [Piaget (222)]. As examples, the child quite early intuits that his identity as a particular individual remains invariant as he grows older and bigger [Piaget (222)]; that straight objects which are inserted into a beaker of water do not really become doubled or broken, in spite of appearances [Elkind (67); Murray (202)]; and that the water which has been poured in a conservation of liquid quantity experiment is still the same water (qualitative identity), although perhaps no longer equal in amount either to what it was (quantitative identity) or to the water in the comparison container (quantitative equivalence, or conservation) [Bruner, Olver & Greenfield (32); Piaget (222)]. One of the most imaginative studies of the genre was carried out by DeVries (57). Children from 3 to 6 years of age were shown a live and very tolerant cat whose "generic identity" appeared to change when he was successively fitted with very realistic masks of a rabbit and a fierce-looking dog. A variety of verbal and nonverbal (e.g., fear) indices showed that the younger children could not manage this particular form of qualitative identity under such transformations, whereas the older but still preoperational ones clearly could.

It may also be that some of the apparent cognitive obstacles to the attainment of concrete-operational invariances could be reconstrued as developmental products in the positive sense. Mehler & Bever (186) report evidence which they interpret as suggesting that very young children actually have number conservation, subsequently lose it as perceptual-cognitive biases develop (e.g., the tendency to index number by length of row), and finally reacquire it on a permanent basis. Their evidence actually supports no such interpretation (the task used was not in fact a conservation test), but it is not implausible to think that the young child's growing ability, for instance, to differentiate and code the attributes and dimensions of stimulus arrays might for a time be increasingly maladaptive for some cognitive problems, while manifestly adaptive for many others. Although "cognitive progress" is admittedly a difficult thing to define, it surely cannot in all instances be equated with problem-solving success.

A less novel but still interesting subarea of Piagetian research concerns the possibility of advancing the child's grasp of fundamental concepts through systematic tuition, particularly of the short-term, laboratory variety. The early Piagetian training studies had largely negative outcomes, but the picture is now changing. If our reading of recent trends is correct, few on either side of the Atlantic would now maintain that one cannot by any pedagogic means measurably spur, solidify, or otherwise further the child's concrete-operational progress. In the first place, some recent nonGenevan training experiments appear to have been remarkably successful in this respect [Gelman (88); Kingsley & Hall (146); Kohnstamm (155)]. In the second place, the Genevans themselves have also begun a program of training studies [Inhelder et al. (134); Inhelder, Bovet & Sinclair (133)], largely in reaction to the work of Bruner [Bruner, Olver & Greenfield (32)] and his students. (Our space limitations and its publication date unfortunately militate against a discussion of this stimulating and controversial book, together with the Genevan reaction to it).

This is not to say, of course, that the important questions about the acquisition of Piagetian concepts have thereby been resolved. On the practical-educational side, there remains the question of how much and what kind of, say, concrete-operational progress can be effected by how much and what kind of pedagogic input. It can also be asked if the formal, programmed training of Piagetian operations is, as seems to have been generally assumed, an unmitigated good; the Genevans, at least, have reservations on this score (Hermione Sinclair, personal communication). The basic research questions raised by such experiments actually have as much to do with the theoretical analysis and experimental diagnosis of cognitive states as with training-induced changes in state. What precisely do we assume the child has acquired in the way of cognitive abilities when we credit him with, for example, a particular conservation concept? What exactly does he have and not have at the various points in his development prior to that concept's attainment? More fundamentally, is "possession of a conservation (or any other) concept" a clear and unambiguous notion, or are there different degrees, and perhaps even kinds, of "possession" which successively manifest themselves in the course of the child's development? And finally, what sorts of tests and probes can give us accurate diagnostic information as to what the child "possesses" before and after the training intervention?

Genevan views notwithstanding [e.g., Piaget (222)], convincing experimental demonstrations that conservation judgments are to be explained with reference to a grouping-structure foundation—involving the ability to carry

out rigorous identity, reversibility, and compensation operations—appear
to be hard to come by [Bruner, Olver & Greenfield (32); Cohen (47); Wallach, Wall & Anderson (290)]. But whatever underlies these judgments, the
acquisition of the capacity to make them is increasingly coming to resemble
a developmental zone rather than a point: the age gap between initial "competence" in the psycholinguistic sense for a given conservation and the
systematic mastery of any and all tasks which test for it is probably greater
than has been suspected. For instance, brief training may through its effects
on attentional selectivity, memory, and other processes serve mainly to remove "performance" obstacles to a latent but genuine conservation "competence" in some nonconserving children [e.g., Gelman (88); Wallach, Wall
& Anderson (290)]. Likewise, there is a vast accumulation of evidence from
assessment as well as training studies that all manner of task variations act
to facilitate or impede the transitional child's ability to give concrete-operational responses to Piagetian-type tasks [Davol et al. (54); Griffiths, Shantz
& Sigel (99); Goldschmid (95); Mermelstein & Schulman (188); Odom &
Coon (206); Pascual-Leone & Bovet (215); Peters (220); Shantz (269);
Sigel, Saltz & Roskind (273); Smedslund (275, 276); Wohlwill & Katz (308)].
Wohlwill & Katz (308) have shown, for example, that class-inclusion problems are more difficult for the transitional child when the class instances are
presented visually rather than verbally. Similarly, Sigel, Saltz & Roskind
(273) have identified both perceptual and conceptual types of performance
obstacles on a "concept conservation" task. An oversimplified but not
wholly inaccurate characterization of the current differences in approach
between Genevan and nonGenevan (especially American) Piagetians would
be the following: the Genevans tend to credit the child with, say, a conservation concept only when that concept is very solidly planted in his cognitive
system (generalizable across tasks, well-rationalized, invulnerable to experimental countersuggestion, etc.); in contrast, nonGenevans are inclined to
believe that the concept may be genuinely in the repertoire at earlier stages,
although fragilely and unstably so, and that test probes which bypass some
of the young child's performance limitations (again in the psycholinguistic
sense) may bring a latent grasp of it to the surface. In short, the first group
appears to see basic competence differences between transitional and fully
operational children, whereas the second emphasizes differences in perfor-
mance-type subsidiary abilities (attention, language, memory, etc.). Our
opinion is that some moderate version of the second position will prove to be
the more scientifically productive one at this point in the history of Piagetian
developmental psychology.

    Other interesting papers related to this psychology will be quickly noted.
Three present unusual results, hard to interpret: preschoolers can visually
estimate relative proportions as well as adolescents (91, 93), and older children perform worse on certain kinds of probability estimation problems than
younger ones do (78). Shantz (268) found only modest intercorrelations
among certain concrete-operational skills which might on theoretical grounds

have been expected to develop concurrently. And finally, Gyr and his associates [Gyr, Brown & Cafagna (101); Gyr & Fleisher (102)] describe some pioneering work on computer-simulation approaches to the testing of Piaget's theory of cognitive-structural growth.

Thought (other research).—Some shibboleths came under fire in the recent IQ literature. It has been widely accepted that Hofstaetter's (126) factor analysis of Bayley's longitudinal data provides evidence for qualitative changes in the nature of intelligence during childhood. However, Cronbach (52) convincingly shows that this evidence results from a methodological artifact, and concludes: "Many sorts of developmental research provide a basis for arguing that the available tests tap different processes at different ages, and for arguing that mental development goes through qualitative stages. Factor analysis of simplexes can introduce nothing but noise into the debate over these important hypotheses" (52, p. 289). Even more widely known is the chronic failure of infant developmental tests to predict later IQ scores. However, Cameron, Livson & Bayley (35) now report the puzzling finding that, for females but not males, a cluster of chiefly language-relevant items from the Bayley Scale (e.g., vocalizes displeasure, uses expressive jargon) shows substantial and increasing correlations with verbal IQ through 26 years of age. Data by Moore (195) and Jerome Kagan (personal communication) also hint that language may play a different and perhaps more important role in the cognitive development of girls versus boys. And finally, Wolff (310) was unable to replicate an earlier finding by Osler & Trautman (209) regarding the interactive effects of IQ and stimulus complexity on concept attainment.

Saltz & Sigel (256) find that young children's identity judgments result in narrower equivalence classes than do older children's and adults'; this is congruent with their often-reported tendency to form small groups on sorting tasks [e.g., Bruner, Olver & Greenfield (32)] and with the finding that they generally have more trouble with "same" judgments than with "different" judgments [e.g., Griffiths, Shantz & Sigel (99)]. The experimenter's instructions have been shown to have powerful effects on similarity judgments [Ginsburg & Gamlin (92)], and it may also be that the subject's self-instructions on categorization and related tasks change with age. Once the young child has formed his equivalence classes within an object array, he finds it very difficult to abandon them in favor of a new sorting [Kofsky & Osler (152)]. Bryant's (33) data suggest that, having come to ignore a given dimension as a consequence of his initial sorting (e.g., having once put blue squares and circles into the same category, he "tunes out" whatever initial attention may have been paid to the now-irrelevant form differences), he cannot easily reinstate that dimension subsequently when asked to resort.

The typical probability-learning task behaves like a projective test for which the popular response is the (fallacious) interpretation that real problem-solving efforts are in order and that successful efforts will lead to payoff on every trial. Weir and others have exploited this property to study developmental changes in problem-solving skills and strategies [see Weir (296) for a very readable review of his and other recent studies]. As the child develops, he comes increasingly to construe the task in these terms, showing a variety of response patterns (e.g., systematic response alternation) which reflect covert hypothesis-generating and hypothesis-testing activities [Derks & Paclisanu (56); Odom (205); Weir (296)]. During the middle childhood years, the child's ability to test hypotheses and pursue strategies may be hampered by memory limitations; provision of memory aids for this age group has been shown to result in superior performance, both on these tasks [Weir (295)] and on concept-learning problems [Pishkin, Wolfgang & Rasmussen (227)]. Memory and other cognitive limitations can also lead the child to keep retesting previously disconfirmed hypotheses, but systematic training may improve his skills in this regard [Wittrock (307)].

Odom & Blanton (204) obtained preliminary experimental support for an intriguing hypothesis regarding a developmental difference between deaf and hearing children, namely, that the latter have acquired a greater sensitivity to temporal order as a cognitive cue through their constant exposure to spoken language. Whiteman (300) adds to the small but growing literature on social-cognitive development by documenting age changes in the child's understanding of human motivation ("psychological causality"). Kaplan (138) presents an interesting summary of the Werner-Kaplan organismic-developmental approach to the study of human growth. And finally, Kendler & Kendler (145) offer a well-written summary of their extensive work on children's performance on a variation of Hull's inference problem. We wonder if the child's developing grasp of the transitivity principle, as described by the Genevans and others, may not play a role in his ability to solve this particular problem. The Kendlers also clarify their sometimes misunderstood position on verbal mediation: while linguistic labels may be particularly well suited to the function of symbolic representation in articulate organisms, they are not the only responses which can serve this function nor would they necessarily constitute the most adaptive mode of representation for all subjects in all task situations. As would be predicted from our previous editorializing about the language-thought question, we find much to applaud in the Kendlers' position.

Learning.—Investigations of both adult and child learning have in recent years come more and more to resemble studies of what might be termed "applied cognition." As the traditional, essentially acognitive learning theories have appeared increasingly inadequate as descriptions of what human beings actually do when confronted with learning tasks, it has been necessary to make theoretical allowance for the intervention of various cognitive activities (perception, language, etc.) in the learning process. While this is perhaps most strikingly apparent in the case of children's probability learning (we experienced no discomfort at all in reviewing this literature under the rubric of "thought"), it is no less true for many other learning tasks and procedures. The field could hope for at least two scientific benefits from this recent convergence of cognition and learning. One would be a detailed understanding of how the various cognitive-developmental changes we already know something about from nonlearning studies get reflected or "applied" in the context of acquiring new information, i.e., in a learning context. A more exciting prospect to many, however, would be the possibility of discovering important new facts about cognitive development itself. It might be, for example, that the special properties of learning tasks would bring to the surface processes not hitherto identified in other testing situations, or that differences in scientific *Weltanschauungen* between psychologists of child learning and other developmental psychologists would make for fresh and original interpretations of whatever processes are observed.

Although the complexities and inconsistencies of the recent data on children's learning are still such as to permit alternative theoretical explanations for many phenonema (e.g., regarding the role of linguistic versus attentional factors in discrimination learning), not many would want to argue that no progress whatever has been made towards the first, applied-cognitive-development objective. As we read the evidence, however, no particularly novel claims about cognitive growth proper seem to be emerging from the child-learning literature. That is, while the cognitive processes currently being inferred from learning data may be new within the domain of learning, they are apt to look disappointingly familiar to those outside that domain.

Discrimination-shift experiments continue to be very popular among students of child learning. These experiments are certainly no fare for anyone who likes his psychology straightforward and simple. Comprehension and short-term retention of their highly intricate designs and evaluation of their usually complex patterns of results [e.g., Mumbauer & Odom (198); Saravo (261)] appear to demand a level of convergent thinking ability not given to many. Since we are far from sure that it is given to us, the reader is warned that our assimilation of recent findings in this area may be off the mark. As best we can discern, in any case, the bulk of the evidence continues to suggest that younger children are in general less given or less able than older ones to code the stimuli presented during original discrimination learning in a categorical or dimensional fashion, i.e., to apprehend the fact that a given pair of stimuli constitute different instances of the same class (e.g., two different colors) or represent different values of the same dimension (e.g., two different sizes) [Saravo (261); Tighe & Tighe (283)]. The most direct experimental support for this interpretation, perhaps, is Johnson & White's (135) finding that the ability to seriate sets of objects by size and brightness is positively related in 6- to 7-year-olds to speed of reversal learning on the transfer portion of a discrimination-shift task. That young children should behave in this fashion on discrimination tasks is quite plausible, in view of longstanding evidence from developmental studies of seriation and classification skills. Developmental status is, of course, not the only variable that affects the child's coding of the stimuli in these tasks, and much of the year's research evidence bears upon other determining factors [Blank (18);

Dickerson (58); Eimas (63); Mumbauer & Odom (198); Saravo (261); Tighe & Tighe (283); Viney & Varner (286)]. Detailed reviews of the literature on developmental and nondevelopmental aspects of shift behavior in children are provided by Shepp & Turrisi (270) and Wolff (311).

Like the discrimination-shift experiment, a transposition study uses transfer performance as an index of how the child might have coded the stimuli during initial learning, i.e., in absolute versus relative terms. Caron's (37) findings suggest that young children are capable of according either a relative or an absolute interpretation to triads of different sized objects; the interpretation which wins control of the child's behavior will depend in part upon the stimuli used, e.g., the size difference between training and test trials. Caron emphasizes the role of attentional versus linguistic-skill determinants of transposition behavior, a view that appears to be gaining ground throughout the field of child learning [e.g., Wolff (311)]. While the pursuit of variables determining stimulus choice on transposition tasks continues to absorb the energies of some [there seems to be an unmanageable number of such variables, according to Zeiler (317) and Zeiler & Salten (318)], little of developmental interest seems to be emerging from the current transposition literature.

There is not a great deal for the developmentalist in the recent studies of children's paired-associate learning either. Interactions between age and stimulus variables are not always assessed and are seldom found when tested for. However, the reported effects of the stimulus variables themselves are of some general interest. Paired-associate learning in children is facilitated when the stimulus member of the pair is the name of a liked versus unliked classmate [Ramirez & Castaneda (230)], when the response member is a concrete versus abstract noun [Klein et al. (147)], and when the two have a strong free-associative connection [Klinger & Palermo (150)]. Facilitation also occurs if the two members are presented within a larger verbal or pictorial context, experimenter-produced or self-produced [Milgram (191)], and the amount of facilitation is a function of the type of context. Thus, an actional link (e.g., "the fork cuts the cake"—or a picture to this effect) usually leads to better recall than a locational one ("the fork is on the cake"); and both have clearly stronger effects than a mere coincidental link ("the fork and the cake") [Rohwer & Lynch (239); Rohwer et al. (240, 241)]. There is disagreement as to whether pictorial and verbal presentation of pair members and their contexts have differential effects on recall when the type of context is controlled [Klein et al. (147); Milgram (192); Rohwer et al. (240, 241)]. While it has been shown that context has most of its facilitating effect at the storage rather than retrieval end of the experimental sequence [Rohwer, Shuell & Levin (242)], the nature of the mediating process responsible for this effect is still far from clear.

Levinson & Reese (164) have done the field's most comprehensive developmental investigation of discrimination learning set (age range of subjects: 3 to 97 years!). As in probability-learning studies, emphasis is given to age changes in the kinds of response biases, strategies, and hypotheses which the subject brings to the discrimination problem, and particularly, to the facility with which he can abandon those which prove nonadaptive or incorrect. Making the odd stimulus in an oddity problem perceptually salient is ineffective if the task is basically beyond the subject's grasp (young preschoolers), superfluous if the problem is easily solvable (second-graders), but distinctly helpful otherwise (kindergarteners) [Gollin, Saravo & Salten (96)]. And finally, an excellent study by Covington (49) shows that repeated exposure to the stimulus items has a marked facilitating effect on the matching-to-sample discrimination performance of lower-class kindergarteners, bringing them up to the level of their higher-status peers.

Socialization of cognitive behavior.—The *International Journal of Psychology* has been serving the useful function in its first two volumes of calling readers' attention to problems of cultural differences and cognitive development. Greenfield & Bruner (98) discuss the constraints placed on cognitive development by value orientations and language: "In short, some environments 'push' cognitive growth better, earlier, and longer than others. What does not seem to happen is that different cultures produce completely divergent and unrelated modes of thought. The reason for this must be the constraint of our biological heritage" (98, p. 105). Peluffo (218) brings together a variety of cross-cultural findings that, in general, support the Greenfield-Bruner thesis. The information cited suggests that resisting perceptual centration-inducing features of stimuli in favor of conceptual processing is in part a cultural product. Witkin (306) reviews several cross-cultural studies of field dependence. The latter is viewed as a perceptual subcomponent of a global-articulated cognitive style dimension. One of the more provocative findings cited is an exception to what has appeared to be a universal sex difference in field dependence-independence: rather than being more field independent, Baffin Island Eskimo males attain the same mean score on the Rod-and-Frame Test as do the females. MacArthur (178) successfully replicates this result for another group of Eskimos. It happens that women are not treated as dependent in this Eskimo culture and, consequently, it is tempting to speculate about possible determinants in socialization of the sex difference in field dependence-independence. Hopefully, speculations of this nature will one day lead to a *nouvelle vague* of cross-cultural studies that goes beyond the simple demonstration of cross-cultural differences to compare processes of socialization.

Freeberg & Payne (85) find a surprising number of studies to include in their review of parental influence on cognitive development. Their call for clearer operational definitions of parental practices is in some respects answered by studies which involve direct observation of parent-child interaction. Bee (13) reports such a study of the correlates, measured in conjoint problem-solving, of distractibility (independently assessed). Parents of nondistractible children give more positive encouragement, pay more attention to the child's comments in making decisions, and make relatively more evaluative comments than suggestions. When suggestions are made they are less specific than those given by parents of distractible children. The Stroop color-naming test was used by Heilbrun, Harrell & Gillard (115) to measure "cognitive control," a variable that shares at least some of the same semantic space as Bee's "distractibility." Female undergraduates were asked to complete the task in the presence of the experimenter and other subjects. They were reinforced negatively for errors ("Wrong") and offered money for correct answers. Some of the findings are similar to those reported by Bee. Daughters who reported child-rearing histories of rejection (high paternal control and low paternal nurturance) showed the greatest degree of impairment of cognitive control in the task. One would not predict from Bee's results that girls with a history of being ignored by their fathers (low nurturance and low control) would do best on the task, as indeed they did.

Probably the most extensive study of parent-child relations and cognitive development in progress is that of Hess [Hess & Shipman (118)]. Observation of parent-child interaction in situations requiring lower- and middle-class Negro mothers to teach their preschool children simple tasks is combined with interviews in this study. Middle-class mothers emit more motivating, orienting, positively reinforcing, and fewer negatively reinforcing comments than lower-class mothers during the teaching tasks. They also provide more specific directions and criticisms, making clear to the child what behaviors are desirable and undesirable. Middle-class mothers more often use regulatory techniques that provide a rationale for disapproval of misbehavior; lower-class mothers appeal to their own status and power and "the rules." Positive relations are reported between cognitive behavior (e.g., IQ, verbalizing a concept) and most of the parent behaviors on which differences favor the middle class. On the whole, it is not clear from this study, as from others that involve comparison of lower- and middle-class performance, which effects of being reared in the lower class are cognitive and which are motivational, which have to do with the child's competence and which with its activation.

Four other papers will be of interest to readers interested in the socialization of cognition. Honzik (127, 128) reports a multivariate, longitudinal study of parental behavior during infancy and its association with IQ from 21 months to 30 years. Some personality characteristics associated with descriptive, relational, and categorical cognitive styles in 4- and 5-year-olds are presented by Sigel, Jarman & Hanesian (272). Wender & Pederson (297) found that boys who were highly socially dependent at age 2 tended as 6-year-olds to have relational (as opposed to inferential-categorical) cognitive styles. They also obtained lower WISC performance scores and were more field dependent than boys who were less dependent as infants.

SOCIAL PROCESSES AND PERSONALITY DEVELOPMENT

Contemporary research on social processes and personality development has a Skinnerian bias, favors the short-term experimental study, is largely nondevelopmental, and, as far as content is concerned, is fixated on nurturance and nurturance withdrawal as antecedent and determinant of practically everything. However, the Piagetians slowly are moving in, observational studies are becoming more popular, CA and other independent variables that might index developmental levels or history more often are incorporated into research designs, and it is all right once again to talk about the self. There are, of course, major exceptions but these are some of the trends as we see them. The research follows.

Social learning processes.—Many current studies of social reinforcement are demonstrations that verbal praise, approval, and attention can modify selected (classes of) responses in one or a (usually small) number of subjects. Reinforcement techniques have been used: to modify language and other social behaviors of "untreatable" schizophrenic children [Lovaas (173); Lovaas et al. (174), Wolf et al. (309)]; to control hyperactivity by strengthening attending behavior [Allen et al. (3); Quay et al. (229)]; to strengthen social approach behavior in withdrawn, shy 8-year-old boys [Clement & Milne (44)]; to change the behavior of brain-injured children [Hall & Broden (106)]; to modify sibling interaction [O'Leary et al. (207)]; to habilitate antisocial retardates [Burchard (34)]; and to modify interpersonal dominance in dyads [Blum & Kennedy (20)].

Relatively few studies of social reinforcement are designed to yield basic information about the determinants of reinforcement efficacy. Few use reinforcement techniques as a means to the solution of developmental problems. Few test competing formulations with the objective of illuminating the concept of reinforcement itself. Some reinforcement studies that bear on issues of these kinds are considered in other sections of this review (60, 75, 115, 140, 141, 190, 217, 288, 289). Here will be discussed studies addressed to basic issues of general interest.

It is a fact that deprivation of social stimuli heightens subsequent responsiveness to them and that social satiation results in lowered responsiveness. For the cue function of stimuli, Canon (36) shows that a prior period of social isolation increases subsequent distractability by a social stimulus. Gewirtz (90) reviews his own previously published and unpublished studies which establish an inverse relation between the number of prior presentations of a social stimulus and its subsequent reinforcing efficacy. Using isolation and interaction rather than varying the number of stimulus presentations, Rosenhan (247) investigated the effects of social deprivation and satiation on responsiveness to subsequent reinforcement in a probability learning task. The reinforcement given was either social or nonsocial and negative or positive. Socially deprived children proved to be indifferent to the valence of reinforcement if it was social. This casts doubt on the validity of simple anxiety interpretations of social deprivation effects since "If it is anxiety and only anxiety that is reduced by social reinforcement, then it is difficult to understand why the avoidance of negative social reinforcement should be as strong as the effects of positive reinforcement" (247, p. 37). Rosenhan also found that socially satiated children are most responsive to nonsocial reinforcement. He suggests that the presence and absence of reinforcement *qua* reinforcement may be less critical than its sociality: when bored by togetherness, the child's responsiveness to nonsocial stimuli increases; when bored by aloneness (nonsocial stimuli), the child's responsiveness to social stimuli increases. Further evidence of the complexity of social reinforcement effects is provided by Hill (123) who investigated high and low test-anxious children's responsiveness to social reinforcers following success and failure on another task. Low test-anxious children were more responsive to supportive comments than nonreinforcement following success but there was no difference in performance following failure. High test-anxious children, on the other hand, were more responsive to social reinforcement than nonreinforcement following failure, but there was only a minimal difference in performance following success.

Drive and nondrive interpretations of social deprivation and satiation phenomena are discussed by Gewirtz (90), whose research and commentary constitute a strong argument for relativistic, context-aware definitions of the stimulus as cue and as reinforcer [cf. Kagan (136)]. A related point is made by Scott, Burton, & Yarrow (262), who warn that the scheduling of a single reinforcer (as in a laboratory study) in a natural setting will vary in its effectiveness as a function of the introduction of stimuli not under the change agent's control. Consequently, the most flexible and effective adaptation of reinforcement principles to natural settings may well occur when a variety of reinforcers can be programmed by a change agent who has assessed the child's history of responsiveness in a variety of situations.

Scott, Burton & Yarrow also turn up evidence for experimenter bias in their study of the operant conditioning of prosocial behavior in a nursery school child. Although the reports of observers who were informed and those who were uninformed about the child's social behavior and adult reinforcement were highly correlated, on 10 of the 12 study days the informed observer's records supported the hypothesis whereas the uninformed observer's records did not. A similar discrepancy is reported for data on the cumulative effects of the reinforcement contingencies. Given these findings and the recent increase in reliance on observational techniques, it would seem prudent for more developmental psychologists to take Rosenthal's (250) work on experimenter bias seriously.

Symbolic interaction theory and role theory have long insisted on the importance of mutual sanctioning behavior in the determination of ongoing social interaction. But such mutual reinforcement phenomena have for the most part proved refractory to experimental analysis. Rosenfeld (246), however, reports a beginning step in his experimental investigation of the reciprocation of common approval responses such as smiling and positive head-nodding. His ninth-grade subjects emitted higher percentages of smiles and head-nods to interviewers who emitted these and other approval behaviors than to disapproving or nonresponsive interviewers. Less verbal disfluency and self-manipulatory behavior also were found in the approval condition.

Imitation may be treated as both a product and a process of social learning. Children with limited behavioral repertoires, e.g., mental retardates or schizophrenics, may be shaped to imitate an adult who provides reinforcement contingent on the child's matching his behavior to that of the experimenter [Baer, Peterson, & Sherman (5); Hingtgen et al. (124); Lovaas (173); Lovaas et al. (174)]. As Baer, Peterson & Sherman suggest, behavioral similarity can be expected to become reinforcing since it is made discriminative with respect to positive reinforcement. Under such circumstances the emphasis is on the development of generalized imitation in exceptional children as a product of contingent reinforcement. A major gap in the social learning literature continues to be the lack of information about the genesis of imitation in normal infants. In older children, where a generalized imitation habit or drive may already be presumed to exist, the emphasis is on imitation as a process of acquiring new responses. The major empirical preoccupation is with the facilitation of such acquisition and the kinds of behavioral phenomena which may be modified by observation of a model.

The hypothesis that prior rewardingness of the model has a facilitative effect was tested, and for the most part confirmed, in a number of studies (108, 248, 267). That the perceived similarity of the model to the observer facilitates imitation of instrumental responses was the hypothesis tested and confirmed by Rosekrans (243). Preadolescent boys who viewed a film in which a male model was depicted as similar in background and interests made more imitative responses than did those who were exposed to a dissimilar model.

A number of classes of responses have been shown to be influenced by exposure to a model. But prior to the study reported by Bandura, Grusec & Menlove (8), there has been no firm evidence that extinction of avoidance responses might be effected by observation of a model's approach behavior. These investigators measured avoidance responses to a dog by asking preschool children to engage in progressively intimate interactions with the animal. Significant increases in approach behavior were found following exposure to a model who, across eight 10-minute treatment sessions, gradually became more direct and intimate in his approaches to the dog. As the authors point out, further research is required to differentiate the contributions of affective, cognitive, and other factors operative in this and similar studies of observational learning.

In another study (7), the interest of the same investigators was in the determination of those conditions under which children would emulate the self-reward behavior of a highly competent model who had stringent criteria for self-reward. Adoption of the most stringent self-reward criteria by a child occurs when an adult model displays low nurturance and is positively reinforced for setting high standards and if competing low peer standards are absent. Mischel & Liebert's (194) study also deals with the influence of characteristics of a social agent on children's self-reward behavior. Children in the control group were exposed to a male adult who had lenient criteria for rewarding himself in a bowling game but imposed a more stringent pattern on the child. Children in the experimental group were given the same treatment but told in addition that the adult might give the child a valuable prize. Greater adherence to a stringent schedule of self-reward was observed in the latter group when the game was played in the absence of the adult. Thus a social agent's power to dispense a valued reward led children, in private, to reward themselves in accord with the agent's stringent prescriptions even though the agent's own self-reward behavior was lenient. Bandura & Perloff (9) found self-monitored reinforcement to be as efficacious as externally imposed reinforcement in maintaining effortful behavior in 7- to 10-year-olds. Both conditions sustained considerably more behavior than occurred when rewards were absent or noncontingent—a necessary demonstration if self-reward is to be considered synonymous to self-reinforcement.

The rapidly growing literature on modeling and self-reward processes was not matched this past year by as much interest in punishment. An excellent review of the punishment literature by Walters & Parke (291) and their empirical monograph (214) may well stimulate more research in this area. It is suggested that punishment is a more effective control technique than has been supposed, especially if it is judiciously timed and if the elicitation and reinforcement of alternative responses is a coexistent process. Much the same conclusion is drawn by Worell (314) in his discussion of ramifications of exposure to conflict.

That the role of time in voluntary delay behavior is different when the delayed events are punishments than when they are rewards is established in a study by Mischel & Grusec (193), who asked children to choose between immediate smaller and delayed larger punishments as well as rewards. Increasing the probability of occurrence of the delayed event led to more delayed reward choices and more immediate punishment choices as predicted. As length of the delay interval was increased for rewards, more immediate choices were made. However, length of delay did not influence choices between immediate and delayed punishments. The study calls into question subjective probability interpretations of voluntary time delay phenomena: increasing the length of a delay period apparently does not act uniformly to reduce the subjective probability of the occurrence of positive and aversive events.

Achievement.—The current practical interest in educating young children from disadvantaged backgrounds [for a review, see Bronfenbrenner (29)] seems to be accompanied by an increased output of basic research on the development of achievement motivation and behavior. That such attention may be warranted on grounds of the stability over time of achievement-related behavior as opposed to other personality characteristics is suggested by Ryder's (254) reanalysis of the mass of longitudinal data reported by Kagan & Moss (137) in their book *Birth to Maturity.* Through the use of canonical correlation techniques, Ryder identified two main clusters of characteristics on which correlations between latency, early adolescent, and adult ratings show moderate stability. One cluster probably is best labeled "adventuresomeness" but the major cluster is saturated with achievement-related behaviors: indirect aggressiveness, competitiveness, and task persistence in 6- to 10-year-olds predicted to independence, aggressiveness, and achievement orientation at adulthood. The analysis of early adolescent-adult correlations also implicates achievement-related characteristics in the stability which is found over this time period.

Sampson & Hancock (259) avoid the methodological deficiencies of most ordinal position studies—lumping of firstborns and only children, neglect of family size, sibling sex, and sibling age-spacing, creating a heterogeneous "laterborn" category—and report that, as high school students, firstborns have higher n Achievement and n Autonomy, tend to have lower test anxiety, and, if they are male, show more achievement-related conformity than second borns.

The McClelland-Atkinson tradition in the study of achievement phenomena consistently has been identified with a conception of achievement motivation that stresses task orientation and self-reward as opposed to social orientation and social reinforcement. The research growing out of this tradition and others is brought together by Heckhausen in his book, *The Anatomy of Achievement Motivation* (114). Heckhausen reviews the evidence, mainly his own studies published in the past 5 years in German journals, for the hypothesis that achievement motivation presupposes a level of cognitive maturation which permits the child to refer outcomes of performance back to the self and thus to be viewed as an effect of his own competence. It is hypothesized that this becomes possible for the child at some time between 3 and 3 and one-half years. Social approval is important but only as it provides a measure of success, and disapproval only insofar as it provides a measure of failure. Child-rearing practices are seen as having "nothing to do with the origin or the existence of achievement motivation per se. It is a universal 'fact of life' just as the maturational steps in cognitive development are" (114, p. 150). The socialization variables studied assiduously by American investigators are important for understanding individual differences but not the general course of development of achievement motivation. Whatever the interpretation, parental demands for early independence and achievement, nurturance, and control continue to serve as a focus of interest for many studies of achievement.

Feld (77), for example, reports a follow-up 6 years later on Winterbottom's (305) Ss, now 14 to 16 years old. While n Achievement was somewhat stable over this period, mothers' expectations for independence and achievement when the boys in the sample were 8 to 10 were not related to n Achievement in adolescence as they had been in the earlier age period. Interestingly enough, the earlier maternal expectations did predict negatively ($r = -.75$) to adolescent test anxiety scores. Baumrind & Black (12) report positive relations between parental granting of independence and dimensions of competence (stability and assertiveness) in preschoolers. Hatfield, Ferguson & Alpert (111), on the other hand, found that parental pressure and reward for independence were not correlated with preschool boys' achievement standards but were negatively related to achievement standards in preschool girls.

The ubiquitous hypothesis that warm, accepting, or nurturant parental behaviors conduce to an achieving child—as indeed, to virtually any culturally valued behaviors in children—also received mixed empirical support in 1967. Positive relations were reported between positive parental behavior and competence [Baumrind (11)] and belief in internal control of reinforcement [Katkovsky, Crandall, & Good (140)]. In his study of fifth and sixth-grade Negro children, Katz (141) found significant differences between high and low achieving boys in paternal but not maternal provision of positive reinforcers; there were no significant differences for girls. Hatfield, Ferguson & Alpert (111) found no relation between maternal warmth and achievement standards for either preschool boys or girls; however, for boys, maternal directiveness and achievement standards were positively correlated. Similarly, Baumrind & Black (12) found warmth a weak predictor of dimensions of competence in upper middle-class preschoolers. Parental control techniques, enforced demands, and consistency of discipline accounted for more of the variance. Some promise of clarifying these mixed results is held out by studies which examine concurrently the effects of parental nurturance and control. Heilbrun, Harrell, & Gillard (116) found that the goal-setting behavior of college students is influenced by maternal nurturance only when the mother is also perceived as having been highly controlling: Ss with self-reported histories of high control and low nurturance were more likely to set low levels of aspiration following social nonreaction than were Ss with histories of high control and high nurturance. These results were in accord with the investigators' "sensed-competence" hypothesis, namely that the combination of high control and disapproval or rejection adversely affects the child's subjective evaluation of his own competence and therefore his achievement behavior. The child with a history of high control is assumed to be more influenced by social reinforcement ("reinforcer-sensitized") than is the child with an autonomy-granting parent. Consonant with this position is the finding by Katkovsky, Crandall & Good (140) that parental dominance, rejection and "criticality" are negatively associated with beliefs in internal control of reinforcement.

While approaches like Heilbrun's may help to clarify the correlates in parental behavior of children's achievement, it is certain that such correlates will differ depending upon whether the achievement variable of interest is defined in terms of or assessed in the presence of social or other tangible reinforcement. Katz (141) argues for studies of achievement motivation which de-emphasize the salience of experimenter surveillance and which, unlike current studies of self-reward, do not provide external resources for immediate self-gratification. His findings from an attempt at implementation of these criteria in a laboratory assessment situation suggest that low-achieving Negro boys have as high standards as high-achievers but are more self-critical. A history of high parental levels of aspiration but low reinforcement for instrumental achievement behavior and negative reinforcement for failure is suggested by Katz to be characteristic of low SES children. However, with IQ controlled, positive correlations between SES and self-estimates of ability, school achievement, scholastic and career aspirations, and perceived parental and peer encouragement for academic achievement are reported by Wylie & Hutchins (316). Their extensive questionnaire study of 4245 7- to 12-year-olds also suggests that Negro children have aspirations equal to or greater than those of white children and perceive themselves as having as much or more encouragement to pursue them from parents and peers. In a related study, Rehberg & Westby (233) used partial correlation techniques in the analysis of information from a large sample of adolescents to demonstrate that parental encouragement, occupation, and education are independent predictors of adolescent educational expectations.

Persistence at a task under nonreward conditions provides a response counterpart to or performance measure of achievement motivation. Semler (264) found stable individual differences in persistence on a nonterminal task in 3-, 4-, and 5-year-olds. Median total persistence scores increased significantly with CA. Weyer & Bednar (299) manipulated preschoolers' success and failure on a pretraining task and measured their perseverance on an objectively easy or objectively hard second task which they were told was easy or hard for others. When the task was objectively hard or hard for others, children who had been exposed to failure persevered longer than those exposed to success. When the task was objectively easy or easy for others, children exposed to success persevered longer than those exposed to failure. The findings are not consistent with those from similar studies of adults [Heckhausen (114)], and trying to interpret them calls attention to developmentalists' relative ignorance of the structure and dynamics of achievement phenomena in young children.

Moral behavior.—While claims for conscience or superego concepts are on the wane, this year's research on moral behavior falls easily into the familiar resistance to deviation and moral judgment categories. Children who observed an adult model yield to the temptation to engage in proscribed movie-watching yielded more than the no-model controls [Stein (279)]; observing a resisting model, however, did not induce more resistance than found in the no-model controls. Parke (213) exposed one group of first- and second-graders to a period of continuous nurturance and another to nurturance followed by nurturance withdrawl. Girls in the latter condition deviated (played with proscribed toys) less frequently than those in the former condition, particularly when paired with a same sex rather than an opposite sex E. Results for boys took the same form but did not attain statistical significance. Parke & Walters (214) report on a related series of studies involving the effects on response inhibition of the timing and intensity of punishment (aversive 96 db and 65 db tones at 710 cps) under high and low nurturance. The effects of intensity and timing of punishment were complex and inconsistent across the three studies reported. Punishment was more efficacious for those Ss who had prior nurturant interaction with the agent of punishment than for those whose interaction was impersonal. The authors suggest that when a nurturant social agent employs punishment techniques involving noxious stimulation, their efficacy may derive more from the nurturance withdrawal implicit in presenting an aversive stimulus than from the noxious character of the stimulus per se. Hoffman & Stalzstein's (125) findings suggest the need for more careful delimitation, especially in correlational studies, of what techniques are categorized as indicative of love withdrawal or are "love oriented" or "nonpower assertive." Techniques consisting of direct but nonphysical expressions of anger ("love withdrawal") were differentiated from those involving a parental focus on the painful consequences for others of engaging in disapproved behavior ("induction"). Frequent use of induction correlated more consistently than love withdrawal with advanced development on several dimensions of moral behavior in this seventh-grade sample. Infrequent use of power assertive techniques was related to the same outcomes and, indeed, love withdrawal proved to be related negatively to a Piaget-type measure of internal moral judgment.

Turning now to moral judgment, the development of intentionality was considered by Breznitz & Kugelmass (26, see also 156). Using a questionnaire constructed on the basis of Guttman's scalogram technique, these authors (26) substantiate hypothesized refinements in the concept of intentionality from 11 to 17. In the first stage, Preverbalized Usage, the child appears to evaluate individual acts according to intention without being able to verbalize the criteria in use. The second stage, Verbalization of the Principle, suggests not only the capacity to specify evaluative criteria but the ability to apply the principle of intentionality to all relevant stimuli rather than confining application to stimuli associated with specific experience in the past. In the third stage, the child can recall the principle without external cues, and finally, in the fourth, the principle can be used in a more refined manner.

Piaget has argued that the transition in children 6 to 10 years old from moral judgments based on consequences of acts (objective responsibility) to judgments based upon intentionality (subjective responsibility) is facilitated by peer group interaction. Kugelmass & Breznitz (156) wanted to find out if this hypothesis could be generalized to the subsequent development of the concept of intentionality from 11 to 17. However, adolescents in the *Kibbutzim*, presumably a more peer oriented lot, proved not to be more accelerated in this aspect of moral development than their city peers.

Understanding of good and bad by children 2 to 6 years old was studied by Rhine, Hill & Wandruff (234). Ss were shown sets of four pictures; each set contained all neutral or one loaded (depicting a good or bad activity) picture. Selection of the loaded pictures was no better than chance at age 2 but approached the point of all correct near age 6. The results suggest that socialization induces earlier understanding of bad than good: from 29 months onward, identification of the bad pictures was more common than identification of the good ones.

Sex role.—Hopefully, the research reported in 1967 will free the field of simple and sovereign "identification-with-the-parent-of-the-same-sex" hypotheses about sex-role learning. If so, Hetherington's excellent studies (119, 120) will have played an important role in bringing this about. Among many provocative contributions are her demonstrations of the importance of the father for the daugher's femininity and her elaboration of the role of parental dominance in sex-role learning. Parental dominance is critical to boys' sex-typing but not to that of girls: masculine sons come from families where the father is dominant. Maternal dominance is disruptive not only to sex-typing but to father-child similarity and father-son imitation and, in fact, enhances mother-son similarity and mother-son imitation. Parental warmth leads to imitation in boys but not to greater masculinity, and to both increased imitation and femininity in girls. The antecedents of "identification," then, depend upon what outcome variable is employed. It cannot be assumed that scores on masculinity-femininity tests, parent-child similarity scores on measures of sex-typed or non-sex-typed characteristics, and the extent of imitation of the parent, provide equivalent operations for identification concepts. As the different relations of warmth and dominance to these three identification-related variables suggest, sex-typing is related neither to similarity nor imitation of either parent for boys. Therefore, sex-typing of boys' behavior cannot be held to be a product of simple modeling of the overt characteristics of the parent of the same sex. That this hypothesis may fare better for girls may be suggested by the significant interrelations among these outcomes. However, Hetherington's work also shows that the girl's relationship with the father is critical for sex-typing. In a study which bears on many of the same issues, Hill (122) found that sons' attitudes toward mathematics were correlated with maternal but not paternal attitudes and that warmth and use of psychological control techniques predicted to mother-son but not father-son similarity. On the other hand, sons were more likely to behave in accord with their fathers' expectations than their mothers'. Paternal warmth and participation in child-rearing predicted to accordant behavior between fathers and sons but not mothers and sons.

Barclay & Cusumano (10) also call attention to the nature of the outcome of identification under study. They found that adolescent boys reared since age 5 in father-absent homes did not differ from father-present boys on such overt characteristics as CPI Masculinity-femininity scores or indices of cross-sex identity, but did score higher on Witkin's measure of field dependency. The latter is interpreted as a more covert or deep-seated characteristic indicative of general passivity in relation to one's environment.

The extension of cognitive theory to the problem of sex-role learning is represented in an interesting monograph by Kohlberg & Zigler (154). It is argued that "the child's basic sex-role identity is largely the result of a self-categorization as a male or female made early in development" (154, p. 103). Having made this categorization, the child comes to value acts and objects consistent with his conceived identity. Imitation and preferences for sex-typed acts and objects proceed from rather than cause basic sex-role identity. Since intellectual growth involves the transformation of the child's perceptions of the environment, it should both facilitate and initiate changes in social attitudes. Thus it may be argued that bright children who advanced from one stage to another before their less-bright peers should also show advanced social development: MA should be correlated positively with maturity of social development. Kohlberg & Zigler tested this proposition by examining differences on sex-role attitude measures for matched bright and average 4- to 8-year-olds. Although the number of different assessment procedures employed make the findings difficult to evaluate and to report here, in general the developmental trends reported are parallel for the two groups but occur earlier for the bright than for the average children.

Aggression.—Patterson, Littman & Bricker (217) argue that early socialization, by strengthening assertive responses, provides the necessary but not sufficient condition for subsequent acquisition of aggressive responses (viewed by these authors as a high amplitude subclass of assertive behavior). Over a nine-month nursery school period, children with initially low rates of aggression showed striking increases in aggression, particularly if they were frequently victims of other children's aggression and managed successful counterattacks. A child reinforced for his aggressive behavior by positive consequences from peers is likely to select the same response and victim the next time he aggresses; either response or victim or both are likely to change in the next round if aggression is followed by negative peer consequences. It is intriguing that turning the other cheek does not assure victimdom. Across Ss, the child's provision of positive reinforcement for aggression does not predict to popularity as a target in nursery school society.

The influence of exposure to verbally aggressive models on subsequent verbal conditioning of hostility was studied by Ditrichs, Simon & Greene (59). Children who heard a model reinforced for constructing sentences with hostile verbs subsequently were conditioned to emit hostile sentences themselves; such conditioning was not obtained without previous exposure to the model. Additional information suggests that such disinhibition of hostile responses through exposure requires that change in the model's own behavior be salient for the observer. Facilitation of conditioning was not obtained when, in a second study, exposure to the model's behavior consisted in the presentation of a block of reinforced hostile sentences as opposed to an acquisition sequence featuring an ascending number of hostile sentences over blocks of five trials.

However the consequences to aggressors from victims turn out to affect aggressors, the hypothesis that such consequences can have important effects on third-party observers continues to be supported. Rosekrans & Hartup (244) exposed 3- to 6-year-olds to an aggressive adult model who was either (*a*) successively rewarded and punished; (*b*) rewarded; or (*c*) punished by the experimenter. Children exposed to the inconsistently reinforced model produced less imitation than those exposed to the consistently rewarded model, but more than the children whose exposure was to a consistently punished model. The authors argue that the effects of successive reward and punishment are additive and, therefore, in this situation cancel one another out. Since the everyday socialization of the child probably involves the observation of sequences of inconsistent reward and punishment of siblings and classmates, the further investigation of this variable is to be encouraged. Studies using children as models who emit novel but nonbizarre responses would be useful. In this study, as in many modeling studies, some skepticism is warranted about the potential for generalizing the findings to situations where models are not engaging in bizarre behavior ("Wham, bam, I'll knock your head off!").

A child's peers evidently are good sources of information about his aggressive behavior. Validation for the Peer Rate Index of Aggesssion is provided by the information that in a laboratory assessment situation structured as requiring cooperation, children rated as high aggressive by their 8-year-old peers made more frequent, intense and longer-lasting aggressive responses, and at shorter latencies, than did *S*s rated by peers as low aggressive [Williams, Meyerson & Eron (303)]. Construct validation for the same scale in the form of negative correlations between aggressiveness and social class, achievement test scores, IQ, and a positive correlation between tardiness and aggression is provided by Semler and associates (266) and in a replication study [Semler & Eron (265)]. Patterson (216) suggests that operant technology may have general utility for childhood assessment problems. He illustrates his point by showing that nursery school children with a known history of victimization showed greater decrements in responding when lever pressing led to exposure to cartoon pictures of victimization than did children who had been victimized less frequently.

In a circumplex reduction of information from their study of parent-child interaction, Hatfield, Ferguson & Alpert (111) found that maternal rejection (in the case of their circumplex, behaviors reflecting a combination of hostile and laissez-faire behavior) is associated with socialized aggression in boys and more outer-directed aggression and restlessness in girls.

Altruism.—Studies of altruism are rare in the developmental literature; this year's studies bear the stamp of social learning theory. The use of social reinforcement to strengthen sharing behavior is reported in preschoolers by Doland & Adelberg (60) and in primary grade children by Midlarsky & Bryan (190). The latter investigators found that neither a warm relationship between the dispenser of social reinforcement and the child nor explicit statements of pleasure following donations of M & M's to needy children was sufficient alone to induce any more sharing than observed in children with no training. Both warmth and explicit approval were necessary to the strengthening of anonymous charity in these young children. Possible mechanisms underlying this relation are discussed by the investigators: owing to the design and procedures employed, modeling as well as direct reinforcement are possibilities. Rosenhan & White (248) invited their fifth- and sixth-grade subjects to a bowling game for gift certificates. Those children who observed a model contribute one-half of his winnings to an orphans' fund during a first game subsequently contributed in a second game when the model was absent. No child who first played without a model contributed during the second game. Most of the subjects who made contributions in the second game had also made contributions in the first game when they alternated with the model in playing the game, thus suggesting that rehearsal (although not in this instance reinforced) as well as observation of a model is necessary for subsequent elicitation of altruism. Hartup & Coates (108) also demonstrate faciliatory effects on altruism of exposure to an altruistic model. Their study, however, makes a novel contribution to both the imitation and altruism literature in that aspects of the models' and observers' reinforcement histories were incorporated into the design, thus providing a different and probably more ecologically valid operation for rewardingness of a model than that encountered in most studies of modeling. Peer reinforcement histories were known to investigators through naturalistic observations of their behavior toward peers in the preschool setting. Children with histories of frequent reinforcement by their peers imitated a rewarding model more than a nonrewarding model. Children with histories of infrequent reinforcement from peers imitated nonrewarding peers significantly more than rewarding ones. The results are interpreted in terms of a dual theory of peer imitation; the incentive value of matching behavior to that of a peer is held to be greater for recipients of frequent social reinforcement. The recipient of infrequent social reinforcement, on the other hand, is presumed to be anxious in the presence of a nonrewarding model and imitation is in the service of anxiety reduction.

Peer relations.—Peer interaction in open field settings has rarely been subjected to the kind of molecular analysis evident in some of this year's research. Wahler (288) instructed the peers of his preschool subjects to ignore certain behavior with high baseline rates, and at other times to attend to or "play with" peers when they emitted behaviors with low baseline rates. Reversals of the same procedure were employed to reinstate baseline contingencies. Through the experimenter's instruction, it did prove possible for peers to alter the strength of high and low rate response classes by means of selective attention.

In an excellent series of studies, Hartup and associates (41, 108, 109) observed preschool children and tabulated the occurrence of generalized social reinforcers—giving positive attention and approval, giving affection and personal acceptance, submission, and token giving. Older children reinforced peers at higher rates than did younger children; about half of the reinforcements were spontaneous and half were responses to peer overtures; the continuation of the recipient's activity at the time of reinforcement was the predominant consequence of it. Amount of positive reinforcement given was positively correlated with the amount received.

In a second study, in which generalized negative reinforcers were also considered, sociometric acceptance scores proved to be positively correlated with the frequency of giving positive reinforcement and rejection scores with giving negative reinforcement. Neither the positive reinforcement-rejection nor the negative reinforcement-acceptance correlation was significant. More positive than negative reinforcement was received from both liked and disliked peers. While children received more positive reinforcement from liked than from disliked peers, receipt of negative reinforcement did not differentiate disliked from liked peers. For a small subset of the children, stability coefficients were calculated, based on fall and spring observations. Giving positive reinforcement and acceptance were relatively stable (r's $=.51$ and $.68$ respectively), but giving negative reinforcement and rejection were not.

In what surely must be the most exhaustive study of peer acceptance-rejection, and probably of peer relations per se, ever undertaken (overall $N = 37,913$), Sells & Roff (263, see also 238) were able to provide many definitive answers about the methodology of sociometric choice and the substance of peer acceptance and rejection. Their elegant 4-year longitudinal design permitted a simultaneous replication study of acceptance-rejection and its important correlates in third- through eighth-graders in Texas and Minnesota. Median split half reliabilities of peer choice (one-half of the classrooms' versus the other half's) average .6 for acceptance and .7 for rejection scores. The reliability of acceptance scores declines with age, while the reliability of rejection scores increases. Acceptance scores are more stable over time than rejection scores; stability coefficients for adjacent years are in the 40's and 50's. Acceptance and rejection scores are negatively correlated ($r = -.50$) but not so highly as to regard them as poles on a single dimension. Teacher ratings of peer relations correlate in the 50's with sociometric acceptance and in the 30's and 40's with sociometric rejection. The correlations between the status of chooser and chosen on both acceptance and rejection dimensions also are statistically significant but, being of the magnitude of .01 to .04 for acceptance and $-.11$ to $-.18$ for rejection, "illustrate very sharply the difference between statistical significance and practical importance" (263, p. 107). The common practice of correcting for the status of the chooser in computing sociometric scores for the chosen in sociometric studies is thus shown to be unnecessary and perhaps misleading. Careful analyses reveal resemblance between a child's sociometric status and that of siblings, including greater resemblance among twins than among other siblings. IQ, school grades, SES, and absence of family pathology are correlated positively with acceptance and negatively with rejection. The study of birth-order effects shows that youngest children are most liked and middle children most disliked.

Self concept.—The empirical study of the self concept does not have an extensive history of experimental or developmental study despite the centrality of the concept in many theories of social relations. The common hypothesis that attitudes toward the self are a function of the reactions of significant others has rarely been tested directly with children but is supported in a study by Ludwig & Maehr (177). Junior high school boys performed some physical tasks before a physical development expert who made either positive or negative evaluative statements. Not only were there persistent increases in self-concept following positive evaluation and decreases following negative evaluations, but preferences for physical activities related to the evaluated activities also showed increases. In a related study, Staffieri (278) provides an empirical basis for the interpretation of self-concept-related studies, particularly those that explain the effects of early and late maturing in terms of negative social feedback. Boys 6 to 10 years old were asked to rate silhouettes of three body types. Significant differences were obtained on 38 of 39 adjectives on which Ss made ratings The boys accorded favorable traits to the mesomorph; unfavorable, socially aggressive traits to endomorphs; and unfavorable, submissive traits to the ectomorph. The boys preferred to look like mesomorphs and for good reason, since boys who were mesomorphic in body build were sociometrically most acceptable to peers. Endomorphic boys received the lowest acceptance scores. Contrary to another common self-concept hypothesis, Katz & Zigler (142) argue that disparity between concepts of self and ideal self is positively related to developmental maturity. Maturity presumably brings a greater capacity to incorporate social expectations, which in turn lead to greater self-demands that cannot be fulfilled, and, consequently, to greater guilt. Commensurately, the more mature the individual the greater his capacity for cognitive differentiation, again leading to greater self-image disparity. Both CA and IQ differences were found in self-image disparity, with older and brighter children having greater disparities. Self-ratings were significantly lower and ideal-self ratings higher for older than younger subjects. As the authors point out, the common assumption that high self-image disparity indexes psychopathology apparently is unwarranted.

Studies of adolescents.—Good studies of adolescents were as rare in 1967 as they have been for the past several years. The kind of translation from psychoanalytic to social learning theory that has instigated and provided substantive content for social learning studies (e.g., of frustration-aggression, identification, conscience) is absent in studies of adolescence. We can think of no nonclinical developmental studies, for example, that directly bear on attachment processes in adolescence despite the fact that psychoanalytic formulations of adolescence, including Blos' most recent paper (19), continue to stress adolescent disengagement from attachment to parents. Perhaps the developmental framework provided by Piagetian theory will lead to more empirical studies of adolescent social behavior, given that the transition to formal operations coincides at least roughly with the events that provide a physical definition of the onset of adolescence. Propaedeutic steps have been taken by Elkind (66, 68), who discusses how some of the phenomena of adolescence—ambivalence, parent-child conflict, self-consciousness, construction of social facades and ideals—might be a function of the child's emergent capacity for propositional thought. In a study related to some of the issues raised by Elkind, Klineberg (149) found that the relation between indices of maladjustment and measures of orientation toward the distant future is positive in childhood but negative in middle adolescence. This correlational pattern was predicted on the general assumption that the child's images of the future are in the service of fantasy wish-fulfillment while the adolescent's anticipations, given formal operations, are under the constraint of logical thought. The more maladjusted the child, the more fantasy about the future serves as an escape; the more maladjusted the adolescent, the greater the threat posed by realistic anticipation of the future.

A well-rationalized new look at the problem of the psychological effects of early- versus late-maturing is taken by Peskin (219). He argues, from the point of view of psychoanalytic ego psychology, that the late-maturer is better prepared cognitively to cope with the somatic changes of puberty. Thus his findings and those of others that indicate greater motility, expressiveness, and flexibility in the late-maturer are taken to reflect greater tolerance for impulses rather than compensatory attention seeking.

Three papers about delinquency require mention, one because its careful reanalysis of the relations between ecological variables and delinquency allows the conclusion that there remains a negative relation between census tract-type SES variables and official delinquency rates when variables indicative of anomie are controlled [Gordon (97)]. Another is the first investigation of the role in subcultural delinquency of symbolic deviance. Lerman (162) devised a vocabulary test consisting of argot endemic to drug, bopping, and unorganized crime subcultures and administered it orally to 555 youths 10 to 19 years old. Knowledge of argot increases with age and peaks in late adolescence. There is an empirically rare but ecologically understandable sex difference: boys are superior to girls on this vocabulary test and maintain their superiority throughout the age range studied. Number of argot words known correlates with official delinquency reports, unofficial (self-reported) delinquency, and with subscription to deviant values (e.g., for toughness, kicks, conning others). Lerman argues not only that youth who share deviant symbols with peers engage in more illegal activities, but that police take cognizance of symbolic as well as value and behavioral deviance in dealing with adolescents. Sells & Roff (263) also make a contribution to the understanding of delinquency. They show that peer status is negatively associated with delinquency at upper SES levels but that the relation between the two is curvilinear at the lowest SES stratum. Here, low and high peer status adolescents both exhibit the same amount of delinquency and more than those with average peer status. This set of results is difficult to explain by means of psychological, disease-oriented theories of delinquency and provides some of the best evidence available for proponents of subcultural delinquency theory.

That adolescents want to be, need to be, are, and should be relatively independent of parental influence is a set of hypotheses that has more mythological than empirical status. Brittain previously (27) had claimed that compliance to peers is greater than compliance to parents in matters of choice central to the peer group, while the opposite is true of matters important to the adolescent's future status as an adult. Now (28) he presents new evidence which suggests that this content distinction is unwarranted and that parent compliance is greater than peer compliance the more important and difficult a choice is perceived to be by the adolescent. Bronfenbrenner (30) reports Soviet and American findings from a larger cross-national study of the differential impact of parents and peers on behavior and personality development. While adult pressure lessens peer group solidarity in both societies, the Bronfenbrenner findings suggest that peer pressure in the USSR strengthens commitment to adult-approved behavior, while in the U.S. it increases behavior deviant from adult standards. It is argued that this is the result of deliberate Soviet policy to use peer groups to implement adult socialization objectives.

Other studies.—The use of the rapid eye movement-interruption technique to study the dreams of 6- to 12-year-old boys is reported by Foulkes and his collaborators (83, 84). In general, the manifest dream content was seldom bizarre and most often was directly related to the major concerns of the boys' social lives. The presleep viewing of an aggressive film reduced dream intensity and the amount of hostile-unpleasant content. Weinstock (293, 294) reports a longitudinal study of the development of defense and coping mechanisms. The use of defenses such as denial and repression in males at age 30 is associated with paternal passivity during infancy, while the use of less primitive defenses is related to rejection during early adolescence. The use of intellectualization and projection is positively correlated with SES; denial correlates negatively with SES. Bronson (31) continues to extend her developmental study of emotional expressiveness and reactivity-control. Ratings on these dimensions made when her subjects were between 5 and 16 were correlated with Q-sort assessment of personality at age 30. Emotional expressiveness has the more stability and the more consistent and less complex adult correlates. Expressive-outgoing boys turn out to be gregarious, expressive men; girls high on this dimension are, as adults, domineering and somewhat pushy. The child accident-repeater, if male, is extraversive, daring, active, exploring, aggressive toward peers, impulsive, careless, unreliable —in short, he has characteristics which expose him more to hazards than his low-accident-liability peers and make him less able to cope with hazards when they are encountered [Manheimer & Mellinger (185)]. Girls who frequently have accidents share some of these characteristics, but attention-getting seems to be more central to their make-up than is the case with boys.

Rosenthal (249) compared attention and proximity-seeking to mothers and to strangers in the presence and absence of anxiety. On the whole, her preschool subjects emitted fewer dependency responses (attention- but not proximity-seeking) to strangers than to mothers and more dependency under high than under low anxiety arousal. Anxiety-induction had a stronger effect on proximity- than on attention-seeking. Wolman (313) embedded "mother" and "father" among the words in the Stanford-Binet Vocabulary subtest and administered it to 180 children from kindergarten to college age. Passive self-referent definitions were characteristic of the younger children. Although confounded in this study with a change from oral to written administration, at puberty a major shift in the nature of the definitions apparently occurs, and nonsubjective, essential characteristics of motherhood and fatherhood commonly emerge. In his presidential address to the American Psychological Association, Lindzey (169) presented some of the evidence for the negative biological consequences of inbreeding and concluded that the consequences are "sufficiently strong and deleterious to make it unlikely that a human society would survive over long periods of time if it permitted, or encouraged, a high incidence of incest" (169, p. 1055). The universally encountered incest taboo, then, may be said to be biologically guaranteed and Freud to be correct in his identification of the Oedipal wishes and their redirection as the core developmental problem.

One of the studies that kept us at our bibliographic task when interest flagged and attention waned was the following. Adler (1) secured drawings from 2906 5- to 12-year-olds of both sexes in 13 countries on 5 continents. The conclusion: "Children from all over the world are more likely to draw apple trees than any other type of fruit tree" (1, p. 19).

References of general interest.—Some recent books of particular interest to developmental psychologists have already been cited in the body of the chapter. The following can be added to the list: Baldwin (6); Hartup & Smothergill (110); Hess & Torney (117); Hill (121); Lambert & Klineberg (157); Lipsitt & Spiker (171); Neisser (203); Piaget (221, 223); Piaget & Inhelder (224); Stolz (281). For an astute characterization of the research habits of today's developmental psychologist by someone who ought to know them, see Siegel's (271) editorial.

POSTSCRIPT

We began this chapter by emphasizing the sheer bulk of a single year's developmental literature. We shall close it by noting, no doubt predictably, that this literature struck us as being of very uneven scientific significance. Some studies were quite exciting to read, full of promise as real and perhaps permanent contributions to our understanding of important developmental processes. Others we found dull and unimaginative, unclear in rationale and, above all, of uncertain implication for any substantive scientific problem. Although no research area had exclusive priorities on studies of either extreme, it was nonetheless our impression that the science of developmental psychology is faring better in some areas than in others. Since there is not enough space to explicate our prejudices in full detail, according to each class of study its due share of bouquets and brickbats, we shall limit this final section to some critical comments about a single area.

The area is that of research on children's learning, especially in its canonical forms (simple discrimination learning and transfer tasks, transposition problems, etc.). It is ironical that methodological criticisms should be leveled at a research enterprise so long esteemed for its scientific rigor and positivistic tough-mindedness, but we think they are justified. Most contemporary learning studies with children appear to be focused on whatever cognitive and other organismic processes have so far developed in the growing child as they are brought into play within a task setting designed specifically to produce organismic change (i.e., learning) as opposed to routine, "steady state" functioning. While this is obviously a worthwhile scientific endeavor, the tasks and procedures used frequently seem most ill-suited to the job.

On the one hand, they characteristically fail to elicit any significant kind and amount of organismic change in the child. What the child typically "learns" is which stimulus (stimulus class, stimulus relation) in the array is the correct one—inexplicably correct and correct for today only in this specific situation only. The "organismic change" thus amounts to a temporary pairing of two items which are already in the cognitive repertoire, rather than any genuine and substantive modification of the repertoire itself. While learning experiments of the noncanonical variety are by no means beyond criticism, the acquisition aimed at is at least either of cognitive (e.g., Piagetian training studies) or practical (e.g., behavior modification studies) significance.

On the other hand, the traditional learning experiment appears to be a very crude instrument for measuring the cognitive processes and abilities that the task situation elicits. As we think our review has shown, there are more direct and sensitive ways to assess, for example, the child's knowledge of classes and relations, his attentional biases, his perceptual skills, and his mnemonic strategies (e.g., rehearsal, clustering) and capacities than, say, by looking at the transfer data of a simultaneous discrimination or transposition task. As we read the situation, many students of children's learning have simply failed to adapt their measurement procedures to the changing definition of the research objectives in this area, and more broadly, to the changing scientific *Zeitgeist* within the field at large. Rigid adherence to traditional tasks and procedures where more innovative and imaginative methods are called for is, of course, an omnipresent danger—in other fields as well as in our own, and in other areas within our own. As one example, a number of recent Piagetian studies strike us as being rigid in precisely the same way; here, too, there are signs of an unthinking and doctrinaire reliance on what are fast becoming "established" testing methods. Nonetheless, we believe that the area of children's learning is, of all those reviewed, most beset by an excess of scientific conservatism.

LITERATURE CITED

1. Adler, L. L. A note on cross-cultural preferences: Fruit-tree preferences in children's drawings. *J. Psychol.*, 65, 15–22 (1967)
2. Ainsworth, M. D. S. *Infancy in Uganda* (Johns Hopkins Press, Baltimore, 471 pp., 1967)
3. Allen, K. E., Henke, L. B., Harris, F. R., Baer, D. M., Reynolds, N. J. Control of hyperactivity by social reinforcement of attending behavior. *J. Educ. Psychol.*, 58, 231–37 (1967)
4. Anisfeld, M., Tucker, G. R. English pluralization rules of six-year-old children. *Child Develpm.*, 38, 1201–17 (1967)
5. Baer, D. M., Peterson, R. F., Sherman, J. A. The development of imitation by reinforcing behavioral similarity to a model. *J. Exptl. Anal. Behav.*, 10, 405–16 (1967)
6. Baldwin, A. L. *Theories of Child Development* (Wiley, New York, 618 pp., 1967)
7. Bandura, A., Grusec, J. E., Menlove, F. L. Some social determinants of self-monitoring reinforcement systems. *J. Pers. Soc. Psychol.*, 5, 449–55 (1967)
8. Bandura, A., Grusec, J. E., Menlove, F. L. Vicarious extinction of avoidance behavior. *J. Pers. Soc. Psychol.*, 5, 16–23 (1967)
9. Bandura, A., Perloff, B. Relative efficacy of self-monitored and externally imposed reinforcement systems. *J. Pers. Soc. Psychol.*, 7, 111–16 (1967)
10. Barclay, A., Cusumano, D. R. Father absence, cross-sex identity, and field-dependent behavior in male adolescents. *Child Develpm.*, 38, 243–50 (1967)
11. Baumrind, D. Child care practices anteceding three patterns of preschool behavior. *Genet. Psychol. Monogr.*, 75, 43–88 (1967)
12. Baumrind, D., Black, A. E. Socialization practices associated with dimensions of competence in preschool boys and girls. *Child Develpm.*, 38, 291–327 (1967)
13. Bee, H. L. Parent-child interaction and distractibility in 9-year-old children. *Merrill-Palmer Quart.*, 13, 175–90 (1967)
14. Beery, J. W. Matching of auditory and visual stimuli by average and retarded readers. *Child Develpm.*, 38, 827–33 (1967)
15. Belmont, J. M. Perceptual short-term memory in children, retardates and adults. *J. Exptl. Child Psychol.*, 5, 114–22 (1967)
16. Bem, S. L. Verbal self-control: The establishment of effective self-instruction. *J. Exptl. Psychol.*, 74, 485–91 (1967)
17. Bernbach, H. A. The effects of labels on short-term memory for colors with nursery school children. *Psychon. Sci.*, 7, 149–50 (1967)
18. Blank, M. Effect of stimulus characteristics on dimensional shifting in kindergarten children. *J. Comp. Physiol. Psychol.*, 64, 522–25 (1967)
19. Blos, P. The second individuation process of adolescence. *Psychoanal. Study Child*, 22, 162–86 (1967)
20. Blum, E. R., Kennedy, W. A. Modification of dominant behavior in school children. *J. Pers. Soc. Psychol.*, 7, 275–81 (1967)
21. Bogartz, R. S. Extension of a theory of predictive behavior in young children to the effects of intertrial interval duration. *Psychon. Sci.*, 8, 521–22 (1967)
22. Bower, T. G. R. The development of object-permanence: Some studies of existence constancy. *Percept. Psychophys.*, 2, 411–18 (1967)
23. Bower, T. G. R. Phenomenal identity and form perception in an infant. *Ibid.*, 74–76
24. Brackbill, Y., Fitzgerald, H. E., Lintz, L. M. A developmental study of classical conditioning. *Monogr. Soc. Res. Child Develpm.*, 32 (8), Ser. No. 116 (1967)
25. Braun-Lamesch, M. Remarques sur le caractère global ou analytique de la comprehension du langage chez l'enfant. *J. Psychol. Norm. Pathol.*, 73–83 (1967)
26. Breznitz, S., Kugelmass, S. Intentionality in moral judgment: Developmental stages. *Child Develpm.*, 38, 469–79 (1967)
27. Brittain, C. V. Adolescent choices and parent-peer cross-pressures. *Am. Sociol. Rev.*, 28, 385–91 (1963)
28. Brittain, C. V. An exploration of the bases of peer-compliance and parent-compliance in adolescence. *Adolesence*, 2, 445–58 (1967)
29. Bronfenbrenner, U. The psychological

costs of quality and equality in education. *Child Develpm.*, **38**, 909–25 (1967)

30. Bronfenbrenner, U. Response to pressure from peers versus adults among Soviet and American school children. *Intern. J. Psychol.*, **2**, 199–207 (1967)

31. Bronson, W. C. Adult derivatives of emotional expressiveness and re-activity-control: Developmental continuities from childhood to adulthood. *Child Develpm.*, **38**, 801–17 (1967)

32. Bruner, J. S., Olver, R. R., Greenfield, P. M. (with others). *Studies in Cognitive Growth* (Wiley, New York, 343 pp., 1966)

33. Bryant, P. E. The causes of failures in children to sort by two different dimensions on successive trials. *Brit. J. Educ. Psychol.*, **37**, 320–28 (1967)

34. Burchard, J. P. Systematic socialization: A programmed environment for the habilitation of antisocial retardates. *Psychol. Rec.*, **17**, 461–76 (1967)

35. Cameron, J., Livson, N., Bayley, N. Infant vocalizations and their relationship to mature intelligence. *Science*, **157**, 331–33 (1967)

36. Canon, L. K. Motivational state, stimulus selection, and distractibility. *Child Develpm.*, **38**, 589–96 (1967)

37. Caron, A. J. Intermediate-size transposition at an extreme distance in preverbal children. *J. Exptl. Child Psychol.*, **5**, 186–207 (1967)

38. Caron, R. F. Visual reinforcement of head-turning in young infants. *J. Exptl. Child Psychol.*, **5**, 489–511 (1967)

39. Carpenter, G. C., Stechler, G. Selective attention to mother's face from week 1 through week 8. *Proc. Ann. Conv. Am. Psychol. Assoc., 75th*, Sept. 1–5, Washington, D.C., **2**, 153–54 (1967)

40. Chance, J., Goldstein, A. G., Schicht, W. Effects of acquaintance and friendship on children's recognition of classmates' faces. *Psychon. Sci.*, **7**, 223–24 (1967)

41. Charlesworth, W. R., Hartup, W. W. Positive social reinforcement in the nursery school peer group. *Child Develpm.*, **38**, 993–1002 (1967)

42. Charlesworth, W. R. *Development of the Object Concept: A Methodological Study* (Presented at Am. Psychol. Assoc. Meeting, New York, 1966)

43. Cirillo, L., Wapner, S., Rand, G. Differentiation of haptic exploration in two age groups. *Psychon. Sci.*, **9**, 467–68 (1967)

44. Clement, R. W., Milne, D. C. Group play therapy and tangible reinforcers to modify the behavior of 8-year-old boys. *Behav. Res. Ther.*, **5**, 301–12 (1967)

45. Cobb, K., Grimm, E. R., Dawson, B., Amsterdam, B. Reliability of global observations of newborn infants. *J. Genet. Psychol.*, **110**, 253–67 (1967)

46. Cohen, D. J. The crying newborn's accommodation to the nipple. *Child Develpm.*, **38**, 89–100 (1967)

47. Cohen, G. M. Conservation of quantity in children: The effect of vocabulary and participation. *Quart. J. Exptl. Psychol.*, **19**, 150–54 (1967)

48. Conners, C. K., Schuette, C., Goldman, A. Informational analysis of intersensory communication in children of different social class. *Child Develpm.*, **38**, 251–66 (1967)

49. Covington, M. V. Stimulus discrimination as a function of social-class membership. *Child Develpm.*, **38**, 607–13 (1967)

50. Cowan, P. A., Weber, J., Hoddinott, B. A., Klein, J. Mean length of spoken response as a function of stimulus, experimenter, and subject. *Child Develpm.*, **38**, 191–203 (1967)

51. Crane, N. L., Ross, L. E. A developmental study of attention to cue redundancy introduced following discrimination learning. *J. Exptl. Child Psychol.*, **5**, 1–15 (1967)

52. Cronbach, L. J. Year-to-year correlations of mental tests: A review of the Hofstaetter analysis. *Child Develpm.*, **38**, 283–89 (1967)

53. Crowell, D. H. Patterns of psychophysiological functioning in early infancy: A preliminary analysis with autonomic lability scores. *Merrill-Palmer Quart.*, **13**, 37–53 (1967)

54. Davol, S. H., Chittenden, E. A., Plante, M. L., Tuzik, J. A. Conservation of continuous quantity investigated as a scalable developmental concept. *Merrill-Palmer Quart.*, **13**, 191–99 (1967)

55. Denner, B., Cashdan, S. Sensory processing and the recognition of forms

in nursery-school children. *Brit. J. Psychol.*, **58**, 101–4 (1967)

56. Derks, P. L., Paclisanu, M. I. Simple strategies in binary prediction by children and adults. *J. Exptl. Psychol.*, **73**, 278–85 (1967)

57. DeVries, R. *Conservation of Generic Identity in the Years Three to Six* (Doctoral thesis, Univ. Chicago, Chicago, Ill., 1967)

58. Dickerson, D. J. Irrelevant stimulus dimensions and dimensional transfer in the discrimination learning of children. *J. Exptl. Child Psychol.*, **5**, 228–36 (1967)

59. Ditrichs, R., Simon, S., Greene, B. Effect of vicarious scheduling on the verbal conditioning of hostility in children. *J. Pers. Soc. Psychol.*, **6**, 71–78 (1967)

60. Doland, D. J., Adelberg, K. The learning of sharing behavior. *Child Develpm.*, **38**, 695–700 (1967)

61. Doris, J., Casper, M., Poresky, R. Differential brightness thresholds in infancy. *J. Exptl. Child Psychol.*, **5**, 522–35 (1967)

62. Drillien, C. M. The incidence of mental and physical handicaps in school age children of very low birth weight. II. *Pediatrics*, **39**, 238–47 (1967)

63. Eimas, P. D. Optional shift behavior in children as a function of overtraining, irrelevant stimuli, and age. *J. Exptl. Child Psychol.*, **5**, 332–40 (1967)

64. Eisenberg, R. B. *The Development of Hearing in Man: An Assessment of Current Status* (Rept. to Subcomm. Hum. Commun. Disord., Natl. Advisory Neurol. Dis. Blindness Council, Sept. 7, 1966)

65. Eisenberg, R. B. *Stimulus Significance as a Determinant of Newborn Responses to Sound* (Presented at Soc. Res. Child Develpm., New York, 1967)

66. Elkind, D. Cognitive structure and adolescent experience. *Adolescence*, **2**, 427–34 (1967)

67. Elkind, D. Conservation across illusory transformations in young children. *Acta Psychol.*, **25**, 389–400 (1967)

68. Elkind, D. Egocentrism in adolescence. *Child Develpm.*, **38**, 1025–34 (1967)

69. Elkind, D. Piaget's conservation problems. *Ibid.*, 15–27

70. Elkind, D., Van Doorninck, W., Schwarz, C. Perceptual activity and concept attainment. *Child Develpm.*, **38**, 1153–61 (1967)

71. Elkind, D., Weiss, J. Studies in perceptual development, III: Perceptual exploration. *Child Develpm.*, **38**, 553–61 (1967)

72. Ellingson, R. J. The study of brain electrical activity in infants. In *Advances in Child Development and Behavior*, III, 53–97 (Lipsitt, L. P., Spiker, C. C., Eds., Academic Press, New York, 272 pp., 1967)

73. Endsley, R. C. Effects of differential prior exposure on preschool children's subsequent choice of novel stimuli. *Psychon. Sci.*, **7**, 411–12 (1967)

74. Ervin-Tripp, S. *Sociolinguistics* (Working Paper no. 3, Lang.-Behav. Res. Lab., Univ. California, Berkeley, Calif., 1967)

75. Etzel, B. C., Gewirtz, J. L. Experimental modification of caretaker-maintained high-rate operant crying in a 6- and a 20-week-old infant (*Infans tyrannotearus*): Extinction of crying with reinforcement of eye contact and smiling. *J. Exptl. Child Psychol.*, **5**, 303–17 (1967)

76. Fantz, R. L., Nevis, S. Pattern preferences and perceptual-cognitive development in early infancy. *Merrill-Palmer Quart.*, **13**, 77–108 (1967)

77. Feld, S. C. Longitudinal study of the origins of achievement strivings. *J. Pers. Soc. Psychol.*, **7**, 408–14 (1967)

78. Fischbein, E., Pampu, I., Minzat, I. L'intuition probabiliste chez l'enfant. *Enfance*, 193–208 (1967)

79. Fitzgerald, H. E., Lintz, L. M., Brackbill, Y., Adams, G. Time perception and conditioning an autonomic response in human infants. *Percept. Mot. Skills*, **24**, 479–86 (1967)

80. Flavell, J. H. Role taking and communication skills in children. *Young Childr.*, **21**, 164–77 (1966)

81. Flavell, J. H., Beach, D. R., Chinsky, J. M. Spontaneous verbal rehearsal in a memory task as a function of age. *Child Develpm.*, **37**, 283–99 (1966)

82. Forsman, R. Age differences in the effects of stimulus complexity and symmetrical form on choice reaction and visual search performance. *J. Exptl. Child Psychol.*, **5**, 406–29 (1967)

83. Foulkes, D. Dreams of the male child:

Four case studies. *J. Child Psychol. Psychiat.*, **8**, 81–98 (1967)

84. Foulkes, D., Pivik, T., Steadman, H. S., Spear, P. S., Symonds, J. D. Dreams of the male child: An EEG study. *J. Abnorm. Psychol.*, **72**, 457–67 (1967)

85. Freeberg, N. E., Payne, D. T. Parental influence on cognitive development in early childhood: A review. *Child Develpm.*, **38**, 65–88 (1967)

86. Furth, H. G. Concerning Piaget's view on thinking and symbol formation. *Child Develpm.*, **38**, 819–26 (1967)

87. Furth, H. G. *Thinking Without Language: Psychological Implications of Deafness* (Free Press, New York, 236 pp., 1966)

88. Gelman, R. S. *Conservation, Attention, and Discrimination* (Doctoral thesis, Univ. California, Los Angeles, Calif., 1967)

89. Gewirtz, H. B., Gewirtz, J. L. Caretaking and background themes for Kibbutz infants: Age and sex trends. *Am. J. Orthopsychiat.*, **37**, 395–97 (1967)

90. Gewirtz, J. L. Deprivation and satiation of social stimuli as determinants of their reinforcing efficacy. In *Minnesota Symposia on Child Psychology*, **I**, 3–56 (Hill, J. P., Ed., Univ. Minnesota Press, Minneapolis, 239 pp., 1967)

91. Ginsburg, H. Children's estimates of simultaneously presented proportions. *Merrill-Palmer Quart.*, **13**, 151–57 (1967)

92. Ginsburg, H., Gamlin, P. Effects of instructions and class contrast on children's and adolescent's similarity judgments. *Percept. Mot. Skills*, **25**, 497–505 (1967)

93. Ginsburg, H., Rapoport, A. Children's estimates of proportions. *Child Develpm.*, **38**, 205–12 (1967)

94. Glucksberg, S., Krauss, R. M. What do people say after they have learned how to talk? Studies of the development of referential communication. *Merrill-Palmer Quart.*, **13**, 309–16 (1967)

95. Goldschmid, M. L. Different types of conservation and nonconservation and their relation to age, sex, IQ, MA, and vocabulary. *Child Develpm.*, **38**, 1229–46 (1967)

96. Gollin, E. S., Saravo, A., Salten, C. Perceptual distinctiveness and oddity-problem solving in children.

J. Exptl. Child Psychol., **5**, 586–96 (1967)

97. Gordon, R. A. Issues in the ecological study of delinquency. *Am. Sociol. Rev.*, **32**, 927–44 (1967)

98. Greenfield, P. M., Bruner, J. S. Culture and cognitive growth. *Intern. J. Psychol.*, **1**, 89–107 (1966)

99. Griffiths, J. A., Shantz, C. A., Sigel, I. E. A methodological problem in conservation studies: The use of relational terms. *Child Develpm.*, **38**, 841–48 (1967)

100. Grim, P. F. A sustained attention comparison of children and adults using reaction time set and the GSR. *J. Exptl. Child Psychol.*, **5**, 26–38 (1967)

101. Gyr, J. W., Brown, J. S., Cafagna, A. C. Quasi-formal models of inductive behavior and their relation to Piaget's theory of cognitive stages. *Psychol. Rev.*, **74**, 272–89 (1967)

102. Gyr, J. W., Fleisher, C. Computer-assisted studies of Piaget's three-stage model of cognitive development. *Psychol. Rept.*, **20**, 165–66 (1967)

103. Haaf, R. A., Bell, R. Q. A facial dimension in visual discrimination by human infants. *Child Develpm.*, **38**, 893–99 (1967)

104. Hagen, J. W. The effect of distraction on selective attention. *Child Develpm.*, **38**, 685–94 (1967)

105. Hagen, J. W., Sabo, R. A. A developmental study of selective attention. *Merrill-Palmer Quart.*, **13**, 159–72 (1967)

106. Hall, R. V., Broden, M. Behavior changes in brain-injured children through social reinforcement. *J. Exptl. Child Psychol.*, **5**, 463–79 (1967)

107. Harris, L. Effects of amount of relative novelty on children's choice behavior. *Psychon. Sci.*, **8**, 319–20 (1967)

108. Hartup, W. W., Coates, B. Imitation of a peer as a function of reinforcement from the peer group and rewardingness of the model. *Child Develpm.*, **38**, 1003–16 (1967)

109. Hartup, W. W., Glazer, J. A., Charlesworth, W. R. Peer reinforcement and sociometric status. *Child Develpm.*, **38**, 1017–24 (1967)

110. Hartup, W. W., Smothergill, N. L., Eds. *The Young Child* (Natl. Assoc.

Educ. Young Childr., Washington, D. C., 302 pp., 1967)

111. Hatfield, J. S., Ferguson, L. R., Alpert, R. Mother-child interaction and the socialization process. *Child Develpm.*, **38**, 365–414 (1967)

112. Hatwell, Y. *Privation sensorielle et intelligence* (Presses Universitaires de France, Paris, 232 pp., 1966)

113. Hayhurst, H. Some errors of young children in producing passive sentences. *J. Verbal Learn. Verbal Behav.*, **6**, 654–60 (1967)

114. Heckhausen, H. *The Anatomy of Achievement Motivation* (Academic Press, New York, 215 pp., 1967)

115. Heilbrun, A. B., Jr., Harrell, S. N., Gillard, B. J. Perceived childrearing attitudes of fathers and cognitive control in daughters. *J. Genet. Psychol.*, **111**, 29–40 (1967)

116. Heilbrun, A. B., Jr., Harrell, S. N., Gillard, B. J. Perceived maternal child-rearing patterns and the effects of social nonreaction upon achievement motivation. *Child Develpm.*, **38**, 267–81 (1967)

117. Hess, R. D., Torney, J. V. *The Development of Political Attitudes in Children* (Aldine Press, Chicago, 288 pp., 1967)

118. Hess, R. D., Shipman, V. Cognitive elements in maternal behavior. In *Minnesota Symposia on Child Psychology*, **I**, 57–81 (See Ref. 90)

119. Hetherington, E. M. The effects of familial variables on sex typing, on parent-child similarity, and on imitation in children. In *Minnesota Symposia on Child Psychology*, **I**, 82–107 (See Ref. 90)

120. Hetherington, E. M., Frankie, G. Effects of parental dominance, warmth, and conflict on imitation in children. *J. Pers. Soc. Psychol.*, **6**, 119–25 (1967)

121. Hill, J. P., Ed. *Minnesota Symposia on Child Psychology*, **I** (See Ref. 90)

122. Hill, J. P. Similarity and accordance between parents and sons in attitudes toward mathematics. *Child Develpm.*, **38**, 777–91 (1967)

123. Hill, K. T. Social reinforcement as a function of test anxiety and success-failure experiences. *Child Develpm.*, **38**, 723–37 (1967)

124. Hingtgen, J. N., Coulter, S. K., Churchill, D. W. Intensive reinforcement of imitative behavior in mute autistic children. *Arch. Gen. Psychiat.*, **17**, 36–43 (1967)

125. Hoffman, M. L., Saltzstein, H. D. Parent discipline and the child's moral development. *J. Pers. Soc. Psychol.*, **5**, 45–57 (1967)

126. Hofstaetter, P. R. The changing composition of "intelligence": A study in T-technique. *J. Genet. Psychol.*, **85**, 159–64 (1954)

127. Honzik, M. P. Environmental correlates of mental growth: Prediction from the family setting at 21 months. *Child Develpm.*, **38**, 337–64 (1967)

128. Honzik, M. P. Prediction of differential abilities at age 18 from the early family environment. *Proc. Ann. Conv. Am. Psychol. Assoc. 75th*, **2**, 151–52 (1967)

129. Howard, I. P., Templeton, W. B. *Human Spatial Orientation* (Wiley, New York, 533 pp., 1966)

130. Huttenlocher, J. Children's ability to order and orient objects. *Child Develpm.*, **38**, 1169–76 (1967)

131. Huttenlocher, J. Discrimination of figure orientation: Effects of relative position. *J. Comp. Physiol. Psychol.*, **63**, 359–61 (1967)

132. Inglis, J., Sykes, D. H. Some sources of variation in dichotic listening performance in children. *J. Exptl. Child Psychol.*, **5**, 480–88 (1967)

133. Inhelder, B., Bovet, M., Sinclair, H. Développement et apprentissage. *Rev. Suisse Psychol.*, **26**, 1–23 (1967)

134. Inhelder, B., Bovet, M., Sinclair, H., Smock, C. D. On cognitive development. *Am. Psychologist*, **21**, 160–64 (1966)

135. Johnson, P. J., White, R. M., Jr. Concept of dimensionality and reversal shift performance in children. *J. Exptl. Child Psychol.*, **5**, 223–27 (1967)

136. Kagan, J. On the need for relativism. *Am. Psychologist*, **22**, 131–42 (1967)

137. Kagan, J., Moss, H. A. *Birth to Maturity* (Wiley, New York, 381 pp., 1962)

138. Kaplan, B. Meditations on genesis. *Hum. Develpm.*, **10**, 65–87 (1967)

139. Kaplan, E., Yonas, P. Communication requirements and children's production of relational words. *J. Exptl. Child Psychol.*, **5**, 142–51 (1967)

140. Katkovsky, W., Crandall, V. C., Good, S. Parental antecedents of children's beliefs in internal-external control of reinforcements in

intellectual achievement situations. *Child Develpm.*, **38**, 765–76 (1967)

141. Katz, I. The socialization of academic motivation in minority group children. In *Nebraska Symposium on Motivation*, **XV**, 133–91 (Levine, D., Ed., Univ. Nebraska Press, Lincoln, 1967)

142. Katz, P., Zigler, E. Self-image disparity: A developmental approach. *J. Pers. Soc. Psychol.*, **5**, 186–95 (1967)

143. Kaye, H. Infant sucking behavior and its modifications. In *Advances in Child Development and Behavior*, **III**, 1–52 (See Ref. 72)

144. Keeney, T. J., Cannizzo, S. R., Flavell, J. H. Spontaneous and induced verbal rehearsal in a recall task. *Child Develpm.*, **38**, 953–66 (1967)

145. Kendler, T. S., Kendler, H. H. Experimental analysis of inferential behavior in children. In *Advances in Child Development and Behavior*, **III**, 157–90 (See Ref. 72)

146. Kingsley, R. C., Hall, V. C. Training conservation through the use of learning sets. *Child Develpm.*, **38**, 1111–26 (1967)

147. Klein, R. E., Hale, G. A., Miller, L. K., Stevenson, H. W. Children's paired associate learning of verbal and pictorial material. *Psychon. Sci.*, **9**, 203–4 (1967)

148. Klima, E. S., Bellugi, U. Syntactic regularities in the speech of children. In *Psycholinguistic Papers: The Proceedings of the 1966 Edinburgh Conference*, 183–208 (Lyons, J., Wales, R. J., Eds., Edinburgh Univ. Press, Edinburgh, 243 pp., 1967)

149. Klineberg, S. L. Changes in outlook on the future between childhood and adolescence. *J. Pers. Soc. Psychol.*, **7**, 185–93 (1967)

150. Klinger, N. N., Palermo, D. S. Aural paired-associate learning in children as a function of free-associative strength. *Child Develpm.*, **38**, 1143–52 (1967)

151. Kofsky, E. The effect of verbal training on concept identification in disadvantaged children. *Psychon. Sci.*, **7**, 365–66 (1967)

152. Kofsky, E., Osler, S. F. Free classification in children. *Child Develpm.*, **38**, 927–37 (1967)

153. Kohen-Raz, R. Scalogram analysis of some developmental sequences of infant behavior as measured by the Bayley Infant Scale of Mental Development. *Genet. Psychol. Monogr.*, **76**, 3–21 (1967)

154. Kohlberg, L., Zigler, E. The impact of cognitive maturity on the development of sex-role attitudes in the years 4 to 8. *Genet. Psychol. Monogr.*, **75**, 89–165 (1967)

155. Kohnstamm, G. A. *Teaching Children to Solve a Piagetian Problem of Class Inclusion* (Mouton, Uitegevers, Netherlands, 155 pp., 1967)

156. Kugelmass, S., Breznitz, S. The development of intentionality in moral judgment in city and Kibbutz adolescents. *J. Genet. Psychol.*, **111**, 103–12 (1967)

157. Lambert, W. E., Klineberg, O. *Children's Views of Foreign Peoples* (Appleton-Century-Crofts, New York, 319 pp., 1967)

158. Leibowitz, H. W., Gwozdecki, J. The magnitude of the Poggendorff illusion as a function of age. *Child Develpm.*, **38**, 573–80 (1967)

159. Leibowitz, H. W., Judisch, J. M. The relation between age and the magnitude of the Ponzo illusion. *Am. J. Psychol.*, **80**, 105–9 (1967)

160. Leibowitz, H. W., Pollard, S. W., Dickson, D. Monocular and binocular size-matching as a function of distance at various age-levels. *Am. J. Psychol.*, **80**, 263–68 (1967)

161. Lenneberg, E. H. *Biological Foundations of Language* (Wiley, New York, 489 pp., 1967)

162. Lerman, P. Argot, symbolic deviance, and subcultural delinquency. *Am. Sociol. Rev.*, **32**, 209–24 (1967)

163. Levine, J., Fishman, C., Kagan, J. Social class and sex as determinants of maternal behavior. *Am. J. Orthopsychiat.*, **37**, 397 (1967)

164. Levinson, B., Reese, H. W. Patterns of discrimination learning set in preschool children, fifth-graders, college freshmen, and the aged. *Monogr. Soc. Res. Child Develpm.*, **32**, 1–92 (1967)

165. Levison, C. A., Levison, P. K. Operant conditioning of head turning for visual reinforcement in three-month infants. *Psychon. Sci.*, **8**, 529–30 (1967)

166. Lewis, M., Goldberg, S., Rausch, M. Attentional distribution as a function of novelty and familiarity. *Psychon. Sci.*, **7**, 227–28 (1967)

167. Liberman, A. M., Cooper, F. S., Shankweiler, D. P., Studdert-

Kennedy, M. Perception of the speech code. *Psychol. Rev.*, **74**, 431–61 (1967)

168. Lichte, W. H., Borresen, C. R. Influence of instructions on degree of shape constancy. *J. Exptl. Psychol.*, **74**, 538–42 (1967)

169. Lindzey, G. Some remarks concerning incest, the incest taboo, and psychoanalytic theory. *Am. Psychologist*, **22**, 1051–59 (1967)

170. Lintz, L. M., Fitzgerald, H. E., Brackbill, Y. Conditioning the eyeblink response to sound in infants. *Psychon. Sci.*, **7**, 405–06 (1967)

171. Lipsitt, L. P., Spiker, C. C., Eds. *Advances in Child Development and Behavior*, **III** (See Ref. 72)

172. Livson, N. Towards a differentiated construct of curiosity. *J. Genet. Psychol.*, **111**, 73–84 (1967)

173. Lovaas, O. I. A behavior therapy approach to the treatment of childhood schizophrenia. In *Minnesota Symposia on Child Psychology*, **I**, 108–59 (See Ref. 90)

174. Lovaas, O. I., Freitas, L., Nelson, K., Whalen, C. The establishment of imitation and its use for the development of complex behavior in schizophrenic children. *Behav. Res. Ther.*, **5**, 171–81 (1967)

175. Lovell, K., Dixon, E. M. The growth of the control of grammar in imitation, comprehension, and production. *J. Child Psychol. Psychiat.*, **8**, 31–39 (1967)

176. Lu, E. G. Early conditioning of perceptual preference. *Child Develpm.*, **38**, 415–24 (1967)

177. Ludwig, D. J., Maehr, M. L. Changes in self concept and stated behavioral preferences. *Child Develpm.*, **38**, 453–67 (1967)

178. MacArthur, R. Sex differences in field dependence for the Eskimo. *Intern. J. Psychol.*, **2**, 139–40 (1967)

179. McCall, R. B., Kagan, J. Attention in the infant: Effects of complexity, contour, perimeter, and familiarity. *Child Develpm.*, **38**, 939–52 (1967)

180. McCall, R. B., Kagan, J. Stimulus-schema discrepancy and attention in the infant. *J. Exptl. Child Psychol.*, **5**, 381–90 (1967)

181. Maccoby, E. E. Selective auditory attention in children. In *Advances in Child Development and Behavior*, **III**, 99–124 (See Ref. 72)

182. Maccoby, E. E., Konrad, K. W. The effect of preparatory set on selective listening: Developmental trends. *Monogr. Soc. Res. Child Develpm.*, **32**(4), Ser. No. 102 (1967)

183. Mahler, M. S., McDevitt, J. B. Observations on adaptation and defense *in statu nascendi*: Developmental precursors in the first two years of life. *Psychoanal. Quart.*, **37**, 1–21 (1968)

184. Mandler, G., Stephens, D. The development of free and constrained conceptualization and subsequent verbal memory. *J. Exptl. Child Psychol.*, **5**, 86–93 (1967)

185. Manheimer, D. I., Mellinger, G. D. Personality characteristics of the child accident repeater. *Child Develpm.*, **38**, 491–513 (1967)

186. Mehler, J., Bever, T. G. Cognitive capacity of very young children. *Science*, **158**, 141–42 (1967)

187. Meneghini, K. A., Leibowitz, H. W. Effect of stimulus distance and age on shape constancy. *J. Exptl. Psychol.*, **74**, 241–48 (1967)

188. Mermelstein, E., Shulman, L. S. Lack of formal schooling and the acquisition of conservation. *Child Develpm.*, **38**, 39–52 (1967)

189. Meyers, W. J., Cantor, G. N. Observing and cardiac responses of human infants to visual stimuli. *J. Exptl. Child Psychol.*, **5**, 16–25 (1967)

190. Midlarsky, E., Bryan, J. H. Training charity in children. *J. Pers. Soc. Psychol.*, **5**, 408–15 (1967)

191. Milgram, N. A. Retention of mediation set in paired-associate learning of normal children and retardates. *J. Exptl. Child Psychol.*, **5**, 341–49 (1967)

192. Milgram, N. A. Verbal context versus visual compound in paired-associate learning by children. *Ibid.*, 597–603

193. Mischel, W., Grusec, J. Waiting for rewards and punishments: Effects of time and probability on choice. *J. Pers. Soc. Psychol.*, **5**, 24–31 (1967)

194. Mischel, W., Liebert, R. M. The role of power in the adoption of self-reward patterns. *Child Develpm.*, **38**, 673–83 (1967)

195. Moore, T. Language and intelligence: A longitudinal study of the first eight years. Part 1–Patterns of development in boys and girls. *Hum. Develpm.*, **10**, 88–106 (1967)

196. Moss, H. A. Sex, age, and state as determinants of mother-infant in-

52   FLAVELL & HILL

teraction. *Merrill-Palmer Quart.*, **13**, 19–36 (1967)

197. Moss, H. A., Robson, K. S. Maternal influences in early social visual behavior. *Am. J. Orthopsychiat.*, **37**, 394–95 (1967)

198. Mumbauer, C. C., Odom, R. D. Variables affecting the performances of preschool children in intradimensional, reversal, and extradimensional shifts. *J. Exptl. Psychol.*, **75**, 180–87 (1967)

199. Munsinger, H. Developing perception and memory for stimulus redundancy. *J. Exptl. Child Psychol.*, **5**, 39–49 (1967)

200. Munsinger, H., Gummerman, K. Identification of form in patterns of visual noise. *J. Exptl. Psychol.*, **75**, 81–87 (1967)

201. Munsinger, H., Weir, M. W. Infants' and young children's preference for complexity. *J. Exptl. Child Psychol.*, **5**, 69–73 (1967)

202. Murray, F. B. *Some Factors Related to the Conservation of Illusion-Distorted Length by Primary School Children* (Presented at Am. Educ. Res. Assoc., New York, 1967)

203. Neisser, V. *Cognitive Psychology* (Appleton-Century-Crofts, New York, 351 pp., 1967)

204. Odom, P. B., Blanton, R. L. Rule learning in deaf and hearing subjects. *Am. J. Psychol.*, **80**, 391–97 (1967)

205. Odom, R. D. Problem-solving strategies as a function of age and socioeconomic level. *Child Develpm.*, **38**, 747–52 (1967)

206. Odom, R. D., Coon, R. C. A questionnaire approach to transitivity in children. *Psychon. Sci.*, **9**, 305–6 (1967)

207. O'Leary, K. D., O'Leary, S., Becker, W. C. Modification of a deviant sibling interaction pattern in the home. *Behav. Res. Ther.*, **5**, 113–20 (1967)

208. Olmstead, D. L. A theory of the child's learning of phonology. *Language*, **42**, 531–35 (1966)

209. Osler, S. F., Trautman, G. E. Concept attainment: II. Effect of stimulus complexity upon concept attainment at two levels of intelligence. *J. Exptl. Psychol.*, **62**, 9–13 (1961)

210. Over, R. Haptic judgment of the Müller-Lyer illusion by subjects of different ages. *Psychon. Sci.*, **9**, 365–66 (1967)

211. Over, R., Over, J. Detection and recognition of mirror-image obliques by young children. *J. Comp. Physiol. Psychol.*, **64**, 467–70 (1967)

212. Over, R., Over, J. Kinesthetic judgments of the direction of line by young children. *Quart. J. Exptl. Psychol.*, **19**, 337–40 (1967)

213. Parke, R. D. Nurturance, nurturance withdrawal, and resistance to deviation. *Child Develpm.*, **38**, 1101–10 (1967)

214. Parke, R. D., Walters, R. H. Some factors influencing the efficacy of punishment training for inducing response inhibition. *Monogr. Soc. Res. Child Develpm.*, **32**(1), Ser. No. 109, 1–45 (1967)

215. Pascual-Leone, J., Bovet, M. C. L'apprentissage de la quantification de l'inclusion et la théorie opératoire. *Acta Psychol.*, **26**, 64–74 (1967)

216. Patterson, G. R. Prediction of victimization from an instrumental conditioning procedure. *J. Consult. Psychol.*, **31**, 147–52 (1967)

217. Patterson, G. R., Littman, R. A., Bricker, W. Assertive behavior in children: A step toward a theory of aggression. *Monogr. Soc. Res. Child Develpm.*, **32**(5), Ser. No. 113, 1–43 (1967)

218. Peluffo, N. Culture and cognitive problems. *Intern. J. Psychol.*, **2**, 187–98 (1967)

219. Peskin, H. Pubertal onset and ego functioning. *J. Abnorm. Psychol.*, **72**, 1–15 (1967)

220. Peters, D. L. Task variations and individual differences in Piaget's conservation of number. *Merrill-Palmer Quart.*, **13**, 295–308 (1967)

221. Piaget, J. *Biologie et Connaissance* (Gallimard, Paris, 430 pp., 1967)

222. Piaget, J. *On the Development of Memory and Identity* (Clark Univ. Press, Worcester, Mass., 42 pp., 1967)

223. Piaget, J. *Six Psychological Studies* (Random House, New York, 169 pp., 1967)

224. Piaget, J., Inhelder, B. *La Psychologie de l'Enfant* (Presses Univ. France, Paris, 128 pp., 1966)

225. Pick, H. L., Jr., Pick, A. D. A developmental and analytic study of the size-weight illusion. *J. Exptl. Child Psychol.*, **5**, 362–71 (1967)

226. Pick, H. L., Jr., Pick, A. D., Klein, R. E. Perceptual integration in chil-

dren. In *Advances in Child Development and Behavior*, **III**, 192–223 (See Ref. 72)

227. Pishkin, V., Wolfgang, A., Rasmussen, E. Age, sex, amount, and type of memory information in concept learning. *J. Exptl. Psychol.*, **73**, 121–24 (1967)

228. Pollack, R. H., Silvar, S. D. Magnitude of the Mueller-Lyer illusion in children as a function of pigmentation of the *Fundus oculi*. *Psychon. Sci.*, **8**, 83–84 (1967)

229. Quay, H. C., Sprague, R. L., Werry, J. S., McQueen, M. M. Conditioning visual orientation of conduct problem children in the classroom. *J. Exptl. Child Psychol.*, **5**, 512–17 (1967)

230. Ramirez, M., Castaneda, A. Paired-associate learning of sociometrically ranked children's names. *Child Develpm.*, **38**, 171–79 (1967)

231. Rapoport, J. L. Attitude and size judgment in school age children. *Child Develpm.*, **38**, 1187–92 (1967)

232. Reed, J. C. Lateralized finger agnosia and reading achievement at ages 6 and 10. *Child Develpm.*, **38**, 213–20 (1967)

233. Rehberg, R. A., Westby, D. L. Parental encouragement, occupation, education and family size: Artifactual or independent determinants of adolescent educational expectations. *Soc. Forces*, **45**, 362–73 (1967)

234. Rhine, R. J., Hill, S. J., Wandruff, S. E. Evaluative responses of preschool children. *Child Develpm.*, **38**, 1035–42 (1967)

235. Robinson, J. S., Higgins, K. E. The young child's ability to see a difference between mirror-image forms. *Percept. Mot. Skills*, **25**, 893–97 (1967)

236. Robson, K. S. The role of eye-to-eye contact in maternal infant attachment. *J. Child Psychol. Psychiat.*, **8**, 13–25 (1967)

237. Rock, I., Harris, C. S. Vision and touch. *Sci. Am.*, **216**, 96–104 (1967)

238. Roff, M., Sells, S. B. The relations between the status of chooser and chosen in a sociometric situation at the grade school level. *Psychol. Sch.*, **4**, 101–11 (1967)

239. Rohwer, W. D., Jr., Lynch, S. Form class and intralist similarity in paired-associate learning, *J. Verbal Learn. Verbal Behav.*, **6**, 551–54 (1967)

240. Rohwer, W. D., Jr., Lynch, S., Levin, J. R., Suzuki, N. Pictorial and verbal factors in the efficient learning of paired-associates. *J. Educ. Psychol.*, **58**, 278–84 (1967)

241. Rohwer, W. D., Jr., Lynch, S., Suzuki, N., Levin, J. R. Verbal and pictorial facilitation of paired-associate learning. *J. Exptl. Child. Psychol.*, **5**, 294–302 (1967)

242. Rohwer, W. D., Jr., Shuell, T. J., Levin, J. R. Context effects in the initial storage and retrieval of noun pairs. *J. Verbal Learn. Verbal Behav.*, **6**, 796–801 (1967)

243. Rosekrans, M. A. Imitation in children as a function of perceived similarity to a social model and vicarious reinforcement. *J. Pers. Soc. Psychol.*, **7**, 307–15 (1967)

244. Rosekrans, M. A., Hartup, W. W. Imitative influences of consistent and inconsistent response consequences to a model on aggressive behavior in children. *J. Pers. Soc. Psychol.*, **7**, 429–34 (1967)

245. Rosenbaum, M. E. The effect of verbalization of correct responses by performers and observers on retention. *Child Develpm.*, **38**, 615–22 (1967)

246. Rosenfeld, H. M. Nonverbal reciprocation of approval: An experimental analysis. *J. Exptl. Soc. Psychol.*, **3**, 102–11 (1967)

247. Rosenhan, D. Aloneness and togetherness as drive conditions in children. *J. Exptl. Res. Pers.*, **2**, 32–40 (1967)

248. Rosenhan, D., White, G. M. Observation and rehearsal as determinants of prosocial behavior. *J. Pers. Soc. Psychol.*, **5**, 424–31 (1967)

249. Rosenthal, M. K. The generalization of dependency behavior from mother to stranger. *J. Child Psychol. Psychiat.*, **8**, 117–33 (1967)

250. Rosenthal, R. Experimenter outcome orientation and the results of the psychological experiment. *Psychol. Bull.*, **61**, 405–12 (1964)

251. Rossi, S. I., Wittrock, M. C. Clustering versus serial ordering in recall by four-year-old children. *Child Develpm.*, **38**, 1139–42 (1967)

252. Rubenstein, J. Maternal attentiveness and subsequent exploratory behavior in the infant. *Child Develpm.*, **38**, 1089–1100 (1967)

253. Rudnick, M., Sterritt, G. M., Flax, M. Auditory and visual rhythm

perception and reading ability. *Child Develpm.*, **38**, 581–87 (1967)

254. Ryder, R. G. Birth to maturity revisited: A canonical reanalysis. *J. Pers. Soc. Psychol.*, **7**, 168–72 (1967)

255. Sackett, G. P. Response to differential visual complexity in four groups of retarded children. *J. Comp. Physiol. Psychol.*, **64**, 200–5 (1967)

256. Saltz, E., Sigel, I. E. Concept overdiscrimination in children. *J. Exptl. Psychol.*, **73**, 1–8 (1967)

257. Salzinger, S., Salzinger, K., Hobson, S. The effect of syntactic structure on immediate memory for word sequences in middle- and lower-class children. *J. Psychol.*, **67**, 147–59 (1967)

258. Sameroff, A. Nonnutritive sucking in newborns under visual and auditory stimulation. *Child Develpm.*, **38**, 443–52 (1967)

259. Sampson, E. E., Hancock, F. T. An examination of the relationship between ordinal position, personality, and conformity: An extension, replication, and partial verification. *J. Pers. Soc. Psychol.*, **5**, 398–407 (1967)

260. Santostefano, S., Stayton, S. Training the preschool retarded child in focusing attention: A program for parents. *Am. J. Orthopsychiat.*, **37**, 732–43 (1967)

261. Saravo, A. Effect of number of variable dimensions on reversal and nonreversal shifts. *J. Comp. Physiol. Psychol.*, **64**, 93–97 (1967)

262. Scott, P. M., Burton, R. V., Yarrow, M. R. Social reinforcement under natural conditions. *Child Develpm.*, **38**, 53–64 (1967)

263. Sells, S. B., Roff, M. *Peer Acceptance-Rejection and Personality Development* (Unpublished final rept., Off. Educ. Project No. OE5-0417, 1967)

264. Semler, I. J. Persistence and learning in young children. *Child Develpm.*, **38**, 127–38 (1967)

265. Semler, I. J., Eron, L. D. Replication report: Relationship of aggression in third grade children to certain pupil characteristics. *Psychol. Sch.*, 356–58 (1967)

266. Semler, I. J., Eron, L. D., Meyerson, L. J., Williams, J. F. Relationship of aggression in third grade children to certain pupil characteristics. *Psychol. Sch.*, **4**, 85–88 (1967)

267. Sgan, M. L. Social reinforcement, socioeconomic status, and susceptibility to experimenter influence. *J. Pers. Soc. Psychol.*, **5**, 202–10 (1967)

268. Shantz, C. U. A developmental study of Piaget's theory of logical multiplication. *Merrill-Palmer Quart.*, **13**, 121–37 (1967)

269. Shantz, C. U. Effects of redundant and irrelevant information on children's seriation ability. *J. Exptl. Child Psychol.*, **5**, 208–22 (1967)

270. Shepp, B. E., Turrisi, F. D. Learning and transfer of mediating responses in discrimination learning. In *International Review of Research in Mental Retardation*, **2**, 85–121 (Ellis, N. R., Ed., Academic Press, New York, 366 pp., 1966)

271. Siegel, A. E. Editorial. *Child Develpm.*, **38**, 901–7 (1967)

272. Sigel, I. E., Jarman, P., Hanesian, H. Styles of categorization and their intellectual and personality correlates in young children. *Hum. Develpm.*, **10**, 1–17 (1967)

273. Sigel, I. E., Saltz, E., Roskind, W. Variables determining concept conservation in children. *J. Exptl. Psychol.*, **74**, 471–75 (1967)

274. Sinclair, H. *Acquisition du Langage et Développement de la Pensée* (Dunod, Paris, 168 pp., 1967)

275. Smedslund, J. Determinants of performance on double classification tasks. I. Effects of covered vs. uncovered materials, labelling vs. perceptual matching, and age. *Scand. J. Psychol.*, **8**, 88–96 (1967)

276. Smedslund, J. Determinants of performance on double classification tasks. II. Effects of direct perception and of words with specific, general, and no reference. *Ibid.*, 97–101

277. Sokolov, A. N. Speech-motor afferentiation and the problem of brain mechanisms of thought. *Sov. Psychol.*, **6**, 3–15 (1967)

278. Staffieri, J. R. A study of social stereotype of body image in children. *J. Pers. Soc. Psychol.*, **7**, 101–4 (1967)

279. Stein, A. H. Imitation of resistance to temptation. *Child Develpm.*, **38**, 157–70 (1967)

280. Stevenson, H. W., Hess, E. H., Rheingold, H. L., Eds. *Early Behavior: Comparative and Developmental Approaches* (Wiley, New York, 303 pp., 1967)

281. Stolz, L. M. *Influences on Parent Behavior* (Stanford University Press, Stanford, Calif., 355 pp., 1967)
282. Strang, H. R. Relationship between focal point, location and inversion perception at three age levels. *J. Genet. Psychol.*, 111, 3–8 (1967)
283. Tighe, T. J., Tighe, L. S. Discrimination shift performance of children as a function of age and shift procedure. *J. Exptl. Psychol.*, 74, 466–70 (1967)
284. Turner, E. A., Rommetveit, R. The acquisition of sentence voice and reversibility. *Child Develpm.*, 38, 649–60 (1967)
285. Uzgiris, I. C., Hunt, J. McV. *Ordinal Scales of Infant Development* (Presented at 18th Intern. Congr. Psychol., Moscow, 1966)
286. Viney, W., Varner, G. A. The effect of overtraining and delay on reversal and nonreversal shifts in kindergarten children. *Psychon. Sci.*, 8, 407–8 (1967)
287. Vurpillot, E. Données expérimentales récentes sur le développement des perceptions visuelles chez le nourrisson. *Année Psychol.*, 66, 213–30 (1966)
288. Wahler, R. G. Child-child interactions in free field settings: Some experimental analyses. *J. Exptl. Child Psychol.*, 5, 278–93 (1967)
289. Wahler, R. G. Infant social attachments: A reinforcement theory interpretation and investigation. *Child Develpm.*, 38, 1079–88 (1967)
290. Wallach, L., Wall, A. J., Anderson, L. Number conservation: The roles of reversibility, addition-subtraction, and misleading perceptual cues. *Child Develpm.*, 38, 425–42 (1967)
291. Walters, R. H., Parke, R. D. The influence of punishment and related disciplinary techniques on the social behavior of children: Theory and empirical findings. In *Progress in Experimental Personality Research*, 4, 179–228 (Maher, B. A., Ed., Academic Press, New York, 1967)
292. Watson, J. S. Memory and "contingency analysis" in infant learning. *Merrill-Palmer Quart.*, 13, 55–76 (1967)
293. Weinstock, A. R. Family environment and the development of defense and coping mechanisms. *J. Pers. Soc. Psychol.*, 5, 67–75 (1967)
294. Weinstock, A. R. Longitudinal study of social class and defense preferences. *J. Consult. Psychol.*, 31, 539–41 (1967)
295. Weir, M. W. Age and memory as factors in problem solving. *J. Exptl. Psychol.*, 73, 78–84 (1967)
296. Weir, M. W. Children's behavior in probabilistic tasks. *Young Child.*, 23, 90–105 (1967)
297. Wender, P. H., Pederson, F. A., Waldrop, M. F. A longitudinal study of early social behavior and cognitive development. *Am. J. Orthopsychiat.*, 37, 691–96 (1967)
298. Werner, E., Simonian, K., Bierman, J. M., French, F. E. Cumulative effect of perinatal complications and deprived environment on physical, intellectual, and social development of preschool children. *Pediatrics*, 39, 490–505 (1967)
299. Weyer, R. S., Jr., Bednar, R. Some determinants of perseverance in achievement-related activity. *J. Exptl. Soc., Psychol.*, 3, 255–65 (1967)
300. Whiteman, M. Children's conceptions of psychological causality. *Child Develpm.*, 38, 143–55 (1967)
301. Wickelgren, L. W. Convergence in the human newborn. *J. Exptl. Child Psychol.*, 5, 74–85 (1967)
302. Willerman, L., Churchill, J. A. Intelligence and birth weight in identical twins. *Child Develpm.*, 38, 623–29 (1967)
303. Williams, J. F., Meyerson, L. J., Eron, L. D., Semler, I. J. Peer-rated aggression and aggressive responses elicited in an experimental situation. *Child Develpm.*, 38, 181–90 (1967)
304. Willner, A. E. Associative neighborhoods and developmental changes in the conceptual organization of recall. *Child Develpm.*, 38, 1127–38 (1967)
305. Winterbottom, M. R. The relation of need for achievement to learning experiences in independence and mastery. In *Motives in Fantasy, Action and Society*, 453–78 (Atkinson, J. W., Ed., Van Nostrand, Princeton, N. J., 1958)
306. Witkin, H. A. A cognitive-style approach to cross-cultural research. *Intern. J. Psychol.*, 2, 233–50 (1967)
307. Wittrock, M. C. Replacement and nonreplacement strategies in children's problem solving. *J. Educ. Psychol.*, 58, 69–74 (1967)

308. Wohlwill, J. F., Katz, M. *Factors in Children's Responses on Class-Inclusion Problems* (Presented at Soc. Res. Child Develpm., New York, 1967)

309. Wolf, M., Risley, T., Johnston, M., Harris, F., Allen. E. Application of operant conditioning procedures to the behavior problems of an autistic child: A follow-up and extension. *Behav. Res. Ther.*, **5**, 103–11 (1967)

310. Wolff, J. L. Concept attainment, intelligence, and stimulus complexity: An attempt to replicate Osler and Trautman (1961). *J. Exptl. Psychol.*, **73**, 488–90 (1967)

311. Wolff, J. L. Concept-shift and discrimination-reversal learning in humans. *Psychol. Bull.*, **68**, 369–408 (1967)

312. Wolff, P. H., Simmons, M. A. Nonnutritive sucking and response thresholds in young infants. *Child Develpm.*, **38**, 631–38 (1967)

313. Wolman, R. N. A developmental study of the perception of people. *Genet. Psychol. Monogr.*, **76**, 95–140 (1967)

314. Worell, L. Some ramifications of exposure to conflict. In *Progress in Experimental Personality Research*, **4**, 91–126 (Maher, B. A., Ed., Academic Press, New York, 1967)

315. Wright, J. C., Smothergill, D. Observing behavior and children's discrimination learning under delayed reinforcement. *J. Exptl. Child Psychol.*, **5**, 430–40 (1967)

316. Wylie, R. C., Hutchins, E. B. School-work-ability estimates and aspirations as a function of socioeconomic level, race, and sex. *Psychol. Rept.*, **21**, 781–808 (1967)

317. Zeiler, M. D. Stimulus definition and choice. In *Advances in Child Development and Behavior*, III, 126–156 (See Ref. 72)

318. Zeiler, M. D., Salten, C. S. Individual gradients of transposition and absolute choice. *J. Exptl. Child Psychol.*, **5**, 172–85 (1967)

319. Zern, D. Effects of variations in question-phrasing on true-false answers by grade-school children. *Psychol. Rept.*, **20**, 527–33 (1967)

BASIC DRIVES[1,2]

By Byron A. Campbell

Princeton University, Princeton, New Jersey

And James R. Misanin

Susquehanna University, Selinsgrove, Pennsylvania

Over the past ten years, since the general topic of motivation (37) was last covered in the *Annual Review of Psychology*, there has been a precipitious decline in research dealing with the theoretical issues generated by the learning theorists of the thirties, forties and fifties. No longer are there hosts of studies on the effects of motivation on habit strength, extinction, generalization, etc. Most of the questions generated by this approach either have been resolved or have reached a position of stalemate where further research brings small return. This is in contrast to research on the learning process itself where new mathematical theories and other new approaches have sustained interest in the old problems and directed attention toward new issues. Within the field of motivation Estes' (63) semiquantitative analysis of motivation has failed either to generate any substantial amount of research or to stimulate development of new quantitative theories of motivation. Similarly, Miller's "go" mechanism (120), which was hailed as an alternative or supplement to drive reduction, has not yet swept up an enthusiastic crowd of supporters bent on extending the theory.

The area of learning-oriented research on motivation receiving the greatest attention in recent years is that of incentive motivation, a topic which was excellently covered in last year's *Annual Review of Psychology* (24). As Brown & Farber noted, this marks the first time that primary and secondary motivation have been covered as separate topics. The present chapter is concerned with the effects of motivation on both learned and unlearned behavior from an atheoretical point of view, and our intent is to cover current developments which have not received extensive coverage in other sources. We have also restricted our coverage to research on infrahuman mammals in order to keep the chapter within bounds.

No new books on motivation have appeared since last year when Brown & Farber (24) listed the major books on motivation published during the past decade. They did, however, fail to mention one recent book, *Animal Behaviour* by Hinde (87), which contains an excellent synthesis of motivational and behavioral research from both this country and Europe.

[1] The survey of literature pertaining to this review was concluded in May 1968.

[2] Preparation of this chapter was aided by National Science Foundation Grant GB-5628.

DEFINITION

Nearly every writer on motivation in the past decade has pointed out that the term "drive" was first introduced to psychology by Woodworth in 1918 (185). While this may be the case, it probably did not constitute as big a step as it is now viewed. The word was used then as it is now to describe highly motivated people, and was also used prior to 1918 by eminent biologists such as Jennings (93) to describe the energetic behavior of hungry invertebrates. And long before that, Milton wrote in *Paradise Lost*: "A prowling wolf, whom hunger drives to seek new haunt for prey" (121). Moreover, Woodworth thought so little of the concept that he did not index the term in his 1938 textbook *Experimental Psychology* (186).

At the same time, far less attention has been paid to how the concept of motivation came to be the equivalent of drive for many theorists. As a term, motive has been used for centuries to describe the reason behind man's behavior, and it is only recently that the two concepts have become more or less synonomous for experimental psychologists [e.g., Hebb (86)]. This placid use of the two terms interchangeably may soon come to a halt, however, if the dichotomy proposed by Teitelbaum (172, 173) receives a favorable welcome from the scientific community. In his text, *Physiological Psychology*, he proposes that we apply the term motive to the activation of all behavior that is learned and drive to all behavior that is unlearned. Teitelbaum apparently reached this dichotomy in a two-stage process. In 1966 he first defined motivation as "the urge to perform a particular act, to obtain a certain object, or to produce a desired outcome," and proposed that we can best infer motivation by requiring the animal to perform an operant response to obtain the desired outcome. The purpose of this definition was to distinguish between reflexive and motivated behavior. In his words: "clearly, if the response is a completely automatic consequence of the stimulus we cannot speak of motivation" (172, p. 566).

Even before this definition of motivation appeared in print it received an ambivalent reaction from Dethier (54). While lauding its value as a means of pointing the way to possible differences that a broader definition might obscure, he hastened to state that learning should be used "as a criterion for motivation and not as a *sine qua non* for its existence" (54, p. 1139). Dethier's concern stemmed from his extensive study of the blowfly which thus far has not demonstrated even the slightest tendency to acquire operant behavior of any kind, and thus, by Teitelbaum's definition, is incapable of displaying motivated behavior. Yet by other criteria, e.g., the lowering of external thresholds and a broadening of the spectrum of adequate stimuli during deprivation and an increasing tendency to become active with increasing food deprivation, the fly is as motivated as the typical hungry laboratory rat.

In apparent response to this criticism, Teitelbaum added the concept of drive. As he puts it:

The internal state (e.g., hunger) of the fly does influence the excitability of its nervous system, and does control its feeding reflexes. Such a state, which is characteristic of all instinctive activities, can be called a drive state. A hunger drive exists: The fly's approach to and acceptance of food are increased automatically, in contrast to motivated behavior, where a central state apart from reflexes can be inferred each time the animal uses an arbitrary act to obtain food (173, p. 59).

This proposed dichotomy between drive and motivation is reminiscent of previous attempts to distinguish between the two terms. Numerous writers, particularly those concerned with human motivation [e.g., Melton (119); Shaffer (158); McClelland et al. (113)], have used drive to describe a pure energizing function and motive to describe behavior containing a directive or associative aspect. Among those concerned with animal behavior [e.g., Hebb (86); Brown & Farber (24); Hinde (87)], the concepts of drive and motivation have been more typically viewed as interchangeable hypothetical constructs which are in some way related to the energization or activation of behavior. As such, they are constructs which have never been firmly anchored by operational definitions. In fact, it is probably because these terms are so loosely defined that they are still widely used. We all recognize that there are times in the development of a science when we know that we are working with real phenomena, yet we are not conceptualizing them properly or concisely, and it is in just that state that the psychology of motivation lies. It is our belief that any attempt to precisely define or delimit the concept of drive or motivation at this time would tend to constrict creative research rather than lead to clarification of the concept. It seems apparent, as a case in point, that Hull's quantitative definition of drive, which led to a substantial amount of research, also restricted the type of research done in this country to an exceptionally limited range of problems.

Teitelbaum's distinction between drive and motivation is distressing at yet another level. In the evolutionary scheme of things we picture a relatively systematic phylogenetic development of the mechanisms and structures which regulate basic mechanisms such as food and water intake, with imbalances in these systems leading to motivating conditions like hunger and thirst. Thus to say that the 'reflexive' behavior of a fly obtaining food is driven, and the behavior of a bee that has learned the location of a succulent flower containing pollen motivated, implies a break in the evolutionary development of the homeostatic regulatory mechanisms that is unwarranted. What has entered into the picture is the ability of the organism to use learned as well as unlearned responses to regulate imbalances; the stimulus or condition for action in both instances is the same and the resultant behavior is what is typically called motivated or driven.

Dethier, in response to Teitelbaum's discussion of motivation, proposed the following alternative definition:

Motivation is a specific state of endogenous activity in the brain which, under the modifying influence of internal conditions and sensory input, leads to behavior resulting in sensory feedback or change in internal milieu, which then causes a change (reduction, inhibition or another) in the initial endogenous activity. The essence of motivation is endogenous activity, in the brain, correlated with a particular kind of behavior (55, pp. 119–20).

In our view this is more of a research credo than a definition of motivation, since knowledge of the neurological changes accompanying motivational states is so limited. It should also be noted that this definition bears a remarkable similarity to the drive reduction hypothesis, the main difference being in the locus of the excitatory activity. As such, Dethier's definition will also have trouble encompassing or predicting the vigorous activity elicited in satiated, quiescent animals by novel stimuli or by highly preferred substances such as saccharin or sucrose.

For the purpose of the present chapter we shall use the two terms, drive and motivation, loosely and interchangeably. But we have not done so with the terms drive and motive since "motive" has been used so often to connote human aspirations and goals. Our nonuse of the word motive is put forth as a preference rather than a theoretical issue.

REGULATION OF FOOD AND WATER INTAKE

Much of the research energy that was once directed at the complex of interactions between motivation and learned behavior is now focused on the analysis of the physiological and neurological variables that control hunger and thirst as well as other basic drives. Many experimental psychologists once concerned only with behavioral variables are now engaged in this type of research, and an ever-increasing number of physiological psychologists as well as physiologists are also directing their attention to this problem. In fact, so much work is now being done in this area that to describe it in even a cursory fashion would more than exhaust the pages allotted for this chapter. Fortunately for the reader interested in this topic, an entire volume of the *Handbook of Physiology* has just been devoted to "Control of Food and Water Intake" (36). The volume encompasses a wide variety of approaches to the problem, although the coverage lacks synthesis and tends to be superficial and idiosyncratic in many instances. Yamamoto & Brobeck (189) and Grossman (80) also provide good reviews of the field. For the remainder of this section we would like to report on a few recent developments which either were not covered in the above sources or that are of more than usual interest.

Regulation of food intake.—The striking feature of research and theorizing in this area is the lack of progress in determining the physiological stimulus for hunger. The earlier glucostatic, thermostatic, lipostatic and osmolarity theories have all acquired a care-worn look, and while all may be involved indirectly in the regulation process, none seems to be the critical stimulus for the onset or offset of hunger.

Lurking over the horizon, however, is the possibility that some component of the ventricular fluid [Myers (134)] may be the primary stimulus for hunger. In an interesting pilot study, Myers found that cerebral spinal fluid pumped from the third ventricle of a hungry monkey to either the third ventricle or the lateral hypothalamus of a satiated monkey produced eating and drinking shortly thereafter. Whether this ingestion was caused by some neurotransmitter, a local change in glucose or electrolyte concentration, or some unknown hormone is yet to be determined.

Another dimension of hunger that is of extreme importance to psychologists is that of long-term regulation of body size and growth. Collier and his associates (41, 43, 44) have emphasized the view that the animal's "genetic potential" determines optimal body size and composition. Furthermore, Collier postulates that any dietary deficiency leads the animal to defend the normal minimum ratio of the deficient component to body size. For example, if animals are placed on a restricted water regimen, the normal ratio of body water to lean body mass remains remarkably constant. No evidence of relative dehydration of any organ or tissue was found even after 12 days of continuous water deprivation. This defense of normal body composition takes place by a loss of body weight to the point where intake of the deficient constituent is sufficient to maintain the normal ratio of that item to body size. Collier also postulates that the best measure of deficiency-induced motivation is percentage of weight lost in relation to an *ad libitum* control group, and he presents impressive evidence showing that rate of bar pressing and spontaneous wheel running are linear log-log functions of percentage of body weight loss (39, 43).

Another development of major importance is the finding that hungry animals respond more to taste cues and less to caloric cues than nondeprived animals. Valenstein (176), for example, has shown that under *ad libitum* conditions rats consume greater quantities of a 3 per cent sucrose solution than of .25 per cent saccharin solution, but when placed on a restricted diet their preference gradually shifts so that they ingest greater quantities of the saccharin solution, an obviously maladaptive response. In related papers, Jacobs (91, 92) has shown over a wide variety of conditions that the metabolic properties of the diet control intake while the animal is in balance or in surfeit, but that during deprivation the sensory properties of food substances receive priority in regulating intake.

Specific hungers.—One of the exciting events of the past few years has been Rozin's re-examination of the basis of specific hungers. For decades psychologists and nutritionists have assumed that preference for a deficient dietary component was either due to learning (e.g., drive reduction) or to an unlearned preference for the missing substance. Rozin and his co-workers (144, 151–155), however, have revealed this to be a myth by showing that as a thiamine deficiency develops rats acquire an aversion to the deficient diet, which results in avid ingestion of novel diets even if the novel diet does not contain thiamine. If the diet does contain thiamine, feeding is continued at a high level, but if the novel diet is also deficient, the animal gradually ceases to ingest it over a three or four-day period. Moreover, the recovered animal continues to avoid the diet on which it became deficient, even if it now contains thiamine.

In an excellent follow-up of this work, Rogers (143) demonstrated that the same principle applied to calcium hunger and magnesium aversion, but that sodium-deficient rats display an unlearned, specific preference for sodium. Regulation of sodium supply in the body has also been studied extensively in recent years (e.g., 159, 181), but a review of that material is beyond the scope of the present chapter.

Regulation of water intake.—Many investigators now believe that there are two types of regulatory thirst: osmotic thirst and hypovolemic thirst. Osmotic thirst results from a deficit in intracellular water, and numerous studies have shown that rats restore normal osmotic pressure after administration of saline loads through any number of routes (e.g., intragastrically, intravenously or interperitoneally) by drinking or by sodium diuresis or both (48, 98). Drinking in response to saline loads is remarkably rapid (46, 99), and deficits in extracellular water as low as 1 per cent elicit drinking (98). Corbit (48) has just formulated a precise mathematical model which posits that drinking during osmotic thirst is proportional to the volume of water required to restore isotonicity. The model takes into account the rate of kidney excretion and predicts, surprisingly, that rate of kidney excretion is greater with saline loads of low concentration than with loads of high concentration, a prediction which was confirmed experimentally.

Another finding of interest is that osmotic thirst is not reduced by injecting isotonic saline solutions intravenously, even when severe hypervolemia results (47). In contrast, intravenous injection of water produces a rapid reduction in thirst produced by water deprivation (136).

Although it has been suspected for some years that the total volume of intravascular fluid might play a role in thirst, it is only recently that extensive research on hypovolemia has been undertaken. As is often the case, the upsurge in research stems from the development of a new technique. In this case, Fitzsimmons (74) and Stricker (164, 168) have found that injections of polyethylene glycol (PG) produce a relatively pure form of hypovolemic thirst. When injected subcutaneously, PG causes a sequestration of protein-free plasma from the intravascular fluid in the form of a localized isosmotic edema, thus removing it from general circulation. Because the sequestered fluid is isosmotic with plasma, osmotic thirst does not result.

In an excellent parametric study, Stricker (166) has determined the rate at which plasma deficit develops after the subcutaneous injection of PG, and has shown further that cumulative water intake is a direct function of plasma deficit. Intubation of isotonic saline is more effective than water in reducing hypovolemic thirst, but surprisingly the animals showed no preference for isotonic saline over distilled water (165).

Current research is directed at identifying the site of the volumetric receptors that signal hypovolemic thirst. Thus far it appears that neither nephrectomy, salivarectomy, nor denervation of the carotid sinus receptors selectively abolish hypovolemic thirst (169).

Psychogenic polydipsia.—In marked contrast to situations in which water ingestion is apparently under homeostatic regulation, is the situation, initially described by Falk (65), in which drinking emerges in the absence of a physiologic need and in opposition to homeostatic requirements (167). Food-deprived rats, given feeding sessions during which a small amount of food is available intermittently, develop a postprandial drinking pattern that leads to excessive water intake, much above that of rats having *ad libitum* access to food and water. Falk (64) has labeled this inordinate drinking psychogenic polydipsia.

Initially this phenomenon was observed in rats trained to bar-press for food on VI schedules, and Clark (34) proposed that polydipsia might be a form of superstitious behavior maintained through adventitious reinforcement. That the drinking develops over sessions (139, 140, 156), is influenced by the proximity of the water reservoir to the bar, and is affected by the proportion of short intervals in the VI schedule, suggest such an interpretation (34). It has been shown (161), however, that the drinking occurs after, not before, a reinforced response and rarely occurs if a bar press is not reinforced (156). It has also been found that the polydipsic pattern is reduced if a liquid meal replaced dry food (161, 167), and develops under FR (70, 161), limited-hold, and other schedules (65, 66) more deterrent to pausing than interval schedules. These findings argue against the superstitious behavior hypothesis, as well as the interpretation of drinking as a timing device (157).

The dry mouth produced by both dry food and the cellular dehydration accompanying eating (161, 172) also have been suggested as the underlying mechanism in psychogenic polydipsia. Obviously, mouth factors play a role, but this interpretation also has its limitations. Hydrating the animal before the session, for example, does not eliminate excessive drinking, and polydipsia has been shown to emerge following small "meals" of high water content and has failed to emerge with some dry foods (70). Also, that polydipsia takes time to develop (139, 156), and decreases with increases in meal size (69), argue against dry mouth as the sole factor involved. These arguments against the dry mouth hypothesis, however, may be more suggestive than conclusive, since the only liquid diet producing polydipsia apparently was not thoroughly emulsified (35); possibly the nonliquified portion was a key component. Other liquid diets such as Metrecal, milk, and 30 per cent sucrose solution eliminated the effect (70). Similarly, it is possible that the two dry foods failing to produce polydipsia—sucrose and dextrose pellets—are substances which do not produce a dry mouth "sensation."

Falk (68, 70), has proposed recently that psychogenic drinking may be "adjunctive behavior," a sort of displacement activity resulting from the thwarting of eating that results from the intermittent food schedule. But from this analysis it is difficult to see why the above-mentioned liquid and dry foods do not also produce the "adjunctive behavior." In support of the displacement hypothesis, it is interesting to note that when a water bottle is replaced with a running wheel, wheel running increases under intermittent food schedules (105). Unlike polydipsia, however, this "psychogenic running" occurs throughout the entire interresponse interval, and it is thus possible that adventitious reinforcement is exerting an influence.

Spontaneous Activity

Concomitant with the upsurge of research on the mechanisms that regulate intake of food and water is renewed interest in the processes that control spontaneous activity during deprivation conditions. Historically, the early studies on activity stemmed from peripheral theories of hunger and thirst [see Rosenzweig (148) for an excellent review of these theories and their development]. Stimuli arising from local sites, e.g., stomach contractions and dry mouth, were assumed to have drive or motivating properties which goaded the animal into activity, and spontaneous activity was often considered the simplest and most direct measure of drive. This view persisted until the middle 1940's and early 50's when two new analyses of spontaneous activity appeared. The first of these was the idea that spontaneous activity might play some homeostatic role in the internal economy of the organism (22, 23) and the second was that deprivation may alter the reactivity of the animal to environmental stimuli (29). Current research on these two views and other recent developments in activity are reported below.

Regulation versus reactivity.—The concept that activity might serve some regulatory function apparently was first introduced by Brobeck in 1945 (22) as a corollary of his thermostatic theory of food intake. In the absence of food, homeotherms were hypothesized to resort to spontaneous activity as a substitute thermoregulatory mechanism. Hamilton (85) has recently reviewed this position uncritically and extended it to account for the normal high levels of running found in nondeprived rats. According to his analysis, the rat occasionally indulges in running instead of eating to keep warm. As evidence Hamilton notes that rats deprived of exercise eat more and gain more weight, and he postulates that "perhaps this is a case in which temperature regulation may have priority over regulation of body weight" (85, p. 291).

In contrast to this notion that *ad libitum* activity might serve some regulatory function is the work of Kavanau (97) on the behavior-eliciting characteristics of wheels. He finds, for example, that deermice prefer square wheels or round wheels with hurdles to plain round wheels, a finding which prompted him to postulate that animals run in order to indulge in "split-second timing, coordination of movements, and quick reflex actions" (97, p. 1630). Running would thus appear to be much more than a simple response which serves to raise body temperature.

Other negative evidence for the thermoregulatory hypothesis (27) showed that food-deprived rats become active in wheels at high environmental temperatures which prevent hypothermia, and that *ad libitum* rats run to the point of severe hyperthermia. In addition, food-deprived rats given a choice between a heated compartment and an activity wheel increased both running and the time spent in the heated compartment (28).

Water-deprived rats, who also became seriously hypothermic, showed an increase in running and a decrease in time spent in the heated compartment. Hypothermic water-deprived animals thus avoid an environment which would raise their body temperature to normal and apparently run in spite of the fact that running raises body temperature.

Collier & Squibb (44) report that a high protein diet both lowers body temperature and decreases running, contrary to the thermoregulatory hypothesis. Temperatures were recorded only twice daily, however, and these results should be viewed cautiously since it is evident from continuous temperature recordings (27) that body temperature varies enormously during the course of day. In a related direct test of the thermoregulatory basis of hunger, Grossman & Rechtschaffen (81) have recently published an elegant study showing a complete absence of correlation between brain temperatures and the onset and offset of food ingestion.

These negative results for the thermoregulatory basis of activity do not rule out the possibility that running serves some other regulatory function. For example, Collier, Squibb & Jackson (45) proposed that running by protein-deficient rats might increase metabolic rate and total amount of food consumed, thereby increasing the amount of protein available per gram of body tissue. This assumes that the carbohydrate portion of the diet is more likely to be metabolized by exercise than the protein component. Unfortunately, a direct test of this hypothesis (44) failed to show any increase in protein synthesis in rats allowed access to running wheels. In related experiments, Collier and his associates (40, 42) reported that work expended rather than distance traveled or time spent running is invariant across wheels of different sizes and treadmills of different slopes. From this they again concluded that "work may serve some function in the regulation of physiological parameters within the organism such as body weight and composition" (40, p. 10). Similarly, there is a remarkable correspondence between the percentage of weight lost during food or water deprivation and the amount of wheel running (39, 175), a finding which could be interpreted as suggesting that running plays some regulatory function.

Paradoxically, recent studies (150, 160) have demonstrated that running has disastrous consequences for animals maintained on restricted diets. Rats housed in activity wheels with an attached living cage eat less, lose weight rapidly, and ultimately die when they are allowed access to food for only one hour per day (during which time they are locked out of the wheel so running does not directly compete with eating) while control rats adapt to the schedule with ease.

In a more general sense, these studies highlight our lack of knowledge of the physiological conditions which lead to heightened activity. Until recently it has been generally assumed that the physiological stimuli which govern the ingestion of food and water also control increases in activity in the absence of those essentials. But two recent papers (79, 178) report that hypertonic salt loads, which induce thirst as a function of dosage, produce a decrement in wheel running proportionate to dosage. Control rats, deprived of water, showed increases in running under the same experimental conditions. Pure osmotic thirst is thus not a stimulus for heightened activity.

In direct contrast to the hypothesis that activity during deprivation serves some regulatory function is the view that deprivation conditions alter the reactions of the animal to environmental stimuli (29). Research and theory related to this approach have been reviewed recently by Baumeister, Hawkins & Cromwell (7), as well as by Bolles (18) and Cofer & Appley (38). One recent finding relevant to this position is contained in a report by Collier & Squibb (44) indicating that protein-deficient rats housed in a communal environment where they can see and hear other rats in adjacent wheels are nearly twice as active as rats housed in individual sound-isolated compartments. This finding both supports the increased reactivity hypothesis and weakens the view that running during a deficiency serves some regulatory function. Similarly, Lát (102, 103) and Frankova (76) have reported that protein deficiency increases "rearing," cage crossings, and other indices of reactivity. More direct tests of the reactivity hypothesis, however, have not been as consistent. Blanchard & Blanchard (15) report no difference in reactivity to foot shock during food deprivation as measured by jumps and flinches; and Bolles & Younger (20), using a direct observation technique, found that food deprivation did not lower auditory response thresholds as measured by startle, exploratory behavior, and disruption of any ongoing behavior.

On the other hand, Tapp (170) and Tapp & Simpson (171) have shown in well-controlled experiments that both food and water deprivation increase the rate of responding for light-onset. At a theoretical level, a resolution of these discrepancies has been offered by Campbell et al. (30, p. 127), who proposed "that the range and variety of stimuli which elicit activity, both in the satiated and deprived organism, vary enormously from species to species as a result of evolutionary development." Elaborating this argument, it appears quite plausible that the rat would become more reactive to changes in light intensity during deprivation because of its nocturnal feeding habits and remain unchanged in responsitivity to pain and auditory stimuli which have no adaptive significances in so far as feeding or drinking are concerned. This hypothesis stemmed from the finding that chicks, rabbits, hamsters, and guinea pigs all showed dramatically different patterns of activity during terminal deprivation in the same activity measuring device (30). Chicks, for example, became active during both hunger and thirst, while rabbits showed a progressive decrease in activity under the same deprivation conditions. Moreover, the patterns of activity were different in wheels and stabilimeter cages for the guinea pigs and hamsters, a finding which had been reported earlier for rats (25).

Direct observation of rats' activity during food and water deprivation also yields a picture different from that obtained using either stabilimeter cages or activity wheels (17, 111). Some understanding of these discrepant results may emerge from the recent finding that in the rat two separate but partially overlapping neural systems appear to regulate spontaneous activity in wheels and stabilimeter cages (107).

Cornish & Mrosovsky (49) investigated species differences in activity of four hibernating and two nonhibernating rodents. Interestingly, only one hibernator, chipmunks, showed a decrease in running activity, while three others showed either slight (dormice and ground squirrels) or substantial (hamsters) increments in wheel running during food deprivation. Nonhibernators, rats and guinea pigs, both showed significant increments. These findings appear to rule out any simple generalization suggesting that the normal response to deprivation in hibernators is inactivity.

The role of reinforcement in the etiology of activity.—Several investigators (e.g. 73, 187) have postulated that the increase in activity seen during food and other deprivation conditions is nothing more than the evocation of previously learned instrumental response sequences acquired under previous deprivation and reinforcement conditions. Wright (187), for example, adulterated rats' diets with two levels of quinine and found that the group receiving the smaller amount of quinine ate more and displayed greater activity in running wheels than the group receiving the more severely debased diet. He interpreted this as indicating that the former group was reinforced more frequently for wheel running and hence ran more. In a second experiment, he fed rats only during the dark period or only during the light period of the light-dark cycle and found that activity tends to increase during the period in which food is available and decrease when it is absent. Anderson & Miles (1) paired a "noise-off" condition with food in mildly deprived rats and found that this increased activity as compared to a "noise-on" nonreinforced condition. They were able to demonstrate discrimination-reversal training, extinction, and spontaneous recovery. Similarly, animals exposed to successive deprivations become more active with each succeeding deprivation experience, suggesting that learning plays some role in deprivation-induced activity (59).

While learning may play some role in the heightened activity observed during deprivation, several studies have shown that specific prior reinforcement of running in the activity wheel is not necessary to produce an increase in running during food deprivation. Finger (72) deprived naive rats of food and then placed them in activity wheels and found that they were more active than the nondeprived controls. Wright, Gescheider & Johnson (188) confirmed this result in rats which had been habituated to wheels but which were prevented from developing reinforced wheel-running by always feeding them in a different setting.

The major study on this topic in recent years, however, is that of Bindra & Palfai (13). In an ingenious experiment they partially immobilized rats in a plastic restraining device which contained a small drinking cup located just beneath the animal's mouth. After habituation, stimuli were paired either with the presentation of water (CS+), the presentation of electric shock applied to the rear legs with fixed electrodes (CS−) or no unconditioned stimulus (CS°). The effects of these stimuli on various types of activity were then measured in a larger cage under conditions of mild water deprivation. CS+ increased activity, CS− decreased it, and CS° produced little or no change. These results demonstrate that incentive-motivational states can influence activity without prior reinforcement or punishment of specific instrumental response sequences. It might still be argued, however, that the pairing of stimuli with positive and negative incentive conditions evokes, under the test conditions, responses that were learned previously by the animal in its normal course of development. Future research on animals without a prior history of reinforcement or punishment, such as the neonatal guinea pig or chick, are necessary to firmly establish the independence of this phenomenon.

Bindra (12) then incorporated these findings, along with many others in the activity and neurophysiological literature, into an important theoretical article on the neuropsychological basis of general and instrumental activity. At the neural level, drive was postulated to activate species-typical consummatory behaviors such as those described by Glickman & Schiff (77); facilitate "selective attention" to relevant consummatory stimuli; energize a nonspecific motivational system; and increase motor readiness through activation of the midbrain reticular system. The paper is an excellent synthesis of current neural and behavioral knowledge and is certain to stimulate further research and theorizing on the neural basis of motivation and activity.

ACTIVATION AND AROUSAL

Activation and arousal are two intertwined and currently interchangeable concepts that are frequently put forth as an alternative to the drive concept (11, 61, 86, 108). Basically, activation theory posits that there is an optimal level of "tonic" background neural activity for any given organized neural activity. Too much background activity (high activation) disrupts sequential or organized neural activity and too little (low activation) provides insufficient support (86, 109). From this neural model they then predict that the relation of performance to activation level (drive) is an inverted U-shaped function.

Currently, this concept is at a stage of crisis on several fronts. Lacey (101) has summarized a large body of evidence primarily from the psychophysiological literature which suggests that autonomic arousal, electrocortical arousal, and behavioral arousal are different forms of arousal, each imperfectly coupled and complexly interacting. Lacey contends that neither interindividual nor intraindividual correlations among autonomic measures are large enough to warrant their utilization as criteria for gauging the activation level, and he contends further that different stimulus-situations reliably produce different patterns of somatic response (situational stereotypy). Finally, evidence is presented suggesting that the autonomic nervous system is not always a passive index of CNS functioning; oftentimes, the

CNS and other "arousal systems" interact cybernetically—thus producing "homeostatic brakes" upon one another.

Malmo & Bélanger (110) have responded vigorously and extensively to these criticisms by first acknowledging the need to revise the basic model and then rebutting in detail many of Lacey's criticisms while accepting others. The net result appears to be that the concept of arousal has lost a good deal of the elegant simplicity typical of newborn theories but that it is still capable of spawning a good deal of important research.

Also relevant to arousal theory and not reviewed by Lacey are a number of papers dealing with the relationship between heart rate, degree of food or water deprivation, and instrumental performance in animals. In Malmo's original papers (108, 109) heart rate, along with a number of other physiological indices, was proposed as a potentially superior measure of motivation (arousal) to the then traditional measures, such as hours of deprivation. In support of this view he cited the Bélanger & Feldman (10) findings showing that heart rate increased linearly with deprivation while bar-pressing for water increased up to 48 hr and then declined. Malmo was careful to note that heart rate increased only when the animal was in the experimental compartment pressing the lever or drinking; outside that compartment heart rate was lower and more variable. Several subsequent studies have confirmed this observation [e.g., Eisman (62); Ducharme (60); Goldstein, Stern & Rothenberg (78)], and other studies have shown that the increase in heart rate was not an artifact of inanition (58, 83) or adaption to a particular deprivation schedule (84). Thirst induced by hypertonic saline also decreases heart rate except when the animal is allowed access to water (137). In contrast, Doerr & Hokanson (58), in a carefully executed study, found that heart rate following various degrees of food deprivation did not increase while the animal was bar-pressing for food during the first 25 min of a 30-min session. Only during the last 5 min of the session was there a positive correlation between degree of deprivation and heart rate, suggesting that repletion of metabolic deficiency may play an important role in the usually obtained increases in heart rate!

On the behavioral side, the inverted U-shaped function is also in question. Collier and his co-workers (39, 43) report that rate of bar-pressing for both food and water is a linear log-log function of per cent weight loss for weight losses up to 30 per cent in animals that are maintained on restricted food or water rations. Since it takes at least 5 to 7 days for totally deprived rats to incur a weight loss of 30 per cent, these results must be viewed as discrepant with those recently summarized by Malmo & Bélanger (110). On the basis of these and other results, it seems quite likely that the function relating degree of deprivation to instrumental performance will vary as a function of type of maintenance schedule, degree of training, reinforcer quality, etc. It is also interesting to note that activation theorists have generally ignored the well-established finding that the form of the function relating drive to learning and/or performance varies as a function of task complexity (21).

The experiments on instrumental escape and avoidance reviewed elsewhere in this chapter also indicate that there is no simple relationship between aversive stimulus intensity and performance.

AVERSIVE MOTIVATION AND LEARNING

In prior years it would have been conventional to consider the effects of appetitive and aversive motivation on learning as a single topic, but the former was treated in some detail in last year's chapter on "Secondary Motivational Systems" and hence will not be considered here.

The most important development in the area of aversive motivation and learning in recent years is the finding that acquisition of avoidance responding in a shuttle-box is inversely related to shock intensity (104, 128). This result is novel in so much as a direct relationship is typically obtained between shock intensity and learning in other situations (174). Moyer & Korn (128) implicated disorganized escape behavior as a factor contributing to this poorer learning at high shock levels, but Theios, Lynch & Lowe (174) found escape behavior to be unaffected by shock intensity in the shuttle-avoidance situation. These investigators suggested that the rat shows a strong tendency not to re-enter the compartment in which it was shocked on the previous trial and thus develops a competing "staying response," the strength of which increases as a direct function of shock intensity. D'Amato & Fazzaro (52) and Bolles & Warren (19) offered similar competing response interpretations for the inverse relationship they later observed between shock intensity and the rate of learning a discriminated bar-press avoidance response. D'Amato & Fazzaro suggested (52) that a disassociation of fear from the competing response would lead to a positive relationship between shock intensity and rate of avoidance learning. "One-way" avoidance conditioning in rats and discriminated bar-press avoidance in gerbils were offered as examples of situations in which this disassociation may obtain. These situations, however, may merely exemplify conditions under which the competing response is removed, rather than conditions under which fear and competing responses are disassociated.

Some of the above studies have also shown that extinction of avoidance responding does not vary with training shock level, even though acquisition was inversely related to intensity. In an analysis of this result, D'Amato, Fazzaro & Etkin (53) suggested that the strong competing responses acquired during acquisition at high shock levels may counterbalance the incremental effect high drive otherwise has on resistance to extinction. In an experiment designed to separate these two factors, they conditioned avoidance in various groups of rats under a favorable shock intensity, varied shock level over only the latter part of training, and then tested for resistance to extinction. Although low shock was advantageous in conditioning, maintenance of the avoidance response and resistance to extinction were directly related to shock intensity.

McAllister & McAllister (112) used a two-stage paradigm to investigate the role of drive and reward in aversive conditioning in order to avoid having two sources of drive and reward (e.g., pain and fear and their reduction) associated with a particular response. In the first stage, drive level was manipulated by varying the number of drive stimuli to which fear was conditioned with inescapable shock. In the second stage, the testing situation, shock (pain) was omitted and fear-drive reduction was varied by using a novel or familiar safe box to which subjects escaped from the previously fear-conditioned stimuli. Thus, high drive was associated with the greater amount of fear-conditioned stimuli, and greater drive reduction with the familiar compartment. Two experiments were run, one employing a high level of shock and one a low level. With the high shock intensity, high drive was superior to low drive, and high drive-high reward group differed from all other groups which did not differ among themselves. These results were interpreted to be consistent with Black's (14) analysis of the interaction of drive and incentive.

Woods, Davidson & Peters (183) and Woods & Holland (184) have recently reported a series of studies showing that a constant reduction in water temperature is equally reinforcing over a wide range of drive (temperature) levels. At first blush, these results appear to contradict the general principle that the reinforcing properties of stimulus reduction follow Weber's law [Campbell (26)], from which it follows that a fixed amount of reinforcement should be less reinforcing at high drive levels. But this interpretation ignores the fact that mammals adapt quickly to temperature extremes and that even small changes in temperature from those levels yield the sensation of warmth or cold (186). In a related study, Woods & Campbell (182) determined the relative aversiveness of cold water and white noise using a spatial preference technique. The most intriguing aspect of this research was that the function relating noise and cold water was a power function with the same exponent that would be predicted if human subjects were asked to match noise to cold (162). Perhaps preference is a means of extending the generality of Steven's power law. In another experiment with a psychophysical twist, Church, Raymond & Beauchamp (33) have shown that the effectiveness of a punisher is directly proportional to intensity of shock (in milliamps) times duration of shock. This is an obvious analogue to the Bunsen-Roscoe law in human psychophysics.

Related to the general question of aversive motivation and learning is a recent series of studies by Kamin (94), who reports that an increase in unconditioned stimulus intensity causes a rat to suppress to a redundant conditioned stimulus in a conditioned emotional response paradigm that would otherwise fail to produce suppression. Kamin postulates that the increase in unconditioned stimulus intensity causes the animal to scan the recent stimulus input, and that this backward scanning results in the formation of a conditioned-unconditioned stimulus association. If this principle is established and extended, it will mark the beginning of a major reconceptualization of Pavlovian principles.

Interaction of Drives

Early experiments on the interaction of drives were performed specifically to test the drive-summation hypothesis which stipulates that a particular behavior at a given time is energized by all motivational factors operative at that time (88). The most common interpretation now is that there is little evidence for this generalized drive notion [e.g., Bolles (18); Hinde (87)]. Although a few of the more recent investigations of drive interactions were still testing Hull's hypothesis, the majority have been more concerned with defining the conditions under which drive summation does occur or delineating the determinants of specific interactions.

Interaction of hunger and thirst.—In 1953 Verplanck & Hayes (177) reported several experiments in which the amount of food eaten by water-deprived rats and the amount of water drunk by food-deprived rats were found to be considerably less than amounts ingested by rats not deprived. Their conclusion was that ". . . thirsty rats are hungry and vice versa" (177, p. 330). Whether this "voluntary" restriction on food and water intake results in an increase in the corresponding drive level is currently a matter of speculation. Several investigators maintain that whereas the hungry animal is not thirsty, the thirsty animal is hungry (16, 71, 114). One rationale for this contention is that food deprivation reduces the need for water, but water deprivation in no way alters the animal's food requirements (18).

Fallon, Thompson & Schild (71) trained rats to press one bar for food and another for water on a VI schedule in a two-bar situation and then recorded the number of responses emitted on each bar by rats deprived of food, water, or food-plus-water for 22 hr. Both food and water were available during the test periods. Under food deprivation few responses were emitted for water, whereas under water deprivation the number of bar presses for food was relatively high. These results were taken to support the notion that food-deprived animals aren't thirsty, but water-deprived animals are hungry. A puzzling thing about this study is that the food-deprived rats responded very little for water in a situation similar to one that typically gives rise to psychogenic polydipsia (67).

McFarland (114, 117), working with the barbary dove, found that although water-deprived doves pecked for food, they did not eat; food-deprived doves did not peck for water unless food was also present. If food was available, the doves drank more than usual during a 3 hr test. This increased responding for water was not, however, considered indicative of a thirst incurred under food deprivation; instead it was taken to indicate that food intake contributes to thirst (114). In a later paper, McFarland & L'Angellier (118) found that the amount of food ingested in the first feeding bout following food deprivation did not vary with the presence or absence of water, but if water was present the doves did consume it in modest quantities. McFarland (115) calls this drinking "displacement activity" because it occurs during a time when the feeding system predominates. No conclusive evidence is presented to indicate that this is not some simple form of regulatory drinking.

In a related study, Morrison et al. (127) found that water intake of food-deprived rats was much in excess of the actual water requirement. However, water intake was reduced to normal levels when acquisition of water required a modest amount of effort, indicating that the animals were not highly motivated to obtain water (126). In a comparative study, Kutscher (100) has reported vast differences among species in water intake during food deprivation. Gerbils and hamsters both showed severe polydipsia while rats and guinea pigs did not. Perhaps hunger leads to displacement drinking in some animals but not in others.

The theoretical framework which bears most directly on this problem is that proposed by Collier (39, 42) described earlier in this chapter. If one assumes that the water-deprived animal restricts food intake to defend the ratio of body water to lean body mass, then the animal can be judged "hungry" only to the extent that body weight is below its genetic potential. By other measures the animal is not hungry. It does not eat and blood sugar level, for example, does not drop as it does in food-deprived animals (122); conversely, the hungry animal is not thirsty because water intake is presumably determined by immediate tissue needs and not by deviations from optimal body size.

In contrast, the food-deprived rat is in no way thirsty. Of course, when food is returned to the hungry animal, its water intake will increase in proportion to the need for water in the digestive process and recovering body size.

Some investigators (71, 118) have reported that animals under food-plus-water deprivation choose to eat first if both food and water are made available. This raises the question as to whether hunger or thirst predominates under conditions of total deprivation. A study by Crawford & James (50) suggests that the predominance of one system over another, as measured by amount consumed during a 1-hr test, may be relative to the length of the total deprivation period. Prior to 72 hr, food intake in rats was greater than water intake, whereas after 72 hr water intake was greater. The point at which the two functions cross will undoubtedly vary as a function of those environmental conditions which influence water loss and metabolic rate, such as temperature and humidity.

Another interesting feature of the Crawford & James (50) data is that over the first 24 hr of deprivation, feeding and drinking were in phase, i.e., as food responding increased, water responding increased. After 72 hr, there was an out-of-phase relationship. Phase relationships have also been studied by McFarland (116, 117), who has applied control theory to the regulation of drinking. He has concluded that there are two main inputs into the drinking system: environmental factors that influence the rate of water loss, and feeding factors which essentially divert water into the gastrointestinal tract for digestive purposes. Dominance of feeding factors, which occurs during steady states or emerges with variations in feeding factors, causes feeding and drinking to vary in phase, while dominance of environmental factors, which occurs following changes in environmental factors, results in an out-of-phase relationship. In agreement with the prediction of his model that feeding factor dominance promotes in-phase relationships, McFarland (114) found that doves which ate more during recovery from food deprivation also drank more. In like agreement is the finding (117) that after a change in temperature or during recovery from water deprivation there is an initial out-of-phase relationship that reverts to an in-phase one as a steady state is reached. It would have been much more persuasive had McFarland (114) reported a correlation between feeding and drinking during recovery from food deprivation over periods shorter than one day, since his model predicts an in-phase relationship both during the initial recovery period and the ensuing steady state, in contrast to the out-of-phase-in-phase prediction during recovery from water deprivation.

The interaction of other drives with hunger or thirst.—A rarely used paradigm for studying the interaction of other drives with hunger or thirst is one in which both drives are relevant. Rollins, Thomas & Remley (145) compared the effects of food deprivation and water temperature on a swimming-escape response in a situation in which some subjects were reinforced with food and some were not. Food deprivation, whether or not food followed the response, did not influence the escape response. Water temperature, however, affected food intake of the reinforced subjects, the lower temperature producing the lesser intake.

Sachs (155) investigated the effects of food deprivation on the various components of the sexual response in mature male rats. He found that although total starvation for as long as nine days had no effect upon the ejaculatory response, it did increase intromission latency and the frequency of mounts without ejaculation.

Dachowski (51) was interested in a more general statement concerning drive interactions. He performed two experiments to test Strange's (163) hypothesis that an irrelevant drive increases responding only if the relevant drive is absent. In both experiments animals were initially trained to bar-press to turn off an aversive light. In the first experiment the effect of irrelevant thirst was assessed during extinction with the light either always on or always off, while in the second experiment thirst was imposed during a continuation of training. The analyses showed that in Experiment 1, extinction performance over two sessions was not influenced by irrelevant thirst, whereas performance was attenuated in Experiment 2. A result more inconsistent with Strange's hypothesis is the finding that acquisition of an escape or avoidance (75, 106) response is augmented as a direct function of the level of food or food-plus-water deprivation respectively.

From the results of the above studies, as well as from those previously reviewed by Bolles (18), Hinde (87), and others, it appears that an additional drive, whether relevant or irrelevant, may facilitate or interfere with a particular response, or affect only one of several responses. Thus, no general rule concerning drive summation or a conflict of drives can be readily formulated when the drives under consideration are both appetitive, or when one is aversive and the other appetitive.

The interaction of aversive drives.—How do aversive drives interact, and what are the behavioral consequences? Campbell (26) performed three experiments in an attempt to answer this question. In the first experiment, responding to turn off an intense white noise stimulus was poorer in the presence of an irrelevant, unescapable electric shock, whether shock was introduced at the beginning or in the middle of training. The irrelevant shock was interpreted as "masking" the reinforcing properties of noise reduction. The second experiment supported this conclusion by showing that the aversion difference limens for noise increased as a function of intensity of irrelevant shock, and the third experiment demonstrated that the aversive properties of noise and shock were additive. The overall conclusions drawn were: (*a*) aversive drives summate to produce a heightened drive level; and (*b*) the reinforcing properties of reducing one aversive stimulus is diminished in the presence of a second aversive stimulus because the proportional reduction in total aversiveness is smaller.

MATERNAL BEHAVIOR AND AGGRESSION

Any treatment of basic drives should include the topic of sex, maternal behavior, and aggression. So much work has been done recently in these areas, however, that entire chapters would have to be devoted to these topics to provide a detailed coverage. Presented here are but some of the highlights of the past few years.

Sex.—Two current books (8, 56) and a review (9) provide excellent coverage of this area, and hence we shall not attempt even a partial review of this field.

Maternal behavior.—Renewed interest in the nonhormonal basis, as well as continued interest in the hormonal origins of maternal behavior has enhanced progress in this area. Pregnancy and parity appear to facilitate responses necessary for the rearing of young (31, 141) but do not seem crucial (147). Virgin hamsters characteristically kill 1 to 6-day pups and attack 6 to 10-day pups, but surprisingly this experience increases the amount of maternal behavior shown on subsequent exposure to pups (135, 141). Equally surprising is Rosenblatt's (147) finding that maternal behavior as measured by retrieving, crouching over the pups, licking, and nest building, can be elicited in normal and castrated male rats and in nulliparous ovariectomized or hypophysectomized females by repeatedly exposing them to rat pups over a 15-day period. These results demonstrate that there is a basic maternal responsivity in rats which is not dependent upon hormones or sex for its arousal!

Parturition also does not appear to be a determining factor in offspring care, since Caesarian delivery apparently has little effect on maternal behavior (125), although rate of presentation of pups following Caesarian delivery and the presence or absence of placenta are important determinants (82). Prior rearing experience also has little effect on maternal behavior (124), although it may facilitate some aspects of retrieval (31). Retrieval, however, is not improved by experience with moveable objects (179).

Self-licking of rodents during pregnancy is apparently not an important prerequisite for offspring care, (32) even though prevention of self-licking inhibits development of the mammary glands (149). In agreement with this, completely mammectomized rats displayed normal maternal behavior including adoption of the typical nursing posture as frequently as sham operates, indicating that mammary engorgement is not necessary for maternal care of offspring (123).

Aggression.—While the most common response to aversive stimulation is the escape-avoidance reaction, attack of both animate and inanimate objects is also frequently observed. This aggressive reaction, first reported by O'Kelly & Steckle (138), has been extensively investigated by Azrin and his associates (2–6, 89, 90). Attack or aggression is typically observed in situations where other responses to aversive stimulation are without effect (4). Attack however, may interfere with the acquisition of these other responses but does not interfere with these reactions once established (4), except possibly in the case where aggression itself is conditioned (3). The characteristics of the object of attack are not critical (5), and aggression can be elicited by "psychologically painful" situations such as withdrawal of reinforcement (3), as well as by physical pain. Pain-induced aggression occurs in a wide range of species and is influenced by such factors as the frequency, duration, and intensity of the painful stimulation (4, 6, 90); the dimension of the confinement space (180); and habituation to the surrounds (142).

Mouse killing in rats is another "aggressive" reaction that has been extensively investigated by Karli and his associates in France (57, 95, 96) and by Myer and co-workers in this country (129–133). This reaction apparently is unrelated to pain-elicited aggression since rats that can be induced to perform one of these responses cannot necessarily be induced to perform the other (95, 132). Nevertheless, the killing response is similar in some respects to pain-induced aggression. It can, for example, be brought under stimulus control (128), and, like attack, be used as a reinforcer (133). The killing response also does not appear predatory in nature. Lesions of the hypothalamus which abolish feeding do not inhibit mouse killing (96), and rats persist in killing mice even when they are not permitted to feed on them (129). Olfaction apparently plays a role in killing since removal of the olfactory bulbs results in a loss of inhibition of rat pup killing (129), and produces mouse killing in rats that were not killers preoperatively (57). In contrast, olfactory bulbectomy decreased aggression (146) which further suggests the unrelatedness of mouse-killing and other aggressive reactions.

OVERVIEW

In retrospect this has been a disquieting chapter to prepare for the *Annual Review* because of the disintegration of the drive concept. Few, if any, psychologists now believe that those conditions once labeled basic drives, such as hunger, thirst, sex, and maternal behavior, are predominantly governed by some common underlying generalized drive state. Even if there is some activating or energizing state common to many basic drives, it is clear that the specific behaviors elicited by those drives are controlled by a complex of interactions among environmental stimuli, hormonal states, physiological imbalance, previous experience, etc., and that the basic drive concept is of little value in unraveling these complexities. Moreover, research on each of the basic drive states covered in this chapter has expanded explosively in recent years with the result that specialists in those fields will no doubt feel that their topic has been treated superficially, which indeed is true. As a result, we recommend that future *Annual Review* chapters on this general subject be devoted to content areas such as "hunger and thirst," "sex and maternal behavior," and the like. Such an organization should prove much more satisfying to the reader and reviewer.

LITERATURE CITED

1. Anderson, R. A., Miles, R. C. Correspondence between "spontaneous" activity and learning. *Can. J. Psychol.*, **20**, 273–79 (1966)
2. Azrin, N. H., Hutchinson, R. R. Conditioning of the aggressive behavior of pigeons by a fixed interval schedule of reinforcement. *J. Exptl. Anal. Behav.*, **10**, 395–402 (1967)
3. Azrin, N. H., Hutchinson, R. R., Hake, D. F. Extinction induced aggression. *J. Exptl. Anal. Behav.*, **9**, 191–204 (1966)
4. Azrin, N. H., Hutchinson, R. R., Hake, D. F. Attack, avoidance and escape reactions to aversive shock. *Ibid.*, **10**, 131–48 (1967)
5. Azrin, N. H., Hutchinson, R. R., Sallery, R. D. Pain-aggression toward inanimate objects. *J. Exptl. Anal. Behav.*, **7**, 223–28 (1964)
6. Azrin, N. H., Ulrich, R. E., Hutchinson, R. R., Norman, D. G. Effect of shock duration on shock induced fighting. *J. Exptl. Anal. Behav.*, **7**, 9–11 (1964)
7. Baumeister, A., Hawkins, W. F., Cromwell, R. L. Need states and activity level. *Psychol. Bull.*, **61**, 438–53 (1964)
8. Beach, F. A., Ed. *Sex and Behavior* (Wiley, New York, 1965)
9. Beach, F. A. Cerebral and hormonal control of reflexive mechanisms involved in copulatory behavior. *Physiol. Rev.*, **47**, 289–316 (1967)
10. Bélanger, D., Feldman, S. M. Effects of water deprivation upon heart rate and instrumental activity in the rat. *J. Comp. Physiol. Psychol.*, **55**, 220–25 (1962)
11. Berlyne, D. E. Arousal and reinforcement. In *Nebraska Symposium on Motivation*, 1–110 (Levine, D., Ed., Univ. Nebraska Press, Lincoln, Neb., 1967)
12. Bindra, D. Neuropsychological interpretation of the effects of drive and incentive-motivation on general activity and instrumental behavior. *Psychol. Rev.*, **75**, 1–22 (1968)
13. Bindra, D., Palfai, T. Nature of positive and negative incentive-motivational effects on general activity. *J. Comp. Physiol. Psychol.*, **63**, 288–97 (1967)
14. Black, R. W. On the combination of drive and incentive motivation. *Psychol. Rev.*, **72**, 310–17 (1965)
15. Blanchard, R. T., Blanchard, D. C. Food deprivation and reactivity to shock. *Psychon. Sci.*, **4**, 317–18 (1966)
16. Bolles, R. C. The interaction of hunger and thirst in the rat. *J. Comp. Physiol. Psychol.*, **54**, 580–84 (1961)
17. Bolles, R. C. Effects of deprivation conditions upon the rat's home cage behavior. *Ibid.*, **60**, 244–48 (1965)
18. Bolles, R. C. *Theory of Motivation* (Harper & Row, New York, 1967)
19. Bolles, R. C., Warren, J. A., Jr. The acquisition of bar press avoidance as a function of shock intensity. *Psychon. Sci.*, **3**, 297–98 (1965)
20. Bolles, R. C., Younger, M. S. The effect of hunger on the threshold of behavioral arousal. *Psychon. Sci.*, **7**, 243–44 (1967)
21. Broadhurst, P. L. Emotionality and the Yerkes-Dodson law. *J. Exptl. Psychol.*, **54**, 345–52 (1957)
22. Brobeck, J. R. Effects of variations in activity, food intake and body temperature on weight gain in the albino rat. *Am. J. Physiol.*, **143**, 1–5 (1945)
23. Brobeck, J. R. Food intake as a mechanism of temperature regulation. *Yale J. Biol. Med.*, **20**, 545–53 (1948)
24. Brown, J. S., Farber, I. E. Secondary motivational systems. *Ann. Rev. Psychol.*, **19**, 99–134 (1968)
25. Campbell, B. A. Theory and research on the effects of water deprivation on random activity in the rat. In *Thirst: First International Symposium on Thirst in the Regulation of Body Water*, 317–34 (Wayner, M. J., Ed., Pergamon, New York, 1964)
26. Campbell, B. A. Interaction of aversive stimuli: Summation or inhibition? *J. Exptl. Psychol.* (In press, 1968)
27. Campbell, B. A., Lynch, G. S. Activity and thermoregulation during food deprivation in the rat. *Physiol. Behav.*, **2**, 311–13 (1967)
28. Campbell, B. A., Lynch, G. S. Influence of hunger and thirst on the relationship between spontaneous activity and body temperature. *J. Comp. Physiol. Psychol.*, **65**, 492–98 (1968)
29. Campbell, B. A., Sheffield, F. D. Relation of random activity to food

deprivation. *J. Comp. Physiol. Psychol.*, **46**, 320–22 (1953)

30. Campbell, B. A., Smith, N. F., Misanin, J. R., Jaynes, J. Species differences in activity during hunger and thirst. *J. Comp. Physiol. Psychol.*, **61**, 123–27 (1966)

31. Carlier, C., Noirot, E. Effects of previous experience on maternal retrieving by rats. *Anim. Behav.*, **13**, 423–26 (1965)

32. Christophersen, E. R., Wagman, W. Maternal behavior in the albino rat as a function of self-licking deprivation. *J. Comp. Physiol. Psychol.*, **60**, 142–44 (1965)

33. Church, R. M., Raymond, G. A., Beauchamp, R. D. Response suppression as a function of intensity and duration of a punishment. *J. Comp. Physiol. Psychol.*, **63**, 39–44 (1967)

34. Clark, F. C. Some observations on the adventitious reinforcement of drinking under food reinforcement. *J. Exptl. Anal. Behav.*, **5**, 61–63 (1962)

35. Clark, F. C. Emulsification of liquid monkey food. *Ibid.*, **8**, 16 (1965)

36. Code, C. F., Ed. *Handbook of Physiology*, **I**, Sect. 6 (Am. Physiol. Soc., Washington, D.C., 1967)

37. Cofer, C. N. Motivation. *Ann. Rev. Psychol.*, **10**, 173–202 (1959)

38. Cofer, C. N., Appley, M. H. *Motivation: Theory and Research* (Wiley, New York, 1964)

39. Collier, G. Body weight loss as a measure of motivation in hunger and thirst. *Ann. N. Y. Acad Sci.* (In press, 1968)

40. Collier, G., Leshner, A. I. An invariant in mouse running wheel behavior. *Psychon. Sci.*, **8**, 9–10 (1967)

41. Collier, G., Levitsky, D. Defense of water balance in rats: Behavioral and physiological responses to depletion. *J. Comp. Physiol. Psychol.*, **64**, 59–67 (1967)

42. Collier, G., Levitsky, D. A. Operant running as a function of deprivation and effort. *Ibid.* (In press, 1968)

43. Collier, G., Levitsky, D., Squibb, R. L. Instrumental performance as a function of the energy content of the diet. *J. Comp. Physiol. Psychol.*, **64**, 68–72 (1967)

44. Collier, G., Squibb, R. L. Diet and activity. *J. Comp. Physiol. Psychol.*, **64**, 409–13 (1967)

45. Collier, G., Squibb, R. L., Jackson, F. Activity as a function of diet: 1. Spontaneous activity. *Psychon. Sci.*, **3**, 173–74 (1965)

46. Corbit, J. D. Effect of intravenous sodium chloride on drinking in the rat. *J. Comp. Physiol. Psychol.*, **60**, 397–406 (1965)

47. Corbit, J. D. Effect of hypervolemia on drinking in the rat. *Ibid.*, **64**, 250–55 (1967)

48. Corbit, J. D. Osmotic thirst: Theoretical and experimental analysis. *Ibid.* (In press, 1968)

49. Cornish, E. R., Mrosovsky, N. Activity during food deprivation and satiation of six species of rodent. *Anim. Behav.*, **13**, 242–48 (1965)

50. Crawford, M. L. J., James, W. T. Effect of acute simultaneous food and water deprivation upon bar-pressing behavior. *Psychol. Rept.*, **15**, 239–42 (1964)

51. Dachowski, L. Irrelevant thirst drive and light aversion. *Psychol. Rept.*, **14**, 899–904 (1964)

52. D'Amato, M. R., Fazzaro, J. Discriminated lever-press avoidance learning as a function of type and intensity of shock. *J. Comp. Physiol. Psychol.*, **61**, 313–15 (1966)

53. D'Amato, M. R., Fazzaro, J., Etkin, M. Discriminated bar press avoidance maintenance and extinction in rats as a function of shock intensity. *J. Comp. Physiol. Psychol.*, **63**, 351–54 (1967)

54. Dethier, V. G. Microscopic brains. *Science*, **143**, 1138–45 (1964)

55. Dethier, V. G. Insects and the concept of motivation. In *Nebraska Symposium on Motivation*, 105–36 (Levine, D., Ed., Univ. Nebraska Press, Lincoln, Neb., 1966)

56. Diamond, M., Ed. *Perspectives in Reproduction and Sexual Behavior* (Indiana Univ. Press, Bloomington, Ind., In press, 1968)

57. Didiergeorges, F., Vergnes, M., Karli, P. Désafférentation olfactive et agressivité inter-spécifique due rat. *J. Physiol. (Paris)*, **58**, 510 (1966)

58. Doerr, H. O., Hokanson, J. E. Food deprivation, performance, and heart rate in the rat. *J. Comp. Physiol. Psychol.*, **65**, 227–31 (1968)

59. Draper, W. A. A behavioral study of the home-cage activity of the white rat. *Behavior*, **28**, 280–306 (1967)

60. Ducharme, R. Effect of internal and external cures on the heart rate of

the rat. *Can. J. Psychol.*, **20**, 97–104 (1966)

61. Duffy, E. *Activation and Behavior* (Wiley, New York, 1962)

62. Eisman, E. Effects of deprivation and consummatory activity on heart rate. *J. Comp. Physiol. Psychol.*, **62**, 71–75 (1966)

63. Estes, W. K. Stimulus response theory of drive. In *Nebraska Symposium on Motivation*, 35–69 (Jones, M. R., Ed., Univ. Nebraska Press, Lincoln, Neb., 1958)

64. Falk, J. L. Production of polydipsia in normal rats by an intermittent food schedule. *Science*, **133**, 195–96 (1961)

65. Falk, J. L. The behavioral regulation of water electrolyte balance. In *Nebraska Symposium on Motivation*, 1–33 (Jones, M. R., Ed., Univ. Nebraska Press, Lincoln, Neb., 1961)

66. Falk, J. L. Studies on schedule-induced polydipsia. In *Thirst*, 95–116 (See Ref. 25)

67. Falk, J. L. The motivational properties of schedule-induced polydipsia. *J. Exptl. Anal. Behav.*, **9**, 19–25 (1966)

68. Falk, J. L. Schedule-induced polydipsia as a function of fixed interval length. *Ibid.*, 37–39

69. Falk, J. L. Control of schedule-induced polydipsia: Type, size, and spacing of meals. *Ibid.*, **10**, 199–206 (1967)

70. Falk, J. L. Conditions producing psychogenic polydipsia in animals. *Ann. N. Y. Acad. Sci.* (In press, 1968)

71. Fallon, D., Thompson, D. M., Schild, M. E. Concurrent food- and water-reinforced responding under food, water, and food-plus-water deprivation. *Psychol. Rept.*, **16**, 1305–11 (1965)

72. Finger, F. W. Effect of food deprivation on running-wheel activity in naive rats. *Psychol. Rept.*, **16**, 753–57 (1965)

73. Finger, F. W., Reid, L. S., Weasner, M. H. Activity changes as a function of reinforcement under low drive. *J. Comp. Physiol. Psychol.*, **53**, 385–87 (1960)

74. Fitzsimons, J. T. Drinking by rats depleted of body fluid without increase in osmotic pressure. *J. Physiol. (London)*, **159**, 297–309 (1961)

75. Franchina, J. J. Combined sources of motivation and escape responding. *Psychon. Sci.*, **6**, 221–22 (1966)

76. Frankova, S. Influence of a changed dietary pattern on the behavior of rats with a different excitability of the C. N. S. *Cesk. Psychologie*, **10**, 13–23 (1966)

77. Glickman, S. E., Schiff, B. B. A biological theory of reinforcement. *Psychol. Rev.*, **74**, 81–109 (1967)

78. Goldstein, R., Stern, J. A., Rothenberg, S. J. Effect of water deprivation and cues associated with water on the heart rate of the rat. *Physiol. Behav.*, **1**, 199–203 (1966)

79. Grimsley, D. L. Effect of water deprivation and injections of hypertonic saline on the activity of rats. *Psychol. Rept.*, **16**, 1081–85 (1965)

80. Grossman, S. P. *A Textbook of Physiological Psychology* (Wiley, New York, 1967)

81. Grossman, S. P., Rechtschaffen, A. Variations in brain temperature in relation to food intake. *Physiol. Behav.*, **2**, 379–83 (1967)

82. Grota, L. J., Denenberg, V. H., Zarrow, M. X. Maternal behavior in the rat: Some parameters affecting the acceptance of young delivered by Caesarean section, *J. Reprod. Fertility*, **13**, 405–11 (1967)

83. Hahn, W. W., Stern, J. A., Fehr, F. S. Generalizability of heart rate as a measure of drive state. *J. Comp. Physiol. Psychol.*, **58**, 305–9 (1964)

84. Hahn, W. W., Stern, J. A., McDonald, D. G. Effects of water deprivation and bar pressing activity on heart rate of the male albino rat. *J. Comp. Physiol. Psychol.*, **55**, 786–90 (1962)

85. Hamilton, C. L. Control of food intake. In *Physiological Controls and Regulations*, 274–94 (Yamamoto, W. S., Brobeck, J. R., Eds., W. B. Saunders, Philadelphia, Pa., 1965)

86. Hebb, D. O. Drives and the C. N. S. (conceptual nervous system). *Psychol. Rev.*, **62**, 243–54 (1955)

87. Hinde, R. A. *Animal Behaviour* (McGraw-Hill, New York, 1966)

88. Hull, C. L. *Principles of Behavior* (Appleton-Century-Crofts, New York, 1943)

89. Hutchinson, R. R., Azrin, N. H., Hake, D. F. An Automatic method for the study of aggression in squirrel monkeys. *J. Exptl. Anal. Behav.*, **9**, 233–37 (1966)

90. Hutchinson, R. R., Azrin, N. H.,

Renfrew, J. W. Effects of shock intensity and duration on the frequency of biting attack by squirrel monkeys. *J. Exptl. Anal. Behav.*, **11**, 83–88 (1968)

91. Jacobs, H. L. Sensory and metabolic regulation of food intake: Thoughts on a dual system regulated by energy balance. *Proceedings of the Seventh International Congress of Nutrition*, 2 (Verlag Friedr. Vieweg, Braunschweig, Germany, 1966)

92. Jacobs, H. L., Sharma, K. N. Taste versus calories: Sensory and metabolic signals in the control of food intake. *Ann. N. Y. Acad. Sci.* (In press, 1968)

93. Jennings, H. S. *The Behavior of Lower Organisms* (Columbia Univ. Press, New York, 1906)

94. Kamin, J. L. Predictability, surprise, attention, and conditioning. In *Punishment and Aversive Behavior* (Campbell, B. A., Church, R. M., Eds., Appleton-Century-Crofts, New York, In press, 1969)

95. Karli, P. The Norway rat's killing response to the white mouse: An experimental analysis. *Behaviour*, **10**, 81–103 (1956)

96. Karli, P., Vergnes, M. Nouvelles donneés sur les bases neurophysiologigue du comportement d'agression interspécifique rat-souris. *J. Physiol. (Paris)*, **56**, 384 (1964)

97. Kavanau, J. L. Behavior of captive white-footed mice. *Science*, **155**, 1632–39 (1967)

98. Kutscher, C. L. An osmometric analysis of drinking in salt injected rats. *Physiol. Behav.*, **1**, 79–83 (1966)

99. Kutscher, C. L. Effect of hypertonic saline injection and water deprivation on drinking, serum osmolarity and gut water. *Ibid.*, 259–68

100. Kutscher, C. L. Species difference in the interaction of feeding and drinking. *Ann. N. Y. Acad. Sci.* (In press, 1968)

101. Lacey, J. I. Somatic response patterning and stress: Some revisions of activation theory. In *Psychological Stress: Issues in Research*, 14–37 (Appley, M. H., Trumbell, R., Eds., Appleton-Century-Crofts, New York, 1967)

102. Lát, J. The relationship of the individual differences in the regulation of food intake, growth, and excitability of the central nervous system.

Physiol. Bohemoslov., **5**, 38–42 (1956)

103. Lát, J. Self selection of dietary components. In *Handbook of Physiology*, I, Sect. 6, 367–86 (See Ref. 36)

104. Levine, S. UCS intensity and avoidance learning. *J. Exptl. Psychol.*, **71**, 163–64 (1966)

105. Levitsky, D., Collier, G. Schedule induced wheel running. *Physiol. Behav.* (In press, 1968)

106. Ley, R. Effects of food and water deprivation on the performance of a response motivated by acquired fear. *J. Exptl. Psychol.*, **69**, 583–89 (1965)

107. Lynch, G. S. *Frontal Control of Spontaneous Activity: An Experimental and Theoretical Inquiry* (Doctoral thesis, Princeton Univ., Princeton, N.J., 1968)

108. Malmo, R. B. Measurement of drive: An unresolved problem in psychology. In *Nebraska Symposium on Motivation*, 229–65 (Jones, M. R., Ed., Univ. Nebraska Press, Lincoln, Neb., 1958)

109. Malmo, R. B. Activation: A neuropsychological dimension. *Psychol. Rev.*, **66**, 367–86 (1959)

110. Malmo, R. B., Bélanger, D. Related physiological and behavioral changes: What are their determinants? In *Sleep and Altered States of Consciousness*, 288–318 (Kety, S. S., Evarts, E. V., Williams, H. L., Eds., Williams & Wilkins, Baltimore, Md., 1967)

111. Mathews, S. R., Jr., Finger, F. W. Direct observation of the rat's activity during food deprivation. *Physiol. Behav.*, **1**, 85–88 (1966)

112. McAllister, W. R., McAllister, D. E. Drive and reward in aversive learning. *Am. J. Psychol.*, **80**, 377–83 (1967)

113. McClelland, D. C., Atkinson, J. W., Clark, R. A., Lowell, E. L. *The Achievement Motive* (Appleton-Century-Crofts, New York, 1953)

114. McFarland, D. J. The effect of hunger on thirst motivated behaviour in the barbary dove. *Anim. Behav.*, **13**, 286–92 (1965)

115. McFarland, D. J. Hunger, thirst and displacement pecking in the barbary dove. *Ibid.*, 293–300

116. McFarland, D. J. Control theory applied to the control of drinking in the barbary dove. *Ibid.*, 478–92

117. McFarland, D. J. Phase relationships

between feeding and drinking in the barbary dove. *J. Comp. Physiol. Psychol.*, **63**, 208–13 (1967)

118. McFarland, D. J., L'Angellier, A. B. Disinhibition of drinking during satiation of feeding behaviour in the barbary dove. *Anim. Behav.*, **14**, 463–67 (1966)

119. Melton, A. W. Learning. In *Encyclopedia of Educational Research*, 2nd ed., 668–90 (Monroe, W. S., Ed., Macmillan, New York, 1950)

120. Miller, N. E. Some reflections on the law of effect produce a new alternative to drive reduction. In *Nebraska Symposium on Motivation*, 65–112 (Jones, M. R., Ed., Univ. Nebraska Press, Lincoln, Nebraska, 1963)

121. Milton, J. *Paradise Lost. A Poem Written in Ten Books.* Book IV, lines 183–84 (Printed and sold by Peter Parker under Creed Church neer Aldgate; and by Robert Boulter at the Turks Head in Bishops Gate-street; and Matthias Walker under St. Dunstons Church in Fleet-street, London, 1667)

122. Misanin, J. R., Smith, N. F., Campbell, B. A. Relation between blood sugar level and random activity during food and water deprivation. *Psychon. Sci.*, **1**, 63–64 (1964)

123. Moltz, H., Geller, D., Levin, R. Maternal behavior in the totally mammectomized rat. *J. Comp. Physiol. Psychol.*, **64**, 225–29 (1967)

124. Moltz, H., Robbins, D. Maternal behavior of primiparous and multiparous rats. *J. Comp. Physiol. Psychol.*, **60**, 417–21 (1965)

125. Moltz, H., Robbins, D., Parks, M. Caesarean delivery and maternal behavior of primiparous and multiparous rats. *J. Comp. Physiol. Psychol.*, **61**, 455–60 (1966)

126. Morrison, S. D. Regulation of water intake by rats deprived of food. *Physiol. Behav.*, **3**, 75–81 (1968)

127. Morrison, S. D., Mackay, C., Hurlbrink, E., Wier, J. K., Nick, M. S., Millar, F. K. The water exchange and polyuria of rats deprived of food. *Quart. J. Exptl. Physiol.*, **52**, 51–67 (1967)

128. Moyer, K. E., Korn, J. H. Effect of UCS intensity on the acquisition and extinction of an avoidance response. *J. Exptl. Psychol.*, **67**, 352–59 (1964)

129. Myer, J. S. Stimulus control of mouse-killing rats. *J. Comp. Physiol. Psychol.*, **58**, 112–17 (1964)

130. Myer, J. S. Punishment of instinctive behavior: Suppression of mouse-killing by rats. *Psychon. Sci.*, **4**, 385–86 (1966)

131. Myer, J. S. Prior killing experience and the suppressive effects of punishment on the killing of mice by rats. *Anim. Behav.*, **15**, 59–61 (1967)

132. Myer, J. S., Baenninger, R. Some effects of punishment and stress on mouse killing by rats. *J. Comp. Physiol. Psychol.*, **62**, 292–97 (1966)

133. Myer, J. S., White, R. T. Aggressive motivation in the rat. *Anim. Behav.*, **13**, 430–33 (1965)

134. Myers, R. D. Chemical mechanisms in the hypothalamus mediating eating and drinking in the monkey. *Ann. N. Y. Acad. Sci.* (In press, 1968)

135. Noirot, E., Richards, M. P. M. Maternal behavior in virgin female golden hamsters: Changes consequent upon initial contact with pups. *Anim. Behav.*, **14**, 7–10 (1966)

136. Novin, D., Hutchins, C., Mundy, P. Effects of intravenous injections of water on the consummatory behavior of rats. *J. Comp. Physiol. Psychol.*, **61**, 473–74 (1966)

137. O'Kelly, L. I., Hatton, G. I., Tucker, L., Westall, D. Water regulation in the rat: Heart rate as a function of hydration, anesthesia, and association with reinforcement. *J. Comp. Physiol. Psychol.*, **59**, 159–65 (1965)

138. O'Kelly, L. I., Steckle, L. C. A note on long enduring emotional responses in the rat. *J. Psychol.*, **8**, 125–31 (1939)

139. Reynierse, J. H. Excessive drinking in rats as a function of number of meals. *Can. J. Psychol.*, **20**, 82–86 (1966)

140. Reynierse, J. H., Spanier, D. Excessive drinking in rats' adaptation to the schedule of feeding. *Psychon. Sci.*, **10**, 95–96 (1968)

141. Richards, M. P. M. Maternal behavior in the golden hamster: Responsiveness to young in virgin, pregnant and lactating females. *Anim. Behav.*, **14**, 310–13 (1966)

142. Roberts C. L., Larson, C. Shock history and adaptation as parameters of elicited aggression in rats. *Psychol. Rec.*, **17**, 425–28 (1967)

143. Rodgers, W. L. Specificity of specific hungers. *J. Comp. Physiol. Psychol.*, **64**, 49–58 (1967)

144. Rodgers, W., Rozin, P. Novel food preferences in thiamine-deficient

rats. *J. Comp. Physiol. Psychol.*, **61**, 1–14 (1966)

145. Rollins, J. B., Thomas, R. K., Remley, N. R. An investigation of drive summation in a water runway. *Psychon. Sci.*, **3**, 183–84 (1965)

146. Ropartz, P. The relation between olfactory stimulation and aggressive behavior in mice. *Anim. Behav.*, **16**, 97–100 (1968)

147. Rosenblatt, J. S. Nonhormonal basis of maternal behavior in the rat. *Science*, **156**, 1512–14 (1967)

148. Rosenzweig, M. R. The mechanisms of hunger and thirst. In *Psychology in the Making*, 73–143 (Postman, L., Ed., Knopf, New York, 1962)

149. Roth, L. L., Rosenblatt, J. S. Mammary glands of pregnant rats: Development stimulated by licking. *Science*, **151**, 1403–4 (1966)

150. Routtenberg, A., Kuznesof, A. W. Self-starvation of rats living in activity wheels on a restricted feeding schedule. *J. Comp. Physiol. Psychol.*, **64**, 414–21 (1967)

151. Rozin, P. Specific hunger for thiamine: Recovery from deficiency and thiamine preference. *J. Comp. Physiol. Psychol.*, **59**, 98–101 (1965)

152. Rozin, P. Specific aversions as a component of specific hungers. *Ibid.*, **64**, 237–42 (1967)

153. Rozin, P., Rodgers, W. Novel-diet preferences in vitamin-deficient rats and rats recovered from vitamin deficiency. *J. Comp. Physiol. Psychol.*, **63**, 421–28 (1967)

154. Rozin, P., Wells, C., Mayer, J. Specific hunger for thiamine: Vitamin in water versus vitamin in food. *J. Comp. Physiol. Psychol.*, **57**, 78–84 (1964)

155. Sachs, B. D. Sexual behavior of male rats after one to nine days without food. *J. Comp. Physiol. Psychol.*, **60**, 144–46 (1965)

156. Segal, E. F. The development of water drinking on a dry-food free-reinforcement schedule, *Psychon. Sci.*, **2**, 29–30 (1965)

157. Segal, E. F., Halloway, S. M. Timing behavior in rats with water drinking as a mediator. *Science*, **140**, 888–89 (1963)

158. Shaffer, L. F. *The Psychology of Adjustment* (Houghton Mifflin, New York, 1936)

159. Smith, M. H., Holman, G. L., Fortune, K. B. Sodium need and sodium consumption. *J. Comp. Physiol. Psychol.*, **65**, 33–37 (1968)

160. Spear, N. E., Hill, W. F. Methodological note: Excessive weight loss in rats living in activity wheels. *Psychol. Rept.*, **11**, 437–38 (1962)

161. Stein, L. Excessive drinking in the rat: Superstition or thirst? *J. Comp. Physiol. Psychol.*, **58**, 237–42 (1964)

162. Stevens, S. S. The psychophysics of sensory function. *Am. Scientist*, **48**, 226–53 (1960)

163. Strange, J. R. The effect of an irrelevant drive on the reaction tendency specific to another drive. *J. Gen. Psychol.*, **51**, 31–40 (1954)

164. Stricker, E. M. Extracellular fluid volume and thirst. *Am. J. Physiol.*, **211**, 232–38 (1966)

165. Stricker, E. M., Wolf, G. Hypovolemic thirst in comparison with thirst induced by hyperosmolarity. *Physiol. Behav.*, **2**, 33–37 (1967)

166. Stricker, E. M. Some physiological and motivational properties of the hypervolemic stimulus for thirst. *Ibid.* (In press, 1968)

167. Stricker, E. M., Adair, E. R. Body fluid balance, taste, and postprandial factors in schedule-induced polydipsia. *J. Comp. Physiol. Psychol.*, **62**, 449–54 (1966)

168. Stricker, E. M., Wolf, G. Hypovolemic thirst in comparison with thirst induced by hyperosmolarity. *Physiol. Behav.*, **2**, 33–37 (1967)

169. Stricker, E. M., Wolf. G. Behavioral control of intravascular fluid volume: Thirst and sodium appetite. *Ann. N. Y. Acad. Sci.* (In press, 1968)

170. Tapp, J. T. Activity, reactivity, and the behavior directing properties of stimuli. In *Reinforcement: Current Research and Theory* (Tapp, J. T., Ed., Academic Press, New York, In press, 1969)

171. Tapp, J. T., Simpson, L. L. Motivational and response factors are determinants of the reinforcing value of light onset. *J. Comp. Physiol. Psychol.*, **62**, 143–46 (1966)

172. Teitelbaum, P. The use of operant methods in the assessment and control of motivational states. In *Operant Behavior: Areas of Research and Application*, 565–608 (Honig, W. K., Ed., Appleton-Century-Crofts, New York, 1966)

173. Teitelbaum, P. *Physiological Psychology* (Foundations of Modern Psychology Series, Lazarus, R. S.,

Ed., Prentice-Hall, Englewood Cliffs, New Jersey, 1967)

174. Theios, J., Lynch, D. A., Lowe, W. F., Jr. Differential effects of shock intensity on one-way and shuttle avoidance conditioning. *J. Exptl. Psychol.*, **72**, 294–99 (1966)

175. Treichler, F. R., Collins, R. W. Comparison of cyclic and continuous deprivation on wheel running. *J. Comp. Physiol. Psychol.*, **60**, 447–48 (1965)

176. Valenstein, E. S. Selection of nutritive and non-nutritive solutions under different conditions of need. *J. Comp. Physiol. Psychol.*, **63**, 429–33 (1967)

177. Verplanck, W. S., Hayes, J. R. Eating and drinking as a function of maintenance schedule. *J. Comp. Physiol. Psychol.*, **46**, 327–33 (1953)

178. Wayner, M. J., Petraitis, J. Effects of water deprivation and salt arousal of drinking on wheel turning activity of rats. *Physiol. Behav.*, **2**, 273–75 (1967)

179. Wehmer, F. Effects of prior experience with objects on maternal behavior in the rat. *J. Comp. Physiol. Psychol.*, **60**, 294–96 (1965)

180. Willis, F. N., Jr. Fighting in pigeons relative to available space. *Psychon. Sci.*, **4**, 315–16 (1966)

181. Wolf, G., Stricker, E. M. Sodium appetite elicited by hypovolemia in adrenalectomized rats: Reevaluation of the "reservoir" hypothesis.

J. Comp. Physiol. Psychol., **63**, 252–57 (1967)

182. Woods, P. J., Campbell, B. A. Relative aversiveness of white noise and cold water. *J. Comp. Physiol. Psychol.*, **64**, 493–95 (1967)

183. Woods, P. J., Davidson, E. H., Peters, R. J., Jr. Instrumental escape conditioning in a water tank: Effects of variations in drive stimulus intensity and reinforcement magnitude. *J. Comp. Physiol. Psychol.*, **57**, 466–70 (1964)

184. Woods, P. J., Holland, C. H. Instrumental escape conditioning in a water tank: Effects of constant reinforcement at different levels of drive stimulus intensity. *J. Comp. Physiol. Psychol.*, **62**, 403–8 (1966)

185. Woodworth, R. S. *Dynamic Psychology* (Columbia Univ. Press, New York, 1918)

186. Woodworth, R. S. *Experimental Psychology* (Holt, New York, 1938)

187. Wright, J. H. Modifications in the rat's diurnal activity pattern as a function of opportunity for reinforcement by ingestion. *J. Comp. Physiol. Psychol.*, **59**, 463–65 (1965)

188. Wright, J. H., Gescheider, G. A., Johnson, M. L. Energizing effects of combined food and water deprivation upon general activity. *Psychon. Sci.*, **5**, 415–16 (1966)

189. Yamamoto, W. S., Brobeck, J. R., Eds. *Physiological Controls and Regulations* (W. B. Saunders, Philadelphia, Pa., 1965)

THE PHYSIOLOGICAL BASIS OF MEMORY[1]   131

By J. A. Deutsch

University of California, San Diego, California

The present review confines itself to recent developments in the physiological bases of memory. The review deals mainly with advances produced by the application of techniques which cause amnesia. There is also a section on experiments using spreading depression as a tool. An attempt has been made to evaluate these topics critically and in depth.

Protein Synthesis Inhibition and Memory

The original impetus to the work with protein synthesis inhibitors was the idea that memory storage was in some way connected with the synthesis of protein molecules. If this was the case, it should be possible to prevent the formation or maintenance of memory after a learning experience by the administration of substances preventing the synthesis of protein. Flexner, one of the earliest and most thorough investigators using this technique, has recently published a valuable review of his work (31).

Flexner and his collaborators teach mice what is essentially an escape task in a Y-maze. After the mice are trained, puromycin is injected intracerebrally 1 to 60 days after training. The mice are typically retested 3 to 4 days after treatment. Memory loss is expressed in terms of a percentage savings score. "These percentages are calculated by subtracting the number of trials or errors to criterion in the retention tests from the number to criterion in training, dividing by the number in training and multiplying by 100" (31). Such a score could produce a serious overestimate of the amount of amnesia if the rate of learning is slowed down by the drug. Unless there is an independent estimate through the use of preinjected controls of the effect of the drug on the rate of learning, the number of trials to criterion during retest does not specify the relative contributions to the total relearning score made by amnesia and by altered rate of learning. Flexner et al. (31) state about puromycin-treated mice, "some reach criterion on second learning in practically the same number of trials with the same number of errors as on first learning; in others, second learning is substantially more difficult than first learning." There is, therefore, reason to believe that rate of relearning was affected in this set of experiments. Given this measure then, it is possible that in these experiments a trivial degree of

---

[1] The survey of literature pertaining to this review was concluded in May 1968.

forgetting would look like a complete amnesia if on retest the mouse learned very slowly.

Flexner et al. (31) infer that the memory trace spreads as it becomes older. Mice injected one day after training with 90 μg of puromycin, using injection into the temporal region of the brain, lose their memory of the habit. On the other hand, with an interval of 11 days between training and injection, injection into the temporal region appears no longer sufficient to cause amnesia. The dose has to be distributed into at least three sites (temporal, ventricular, and frontal) bilaterally symmetrical. This is taken to be evidence of the spread of the memory trace with time after learning. However, there are alternative conclusions that can be drawn. No preinjected controls are ever run. Consequently, we do not know whether the widely injected mice are more impaired in their capacity to learn than their counterparts injected only in the temporal region. Further, the difference obtained may be attributed to effective dose rather than spread of the memory trace. We could suppose that the memory trace is scattered over a large number of sites and that soon after learning the memory substrate is sensitive to a lower level of drug. It has been shown that an injection of puromycin into the temporal cortex produces only low protein synthesis inhibition in all other sampled areas of the brain (31). This low effect might therefore be sufficient to block memory initially. However, a combined set of injections (temporal, ventricular, and frontal) causes a very much higher puromycin inhibition of protein synthesis in other areas besides the temporal. Thus while a temporal injection may no longer cause amnesia because the traces in other sites require a larger depression to be blocked, this can be achieved by a different spatial distribution of the injection.

Subsequent to these results with puromycin which support the idea that protein synthesis is necessary for the formation and maintenance of memory, Flexner & Flexner (29) have reported that intracerebral injections of small quantities of saline at various times after puromycin treatment abolished the puromycin-induced amnesia. It therefore seems that puromycin simply blocked retrieval in some way and that the memory trace itself was in fact unimpaired by puromycin. In this experiment, puromycin injections were made one day after training, with the exception of subsidiary groups where injection was made after a longer interval. Saline was then injected at intervals varying between 4 hr and 60 days.

It could be argued that Flexner's experiments have a bearing on the maintenance of memory but not on its formation because they have only made injections one day or more after training. Barondes & Cohen (5) trained mice in a situation similar to Flexner's, either in the presence of puromycin or with puromycin injected immediately after learning. They found in both cases that memory was present for 45 min after training but was almost lost after 3 hr. Therefore, puromycin also seems to have an effect on the formation of memory. Flexner & Flexner (30) attempted to discover whether this effect of puromycin on presumed memory formation was also reversible by saline injection. They found that "in the presence of puromycin, our mice, when naive to the maze, are exceptionally difficult to train." They were compelled then to use a training schedule which makes the mice trained in such a manner difficult to compare with other groups. However, a second group injected with puromycin immediately after training can be compared. Flexner & Flexner (30) summarize the results of their studies with puromycin followed by saline as follows:

It was shown that puromycin administered to mice one or more days after maze-learning blocks expression of memory; the blockage can be removed by intracerebral injections of saline. We present evidence that intracerebral injections of saline are relatively ineffective in restoring memory when puromycin is administered either before or immediately after training; in these two situations puromycin appears to interfere with consolidation of memory.

Such an important conclusion should be examined further. We shall consider only the group injected after training, as it is the only one which is comparable to other groups which have been run. This group was trained, injected with puromycin immediately upon being trained, injected with saline 5 days later, and then retested 10 days after original training. The difference in retention between the mice treated with saline and those treated only with puromycin was clearly significant.

Injection of saline seems therefore to reverse the amnesia produced by puromycin injected immediately after training. The question is then asked whether such a reversal is as effective as when saline is injected into animals treated with puromycin one day after training. Flexner & Flexner (30) answer their question as follows:

Our earlier results on the efficacy of saline in restoring memory after treatment with puromycin referred to 47 mice in which puromycin was given one or more days after training and followed 30 hr to 60 days later by intracerebral injections of saline. . . . These savings are marginally significantly greater (p<.05) than those obtained when puromycin, given immediately after training, was followed 5 days later by saline (p. 311).

It is doubtful if the group of 47 animals mentioned is in fact a proper control group, because it differs in other ways besides the time after training when puromycin was injected.

One of these differences which seems important concerns the time between the puromycin and saline injections. Inspection of Table II in the previous experiment (29) describing this group shows that there seems to be an interaction between time between puromycin injection and saline injection and subsequent recovery from amnesia. For instance, when the interval is 30 hr, no mice lose their memory, one has impaired memory, and 7 retain their memory. On the other hand, when the intervals between puromycin and saline injections are from 2 to 12 days, one animal loses its memory, 9 have impaired memory, and 13 retain their memory. Both the 30-hr group and the 2-to-12-day group were injected with puromycin at the same time after training and were used as a part of the same baseline comparison group of 47 mice. Yet the probability that the 30-hr and 2-to-12-day groups are different is greater than the probability that the 2-to-12-day group and the group injected with puromycin immediately after training are different. (I thank Dr. P. H. Lindsay for calculating this from the published data.)

The marginal difference between the mice injected with puromycin immediately after training and those injected one day later could therefore be due to the fact that they were also injected with saline at different times after puromycin. Furthermore, the group of 47 mice injected at least 1 day after training, used as a baseline of comparison of the mice injected immediately after training and with saline 5 days later, is also heterogeneous in another way. One subgroup was given 6 intracerebral injections of puromycin 13 to 15 days after training. The Ns in each group are quite unequal, so that the total baseline becomes completely arbitrary. Therefore, it cannot be concluded safely that saline is relatively less effective in restoring memory when puromycin has been administered immediately after learning. Thus the experiments suggesting reversal of puromycin amnesia with saline should be examined with caution when it is claimed that memory storage rather than retrieval has been affected by a treatment.

Flexner et al. (31) also report that acetoxycycloheximide, an extremely potent protein synthesis inhibitor, does not have an amnesic effect when injected one day or more after training. However, when acetoxycycloheximide is injected in mixture with puromycin, it protects against the amnesic effects of puromycin. Flexner et al. (31) attempt to explain this in terms of the ways in which the two drugs inhibit protein synthesis. On the other hand, it has never been demonstrated that puromycin or any other protein synthesis inhibitor has its action on memory through a direct effect on protein synthesis rather than through some indirect or side effect. Koenig (36), for instance, has shown that puromycin depresses cholinesterase synthesis and that actinomycin-D has the opposite effect (37). Puromycin blocks the increase of acetylcholinesterase by actinomycin-D. Dahl and Leibowitz, together with the reviewer (quoted in 21), have shown a remarkable similarity in the time course of amnesic effect between puromycin and anticholinesterases.

Barondes & Cohen (6) have reported recently that subcutaneous injection of 240 μg of acetoxycycloheximide in mice 5 min to 5 hr before training in a T-maze produces amnesia for the habit. The mice were trained to a criterion of 5 out of 6 correct. This result is in marked contrast with previously reported results by these workers (15), where intracerebral injections of the same substance which produced at least as high protein synthesis inhibition at the time of training were without effect on a well trained habit. (However, an amnesic effect on a habit learned to a criterion of 3 out of 4 correct was observed.) Barondes & Cohen (6) also found that memory was unimpaired at 3 hr, although amnesia set in 6 hr after training. From this it is argued "that a different process is utilized for memory storage during this period and that the absence of a long-term process, which is apparently dependent on cerebral protein synthesis, does not become manifest until the short-term process has decayed sufficiently" (6).

The inadequacy of such an argument to establish different memory processes is best shown by quoting from Flexner et al. (31): "In mice trained to criterion both recent and longer-term memory are maintained for 10 to 20 hr after injection of puromycin, then they disappear permanently." From such evidence it can be argued more plausibly that it takes some time for a single process to become irretrievable. Though belief in different stages and processes in memory has become popular, the fact is that no one has devised an experiment capable of deciding between a single process and a multiple process theory.

Another group of studies on amnesia and protein synthesis inhibition has been performed by Agranoff and his associates. Goldfish are taught to avoid shock in a shuttle-box apparatus. They are given a fixed number of trials, at the end of which only a little learning has occurred. Treatment is given either before or soon after training, and retesting is done at different times after training. Agranoff & Klinger (3) have found that injection with puromycin immediately after training causes goldfish to forget after 3 days. Potts & Bitterman (47) added an element of discrimination to the shuttle-box situation used by Agranoff. Instead of using a white light as a warning stimulus, the goldfish could discriminate what color light was followed by shock. They trained the goldfish giving 20 trials a day on 6 training days one week apart. Each set of trials was followed by an injection of 170 μg of puromycin intracranially. The results show that the puromycin-injected goldfish learned to avoid though at a slower rate than the controls. However, it seems that the relative efficiency of discrimination (given different baselines of responding) was about the same for the experimental as for the control fish. Potts & Bitterman (47) suggest that puromycin does not interfere with the consolidation of memory in general but with the consolidation of conditioned fear.

An alternative explanation may be suggested. As the ECS experiment of Schneider & Sherman (59) indicates, the effect may be due to an obliteration or diminution of fear by an interaction between fear arousal and treatment when these are temporally contiguous. Memory consolidation may not be involved in the puromycin effect at all.

That the effect of puromycin resembles that of ECS extremely closely in the parameters of retrograde amnesia it produces in goldfish has been shown by Davis, Bright & Agranoff (19). Agranoff et al. (2) report that actinomycin-D injected intracranially immediately after learning produces partial amnesia. An injection of the drug 3 hr after training does not produce amnesia. A similar effect is reported with injections of acetoxycycloheximide. It is not reported how long memory persists after the injection. The authors state: "Since protein synthesis is not significantly inhibited for several hours after the injection of actinomycin-D, we suggest that this drug impairs memory not by blocking protein synthesis but by some other means, presumably by its well-known role in blocking DNA-mediated RNA synthesis."

Agranoff has recently reported (1) that intracranial injections of 6 per cent KCl into the goldfish produce retrograde amnesia for 12 to 18 hr, a much longer time span than affected by protein synthesis inhibitors. Memory apparently also takes 12 to 18 hr to disappear after treatment. There is no suggestion that such disappearance of memory after treatment is more rapid with any of these agents the longer the interval between training and drug treatment. However, this is what we would expect if the two-stage theory were correct. The persistence of memory after treatment is attributed to a decaying short-term memory process. The later in the life of this process treatment to knock out the long-term memory is given, the shorter the time over which memory should be observed. A single-stage model would predict the opposite, if anything.

Davis (17) has reported further on his previously described evidence (18) for an environmental trigger to memory fixation in the goldfish. It has been shown (see above) that puromycin has gradually less effect the longer after the learning experience it is injected. Davis reports that if the goldfish is left in the training environment after training, the time is extended during which the memory is vulnerable to puromycin. Davis interprets this to mean that memory fixation is suppressed by conditions in the training environment. This conclusion must be accepted with caution. It can be seen from Davis' data that uninjected controls show a memory deficit which rapidly increases with the time they are left in the training environment. Such a deficit does not occur if such controls are returned to their home tanks. It can be argued then that puromycin injections, given to fish that have been left in the training environment for increasing times, are acting on a rapidly decreasing memory substrate as indicated by a behavioral impairment of memory. For instance, a puromycin injection made immediately after training affects a memory where the normal retention index 72 hr later would be $-.38$. The same injection made 3.5 hr after training affects a memory where the normal retention index would be -1.22, significantly different from the case where the goldfish is removed immediately from the training environment. After 24 hr in the training environment, retention deficits of controls are very large and not significantly different from deficits shown by the groups which received puromycin after 24 hr in the same environment. It is possible that a weaker memory remains susceptible to puromycin for a longer time than a stronger one, and Davis has not excluded this possibility. Until the nature of the decrement observed in untreated fish kept in the training environment is clarified, the fact that puromycin remains an effective agent for longer after training when fish are kept in the training environment can hardly be taken as evidence for an environmental trigger of memory fixation. Another possible explanation of the result is that puromycin, like ECS in Schneider & Sherman's experiment (59), is effective while the animal is in a state of fear. Such fear would be sustained by the training environment. Potts & Bitterman (47) have criticized the environmental trigger explanation by showing that goldfish trained to a much higher criterion do not suffer from amnesia even though injected immediately upon being taken out of the training environment. This exposure to the training environment should on Davis' argument have postponed fixation, thus rendering the memory vulnerable to puromycin. However, this experiment of Potts & Bitterman does show that memory strength is an important variable in susceptibility to puromycin.

The work with protein synthesis inhibitors seems to face major unsolved problems. Flexner's work with puromycin indicates that the effect is not on memory storage but on retrieval. The question must be asked whether such is not the effect of other protein synthesis inhibitors also. A more severe problem is posed for the protein synthesis inhibitors shown to be effective only when they are administered close to learning. It must be shown that they affect memory at all, let alone whether they affect retrieval or storage. The possibility of an interaction between motivational effects and drug treatment remains open, especially in view of recent results with ECS. Even if a real effect on memory is substantiated, there remains the question whether such an effect is due directly to protein synthesis inhibition or to some indirect or side effect of the drug.

CHOLINERGIC DRUGS AND MEMORY

A series of experiments has shown that cholinergic agents can alter recall in various ways (20). In the initial experiment, DFP (diisopropyl fluorophosphate) was injected intracerebrally various times after training. Rats had been trained to escape a shock by running to the lit arm of a Y-maze. Retest was always conducted the same time after injection. In this way any differences found in recall could not be due to differences in effective drug dosage at time of testing. It was found that there was a small degree of amnesia when injection was made half an hour after training. At 3 days after training, the drug had no effect. On the other hand, there was considerable amnesia at 7 and 14 days after training. A very similar time course was obtained with intraperitoneal injections of physostigmine (22). Both DFP and physostigmine are anticholinesterases. Therefore, they slow down the destruction of acetylcholine by combining with cholinesterase. At low levels of synaptic conductance, such drugs will facilitate transmission by preventing the destruction of acetylcholine and thus aiding the depolarization of the postsynaptic membrane. At high levels of synaptic conductance, synaptic transmission is blocked because of the accumulation of acetylcholine. It was therefore concluded that with the exception of a short time after initial learning, the conductance of a synapse increased with time after training. In this way an anticholinesterase would have no effect soon after learning but would cause a block as synaptic conductance improved with time. To test this, parallel experiments were performed with scopolamine, an anticholinergic agent. Such a drug diminishes the effective amount of acetylcholine. It would therefore be expected that this drug would have its maximum effect on memory when anticholinesterases had no effect (when conductance was low) but would have no effect when anticholinesterases blocked memory. That this is the case was verified in two experiments. In the first (25), exactly the same escape habit was used as in the experiments with anticholinesterases. In the second (61), an appetitive habit was employed, and both DFP and scopolamine were used within the same experimental design. The results were very similar to those obtained with the escape habit. The effects of the injection of DFP were also tested when the escape and appetitive habits were almost forgotten (23, 61). Rats injected with a control injection 28 days after training had almost forgotten the escape habit. However, when injected with DFP at this time, they showed almost complete retention. A similar facilitation was obtained with the almost forgotten appetitive habit when it was 21 days old. Forgetting in the case of the appetitive habit was faster. The dose of DFP producing facilitation of an almost forgotten habit is the same as that which blocks the recall of the same habit when it normally is well remembered. These results suggest that forgetting is due to a lowering of synaptic conductance, because anticholinesterases facilitate synaptic transmission where synaptic conductance is low.

While the drug data suggested that there was an increase in the substrate of memory between 3 and 7 days after training, no improvement in the performance of undrugged controls was detected from 3 to 7 days after training. In other words, anticholinesterase has two different effects on memory, no block at 3 days and a block at 7. However, habits were as well performed after 3 days as they were after 7. This could have been due to a "ceiling" effect, as the rats had been trained to a high criterion and therefore could show no behavioral evidence of improvement from 3 days to a week because their performance was almost perfect. Consequently, rats were undertrained (34) and retention measured at various times after training. Retention without any injection was much better at 7 or 10 days than at 1 or 3 days. This confirmed the inference made from the drug studies.

It has also been found (22, 23) that the amnesic effect due to DFP is temporary. This agrees with the idea that the amnesia is due to synaptic block. Amnesia should only be observed in the presence of sufficient quantities of anticholinesterase when excessive acetylcholine is present. A way of diminishing the pile-up of acetylcholine when anticholinesterase is present is to give the rat longer pauses between trials during retest. This is because, with the rate of destruction of acetylcholine slowed down by phosostigmine, it takes longer for an excessive or blocking amount of acetylcholine to be cleared away. Under physostigmine, when trials during retest are spaced (50) there is almost no amnesia, though amnesia is severe when trials are massed. On the other hand, reversal learning under physostigmine is easier when trials are massed than when they are spaced. Reversal is easier when there is no memory of the original habit.

An interaction has been found between the degree of original training

THE PHYSIOLOGICAL BASIS OF MEMORY

and the effects of anticholinesterase on memory (24). Weakly learned habits are strongly facilitated, whereas well learned habits are blocked by the same dose of DFP. The drug has no effect on habits learned to an intermediate degree. This relationship has been demonstrated by varying the number of trials given on the same task. The same relation holds if instead of varying the number of trials on the same task we hold number of trials constant but vary task difficulty. The easier task is then better learned than the difficult task at the end of the same number of trials (40). Difficulty was increased by dimming the light to be discriminated. DFP produced memory block with the easy task, whereas it caused strong facilitation with the difficult task. Again exactly the same dose of drug was used to produce these opposite effects. These results suggest that conductance in a set of synapses increases with degree of training.

As has been stated above, it is possible with anticholinesterase injections to produce amnesia for 7-day-old habits while leaving the memory for 3-day-old habits unblocked. This property has been utilized to analyze the nature of extinction (26). If extinction is a separate habit, it should be possible to leave it intact, so that it should be remembered on retest while the original habit is unavailable. A rat in this condition should therefore find it much more difficult to relearn the original habit on retest than preinjected control rats, or rats which were extinguished soon after learning. In the rats extinguished soon after learning, both the memory of original learning and of extinction should be blocked. To test these predictions, rats were trained to approach a light for a reward of sugar-water in a modified Y-maze 7 days before an injection of physostigmine. Then at various times after initial training they were placed in the maze and not rewarded for approaching the light, until a criterion of nonresponding was reached. The rats which were extinguished 3 days before injection took almost twice the number of trials to relearn on retest when compared with controls and rats extinguished 6 days before injection. On the other hand, they learned a reversal of the original habit more quickly than such control groups. This suggests that during extinction a separate habit is learned which opposes the performance of the initially rewarded habit. From the results on reversal it seems plausible that such an opposing habit is an aversion to the initially rewarding stumuli. This supports the theory of extinction put forward by Miller & Stevenson (43).

INTERHEMISPHERIC TRANSFER OF MEMORY

A very large number of experiments have now been carried out to study characteristics of the memory process by means of spreading depression since Bureš (9) first used such a technique for this purpose. The technique of spreading depression can selectively abolish most neural activity in the cortex covering one hemisphere of a rat. Such an inactivation is reversible. In an initial set of experiments, rats were trained with, say, the left half of the cortex depressed, and then tested with only the right side depressed. If the rats could not perform the original habit, it was concluded that the memory trace had been stored in the originally nondepressed hemisphere. When this hemisphere was depressed during test, the stored memory was unavailable. In a second generation of experiments, the characteristics of the transfer of a memory trace from hemisphere to hemisphere were studied. It was found that if the animal was given the opportunity to make one or two rewarded responses with neither hemisphere depressed, after it had been trained with one hemisphere depressed and before it was tested with the other hemisphere depressed, it performed well during test. This was interpreted to mean that the trials when neither hemisphere was depressed enabled the memory trace to move from the educated hemisphere to the ignorant one.

In a further refinement, an attempt was made to measure the time necessary for transmission to take place from the trained hemisphere to the untrained after the trial with both hemispheres undepressed. This was done by producing spreading depression in the previously trained hemisphere at various times after the trial with both hemispheres undepressed. It was found that the degree of transfer decreased as the time between the trial with both hemispheres undepressed and the subsequent depression of the originally trained hemisphere were brought closer together. A similar attempt was made to measure how long it would take the receiving hemisphere (i.e., the originally depressed and so untrained half) to consolidate the memory trace transmitted to it by the trained hemisphere. For this purpose experimenters varied the interval between the first time one hemisphere was depressed and its subsequent depression. As spreading depression can also produce retrograde amnesia, it was thought that the period during which the transferred trace was vulnerable to spreading depression would give a measure of the time that the trace took to consolidate.

While such experiments have been elegant and their interpretation in terms of the anatomy of memory enticing, difficulties have begun to appear. Some habits appeared not to be confined to one hemisphere, and so a subcortical locus of storage had to be posited (10). Even more perplexing is the finding that rats trained to go, say, to the left when one hemisphere is depressed, go right when the other hemisphere is depressed (49 a, b). While it is true that the rats did not perform the original habit of going left when spreading depression was shifted to the other hemisphere, it is somewhat surprising that their behavior deviated from random performance to the same extent as before the hemispheres were switched. While this was claimed as a loss of the learned habit, it could equally well be interpreted as an acquisition of the mirror image habit by some mysterious means. However, a simpler explanation is that the rats during initial training had learned by orienting themselves with respect to the lateralized symptoms to which unilateral spreading depression gives rise. Then when the side of the cortex which is depressed is switched, the rats will perform the mirror-image habit. No forgetting has taken place.

Such considerations prompted Schneider (53) to reinterpret the results obtained with the use of spreading depression. As was stated above, the basic assumption of this work was that if an animal has been trained with one hemisphere depressed, it cannot then perform when the state of the two hemispheres is reversed; this shows that the memory of the habit must have been confined to the hemisphere which was nondepressed during original learning. Though this is an appealing argument, it is by no means a compelling one, and Schneider has set about showing why it is often wrong. Schneider's alternative hypothesis is that the rat's inability to transfer is due to generalization decrement. It is probable that there is a change in the stimulus complex concomitant with changes of cortical depression. It is also known that changes in stimulus conditions between training and test conditions can lead to apparent forgetting on the part of the animal.

To support his thesis, Schneider has to show that certain propositions are true. The first is that spreading depression can act as a stimulus to the rat. Schneider & Kay (58) trained rats in an operant situation, reinforcing responses emitted under unilateral spreading depression but not reinforcing those with cortex normal. It was found that during extinction more responses were emitted under unilateral spreading depression than without depression. The second proposition which then has to be demonstrated is that stimulus change due to spreading depression does act to interfere with performance. To test this, Schneider (54) trained rats to perform an avoidance task. Some rats were trained under unilateral spreading depression while others were trained with the entire cortex undepressed. Later transfer of both groups to a condition where the cortex was bilaterally depressed showed much larger savings in the case of the animals trained originally under unilateral spreading depression. Schneider (54) interprets this to show that transfer to a state of bilateral spreading depression involves much less of a stimulus change for the animals trained under unilateral spreading depression than for the animals which had not had experience of spreading depression at all.

However, this experiment may be criticized on two grounds. First, no controls were run for the effects of repeated spreading depression. There may be physiological effects due simply to repeated treatment. Second, Schneider (53) purports to show that unilateral spreading depression produces subcortical memory storage. Such subcortical storage, according to him, does not occur when the cortex is undepressed. It seems that this, rather than degrees of stimulus change, could explain his experiment, as he himself states (53).

To counter this objection, Schneider (53) ran another experiment in which he trained rats in a passive avoidance task of the step-down variety. Two groups were trained under unilateral spreading depression. One was subsequently tested under the same unilateral depression, whereas the other was tested with cortex normal. During this test the performance of the rats tested with cortex normal was greatly inferior to those tested under unilateral depression.

Schneider's conclusion has been criticized by Squire & Liss (60) on the grounds that unilateral spreading depression normally increases latencies and that the longer latencies, and so "better" performance, of the unilaterally depressed rats are a result of motor depression. However, Schneider correctly points out that the two other groups in his experiment which were tested under unilateral spreading depression had even shorter latencies than the normal group whose superior performance Squire & Liss (60) seek to explain on grounds of motor noninvolvement. However, the role of repeated treatment with spreading depression was not evaluated.

It is when we come to his experimental critique of memory transfer from one hemisphere to the other that Schneider's case becomes watertight. The experiment we may consider as a paradigm was carried out by Russell & Ochs (52). They trained rats to lever-press to obtain food while one hemisphere was depressed. This habit did not transfer to the originally depressed hemisphere even after a two-week interdepression period. However, if the animals were given a single rewarded lever-press with both hemispheres nondepressed, the response apparently "transferred" to the originally depressed hemisphere. A number of experiments based on this paradigm have been performed and remarkable inferences about memory trace movements have been drawn.

Schneider & Hamburg (57) trained rats in a shuttle box under unilateral spreading depression. No savings were observed when the rats were retested with the opposite hemisphere depressed. Savings were observed when a trial with unavoidable shock was given between the two sessions with unilateral spreading depression. This is in accord with the previous hypothesis that one trial is needed with both hemispheres undepressed to induce the memory trace to transfer from one hemisphere to the other. However, another group given the unavoidable shock prior to all training and not in the interval between the depression of one hemisphere and then the other showed transfer between the two separately trained hemispheres on a subsequent test. That is, it does not seem to matter whether training in the situation with two hemispheres undepressed takes place before any memory trace has been laid down or after it has been unilaterally laid down. Transfer of training from the condition of one hemisphere depressed to the other depressed takes place in both conditions. This indicates that such transfer cannot be due to the memory trace moving from one hemisphere to the other because of a single reinforced trial conducted in the interval between the depression of one hemisphere and that of the other.

An even more damaging experiment to the interpretation of interhemispheric memory transfer was carried out by Schneider & Ebbesen (56). Their experiment was very similar to that of Russell & Ochs except that they added a control group. Besides the group which was given a rewarded trial with both hemispheres undepressed, another group was given the rewarded trial under identical circumstances except that the rewarded trial was given with the trained hemisphere depressed. Both groups were then tested for responding during extinction with the trained hemisphere depressed. Transfer from the trained to the untrained hemisphere was observed for both groups. However, the group given the single intervening trial with the trained hemisphere depressed showed very much more transfer than the group given the intervening rewarded trial with both hemispheres undepressed. Here it is difficult to see how a memory trace could have been induced to transfer from a depressed hemisphere to the undepressed hemisphere by the rewarded trial. On the other hand, the result is much more comprehensible in terms of the stimulus generalization hypothesis of Schneider (53).

It seems then that Schneider has cast serious doubt on the conventional explanations of experiments using spreading depression to study memory. Squire & Liss claim (60), however, that he cannot readily explain the results of Albert (4). Albert used the same paradigm as Russell & Ochs (52). That is, he trained a single undepressed hemisphere, then gave an intervening rewarded trial with both hemispheres undepressed, and finally used unilateral spreading depression to produce retrograde amnesia in a single hemisphere. In one set of experiments such depression was applied to the previously trained hemisphere (the transmitting hemisphere); in another set to the previously untrained hemisphere. Albert claimed to measure the consolidation time of the transferred trace. However, though spreading depression causes retrograde amnesia, Bureš (8) has recently shown that such amnesia is only temporary and therefore cannot be considered to prevent consolidation. Schneider (55) attempts an intricate analysis of Albert's experiment to refute Squire & Liss' criticism. The matter can be dealt with more simply. If the original Russell & Ochs' (52) interpretation is erroneous, as Schneider has certainly shown, then Albert's interpretation of his own work which uses Russell & Ochs' basic paradigm and theory must also be fallacious. Further, Schneider does not need to interpret all the data on spreading depression in terms of a single detailed theory based on the notions of generalization decrement and stimulus generalization. Spreading depression has never been a tool of choice for studying such phenomena and one may confidently say it never will be. There are too many unknown confounding factors. The important contribution of Schneider is his demonstration that spreading depression is not a tool of choice for studying memory trace dynamics. The burden of proof is not on Schneider to show that he can explain all the data on his hypothesis, as seems to be assumed by Squire & Liss (60) and Carlson (12). Rather, those wishing to use the method to draw inferences about memory must prove that their results are not due to the serious confounding factors demonstrated by Schneider.

Memory localization—cortical or subcortical.—Inferences from the method of spreading depression have been drawn about whether a particular habit is stored cortically or subcortically (10). If a habit transfers between the condition where one hemisphere is depressed to the condition where the other is depressed, it is concluded that storage must have been subcortical. If the habit does not transfer, the conclusion is drawn that the habit is cortically stored.

Continuing this tradition, Carlson (12) in a series of experiments trained

rats in a box, one half of which was white and the other black. In her first
experiment, rats were shocked in one compartment under unilateral spreading depression. In the subsequent test, Carlson measured the time spent in
the nonshocked compartment as a index of the memory of emotional and
cue aspects, and the latency of entry into the shocked compartment as a
measure of the response of passive avoidance. It was found that even when
the spreading depression was switched from one hemisphere to the other
between training and test, rats would spend more time in the side in which
they had not been shocked, indicating memory of emotional and cue aspects.
Though there was a large difference in the means of the latencies of entry into
the shocked side between experimentals and controls (6.50 to 33.12), this
difference in passive avoidance did not reach statistical significance. This is
not surprising, as there were only four rats in the control group and eight in
the experimental group. What is more surprising is the author's conclusion:
"From this it would appear that subcortical structures can store information
about emotional and cue aspects of the situation but that 'trained' hemicortex must be functional . . . . for S to perform even as simple a response
as passive avoidance" (12, p. 425).

In a second experiment, Carlson trained three groups ($N=5$) of rats in
avoidance, shocking them in the black compartment until they escaped to
the white. One group (S) was trained and tested with unilateral spreading
depression always on the same side. A second group (E) was trained with
spreading depression on one side and tested under contralateral spreading
depression. A third group (C) was given spreading depression on one side
but not trained, and then tested under contralateral spreading depression.
Group S showed retention both by the time spent in the black side and also
by the latency of entry into that side. To assess the test behavior of group
E, E could be compared either with its own performance before treatment or
with group C. Carlson is not consistent about which comparison is made.
Group C was compared with group E to show that side preference had
changed for group E as a result of the training of the opposite hemicortex.
The change in group E's score before and after treatment was smaller than
the difference between E and C. Here a comparison between E and C was
made, and it was concluded that emotional and cue aspects were retained
and therefore stored subcortically. However, when changes in latency of
entry into the black side were assessed, group E was compared against itself.
Here the change in latency in group E before and after treatment was small,
but the difference between group E and group C was more than threefold.
This large difference might support the notion that complex motor responses
could also be stored subcortically and contradict Carlson's thesis.

> Thus although Ss in group E clearly retained information about the emotional and
> cue aspects, sufficient to enable them to spend less time overall in the black side,
> they did not delay their first entry into that side. . . Thus these results support . . .
> (the) hypothesis that subcortical structures are important in the storage of emo-

tional and cue components, and that the complex motor response must be cortically integrated [Carlson (12), p. 425–26].

Not only are questionable logical methods used to bolster a preconceived hypothesis, but it is also clear that the interpretation of experiments like this can be made in terms of generalization decrement. It may be simply that different degrees of generalization decrement operate for different components of a task and for different tasks and under different motivational conditions.

Schneider (53) has employed another approach to this problem of localizing the memory trace. He has used the fact that spreading depression applied soon after learning produces retrograde amnesia. He reasoned that he could produce retrograde amnesia only in one cortical hemisphere if he applied spreading depression to that hemisphere alone. From results obtained by employing a combination of spreading depression during and just after learning, he concludes that there is subcortical storage if there is spreading depression during training. Otherwise, according to him, the trace resides only in the cortex. However, there are insufficient controls on the role of unilateral or repeated spreading depression on susceptibility to such treatment to permit a conclusive evaluation of Schneider's study. There seems to be no good evidence at present that memory storage in the rat is ever cortical.

ELECTROCONVULSIVE SHOCK AND AMNESIA

The hope behind the many investigations employing ECS seemed to be that "consolidation" of the memory trace could be studied. The notion was that the memory trace shortly after being laid down was labile and susceptible to destruction, but that it soon changed state and became impervious to disruption. If the time that it took the memory trace to consolidate could be measured, some clue to its physical identity might be found. However, no constant time over which ECS disrupts memory after training has been found. For instance, Quartermain, Paolino & Miller (48) and Chorover & Schiller (14) have found an interval in the order of seconds. On the other hand, Kopp, Bohdanecky & Jarvik (39) have found effects 6 hr after training, and McGaugh (42) reports effects on memory 3 hr after training. Some of these discrepancies are due to amount of current passed through the animal. McGaugh (42) demonstrates that length of electroshock is a factor. Jarvik & Kopp (35) show that increased current intensity produces increasing amnesia.

Whether ECS effects are seen at all may be influenced by competing responses. Gerbrandt et al. (33) report failure to find an effect of ECS on memory of a discrimination training using hooded rats. In a subsequent experiment, Bureš and co-workers (11) found such an effect only in albino rats. They did find an adverse effect of ECS on the memory of a reversal habit when overtraining was given on the original habit. This effect was observed both in hooded and albino rats.

The picture of two qualitatively different processes—one susceptible to ECS and the other an invulnerable consolidated memory trace—seems no longer so plausible. That some change is occurring during the footshock-ECS interval has been made clear. However ECS seems to be capable of interfering with memory up to an ill-defined point on a merely quantitatively changing continuum. The notion of a quantitatively changing continuum is supported by the amnesic effects of other agents. For instance, flurothyl (hexafluorodiethyl ether), when compared in efficacy to ECS by Bohdanecky, Kopp & Jarvik (7), showed an effect longer after training than did ECS. The curves of amnesic effect of these two agents presented by Bohdanecky, Kopp & Jarvik (7) run parallel and except for the degree of amnesic effect seem qualitatively similar.

Turning back again to the original hypothesis which appeared to motivate research with ECS, it was hoped to show that there was a phase during which memory was labile and so subject to destruction by ECS. If this were the case, the application of ECS at some interval after learning should lead to a permanent amnesia for the habit learned [Duncan (28)]. Chevalier (13) found no diminution of ECS amnesia after a month. Zinkin & Miller (62) found an apparent recovery of memory after ECS under conditions of repeated testing of a single group. Luttges & McGaugh (41) found no such effect if separate groups were tested at different time intervals, so that each mouse was retested only once. No apparent recovery of memory occurred after one month, even though control animals had not forgotten the task. Kohlenberg & Trabasso (38) on the other hand, found that mice given ECS performed at the same level as controls 48 hr after treatment, but were markedly inferior after only 24 hr. It is to be noted here that there was a considerable degree of forgetting in the controls after 48 hr. Such a trend can also be seen in the data of McGaugh and Alpern [quoted by McGaugh (42)]. Almost complete forgetting in a one-trial escape task after one week has been observed by Deutsch & Yeomans (27). There are, therefore, discrepancies both in the time course of memory after ECS and without ECS.

Some of the differences with respect to recovery of memory after ECS are resolved by Peeke & Herz (46), who showed an apparent recovery in mice 72 hr after learning when such mice had been tested 24 and 48 hr after learning, but no such recovery when mice were tested only 72 hr later. Schneider & Sherman (59) present data which suggest that recovery of memory after ECS occurs when there is stronger initial learning, as produced by increasing the number of footshocks, but not when such learning is weaker. Another possible reason for this discrepancy in the ECS data has been given by Pagano et al. (45). They have shown that whether memory returns after ECS treatment depends upon the intensity of ECS. Relatively low ECS intensity permitted a return of memory of a step-down task within 24 to 48 hr. There was amnesia at one hour after ECS, in contrast with the results of Geller & Jarvik (32). Such amnesia was only observed when ECS was administered 0.5 sec after footshock. No amnesia was observed when the footshock-ECS interval was 30 sec. On the other hand, high ECS intensity led to an amnesia which lasted for 48 hr, the longest time after ECS that the rats were tested.

An interesting sidelight on the initial hypothesis of consolidation which motivated work with ECS is cast by a study of Geller & Jarvik (32). These workers found that memory remains for a few hours after ECS but disappears by 24 hr, the interval after which animals treated with ECS have been traditionally tested. This creates somewhat of a paradox for the simple consolidation model. It is difficult to see how memory could persist after the labile stage of memory has been destroyed by ECS. There are alternate possibilities to explain Geller and Jarvik's result. The first would be to suppose that there were two processes involved, both beginning with the learning experience. The first would be transient and immune to ECS. The second process would normally be long-lasting but ECS could prevent its initiation. This type of explanation has been suggested in connection with the protein synthesis data. A second possible explanation would be to assume that there was a single process and that ECS accelerates forgetting. The data do not compel us to accept a two-stage model.

Perhaps the most damaging criticism of ECS as a tool is that it does not produce a retrograde memory deficit at all. Routtenberg & Kay (51) and Kopp et al. (39) have provided evidence that ECS causes decreased latencies and thus could produce an appearance of amnesia in tests where an increase in latency is taken as evidence of retention. However, such findings by themselves could not explain why somewhat small differences in time of ECS after learning (the retrograde effect) should produce differences in amount of amnesia. However, Schneider & Sherman (59) have now shown why this explanation in terms of reduced latency could fit the retrograde effect. Schneider & Sherman found that the critical variable to produce an appearance of amnesia was the interval between footshock and ECS. When rats were shocked upon stepping off a platform, ECS 0.5 sec later produced amnesia 24 hr later. ECS administered 30 sec or 6 hr later produced no amnesia. However, if a second footshock was given 0.5 sec before the ECS (given either 30 sec or 6 hr later), "amnesia" was produced.

Schneider (personal communication) states that the combination of footshock and ECS can be given outside the test situation, either before or after the step-off task, and apparent amnesia for the step-off task will still result. It seems that some interaction between footshock and ECS is responsible for the quasi-retrograde amnesia normally observed. It is difficult to see how this explanation could be extended to situations where there is an apparent amnesic effect of ECS even where shock is not used before ECS, such as in the study of Peeke & Herz (46). However, the "amnesia" in their experiment may have been a simple performance decrement due to ECS, as no retrograde action of the ECS was demonstrated. There does seem to be an interaction between ECS and footshock. Coons & Miller (16) showed that ECS side-effects were greater if ECS was administered sooner after footshock.

Another experiment casting doubt on the retrograde amnesic nature of

ECS was performed by Misanin, Miller & Lewis (44), who propose a hypothesis which would cover ECS results found in appetitive situations. They trained rats to lick when thirsty. The rats were then exposed to a burst of intense white noise. The offset of this noise coincided with footshock. A control group showed that 24 hr later such noise depressed the rate of licking. The rate of licking was equally unaffected in the group given ECS immediately after the noise-footshock training and in the group where ECS was administered 24 hr later, immediately after a second exposure to the noise. When the white noise was omitted just prior to ECS treatment 24 hr later, memory was not significantly affected, as judged by depression in the rate of licking. The authors explain the result by assuming that ECS has an effect on memory when the memory trace is activated and "that the memory system must be in a state of change at the time of ECS."

The studies just reviewed show how the use of ECS as a technique for the study of consolidation of memory has recently been called into serious question by the experimental evidence. It is not even clear at present in what way, if any, memory is affected by ECS. Earlier we saw how the use of inhibitors of protein synthesis and the use of spreading depression have also run into major problems. However, in spite of, or rather perhaps because of, recent discoveries which are forcing a re-evaluation of old ideas, the study of the physiological bases of memory is entering a new and exciting phase.

LITERATURE CITED

1. Agranoff, B. W. Recent studies on the stages of memory formation in the goldfish (Presented at the 134th Ann. Meeting of AAAS, 1967)
2. Agranoff, B. W., Davis, R. E. Casola, L., Lim, R. Actinomycin-D blocks formation of memory of shock-avoidance in goldfish. *Science,* **158,** 1600–1 (1967)
3. Agranoff, B. W., Klinger, P. D. Puromycin effect on memory fixation in the goldfish. *Science,* **146,** 952–53 (1964)
4. Albert, D. J., The effect of spreading depression on the consolidation of learning. *Neuropsychologia,* **4,** 49–64 (1966)
5. Barondes, S. H., Cohen, H. D. Puromycin effect on successive phases of memory storage. *Science,* **151,** 594–95 (1966)
6. Barondes, S. H., Cohen, H. D. Memory impairment after subcutaneous injection of acetoxycycloheximide. *Science,* **160,** 556–57 (1968)
7. Bohdanecky, Z., Kopp, R., Jarvik, M. E. Comparison of ECS and flurothyl-induced retrograde amnesia in mice. *Psychopharmacologia* (Berlin), **12,** 91–95 (1968)

8. Bureš, J. In *Neurosciences Research Program* on consolidation of memory (In press)
9. Bureš, J., Burešová, O. The use of Leão's spreading cortical depression in research on conditioned reflexes. *EEG Clin. Neurophysiol.,* Suppl. 13, 359–76 (1960)
10. Bureš J., Burešová, O., Fifková, E. Interhemispheric transfer of a passive avoidance reaction. *J. Comp. Physiol. Psychol.,* **57,** 326–30 (1964)
11. Burešová, O., Bureš, J., Gerbrandt, L. K. The effect of an electroconvulsive shock on retention of a spatial discrimination or its reversal. *Physiology and Behavior,* **3,** 155–59 (1968)
12. Carlson, K. R. Cortical spreading depression and subcortical memory storage. *J. Comp. Physiol. Psychol.,* **64,** 422–30 (1967)
13. Chevalier, J. A. Permanence of amnesia after a single post-trial electroconvulsive seizure. *J. Comp. Physiol. Psychol.,* **59,** 125–27 (1965)
14. Chorover, S. L., Schiller, P. H. Short-term retrograde amnesia in rats. *J. Comp. Physiol. Psychol.,* **59,** 73–78 (1965)

15. Cohen, H. D., Barondes, S. H. Relationship of degree of training to the effect of acetoxycycloheximide on memory in mice. *Proc. 75th Ann. Conv. Am. Psychol. Assoc.*, **2**, 79–80 (1967)

16. Coons, E. E., Miller, N. E. Conflict versus consolidation of memory traces to explain "retrograde amnesia" produced by ECS. *J. Comp. Physiol. Psychol.*, **53**, 524–31 (1960)

17. Davis, R. E., Environmental control of memory fixation in goldfish. *J. Comp. Physiol. Psychol.*, **65**, 72–78 (1968)

18. Davis, R. E., Agranoff, B. W. Stages of memory formation in goldfish: evidence for an environmental trigger. *Proc. Natl. Acad. Sci. U.S.*, **55**, 555–59 (1966)

19. Davis, R. E., Bright, P. J., Agranoff, B. W. Effect of ECS and puromycin on memory in fish. *J. Comp. Physiol. Psychol.*, **60**, 162–66 (1965)

20. Deutsch, J. A. Substrates of learning and memory. *Dis. Nerv. Sys.*, **27**, 20–24 (1966)

21. Deutsch, J. A., Deutsch, D. *Physiological Psychology* (Dorsey Press, 1966)

22. Deutsch, J. A., Hamburg, M. D., Dahl, H. Anticholinesterase-induced amnesia and its temporal aspects. *Science*, **151**, 221–23 (1966)

23. Deutsch, J. A., Leibowitz, S. F. Amnesia or reversal of forgetting by anticholinesterase, depending simply on time of injection. *Science*, **153**, 1017 (1966)

24. Deutsch, J. A., Lutzky, H. Memory enhancement by anticholinesterase as a function of initial learning. *Nature*, **213**, 742 (1967)

25. Deutsch, J. A., Rocklin, K. Amnesia induced by scopolamine and its temporal variations. *Nature*, **216**, 89–90 (1967)

26. Deutsch, J. A., Wiener, N. I. Analysis of extinction through amnesia (Submitted for publication)

27. Deutsch, J. A., Yeomans, J. (Unpublished data)

28. Duncan, C. P. The retroactive effects of shock on learning. *J. Comp. Physiol. Psychol.*, **42**, 32–34 (1949)

29. Flexner, J. B., Flexner, L. B. Restoration of expression of memory lost after treatment with puromycin. *Proc. Natl. Acad. Sci. U. S.*, **57**, 1651–54 (1967)

30. Flexner, L. B., Flexner, J. B. Intracerebral saline: effect on memory of trained mice treated with puromycin. *Science*, **159**, 330–31 (1968)

31. Flexner, L. B., Flexner, J. B., Roberts, R. Memory in mice analyzed with antibiotics. *Science*, **155**, 1377–83 (1967)

32. Geller, A., Jarvik, M. E. The time relations of ECS induced amnesia. *Psychon. Sci.*, **12**, 169–70 (1968)

33. Gerbrandt, L. K., Burešová, O., Bureš, J. Discrimination and reversal learning followed by a single electroconvulsive shock. *Physiology and Behavior*, **3**, 149–53 (1968)

34. Huppert, F. A., Deutsch, J. A. Improvement in memory with time (Submitted for publication)

35. Jarvik, M. E., Kopp, R. Transcorneal electroconvulsive shock and retrograde amnesia in mice. *J. Comp. Physiol. Psychol.*, **64**, 431–33 (1967)

36. Koenig, E. J. Synthetic mechanisms in the axon. I. Local axonal synthesis of acetylcholinesterase. *J. Neurochem.*, **12**, 343–55 (1965)

37. Koenig, E. J. Synthetic mechanisms in the axon. III. Stimulation of acetylcholinesterase synthesis by actinomycin-D in the hypoglossal nerve. *J. Neurochem.*, **14**, 429–35 (1967)

38. Kohlenberg, R., Trabasso, T. Recovery of a conditioned emotional response after one or two electroconvulsive shocks. *J. Comp. Physiol. Psychol.* (In press)

    Kopp, R., Bohdanecky, Z., Jarvik, M. E. Proactive effect of a single ECS on step-through performance on naive and punished mice. *J. Comp. Physiol. Psychol.*, **64**, 22–25 (1967)

40. Leibowitz, S. F. *Memory and Emotionality after Anticholinesterase in the Hippocampus: Reverse Function of Prior Learning Level* (Doctoral thesis, New York Univ., June 1968)

41. Luttges, M. W., McGaugh, J. L. Permanence of retrograde amnesia produced by electroconvulsive shock. *Science*, **156**, 408–10 (1967)

42. McGaugh, J. L. Time-dependent processes in memory storage. *Science*, **153**, 1351–58 (1966)

43. Miller, N. E., Stevenson, S. S. Agitated behavior of rats during experimental extinction and a curve of spontaneous recovery. *J. Comp. Psychol.*, **21**, 205–31 (1936)

44. Misanin, J. R., Miller, R. R., Lewis, D. J. Retrograde amnesia produced by electroconvulsive shock

after reactivation of a consolidated memory trace. *Science*, **160**, 554–55 (1968)

45. Pagano, R. R., Bush, D. F., Martin, G., Hunt, E. B. *Duration of Retrograde Amnesia as a Function of Electroconvulsive Shock Intensity* (Tech. Rept. No. 68-1-09, Univ. Washington, 1968)

46. Peeke, H. V. S., Herz, M. J. Permanence of electroconvulsive shock-produced retrograde amnesia. *Proc. 75th Ann. Conv. Am. Psychol. Assoc.*, **2**, 85–86 (1967); Herz, M. J., Peeke, H. V. S. Permanence of retrograde amnesia produced by electroconvulsive shock. *Science*, **156**, 1396–97 (1967)

47. Potts, A., Bitterman, M. E. Puromycin and retention in the goldfish. *Science*, **158**, 1594–96 (1967)

48. Quartermain, D., Paolino, R. M., Miller, N. E. A brief temporal gradient of retrograde amnesia independent of situational change. *Science*, **149**, 1116–18 (1965)

49a. Ray, O. S., Emley, G. Time factors in interhemispheric transfer of learning. *Science*, **144**, 76–78 (1964)

49b. Ray, O. S., Emley, G. Interhemispheric transfer of learning. *Life Sci.*, **4**, 271–79 (1965)

50. Rocklin, K. W., Deutsch, J. A. (Unpublished data)

51. Routtenberg, A., Kay, K. E. Effect of one electroconvulsive seizure on rat behavior. *J. Comp.. Physiol. Psychol.*, **59**, 285–88 (1965)

52. Russell, I., Ochs, S. One-trial interhemispheric transfer of a learning engram. *Science*, **133**, 1077–78 (1961)

53. Schneider, A. M. Control of memory by spreading cortical depression: a case for stimulus control. *Psychol. Rev.*, **74**, 201–15 (1967)

54. Schneider, A. M. Retention under spreading depression: a generalization-decrement phenomenon. *J. Comp. Physiol. Psychol.*, **62**, 317–19 (1966)

55. Schneider, A. M. Stimulus control spreading cortical depression: some problems reconsidered. *Psychol. Rev.* (In press)

56. Schneider, A. M., Ebbesen, E. Interhemispheric transfer of lever pressing as stimulus generalization of the effects of spreading depression. *J. Exptl. Anal. Behav.*, **7**, 350 (1964)

57. Schneider, A. M., Hamburg, M. Interhemispheric transfer with spreading depression: a memory transfer or stimulus generalization phenomenon? *J. Comp. Physiol. Psychol.*, **62**, 133–36 (1966)

58. Schneider, A. M., Kay, H. Spreading depression as a discriminative stimulus for lever pressing. *J. Comp. Physiol. Psychol.*, **65**, 149–51 (1968)

59. Schneider, A. M., Sherman, W. Amnesia: a function of the temporal relation of footshock to electroconvulsive shock. *Science*, **159**, 219–21 (1968)

60. Squire, L. R., Liss, P. N. Control of memory by spreading cortical depression: a critique of stimulus control. *Psychol. Rev.*, **75**, 347–52 (1968)

61. Wiener, N. I., Deutsch, J. A. Temporal aspects of anticholingeric and anticholinesterase induced amnesia. *J. Comp. Physiol. Psychol.* (In press)

62. Zinkin, S., Miller, A. J. Recovery of memory after amnesia induced by electroconvulsive shock. *Science*, **155**, 102–3 (1967)

AUDITION

By David M. Green

Department of Psychology, University of California, San Diego
La Jolla, California

AND

G. Bruce Henning

Defence Research Establishment Toronto
Downsview, Ontario, Canada

During the past five years there has been a series of very competent and thorough reviews of current auditory research. Thurlow said, in his 1964 review, that he intended to cover "all areas which are of current concern to the psychologist who is interested in understanding the nature of reactions to auditory stimuli." Even when other recent reviewers did not explicitly adopt such catholic objectives, their reviews were very thorough and complete. Therefore, the active researcher in audition, as well as the general psychological community, will not become outrageously out of date if we depart from this objective of broad coverage and select a special topic to treat in depth. Specifically, this chapter will review the area of binaural hearing with special emphasis on the topic of binaural masking. Despite this specialization, we have omitted comment on some of the current papers in the area. The authors of the works that are slighted may be consoled by the observation that truly original contributions are seldom quickly appreciated.

One specific area of omission is any comprehensive coverage of the anatomical or physiological literature on binaural interaction. Deatherage's (4) review paper is the most comprehensive current survey of the literature in that very active and changing area. Rosenzweig's (51) paper contains a good review of much of the older literature.

SOUND LOCALIZATION AND BINAURAL ANALYSIS
INTRODUCTION

Sound localization is an old topic in audition, and while some of the basic and fundamental issues have been resolved, we are still uncertain of many of the details of the process. There is still considerable ambiguity about how one localizes a source in a realistic environment with acoustic reflections, transient signals, head movement, and the complication of integrating information sampled at different moments in time. In addition to localizing a source, however, the general binaural apparatus also allows us to make distinctions among the sources, to pay attention to one source and to exclude others. This ability to analyze complex waveforms depends, in part, on differences in the waveforms arriving at the two ears; we call this ability binaural analysis. This selection of one source from a group of similar, competing sources is most obvious at a cocktail party where one selectively attends to one of a number of simultaneous conversations, [Kaiser & David (33)]. In such cases, the listener is not primarily concerned with the location of the source but with how one source or signal can be distinguished from a background of other, competing, acoustic energy. There has been a considerable body of research in this general area, and more than half our review will be devoted to this topic of binaural analysis. Let us consider first the more orthodox topics of sound localization.

<h2 style="text-align:center">SOUND LOCALIZATION</h2>

Background and earlier work.—The first and simplest question is: "What aspects of the physical stimulus enable the observer to locate the sound source?" Early work was devoted to a careful analysis of the cues actually present at the two ears, and to a determination of the cues that determine the localization judgment. The obvious candidates are either (*a*) temporal information—the waveform in the ear nearer the source leads, in time, the waveform at the farther ear; or (*b*) intensive information—the intensity of the sound is greater at the nearer ear. Historically, research in this area was of interest both in its own right and because of the implications such research had for classical theories of hearing. Ohm and Helmholtz earlier had emphasized that the ear was a spectrum analyzer and paid little, if any, attention to phase. But if small temporal differences between the waveforms arriving at the two ears are important cues for localization, then subtle timing information is present in the auditory system. Might not similar mechanisms preserve monaural time differences? Careful studies of the physical cue occupied the period from about 1920 to 1935. This mode of attack is represented by Stewart (57, 58, 59), Hartley & Fry (21), later papers of Firestone (17), Steinberg & Snow (55), and, in more recent times, the papers of Wiener (70, 71) and Wiener & Ross (72).

An object, such as a head, casts a sound shadow only when the wavelength of the sound is small compared with the dimensions of the head. Since the velocity of sound in air is 1100 ft/sec or about 34,500 cm/sec, and since the average head has a linear dimension of about 17 cm. variations in the direction of the source introduce significant intensive differences between the two ears only at frequencies above about 2000 cps. Firestone's (17) measurements of sound diffraction were made on a dummy head in a free sound field. He found a difference between the two ears of nearly 10 db at 4000 cps. When the source is located at the side of the head, 90° azimuth, it produces a greater difference in intensity at the two ears than when it is straight ahead, 0° azimuth. But the specific relation between the difference in level at the two ears and the azimuth of the source depends on frequency and is not easy to summarize. Firestone's measurements of the difference in timing or phase information are more easily summarized.

One can try to deduce the phase (time) difference between the two ears as a function of the azimuth of the source based upon simple geometric assumptions. Specifically, consider the difference in distance the sound wave has to travel around a sphere to reach "ears" located at each side. Woodworth & Schlosberg (75) illustrate a very simple scheme for calculating the differences in path length given the azimuth of the source θ. The difference in distance is $r(\theta + \sin \theta)$, where θ is the azimuth, measured in radians, and r is the radius of the sphere. The distance formula, you will note, ignores the frequency of the source and any reflections of the sound off the head itself. The correct solution to this problem was first solved by Rayleigh, but only rather lengthy and tedious calculations can provide the numerical answers of interest. The exact solutions have been compared with empirical measurement by Wiener (71) for spheres and cylinders, and by Firestone (17) for a dummy of the human head. This simple geometric argument, however, provides fairly accurate predictions. Firestone's results can be predicted with moderate accuracy, and probe tube measurements on live, human heads by Fedderson and co-workers (16) agree very well with the simple formula. The maximum time difference occurs when the source has an azimuth of $\pm 90°$. At this azimuth the time difference is about two-thirds of a millisecond. Compared with the absolute refractory period of a neuron, this time may seem brief, but it is an enormous delay when compared with data on the perception of a small time difference between the two ears, where the threshold is about 30 μsec for a single click [Klumpp & Eady (35)].

If transients such as clicks or sharp onsets for tonal stimuli are ignored, then the only indication of a temporal discrepancy between the two ears is the phase of the sinusoid. Since a phase delay of more than a cycle is ambiguous (was the left ear a cycle ahead or a cycle behind?) we would expect phase to be a less reliable indicator of location once the period of the pure tone is less than 1 msec. This expectation is confirmed by empirical data on judgments of localization using sinusoidal stimuli in an essentially free field. The classical paper of Stevens & Newman (56) provides one of the earliest sources of information about localization in such an environment. They used three different stimuli: sinusoids with slow onset and offset, a click, and two broadband noise stimuli. Their basic data were presented in a graph of error in localization (averaged over several azimuths and ignoring 180° reversals) as a function of the frequency of the pure tone. The data show relatively small average error, about 10° at both the very low and very high frequencies, with an increase in the average error to about 20° in the mid-frequency range, about 2000 to 5000 cps. Finally, they found that both the impulsive "click" stimulus and the two noise sources were localized very reliably, the average error being about 5°.

Stevens & Newman's discussion of the results is a convincing presentation of the duplex theory of localization, a view still current today and generally believed to be a correct summary of the way in which nontransient tones are localized. Briefly, the duplex theory of localization maintains that two sets of cues operate: the temporal cues at low frequencies, and the intensive cues at high frequencies. In the mid-frequency range, at the boundary of the two cue systems, neither time nor intensity is effective and localization errors, therefore, increase. If a more complex stimulus is employed, such as an impulse or noise, then both types of cues are available simultaneously; thus the theory also explains why complex stimuli are easier to locate than a single sinusoidal component.

The continuation of the work of Stevens & Newman is represented in a series of experiments reported by Zwislocki & Feldman (76) and Mills (43, 44). In general, Mills' measurements support almost every assumption of the duplex theory of localization. His data on the minimum audible angle provide a set of detailed measurements of the basic discriminatory capacity to discern differences in intensity and phase at the two ears as a function of frequency.

Sound localization in nonfree fields.—The preceding experiments, utilizing a free acoustic field, have greatly contributed to our understanding of the physical cues effective in localization. Unfortunately, there has been a tendency among the unsophisticated to use these results in a rather naive discussion of how sounds are localized in more realistic sound fields. If the observer is surrounded by sound-reflecting surfaces, then the problem of localization is greatly complicated and any simple extension of the duplex theory may be misleading. First, intensive cues become particularly unreliable, since an intensity difference between the two ears is determined as much by the geometry of the surrounding space as by the location of the sound source. Similarly, the phase difference produced by a pure tone is simply the phase difference of two resultant vectors, one vector for each ear. The resultant vector is in turn determined by the different components reaching the two ears by their various paths. Again the geometry of the room is as important as the actual locus of the source. The preceding statements are not intended in any way as a criticism of the duplex theory but only to point out that its application in more realistic sound fields is extremely complicated.

Given a realistic sound field with nodes and antinodes, multiple reflections, and the rest, how can reliable judgments of location be made? One important aspect of localization in real space is head movement, as Wallach has pointed out in several brilliant experimental demonstrations (64, 65). Recently, there have been two studies on how head movements are used by typical subjects and on the movements which are most effective, [Thurlow & Runge (62); Thurlow, Mangels & Runge (61)]. Without head movements, reliable inferences about the location of a sound source must be based on the waveforms sampled at only two points in the field, namely, the two ears. One might try to deduce the locus of the source from simultaneous solutions based on comparison of several fallible cues; for example, phase differences at a variety of different frequencies. However, a single reliable cue to the location of the source may be based on comparisons of the time of arrival of transients in the waveforms. Even these comparisons are complicated, since only the initial (direct) wavefront is a reliable indicant of location; the later echoes may yield erroneous information, since they are determined by the reflecting surface in the neighborhood of the head and source.

Interestingly enough, there is evidence to indicate that for impulsive stimuli the ear forms the judgment of location from the arrival of the first transient information, and that the information arriving later in time is not given much weight. This is the so-called precedence effect, or Haas effect. Gardner (18) has recently published a thorough review of this effect, also called the "Law of the First Waveform," "auditory suppression effect," and "first arrival effect." Gardner credits Henry, in 1849, with being one of the first to notice the phenomenon. The article by Wallach, Newman & Rosenzweig (66) provides a good summary of the major experimental findings.

The concluding section of the Wallach, Newman & Rosenzweig paper gives some quantitative estimate of the size of the precedence effect. Consider delivering two clicks in succession to both of the observer's earphones. Call the first click the initial click and the second of the pair the echo. If one keeps the time between the initial and the echo click less than 2000 μsec, the clicks fuse and yield the impression of one brief impulsive stimulus. Now consider the effects of varying the times at which the clicks can arrive at each of the earphones. If both the initial and the echo arrive earlier at the right earphone, the source will appear to be located to the right. However, the interaural times can also be arranged so that the initial click leads in the left ear and the echo click leads in the right ear. The source is then localized at some intermediate location. In fact, the interaural delays of the initial and echo clicks can be balanced so that the source appears to be located straight ahead. In this way the relative importance of the interaural time difference for the initial and the echo clicks can be determined and compared.

The results show that the first or initial transient is, in some conditions, given almost an order of magnitude more weight than the second or echo transient. That is, a 500 μsec lag in the second pair of clicks is needed to offset a lag of 50μsec in the opposite direction for the first pair of clicks. Clearly the information in the initial click is more heavily weighted. The advantage of such a system of localization in realistic situations, where objects and walls produce numerous unreliable echoes, is obvious.

Lateralization.—The experiment by Wallach, Newman & Rosenzweig (66) demonstrates that a convenient way to attack many of the problems of binaural listening is with headphones. They allow one to produce specific and different waveforms at each ear and thus to generate stimuli that are difficult to achieve in free space. Further, the duplex theory of localization, based as it is on the differences of interaural time and intensity, also invites research with headphones, since with headphones independent control of these two aspects of the stimulus is easy to achieve. Situations can be studied in which the intensity cues and the temporal cues "point" in different directions. By systematically opposing these two sets of cues, one can more fully

understand how each works separately and thus assess the relative importance of each as a function of frequency, signal complexity, and other
parameters.

However, at least two critical features of realistic sound localization are
sacrificed when one uses headphones to study localization. First, head movements are useless with earphones, although as we previously mentioned
head movements are important in localizing a source in real space [Wallach
(64, 65)]. Second, headphones do not create the same impression as produced by real sounds in free space. The sound image induced by earphones
is generally described as within the head. Despite its appearance within the
head, the sound image can appear in a number of different locations; for
example, it can appear in the center of the head or at various points toward
one or the other ear. This "localization" of a sound image within one's head
is called lateralization.

There are at least two general methods used to study the lateralized
sound image, and several variants of each general method. Regrettably,
these different methods do not always produce the same results. One general
approach is simply to ask the subject to indicate where the source appears
to be, using some kind of pointer. The pointer may be simply an air stream
directed at some point on the forehead [von Békésy (63)], or a line drawn
on a picture of the head [Teas (60)]. The pointer might also be another
sound; for example, a noise source with variable delay between the waveforms driving each earphone. In the latter case, the subject's task is to adjust the delay of the noise so that its locus within the head is the same as
that of the test stimulus [Moushegian & Jeffress (45)]. The accuracy of these
lateralization judgments appears to be about that of the localization of external sources [Jeffress & Taylor (32)].

The second general class of methods requires the observer to "center"
the sound image. That is, the subject is instructed to adjust some parameter
of the binaural stimulus (such as the difference in intensity between the two
ears) until the sound image appears to be in the "center" of his head. While
it might seem that the exact position of "center" is ill-defined, even this difficulty can be avoided if we allow the subject to interchange (commutate)
the waveforms on the two earphones. Obviously, if the image moves when
the waveforms on the phones are interchanged, then the image is not centered. This technique was first introduced by Kikuchi (34). Jeffress & Blodgett (28) have presented data showing that this procedure, or a simple variant of it, greatly increases the accuracy of the "centering" judgment. In
practice, the technique of centering is not as neat or simple as this description
may imply. First, there appear to be two images, a "time" image and an
"intensity" image [Whitworth & Jeffress (69)]. Secondly, the time-intensity
trade may well be different when the time and intensity cues are in opposition and when the two cues are consistent [Moushegian & Jeffress (45)]. The
subjective experience is nicely summarized by Jeffress (27):

If you listen to a noise that is switched (commutated) between the headphones, and try to offset a difference of level by a difference of time, you can never get rid of the fluctuation—something keeps changing in your head. You can minimize this effect and get a reasonable trading ratio, but you are not really cancelling time with intensity.

While the last observation might be explained by the assumption of different trading ratios at different frequencies, it is also consistent with the hypothesis that there is a variety of systems involved in this process of lateralization, and only some part of the binaural system actually trades time and intensity. The latter viewpoint seems to be most consistent with the latest physiological evidence.

In principle, the procedure of centering the lateralized sound image is similar to a null reading or a judgment of equality. Since it is possible to cancel one difference between the two ears—for example, a phase or time delay—with another difference—for example, an intensity difference—one can construct graphs relating one parameter of the stimulus to another and establish trading relationships (μsec/db) between the two.

Shaxby & Gage (54), using sinusoidal stimuli, were among the first to employ this "centering" technique. They asked their observers to offset a temporal difference with an intensive one to achieve a centered image. While the use of this technique to establish the relative importance of time and intensity as a function of frequency seems rather obvious in retrospect, it was not until recently that extensive data employing this technique have been available.

Much of the impetus for the recent studies has been physiologically inspired. Electrophysiological records showed that the latency or delay between the acoustic stimulus and the resulting neural response depends on the intensity of the acoustic stimulus. This leads naturally to the hypothesis that the mechanism whereby time and intensity are traded is exactly this relation between the intensity of the signal and the latency of the neural response to it. Deatherage & Hirsh (5) concluded:

We believe that discussion of the relative roles of time and intensity as physical factors in auditory localization is proper in a psychophysical orientation, but once the frame of reference becomes neural, we would hypothesize that intensity, having made its contribution to neural 'time' may drop out of consideration, leaving the judgment of localization almost entirely dependent upon the results of a comparison of neural times.

Thus, according to Deatherage & Hirsh, the sole determinant of localization may be simply a comparison of temporal neural events. Intensity enters the picture only as it affects latencies. In the experiments of Deatherage & Hirsh, the stimulus was a click filtered by a 2400-cps low-pass filter. Their principal finding, in addition to confirming that time and intensity could indeed be traded, was that the trading ratio depends on the overall intensity level of the stimuli. Increasing the intensity level by 40 db reduced the $\Delta T/\Delta I$ ratio from 0.1 to 0.02 msec/db, a factor of 5. They also found that introducing high-frequency-bandpass noise into one ear has the same effect as delaying the signal in that ear. Both the dependence of the time-intensity trade on the overall level of stimulation and the effect of the masking noise are consistent with physiological studies of the latency of the action potential.

In a later paper, David, Guttman & van Bergeijk (3) used a click stimulus filtered through a 2000-cps high-pass filter. They varied the overall level of the stimulus and also found the time-intensity trade to depend on the overall level. Their values for $\Delta T/\Delta I$ were about 0.1 msec/db at the lower level and about 0.06 msec/db at the higher level. They present a rather elaborate schematic picture of the binaural mechanism containing three to four separate systems. For high-frequency sinusoidal signals they see no other possibility than a direct intensity comparator. In addition, they point out that for impulsive stimuli the envelope of the high-frequency wave may contain timing information. Their data indicate that this temporal mechanism does trade time and intensity, At low frequencies they postulate another temporal mechanism, also capable of trading time for intensity. They suggest that the trading relation for the low-frequency system is different from that found at high frequencies. The basis for this inference is, aparently, the ratio $\Delta T/\Delta I$ found by Shaxby & Gage (54), who used pure tones of 500, 800, and 1200 cps. They found the ratio $\Delta T/\Delta I$ to be about 0.0017 msec/db. This ratio (about 2μsec/db) is more than an order of magnitude smaller than the ratio found using click stimuli. Because of the many differences in the two experiments, there was uncertainty about the crucial variables until Harris' comprehensive study.

Harris (20) used clicks and systematically varied the low-frequency cutoff from 200 to 7000 cps. He also employed impulses filtered through high-pass filters and low-frequency sinusoids. Although there are differences among the results from the various stimulus conditions, the ratio of 0.04 msec/db is close to much of the data. Harris repeated Shaxby & Gage's experiment except that he allowed the subject to manipulate the phase or time delay over a much larger range. With this and other small changes in experimental technique, he obtained values for the trading ratio similar to those obtained with the click data, and therefore inconsistent with Shaxby & Gage's earlier measurement.

The inconsistency might rest there were it not for two separate experiments from the Texas group confirming Shaxby & Gage's results [Moushegian & Jeffress (45); Whitworth & Jeffress (69)]. Although consensus is far from perfect on this issue, this gross difference between transient and sinusoidal signals is probably explained by the arguments advanced in the latter paper.

A brief mathematical formulation of the arguments of Whitworth & Jeffress runs as follows. Consider a neural element with a fixed amplitude threshold and call it k. Let such an element be stimulated by two sinusoids of different amplitude, A_1 and A_2, with $A_2 > A_1$. There is a difference in time from a zero crossing of the sinusoid until it rises and reaches the threshold amplitude k, with the larger sinusoid clearly reaching this level in a shorter period of time. In fact, the difference in latency, Δt, is approximately (k/A_1) $(1/2\pi f)$ $(1 - A_1/A_2)$ where f is the frequency of the sinusoid and $k/A_1 < <1$. If $A_1/A_2 < <1$, then $\Delta t = (k/A_1)$ $(1/2\pi f)$. The ratio k/A_1 is the ratio of the absolute threshold of the neuron to the amplitude of the weaker of the two sinusoids. At a sensation level of 60 db, for example, the ratio is 1/1000. Thus, the time difference Δt is three orders of magnitude less than the period of the sinusoid divided by 2π. For a 500 cps waveform the period is 2 msec, and if loud signals are compared, it is easy to see that $\Delta t \approx 1\mu\text{sec}$. This argument then provides one rationale for the incredibly small trading ratio obtained by Shaxby & Gage.

An interesting finding of Whitworth & Jeffress was that their subjects "perceive the signal in two places, one strongly affected by the difference of level at the two ears, the other almost wholly dependent upon the difference of time." By instructing the subject to pay attention to one or the other image, they obtained data that closely followed the Shaxby & Gage results (intensity image) or the transient data (time image), depending upon the instruction set used. The time judgments were easier to make and somewhat less variable. The use of the intensity image in situations of practical interest seems dubious.

But what of Harris' data? Two explanations are possible. First, he used the centering technique, and thus the subject may have been forced to adjust the more salient time image rather than the intensity image. Harris also used less intense signals than Whitworth & Jeffress, the k/A_1 ratio being about 1/100. The calculated Δt is therefore about 10 to 20 μsec, a value similar to that obtained with the transient signals.

Probably the most important implication for localization in a realistic situation is stated at the conclusion of the Harris article. He points out that the dependence of temporal differences on intensity differences, in effect increases the distance between the two ears. Consider two cases: If the transient is largely composed of low frequencies, there is little sound shadow and hence little difference between the time difference and that inherent in the acoustic waves. At high frequencies, however, there is considerable difference in the intensity of the sound at the two ears. This means that whatever delay is present in the acoustic waves is augmented by the difference in intensity and therefore latency at the two ears. Since the neural delay may exceed the acoustic delay at the higher frequencies, the ears are effectively separated by two or three times their actual physical separation. This factor, working as it does only at high frequencies, probably explains why the high-frequency transients of actual sounds in real environments are given considerable weight in the judgements of location.

In summary, then, the work on lateralization has contributed substantially to our understanding of the process of localization. Whereas initially the impetus to study lateralization was to assess the relative importance of time and intensity cues, these two factors are now seen to be complementary rather than separate or independent. It may well be that most of localization is based on a single dimension, namely the relative arrival time of certain neural impulses, and that intensity differences simply serve to augment the time differences rather than operating as a separate and independent cue system. In any case, the work on lateralization, as well as that on the precedence effect, has emphasized the importance of transient cues and especially the high frequency components of these transient waveforms. The timing information present in these high-frequency components, augmented by interaural intensity differences, may be the most reliable and hence the most important cue to location.

We now turn to a somewhat different aspect of the binaural process, the topic of binaural analysis or masking-level differences.

BINAURAL ANALYSIS

Masking level difference (*MLD*).—Thus far, we have discussed the ability of the binaural system to localize sounds in space. Another, and perhaps more important, use of the binaural system is in communication, particularly in selecting some specific acoustic source out of the interference of other unwanted sounds. Anyone who has attempted to listen to a single source and ignore the interfering effects of some other acoustic energy has experienced this aspect of the binaural system. The systematic exploration of this ability depends upon being able to control and independently manipulate the waveforms arriving at the two ears.

Let us call the waveform we want to hear the "signal" and the remaining acoustic stimulus "noise." The first and easiest demonstration of the ability to accomplish binaural analysis is to put noise in both earphones and to simply add a signal to only one of the phones. Remarkably, the signal is easier to hear in this situation than with either a single phone or with the signal added, in-phase, to both phones. Thus the presence of only noise in one ear allows us to somehow separate the signal in the other ear from that same noise waveform and thus to decrease the masking effectiveness of the noise. Licklider (37) and Hirsh (23) were the first to discover this effect, and Webster (67) presented one of the first general theories to account for the phenomenon.

A convincing and spectacular set of demonstrations of this phenomenon has been outlined by Jefferess (26). Start with a single earphone and turn on a broadband noise. Add to that noise a low frequency sinusoid, say 250 cps, and adjust the amplitude of the sinusoid so that it is just detectable in the noise. Now add just the noise to the second earphone. Immediately, the signal becomes evident in the noise. Next add the signal to the noise in the second earphone; The signal again becomes very difficult to hear. This is called a homophasic condition since the noise and signal have the same interaural phase relations. If the noise is reasonably loud, say 35 db spectrum level, then the threshold for the tone in the binaural condition is equal to the threshold in the monaural condition. Now reverse the phase of the signal so that it is 180° out of phase at the two ears, the noise being still in phase. The signal is now easily heard. This last condition is called an antiphasic condition since the noise and signal have different interaural phase relations. The difference between the threshold of the signal in the antiphasic condition and homophasic or monaural condition is as much as 25 db for narrow band width noise (7 cps wide) and short duration signal (1/100 sec).

A systematic exploration of this phenomenon obviously entails a comparison of two signal levels: the level of the signal in the monaural or homophasic condition compared to the usually lower signal level needed for the same degree of detectability in the binaural, antiphasic, condition. The difference in these signal levels is called the masking level difference (MLD) or sometimes binaural masking level difference (BMLD). It is regrettable to report that this name for a dependent variable also is used to designate the phenomenon itself. Some authors refer to the phenomenon as binaural unmasking, but this usage is not general and we have in this review suggested "binaural analysis" for the general phenomenon.

While we are discussing nomenclature we might also review the designations used for various phase conditions. Obviously, these can become quite complicated since there are two ears, a signal and noise, and a variety of interaural phase relations, but we shall employ only the most elementary notation: S is signal, N is noise, the subscript refers to the interaural phase relation. The following examples illustrate some of the binaural phase relations that we will consider in the remainder of the paper:

S_o = signal in-phase at the two ears

S_m = signal monaural, no signal in the other ear

S_π = signal at one ear 180° out-of-phase with signal at other ear.

N_o = noise in-phase at two ears

N_π = noise waveform at one ear is inverted with respect to waveform at the other ear

N_u = noise uncorrelated at the two ears.

Thus $N_\pi S_o$ means the same as $S_o N_\pi$, namely, that the signal is in-phase at the two ears but the noise waveform is inverted at one ear with respect to the waveform at the other ear. The remainder of the discussion is a brief review of some of the most important empirical relations and the main theoretical positions proposed to account for these relations. We close this section by outlining the main weaknesses of these theories.

Empirical results.—The task of describing the many results obtained in the study of binaural analysis is difficult, both because of the large number of studies (about 70 are directly relevant), and because there is as yet no completely successful theoretical account that would serve as a convenient organizational scheme. One very simple and obvious mnemonic is to consider the binaural condition in terms of localizing the signal and noise. If, in the binaural condition, the interaural phases of the signal and noise are such that they can be localized in different places, then it is possible that the signal will be more dectable in the binaural situation than in the monaural situation. If signal and noise are not localized differently, then probably there is no masking-level difference. There is evidence to indicate that the localization process and the process of binaural analysis are at least partially different [Egan & Benson (15); Robinson & Egan (49)]. Nevertheless, it is still a convenient mnemonic and it may be helpful, initially, in trying to structure a rather large and apparently unrelated set of results.

Fortunate for this review, two chapters have recently been prepared on this general topic by two experts in the area. Jeffress' chapter (26) is somewhat tutorial and is recommended as an introduction. Durlach's chapter (13) is more detailed and comprehensive. We will review three general areas of empirical results to present the substantive data available concerning the phenomenon of binaural analysis so that subsequently the theoretical work may be evaluated in the light of the empirical findings.

The MLD as a function of signal frequency.—Consider, for simplicity, two binaural conditions: a homophasic condition N_oS_o, noise and signal in phase at the two ears; and an antiphasic condition N_oS_π, signal inverted but noise in phase at the two ears. In each condition we measure the signal level that is needed to obtain constant level of detectability. The difference in these levels is the MLD; the question we wish to consider is how the MLD depends on the frequency of the signal. Since we know that the auditory nerve exhibits phase-locked firing only at relatively low frequencies, we might anticipate the results; namely, the MLD is large at low frequencies and grows smaller as the frequency of the signal increases. For broadband noise and 1/10 sec signal, the MLD is about 15 db at a signal frequency of 250 cps. The asymptote of this function relating the size of the MLD as a function of signal frequency is not zero, however, but about 3db. For signal frequencies of 2000 cps and above, the MLD is essentially constant at about 3 db. Several authors have apparently found this fact surprising and have taken new data at the higher frequencies to confirm this fact, first reported by Hirsh (22) and Webster (67). These later replications included Hirsh & Burgeat (25), Durlach (13), Schenkel (52), Green (19), Wilbanks & Whitmore (74).

The general increase in the size of the MLD as the frequency of the signal decreases may indicate that the temporal aspect of the waveforms is especially crucial in binaural analysis. We might expect, therefore, that the size of the MLD would continue to increase as the frequency of the signal is lowered. This increase does occur down to about 250 cps but at still lower signal frequencies the experimental results are often contradictory. Below about 200 cps some investigators find that the MLD seems to decrease as a function of signal frequency. In the region near 100 cps Webster (67) and Durlach (13) found the MLD to be about 15 db. Hirsh (22) and Schenkel (52), however, found an MLD of about 5 db. Rabiner, Laurence & Durlach (48) also found a tendency for the MLD to decrease at 200 cps and measured an MLD of about 8 db at 160 cps.

The reasons for these discrepancies at very low signal frequencies are not entirely clear. Obviously, there are some parameters of the experimental situation that are not fully understood. One possibility is that the intensity of the noise is an especially crucial factor at these low frequencies. Dolan (8) has just obtained data at signal frequencies of 150 cps and 300 cps as a function of the intensity of the background noise level. He found an MLD of about 10 db at 300 cps and 5 db at 150 cps when using a low noise level, about 20 db spectrum level. However, at the higher noise levels, for example, a spectrum level of 65 db, both signal frequencies yielded MLDs of about 15 db.

Another strong candidate for the decline of the MLD at very low frequencies is an increase in variability of time at which the nerve fires, caused by the decrease in the slope of the sinusoid as its frequency is lowered. Suppose the nerve fires at a relatively fixed point on the pressure waveform. Then any variability in this amplitude threshold produces a corresponding variability in the exact time at which the neural burst is initiated. The argument is exactly parallel to the one outlined earlier in the discussion of the time-intensity trading ratio. As the frequency of the sinusoid is lowered, the variability increases as the reciprocal of frequency. If temporal coincidence of neural burst between the two ears is heavily involved in producing the MLD, then one might expect the size of the MLD to diminish with signal frequency. We say "might," since the details of this argument have not been fully explored. The relative temporal error, the ratio of firing time variability to the period of the wavetone, is independent of the signal frequency. Only the absolute variability in firing time increases with decreases in signal frequency, and whether the relative or absolute variability is the crucial quantity depends on the specific assumptions of the theory.

Finally, we should note that the effect of signal frequency would be essentially the same were we to define the MLD in other ways, for example, the difference between $N_\pi S_o$ and $N_m S_m$. Naturally the size of the MLD is not the same for all the various pairings of binaural and monaural conditions. In fact, the relative detectability of the signal in the various monaural, binaural, homophasic, antiphasic, and mixed conditions is one of the oldest topics in the area of binaural analysis. Hirsh (22) in his original paper suggested a ranking or hierarchy of the various conditions, and Jeffress et al. (30) and Blodgett, Jeffress & Taylor (1) have thoroughly investigated this matter. If we rank the various conditions according to how difficult the signal is to hear in a high-level noise, then $N_\pi S_\pi$, $N_o S_o$, and $N_m S_m$ are all roughly the same. $N_u S_\pi$, $N_u S_o$, and $N_\pi S_m$, $N_o S_m$ would be the next four conditions, the former pair being considerably lower than the latter pair. In the final positions are $N_\pi S_o$ and $N_o S_\pi$, with the latter generally producing the most detectability. These rankings, however, are only true at high levels of noise. The effect of noise level is considered in the next section.

The MLD as a function of intensity.—In this section we describe two sets of results: (a) the dependence of the MLD on the absolute level of sound in the two ears; and (*b*) the dependence of the MLD on the relative level of sound in the two ears. Throughout the description that follows, the phrase, "a change in the level of the sound," at a given ear means both signal and noise are attenuated by the same amount. It is convenient to think of the MLD as the difference in signal level needed for a given level of detectability in the $S_\pi N_o$ condition as opposed to the $S_m N_m$ condition. Consider first an extreme condition, namely, the largest possible interaural ratio—that is, when the level of sound in one ear is zero. We then have sound in only one ear and hence the $S_\pi N_o$ condition has been converted into an $S_m N_m$ condition. There is, therefore, no MLD. As we raise the level of the sound in the weaker ear, raising both signal and noise together, a difference between the monaural and binaural condition emerges once the spectrum level of the broadband noise is only a little above threshold. At that point, the MLD increases in a nearly linear fashion with the level of sound in the weaker ear. The maximum MLD (15 db for a low-frequency signal) occurs when the sound in the weaker ear is within about 10 db of the level in the stronger ear. The particular relation just described is clearly summarized in a series of experiments by McFadden (42). The same general relation obtains if we contrast $N_o S_m$ with $N_\pi S_m$, and vary only the noise level in the nonsignal ear, as shown in the papers by Blodgett, Jeffress & Whitworth (2); Mulligan & Wilbanks (46); Weston & Miller (68); Egan (14); Dolan (7); and Dolan & Robinson (9).

The second set of results concerns the effect of absolute noise level. Here the two ears receive the same level of stimulation but this level is varied. If we start at a high noise level (about 35 db spectrum level), the MLD will be about 15 db. Below this level the MLD decreases, reaching about 11 db at a spectrum level of 15 db. As we continue to decrease the noise level, the MLD appears to asymptote at about 3 or 4 db. Finally, in the extreme condition the noise is no longer audible, and we are simply comparing the detectability of a monaural signal S_m with the detectability of a binaural signal S_π (180° out of phase). As has been known for some time, the binaural threshold is some 3 to 4 db better than the monaural threshold [Hirsh (24); Licklider (38); Pollack (47)]. An additional fact is that the phase of the binaural signal seems to be important. The signal is easier to detect when S_π than when S_o at absolute threshold condition [Diercks & Jeffress (6)].

In this absolute threshold condition it is probable that the limit of detectability for this low-frequency signal is physiological or neural noise or both. Both the spectrum characteristics and level of physical noise generated in the external ear channel have been studied by Shaw & Piercy (53). In effect, the absolute threshold condition is the same as if we place a binaural signal in external noise that is largely independent at the two ears. If a high noise level is used, there is a small MLD of about 3 db, if we compare $S_m N_m$ to either $S_o N_u$ or $S_\pi N_u$ [Robinson & Jeffress (50)]. The absolute theshold condition probably produces a slightly larger MLD (4 db for the S_π rather than 3 db for the S_o), presumably because the physiological noise in the ear channels is slightly correlated. The correlation in the physiological noise probably arises because the source of the noise is the circulatory system and some of the noise is synchronized via the heart.

One can argue that the general increase in the size of the MLD with absolute level is simply the result of adding a large external source of noise to a constant level of physiological and neural noise [McFadden (42); Dolan & Robinson (9); Diercks & Jeffress (6)]. The predictions generated by these considerations depend on the function relating the MLD to the interaural correlation of the noise waveform. This relation will be discussed in the following section.

The MLD as a function of interaural correlation.—In both of the preceding sections, we discussed situations in which the noise waveforms at the two ears were perfectly correlated. Let us now consider two situations in which this correlation is changed. In the first, we systematically vary the interaural correlation by adding two uncorrelated noises, one source to each ear, to correlated noise already present at the two ears. If the power level of the mixture is held at a constant level, the correlation between the noise waveforms present at the two ears is simply the power of the common source divided by the sum of the powers of the common plus the uncorrelated source [Licklider & Dzendolet (40)]. Robinson & Jeffress (50) used this technique to vary systematically the interaural correlation and to determine how the MLD depended on its magnitude. They found slight differences in the MLDs obtained, depending on the psychophysical method that they used. There are also slight differences, depending on whether the signal is in phase at the two ears—S_o or inverted S_π. These differences are slight however, compared to the change in the MLD from essentially zero, when the noise has a perfect correlation and the same phase as the signal (N_oS_o or $N_\pi S_\pi$) through about 3 db when the noise waveforms are independent (N_uS_o or N_uS_π) to about 12 to 14 db when the noise correlation is unity but opposite that of the signal ($N_\pi S_o$ or N_oS_π). In both the S_o and S_π condition, the MLD decreases rapidly as the correlation is changed from that one producing the largest MLD.

A second way to change the interaural correlation of the noise, and one closely related to the process of localization, is to delay the noise in one ear, as was done by Langford & Jeffress (36). Call this delay in the noise waveform T_n. Suppose for a moment that the signal is in phase at the two ears, S_o. With no delay, $T_n = 0$; there is no MLD since the S_oN_o and S_mN_m conditions yield essentially the same detectability for the signal. When the noise is delayed by half the period of the signal, then the components of the noise near the signal frequency are approximately 180° out of phase. The binaural condition is then essentially S_oN_π and a large MLD results. When the delay is a full period of the signal we are back to the N_o condition and no MLD occurs. As the delay increases to the second half-period of the signal, an increase in the MLD occurs once again, but this time it is somewhat smaller than the MLD associated with the first half-period delay. In general then the MLD oscillates as a function of delay, the maxima occurring at integral multiples of the half-period of the signal. The size of these maxima decreases at each successive half-period until, after about four or five half-periods, the MLD approaches an asymptote of about 3 db, about the amount of MLD associated with independent noise sources ($N_u S_o$). If the signal is S_π rather than S_o, a similar result occurs except, as one would expect, the maxima occur at delays associated with full periods of the signal. Similar results have been obtained by a number of investigators; for example, Jeffress, Blodgett & Deatherage (29), and Rabiner, Laurence & Durlach (48).

THEORETICAL POSITIONS

There are two major theories that attempt to explain how binaural analysis is accomplished and to predict the size of the MLD in a variety of experimental conditions. The first of these is the Webster-Jeffress theory or what we will call the time-difference (T-D) model. The second theory is Durlach's Equalization and Cancellation (EC) Model.

In the next two sections we briefly review each theory and indicate some of the predictions easily derived from the theories. We will then contrast the theories, comparing them with some of the empirical data just reviewed, and finally present a general criticism of both theories.

TIME DIFFERENCE (T-D) THEORY

Webster's hypothesis.—Webster's hypothesis (67) stems primarily from the fact that the MLD changes markedly with signal frequency. Webster suggested that the crucial quantity "is the time-divergence between the two ears that is produced by the signal whenever it is neither exactly in phase with the masking tone, nor exactly out of phase with it." The phrase "masking tone" may require some comment. The masking stimulus is, in fact, noise. But, as Webster put it, "as a simplifying assumption, we shall . . . consider the signal and masker to be identical in frequency over a short interval (e.g. 10 or 20 milliseconds)."

This simplifying assumption is made so that it is possible to compute exactly the time difference between the ears. To see how this is done, recall that it is a simple matter to estimate, using vector diagrams, a phase difference, and hence a time difference, between two vectors. The two vectors in this case represent the resultants produced at the two ears by adding one sinusoid, the signal, s, and another sinusoid, the noise, n. The resultants depend on the amplitude of signal and noise and the relative phase of the signal and noise. The signal amplitude is directly measured; the average noise amplitude is calculated from the spectrum level of the noise and the presumed width of the critical band. Webster estimated the time difference by assuming that the phase between signal and noise was 90°.

Whatever the initial interaural phase of the noise vectors, the addition of the signal to one ear only (S_m) will produce a resultant with a different phase. It is this change in interaural phase that produces the MLD, according to the Webster hypothesis. Since a given change in phase is a small time difference at high frequencies and a large time difference at low frequencies, the MLD should be large at the lower frequencies and small at high frequencies, as it is.

Jeffress' hypothesis.—Jeffress (26) has extended the hypothesis advanced by Webster and embedded it within a general theory of localization. Put very simply, Jeffress envisions a set of two filter systems, one for each ear. The incoming acoustic waveform is filtered by a set of bandpass filters. Each successive filter is tuned to a lower frequency and the action is designed to mimic the filtering accomplished in the cochlea and first-order neural structures. The width of each filter might be about the size of a critical band.

Since each filter in the right ear has a similar corresponding filter in the left ear, imagine the filters of the same frequency opposite each other along the rows of a square matrix. At the output of each filter is an "axon" extending almost to the corresponding filter on the opposite side. As the like axons pass each other they extend numerous collaterals that converge on a number of other "higher order neurons" located at various distances in the center of the matrix. Each "higher order neuron" is fed by two collaterals, one from each ear. It is further assumed that only the simultaneous or nearly simultaneous excitation by two collaterals stimulates these "higher order neurons." If the waveforms are identical at the two ears, the successive impulses will tend to meet in the center of the matrix and the neurons located in the median plane will be excited. If the sound in the right ear leads that in the left ear, the impulses will travel almost all the way across the matrix and meet near the ear that is lagging. Thus the neural activity will tend to arise near the lagging ear, and we have a simple correspondence between locus of the source and locus of maximal excitation. Formally the mechanism is a filter system with delay lines as outputs and some sort of AC coupled "and" gate detecting the place where the excitation on the two delay lines cross. It is identical to one of the systems suggested by Licklider (39) in his triplex theory.

Jeffress assumes that there is greater density of the "higher order neurons" in the median plane to account for the greater accuracy of localization judgments when the source is near $0°$ azimuth. He also assumes that the density diminishes as we move toward either ear. If the system of localization were extremely precise, a subject could detect an antiphasic signal no matter how small. Instead, Jeffress suggests there is some random variation in the timing signals so that even under identical circumstances the localization of the sound in the median plane changes from moment to moment. Jeffress assumes the errors are symmetric about zero and probably gaussian since they are the result of numerous independent and finite errors.

One must compute the time difference between the two ears to predict the detectability of an antiphasic signal in Jeffress' model just as in Webster's. Jeffress, however, uses a more elaborate model of the noise process than Webster's assumption that the signal and noise are in quadrature. Jeffress assumes the noise has a phase that is random with respect to the sinusoidal signal and an amplitude that is given by the Rayleigh distribution.

He then integrates overall amplitude and phase angles to arrive at an average time difference produced by adding the signal to the noise. This average time difference compared with the random variation on the timing signals is what determines the detectability of the signal in the antiphasic conditions.

Durlach's equalization and cancellation model.—In 1960 Durlach (10) published a note on an extremely simple model explaining the phenomena of binaural analysis and predicting the size of the MLD in several situations. During the following years, he has investigated various aspects of this model and explored many of its implications. The best summary is Durlach (13). Basically, the model assumes that the waveforms presented at the two ears are first filtered, then amplified or attenuated, and then shifted in time. The amount of attenuation or time shifting depends on the nature of the task. Finally, the scaled and perhaps time-shifted signals from each ear are either added or subtracted in a cancellation device. In all cases the specific mode of operation or parameter value is chosen to optimize the signal-to-noise ratio. For example, given a binaural situation such as $N_\pi S_o$, it is assumed that the cancellation device will add the two waveforms since this will tend to make the noise zero and double the signal level. Similarly, if the level of one ear is less than another, it is assumed the levels are "equalized" before the addition or subtraction takes place. Implicit in this system is the ability to listen to the monaural signal alone. This assumption excludes the possibility that the binaural masked threshold will ever be worse than the monaural threshold (a negative MLD).

The model, as explained to this point, has no free parameters since, by assumption, the cancellation operation and parameter values (amplitude and time shift) are always chosen in an optimal sense. That is, they are chosen so as to maximize the signal-to-noise ratio. The model, at this stage, is obviously incomplete since it would predict perfect performance in a variety of binaural conditions. To avoid this kind of absurdity, Durlach assumes two kinds of processing errors. First, he assumes that there is a slight, random time difference between the waveforms as processed by the left and right ears. At low frequencies then, where small time differences do not alter the phase significantly, there is essentially perfect addition or subtraction. At high frequencies, however, this temporal jitter destroys the coherence between the waveforms at the two ears. The second source of error is the assumption of some slight instability in processing the amplitude of the signal. Thus, even at low frequencies where the time jitter is unimportant, the noise cannot always be exactly cancelled. These two sources of error constitute the free parameters of the equalization and cancellation (E-C) model.

Comparison of the two theories and data.—The obvious contrast between Durlach's E-C model and the Time-Difference model is that the E-C model is essentially a black box approach, whereas the Time-Difference model is more physiologically oriented. The E-C model is generally more specific and quantitative predictions can be derived. Several aspects of the Time-Difference model are rather vague, however, and this makes specific quantitative prediction impossible. For example, what is the random variation in the comparison of time of arrival from the two ears? This temporal error is an essential part of the Time-Difference theory since it prevents the theory from predicting perfect detectability in the various binaural conditions. Jeffress suggests that these time errors are probably gaussian, but even this assumption has been made specifically only for the central condition. Since the explicit assumption of asymmetries between the center and off-center positions is part of the theory, one wonders whether the temporal errors are the same at all positions. Further, is the amount of this temporal error the same at all frequencies?

The E-C model, on the other hand, has tried to account for a great deal of data on the basis of a very simple theory and with few parameters. No assumption of the theory violates any physiological principle, but it is a theory that treats the nervous system as a general purpose computer. No part of the model is directly inspired by any of our present-day understanding of binaural anatomy or neurophysiology.

Let us briefly contrast the predictions of the two models as they try to explain how the MLD is affected by the following variables:

Signal frequency.—Both theories account for the decrease in the MLD at higher frequency signals by assuming some finite timing error in the processing of the waveforms from the two ears. Both theories are incorrect in detail because of the small MLD (3 db) even at the higher frequencies. Each theory is easily modified to account for this small discrepancy [Durlach (11)].

At low signal frequencies the E-C model assumes that temporal instability is no longer relevant and assumes a small, constant-amplitude instability. Thus the E-C model predicts that the MLD will asymptote at some low signal frequency. The T-D model predicts quite differently. Since a given phase difference means a greater and greater time difference, the MLD should increase monotonically with lower signal frequency. Just exactly how this paradox is to be avoided has never been precisely clarified. One approach would emphasize the increase in variability of firing times as the frequency decreases. As we pointed out earlier, another possible explanation rests upon the assumption that the density of binaural cells depends upon frequency and, therefore, limits the resolution of time difference at the low frequencies. In any case, the time-difference hypothesis has never predicted the exact shape of the curve relating the size of the MLD to frequency since Webster's original paper, and nothing more than a qualitative account of the functions has been given.

Interaural or absolute noise level.—Neither theory can directly predict the effects of either interaural intensity differences or absolute intensity level. According to the E-C model, the ears should be equalized and hence the interaural ratio should not be an important variable. Similarly, the Time-Difference model would compute the same time difference from vectors showing the phase changes caused by adding the signal to the noise. This diagram would be changed only in size if both noise and signal were attenuated.

It is apparent, however, how one might modify the models to account for these results. Dolan & Robinson (9) show the very close correspondence between the data on changes in interaural intensity and the data on changes in interaural correlation of the noise. They assume a small internal noise that is added linearly with the external noise. Dropping the level of the noise in one ear then is treated as a reduction in interaural correlation. Dolan & Robinson show that one can predict the results of changes in interaural correlation from changes in interaural intensity level or the reverse. Both sets of data are consistent with such a theory.

McFadden (42) has taken the same basic theory and applied it to the data on MLD as a function of the absolute level of the noise. Again, the data on correlation and absolute intensity difference are mutually consistent if this simple hypothesis is adopted. McFadden also presents data that confirm the findings of Dolan & Robinson on the correspondence of correlation and interaural intensity differences.

Interaural correlation.—The question now becomes: How can one account for the changes in MLD with changes in interaural correlation? There is little doubt that the E-C model can handle these data in a much more quantitative and rigorous fashion than the T-D model. Durlach (12) again has outlined in detail how the E-C model would handle the effect of interaural correlation. The E-C model can directly predict the results with only one free parameter. This parameter depends on the value of the two other parameters, the time jitter, and the amplitude error. If one uses the same constants as measured in the previous experiments, one can predict the interaural correlation result to within about 2 db over most of the range. The major discrepancy is, in fact, at a correlation of unity, where the theory seems to predict too small an effect (about 4 db). Even this discrepancy can be corrected if the free parameter is chosen as a constant and not based on previous estimates of the error and jitter parameters.

The Time-Difference model might, of course, be able to predict the effects of a change in interaural correlation. To do so it would have to become specific about a number of details. Specifically, the form of the internal error would have to be spelled out and the exact representation of the external noise, bandwith, and level would have to be specified. Such a detailed analysis would prove useful since it would further clarify any discrepancy between the Time-Difference and the Equalization and Cancellation models.

General criticism of both models.—Both theories base their prediction on static quantities, quantities that represent the average over some interval of time. In fact, the most salient cues in the binaural conditions may not be the average change but the amount and rate of change during the stimulus interval. As Jeffress, Blodgett & Wood (31) put it, in binaural listening "we hear the sound move when the signal is added to the noise."

This general concern about the relative position of signal and noise brings us to an awkward detail of the Time-Difference model. The use of a vector to represent the noise, and especially the assumption that the amplitude of that vector has a Rayleigh distribution, are tantamount to the assumption that the bandwidth of the noise is less than the reciprocal of the signal duration. This implies that for a 1/10 sec signal duration the bandwidth of the noise is 10 cps wide. If it is wider than this value, then the noise will change appreciably in amplitude during the signal interval. Therefore the relative phase difference between the signal and noise will vary, and hence the time difference will also vary during the signal interval. How or why the Rayleigh assumption is justified in calculating the average time difference is far from clear.

There is some evidence besides introspection to support this emphasis on dynamic cues. Consider a situation in which all details of the Time-Difference model are correct, namely, a situation where the masker is a sinusoid of fixed amplitude and of the same frequency as the signal. If care is taken to reduce onset cues, then the only remaining cue is exactly the time-difference one. The MLD in this tonal masking situation is extremely small, about half that obtained with wideband noise. Similar evidence is available if one contrasts the MLD obtained when the masker is continuous as opposed to that obtained when the masker is gated on only during the observation interval. In the continous condition there are dynamic cues at onset and offset of the signal that are not present in the gated condition. Using either noise [McFadden (41)] or sinusoids [Wightman (73)] as the masker, one finds that the continous condition produces larger MLDs than the gated condition.

Even if there is considerable change in the binaural cues during the signal interval, this fact by itself may not change many of the predictions generated by a static analyis. The time difference may change during the signal interval, but one still would expect a strong correlation between a calculation of the "average" change and the rate and range of the change during the signal interval.

Perhaps this correlation is responsible for the success enjoyed by the static models. A careful analysis of the dynamic cues might well leave many predictions of the models unchanged. However, inclusion of the dynamic cues may explain some phenomena that now appear mysterious and lead us to a more realistic model of the process of binaural analysis.

ACKNOWLEDGMENTS

The authors are particularly indebted to several people who patiently read and criticized earlier drafts of this paper. They were N. I. Durlach, L. A. Jeffress, G. Mandler, D. McFadden, and D. E. Robinson. The preparation of this review was supported, in part, by the National Institutes of Health, Public Health Service, U. S. Department of Health, Education, and Welfare.

LITERATURE CITED

1. Blodgett, H. C., Jeffress, L. A., Taylor, R. W. Relation of masked threshold to signal-duration for various interaural phase combinations. *Am. J. Psychol.*, **71**, 283–90 (1958)
2. Blodgett, H. C., Jeffress, L. A., Whitworth, R. H. Effect of noise at one ear on the masked threshold for tone at the other. *J. Acoust. Soc. Am.*, **34**, 979–81 (1962)
3. David, E. E., Jr., Guttman, N., van Bergeijk, W. A. Binaural interaction of high-frequency complex stimuli. *J. Acoust. Soc. Am.*, **31**, 774–82 (1959)
4. Deatherage, B. H. Examination of binaural interaction. *J. Acoust. Soc. Am.*, **39**, 232–49 (1966)
5. Deatherage, B. H., Hirsh, I. J. Auditory localization of clicks. *J. Acoust. Soc. Am.*, **31**, 486–92 (1959)
6. Diercks, K. J., Jeffress, L. A. Interaural phase and the absolute threshold for tone. *J. Acoust. Soc. Am.*, **34**, 981–84 (1962)
7. Dolan, T. R. *Masking-Level Differences for Monaural Signals Binaurally Masked.* (Doctoral Thesis, Univ. Texas, Austin, Texas, 1966)
8. Dolan, T. R. Center for Neural Sciences, Univ. Indiana, Bloomington, Indiana (Personal communication, 1968)
9. Dolan, T. R., Robinson, D. E. An explanation of masking-level differences that result from interaural intensive disparities of noise. *J. Acoust. Soc. Am.*, **42**, 977–81 (1967)
10. Durlach, N. I. Note on the equalization and cancellation theory of binaural masking level differences. *J. Acoust. Soc. Am.*, **32**, 1075–76 (1960)
11. Durlach, N. I. Note on binaural masking-level differences at high frequencies. *Ibid.*, **36**, 576–81 (1964)
12. Durlach, N. I. Note on binaural masking-level differences as a function of the interaural correlation of the masking noise. *Ibid.*, 1613–17
13. Durlach, N. I. Binaural signal detection: Equalization and cancellation theory. (1968) To appear in *Modern Foundations of Auditory Theory* (Tobias, J. V., Schubert, E. D. Eds., Academic Press)
14. Egan, J. P. Masking-level differences as a function of interaural disparities in intensity of signal and of

noise. *J. Acoust. Soc. Am.*, **38**, 1043–49 (1965)
15. Egan, J. P., Benson, W. Lateralization of a weak signal presented with correlated and with uncorrelated noise. *J. Acoust. Soc. Am.*, **40**, 20–26 (1966)
16. Feddersen, W. E., Sandel, T. T., Teas, D. C., Jeffress, L. A. Localization of high frequency tones. *J. Acoust. Soc. Am.*, **29**, 988–91 (1957)
17. Firestone, F. A. The phase difference and amplitude ratio at the ears due to a source of pure tone. *J. Acoust. Soc. Am.*, **2**, 260–68 (1930)
18. Gardner, M. B. Historical background of the Hass and/or precedence effect. *J. Acoust. Soc. Am.* (To be published, 1968)
19. Green, D. M. (Unpublished research, 1965)
20. Harris, G. G. Binaural interactions of impulsive stimuli and pure tones. *J. Acoust. Soc. Am.*, **32**, 685–92 (1960)
21. Hartley, R. V. L., Fry, T. C. The binaural location of pure tones. *Phys. Rev.*, **18**, 431–42 (1921)
22. Hirsh, I. J. The influence of interaural phase on interaural summation and inhibition. *J. Acoust. Soc. Am.*, **20**, 536–44 (1948)
23. Hirsh, I. J. Binaural summation and interaural inhibition as a function of the level of the masking noise. *Am. J. Physiol.*, **56**, 205–13 (1948)
24. Hirsh, I. J. Binaural summation—a century of investigation. *Psychol. Bull.*, **45**, 193–206 (1948)
25. Hirsh, I. J., Burgeat, M. Binaural effects in remote masking. *J. Acoust. Soc. Am.*, **30**, 827–32 (1958)
26. Jeffress, L. A. Masking and binaural phenomena. DRL Acoust. Rept. No. 245 (1965); Also to appear in *Modern Foundations of Auditory Theory* (Tobias, J. V., Schubert, E. D., Eds., Academic Press)
27. Jeffress, L. A. Dept. Psychol., Univ. Texas, Austin, Texas (Personal communication, 1968)
28. Jeffress, L. A., Blodgett, H. C. Effect of switching earphone channels upon the precision of centering. *J. Acoust. Soc. Am.*, **34**, 1275–77 (1962)
29. Jeffress, L. A., Blodgett, H. C., Deatherage, B. H. The masking of tones by white noise as a function of the interaural phases of both

components. *J. Acoust. Soc. Am.*, **24**, 523–27 (1952)

30. Jeffress, L. A., Blodgett, H. C., Sandel, T. T., Wood, C. L., III. Masking of tonal signals. *J. Acoust. Soc. Am.*, **28**, 416–26 (1956)

31. Jeffress, L. A., Blodgett, H. C., Wood, C. L., III. Detecting a signal in noise. *J. Acoust. Soc. Am.*, **30**, 802 (1958)

32. Jeffress, L. A., Taylor, R. W. Lateralization vs. localization. *J. Acoust. Soc. Am.*, **33**, 482–83 (1961)

33. Kaiser, J. F., David, E. E., Jr. Reproducing the cocktail party effect. *J. Acoust. Soc. Am.*, **32**, 918 (1960)

34. Kikuchi, Y. Objective allocation of sound-image from binaural stimulation. *J. Acoust. Soc. Am.*, **29**, 124–28 (1957)

35. Klumpp, R. G., Eady, H. R. Some measurements of interaural time difference thresholds. *J. Acoust. Soc. Am.*, **28**, 859–60 (1956)

36. Langford, T. L., Jeffress, L. A. Effect of noise crosscorrelation on binaural signal detection. *J. Acoust. Soc. Am.*, **36**, 1455–58 (1964)

37. Licklider, J. C. R. The influence of interaural phase relations upon the masking of speech by white noise. *J. Acoust. Soc. Am.*, **20**, 150–59 (1948)

38. Licklider, J. C. R. In *Handbook of Experimental Psychology* (S. S. Stevens, Ed., John Wiley, New York, 1436 pp., 1951)

39. Licklider, J. C. R. Three auditory theories. In *Psychology: A Study of a Science, Study I*. (E. S. Koch, Ed., 710 pp., 1959)

40. Licklider, J. C. R., Dzendolet, E. Oscillographic scatterplots illustrating various degrees of correlation. *Science*, **107**, 121–24 (1948)

41. McFadden, D. Masking-level differences with continuous and with burst masking noise. *J. Acoust. Soc. Am.*, **40**, 1414–19 (1966)

42. McFadden, D. Masking-level differences determined with and without interaural disparities in masker intensity. *J. Acoust. Soc. Am.*, **44**, 212–23 (1968)

43. Mills, A. W. On the minimum audible angle. *J. Acoust. Soc. Am.*, **30**, 237–46 (1958)

44. Mills, A. W. Lateralization of high-frequency tones. *Ibid.*, **32**, 132–34 (1960)

45. Moushegian, G., Jeffress, L. A. Role of

interaural time and intensity differences in the lateralization of low-frequency tones. *J. Acoust. Soc. Am.*, **31**, 1441–45 (1959)

46. Mulligan, B. E., Wilbanks, W. A. Effect of noise at one ear on the detection of signals at the other ear. *J. Acoust. Soc. Am.*, **37**, 1179 (1965)

47. Pollack, I. Monaural and binaural threshold sensitivity for tones and white noise. *J. Acoust. Soc. Am.*, **20**, 52–57 (1948)

48. Rabiner, L. R., Laurence, C. L., Durlach, N. I. Further results on binaural unmasking and the EC model. *J. Acoust. Soc. Am.*, **40**, 62–70 (1966)

49. Robinson, D. E., Egan, J. P. Lateralization of an auditory signal in correlated noise and in uncorrelated noise as a function of signal frequency. *J. Acoust. Soc. Am.*, **42**, 1180 (1967)

50. Robinson, D. E., Jeffress, L. A. Effect of varying the interaural noise correlation on the detectability of tonal signals. *J. Acoust. Soc. Am.*, **35**, 1947–52 (1963)

51. Rosenzweig, M. R. Development of research on the physiological mechanisms of auditory localization. *Psychol. Bull.*, **58**, 376–89 (1961)

52. Schenkel, K. D. Über die Abhängigkeit der Mithörschwelle von der interauralen Phasenlage des Testschalls. *Acustica*, **14**, 337–46 (1964)

53. Shaw, E. A. G., Piercy, J. E. Physiological noise in relation to audiometry. *J. Acoust. Soc. Am.*, **34**, 745 (1962)

54. Shaxby, J. H., Gage, F. H. *Medical Research Council* (Brit.). (Spec. Rept., Ser. No. 166, 1–32, 1932)

55. Steinberg, J., Snow, W. Physical factors in auditory perspective. *Bell System Tech. J.*, **13**, 247–60 (1934)

56. Stevens, S. S., Newman, E. B. The localization of actual sources of sound. *Am. J. Psychol.*, **48**, 297–306 (1936)

57. Stewart, G. W. The acoustic shadow of a rigid sphere, with certain applications in architectural acoustics and audition. *Phys. Rev.*, **33**, 467–79 (1911)

58. Stewart, G. W. The function of intensity and phase in the binaural location of pure tone. I. Intensity. *Phys. Rev.*, 425–31 (1920)

59. Stewart, G. W. The function of intensity and phase in the binaural lo-

cation of pure tones. II. Phase. *Ibid.*, 432–45.

60. Teas, D. C. Lateralization of acoustic transients. *J. Acoust. Soc. Am.*, **34**, 1460–65 (1962)

61. Thurlow, W. R., Mangels, J. W., Runge, P. S. Head movements during sound localization. *J. Acoust. Soc. Am.*, **42**, 489–93 (1967)

62. Thurlow, W. R., Runge, P. S. Effect of induced head movements on localization of direction of sounds. *J. Acoust. Soc. Am.*, **42**, 480–88 (1967)

63. von Békésy, G. *Experiments in hearing* (McGraw-Hill, New York, 745, 1960)

64. Wallach, H. On sound localization. *J. Acoust. Soc. Am.*, **10**, 270–74 (1939)

65. Wallach, H. The role of head movements and vestibular and visual cues in sound localization. *J. Exptl. Psychol.*, **27**, 339–68 (1940)

66. Wallach, H., Newman, E. B., Rosenzweig, M. R. The precedence effect in sound localization. *Am. J. Psychol.*, **52**, 315–36 (1949)

67. Webster, F. A. The influence of interaural phase on masked thresholds: I. the role of interaural time-deviation. *J. Acoust. Soc. Am.*, **23**, 452–61 (1951)

68. Weston, P. B., Miller, J. D. Use of noise to eliminate one ear from masking experiments. *J. Acoust. Soc. Am.*, **37**, 638–46 (1965)

69. Whitworth, R. H., Jeffress, L. A. Time vs. intensity in the localization of tones. *J. Acoust. Soc. Am.*, **33**, 925–29 (1961)

70. Wiener, F. M. On the diffraction of a progressive sound wave by the human head. *J. Acoust. Soc. Am.*, **19**, 143–46 (1947)

71. Wiener, F. M. Sound diffraction by rigid spheres and circular cylinders. *Ibid.*, 444–51

72. Wiener, F. M., Ross, D. A. The pressure distribution in the auditory canal in a progressive sound field. *J. Acoust. Soc. Am.*, **18**, 401–8 (1946)

73. Wightman, F. L. Binaural masking with sinewave maskers (Paper in preparation, Dept. Psychol., Univ. Calif. at San Diego, La Jolla, Calif.)

74. Wilbanks, W. A., Whitmore, J. K. Detection of monaural signals as a function of interaural noise correlation and signal frequency. *J. Acoust. Soc. Am.*, **43**, 785–97 (1968)

75. Woodworth, R. S., Schlosberg, H. *Experimental Psychology* (Henry Holt Co., New York, 1958)

76. Zwislocki, J., Feldman, R. S. Just noticeable difference in dichotic phase. *J. Acoust. Soc. Am.*, **28**, 860–64 (1956)

THE CHEMICAL SENSES[1]

133

By Don Tucker and James C. Smith[2,3]

Florida State University, Tallahassee, Florida

We were encouraged by the editor to be selective and indeed learned that it is the only practical approach. However, we regret that we have included only a small fraction of the number of papers we originally considered. Many other topics are covered in reviews and symposia from which we have cited literature (2, 5, 10, 11, 12, 35, 52, 54, 55, 57, 89, 93, 97, 103, 130, 166, 171).

Anatomy of the Receptor Organs

Electron microscopy is the major source of new information, with conventional histology playing a prominent ancillary role. Attention is focused on the surface of receptor organs because it is felt that the exposed terminals of receptor cells are obviously the first parts to contact stimulating substances and, therefore, probably embody the postulated receptive membranes. One might be alert for evidence bearing on the thesis of Vinnikov (163) that all receptors include some ciliary or paraciliary structures and that the mechanism of stimulation-response involves some form of movement. Duncan's (54) postulation of a similar scheme basic to all receptor cells apparently drops the requirement for movement in gustatory receptors but retains the mechanism of energy-yielding reactions mediated by enzymes which are somehow affected by diverse chemical stimuli.

Taste buds.—These organs are often located on outside body surfaces of fish, but in mammals they are mainly restricted to the palate and the tongue. They are borne on the projecting fungiform papillae, diffusely scattered over about the anterior two-thirds of the tongue, and embedded in folds of the foliate and circumvallate papillae toward the back of the tongue. It has been shown that cells in taste buds of rat fungiform papillae have a limited lifetime and are replaced by new cells (14). Therefore, it is assumed that probably all taste bud cells undergo turnover. Farbman (58) studied the normal development of the rat fungiform taste bud and found the sequence of rudimentary papillae, appearance of nerve fibers at the base, and then, differentiation of precursor cells for the bud. On the other hand, when the chorda tympani nerve is cut in the adult, the fungiform papillae and taste buds degenerate. Upon regeneration of chorda tympani fibers to the tongue

---

[1] The survey of literature pertaining to this review was completed in April 1968.

[2] Supported by NIH Research Grant No. NB-01083-12 and U.S. Atomic Energy Commission Contract AT-(40-1)-2903.

[3] In this chapter, electro-olfactogram will be referred to as EOG and electroencephalogram will be referred to as EEG.

the fungiform papillae and taste buds reappear, which suggests that appearance of the nerves induced the formation of the papillae. Bradley & Stern (28) found that human taste buds appear well developed at 13 to 15 weeks fetal age and suggested that they are functional because it appears that the fetus can be induced to swallow amniotic fluid by introduction of saccharin.

Taste buds of rabbit foliate papillae have been studied extensively (106, 108, 132). The cells in the interior of the bud have apical prolongations which terminate in bundles of microvilli, extending into a chamber which communicates via a channel to the taste pore on the surface. The space around the microvilli is occupied by an amorphous osmiophilic material which has been histochemically defined as a neutral mucopolysaccharide (132). The classical histologically derived picture of supporting and receptor cells persists in the form of dark and light cells. The cells are connected by junctional complexes below the shafts bearing the microvilli; called a tight junction (68), *zonula occludens* or tight junction (106) and *zonula occludens* followed by a *zonula adhaerens* (132). The dark cells contain membrane-bounded granules which appear to be secretory precursors of the amorphous material around the microvilli. A probable sequence of cellular types is perigemmal to dark, to light, to degeneration (106, 132). Farbman (57) found similar results for rat circumvallate taste buds, but the dark secretory granules do not appear in rat fungiform bud cells which, however, do contain dense bodies.

Dark and light cells contain centrioles (106, 132) which are indistinguishable from ciliary basal bodies, and in the dark cells they frequently have striated rootlets (132). Whether both light and dark cells function as receptors is debated (57, 106, 132) because both are associated with nerves, but structures characteristic of synapses are rarely observed. However, Gray & Watkins (68) did find some evidence for synapses in rat circumvallate taste buds. The Murrays (106) argue that the light cells are likely candidates as receptors. The nerve endings relative to them are more like that expected for synapses, whereas the dark cells envelop the nerves in a manner suggestive of Schwann cells. Also, the light cells are commonly isolated from each other by the dark cells, which is suggestive of the receptor-supporting cell relationship. However, the microvilli of the light cells do not usually extend through the dense substance, but it may not be a barrier to stimulating materials. Possibly the dark cells also serve as gustatory receptors (106).

Farbman (57) suggested the possibility that the light and dark cells differentiate from a common precursor and even that, perhaps, only one population is subject to turnover.

Olfactory mucosae.—Olfactory-type receptors are primitive bipolar neurons whose axons synapse within the central nervous system. No anatomical specializations have been found that would indicate any functional interactions at the peripheral level. Bloom's (20) study, though older, has a valuable introduction that relates the history and histology to electron microscope results. The early microscopists observed the movements of normally long olfactory "hairs" and already speculated that they were the receptive portions of the cells. In modern papers it is often not clear how the reported lengths of cilia were determined. However, small pieces of olfactory mucosa from amphibians or reptiles on cover-slipped slides will have fields of view tangential to the surface from which the cilia will extend out into the surrounding Ringer's solution (81). It is commonly reported that there are short motile cilia and long immotile ones (122, Fig. 5, is an excellent phase micrograph illustration), but Bronstein (29) stated that they all move. In fact, from reading Hopkins' (81) description and looking at his drawings, one is prepared to accept an optical illusion. Although the cilia can break off at different lengths (122), one can find fields in which they are all long and the proximal portions of them execute sinuous, uncoordinated movements. The peripheral portions execute more or less small longitudinal displacements depending on the amount and viscosity of the mucus in which they are enmeshed. When the mucus is removed by vigorous washing (155), the movements of the peripheral portions of the cilia become much more prominent.

Scanning electron microscopy, in contrast to conventional transmission, has been employed recently to look at cilia, washed free of mucus, which normally are rather short (8). In the rabbit, olfactory cilia of two different lengths on different receptors and supporting cell microvilli were revealed clearly. Similar results were obtained for goldfish microvilli, olfactory cilia, and "motile cilia," i.e., those of ciliated epithelial cells that beat with a metachronous rhythm.

Many writers have commented on the contribution of the supporting (sustentacular) cells to the secretion bathing the surface of the olfactory mucosa, subsequent to Reese's (122) report that they are packed with large secretory droplets. However, this relation is not so obvious in mammals and birds, and it seems likely that their numerous Bowman's glands may contribute the bulk of the secretions. The interesting topic of olfactory pigment was reviewed (103) recently, but subsequently Kurihara (92) determined that the pigment is principally an insoluble chromoprotein existing in granules.

Mammalian olfactory cilia tend to be short and apparently are enmeshed in numerous microvilli of the supporting cells. As in the frog, there is a proximal segment exhibiting the typical ciliary cross-sectional profile of nine paired fibrils around a pair of singlets and a peripheral segment containing single fibrils of varying number (4, 60, 111, 136).

In the lamprey (154, 30), cilia have been found on supporting cells also, and within invaginations of the basal cells (154). On the other hand, microvilli plus cilia have been found on receptors of the duck (69), black vulture (31), and carp (165). Bannister (7) described receptors with microvilli instead of cilia in the minnow, but numerous centrioles suggestive of an immature stage were present. The ciliary outer fibrils originate from basal bodies, which otherwise appear indistinguishable from centrioles. Centrioles appear frequently in the receptor cell dendrites of young animals (4, 136).

Whether a typical tight junction is present between cells of the mucosa is doubtful, but Thornhill (154) raises the possibility that the adhering band between cells in the lamprey might function as a barrier against excessive inflow of water and loss of electrolytes. Fibrous bands or layers have been seen between junctional complexes within the supporting cells of mouse (136), black vulture (31), and lamprey (154). Mucous cells and extremely unusual "foliaceous" cells were described in the carp (165). Supporting cells were much fewer in number, so that contiguity of receptor cells was a common feature in this fish.

The closely related receptors of the vomeronasal organ in the slow worm were found by Bannister (6) to be without cilia. Similarly, vomeronasal receptors were found to be without cilia in the box turtle and the gopher tortoise (70). These receptors bear rather complicated microvilli and in general are devoid of centrioles. Additionally, many of these receptors are in direct contact with one another rather than being completely separated by supporting cells.

FUNCTIONAL ANATOMY AND PHYSIOLOGY

Although interest centers on gustation and olfaction, trigeminal modalities that include chemical sensitivity and other modalities also contribute importantly to the compound experiences associated with tasting and smelling. Trigeminal innervation is extensive in both the nasal and oral mucosae. There are no ancillary receptor cells associated with these free nerve endings whose parent cell bodies are located far away.

The oral cavity.—In mammals the anterior portion of the tongue is innervated by the lingual nerve, which is a branch of the mandibular portion of the trigeminus. Gustatory afferents and autonomic efferents join the lingual nerve by way of the chorda tympani nerve which passes through the middle ear cavity on its way from the facial nerve. The glossopharyngeal nerve innervates the back of the tongue and contains gustatory afferents as well as many other kinds. Although there are species differences in responsiveness to various taste stimuli, within a given species there are characteristic differences between chorda tympani and glossopharyngeal responses (130, 86, 119, 168). Some inconsistencies in these results are clearly attributable to differences in method of stimulation.

A remarkable study by Oakley (109) investigated the character of the responses that could be recorded from whole nerves of the rat after cross-regeneration. It was established that the normal glossopharyngeal or IX*th* nerve was much more responsive to cooling of the tongue than was the tympani. In experimental preparations the proximal portion of the chorda tympani was sutured to the peripheral IX*th* nerve and vice versa. After regeneration the chorda tympani was much more responsive to cooling of the tongue, although not so much as the normal IX*th* nerve and the regenerated IX*th* was not much more sensative to cooling than the normal chorda tympani. Taste responses to various stimuli were compared relative to those to $0.3M$ NH₄Cl. Ringer's solution and NaCl were much better stimuli for the normal chorda tympani, while quinine and saccharin were more effective for the normal IX*th* nerve. Taste responses of the cross-regenerated nerves were much more like those of the nerves that originally innervated the re-innervated areas. Instead of the nerve being an important determinant of the nature of the response as might have been expected, the area of the tongue to which it regenerated seemed considerably more important in determining the response characteristics of the regenerated nerve.

These operations (109) were performed unilaterally, and, when possible the other side served as the control. Guth (72) found that after unilateral section of the glossopharyngeal nerve only about 12 per cent of the rat circumvallate taste buds disappeared, but bilateral transection caused all of them to disappear. However, there is very little evidence for bilateral in-nervation of fungiform papillae in the chorda tympani field. Therefore, the possibility that the regenerating nerve fibers grew out to taste cells which were maintained by normal contralateral innervation is remote in this in-stance.

Experiments on nerve regeneration in the tongue of the frog were done by Robbins (125). The glossopharyngeal nerve is the principal source of gusta-tory innervation in this animal, by way of its major branch, the lingual nerve. Cutaneous branches of the V*th* and VII*th* cranial nerves were used to reinnervate the lingual nerve field. Temporal response patterns to taste stimuli in many of the preparations were similar to those of the normal lingual or regenerated control lingual nerve preparation. Threshold con-centrations were much nearer to those for normal lingual innervation than to those for stimulation of the skin with normal cutaneous innervation. Robbins (126) found that turnover of the taste bud cells is very much slower in the frog than in the rat, and remnants of the taste buds persist for very many weeks after denervation. Thus one might suspect that these receptor cells maintained their response identity and were apparently capable of responding to the trophic influence of nongustatory afferent fibers.

The so-called water taste is of interest because the chorda tympani nerve of many mammals, e.g., rabbit, cat, dog, and monkey, responds to stimula-tion of the tongue with water, but this is not found in other mammals, e.g., rat, hamster, sheep, and human. Beidler (11) discussed some theoretical possibilities to account for these differences. Since the oral mucosa is nor-mally bathed in salivary secretions, it is not surprising that in some animals the neutral stimulus is Ringer's solution or near-isotonic NaCl solution. The perceptual consequences of adaptation to such levels of salt concentra-tion have been shown by Bartoshuk, McBurney & Pfaffmann (9, 118). It thus appears possible that animals without the water taste exhibit a baseline neural activity in response to their own salivary secretions.

What about fresh-water fish, where the taste buds are continuously bathed in the aqueous environment in which they live? Konishi (91) found this to be a complex question, with his results indicating fundamental importance of the electrical double layer, or zeta potential, which exists at surfaces in solutions of low ionic strength. Concentration variation of various salts typically revealed responses at high concentrations and again over a range of low concentrations. Distilled water rinses, following application of the less effective intermediate concentrations, resulted in large responses to the water. Single-fiber analysis and electrical polarization study indicated that different receptors were involved.

There seem to be many more nerve fibers *in toto* to the fungiform papillae than there are in the chorda tympani nerve, which suggests branching of nerve fibers or else innervation from other sources (13). Rapuzzi & Casella (121) studied this in the frog by sucking the papillae into capillary pipette electrodes. Recording from one papilla and mechanically stimulating neighboring papillae revealed that one tactile fiber normally innervates a few papillae. However, no papilla ever receives branches from more than one tactile fiber. The other fibers of the glossopharyngeal nerve, on the other hand, divide into a mean number of five to six branches going to different papillae. With several fibers of this type to each papilla, one finds extensive maps of papillae that are interconnected with a given papilla. Rapuzzi & Casella were not able to determine the amount of branching of fibers that responded to taste stimuli. At the finer level, we have no idea of how many receptor cells may be functionally connected to one nerve fiber branch.

An electrophysiological study by Hellekant (77) revealed that mammalian lingual nerve afferents were more sensitive to ethyl alcohol than the gustatory afferents. However, at concentrations of alcohol below those eliciting chorda tympani responses, responses to quinine mixed with alcohol were inhibited. Although a substance may not reveal an effect on receptors by inducing a response, the presence of an effect may be revealed by testing with other substances.

In the *Contributions to Sensory Physiology* series, Sato (130) presents a well-written account of extensive research that he carried out with various collaborators on the effects of temperature variation on neural responses from the tongue. Temperature dependence of gustatory response was studied by preadapting the tongue to temperature ranging from 10° to 45° C. The integrated responses of taste nerves of rat, cat, and frog exhibited a rather broad maximum which was often centered around 25° to 35° C.

Hardiman (75) made a similar study in the hamster in which the tongue was adapted to the test temperature for 5 min before application of the gustatory stimulus, but it was always returned to 25° C before the next test. The gustatory responses were greatest at 25° C.

The nasal cavity.—The nasal mucosae are extensively innervated by the I*st* and V*th* cranial nerves, and in most instances a wealth of glands of various types are present. The study of Bojsen-Møller (24) of the topography of the nasal glands also contains excellent illustrations of the topography of neural innervation in a whole mount of the rat nasal septum stained by the periodic-acid-Schiff technique. The vomeronasal nerve bundles and branches from the maxillary division of the trigeminus are easily seen. The vomeronasal nerve is considered as part of cranial nerve I, but it extends far forward and ventrally to the organ of Jacobson. The olfactory mucosa is revealed by the stained Bowman's glands and it extends quite far anterodorsally. The dorsal trigeminal innervation is by way of the ethmoidal nerve, derived from the ophthalmic branch of the trigeminus, which enters the region through some of the foramina in the cribriform plate.

It has been shown (157, 158) that olfactory and vomeronasal receptors in turtles respond to inspired odorants, but with characteristic differences analogous to those for chorda tympani and glossopharyngeal responses to taste stimuli. Additionally, trigeminal afferents in the dorsum of the nose of rabbits and turtles were found to respond to many odorants. Vomeronasal receptors in the rabbit did not respond to inhaled odorants (158). According to Parsons (116), however, all amniotes except turtles have the vomeronasal epithelium in a ventromedial outpocketing of the nose, the Jacobson's organ. In most amphibians and turtles there are two exposed sensory areas. One is lined by olfactory epithelium with nerve fibers leading to the main olfactory bulb and the other by vomeronasal epithelium with fibers leading to the accessory olfactory bulb.

An implanted-canulae preparation in the rabbit was developed for reversible blocking of the trigeminal nerves, and the results were checked with one animal in which the nerves were chronically lesioned (146). Recording electrodes were implanted in the sensorimotor cortex and the olfactory bulb, and respiration and electrocardiogram were recorded. If one were to study the published records and disregard the text, a likely conclusion would be that all of the observed responses to inhaled octane and isopropyl alcohol were mediated solely by the trigeminus. The changes in baseline, evident in the records after xylocaine block, illustrate the dramatic influence of the massive trigeminal afferent inflow to the brain.

Although trigeminal nerve fibers can regenerate, olfactory neurons undergo retrograde degeneration after section of their axons. Contrary to earlier reports that not all of the receptors degenerate, Sen Gupta (137) found complete degeneration after removal of the olfactory bulbs in the rat. After 25 days the transformed olfactory mucosa consisted of only one row of low columnar cells with a distinct basement membrane. Takagi & Yajima (149) sectioned the olfactory nerve in the bullfrog to study the effect of receptor degeneration on the slow potential response that can be recorded from the olfactory mucosa with odorous stimulation. The receptor cells and slow potential response gradually disappeared together, and thus it was concluded that the receptors generate this response.

Tucker & Shibuya (159) eliminated the air space in the turtle's nose by increasing the thickness of the layer of mucus, so to speak, with nasal perfusion of salt solution simulating the essential properties of mucus. Typical slow potential responses were recorded "underwater" in response to various concentrations of different odorants introduced into the flowing salt solution from the conventional air olfactometer. This system has been employed with detergents and mechanical agitation of the perfusing solution to remove the olfactory cilia in box turtles (155). Responses recorded from small twigs of the primary olfactory nerve often made substantial recovery toward the control values recorded before such drastic treatment. The role of cilia is made questionable because a high percentage of them can be removed, but all of their basal bodies seem to be retained within the receptor cells. Since the related vomeronasal receptors have no cilia, and rarely centrioles (70), it seems quite probable that a ciliary rudiment is not necessarily involved in the mechanism of chemical stimulation.

The results from experiments on the removal of olfactory cilia must be considered preliminary for reasons that will become apparent. Shibuya (138) wondered about the role of the mucus and thought of applying a piece of absorbent paper to blot some up. He traced a twig of the olfactory nerve to its origin in the mucosa and recorded simultaneously the electro-olfactogram (EOG) and the neural response. The EOG could be reduced to practically nil and the neural response hardly affected after appropriate treatment with the paper. Microelectrode penetration of the treated area did not reveal a remnant of the negativegoing EOG but did reveal unit receptor activity, as would be expected from the undiminished neural response. Examination of treated material with the light microscope revealed the usual profusion of cilia with characteristic movement in the proximal zone, and mucus thickness appeared reduced. Shibuya's suggestion that the slow potential may originate from the superficial mucous layer reflected his preoccupation with the mucus. Removal of the mucus with vigorous washing does not change the "underwater" EOG (155). Although there have been speculations (94), it is still not understood how the paper treatment can attenuate the EOG so dramatically.

It has been claimed recently (114) that Shibuya made serious errors in the experiment just described. The point is made that an odor puff will affect the whole mucosal area, and any untreated receptor area which sends axons to the nerve twig would still contribute to the response recorded there. Ottoson & Shepherd suggested that an essential control is to treat the entire mucosa and see if the nerve discharge remains. They reported that no response whatsoever could be obtained from the olfactory bulb of the frog after the whole sensory area was treated using Shibuya's method. Several points of interest can be developed here: (a) The implication that an undamaged area of mucosa contributed to the twig response does not account for the lack of reduction in the twig response or for the observation with microelectrodes of unit responses in the treated area. (b) Shibuya indicated clearly that the effect could be graded through reduction of the slow potential response with maintenance of neural response and finally to injury of the epithelium, as one would expect from repeated applications of dry paper on a mucosal epithelium. (c) The supposedly simple and essential control is not easily applied in the gopher tortoise because of the relative inaccessibility of much of the olfactory mucosa. (*d*) One can be sure that the whole of the frog's olfactory mucosa was not treated, because Ottoson's preparation is an exposure of the olfactory eminence by removal of olfactory mucosa along with the dorsal nasal structures. This is made clear by the following quotation from Bloom (20):

At first the so-called *eminentia olfactoria* was regarded as the true olfactory region, but Exner (1877) a. o. showed that the olfactory region included practically the whole of the nasal cavity with the exception of a small strip from the outer to the inner opening. In this furrow, where the air passes with great speed at breathing, only respiratory epithelium and myelinated nerve fibers are found.

Therefore the surviving olfactory neural connections to the bulb undoubtedly had a ventral distribution. (*e*) The control procedure that is practicable in the recording experiment with the neural twig is to occlude the site of origin in the mucosa with a piece of plastic membrane and see whether the twig response is completely blocked. Ottoson (113) and Shibuya (138) showed that this procedure does not damage the mucosal response.

The fairly close parallelism between the neural and mucosal responses (159) heightens interest in Ottoson's (113) proposal that the EOG is a record contributed to by the generator potentials of many receptor cells. Contrary to the effect on the EOG just described, it was most interesting to find that the "underwater" EOG could be enhanced markedly by reduction of the calcium ion content in the perfusing solution. The neural response tended toward the same absolute height, but the baseline activity increased with reduction of calcium concentration.

It has been indicated that animal olfactory receptors are insensitive to moderate changes of temperature (67) and that their responses to odorants are similarly insensitive (157). However, studies of human olfactory thresholds in which there was temperature preadaptation, although no measurements were attempted of any nasal mucosal temperatures, have shown a dependence if the stimulus was specified in terms of molarity, i.e., moles/liter. A potentially significant result, however, was temperature independence if relative vapor pressure was the measure of stimulus intensity. The threshold for ethanol at high relative humidity was about 6×10^{-6} of vapor saturation (71), which seems rather low in comparison with other studies (93, 147). Bocca & Battiston (21) obtained constancy of the ratios of threshold partial pressure to saturated vapor pressure for butyric acid, valeric acid, and citral. However, the ratio was a strongly increasing function of the relative humidity for valeric acid, which was the only substance studied with this variable. The data appeared to be rather different between subjects.

Receptor and generator potentials.—Kimura & Beidler (90) and Tateda & Beidler (151) introduced capillary pipette microelectrode tips into taste buds of rat fungiform papillae and recorded slow potential responses upon application of sapid solutions. This seems likely to be a receptor potential which, in a general scheme, would accompany the release of a chemical transmitter at synaptic regions.

Takagi (148) discussed the question of whether EOG's are generator potentials. Considering the possibility of secretory activity in supporting cells and an associated secretory potential, he decided that disappearance of the EOG response upon retrograde degeneration of the receptor cells might be because they induce such activity in supporting cells. On the other hand, considering that the sustentacular cell is supposed to be a kind of glial cell and may exhibit electrical response behavior (112), he concluded that his study of ionic mechanisms of the EOG are not enough to reveal its origin. If the supporting cells are stimulated directly by odorants, the nerve degeneration experiment (149) indicates a trophic influence exerted by the receptor cells.

Higashino & Takagi (80) studied the effect of electrial polarization of the olfactory mucosa on slow potential responses, and they concluded that there are two receptive processes in the olfactory cell: an excitatory one which produces the usual electronegative slow potential, and one activated only by vapor of an organic solvent of high concentration which reacts oppositely to the applied electrotonic current. They identified the "off"-slow potential induced by vapors of organic solvents of high concentration with the same mechanism that produces the usual "on"-slow potential response. This agrees with the intrepretation of Gesteland, Lettvin & Pitts (66) that the off response represents a release of the negative-driving process that falls more slowly than a positive-driving or resting-level seeking process which is inhibitory.

It seems likely that a "spurious" response observed by Higashino & Takagi was due to a change in resistance caused by deformation of the mucous surface at the electrode by the air puff. It was also obtained from nerve-degenerated olfactory epithelium. However, the impedance changes studied by Gesteland and co-workers appear to have been much smaller. Their technique, though, was to inject the odorant into a continuosly flowing stream of air directed at the electrodes. The stimulus perturbation may have been so small that it forced them to resort to the coherent detector to observe an impedance change. They emphasized the differential effects observed on the two components required to specify an impedance, but surface-active effects of high concentrations (159) of the variety of compounds used could have yielded the required second degree of freedom. In both studies (66, 80) instabilities appeared in the records when voltage applied to the surface of the mucus exceeded about 2 mV; this appeared to be caused by the responding of receptors.

The generator current-potential scheme has its basis in the fact that propagated action potentials are usually initiated in the axon-soma region. There is a mechanoreceptor in the crayfish, the thoracic pit receptor studied by Mellon & Kennedy (99), which is strictly a bipolar neuron. It was large enough to be studied intracellularly with microelectrode techniques, and the receptor potential in the thoracic sensory cell was so attenuated at the soma as to be absent. Direct current stimulation of the dendritic region did produce spike trains. Is the site of impulse initiation in olfactory receptors the axon soma? The problem is whether the generator circuit is extensive enough for the potential to be picked up with the recording methods used, and, if not, what is the EOG? On the assumption that receptor sites are on the cilia, alternative mechanisms for stimulus transmission were suggested (94), but calculations by Ottoson & Shepherd (114) indicate that the electrotonic mechanism is probably feasible. There is undoubtly a generator mechanism in the nerve endings of the trigeminal afferents, but no one appears to have observed the corresponding potentials.

THE CODING PROBLEM

After discussing the complexity of flavor experience and the general human tendency to employ small numbers of categories, Beidler (12) stated that most taste scientists use the concept of four taste qualities but do not for a moment believe that four can completely describe all tastes. However, the concept of fundamental or specific qualities in olfaction and taste has been defended with vigor by Amoore and von Békésy. The problem is whether the correlates of such categorization can be recognized in afferent neural activity or properties of stimulating compounds with present experimental methods. Simply defined stimuli of one chemical at a time are normally employed, although complex mixtures and on-going behavior are the rule in normal experience. Chemicals singly have been employed to keep experimentation within manageable proportions, but there is little evidence to compel belief in the likelihood of simple addition of responses for a mixture (94).

Taste.—Pfaffmann (118) related his failure to find the primary taste receptors that experimental psychologists had hypothesized while working under one of the pioneers of electrophysiology, Lord Adrian. Since the discharge of a multisensitive fiber by itself could not be an unequivocal signal, it became apparent that a significant feature of the taste input to the brain may be the ratio of activities in parallel afferent channels as a basis for taste discrimination.

However, Zotterman (171), another pioneer in electrophysiology, seized upon the existence of fibers that apparently are specific for only one taste quality. He argued that even if the number of more strictly specific fibers is fairly small compared with the more or less unspecific fibers which respond to two or more classes of sapid substances, it is easy to imagine that distribution of afferent impulses can be automatically biased in exactly the right way to excite preferentially the center that corresponds to the particular class of chemical compounds that happens to be the external stimulus at the moment. The situation would be clearest near threshold and the bringing in of "unwanted" impulses at higher stimulus strength would be made ineffective centrally by a kind of lateral inhibition. Nevertheless, subjective magnitude appears to be directly proportional to all the impulse traffic in the human chorda tympani nerve, according to results obtained from three patients (26).

The strong influence of point of view emerges in the technically excellent single fiber study by Iggo & Leek (86) of the various sensory modalities represented in chorda tympani, lingual, and glossopharyngeal innervation of the sheep's tongue. They stated that no unexpected results emerged in the work, which confirmed the existence in the sheep of taste afferent units that can be grouped into classes on the basis of the relative sensitivity to salt, acid, sweet, and bitter solutions.

Startling findings with electrical stimulation of single fungiform papillae in the human were reported by von Békésy (17). Subjects experienced only four qualities of taste sensation. Electrically induced qualities were purer than those obtained with chemical stimulation, hence the recurrent theme of overtastes associated with compounds. Few would disagree with the observation that sweet substances taste differently, but the amino acid glycine was found to be most like "monogustatory sweetness." At the same time, von Békésy (18, 19) described localization phenomena with gustatory and olfactory stimuli, which must be caused by neural interactions within the central nervous system. Later, he described methods for chemically and electrically stimulating and studying single fungiform papillae over a long period of time (15). The experimental difficulties were emphasized, but for some subjects there was complete agreement between the maps obtained by chemical and electrical stimulation. Even so, it was indicated the results seem to show that individual papillae have sensitivities for specific taste qualities, but the great importance of neural interaction for appreciation of complex (therefore natural) stimulation was always emphasized (16).

Harper, Jay & Erickson (76) designed a stimulating chamber that could be clamped to the human tongue by suction and had an opening that was supposed to be just large enough to admit a single papilla. Sensations were qualitatively accurate from 10 of the 23 papillae tested, but only 4 of these were restricted to the mediation of a single stimulus quality. Stimulus concentrations were much greater than those used by von Békésy, but it seems difficult to imagine that adaptation for the major taste could outstrip adaptation for the overtastes associated with a stimulus substance.

There is insufficient space to consider in detail Erickson's (55) ingenious attempts to deduce a gustatory neural response function. The question is whether this can be done by working backward in a system that is presumably already known. The best analogous system that he could find, apparently, consisted of data on difference absorption spectra of individual goldfish cones. The results may be considered plausible. The methods were then applied to responses of rat chorda tympani fibers. Normalization of the data to obtain the same total response to each compound may be of questionable validity. However, no evidence for separate stimulus primaries was seen.

The across-fiber pattern approach was employed by Sato, Yamashita &

Ogawa (131) to study taste potentiators. Potentiation of responses to 0.27 per cent monosodium glutamate by the addition of 0.03 per cent 5'-ribonucleotides was uniformally depressed when 0.1 per cent NaCl was present in the solutions. On the assumption that highly correlated stimuli taste alike, it was predicted that the mixture of monosodium glutamate and sodium 5'-guanylate should taste something like sucrose to the rat. The potentiation between the glutamate and 5'-ribonucleotides was found to be correlated to the sucrose/NaCl response ratio.

Marshall (98) repeated Erickson's (56) original experiment in more detail, using the opossum instead of the rat. Reliability coefficients of 0.88 and 0.75 were obtained for the first and second presentations of a series of stimuli. Analysis of a subset of the data for half-second intervals indicated that across-fiber patterns for different stimuli may become "best representations" at different times after the onset of discharge activity. For the complete set of data, correlation coefficients were computed for the first and second seconds of response activity. The second across-fiber pattern thus obtained was most relevant for the behavioral responses of the animals. This result points up graphically the dilemma of deciding what should be a measure of response.

The concept that stimulating compounds are bound to receptor sites to form complexes (11) suggests that if only biochemists could isolate the receptive substances one could study readily the specificities involved. A start in this direction has been made by Dastoli, Lopiekes & Price (44), who isolated from bovine tongue epithelium a protein which binds weakly various sweet-tasting compounds.

Olfaction.—Gesteland et al. (67) obtained unit responses with metal microelectrodes from exposed olfactory mucosa of the grass frog. They discussed four possible receptor models based on the assumption that the resting discharge rate for the receptors is either small or zero, which appeared reasonable from their data (67, p. 33). Cells differed in the model they favored by having different ratios of different receptor site types distributed over each one. However, thay attempted to categorize units and obtained eight groups with considerable overlapping of responsiveness to different odorants. This result was eagerly accepted by many, and some even said that existence of the seven primary receptor sites postulated earlier by Amoore (2) had been independently confirmed.

Meanwhile, responses to odorants were recorded from insect receptors (23). Highly specialized receptors were found for the sex pheromones, but "generalist" receptors were found which responded to many odorants. Appreciable baseline activity was commonly observed and inhibitory responses were frequent. Thus, insect generalist receptors came in a great variety of patterns of response which could be coded +, 0 or −.

By 1965 Gesteland, Lettvin & Pitts (66) decided that every olfactory cell in the grass frog was affected by many odors: some excitatory, some inhibitory, some ineffective; and that there are many kinds of receptors when classified by a spectrum of odors, as was found in insects. They came up with the hologram analogy instead of an across-fiber pattern. The paper, called "Speculations on Smell" (94), is most entertaining and revealing. Lettvin unabashedly stated that they had hoped to bring off a coup like that involving the frog's eye, i.e., "what the frog's eye tells the frog's brain." Although they were able to record from unmyelinated fibers in the optic nerve with their special electrode, they had to place the electrode in the mucosa rather than in the olfactory nerve (67) and thus the integrity of the olfactory organ had to be corrupted. However, a more fundamental and perhaps key difference is that they were looking at responses of primary neurons in the olfactory system, unlike their study of the visual system. The possibility that receptors cannot be grouped or categorized in terms of operations on odors was rejected and the conclusion made that they had simply failed to discover them.

Altner & Boeckh (1) studied primary olfactory units in the water frog. Baseline activity was low and they observed only increases in impulse frequency; thus the response spectrum they obtained contained only + or 0 elements. In a study on single units of vultures, Shibuya & Tucker (139) could not agree between themselves on the incidence of baseline activity. On the one hand a sampling problem is involved, and on the other baseline activity can be modulated with adjustments of the microelectrode. Concentration dependence of unit responses was emphasized in relation to integrated (summated) multi-unit responses from twigs of the olfactory nerve. The variety of unit response behavior found was unexpected in comparison with the regularity of the integrated neural response.

It was implied earlier that olfactory responses should be examined at neural levels higher than the primary receptors. This has been done in a number of instances.

Responses in the olfactory bulb of the water frog were studied by Döving (53) with microelectrodes, and such units commonly had appreciable baseline activity. A variety of temporal response patterns was evoked with different stimuli or with different concentrations of one stimulus. In one example, stimulation with $0.01 M$ butanol gave a weak discharge, while stronger stimulations produced an early inhibition which became gradually more pronounced as the concentration was raised. No units were inhibited by low concentrations and excited by higher concentrations of odor. The anatomy of the olfactory bulb is fairly complex and inhibitory phenomena are well known. The receptor cell axons enter structures called glomeruli and synapse with the terminations of long dendrites from mitral cells. The mitral cell axons constitute the lateral olfactory tract which proceeds to olfactory cortical areas. In the rabbit there is a convergence ratio of about 1000 primary nerve fibers for each mitral cell. Lateral dendrites on the mitral cells are enmeshed with ascending dendrites of granule cells. A combined theoretical and electron microscope study by Rall et al. (120) is especially enlightening. Two-way dendrodendritic synapses were observed between mitral and granule cells. The mitral to granule synapse appears to be excitatory and the oppositely directed synapse inhibitory. These connections seem to be extremely numerous, lying in the external plexiform layer just beneath the layer of glomeruli.

Subsequent studies by Döving (49, 51, 52) have been concerned mainly with odor similarities estimated by means of a chi-square statistic. His method may be better understood by comparison with that employed in a study of multi-responsiveness of neurons in the visual cortex of the cat to various sensory modalities of stimulation (105). Typically, Döving classified responses as +, −, or 0. Stimulus strength was adjusted by regulating the amount of odorous air delivered to the mucosa so as to obtain approximately equal EOG amplitudes, presumably indicating that the stimulating efficiency was about equal for all odors in a series. The finding that musks failed to affect a large number of bulbar units was related to the relatively small amplitude of the EOG elicited by these stimuli (49). In consideration of the response pattern dependence on concentration that was established earlier (53), one wonders how ephemeral these results might be.

Döving (50) made single fiber recordings from the olfactory tract of a fish, the burbot. A variety of response patterns was illustrated. Similar methods were used by Nanba et al. (107) in studies of the carp and goldfish. They described several patterns of response, including one of rhythmic bursting. They also noted extreme sensitivity to flow rate of water over the olfactory mucosa. Mechanical stimulation with a bristle inhibited baseline activity unless the stimulation was in the area synaptically connected to the fiber. During odor stimulation, mechanical stimulation suppressed olfactory adaptation. Hara (74) recorded from olfactory bulb neurons in the goldfish with microelectrodes and described six patterns of response to chemical stimulation of the olfactory mucosa. Incredibly, his chemical stimuli consisted only of NaCl solutions. However, macroelectrode recordings from the olfactory bulbs of spawning salmon revealed responses that were greater for water from home streams than from other streams in the neighborhood (160).

Spatial and temporal coding represent concepts that are formulated differently by some (16, 107). However, the spatiotemporal patterning of olfactory responses studied by Mozell (104) at the primary nerve level, and by Moulton (102) at the bulbar level, are thought to be due, at least in part, to simple chromatographic-like distributions of odorous stimuli over the olfactory organ and to be important in discrimination. Schneider & Schmidt (134) accepted the results of von Békésy's (19) olfactory analogue to directional hearing, but concluded that discriminations were probably mediated by trigeminal sensitivity to the odorants used. Von Békésy (19) reported a remarkable interaction between smell and taste in which sensation could be made to move back and forth from the nose and the tongue through the back of the throat by variation of timing between the two stimuli. It was stated that no vibrations were transmitted to the tubes leading to the nose. However, the same type of switching device was used for taste localization, and it was stated that the pressure pulse arrived before the taste solution and that subjects learned to ignore the mechanical sensation (18).

Leveteau & MacLeod (95) inserted bipolar microelectrodes into the glomerular layer in the olfactory bulb of the curarized rabbit. Slow potential responses were evoked by odor stimulation and probably represented complex averages of postsynaptic potentials. There were various combinations of different glomeruli responding or not responding to different odors. They concluded that the 10^8 point olfactory pattern in the olfactory mucosa is converted to a homologous pattern of only 2000 points at the glomerular level. Hughes & Hendrix (83) implanted electrodes in olfactory bulbs of the rabbit to study induced wave responses to odors. Frequency analyses were performed with an electronic wave analyzer, and a frequency component hypothesis in relation to the coding mechanism in the olfactory bulb was adduced. Excitatory and inhibitory types of responses appeared, and a prominent frequency component appearing for a given category of stimuli varied according to electrode site within the olfactory bulb. It was concluded that the data provided evidence for the frequency component hypothesis and the stereochemical theory of Amoore.

Amoore (2) abandoned the "classical site-fitting concept" and therefore the seven sites he had deduced from study of the molecules associated together by frequency of commonly applied odor names. However, he resorted to a study of odor similarities by means of a panel of human judges and of similarity of molecular shapes relative to certain standards. The results were said to provide strong experimental evidence that the psychophysical basis of odor is primarily molecular size and shape. This is reminiscent of the "profile-functional group" concept of Beets (10), developed from the point of view of the professional perfumer.

Recently, Amoore (3) has turned to a study of specific anosmia. The terminology is misleading because he selected subjects whose thresholds for isobutyric acid were somewhat higher than those for normal subjects. The deficiency in sensitivity was broadly distributed over the straight chain carboxylic acids, but the greatest deficiency observed was for isovaleric acid, being about a hundredfold. This compound was considered to be the primary odorant corresponding to the quality of "sweatiness." The relation between threshold difference or deficiency on a $\log_2$ scale was plotted against molecular similarity to the shape of isovaleric acid. The fourteen other acids varied from 0.5 to 0.65 compared to 1 for the standard on the similarity scale. Presumably such deficiencies in olfactory ability are analogous to well-known examples of deficiency in taste (46). Questions were raised recently (32) concerning the belief that the commonly occurring impairment of ability to smell HCN has a simple genetic basis.

Attempts have been made to correlate molecular properties revealed by infrared spectra to odor qualities. Wright's book (166) chronicles his early attempts and is recommended also as an interesting account of olfaction. The recent emphasis is on low-frequency molecular vibrations which can be studied in the far infrared spectrum. A lively debate between Demerdache & Wright (47) centers around the physical properties of certain molecules whose odors are said to resemble that of HCN. Wright, Hughes & Hendrix reach a joining of forces leading to the amazing conclusion that frequency components of the induced wave response in the olfactory bulb can be correlated against molecular frequencies of the stimulating substances (167). Correlation curves were drawn through data obtained from rabbit and human. Let one criticism be voiced by the authors (167, p. 406): "These correlation curves are not the only smooth curves which can be drawn when all of the frequency components are plotted against all of the molecular vibration frequencies . . . ." In olfaction, at least, we now have a stimulus continuum. In analogy with overtastes, oversmells are rampant.

The membrane puncturing theory of Davies (45) has an appealing immediacy of action between the effect of odorant molecules and the flow of generator current. The stereotyped concept of receptor sites is replaced with variation in the fluid properties of receptor cell membranes, thus conferring a broad, qualitative selectivity upon different receptors. Easily related to and extending this theory is the proposal that charge-transfer complexes between odorants and certain carotenoid pigments influence receptor membrane conductivity (92, 103, 128).

MECHANICAL FACTORS IN CHEMORECEPTOR STIMULATION

The tongue is noted for its exquisite sensitivity to mechanical stimulation, and taste experiments are usually arranged to minimize mechanical stimulation so that the response records will not be contaminated with distracting deflections. However, it has been known for some time that the gustatory response of the glossopharyngeal nerve is enhanced by mechanical stimulation of the back of the tongue.

Passive stretch of the cat's tongue (88) had no effect on gustatory responses of the chorda tympani nerve, but a distinct enhancement of glossopharyngeal responses was seen. A so-called water response was revealed and even a response to Ringer's solution, which is commonly regarded as neutral for the receptor field of the cat chorda tympani. Movement of the cat's tongue (87) in response to electrical stimulation of the motor nerve could be adjusted to produce very little mechanoreceptor activity in the chorda tympani nerve, but any movement was always reflected in activity of the glossopharyngeal nerve. Surprisingly, movement of the tongue enhanced gustatory response of the chorda tympani, the effect being confined to the tonic component. It is easy to visualize how stretch and movement of the tongue could facilitate entrance of stimulating solutions into the deep trench of the circumvallate papilla, in the wall of which are located taste buds. However, the chorda tympani taste buds are on the relatively exposed fungiform papillae. It seems likely that repetitious movements disturb concentration gradients near the receptors and thus free them from exposure to a continuous adapting concentration (17).

Pfaffman, Fisher & Frank (119) introduced the tip of a small pipette in the moat of the rat circumvallate papilla and demonstrated the dramatic dependence of the responses on transport of the stimulus to the taste buds. Iggo & Leek (86) directed a jet of stimulating solution at the papillae or mechanically displaced them in sheep during stimulation with a glass stylus. One can appreciate the difficulty of trying to record from the behaving animal, in which the conditions are appreciably different from those for the usual electrophysiological preparations.

A mechanical factor has frequently been invoked as a requirement for physiological stimulation of olfactory receptors with odors. However, it seems likely that this idea has its seat in the requirement for transport of stimulating molecules to the receptors, which is normally brought about by inspiration during normal breathing or by some mechanism in fishes for moving water through the nasal sac. In one study (22) it was said that mechanical stimulation appears to make odorous perception possible and that in the absence of a mechanical stimulus no odorous sensation arises, however high the concentration of odorous substance in the mucus may be. It is clear that mechanical stimulation means movement of air over the olfactory mucosa. When certain odorants are injected into the arm vein, no odor sensation is perceived if the subject resorts to mouth breathing or is a tracheotomized patient. In the instance of ethyl ether, an odor sensation may be perceived 12 to 14 sec after injection, but it was argued that the vascular pulse could cause a sufficiently strong mechanical stimulation.

Electroencephalographic investigators, studying the relation of more central nervous structures to wave activity of the olfactory bulb, are frequently in disagreement about the role of the primary olfactory nerve activity. Pagano (115) stated that the adequate stimulus is nasal air flow and that the induced wave activity of the olfactory bulb increases with increased rate of nasal flow. Experiments on chronic and acute cat preparations (65) indicated that this activity of the olfactory bulb cannot be elicited independently of nasal air flow.

A more recent experiment (117) employed tracheotomized cats with implanted cannulae and electrodes. The most remarkable finding was bursting activity of olfactory bulb waves in response to auditory, visual, or tactile stimuli of "adequate intensity" when the nares of the animals were occluded. The authors felt that air flow through the nose plays an important but not the main or exclusive role, even though studies were cited showing that the bursting activity of the olfactory bulb persists after severance of its connections with the brain. Yamamoto & Iwama (169) destroyed the olfactory epithelium of the rabbit and found that the intrinsic activity of the olfactory bulb persisted and could still be suppressed by stimulation of the reticular formation. Although they reported no responses of bursting activity from the olfactory bulb of this preparation, one wonders with some doubt whether nonodorous stimuli would have been effective.

Schneider, Schmidt & Costiloe (135) studied human perception of butane odorant and determined thresholds expressed as odor concentration, total quantity of odor, and odor delivery rate for variations of nasal flow rate from 10 to 80 ml/sec. No one quantity was constant. However, Svyataya (147) found that with ethanol the product of concentration times inspired flow rate over the range of 20 to 200 ml/sec was a constant. This latter result probably stems from the aqueous solubility of ethanol and the limited range of flow rate variation.

In summary, chemoreceptor responses depend on the delivery of stimulating substances to them, and this is normally achieved by mechanically effected flows. A complication often unappreciated is that the receptor response is not time independent, just as is true of receptors in general. Response cannot be predicted for a specified stimulus value without knowledge of the immediate history of how this value of stimulation was achieved.

PREFERENCES AND AVERSIONS

Considerable work has been done with taste preferences and aversions, but the olfactory work is less extensive. Several representative studies have reported the importance of olfaction in food detection (82), mating behavior (27, 34), and aggression (127). Long & Tapp (96) found that odors could be used as reinforcers to rats for bar-pressing behavior. Moncrieff (100) studied human reactions to a variety of odorants with respect to age, sex, etc.; the book is summarized with 124 rules of odor preference.

In the study of taste preferences and aversions one must take into consideration the olfactory, gustatory, and other afferent inputs, the immediate postingestive feedback, and the metabolic consequences which follow changes in the nutritional state of the organism (119). Additionally, methods used are extremely influential on the results of the test. For example, Fisher (59) found a significant difference in preference for $0.1 M$ NaCl over distilled water when the solution was presented alternately at a single aperture versus simultaneously at a pair. Collier et al. (38) found that rats pressed more often on the lever reinforced with the higher concentration of sucrose, when a pair of levers and solutions was available, but this was true only when a continuous reinforcement schedule was used; there was no preference when a 1-min fixed interval schedule was used. However, although a reinforcement on only one bar could be obtained in any given minute, this does not constitute a "changeover delay" in the schedule. Catania (35) points out the importance of separation of the two operants in concurrent scheduling designs when using interval schedules. If the subject is reinforced on the first lever press after a changeover from one lever to the other, this favors frequent changeovers, as Collier reported. It is likely that the 1-min fixed interval schedule would yield differential response to the two concentrations if a changeover delay were introduced. The length of the taste test is also very important in determining the preference. Young (170) and co-workers typically use a very short duration test in an attempt to reveal only the influence of consumatory afferent responses.

In spite of the influence of the postingestional feedback on taste preferences and aversions, the role of the sensory afferents is extremely important. Pfaffmann (118) states that he would "maintain it is the taste stimulus itself and the degree of sensory activation aroused that determines behavior." Borer (25), using a nasopharyngeal gastric tube, could place taste substances directly into the stomach or allow the rat to drink by mouth. She found that in 24-hr tests the animals showed no preferences for NaCl, glucose, sucrose, and saccharin in a variety of concentrations if the reinforcement was presented via the gastric tube. When the animals were ingesting the taste substances orally, typical nonmonotonic intakes as a function of concentration were observed. When the substances were presented via the gastric tube, both limbs of the preference curves were flattened. Vance (162) reported a similar flattening of the curves for rats which had olfactory bulb lesions and bilateral divisions of the lingual, glossopharyngeal, and pharyngeal branch of the vagus nerves. However, there was a residual preference for salt and sucrose over water. In the curves reported by Vance for sucrose, the fluid intake rose slightly as the concentration of the sucrose was increased in the operated animals. Borer reports no change in level of intake as a function of increased sucrose concentrations; this indicates the likelihood that postingestional factors are not contributing to the preferences reported by Vance, but trigeminal afferents possibly are. In both experiments the intake of the sucrose mixture did not decrease as the concentration of the solution increased; hence the absolute amount of solute ingested increases at least in direct proportion with concentration.

Collier and co-workers (36, 37) compared intakes of saccharin and sucrose in various combinations at different concentrations with two-bottle long-term tests. Curves that peaked as a function of concentration were obtained for choices between water and sucrose or saccharin. However, in choosing between all possible pairs of 4, 8, 16, and 32 per cent sucrose, rats consumed far more of the higher concentrations. In a similar experiment with six concentrations of saccharin, the largest volumes ingested were at an intermediate value. Thus for saccharin, the preference curve obtained by pairing various concentrations with water is a good prediction of what the animal will take if he receives two concentrations of saccharin simultaneously, but this is not true for sucrose. This method of testing does not support the notion that higher concentrations of sucrose are aversive. When sucrose and saccharin were paired, the rats consumed more sucrose in every combination except for the lowest concentration of sucrose versus the optimal concentration of saccharin.

Even more profound evidence for the importance of the gustatory afferents comes from the work of Valenstein et al. (161). Normal rats consumed excessive quantities of a mixture of 3 per cent glucose and one-eighth of 1 per cent saccharin, and some actually exceeded their body weight in daily consumption of this fluid. Preference for the mixture was not built up gradually; rather, sated rats showed excessive intake (10.3 ml) of the solution in the first 30 min of exposure. Tateda (150) has demonstrated electrophysiologically a synergistic action with sucrose and glycine or fructose in the chorda tympani nerve of the rat. Dare one predict a similar result for glucose and saccharin?

Other investigators have demonstrated the profound importance of taste in the development of preferences and aversions (73, 110, 153). However, the role of postingestional effects is illustrated forcefully by Rozin's (129) study of thiamine-deficient rats. Such animals engage in vigorous feeding on novel foods, but the preference is lost in a few days if thiamine is absent. The association of cue odors or flavors with the beneficial effects of thiamine was documented. On the other hand, Garcia et al. (62) demonstrated the conditioning of gustatory aversions with injections of apomorphine separated from the taste stimuli by as long as an hour. The bait shyness of rats that survived poisoning appeared to Rozin (129) as the reverse of the attraction of thiamine-deficient rats to novel foods, and he formalized this as a novelty-specific-aversion hypothesis. Through specialized abilities to learn about foods and their consequences, rats are capable of making precise adjustments of their intake on the basis of events occurring hours after the ingestion.

DIVERSE EFFECTS OF X RAYS ON TASTE AND OLFACTION

Two rather different topics, both involving X rays, are of current interest. The reversal of innate preferences for certain taste stimuli associated with X rays and the immediate detection of ionizing radiation are distinctly different phenomena, although Le Magnen's (97) demonstration that the rat can use olfactory cues to regulate caloric intake suggests a possible connection.

X-ray-conditioned aversion.—It has been known for more than 12 years that small doses of ionizing radiation can serve as the unconditioned stimulus in conditioning an aversion to a previously preferred taste solution. The conditions under which this taste aversion occurs have been thoroughly reviewed (85, 89, 141). Although aversion to saccharin-flavored water has received the most extensive attention, an aversion has been conditioned to NaCl, sucrose, glucose, combinations of glucose and saccharin, and other solutions. In order to condition the taste aversion, the radiation (X ray, gamma ray or neutron bombardment) needs to be paired only once with the taste solution. Energies ranging from 50 kV to 3 MeV and doses as small as 10r and less have proved effective as the unconditioned stimulus (89).

As pointed out in Rozin's hypothesis (129), it has been found that the temporal juxtaposition of the presence of the taste substance and the irradiation can be quite varied. Saccharin presented as long as 12 hr prior to exposure and from 2 to 12 hr following exposure results in a subsequent aversion to saccharin-flavored water (123, 133, 142). These studies indicate that the time when the postirradiation preference test is initiated is important, since a distinctively novel taste substance presented too close to the X-ray exposure can become conditioned to the irradiation and subsequently will be avoided (143).

The analogy of this X-ray conditioning with the learning of food aversions has been made (61, 124). The absence of a requirement for the conditioned stimulus (saccharin) and the unconditioned stimulus (X ray) to be presented in immediate temporal contiguity is analogous to the "bait-shy" behavior of a wild rat which has survived poisoning (129). Revusky & Bedarf (124) stressed the importance of the novelty of the gustatory stimulus in the formation of the X-ray aversion, which furthers the analogy to food aversions associated with toxic substances.

Garcia, Ervin & Koelling (62) and Revusky & Bedarf (124) conclude that aftertastes are not responsible for the ability of the rat to associate the ingestion of a novel taste stimulus with later illness. It is interesting that Smith & Roll (142) found that an aversion to saccharin could be conditioned when the saccharin was separated by as long as 12 hr from the X-ray exposure, but that sucrose aversion could be produced by a separation of the stimuli up to 6 hr only.

The strength of the averse motivation induced by X-ray exposure has been demonstrated in an experiment by Smith (141). Rats were exposed once to 100r gamma rays while they were drinking the glucose and saccharin mixture described by Valenstein et al. (161). On subsequent two-bottle preference tests where the mixture of glucose and saccharin versus water was available, the average intake for 24 hr of the glucose and saccharin was 5 ml. Sham-exposed animals had an average 24-hr intake of approximately 200 ml of the mixture.

The radiation-induced motivation evidenced by the saccharin aversion problem has been demonstrated to be dependent on humoral factors (85). Pairs of rats joined by parabiotic anastomosis were subjected to the saccharin aversion design. If saccharin-flavored water is available to the shielded rat as the partner is receiving X rays, the nonirradiated rat will demonstrate a subsequent aversion to the sweetened water.

Olfactory mediation of X-ray detection.—For several years it has been known that ionizing radiation can be used as a discriminative stimulus for a variety of animals (89). Partial body exposures delimited this sensitivity in the rat to the specific region of the olfactory bulbs (84). It was demonstrated that sensitivity is dependent on dose rate of the exposure in rats (101), pigeons (145), and rhesus monkeys (144). In the rats and monkeys the threshold dose rate for detection is approximately 3 to 15 milliroentgens/sec. Thresholds in the pigeon are probably much higher but have not been precisely measured. Evidence for immediate X-ray detection has come from three main types of experiments: (*a*) desynchronization of the EEG pattern; (b) behavioral arousal from sleep; and (c) the use of X rays as a discriminative stimulus in various conditioning designs (89).

The role of the olfactory system has been studied extensively. Rats which previously suppressed responding to X-ray stimulation in a conditioned suppression design lost this suppression response after removal of the olfactory bulbs (33, 48). It has also been shown that rats which have had the the olfactory bulbs removed cannot learn to suppress to X-ray stimulation, whereas sham-operated controls learn this response within ten pairings of X ray or shock (48). Pigeons lose their X-ray sensitivity when the primary olfactory nerve is sectioned (145). Monkeys trained to suppress lever-pressing when X-irradiated lose this detection capability after sectioning of the olfactory bulb peduncles (152).

The manner in which X rays are detected is not clear. Hull et al. (84) reported that X-ray detection did not appear to depend on the smelling of ozone. They ran rats with chronic tracheotomies which prevented nasal inhalation and found all animals responded to X rays. Work reported early by Cooper & Kimeldorf (42) with 100 KVP and 35 KVP X rays led to the conclusion that peripheral sensory stimulation was not essential to the EEG desynchronization. Later, however, Cooper & Kimeldorf reported that olfactory bulb neurons in the dog, rabbit, cat, and rat respond to X-ray stimulation (40, 41), and they concluded from the effects of nasal insufflation of certain substances that the response was probably the result of the effects of X rays on the olfactory receptors (43).

Gasteiger & Helling (64) reported that ozone would mask a conditioned response to X rays in the rat and further that this response was dependent on the relative humidity in the animal's chamber (63), which suggests inhalation of odorants produced in the irradiated environment. The "conditioned suppression" behavior which they describe is misleading, since it is really an avoidance design, unlike the conditioned suppression work where learning is usually complete during the first session (48, 101). The avoidance learning took 4 to 5 weeks with six exposures each day. Their criterion for suppression is so rigid (no responding during the X ray treatment) and for no suppression is so loose (no suppression can mean 1 lick or 70 licks) that the magnitude of the suppression cannot be quantified; thus the reader cannot determine the extent of the effect of the ozone. It is also difficult to assess the effect of the ozone because dosages were specified with the unusual concentration units of milligrams per hour, pumped at an unknown volume flow rate into a box of unknown dimensions without provision for rapid mixing and for unknown lengths of time.

Cooper (39) recently reported that electrophysiological responses could be recorded with beta-irradiation on the exposed mucosa. The short latency of the onset and termination of the responses relative to X-ray bursts leads one to suspect a direct effect in the mucus or the olfactory mucosa itself.

The demonstration (145) that pigeons lost the ability for X-ray detection when the primary olfactory nerves were sectioned raises again the controversial issue of the sense of smell in birds. During this reporting period, several research projects have established that birds are capable of responding differentially in the presence of olfactory stimuli. Bang & Cobb (5) have described clearly the avian olfactory anatomy. Tucker (156) recorded responses to odor stimulation, from a twig of the primary olfactory nerve in 14 species of birds and unit responses were recorded from the olfactory mucosa of vultures (139). Wenzel (164) observed changes in heart and respiratory rates to odor stimuli in pigeons, shearwaters, and a turkey vulture. Henton, Smith & Tucker (79) demonstrated odor discrimination in the pigeon, using a conditioned suppression technique. In addition, Henton (78) has used the same technique to demonstrate that the pigeon can discriminate between amyl and butyl acetate, and Shumake, Smith & Tucker (140) have obtained intensity difference thresholds with amyl acetate.

LITERATURE CITED

1. Altner, H., Boeckh, J. Über das Reaktionsspektrum von Rezeptoren aus der Riechschleimhaut von Wasserfröschen (*Rana esculenta*). *Z. Vergleich. Physiol.*, **55**, 299–306 (1967)
2. Amoore, J. E. Psychophysics of odor. *Cold Spring Harbor Symp. Quant. Biol.*, **30**, 623–37 (1965)
3. Amoore, J. E., Venstrom, D., Davis, A. R. Measurement of specific anosmia. *Percept. Mot. Skills*, **26**, 143–64 (1968)
4. Andres, K. H. Der Feinbau der *regio olfactoria* von Makrosmatikern. *Z. Zellforsch.*, **69**, 140–154 (1966)
5. Bang, B. G., Cobb, S. The size of the olfactory bulb in 108 species of birds. *Auk*, **85**, 55–61 (1968)
6. Bannister, L. H. Fine structure of the sensory endings in the vomeronasal organ of the slow-worm *Anguis fragilis. Nature*, **217**, 275–76 (1968)
7. Bannister, L. H. The fine structure of the olfactory surface of teleostean fishes. *Quart. J. Microscop. Sci.*, **106**, 333–42 (1965)
8. Barber, V. C., Boyde, A. Scanning electron microscopic studies of cilia. *Z. Zellforsch.*, **84**, 269–84 (1968)
9. Bartoshuk, L. M., McBurney, D. H., Pfaffmann, C. Taste of sodium chloride solutions after adaptation to sodium chloride: Implications for the "water taste." *Science*, **143**, 967–68 (1964)
10. Beets, M. G. J. A molecular approach to olfaction. In *Molecular Phar-*
macology, 2–51 (Ariens, E. J., Ed., Academic Press, New York, Vol. 2, 1964)
11. Beidler, L. M. Anion influences on taste receptor response. In *Olfaction and Taste II*, 509–34 (Hayashi, T., Ed., Pergamon Press, New York, 835 pp., 1967)
12. Beidler, L. M. Chemical excitation of taste and odor receptors. *Advan. Chem. Ser.*, **56**, 1–28 (1966)
13. Beidler, L. M. Comparison of gustatory receptors, olfactory receptors, and free nerve endings. *Cold Spring Harbor Symp. Quant. Biol.*, **30**, 191–200 (1965)
14. Beidler, L. M., Smallman, R. L. Renewal of cells within taste buds. *J. Cell Biol.*, **27**, 263–72 (1965)
15. von Békésy, G. Taste theories and the chemical stimulation of single papillae. *J. Appl. Physiol.*, **21**, 1–9 (1966)
16. von Békésy, G. Inhibition and the time and spatial patterns of neural activity in sensory perception. *Ann. Otol. Rhinol. Laryngol.*, **74**, 445–62 (1965)
17. von Békésy, G. Sweetness produced electrically on the tongue and its relation to taste theories. *J. Appl. Physiol.*, **19**, 1105–13 (1964)
18. von Békésy, G. Rhythmical variations accompanying gustatory stimulation observed by means of localization phenomena. *J. Gen. Physiol.*, **47**, 809–25 (1964)
19. von Békésy, G. Olfactory analogue to directional hearing. *J. Appl. Physiol.*, **19**, 369–73 (1964)

20. Bloom, G. Studies on the olfactory epithelium of the frog and the toad with the aid of light and electron microscopy. *Z. Zellforsch.*, **41**, 89–100 (1954)

21. Bocca, E., Battiston, M. N. Odour perception and environment conditions. *Acta Oto-Laryngol.*, **57**, 391–400 (1964)

22. Bocca, E., Antonelli, A. R., Mosciaro, O. Mechanical co-factors in olfactory stimulation. *Acta Oto-Laryngol.*, **59**, 243–47 (1965)

23. Boeckh, J., Kaissling, K. E., Schneider, D. Insect olfactory receptors. *Cold Spring Harbor Symp. Quant. Biol.*, **30**, 263–80 (1965)

24. Bojsen-Møller, F. Topography of the nasal glands in rats and some other mammals. *Anat. Record*, **150**, 11–24 (1964)

25. Borer, K. T. Disappearance of preferences and aversions for sapid solutions in rats ingesting untasted fluids. *J. Comp. Physiol. Psychol.*, **65**, 213–21 (1968)

26. Borg, G., Diamant, H., Ström, L., Zotterman, Y. The relation between neural and perceptual intensity: A comparative study on the neural and psychophysical response to taste stimuli. *J. Physiol. (London)* , **192**, 13–20 (1967)

27. Bowers, J. M., Alexander, B. K. Mice: individual recognition by olfactory cues. *Science*, **158**, 1208–10 (1967)

28. Bradley, R. M., Stern, I. B. The development of the human taste bud during the foetal period. *J. Anat.*, **101**, 743–52 (1967)

29. Bronstein, A. A. Intravital observations of hair movement of olfactory cells. *Dokl. Akad. Nauk SSSR*, **156**, 715–18 (English transl., 371–74) (1964)

30. Bronstein, A. A., Ivanov, V. P. Electron microscopic investigation of the olfactory organ in the lamprey. *J. Evol. Biochem. Physiol.*, **1**, 251–61 (1965)

31. Brown, H. E., Beidler, L. M. The fine structure of the olfactory tissue in the black vulture. *Federation Proc.*, **25**, 329 (1966)

32. Brown, K. S., Robinette, R. R. No simple pattern of inheritance in ability to smell solutions of cyanide. *Nature*, **215**, 406–8 (1967)

33. Brust-Carmona, H., Kasprzak, H., Gasteiger, E. L. Role of the olfactory bulbs in X-ray detection.

Radiation Res., **29**, 354–61 (1966)

34. Carr, W. J., Loeb, L. S., Wylie, N. R. Responses to feminine odors in normal and castrated male rats. *J. Comp. Physiol. Psychol.*, **62**, 336–38 (1966)

35. Catania, A. C. Concurrent operants. In *Operant Behavior: areas of research and application*, 213–70 (Honig, W. K., Ed., Appleton-Century-Crofts, New York, 865 pp., 1966)

36. Collier, G., Bolles, R. Some determinants of the intake of sucrose solutions. *J. Comp. Physiol. Psychol.*, **65**, 379–83 (1968)

37. Collier, G., Novell, K. Saccharin as a sugar surrogate. *J. Comp. Physiol. Psychol.*, **64**, 404–8 (1967)

38. Collier, G., Vogel, J., Rega, F. Two-bar sucrose preference. *Psychon. Sci.*, **6**, 203–4 (1966)

39. Cooper, G. P. Responses of olfactory bulb neurons to X- and beta-irradiation. *Radiation Res.*, **35**, 528 (1968)

40. Cooper, G. P., Kimeldorf, D. J. Responses of single neurons in the olfactory bulbs of rabbits, dogs, and cats to X-rays. *Experientia*, **23**, 137–41 (1967)

41. Cooper, G. P., Kimeldorf, D. J. The effect of X-rays on the activity of neurons in the rat olfactory bulb. *Radiation Res.*, **27**, 75–86 (1966)

42. Cooper, G. P., Kimeldorf, D. J. Effects of brain lesions on electroencephalographic activation by 35 KVP and 100 KVP X-rays. *Intern. J. Radiation Biol.*, **9**, 101–5 (1965)

43. Cooper, G. P., Kimeldorf, D. J., McCorley, G. C. The effects of various gases within the nasal cavities of rats on the response of olfactory bulb neurons to X-irradiation. *Radiation Res.*, **29**, 395–402 (1966)

44. Dastoli, F. R., Lopiekes, D. V., Price, S. A sweet-sensitive protein from bovine taste buds. Purification and partial characterization. *Biochemistry*, **7**, 1160–64 (1968)

45. Davies, J. T. A theory of the quality of odors. *J. Theoret. Biol.*, **8**, 1–7 (1965)

46. Dawson, W., West, G. B., Kalmus, H. Taste polymorphism to anethol-trithione and phenylthiocarbamate. *Ann. Hum. Genet., London*, **30**, 273–76 (1967)

47. Demerdache, A., Wright, R. H. Low

frequency molecular vibration in relation to odor. In *Olfaction and Taste II*, 125–65 (See ref. 11)

48. Dinc, H. I., Smith, J. C. Role of the olfactory bulbs in the detection of ionizing radiation by the rat. *Physiol. Behav.*, 1, 139–44 (1966)

49. Döving, K. B. Analysis of odour similarities from electrophysiological data. *Acta Physiol. Scand.*, 68, 404–18 (1966)

50. Döving, K. B. The influence of olfactory stimuli upon the activity of secondary neurones in the burbot (*Lota lota* L.). *Acta Physiol. Scand.*, 66, 290–99 (1966)

51. Döving, K. B. An electrophysiological study of odour similarities of homologous substances. *J. Physiol.* (*London*), 186, 97–109 (1966)

52. Döving, K. B. Studies on the responses of bulbar neurons of frog to different odour stimuli. *Revue de Laryngologie, d'Otologie et de Rhinologie* (*Bordeaux*), 86, 845–54 (1965)

53. Döving, K. B. Studies of the relation between the frog's electroolfactogram (EOG) and single unit activity in the olfactory bulb. *Acta Physiol. Scand.*, 60, 150–63 (1964)

54. Duncan, C. J. *The Molecular Properties and Evolution of Excitable Cells* (Pergamon Press, New York, 253 pp., 1967)

55. Erickson, R. P. Neural coding of taste quality. In *The Chemical Senses and Nutrition*, 313–27 (Kare, M. R., Maller, O., Eds., Johns Hopkins Press, Baltimore, 495 pp., 1967)

56. Erickson, R. P. Sensory neural patterns and gustation. In *Olfaction and Taste I*, 205–13 (Zotterman, Y., Ed., Pergamon Press, New York, 396 pp., 1963)

57. Farbman, A. I. Structure of chemoreceptors. In *Chemistry and Physiology of Flavors*, 25–51 (Schultz, H. W., Day, E. A., Libbey, L. M., Eds., Avi Publ. Co., Westport, Conn., 552 pp., 1967)

58. Farbman, A. I. Electron microscope study of the developing taste bud in rat fungiform papilla. *Develop. Biol.*, 11, 110–35 (1965)

59. Fisher, G. L. Measured saline preference in the albino rat: the role of non-gustatory factors. *Psychon. Sci.*, 1, 45–46 (1964)

60. Frisch, D. Ultrastructure of mouse olfactory mucosa. *Am. J. Anat.*, 121, 87–120 (1967)

61. Garcia, J., Koelling, R. A. Relation of cue to consequence in avoidance learning. *Psychon. Sci.*, 4, 123–24 (1966)

62. Garcia, J., Ervin, F. R., Koelling, R. A. Learning with prolonged delay of reinforcement. *Psychon. Sci.*, 5, 121–22 (1966)

63. Gasteiger, E. L. Modification of stimulus-response curves for olfactory detection of X-ray by rats. *Federation Proc.*, 27, 583 (1968)

64. Gasteiger, E. L., Helling, S. A. X-ray detection by the olfactory system: ozone as a masking odorant. *Science*, 154, 1038–41 (1966)

65. Gault, F. P., Coustan, D. R. Nasal air flow and rhinencephalic activity. *Electroenceph. Clin. Neurophysiol.*, 18, 617–24 (1965)

66. Gesteland, R. C., Lettvin, J. Y., Pitts, W. H. Chemical transmission in the nose of the frog. *J. Physiol.* (*London*), 181, 525–59 (1965)

67. Gesteland, R. C., Lettvin, J. Y., Pitts, W. H., Rojas, A. Odor specificities of the frog's olfactory receptors. In *Olfaction and Taste I*, 19–34 (See ref. 56)

68. Gray, E. G., Watkins, K. C. Electron microscopy of taste buds of the rat. *Z. Zellforsch.*, 66, 583–95 (1965)

69. Graziadei, P., Bannister, L. H. Some observations on the fine structure of the olfactory epithelium in the domestic duck. *Z. Zellforsch.*, 80, 220–28 (1967)

70. Graziadei, P. P. C., Tucker, D. Vomeronasal receptors' ultrastructure. *Federation Proc.*, 27, 583, (1968)

71. Grundvig, J. L., Dustman, R. E., Beck, E. C. The relationship of olfactory receptor stimulation to stimulus-environmental temperature. *Exptl. Neurol.*, 18, 416–28 (1967)

72. Guth, L. Histological changes following partial denervation of the circumvallate papilla of the rat. *Exptl. Neurol.*, 8, 336–49 (1963)

73. Hammer, L. R. Saccharin and sucrose intake in rats: long- and short-term tests. *Psychon. Sci.*, 8, 367–68 (1967)

74. Hara, T. J. Electrophysiological studies of the olfactory system of the goldfish, *Carassius auratus* L.—II. Response patterns of the olfactory

bulb neurons to chemical stimulation and their centrifugal control. *Comp. Biochem. Physiol.*, **22**, 199–208 (1967)

75. Hardiman, C. W. Rat and hamster chemoreceptor responses to a large number of compounds and the formulation of a generalized chemosensory equation. (Doctoral thesis, Florida State Univ., Tallahassee, 1964)

76. Harper, H. W., Jay, J. R., Erickson, R. P. Chemically evoked sensations from single human taste papillae. *Physiol. Behav.*, **1**, 319–25 (1966)

77. Hellekant, G. Action and interaction of ethyl alcohol and some other substances on the receptors of the tongue. In *Olfaction and Taste II*, 465–79 (See ref. 11)

78. Henton, W. W. Suppression behavior to odorous stimuli in the pigeon. (Doctoral thesis, Florida State Univ., Tallahassee, 1966)

79. Henton, W. W., Smith, J. C., Tucker, D. Odor discrimination in pigeons. *Science*, **153**, 1138–39 (1966)

80. Higashino, S., Takagi, S. F. The effect of electrotonus on the olfactory epithelium. *J. Gen. Physiol.*, **48**, 323–35 (1964)

81. Hopkins, A. E. The olfactory receptors in vertebrates. *J. Comp. Neurol.*, **41**, 253–89 (1926)

82. Howard, W. E., Marsh, R. E., Cole, R. E. Food detection by deer mice using olfactory rather than visual cues. *Animal Behav.*, **16**, 13–17 (1968)

83. Hughes, J. R., Hendrix, D. E. The frequency component hypothesis in relation to the coding mechanism in the olfactory bulb. In *Olfaction and Taste II*, 51–87 (See ref. 11)

84. Hull, C. D., Garcia, J., Buchwald, N. A., Dubrovsky, B., Feder, B. H. Role of the olfactory system in arousal to X-ray. *Nature*, **205**, 627–28 (1965)

85. Hunt, E. L., Kimeldorf, D. J. The humoral factor in radiation-induced motivation. *Radiation Res.*, **30**, 404–19 (1967)

86. Iggo, A., Leek, B. F. The afferent innervation of the tongue of the sheep. In *Olfaction and Taste II*, 493–507 (See ref. 11)

87. Ishiko, N., Amatsu, M. Changes in the chorda tympani nerve responses to taste stimuli associated with movement of the tongue in cat. *Japan. J. Physiol.*, **15**, 623–37 (1965)

88. Ishiko, N., Amatsu, M. Effects of stretch of the tongue on taste responses in glossopharyngeal and chorda tympani nerves of cat. *Kumamoto Med. J.*, **17**, 5–17 (1964)

89. Kimeldorf, D. J., Hunt, E. L. *Ionizing radiation: neural function and behavior.* (Academic Press, New York, 331 pp., 1965)

90. Kimura, K., Beidler, L. M. Microelectrode study of taste receptors of rat and hamster. *J. Cell. Comp. Physiol.*, **58**, 131–40 (1961)

91. Konishi, J. Studies on the stimulation of chemoreceptors of freshwater fish by dilute solutions of electrolytes. In *Olfaction and Taste II*, 667–92 (See ref. 11)

92. Kurihara, K. Isolation of chromoproteins from bovine olfactory tissues. *Biochim. Biophys. Acta*, **148**, 328–34 (1967)

93. Laffort, P. Essai de standardisation des seuils olfactifs humains pour 192 corps purs. *Arch. Sci. Physiol.*, **17**, 75–105 (1963)

94. Lettvin, J. Y., Gesteland, R. C. Speculations on smell. *Cold Spring Harbor Symp. Quant. Biol.*, **30**, 217–25 (1965)

95. Leveteau, J., Mac Leod, P. Olfactory discrimination in the rabbit olfactory glomerulus. *Science*, **153**, 175–76 (1966)

96. Long, C. T., Tapp, J. T. Reinforcing properties of odors for the albino rat. *Psychon. Sci.*, **7**, 17–18 (1967)

97. Le Magnen, J. Habits and food intake. In *Handbook of Physiology*, 11–30 (Am. Physiol. Soc., Washington, D.C., **1**, Sect. 6, 1967)

98. Marshall, D. A. A comparative study of neural coding in gustation. *Physiol. Behav.*, **3**, 1–15 (1968)

99. Mellon, D., Jr., Kennedy, D. Impulse origin and propagation in a bipolar sensory neuron. *J. Gen. Physiol.*, **47**, 487–99 (1964)

100. Moncrieff, R. W. *Odour Preferences.* (Leonard Hill, London, 357 pp., 1966)

101. Morris, D. D. Threshold for conditioned suppression using X-rays as the pre-aversive stimulus. *J. Exp. Anal. Behav.*, **9**, 29–34 (1966)

102. Moulton, D. G. Spatio-temporal patterning of response in the olfactory

156   TUCKER & SMITH

system. In *Olfaction and Taste II*, 109–16 (See ref. 11)

103. Moulton, D. G., Beidler, L. M. Structure and function in the peripheral olfactory system. *Physiol. Rev.*, **47**, 1–52 (1967)

104. Mozell, M. M. The spatiotemporal analysis of odorants at the level of the olfactory receptor sheet. *J. Gen. Physiol.*, **50**, 25–41 (1966)

105. Murata, K., Cramer, H., Bach-y-Rita, P. Neuronal convergence of noxious, acoustic and visual stimuli in the visual cortex of the cat. *J. Neurophysiol.*, **28**, 1223–39 (1965)

106. Murray, R. G., Murray, A. Fine structure of taste buds of rabbit foliate papillae. *J. Ultrastruct. Res.*, **19**, 327–53 (1967)

107. Nanba, R., Djahanparwar, B., Baumgarten, R. von. Erregungsmuster einzelner Fasern des *tractus olfactorius lateralis* des Fisches bei Reizung mit verschiedenen Geruchsstoffen. *Pflügers Archiv Ges. Physiol.*, **288**, 134–50 (1966)

108. Nemetschek-Gansler, H., Ferner, H. Über die Ultrastruktur der Geschmacksknospen. *Z. Zellforsch.*, **63**, 155–78 (1964)

109. Oakley, B. Altered temperature and taste responses from cross-regenerated sensory nerves in the rat's tongue. *J. Physiol. (London)*, **188**, 353–71 (1967)

110. Oakley, B. Impaired operant behavior following lesions of the thalamic taste nucleus. *J. Comp. Physiol. Psychol.*, **59**, 202–10 (1965)

111. Okano, M., Weber, A. F., Frommes, S. P. Electron microscopic studies of the distal border of the canine olfactory epithelium. *J. Ultrastruct. Res.*, **17**, 487–502 (1967)

112. Orkand, R. K., Nicholls, J. G., Kuffler, S. W. Effect of nerve impulses on the membrane potential of glial cells in the central nervous system of amphibia. *J. Neurophysiol.*, **29**, 788–806 (1966)

113. Ottoson, D. Analysis of the electrical activity of the olfactory epithelium. *Acta Physiol. Scand.*, **35** (Suppl. 122), 1–83 (1956)

114. Ottoson, D., Shepherd, G. M. Experiments and concepts in olfactory physiology. *Prog. Brain Res.*, **23**, 83–138 (1967)

115. Pagano, R. R. The effects of central stimulation and nasal air flow on induced activity of olfactory structures. *Electroenceph. Clin. Neurophysiol.*, **21**, 269–77 (1966)

116. Parsons, T. S. Evolution of the nasal structure in the lower tetrapods. *Am. Zoologist*, **7**, 397–413 (1967)

117. Peñaloza-Rojas, J. H., Alcocer-Cuarón, C. The electrical activity of the olfactory bulb in cats with nasal and tracheal breathing. *Electroenceph. Clin. Neurophysiol.*, **22**, 468–72 (1967)

118. Pfaffmann, C. De gustibus. *Am. Psychologist*, **20**, 21–33 (1965)

119. Pfaffmann, C., Fisher, G. L., Frank, M. K. The sensory and behavioral factors in taste preferences. In *Olfaction and Taste II*, 361–81 (See ref. 11)

120. Rall, W., Shepherd, G. M., Reese, T. S., Brightman, M. W. Dendrodendritic synaptic pathway for inhibition in the olfactory bulb. *Exptl. Neurol.*, **14**, 44–56 (1966)

121. Rapuzzi, G., Casella, C. Innervation of the fungiform papillae in the frog tongue. *J. Neurophysiol.*, **28**, 154–65 (1965)

122. Reese, T. S. Olfactory cilia in the frog. *J. Cell Biol.*, **25** (Part 2), 209–30 (1965)

123. Revusky, S. H. Aversion to sucrose produced by contingent X-irradiation: Temporal and dosage parameters. *J. Comp. Physiol. Psychol.*, **65**, 17–22 (1968)

124. Revusky, S. H., Bedarf, E. W. Association of illness with prior ingestion of novel foods. *Science*, **155**, 219–20 (1967)

125. Robbins, N. Peripheral modification of sensory nerve responses after cross-regeneration. *J. Physiol. (London)* **192**, 493–504 (1967)

126. Robbins, N. The role of the nerve in maintenance of frog taste buds. *Exptl. Neurol.*, **17**, 364–80 (1967)

127. Ropartz, P. The relation between olfactory stimulation and aggressive behavior in mice. *Animal Behav.*, **16**, 97–100 (1968)

128. Rosenberg, B., Misra, T. N., Switzer, R. Mechanism of olfactory transduction. *Nature*, **217**, 423–27 (1968)

129. Rozin, P. Thiamine specific hunger. In *Handbook of Physiology*, 411–31 (Am. Physiol. Soc., Washington, D.C., **1**, Sect. 6, 1967)

130. Sato, M. Gustatory response as a temperature-dependent process. In *Contributions to Sensory Physiology*,

223-51 (Neff, W. D., Ed., 2, Academic Press, New York, 1967)

131. Sato, M., Yamashita, S., Ogawa, H. Patterns of impulses produced by MSG and 5'-ribonucleotides in taste units of the rat. In *Olfaction and Taste II*, 399-410 (See ref. 11)

132. Scalzi, H. A. The cytoarchitecture of gustatory receptors from the rabbit foliate papillae. *Z. Zellforsch.*, 80, 413-35 (1967)

133. Scarborough, B. B., Whaley, D. L., Rogers, J. G. Saccharin avoidance behavior instigated by X-irradiation in backward conditioning paradigms. *Psychol. Rept.*, 14, 475-81 (1964)

134. Schneider, R. A., Schmidt, C. E. Dependency of olfactory localization on non-olfactory cues. *Physiol. Behav.*, 2, 305-9 (1967)

135. Schneider, R. A., Schmidt, C. E., Costiloe, J. P. Relation of odor flow rate and duration to stimulus intensity needed for perception. *J. Appl. Physiol.*, 21, 10-14 (1966)

136. Seifert, K., Ule, G. Die Ultrastruktur der Riechschleimhaut der neugeborenen und jugendlichen weissen Maus. *Z. Zellforsch.*, 76, 147-69 (1967)

137. Sen Gupta, P. Olfactory receptor reaction to the lesion of the olfactory bulb. In *Olfaction and Taste II*, 193-201 (See ref. 11)

138. Shibuya, T. Dissociation of olfactory neural response and mucosal potential. *Science*, 143, 1338-40 (1964)

139. Shibuya, T., Tucker, D. Single unit responses of olfactory receptors in vultures. In *Olfaction and Taste II*, 219-33 (See ref. 11)

140. Shumake, S. A., Smith, J. C., Tucker, D. Olfactory intensity difference thresholds in the pigeon. *J. Comp. Physiol. Psychol.* (In press, 1968)

141. Smith, J. C. Radiation as an aversive stimulus. *Am. Zoologist*, 7, 402 (1967)

142. Smith, J. C., Roll, D. L. Trace conditioning with X-rays as an aversive stimulus. *Psychon. Sci.*, 9, 11-12 (1967)

143. Smith, J. C., Schaeffer, R. W. Development of water and saccharin preferences after simultaneous exposures to saccharin solution and gamma rays. *J. Comp. Physiol.*, 63, 434-38 (1967)

144. Smith, J. C., Taylor, H. L. Factors influencing the immediate response

of rhesus monkeys to brief X-ray exposures. *Radiation Res.*, 34 (In press, 1968)

145. Smith, J. C., Hendricks, J., Morris, D. D., Powell, R. Immediate response in the pigeon to brief X-ray exposure. *Radiation Res.*, 22, 237 (1964)

146. Stone, H., Carregal, E. J. A., Williams, B. The olfactory-trigeminal response to odorants. *Life Sciences*, 5, 2195-2201 (1966)

147. Svyataya, L. P. Absolute threshold of human olfactory sensitivity. *Biofizika*, 12, 366-68 (English transl., 421-24) (1967)

148. Takagi, S. F. Are EOG's generator potentials? In *Olfaction and Taste II*, 167-80 (See ref. 11)

149. Takagi, S. F., Yajima, T. Electrical activity and histological change in the degenerating olfactory epithelium. *J. Gen. Physiol.*, 48, 559-69 (1965)

150. Tateda, H. Sugar receptor and α-amino acid in the rat. In *Olfaction and Taste II*, 383-97 (See ref. 11)

151. Tateda, H., Beidler, L. M. The receptor potential of the taste cell of the rat. *J. Gen. Physiol.*, 47, 479-86 (1964)

152. Taylor, H. L., Smith, J. C., Wall, A. H., Chuddock, B. Role of the olfactory system in the detection of X-rays by the rhesus monkey. *Physiol. Behav.* (In press, 1968)

153. Teitelbaum, P. Motivation and control of food intake. In *Handbook of Physiology*, 319-35 (Am. Physiol. Soc., Washington, D.C., 1, Sect. 6, 1967)

154. Thornhill, R. A. The ultrastructure of the olfactory epithelium of the lamprey *Lampetra fluviatilis*. *J. Cell Sci.*, 2, 591-602 (1967)

155. Tucker, D. Olfactory cilia are not required for receptor function. *Federation Proc.*, 26, 544 (1967)

156. Tucker, D. Electrophysiological evidence for olfactory function in birds. *Nature*, 207, 34-36 (1965)

157. Tucker, D. Physical variables in the olfactory stimulation process. *J. Gen. Physiol.*, 46, 453-89 (1963)

158. Tucker, D. Olfactory, vomeronasal and trigeminal receptor responses to odorants. In *Olfaction and Taste I*, 45-69 (See ref. 56)

159. Tucker, D., Shibuya, T. A physiologic and pharmacologic study of olfactory receptors. *Cold Spring Harbor*

Symp. Quant. Biol., **30**, 207–15 (1965)

160. Ueda, K., Hara, T. J., Gorbman, A. Electroencephalographic studies on olfactory discrimination in adult spawning salmon. *Comp. Biochem. Physiol.*, **21**, 133–43 (1967)

161. Valenstein, E. S., Cox, V. C., Kakolewski, J. W. Polydipsia elicited by the synergistic action of a saccharin and glucose solution. *Science*, **157**, 552–54 (1967)

162. Vance, W. B. Hypogeusia and taste preference behavior in the rat. *Life Sciences*, **6**, 743–48 (1967)

163. Vinnikov, J. A. Principles of structural, chemical, and functional organization of sensory receptors. *Cold Spring Harbor Symp. Quant. Biol.*, **30**, 293–99 (1965)

164. Wenzel, B. M. Olfactory perception in birds. In *Olfaction and Taste II*, 203–17 (See ref. 11)

165. Wilson, J. A. F., Westerman, R. A. The fine structure of the olfactory mucosa and nerve in the teleost

Carassius carassius L. *Z. Zellforsch.*, **83**, 196–206 (1967)

166. Wright, R. H. *The Science of Smell.* (Basic Books, Inc., New York, 164 pp., 1964)

167. Wright, R. H., Hughes, J. R., Hendrix, D. E. Olfactory coding. *Nature*, **216**, 404–6 (1967)

168. Yamada, K. The glossopharyngeal nerve response to taste and thermal stimuli in the rat, rabbit and cat. In *Olfaction and Taste II*, 459–64 (See ref. 11)

169. Yamamoto, C., Iwama, K. Arousal reaction of the olfactory bulb. *Japan. J. Physiol.*, **11**, 335–45 (1961)

170. Young, P. T., Trafton, C. L. Activity contour maps as related to preference in four gustatory stimulus areas of the rat. *J. Comp. Physiol. Psychol.*, **58**, 68–75 (1964)

171. Zotterman, Y. The neural mechanism of taste. *Prog. Brain Res.*, **23**, 139–54 (1967)

PERCEPTION[1]

134

By Kai von Fieandt
University of Helsinki, Finland
AND
Michael Wertheimer
University of Colorado, Boulder, Colorado

Introduction

Because the literature in perception is vast, any review must necessarily be highly selective. Much that should have been included simply had to be left out. The focus of this survey is upon major trends since early 1966, with special emphasis upon some less well-known developments outside the United States. Perceptual topics which are covered in other chapters in the Annual Review, such as psychophysics, audition, visual acuity, comparative animal research, color, the chemical senses, perception and personality, and perception and psychopathology, are either omitted here or are touched on only very briefly.

Books and reviews.—This has been a period of consolidation for the field of perception. Several books have appeared, including both general surveys and specialized monographs concentrating on particular subfields. Perception also has been reviewed in chapters in various survey books.

Gibson (188) published a new systematic advanced text which develops the thesis that the sensory input provides rich perceptual information concerning the ecology, and von Fieandt (151) came out with a more traditional textbook which emphasizes intermodal interaction, presents representative studies from all over the world, and includes material on the perception of art. Corso (81) has a thorough new text on sensory psychology. A recent general textbook on perception, in French, was published by Francès (171).

Akishige (4) edited a compendium of Japanese perceptual research which is similar to earlier careful experimental treatments of perceptual constancies and the perception of motion in Europe and America; this work can be seen as bridging the gap between Hering's classical constancy studies and Gibson's view of perception as an active search for information. Another volume in this series was published just before this article had to go to press; it contains work on such phenomena as contrast, constancies, and the Land effect (5).

Among briefer surveys is a chapter on perception by Day (91) for the

---

[1] The literature surveyed for this review was selected primarily from the period between January 1966 and December 1967, with a small number of references before and after these limits.

Brown series, and an elementary paperback introduction to perception by Weintraub & Walker (388) which is accompanied by an inexpensive series of perceptual demonstrations. Gregory (196) and Wilman (395) have written interesting brief introductions to visual perception. Hurvich & Jameson (221) wrote a short volume on the perception of brightness and darkness. A condensed survey of sensory processes by Alpern, Lawrence & Wolsk (7) has appeared. More restricted in scope are Holland's (217) review of the spiral aftereffect and a new English translation of Yarbus' (399) monograph on stabilized retinal images.

Epstein (131) has published a systematic volume on the varieties of perceptual learning, Green & Swets (195) wrote on signal detection theory and psychophysics, and Rock (312) has presented a detailed visual theory of adaptation to optical distortion. All three of these volumes introduce and summarize competently several major recent research foci. Malhotra (263) has prepared a thorough monograph on figural aftereffects.

Segall, Campbell & Herskovits (324) published a monograph presenting in detail the results of a large-scale cross-cultural study of the effect of culture on the perception of a variety of geometric illusions.

Uhr (373) edited a set of readings on pattern recognition and Haber (201) prepared a large, and Vernon (376) a briefer, set of readings on visual perception. The proceedings of a symposium on models for the perception of speech and visual form, with contributions by many mathematically sophisticated researchers in the field of perception, were edited by Wathen-Dunn (384). Perceptual development in children is the topic of a substantial volume edited by Kidd & Rivoire (235), composed of contributions by many of the leading figures in that field; and Brackbill (46) has edited a handbook on infancy and early childhood which contains perceptual material.

A major landmark during the period of this review was the publication of von Békésy's book on sensory inhibition (31), which summarizes a theory and some research which has become highly influential. Restrictions in the range of sensory sensitivity, Mach bands, and various other phenomena are elegantly handled by the inhibitory mechanisms he proposes.

Perceptual problems receive extensive space in the first volume of Thomae's handbook (368), which appeared in Germany in 1966. Reviewed is both European and American research, with writers like Metzger, Witte, Kohler, Graumann and Rausch from Europe and Hurvich and Jameson, Nafe and Kenshalo, and Werner from the United States. The overall tone is traditional and metric, and there is still a strong use of gestalt concepts. The topics covered include many traditional problems, and also the work of I. Kohler, Kanizsa, Fraisse, Michotte in Europe, and in the U. S. and elsewhere the Ames demonstrations, figural after-effects in the Köhler-Wallach tradition, Helson and Bevan's adaptation level research, Bruner's work and the studies of Brunswik and his students. In general, the chapters are well written, have excellent bibliographies, and can serve as thorough introductions for the graduate student. Another new handbook of somewhat smaller scope, edited by Helson & Bevan (214), contains several chapters on sensory processes, psychophysics, and perception, with much of the perceptual discussions oriented around Helson's own adaptation level theory. A *Denkschrift* for Brunswik, edited by Hammond (205), contains some excellent material relevant to perception by Brunswik himself and by some prominent psychologists who have been influenced by the Brunswikian mode of thought.

White (390), in a chapter in a Minnesota symposium volume, presents some of his continuing research on perceptual and motor consequences of infant experience, and a detailed review of infant perception was compiled by Fantz (147). Day (92), in his presidential address to the Australian Psychological Society, summarizes some of his influential research on perception.

The Geography of Perceptual Research

While the United States continues to be the most active contributor to psychological research and to studies in perception in particular, major centers for perceptual studies exist all over the world. Japan has long contributed elegant, precise psychophysical studies of classical problems, many universities in continental Europe have traditions of continuous contributions, and recently Scandinavia has become more and more a major center of perceptual research, with four main substantive foci: the perception of form, of color, of space, and of movement. Before we examine some of the chief topics in the field of perception, let us consider briefly some representative research in countries other than the United States, with special attention to the newer developments in Scandinavia.

Scandinavia.—In Denmark, the phenomenological tradition of Edgar Rubin continues to flourish in the work of men like Moustgaard (277) with autokinesis, M. Johansen (229) with stereoscopic tridimensional form, and Holt-Hansen (218) with free descriptions of the perception of simple stimuli like a straight line or a circle.

In Norway, Lie has continued in the tradition of his mentor Saugstad, who has recently worked on the effects of food deprivation (318) and of value (319) on perception. In a study of the gestalt factor of proximity (255) Lie found that vertical grouping of dots is more readily achieved than horizontal, and in a study of convergence (256) he found that this process can provide amazingly accurate perception of distance, reaffirming the important role that the ocular muscles can play in depth perception. An ingenious experiment by Rommetveit (314) demonstrated that a generative process can be involved in word recognition. Slightly different typed rows of letters were presented stereoscopically for 170 msec; when S O U P was exposed to one eye and S O U R to the other, either English word was reported in the fused image, but when S H A P and S H A R were presented, the longer word S H A R P was usually seen.

Sweden has several centers of perceptual research. At Uppsala, perhaps the leading one, Johansson is continuing his long-standing interest in perception, including a recent monograph on vision without contours (230) and a collaborative study on the perceived angle of oscillatory motion (132). Recently, his well-known work in the perception of movement has been applied by himself (231) and by Rumar (316) to the practical problems of driving in traffic. Bergström (32–34) has concentrated upon luminance gradients in the now very popular Mach bands, suggesting in detail how retinal interaction may be the responsible mechanism, and raising some questions about the adequacy of von Békésy's theory. Dureman (116) found that duration and velocity of a visual motion aftereffect are positively related to CFF. At Umeå, a new university in northern Sweden, Borg (45) has been working with Stevens' power law, developing his own form of it and building an active psychophysical research laboratory. Ekman and his team at the University of Stockholm are studying perceived brightness as a function of duration of dark adaptation (125) and are continuing his work in scaling, using such sensory modes as odor (124); Künnapas (240–242) continues his scaling research too, and Sjöberg (337) has worked on similarity. Brandt & Fluur (47–49) are engaged in research on postural perception. At Lund, Andersson (8–10) is working on visual aftereffects, Bokander (41, 42) on stereoscopic perceptual conflict, and Smith & Kragh (343) on serial afterimages.

Perception is a major focus of psychological research in Finland. At Helsinki, von Fieandt and his associates have conducted a series of studies on color, especially color constancy, contrast, and localization in depth under various conditions of illumination (154, 300). Some of the earlier scaling work (e.g., 152) was criticized on methodological grounds (301), but later research by the same group (153) reaffirmed the adequacy of the new scaling method for yielding ordinal ranks of hues, which retain their ranks under a wide variety of illuminations other than white, demonstrating the strength of the relational stimulus framework in maintaining color constancy. Representative of the research of the Helsinki group is a monograph by Weckroth (386), reporting experiments on color afterimages in the light and dark adapted eye and presenting an equilibrium theory of color perception. Space perception, too, within the Gibson tradition of slant perception, continues as a major focus of research at Helsinki (e.g., 155, 228, 285), and there have been studies of selective attention and evoked EEG potentials (279), and of sources of error, in the form of response bias, in large-scale tests of ESP (257). At Turku, another center of Finnish perceptual research, von Wright and his associates have studied form perception (397) and, within an adaptation-level framework, the reproduction of weight (398); Nurminen (284) has developed a spatial technique for scaling subjective similarity. Virsu has engaged in extensive research on perceptual illusions (302, 377–380), with the eventual aim of developing a general theory for the veridicality of the perceptual world.

Continental Europe.—Germany continues to be a major center of perceptual research under the leadership of workers like Metzger, Rausch and Witte, but with other researchers also making significant contributions. Holzkamp (219, 220) at Berlin is working on perceived size, and Vatter found an operational distinction between two sensations of roughness, with horizontally stroked touch stimuli producing more unpleasant sensations whose sensory thresholds are lower and which have a larger aftereffect than vertical stimuli (374). Ertel (141), at Münster, in an extension of the classical studies of the effect of motivation on the perceived size of coins, was unable to replicate the earlier reported findings. At the same university, Prinz (306) undertook quantitative investigations of the *prägnanz* of dot patterns. At Marburg, Düker (111) is resuming research on eidetic imagery, and Hajos (202) is continuing research in perceptual distortions, primarily within the Kohler tradition. Franks (172), at Munich, suggests that signal detection theory can remove some of the ambiguities in the subliminal perception literature.

In Austria, Rohracher's assistants and students are continuing his research on physiological correlates of mental activity; representative of this work is Guttman's (199) study of EEG correlates of simple sensory functions. At Innsbruck, I. Kohler and his students are engaged in further work on distorted perception, work for which Innsbruck has long been world renowned. Among the studies by his former students is one by Hajos & Ritter (203), who demonstrated interocular transfer of the spatial location distortion induced by wearing a prism in front of one eye to the other eye when it is uncovered, and who found that it was possible to induce opposite aftereffects simultaneously in both eyes.

In Czechoslovakia, Kovač at Bratislava has studied perceptual changes as a function of age (236) and has used information theory in investigations of the perception of alterations in simple visual stimuli (237). Dornič has performed research on the central determinants of perceptual reversal of figures and of stereoscopic stimuli (109, 110), and Soudková (346, 347) is working on the vertical-horizontal illusion.

In Poland, Nowakowska (283) has developed a quantitative model for some aspects of the aesthetics and dynamics of perception, and in Yugoslavia, Pečjak (298) has been working on various complex perceptual phenomena and synaesthesias.

England also continues as a major center for perceptual research. Thus at Cambridge, Gregory has undertaken a study with Ross (197) on the effect of addition of a heavy weight to the arm on weight discrimination, and Broadbent (51) has analyzed the literature on the word-frequency effect and response bias. Many other British contributions are mentioned below.

Since the days of Révész, Holland has made contributions to perception. Thus Michon (271) has worked on the time sense, Moed (274) has shown a continuity between the traditionally different phenomena of constancy and contrast, and Buis (64) is studying the perception of perspective change of three-dimensional objects in rotatory motion.

In France, a major center for perceptual research is the Sorbonne, where Fraisse and his associates are studying perceptual recognition as a function of uncertainty in the stimulus (169) and of uncertainty of both stimulus and response (166, 170). He has also demonstrated (167) that perceptual integration and masking depend upon different processes and is continuing his work (e.g., 168) on time perception.

At Milan, in Italy, Funari (180, 181) is engaged in studies of motion perception, to mention but one investigator.

There is, of course, perceptual research in other countries as well. Rather than giving further examples of work in Australia, India, Italy, Spain, the Near East, the Far East, etc., we might consider the foregoing highly selected material as evidence that research in perception is broadly international. The remainder of this article summarizes some selected recent literature according to substantive area and without regard to the country in which it was performed. Most of it was done in the United States, but much also in England, Scandinavia, continental Europe, Japan and the rest of the world. When going through the discussion which follows, the conscientious reader is advised to keep in mind the material already presented so far, since for the sake of economy of space it will not be repeated in those sections where it would be substantively relevant.

FORM PERCEPTION

The perception of form is still the single area receiving the most attention of all subfields in perception. Although many different methods, viewpoints, *Ortgeister* are to be found, the *Zeitgeist* remains predominantly mensurational and quantitative, and perhaps paradoxically, both elementistic and gestalt oriented. Most of the work is on visual form, but tactual form, too, is receiving some attention.

Visual form perception.—Evans (146) has reviewed the literature on redundancy as a variable in pattern perception and has developed quantitative techniques, in an extension of schema theory, for generating stimuli for pattern perception studies (145). Webster (385) reviewed research on the effects of fill, noise, and distortion on pattern perception, and Payne (296) found a substantial correlation between a measure of the organization of visual patterns and their judged complexity. Stenson (352) performed a similar study. Thurmond & Alluisi (371) work with an informational analysis of form. Fantz & Nevis (148) present a useful review of the development of pattern perception in early human infancy, and Ganz & Wilson (183) found evidence of innate generalization of a form discrimination in monkeys. Hershenson (215) reviews the development of the perception of form.

Pairs of identical stimuli viewed under reduced stimulation conditions disappear more rapidly than single stimuli or paired different stimuli (108, 363); Tees & More (363) consider this finding as further support for Hebb's (213) theory, which has generated so much research over the last two decades. However, the results of studies of figure fading and disappearance continue to be somewhat inconsistent. Thus Evans (142, 143) reported that 10 per cent of the disappearances of a stabilized retinal image were total, while 15 per cent were patterned or structured; these percentages were characteristic of almost all subjects. Schuck & Leahy (322), however, found that verbal report of disappearances of parts or all of a luminous HB figure facilitated the report of disappearance of various elements like H, h, B, b, 1, 11 and +; they concluded that rather than perceptual organization, response bias may be responsible for the apparent meaningfulness of the disappearances. Eagle, Bowling & Klein (117) also studied fragmentation phenomena in luminous designs, finding that meaningfulness had little effect, angular figures fragment more than rounded, that whole lines tend to appear and disappear as separate units, and that the fixated and immediately adjacent area suffered the most fragmentation. Minard & Batcher (273) found other phenomena accompanying disappearance of luminous fixated stimuli. Fender & Julesz (149) studied binocularly stabilized vision.

Seiler & Zusne (325) discovered that the number of sides of random polygons was underestimated more the briefer the tachistocopic presentation (between .01 and 1 sec) and the larger the actual number of sides (using seven different numbers of sides, from 3 to 24), and Day (90) studied the effect of number of sides of polygons on their judged pleasingness and interestingness. Eye movements can decrease the judged straightness of a rectilinear dot progression; Holden (216) found that judged straightness increases with presentation rate.

Fox and his collaborators have studied suppression and rivalry in binocular presentations, finding that suppression substantially reduced recognition while rivalry did not (164) and that complex fused targets can suffer from suppression (165). Crovitz & Lochkead (87) suggest that the suppression hypothesis may not be necessary to explain binocular contour rivalry, since various established monocular variables may be sufficient. Cogan & Goldstein (74) found that binocular rivalry rates increased more under spaced than massed viewing.

Much research effort continues to be expended upon temporal factors in form perception (e.g., 1) and results continue to be less than perfectly consistent. Thus Bryden (62) did not find any increase in accuracy of report as tachistoscopic exposure duration increased from 15 to 1500 msec, while Raymond & Glanzer (308) did find an increase in the number of stimuli reported as a function of the same range of tachistoscopic exposure times. Mayzner and his co-workers (264, 265) found that the first half of a sequentially presented list of ten stimuli is not reported when the presentation duration and the interstimulus interval are between 200 and 300 msec. Nesmith & Rodwan (281) working within the microgenetic problem, reported that form and size discrimination did not improve with longer stimulus duration but that form discrimination was consistently superior to size discrimination.

Perceptual organization and figural goodness continue to become more thoroughly understood and more clearly specified. Thus Berlyne & Peckham (35) have used the semantic differential to quantify figural complexity. Festinger et al. (150) propose a broad theory concerning the effect of efference on an array of perceptual functions such as contour perception, and the work of Julesz and his associates with random dot patterns continues (e.g., 178). Goldstein (193) studied threshold and discriminability as a function of the gestalt similarity of test forms in a visual array, and Handel & Garner (206) studied the structure of visual patterns and related it to figural goodness. Brown and his collaborators (60, 61) are studying the determinants of attention and viewing time. Royer (315) constructed a series of binary figures in which uncertainty was held constant but figural "goodness" was varied, and found that the "good" or simple figures were easier to sort in a card-sorting task. Judged similarity was less successful as a predictor of perceptual grouping than were differences in the orientation of the lines in a series of two-line figures varying in orientation and shape studied by Beck (26, 29). In another study, Beck (25) found that increasing the size of the surround against which familiar symbols were presented resulted in increased discriminability of the symbols, with the shape of the function varying under different conditions of symbol size, exposure time, and symbol embedding in the background checkerboard pattern. In a third study, Beck (30) found that changes which alter the orientation of the component lines of two- or three-line figures to 45° or 135° affect grouping more than changes which maintain a horizontal or vertical orientation. Harcum & Smith (207) were unable to find evidence for an isolation effect in pattern perception unless the subjects were informed beforehand of the locus of the isolation in tachistoscopically presented patterns; thus the effect of isolation in pattern perception turned out to be quite analogous to the isolation effect in serial learning. Munsinger & Gummerman (278) undertook a study of the identification of form in patterns of visual noise.

Perceptual masking continues to be a major focus of interest, following upon Eriksen & Collins' (135) finding that forward and backward masking effects of ring on letter are highly similar. Dember & Neiberg (99) found that individual differences in susceptibility to visual backward masking are highly reliable. Masking is substantially affected by delay; an annulus presented concurrently with or as long as 68 msec later than the letter A, T or U interfered with recognition of the letter. In view of the general confusion in other studies on masking phenomena, and of the inadequacy of the concept of summation to account for much of the data, Eriksen and his collaborators (133, 134, 136–140) have suggested a theory of perceptual independence to explain the phenomena of visual masking. There is perceptual independence when the information received from successive form stimuli does not interact and when the internal perceptual error on separate stimulations is uncorrected; if perceptual independence does not obtain, that is, if the form stimulations interact, masking occurs. Recognizing that summation does serve an adequate explanatory function in many cases, Eriksen nevertheless indicates that the perceptual independence hypothesis works better. Later studies that further confirm the usefulness of a perceptual independence approach include one by Collins & Eriksen (77). Other studies on visual masking have been performed by Fitzgerald & Kirkham (158),

Schiller (321), Smith & Schiller (344), Streicher & Pollack (356), Weisstein (389), Sekuler (326), Gilinsky (191), and Robinson (311), the last finding that it is possible to mask a backward masking stimulus so as to produce a disinhibition of the original masking effect.

Vaught and his collaborators (e.g., 375) have been studying the relationship between field-dependence and form discrimination in a series of recent investigations.

Classical geometrical illusions, too, continue to receive research attention. Thus Mountjoy (276) persists in his long series of thorough studies of the Müller-Lyer figure. Hamilton (204) failed to find a correlation between susceptibility to the Müller-Lyer and accuracy in size constancy estimates, and Dewar (102) found simple linear relationships between the size of the illusion on the one hand and the angle between and the length of the oblique lines on the other. Wallace (381) showed that the size of the Zöllner illusion depends upon the pattern of the background. Susceptibility to the Poggendorff illusion was found to be significantly related to performance on both the embedded figures test and the rod and frame in men, and on the embedded figures test in women by Pressey (304). The same illusion was studied by Leibowitz & Gwozdecki (246) as a function of age, and by Novak (282), who found that the illusion varied as a function of the angle and that addition of a fixation point reduced the measured size of the illusion, but did not abolish it, for angles of 22.5°, 45.0° and 67.5°.

Olson & Orbach (288) continue in a series of studies of the Necker cube. Both the effect of stimulus characteristics and of individual differences on Necker cube reversal have been the focus of attention of a series of studies by Wieland & Mefferd (392–394), and Thetford & Klemme (366) found that arousal reduced the Necker cube reversal rate. Cappone (65) and Carlson (66) studied the effect of instruction on various illusions, and Chapanis & Mankin (69) showed that the horizontal-vertical illusion exists for real objects in a visually rich environment. Chyatte & Chyatte (71) suggested a new neurological explanation for the well-known phenomenon that a figure composed of small black squares separated by white strips shows gray patches at all white intersections but the visually fixated intersection. Cleary (72) proposed a binocular parallax theory to account for some geometric illusions, and Coen-Gelders (73) described a new illusion.

Tactual form perception.—This has received much less attention than visual form perception. Sen (329) found that the effect of set on a two-point threshold could be accounted for well by adaptation level theory. Evans & Howarth (144) discovered that descending judgments typically resulted in overestimation, ascending judgments in underestimation of tactile width, and that increasing tension of grip reduced the accuracy of the width judgments. Bliss et al. (38) and Bliss, Crane & Link (39) engaged in sophisticated studies of the recognition of tactually presented alphabetical shapes. Kinesthetic size judgments have been shown to be related to pain tolerance by Blitz, Dinnerstein & Lowenthal (40), and Over (290–292) has studied a haptic illusion and contributed studies of the effect of actual and apparent tilt of the inspection figure on kinesthetic aftereffects.

Cutsforth (89) has shown that the tactual field does not function separately from the visual in seeing individuals. Dinnerstein, Gerstein & Michel (106) and Dinnerstein, Curcio & Chinsky (105) found a substantial context effect of a weight held in one hand upon judgments of the apparent weight of another weight held in the other hand, and Fisher (157) has demonstrated a tactile version of the Poggendorff illusion and (156) of autokinesis. Natsoulas (280) investigated the perception of cutaneous figures traced on the subject's head. Lobb & Friend (258) investigated tactual form discrimination, finding that while stimulus size had only a small effect, duration of exposure had a substantial one. Gescheider (185, 186) has studied apparent successiveness in both hearing and touch, and a tactile aftereffect has received further attention from Gilbert (189).

SPACE PERCEPTION

Traditionally, space perception is a broad field, including all that is perceived as belonging to space or in relation to space: problems of the structure, dimensions, and directions of visual space, depth and distance, and size and shape constancy. Here we shall consider only a few questions which have been the focus of considerable research during the last few years.

Braunstein (50) proposed a psychophysics of depth perception based upon a mathematical analysis of transformations of the visual field. Epstein (130) suggested that perceived depth depends upon optical adjacency. Hay (210) provided a broad new theoretical base for the role of optical transformation in space perception, attempting to encompass the effect of two-dimensional transformation of retinal projections produced by moving three-dimensional objects, and the recent substantial literature on various aftereffects, like figural aftereffects, and the effects of distorting lenses, prisms, and mirrors. Eichengreen, Coren & Nachmias (123) have reopened the question of what cues are employed on the visual cliff in studies of monocular tests on rats raised in enriched and normal environments. Foley (161) reports data on perceived equidistance which raise serious questions about Luneburg's theory of space perception.

Anisotropy of space.—Weene & Held (387) found that bisections of a 90° angle rotating around its apex in the frontal plane suffered from systematic constant errors which could be accounted for in terms of the cardinal role of the vertical and horizontal dimensions. Perceived verticality as a function of various abnormal stimulus conditions continues to interest researchers like Brosgole & Cristal (55), Ebenholtz (118), Harker & McLean (208), Kajitsuka (232), Morant & Aronoff (275) and Rierdan & Wapner (310). Hay & Pick (211) found that looking at one's own body produced different distortions than looking at surrounding objects in a distorting spectacles experiment, a finding analogous to Rierdan & Wapner's (310) discovery that both apparent verticality and apparent body position could be affected in a 20° rotated visual field, depending upon whether the subject paid attention to his body or to the objects surrounding him. Miller & Graybiel (272) have demonstrated the dependence of the visual horizontal upon gravitational force. Agee & Gogel (2) found that the space surrounding the binocularly viewed Ames trapezoidal window is distorted when the window's apparent orientation is reversed, and Attneave & Olson (12) found that horizontal or vertical stimuli are more discriminable than stimuli tilted 45° right or left.

Monocular and binocular vision.—The apparent three-dimensionality of monocular space has been restressed by Metzger (270), but Barrett & Williamson (21) found that the judged quality of depth was significantly better under binocular than monocular viewing conditions. In their study, however, the monocularly viewed scene was judged to have equal or better depth quality in almost one third of the trials. Attneave and Olson (11) found that radial patterning produces a stronger monocular depth effect than relative length. That successive alternate presentation of two stereoscopic stimuli monocularly to the same eye does not produce apparent depth was shown by Engel (129); this finding, with a pair of Julesz stereo random brightness fields, was predictable, since the stimuli contained no monocular depth cues. On the other hand, again predictably, even small head movements can improve the accuracy of monocular depth perception, as demonstrated in a study by Redding, Mefferd & Wieland (309).

Size and distance.—Harvey & Leibowitz (209) studied size matching at short distances, finding that monocular and binocular matches did not differ, and Leibowitz & Dato (245) studied size constancy in temporarily and permanently monocular observers. Leibowitz and his associates (247, 248, 250, 251) continue in their extensive research program on the perception of size.

Size and distance judgments have been subjected to a power law analysis by Baird & Biersdorf (15) and by Stanley (350). Garner, Kaplan & Creelman (184) showed that the effects of stimulus range, duration and contrast on absolute judgments of size are comparable to one another. That filled space produces greater apparent distance than empty space was corroborated in an experiment by Luria, Kinney & Weissman (261), and Baird (13, 14) found that reduction of the numerosity and heterogeneity of the stimuli in a visual field resulted in reduced distance estimates. Dees has investigated size and distance in several studies (97, 98). In one report (96), observing that the actual distance of a series of targets of constant visual angle could be badly misjudged during a set of training trials, Dees suggested that the moon illusion may in part be due to the well-known size-distance invariance: something looks larger because it looks farther away or closer because it looks larger. Blessing, Landauer & Coltheart (37) provided further substantial evidence that the size-distance invariance holds well within individual subjects, but Carlson & Tassone (67) obtained equivocal results. Schiffman (320) found that size estimates of familiar objects depend upon the visual information available. In a well-designed study of errors in distance judgments, Smith & Smith (345) found that judgment in natural units produced smaller errors than judgment in arbitrary units and that response-produced visual stimuli for visual distance also resulted in smaller errors than nonresponse-produced visual stimuli, but that distance judgments were, in their child and adult subjects, surprisingly independent of improvement with experience. By contrast, however, the accuracy of absolute judgments of the size of visual stimuli in an otherwise stimulus-free field improved with knowledge of results in a study by Steedman (351), and the accuracy of absolute judgments of distance was improved by knowledge of results, longer stimulus duration, and induced muscle tension in a study by Agnew, Pyke & Pylyshyn (3). Biersdorf (36) also studied apparent size and apparent distance.

The apparent orientation of trapezoidal retinal projections was studied in a number of investigations. Thus Dunn and his associates (112–115) have studied slant in a number of investigations. In one (114), it was found that perceived tilt of trapezoids increased approximately linearly as the height of the midpoint of the shorter vertical edge in the frontal plane increased. This was true of a series of trapezoids whose horizontal edge and right vertical edge subtended constant visual angles. Flock et al. (159, 160) have also continued in a program of research on depth and slant. In a study by Epstein (130), perceived depth increased as the specificity of the background was increased. Ogasawara (287), working like Epstein within the framework of Gibson's theory of depth perception, proposed a set of formulas for specifying the density gradient of stimuli in depth perception.

Shape, slant, and shape constancy.—Freeman (176) has written a theoretical paper suggesting that perspective theory does a better job than texture-gradient theory in accounting for phenomena of slant. In several studies, Smith supported the slant-shape invariance hypothesis (339, 341), but in another (342) he found a series order effect in judgment of shape and slant which was inconsistent with a simple slant-shape invariance and which he interpreted in terms of adaptation level theory. Using a circle and two ellipses at various slants, Leibowitz & Meneghini (249) found that shape constancy was not a matter of responding to a familiar circular shape as much as a tendency to approximate the true shape of the object, once again emphasizing the importance of cues as mediators of shape constancy. Freeman (175) is continuing his series of investigations of slant perception. Kraft & Winnick (238) studied the effect of pattern and texture gradients on slant and shape judgments, and Winnick & Rosen (396) investigated shape-slant relations under reduction conditions. In an experiment by Meneghini & Leibowitz (269), shape constancy was minimal even when the test object was as close as three feet to the observer, the matches at three feet representing a compromise between true and projected shape with binocular vision, and the matches being closer to retinal shape with monocular vision. Suzuki, Ueno & Tada (358) report an interesting result: shape constancy was strengthened by sensory deprivation. Lichte & Borresen (254) found that instruction to respond to the real shape produced almost perfect constancy, that responding to the silhouette did not fully eliminate constancy, and that conventional apparent instructions produce ambiguous results. Both a modified nativist view (338–342) and an empirist view (e.g., 175) of constancy phenomena continue to be held.

Spatial distortions and aftereffects of displacements.—Interest in displacements and distortions continues at a high level. Foley & Abel (162) studied vision under alternately normal and distorted conditions, and Sekuler & Bauer (327) studied the effect of hand position and target location on adaptation to prismatic displacement. Coren (80) found greater prism adaptation if the arm was free than when it was constrained, and Day, Singer & Keen (94) reported a monocular distorting effect analogous to prism adaptation effects. Day & Wade (95) also found a visual spatial aftereffect resulting from prolonged head tilt. Kravitz & Wallach (239) discovered that adaptation to prismatically displaced vision is enhanced by vibrating the viewed hand during exposure. Mack (262) found that adaptation to a tilted retinal image is enhanced by movement, and Thomas & Lyons (369) are working on sensory-tonic displacement of the apparent vertical in pigeons.

Cohen (75), using a prism technique in a study within the Ivo Kohler tradition, found that when the hand reaching for a visible target was viewed continuously, aftereffects were restricted to that hand, but that when the reaching hand was viewed only after each reaching movement had been completed, aftereffects were obtained in both hands. Kalil & Freedman (233) also obtained an intermanual transfer. Their first explanatory proposal, that there is central interaction in the motor innervation areas of the CNS, is contradicted by Singer & Day's (332) failure to find any interlimb transfer of a kinesthetic spatial transformation, but their second interpretation, that there are changes in the reaction system represented by both areas together, and that such motor dispositions could change with training without involving transfer, remains plausible. Efstathiou et al. (120) found that shifts in reaching for a visible target generalize to nonvisible targets.

Kalil & Freedman (234) obtained photographic evidence of compensatory persistent ocular rotations following prismatic visual displacement, of which the subjects seemed unaware. The authors suggested that these rotations could account for the errors in reaching when the prisms are present as well as for distortions afterwards. This position becomes all the more interesting in view of recent successful attempts, such as that by Templeton, Howard & Lowman (365) and by Singer & Day (333, 334), to obtain adaptation under passive exposure conditions; such adaptation should not be possible if the influential reafference hypothesis of Held, previously the most widely accepted one, were correct. Day & Singer (93) summarize the current status of the whole field of sensory adaptation with spatial transformations, and Rock & Harris (313) present an overview of vision-touch interaction, suggesting that vision may dominate touch: they use this hypothesis to account for the results of a wide variety of distortion studies.

That central processes are involved in prismatic adaptation was demonstrated by Pick, Hay & Willoughby (299), who obtained evidence for interocular transfer of prism adaptation by the third day of exposure; Craske &

Gregg (83) found identical results for visual targets and the unexposed limb. Hay & Pick (212) had half of their subjects wear vertically oriented prisms, so that shearing was associated with horizontal eye movements and stretching with vertical eye movements; half wore horizontally oriented prisms to give the reverse relations. They concluded on the basis of the resulting adaptation phenomena that the adaptation to prismatic image shearing is a rotation, probably a change in the patterning of torsional eye movements; they also obtained further evidence for interocular transfer.

Ebenholtz (118, 119) is also engaged in a program of research on optical tilt, and Freedman, Wilson & Rekosh (174) have studied disarranged hand-ear coordination.

Research on visual figural aftereffects also continues, as in Crawford & Klingaman's (86) study of the effect of hue on aftereffects, in Gibb, Freeman & Adam's (187) demonstration that luminance contrast influences figural aftereffects induced by short fixation periods, and in Pressey & Kelm's (305) discovery that sleep deprivation reduces visual aftereffects. Landauer, Singer & Day (243), studying the old problem of correlations among aftereffects in various modalities, did find a significant relationship between kinesthetic and visual aftereffects using similar tasks for both: a slanted inspection object and judgments of horizontality; the correlation was reduced, but still significantly present, when the effect of adjustment time on the two tasks was partialled out. Sweeney (359) found a negative relationship between susceptibility to a kinesthetic figural aftereffect and pain reactivity, and Bakan & Thompson (16) studied kinesthetic figural aftereffects as a function of number and distribution of inspection trials; Collins (76) studied the effect of restriction of the limbs upon a kinesthetic aftereffect. Immergluck (223–225) is continuing his studies of correlates of individual differences in figural aftereffects, with special emphasis on field dependence. That the extent of the spiral aftereffect depends upon whether the inducing motion was centrifugal or centripetal was demonstrated by Scott et al. (323), and by Costello (82). Stager (349) proposed a neurological theory of the spiral aftereffect. Panagiotou & Roberts (294) studied the effect of order of presentation, finding among other things that latency of the spiral aftereffect is inversely related to its duration. Ganz (182) has presented an ingenious general mathematical model of figural aftereffects, basing his theory on the assumption that the aftereffects might be a kind of simultaneous illusion, with the afterimage of the inspection object acting as an inducing figure and displacing the test contour in phenomenal space because the inducing contour exerts an inhibitory effect upon the test contour. Pollack, in addition to continuing his own program of perceptual research, has developed some criticisms of Ganz's theory (303).

Perception of Time and Movement

Perception of time and of motion have often been discussed together because they are clearly related. Time and space are fused in movements. As has been typical in the past, less new material is available on time perception than on motion perception.

Time perception.—McGrath & O'Hanlon (266) proposed and validated a method for measuring the rate of subjective time in a thorough investigation. Thor & Crawford (370) studied the subjective passage of time during a two-week confinement of 30 men, women, and children in a simulated fallout shelter which lacked all reliable means for determining the actual passage of time. The influence of subjective time on the apparent speed of movement was investigated by Bonnet (43). Orme (289) related individual differences in time estimation to psychiatric diagnoses and other personality variables; but Banks, Cappon & Hagen (19) found that a time estimation procedure was unable to differentiate patients reporting time distortions from controls. Baldwin, Thor & Wright (17) were unable to replicate an earlier report of a sex difference in time estimation.

Other studies of time perception include one by Chatterjea & Rakshit (70) on estimation of short intervals bounded by white light, colored light and sound. El'kin & Kozina (126) found that alcohol produced underestimation of time intervals initially, overestimation after one hour. Fox et al. (163) corroborated and extended earlier findings on the effect of body temperature on time judgment. Lockhart (259) found an effect of ambient temperature on time estimation. Whyman & Moos (391) reported an effect of anxiety, but Singh (335) found no effect of need tension on time estimation.

Visual motion perception.—Brosgole and his collaborators (53, 56–58) are engaged in a program of interesting research on apparent motion. In ingenious experiments, Brosgole (52) and Brosgole & Cristal (54) demonstrated that apparent motion can be induced in a target by an apparent change in its position relative to the observer, showing that actual displacement relative to an actual framework is not essential for the perception of motion. Alexander & Cooperband (6) found that the ability to detect a rotary motion superimposed upon translational motion depends upon the rate of change of the relative bearing of the two moving objects.

Gogel & Mertens (192) devised a method to simulate objects moving in depth at any desired linear speed or acceleration by moving a photographic transparency between a point source of light and a screen, which remained at a constant distance from the observer. Ball & Wilsoncroft (18) have reported a new apparent motion phenomenon with complex stimuli. Mefferd et al. (267, 268) and Cook, Mefferd & Wieland (79) studied perspective reversals with a variety of actually moving three-dimensional forms, showing that depth as such is perceived rather veridically, but that reversals occur in the spatial ordering of objects or of points on objects, usually in the form of abrupt apparent reversals of orientation in depth. These reversals are typically systematic and can readily occur in the absence of misleading perspective cues and in the presence of valid depth cues.

Dixon & Meisels (107) found that the information content of the stimulus figure is an important determinant of both the perception of a rotating field and the motion aftereffect. Sumi (357) and Scott et al. (323) also have studied motion aftereffects, the first in relation to the phenomenal path of the inducing motion, showing that the two tended to curve in opposite directions, and the latter reporting some interesting directional asymmetries in the aftereffects. Sekuler & Pantle (328) proposed a quantitative physiologically based model for aftereffects of seen movement. Denton (100) describes a device for simulating some of the visual aspects of driving, suitable for studying various speed phenomena, including motion aftereffects.

Ellingstad (127) studied estimates of the velocity of briefly displayed targets, and Rachlin (307) scaled subjective velocity. Thines & Jenart (367) have undertaken detailed studies of the perception of rotation and pivoting. Guastella (198) has proposed a new theory to explain the difference between true and apparent motion. Pearce & Matin (297) devised an inventive new technique for measuring autokinetic speed: compensation for the apparent motion by physical motion in the opposite direction so as to result in the phenomenal absence of motion; and Gilbert (190) factor-analyzed five different measures of autokinesis which did not give clearly comparable results. Shaffer & Wallach (330) investigated motion extent thresholds for movement relative to the subject and for movement involving displacement relative to another object. Zapparoli (401) produced simultaneous stroboscopic movements in different directions.

Kinesthetic motion perception.—Estimations of angular velocity by subjects rotated in a chair were subjected to a Stevens scaling technique by Brown (59), further validating the power law, which Yilmaz (400) tried to derive from evolutionary adaptation. Cratty & Williams (85) required standing blindfolded subjects wearing earplugs to execute facing movements of 90°, 180° and 360°, and found that 90° turns were overestimated and the other two turns underestimated.

PERCEPTION OF COLORS

Tanaka, Uemura & Torii (362) demonstrated that a contiguous annular field can induce increases and decreases in the threshold luminance of a surrounded test field, and Stevens (354) studied the effect of size of surround on the brightness inhibition of a test field. A larger scale study of perceived brightness as a function of dark adaptation was carried out by Ekman, Hosman & Berglund (125), who used a direct psychophysical scaling method to measure the increase in brightness as dark adaptation increased. These investigators found that the curve could be characterized as composed of two separate functions, both growing at a decelerated rate and intersecting at about 8 min. Bartleson & Breneman (22), in a thorough study of brightness perception in complex fields, concluded that brightness does not appear to follow a simple power law. Beck (27, 28) studied the effects of age, assimilation and contrast on brightness judgments. Warren & Poulton (383) investigated brightness contrast, and Freeman (177) summarized contrast theories of brightness constancy.

Oyama & Hsia (293) reported a thorough study of color contrast, corroborating that contrast decreases as the separation between test and inducing field increases. Takasaki studied both brightness (360) and chromatic (361) contrast phenomena. Teller & Galanter (364) studied the brightness of colors under monocular and binocular simultaneous contrast and varying levels of adaptation. Color contrast was found by De Valois & Walraven (101) to be a retinal phenomenon and not a central one.

Sternheim & Boynton (353) found that a continuous numerical set of designations for hues produced reliable assignments that included more information than the more usual discrete naming techniques. Luria (260) studied the effect of stimulus intensity (from 0.15 to 15.0 ft-L) and duration (from 2 to 300 msec) on color naming in color normals and a deuteranope, finding that higher scores were more consistently obtained in the brightest, longest condition than in the dimmest and shortest. That instructions and potential response categories can markedly influence color naming was demonstrated in an experiment by Beare & Siegel (24). Warren (382) corroborated Fechner's square root rule in his finding that ratings of color saturation, on a scale ranging from white at one end to the appropriate color name at the other, were proportional to the square root of the proportion of white in a mixture of white and colored paper exposed on a color mixer. Jacobs (227) undertook a technically excellent investigation of the effect of chromatic adaptation upon subsequent estimates of saturation, and Indow (226) compared four different methods for scaling saturation.

Further work in the Innsbruck tradition, along the lines discussed above under spatial distortion and aftereffects of displacements, has continued with color distortions as well. Thus Leppmann & Wieland (252) replicated a study with split-half two-color lenses worn for an 11-day period, finding that adaptation to the intensity difference was more rapid than adaptation to the chromatic difference.

PERCEPTUAL SET

The term "perceptual set" is used here to refer to studies within the tradition that used to be called the new look in perception, studies of the effect of motivation, attitude, value, set, etc. on perceptual processes. Interest in this kind of research and in perception without awareness (e.g., 20, 128) continues at a high level, and the present section selects only a very small number of representative studies. A few others have already been mentioned above in other contexts.

The effect of cognitive variables like field dependence and flexibility upon the recognition of both visual and auditory ambiguous stimuli was demonstrated by Frederiksen (173). Landis, Jones & Reiter (244), in two experiments on the apparent size of coins and of discs, showed that overestimation of size was more a function of the actual size of the stimulus object than of its value. Thus while larger coins were overestimated more than control discs of the same size, the reverse was true for smaller coins.

Verbal reinforcement turned out to be less effective than variation in instructions in influencing accuracy of performance in a size constancy task studied by Levy (253). In a study by Crumpton, Wine & Drenick (88), the probability of food completions of skeleton words was enhanced by food deprivation, but increased deprivation for more prolonged periods did not produce a further increase in food responses. Gordon & Spence (194) found that food set and food deprivation facilitated perception of a subliminal food stimulus.

Continuing in the long-standing attempt to find out whether perceptual defense or perceptual vigilance (see, e.g., 63) can be demonstrated to exist after all possible artifactual effects are controlled out is a theoretical analysis by Broadbent (51) and a paper by Sarbin & Chun (317). The latter argue that some of the correction procedures proposed before contain a logical flaw and suggest a revised correction procedure. Bootzin & Stephens (44) obtained equivocal results in a study of perceptual defense in the absence of response bias.

Didato (103) found that the perceived size of discs carrying words varying in value was positively related to the strength of the value in individuals, as measured by the Allport-Vernon-Lindzey Scale of Values. Sinha & Sinha (336) found an inverse relationship between anxiety as measured by the Taylor Manifest Anxiety Scale and susceptibility to the Müller-Lyer illusion. Stoegbauer (355), however, did not find any appreciable relationship between susceptibility to the Ames trapezoidal window illusion and a variety of personality traits measured by the Guilford-Zimmerman Temperament Survey.

Egeth & Smith (122) were able to demonstrate that set could produce perceptual selectivity in a visual recognition task. Their experiment showed the sophistication of design which the literature of the last two decades in this field has demonstrated to be necessary if artifactual explanations are to be avoided. Comparably, Dielman & David (104) found that instructional set had a substantial effect on the apparent motion of an autokinetic point, but that induction of the set before the light spot appeared was more effective than presenting the set-inducing instructions after it was on. Set also influenced simultaneous brightness contrast in a study by Parrish & Smith (295). Brosgole (53, 54) reports on the effect of shifting the apparent median plane by induced movement, indicating that a change in egocentric location can produce what he called "induced autokinesis."

Egeth (121) has performed a useful service in summarizing the research on selective attention, and Haber (200) reviewed extensively the research on the effects of set on perceptual experience. Spence (348) analysed the relationship between subliminal perception and perceptual defense.

BODY PERCEPTION

Perception of the size, shape, or outline of one's own body has only recently become accepted as an appropriate subarea of perception. Interest in this field has increased in recent years. Thus Shontz (331) undertook an extensive investigation of various distances on the body, using several different methods for judging bodily dimensions. Among other things, the width of the head and the length of the forearm are consistently overestimated while the length of hands and feet is typically underestimated. Fuhrer & Cowan (179) found that active movement of a body part tends to reduce the underestimation of its size.

Bauermeister, Wapner & Werner (23) tilted subjects sitting in a chair in a dark room to the right or left and permitted them simultaneously to see a luminous line which could be turned to any angle. Using two different methods for assessing apparent tilt, they found systematic but small deviations of apparent body tilt in the direction of the actual tilt. Another study within the sensory-tonic tradition by Comalli (78) was performed with above-the-knee unilateral amputees, for whom the apparent vertical turned out to be displaced in the direction opposite to the amputation. O'Connell et al. (286), however, raise the question of whether apparent sensory-tonic effects in perceived verticality may not be artifacts due to psychophysical error. Ueno (372) reports that patients suffering from symptoms in particular peripheral parts of their bodies feel as though that part is, in effect, protected by a surrounding shell, while patients with internal diseases lack this experience.

Cratty (84), in an interesting study of the perception of the slant of planes upon which blind and blindfolded normal subjects walked, found that the threshold for descending slant was lower than for ascending. Furthermore the threshold for the blind subjects was substantially lower than for the normal seeing subjects. Hutton (222) found a kinesthetic aftereffect from walking on an inclined plane.

Cassell (68) is undertaking a program of research on tachistoscopic recognition of different body parts, relating these measures to Rorschach indices.

An Evaluation

The study of perception appears to be undergoing a period of renewed growth and vitality. Fifty to 75 years ago perception was perhaps the chief research area in psychology, but then it became relatively less important as other fields grew and prospered. Now perception seems to be regaining its position as a rapidly moving, exciting, ever-changing and ever-young field, attracting many dedicated research workers. Perhaps the main contemporary trend, composed of several interrelated subtrends, could be characterized by the term sophistication. Methodology has reached a high level of technical competence. The attempt to construct realistic neurophysiological and quantitative models illustrates the concern with what could be called a micromechanistic orientation, which can also be seen in the direct facing of issues that can be extremely complex and intricate. The interrelations among previously distinct fields are beginning to receive recognition, but simultaneously problems which once looked simple have been found to be not so straightforward after all. New, complex phenomena are no longer shied away from, and intricate relational and interactive processes are being studied.

ACKNOWLEDGMENTS

The assistance of the University of Colorado's Council on Research and Creative Work in helping to defray some of the expenses in preparation of this article is gratefully acknowledged. The authors also wish to express appreciation to the following people for their contribution toward preparation of the material: Charles A. Sheets, Jr., Hazel Visvader, Madalyn Bentley, Solveig Watterback, Judy Bowman, and Pekka Korkala.

LITERATURE CITED

1. Aaronson, D. Temporal factors in perception and short-term memory. *Psychol. Bull.*, **67**, 130–44 (1967)
2. Agee, F. L., Jr, Gogel, W. C. Equidistance judgments in the vicinity of a binocular illusion. *J. Exptl. Psychol.*, **74**, 87–92 (1967)
3. Agnew, N. M., Pyke, S., Pylyshyn, Z. Absolute judgment of distance as a function of induced muscle tension, exposure time, and feedback. *J. Exptl. Psychol.*, **71**, 649–54 (1966)
4. Akishige, Y., Ed. *Experimental Researches on the Structure of Perceptual Space* IV (The Faculty of Literature, Kyushu Univ., Fukuoka, Japan, 314 pp., 1961)
5. Akishige, Y. *Ibid.*, VI (1967)
6. Alexander, L. T., Copperband, A. S. Visual detection of compound motion. *J. Exptl. Psychol.*, **71**, 816–21 (1966)
7. Alpern, M., Lawrence, M., Wolsk, D. *Sensory Processes* (Brooks-Cole, Belmont, Calif., 151 pp., 1967)
8. Andersson, A. L. Stability and equivalence of adaptive figural and spiral after-effect processes. *Psychol. Res. Bull.*, **6**, 22 pp. (1966)
9. Andersson, A. L. Adaptive visual after-effect processes as related to patterns of colour-word interference serials. *Ibid.*, **32** pp.
10. Andersson, A. L. Variations in percept-intensity: An attempt at relating adaptive visual after-effect processes to personality. *Ibid.*, 25 pp.
11. Attneave, F., Olson, R. K. Inferences about visual mechanisms from monocular depth effects. *Psychon. Sci.*, **4**, 133–34 (1966)
12. Attneave, F., Olson, R. K. Discriminability of stimuli varying in physical and retinal orientation. *J. Exptl. Psychol.*, **74**, 149–57 (1967)
13. Baird, J. C. Effects of stimulus-numerosity upon distance estimates. *Psychon. Sci.*, **6**, 133–34 (1966)
14. Baird, J. C. Effects of stimulus-heterogeneity upon distance estimates. *Ibid.*, 135–36
15. Baird, J. C., Biersdorf, W. R. Quantitative functions for size and distance judgments. *Percept. Psychophys.*, **2**, 161–66 (1967)
16. Bakan, P., Thompson, R. W. Induction and retention of kinesthetic after-effects as a function of number and distribution of inspectoni trials. *Percept. Psychophys.*, **2**, 304–6 (1967)
17. Baldwin, R. O., Thor, D. H., Wright, D. E. Sex differences in the sense of time: Failure to replicate a 1904 study. *Percept. Mot. Skills*, **22**, 398 (1966)
18. Ball, T. S., Wilsoncroft, W. E. Complex stimuli and apparent motion. *Psychon. Sci.*, **6**, 187–88 (1966)
19. Banks, R., Cappon, D., Hagen, R. Time estimation by psychiatric patients. *Percept. Mot. Skills*, **23**, 1294 (1966)
20. Bánréti-Fuchs, K. M. Perception without awareness. *Acta Psychol.*, **26**, 148–60 (1967)
21. Barrett, G. V., Williamson, T. R. Sensation of depth with one or two eyes. *Percept. Mot. Skills*, **23**, 895–99 (1966)
22. Bartleson, C. J., Breneman, E. J. Brightness perception in complex fields. *J. Opt. Soc. Am.*, **57**, 953–57 (1967)
23. Bauermeister, M., Wapner, S., Werner, H. Method of stimulus presentation and apparent body position under lateral body tilt. *Percept. Mot. Skills*, **24**, 43–50 (1967)
24. Beare, A. C., Siegel, M. H. Color name as a function of wavelength and instructions. *Percept. Psychophys.*, **2**, 521–27 (1967)
25. Beck, J. Effect of surround size on the perception of texture patterns. *J. Exptl. Psychol.*, **72**, 58–75 (1966)
26. Beck, J. Effect of orientation and of shape similarity on perceptual grouping. *Percept. Psychophys.*, **1**, 300–2 (1966)
27. Beck, J. Contrast and assimilation in lightness judgments. *Ibid.*, 342–44
28. Beck, J. Age differences in lightness perception. *Psychon. Sci.*, **4**, 201–2 (1966)
29. Beck, J. Perceptual grouping produced by changes in orientation and shape. *Science*, **154**, 538–40 (1966)
30. Beck, J. Perceptual grouping produced by line figures. *Percept. Psychophys.*, **2**, 491–95 (1967)
31. von Békésy, G. *Sensory Inhibition* (Van Nostrand, Princeton, N. J., 265 pp., 1967)
32. Bergström, S. S. A paradox in the perception of luminance gradients:

I. *Scand. J. Psychol.*, **7**, 209–24 (1966)

33. Bergström, S. S. A paradox in the perception of luminance gradients: II. *Ibid.*, **8**, 25–32 (1967)

34. Bergström, S. S. A paradox in the perception of luminance gradients: III. *Ibid.*, 33–37

35. Berlyne, D. E., Peckham, S. The semantic differential and other measures of reactions to visual complexity. *Can. J. Psychol.*, **20**, 125–35 (1966)

36. Biersdorf, W. R. Convergence and apparent distance as correlates of size judgments at near distances. *J. Gen. Psychol.*, **75**, 249–64 (1966)

37. Blessing, W. W., Landauer, A. A., Coltheart, M. The effect of false perspective cues on distance and size judgments: An examination of the invariance hypotheses. *Am. J. Psychol.*, **80**, 250–56 (1967)

38. Bliss, J. C., Crane, H. D., Link, S. W., Townsend, J. T. Tactile perception of sequentially presented spatial patterns. *Percept. Psychophys.*, **1**, 125–30 (1966)

39. Bliss, J. C., Crane, H. D., Link, S. W. Effect of display movement on tactile pattern perception. *Ibid.*, 195–202

40. Blitz, B., Dinnerstein, A. J., Lowenthal, M. Relationship between pain tolerance and kinesthetic size judgment. *Percept. Mot. Skills*, **22**, 463–69 (1966)

41. Bokander, I. The importance of collative-affective and intensive arousal potential in stereoscopically induced perceptual conflict. *Scand. J. Psychol.*, **7**, 234–38 (1966)

42. Bokander, I. *Stereoscopically Induced Perceptual Conflict Between Facial Photographs* (Studia Psychologica et Paedagogica, Inv. XII, Lund, 29 pp. 1968)

43. Bonnet, C. Influence de la vitesse du mouvement et de l'espace parcouru sur l'estimation du temps. *Année Psychol.*, **67**, 51–60 (1967)

44. Bootzin, R. R., Stephens, M. W. Individual differences and perceptual defense in the absence of response bias. *J. Pers. Soc. Psychol.*, **6**, 408–12 (1967)

45. Borg, G. Om estimering av 'idealmått,' t. ex. en allmän exponent i psykofysisk potensfunktion. *Rapp. Psychol. Und.*, Klin. Psyk. Lab., Umeå Univ., 13 (1967)

46. Brackbill Y., Ed. *Infancy and Early Childhood*. (Free Press, New York, 1967)

47. Brandt, U., Fluur, E. Postural perceptions and compensatory displacements of the eye in respect to a presented force field. *Acta Oto-Laryngologica*, **62**, 252–64 (1966)

48. Brandt, U., Fluur, E. Postural perceptions and eye displacements during the variation of a force field acting in the mid-frontal plane. *Ibid.*, **63**, 49–64 (1967)

49. Brandt, U., Fluur, E. Postural perceptions and eye displacements produced by a resultant vector acting in the median sagittal plane of the head. *Ibid.*, 489–502

50. Braunstein, M. L. Sensitivity of the observer to transformations of the visual field. *J. Exptl. Psychol.*, **72**, 683–89 (1966)

51. Broadbent, D. E. Word-frequency effect and response bias. *Psychol. Rev.*, **74**, 1–15 (1967)

52. Brosgole, L. Change in phenomenal location and perception of motion. *Percept. Mot. Skills*, **23**, 999–1001 (1966)

53. Brosgole, L. Induced autokinesis. *Percept. Psychophys.*, **2**, 69–73 (1967)

54. Brosgole, L., Cristal, R. M. Vertically induced autokinesis. *Psychon. Sci.*, **7**, 337–38 (1967)

55. Brosgole, L., Cristal, R. M. The role of phenomenal displacement on the perception of the visual upright. *Percept. Psychophys.*, **2**, 179–88 (1967)

56. Brosgole, L., Whalen, P. M. The effect of enclosure on the allocation of visually induced movement. *Psychon. Sci.*, **8**, 69–70 (1967)

57. Brosgole, L., Whalen, P. M. The effect of past experience on the distribution of visually induced motion. *Ibid.*, 81–82

58. Brosgole, L., Whalen, P. M. The effect of meaning on the allocation of visually induced movement. *Percept. Psychophys.*, **2**, 275–77 (1967)

59. Brown, J. H. Magnitude estimation of angular velocity during passive rotation. *J. Exptl. Psychol.*, **72**, 169–72 (1966)

60. Brown, L. T., Farha, W. Some physical determinants of viewing time under three instructional sets. *Percept. Psychophys.*, **1**, 2–4 (1966)

61. Brown, L. T., O'Donnell, C. R. At-

tentional response of humans and squirrel monkeys to visual patterns varying in three physical dimensions. *Percept. Mot. Skills*, **22**, 707–17 (1966)

62. Bryden, N. Accuracy and order in tachistoscopic recognition. *Can. J. Psychol.*, **20**, 262–72 (1966)

63. Buck, L. Reaction time as a measure of perceptual vigilance. *Psychol. Bull.*, **65**, 291–304 (1966)

64. Buis, C. Een onderzoek naar de wisseling van perspectief bij driedimensionele draaiende objecten. *Ned. Tijdschr. Psychol. Grensgebieden*, **21**, 525–38 (1966)

65. Cappone, M. K. The effect of verbal suggestion on the reversal rate of the Ames Trapezoid Illusion. *J. Psychol.*, **62**, 211–19 (1966)

66. Carlson, J. A. Effect of instructions and perspective-drawing ability on perceptual constancies and geometrical illusions. *J. Exptl. Psychol.*, **72**, 874–79 (1966)

67. Carlson, V. R., Tassone, E. P. Independent size judgments at different distances. *J. Exptl. Psychol.*, **73**, 491–97 (1967)

68. Cassell, W. A. A tachistoscopic index of body perception: I. Body boundary and body interior awareness. *J. Proj. Tech. Pers. Assess.*, **30**, 31–36 (1966)

69. Chapanis, A., Mankin, D. A. The vertical-horizontal illusion in a visually-rich environment. *Percept. Psychophys.*, **2**, 249–55 (1967)

70. Chatterjea, R., Rakshit, P. Estimation of temporal interval. *Percept. Mot. Skills*, **22**, 176 (1966)

71. Chyatte, D., Chyatte, C. Brain bloodshift theory: A note on the abortion of visual closure. *J. Psychol.*, **65**, 153–55 (1967)

72. Cleary, A. A binocular parallax theory of the geometric illusions. *Psychon. Sci.*, **5**, 241–42 (1966)

73. Coen-Gelders, A. Une singulière illusion visuelle: L'effect piston apparent. *Acta Psychol.*, **26**, 130–47 (1967)

74. Cogan, R., Goldstein, A. G. The stability of binocular rivalry during spaced and massed viewing. *Percept. Psychophys.*, **2**, 171–74 (1967)

75. Cohen, M. M. Continuous versus terminal visual feedback in prism after-effects. *Percept. Mot. Skills*, **24**, 1295–1302 (1967)

76. Collins, J. K. Freedom and restriction of the limbs in the kinesthetic spatial aftereffect. *Australian J. Psychol.*, **19**, 63–67 (1967)

77. Collins, J. F., Eriksen, C. W. The perception of multiple simultaneously presented forms as a function of foveal spacing. *Percept. Psychophys.*, **2**, 369–73 (1967)

78. Comalli, P. E., Jr. Effect of unilateral above-the-knee amputation on perception of verticality. *Percept. Mot. Skills*, **23**, 91–96 (1966)

79. Cook, T. H., Mefferd, R. B., Jr., Wieland, B. A. Apparent reversals of orientation (perspective reversals) in depth as determinants of apparent reversals of rotary motion. *Percept. Mot. Skills*, **24**, 691–702 (1967)

80. Coren, S. Adaptation to prismatic displacement as a function of the amount of available information. *Psychon. Sci.*, **4**, 407–8 (1966)

81. Corso, J. F. *The Experimental Psychology of Sensory Behavior* (Holt, Rinehart & Winston, New York, 1967)

82. Costello, C. G. Direction of rotation and decay of the spiral aftereffect *Percept. Mot. Skills*, **23**, 779–82 (1966)

83. Craske, B., Gregg, S. J. Prism aftereffects: identical results for visual targets and unexposed limb. *Nature*, **212**, 104–5 (1966)

84. Cratty, B. J. Perception of inclined plane while walking without vision. *Percept. Mot. Skills*, **22**, 547–56 (1966)

85. Cratty, B. J., Williams, H. Accuracy of facing movements executed without vision. *Percept. Mot. Skills*, **23**, 1231–38 (1966)

86. Crawford, F. T., Klingaman, R. L. Figural aftereffects as a function of hue. *J. Exptl. Psychol.*, **72**, 916–18 (1966)

87. Crovitz, H. F., Lockhead, G. R. Possible monocular predictors of binocular rivalry of contours. *Percept. Psychophys.*, **2**, 83–85 (1967)

88. Crumpton, E., Wine, D. B., Drenick, E. J. Effects of prolonged food deprivation on food responses to skeleton words. *J. Gen. Psychol.*, **76**, 179–82 (1967)

89. Cutsforth, T. D. An analysis of the relationship between tactual and visual perception. *Am. Found. for Blind Res. Bull.*, **12**, 23–47 (1966)

90. Day, H. Evaluations of subjective

complexity, pleasingness and interestingness for a series of random polygons varying in complexity. *Percept. Psychophys.*, **2,** 281–86 (1967)

91. Day, R. H. Perception. In *Introduction to Psychology: A Self-Selection Textbook.* (Vernon, J. A., Ed. Brown, Dubuque, Iowa, 1966)

92. Day, R. H. Studies in perception. *Australian Psychol.*, **2,** 109–26 (1968)

93. Day, R. H., Singer, G. Sensory adaptation and behavioral compensation with spatially transformed vision and hearing. *Psychol. Bull.*, **67,** 307–22 (1967)

94. Day, R. H., Singer, D., Keen, K. Behavioral compensation with monocular vision. *Science,* **156,** 1129–30 (1967)

95. Day, R. H., Wade, N. J. Visual spatial aftereffect from prolonged headtilt. *Science,* 154, 1201–2 (1966)

96. Dees, J. W. Moon illusion and size-distance invariance: An explanation based upon an experimental artifact. *Percept. Mot. Skills,* **23,** 629–30 (1966)

97. Dees, J. W. Relative contributions of convergence and retinal disparity in the stereopsis cue of size and distance. *Ibid.*, 645–6

98. Dees, J. W. Accuracy of absolute visual distance and size estimation in space as a function of stereopsis and motion parallax. *J. Exptl. Psychol.*, **72,** 466–67 (1966)

99. Dember, W. N., Neiberg, A. Individual differences in susceptibility to visual backward masking. *Psychon. Sci.,* **6,** 49–50 (1966)

100. Denton, G. G. "Moving road simulator:" A machine suitable for the study of speed phenomena including motion after-effect. *Ergonomics,* **9,** 517–20 (1966)

101. De Valois, R. L., Walraven, J. Monocular and binocular aftereffects of chromatic adaptation. *Science,* **155,** 463–65 (1967)

102. Dewar, R. E. Stimulus determinants of the magnitude of the Mueller-Lyer illusion. *Percept. Mot. Skills,* **24,** 708–10 (1967)

103. Didato, S. Influence of value-strength on perceptual distortion. *Percept. Mot. Skills,* **24,** 330 (1967)

104. Dielman, T. E., David, K. H. Temporal arrangement and specificity of set in an autokinetic situation.

Am. J. Psychol., **80,** 426–29 (1967)

105. Dinnerstein, D., Curcio, F., Chinsky, J. Contextual determination of apparent weight as demonstrated by the method of constant stimuli. *Psychon. Sci.,* **5,** 251–52 (1966)

106. Dinnerstein, D., Gerstein, I., Michel, G. Interaction of simultaneous and successive stimulus groupings in determining apparent weight. *J. Exptl. Psychol.*, **73,** 298–302 (1967)

107. Dixon, N. F., Meisels, L. The effect of information content upon the perception and after-effects of a rotating field. *Quart. J. Exptl. Psychol.,* **18,** 310–18 (1966)

108. Donderi, D. C. Visual disappearances caused by form similarity. *Science,* **152,** 99–100 (1966)

109. Dorničč, S. Reverzibilita trojrozmerných objektov. *Studia Psychol.,* **8,** 46–53 (1966)

110. Dorničč, S. Measurement of satiation in reversible figures. *Ibid.,* **9,** 18–24 (1967)

111. Düker, H. Hat Jaenschs Lehre von der Eidetik heute noch Bedeutung? *Psychol. Beiträge,* **8,** 237–53 (1965)

112. Dunn, B. E. Perceived slant as a function of direction of regard. *Psychon. Sci.,* **4,** 297–98 (1966)

113. Dunn, B. E. Some geometric bases for perceived slant. *Ibid.,* **6,** 147–48 (1966)

114. Dunn, B. E., Thomas, S. W. Relative height and relative size as monocular depth cues in the trapezoid. *Percept. Mot. Skills,* **22,** 275–81 (1966)

115. Dunn, B. E., Thompson, D., Thomas, S. Relationship of certainty to amount of perceived slant. *Can. J. Psychol.,* **21,** 132–40 (1967)

116. Dureman, I. Relationships between flicker-fusion threshold and two parameters of visual motion aftereffect. *Scand. J. Psychol.,* **6,** 254–56 (1965)

117. Eagle, M., Bowling, L., Klein, G. S. Fragmentation phenomena in luminous designs. *Percept. Mot. Skills,* **23,** 143–52 (1966)

118. Ebenholtz, S. M. Adaptation to a rotated visual field as a function of degree of optical tilt and exposure time. *J. Exptl. Psychol.,* **72,** 629–34 (1966)

119. Ebenholtz, S. M. Transfer of adaptation as a function of interpolated optical tilt to the ipsilateral and

contralateral eye. *Ibid.*, **73**, 263–67 (1967)

120. Efstathiou, A., Bauer, J., Greene, M., Held, R. Altered reaching following adaptation to optical displacement of the hand. *J. Exptl. Psychol.*, **73**, 113–20 (1967)

121. Egeth, H. Selective attention. *Psychol. Bull.*, **67**, 41–57 (1967)

122. Egeth, H., Smith, E. E. Perceptual selectivity in a visual recognition task. *J. Exptl. Psychol.*, **74**, 543–49 (1967)

123. Eichengreen, J. M., Coren, S., Nachmias, J. Visual-cliff preference by infant rats: Effects of rearing and test conditions. *Science*, **151**, 830–31 (1966)

124. Ekman, G., Berglund, B., Berglund, U., Lindvall, T. Perceived intensity of odor as a function of time of adaptation. *Scand. J. Psychol.*, **8**, 177–86 (1967)

125. Ekman, G., Hosman, J., Berglund, U. Perceived brightness as a function of duration of dark-adaptation. *Percept. Mot. Skills*, **23**, 931–43 (1966)

126. El'kin, D. G., Kozina, T. M. O vliyanii alkogolya na otschet vremeni. *Vopr. Psikhol.*, **2**, 147–52 (1966)

127. Ellingstad, V. S. Velocity estimation for briefly displayed targets. *Percept. Mot. Skills*, **24**, 943–47 (1967)

128. Emrich, H., Heinemann, L. G. EEG bei unterschwelliger Wahrnehmung emotional bedeutsamer Wörter. *Psychol. Forsch.*, **29**, 285–96 (1966)

129. Engel, G. R. A test of the existence of monocular stereoscopic depth perception. *Percept. Mot. Skills*, **23**, 235–38 (1966)

130. Epstein, W. Perceived depth as a function of relative height under three background conditions. *J. Exptl. Psychol.*, **72**, 335–38 (1966)

131. Epstein, W. *Varieties of Perceptual Learning.* (McGraw-Hill, New York, 1967)

132. Epstein, W., Jansson, G., Johansson, G. Perceived angle of oscillatory motion. *Percept. Psychophys.*, **3**, 12–16 (1968)

133. Eriksen, C. W. Independence of successive inputs and uncorrelated error in visual form perception. *J. Exptl. Psychol.*, **72**, 26–35 (1966)

134. Eriksen, C. W. Temporal luminance summation effects in backward and forward masking. *Percept. Psychophys.*, **1**, 87–92 (1966)

135. Eriksen, C. W., Collins, J. Backward masking in vision. *Psychon. Sci.*, **1**, 101–2 (1964)

136. Eriksen, C. W., Collins, J. F. Some temporal characteristics of visual pattern perception. *J. Exptl. Psychol.*, **74**, 476–84 (1967)

137. Eriksen, C. W., Greenspon, T. S., Lappin, J., Carlson, W. A. Binocular summation in the perception of form at brief durations. *Percept. Psychophys.*, **1**, 415–19 (1966)

138. Eriksen, C. W., Lappin, J. S. Selective attention and very short-term recognition memory for nonsense forms. *J. Exptl. Psychol.*, **73**, 358–64 (1967)

139. Eriksen, C. W., Lappin, J. S. Independence in the perception of simultaneously presented forms at brief durations. *Ibid.*, 468–72

140. Eriksen, C. W., Munsinger, H. L., Greenspon, T. S. Identification versus same-different judgment: An interpretation in terms of uncorrelated perceptual error. *J. Exptl. Psychol.*, **72**, 20–25 (1966)

141. Ertel, K. Untersuchungen zur motivierten Wahrnehmung. *Studia Psychol.*, **5** (1963)

142. Evans, C. Some studies of pattern perception using a stabilized retinal image. *Brit. J. Psychol.*, **56**, 121–33 (1965)

143. Evans, C. *Studies of Pattern Perception Using an Afterimage as a Method of Stabilization.*, (Proc. 75th Ann. APA Convention, 65–66, 1966)

144. Evans, G. B., Howarth, E. The effect of grip-tension on tactile-kinaesthetic judgement of width. *Quart. J. Exptl. Psychol.*, **18**, 275–77 (1966)

145. Evans, S. H. A brief statement of schema theory. *Psychon. Sci.*, **8**, 87–88 (1967)

146. Evans, S. H. Redundancy as a variable in pattern perception. *Psychol. Bull.*, **67**, 104–13 (1967)

147. Fantz, R. L. Visual perception and experience in early infancy: A look at the hidden side of behavior development. In *Early Behavior: Comparative and Developmental Approaches*, 181–224. (Stevenson, H. W., Ed., Wiley, New York, 1967)

148. Fantz, R. L., Nevis, S. Pattern preferences and perceptual-cognitive development in early infancy. *Mer-*

rill-*Palmer Quart.*, **13**, 77–108 (1967)
149. Fender, D., Julesz, B. Extension of Panum's fusional area in binocularly stabilized vision. *J. Opt. Soc. Am.*, **57**, 819–30 (1967)
150. Festinger, L., Ono, H., Burnham, C. A., Bamber, D. Efference and the conscious experience of perception. *J. Exptl. Psychol.*, **74**, 1–36 (1967)
151. von Fieandt, K. *The World of Perception* (Dorsey, Illinois, 418 pp., 1966)
152. von Fieandt, K., Ahonen, L., Järvinen, J. A scaling method for measuring color constancy. *Scand. J. Psychol.*, **5**, 10–16 (1964)
153. von Fieandt, K., Ahonen, L., Järvinen, J. Color constancy and the method of categorical judgment. Some remarks on J. Pietarinen's criticism. *Ibid.*, **8**, 123–26 (1967)
154. von Fieandt, K., Ahonen, L., Järvinen, J., Llan, A. Color experiments with modern sources of illumination. *Percept. Mot. Skills*, **20**, 555–56 (1965)
155. von Fieandt, K., Järvinen, J. Experiments on orthogonal localization, I. *Rept. Psychol. Inst.*, Univ. Helsinki, 2 (1965)
156. Fisher, G. H. Autokinesis in vision, audition and tactile-kinesthesis. *Percept. Mot. Skills*, **22**, 470 (1966)
157. Fisher, G. H. A tactile Poggendorff illusion. *Nature*, **212**, 105–6 (1966)
158. Fitzgerald, R. E. Kirkham, R. Backward visual masking as a function of average uncertainty of the masking pattern. *Psychon. Sci.*, **6**, 469–70 (1966)
159. Flock, H. R., Graves, D., Tenney, J., Stephenson, B. Slant judgments of single rectangles at a slant. *Psychon. Sci.*, **7**, 57–58 (1967)
160. Flock, H. R., Tenney, J. H., Graves, D. Depth information in single triangles and arrays of triangles. *Psychon. Sci.*, **6**, 291–92 (1966)
161. Foley, J. M. Locus of perceived equidistance as a function of viewing distance. *J. Opt. Soc. Am.*, **56**, 822–27 (1966)
162. Foley, J. E., Abel, S. M. A study of alternation of normal and distorted vision. *Can. J. Psychol.*, **21**, 220–30 (1967)
163. Fox, R. H., Bradbury, P. A., Hampton, I. F., Legg, C. F. Time judgment and body temperature. *J. Exptl. Psychol.*, **75**, 88–96 (1967)
164. Fox, R., Check, R. Forced-choice form recognition during binocular rivalry. *Psychon. Sci.*, **6**, 471–72 (1966)
165. Fox, R., McIntyre, C. Suppression during binocular fusion of complex targets. *Psychon. Sci.*, **8**, 143–44 (1967)
166. Fraisse, P. Neopredelennost' razdrazhitelya i neopredelennost' reaktsii pri pertseptivnom uznavanii. *Vopr. Psikhol.*, **4**, 8–21 (1966)
167. Fraisse, P. Visual perceptive simultaneity and masking of letters successively presented. *Percept. Psychophys.*, **1**, 285–87 (1966)
168. Fraisse, P. Le seuil différentiel de durée dans une suite régulière d'intervalles. *Année Psychol.*, **67**, 43–49 (1967)
169. Fraisse, P. Le rôle de l'incertitude et de la discriminabilité dans la reconnaissance perceptive. *Ibid.*, 61–72
170. Fraisse, P., Voillaume, C. Incertitude du stimulus, et incertitude de la réponse dans la reconnaissance perceptive. *Année Psychol.*, **66**, 397–416 (1966)
171. Francès, B. *La Perception* (Paris, Presses Universitaires de France, 128 pp. 1967)
172. Franks, H. Bemerkungen zur Problematik der sogenannten unterschwelligen Wahrnehmung. *Zeit. Exptl. Ang. Psychol.*, **13**, 378–89 (1966)
173. Frederiksen, J. R. Cognitive factors in the recognition of ambiguous auditory and visual stimuli. *J. Pers. Soc. Psychol.*, **7**, 1–17 (1967)
174. Freedman, S. J., Wilson, L., Rekosh, J. H. Compensation for auditory re-arrangement in hand-ear coordination. *Percept. Mot. Skills*, **24**, 1207–10 (1967)
175. Freeman, R. B., Jr. Function of cues in the perceptual learning of visual slant: An experimental and theoretical analysis. *Psychol. Monogr. Gen. Appl.*, **80**, 1–29 (1966)
176. Freeman, R. B., Jr. Optical texture versus retinal perspective: A reply to Flock. *Psychol. Rev.*, **73**, 365–71 (1966)
177. Freeman, R. B., Jr. Contrast interpretation of brightness constancy. *Psychol. Bull.*, **67**, 165–87 (1967)
178. Frisch, H. L., Julesz, B. Figure-ground perception and random

geometry. *Percept. Psychophys.*, **1,** 389–98 (1966)

179. Fuhrer, M. J., Cowan, C. O. Influence of active movements, illumination, and sex on estimates of body-part size. *Percept. Mot. Skills*, **24,** 979–85 (1967)

180. Funari, E. A., Romano, D. F. Studio genetico sulla percezione del movimento. *Rivista di Psicol.*, **60,** 3–14 (1966)

181. Funari, E. Influenze delle ripetizioni di stimoli sulla percezione del movimento stroboscopico e della successione. *Rivista di Psicol.*, **60,** 401–12 (1966)

182. Ganz, L. Is the figural aftereffect an aftereffect? A review of its intensity, onset, decay, and transfer characteristics. *Psychol. Bull.*, **66,** 151–65 (1966)

183. Ganz, L., Wilson, P. D. Innate generalization of a form discrimination without contouring eye movements. *J. Comp. Physiol. Psychol.*, **63,** 258–69 (1967)

184. Garner, W. R., Kaplan, G., Creelman, C. D. Effect of stimulus range, duration, and contrast on absolute judgments of visual size. *Percept. Mot. Skills*, **22,** 635–44 (1966)

185. Gescheider, G. A. Resolving of successive clicks by the ears and skin. *J. Exptl. Psychol.*, **71,** 378–81 (1966)

186. Gescheider, G. A. Auditory and cutaneous apparent successiveness. *J. Exptl. Psychol.*, **73,** 179–86 (1967)

187. Gibb, M., Freeman, I., Adam, J. Effects of luminance contrast factors upon figural aftereffects induced by short fixation periods. *Percept. Mot. Skills*, **22,** 535–41 (1966)

188. Gibson, J. *The Senses Considered as Perceptual Systems* (Houghton Mifflin, Boston, 335 pp., 1966)

189. Gilbert, A. J. Tactile spatial aftereffect or adaptation level? *J. Exptl. Psychol.*, **73,** 450–55 (1967)

190. Gilbert, D. C. A factor analytic study of autokinetic responses. *J. Exptl. Psychol.*, **73,** 354–57 (1967)

191. Gilinsky, A. S. Masking of contour-detectors in the human visual system. *Psychon. Sci.*, **8,** 395–96 (1967)

192. Gogel, W. C., Mertens, H. W. A method of simulating objects moving in depth. *Percept. Mot. Skills*, **23,** 371–77 (1966)

193. Goldstein, A. G. Gestalt similarity principle, difference thresholds and pattern discriminability. *Percept. Psychophys.*, **2,** 377–82 (1967)

194. Gordon, C. M., Spence, D. P. The facilitating effects of food set and food deprivation on responses to a subliminal food stimulus. *J. Pers.*, **34,** 406–15 (1966)

195. Green, D. M., Swets, J. A. *Signal Detection Theory and Psychophysics* (Wiley, New York, 455 pp., 1966)

196. Gregory, R. L. *Eye and Brain: The Psychology of Seeing* (McGraw-Hill, New York, 254 pp., 1966)

197. Gregory, R. L., Ross, H. E. Arm weight, adaptation, and weight discrimination. *Percept. Mot. Skills*, **24,** 1127–30 (1967)

198. Guastella, M. J. New theory on apparent movement. *J. Opt. Soc. Am.*, **56,** 960–66 (1966)

199. Guttman, G. *Hirnelektrische Korrelate einfacher Wahrnehmungen.* (Presented at the I. Zusammenkunft der Psychologen aus den Donauländern, Bratislava, Sept. 14–18, 1967)

200. Haber, R. N. Nature of the effect of set on perception. *Psychol. Rev.*, **73,** 335–51 (1966)

201. Haber, R. N. *Contemporary Theory and Research in Visual Perception* (Holt, Rinehart & Winston, New York, 1968)

202. Hajos, A. *Sensumotorische Koordinationsprozesse bei Richtungslokalization.* (Referat, Marburg, unpublished, 1967)

203. Hajos, A., Ritter, M. Experiments to the problem of interocular transfer. *Acta Psychol.*, **24,** 81–90 (1965)

204. Hamilton, V. Susceptibility to the Müller-Lyer illusion and its relationship to differences in size constancy. *Quart. J. Exptl. Psychol.*, **18,** 63–72 (1966)

205. Hammond, K. R., Ed. *The Psychology of Egon Brunswik.* (Holt, Rinehart & Winston, New York, 549 pp., 1966)

206. Handel, S., Garner, W. R. The structure of visual pattern associates and pattern goodness. *Percept. Psychophys.*, **1,** 33–38 (1966) . .

207. Harcum, E. R., Smith, N. F. Stability of error distributions within tachistoscopic patterns. *Psychon. Sci.*, **6,** 287–88 (1966)

208. Harker, G. S., McLean, J. A. Retinal correspondence and the perceived vertical. *Percept. Mot. Skills*, **23,** 347–60 (1966)

209. Harvey, L. O., Jr., Leibowitz, H. W. Effects of exposure duration, cue reduction, and temporary monocularity in size matching at short distances. *J. Opt. Soc. Am.*, **57,** 249–53 (1967)

210. Hay, J. C. Optical motions and space perception: An extension of Gibson's analysis. *Psychol. Rev.,* **73,** 550–65 (1966)

211. Hay, J. C., Pick, H. L., Jr. Gazecontingent prism adaptation: Optical and motor factors. *J. Exptl. Psychol.,* **72,** 640–48 (1966)

212. Hay, J. C., Pick, H. L., Jr. Visual and proprioceptive adaptation to optical displacement of the visual stimulus. *Ibid.,* **71,** 150–58 (1966)

213. Hebb, D. O. *The Organization of Behavior: A Neuropsychological Theory* (Wiley, New York, 355 pp., 1949; 3rd printing, 1955)

214. Helson, H., Bevan, W. *Contemporary Approaches to Psychology.* (Van Nostrand, Princeton, 596 pp., 1967)

215. Hershenson, M. Development of the perception of form. *Psychol. Bull.,* **67,** 326–36 (1967)

216. Holden, E. A., Jr. Eye movements and the perception of rectilinear dot progressions. *Psychon. Sci.,* **7,** 219–20 (1967)

217. Holland, H. C. *International Series of Monographs in Experimental Psychology: II. The Spiral After-effect* (Pergamon, New York, 128 pp., 1966)

218. Holt-Hansen, K. Kinds of experiences in the perception of a circle. *Percept. Mot. Skills,* **24,** 3–32 (1967)

219. Holzkamp, K. Zum Problem der Beziehung zwischen anschaulicher Grösse und anschaulicher Entfernung. *Zeit. Exptl. Ang. Psychol.,* **13,** 39–72 (1966)

220. Holzkamp, K., Perlwitz, E. Absolute oder relative Grössenakzentuierung? *Zeit. Exptl. Ang. Psychol.,* **13,** 390–405 (1966)

221. Hurvich, L. M., Jameson, D. *The Perception of Brightness and Darkness* (Allyn & Bacon, Boston, 1966)

222. Hutton, R. S. Kinesthetic after-effect produced by walking on a gradient. *Res. Quart.,* **37,** 368–74 (1966)

223. Immergluck, L. Figural after-effects, rate of "figure-ground" reversal, and field dependence. *Psychon. Sci.,* **6,** 45–46 (1966)

224. Immergluck, L. Resistance to an optical illusion, figural aftereffects, and field dependence. *Ibid.,* 281–82

225. Immergluck, L. Visual figural aftereffects and field dependence. *Ibid.,* **4,** 219–20 (1966)

226. Indow, T. Saturation scales for red. *Vision Res.,* **7,** 481–95 (1967)

227. Jacobs, G. H. Saturation estimates and chromatic adaptation. *Percept. Psychophys.,* **2,** 271–74 (1967)

228. Järvinen, J. On the perception of slant on the basis of systems of relations among the elements of surface. *Rept. Psychol. Inst.,* Univ. Helsinki, **2** (1962)

229. Johansen, M. The experienced continuations of some three-dimensional forms. *Acta Psychol.,* **13,** 1–26 (1956)

230. Johansson, G. *Vision Without Contours.* (Reports from the Psychol. Lab., Univ. Uppsala, Sweden, 1967)

231. Johansson, G., Rumar, K. Visible distances and safe speeds during night driving car meetings. *Rept. Psychol. Dept.,* **38,** Univ. Uppsala (1966)

232. Kajitsuka, T. Effects of skin pressure on the perception of verticality. *Tohoku Psychol. Folia,* **25,** 124–31 (1967)

233. Kalil, R. E., Freedman, S. J. Intermanual transfer of compensation for displaced vision. *Percept. Mot. Skills,* **22,** 123–26 (1966)

234. Kalil, R. E., Freedman, S. J. Persistence of ocular rotation following compensation for displaced vision. *Percept. Mot. Skills,* **22,** 135–39 (1966)

235. Kidd, A. H., Rivoire, J. L., Eds. *Perceptual Development in Children* (International Universities Press, New York, 1966)

236. Kovač, D. *Wahrnehmung und Alter* (Referat, Marburg, Unpublished, 1967)

237. Kovač, D., Kosinar, V. The perception of discrete changes in simple visual stimuli. *Studia Psychol.,* **7,** 98–113 (1965)

238. Kraft, A. L., Winnick, W. A. The effect of pattern and texture gradient on slant and shape judgments. *Percept. Psychophys.,* **2,** 141–47 (1967)

239. Kravitz, J. H., Wallach, H. Adaptation to displaced vision contingent upon vibrating stimulation. *Psychon. Sci.,* **6,** 465–66 (1966)

240. Künnapas, T. Intensity of the under

lying figural process. *Percept. Psychophys.*, **1**, 288–92 (1966)

241. Künnapas, T. Visual memory of capital letters: Multidimensional ratio scaling and multidimensional similarity. *Percept. Mot. Skills*, **25**, 345–50 (1967)

242. Künnapas, T. Visual perception of capital letters: Multidimensional ratio scaling and multidimensional similarity. *Scand. J. Psychol.*, **7**, 189–96 (1966)

243. Landauer, A. A., Singer, G., Day, R. H. Correlation between visual and kinesthetic spatial aftereffects. *J. Exptl. Psychol.*, **72**, 892–94 (1966)

244. Landis, D., Jones, J. M., Reiter, J. Two experiments on perceived size of coins. *Percept. Mot. Skills*, **23**, 719–29 (1966)

245. Leibowitz, H. W., Dato, R. A. Visual size-constancy as a function of distance for temporarily and permanently monocular observers. *Am. J. Psychol.*, **79**, 279–84 (1966)

246. Leibowitz, H. W., Gwozdecki, J. The magnitude of the Poggendorff illusion as a function of age. *Child Develpm.*, **38**, 573–80. (1967)

247. Leibowitz, H. W., Harvey, L. O., Jr. Size-matching as a function of instructions in a naturalistic environment. *J. Exptl. Psychol.*, **74**, 378–82 (1967)

248. Leibowitz, H. W., Judisch, J. M. Size-constancy in older persons: A function of distance. *Am. J. Psychol.*, **80**, 294–96 (1967)

249. Leibowitz, H. W., Meneghini, K. A. Shape perception for round and elliptically shaped test objects. *J. Exptl. Psychol.*, **72**, 244–49 (1966)

250. Leibowitz, H. W., Moore, D. Role of changes in accommodation and convergence in the perception of size. *J. Opt. Soc. Am.*, **56**, 1120–29 (1966)

251. Leibowitz, H. W., Pollard, S. W., Dickson, D. Monocular and binocular size-matching as a function of distance at various age-levels. *Am. J. Psychol.*, **80**, 263–68 (1967)

252. Leppmann, P. K., Wieland, B. A. Visual distortion with two-colored spectacles. *Percept. Mot. Skills*, **23**, 1043–48 (1966)

253. Levy, L. H. The effects of verbal reinforcement and instructions on the attainment of size constancy. *Can. J. Psychol.*, **21**, 81–91 (1967)

254. Lichte, W. H., Borresen, C. R. Influence of instructions on degree of shape constancy. *J. Exptl. Psychol.*, **74**, 538–42 (1967)

255. Lie, I. The factor of proximity. An attempt to specify its critical conditions. *Scand. J. Psychol.*, **5**, 129–35 (1964)

256. Lie, I. Convergence as a cue to perceived size and distance. *Ibid.*, **6**, 109–16 (1965)

257. Lindholm, G. *Fehlerquellen der sog. ASW-Versuche.* *Ann. Acad. Sci. Fenn.*, B 145, 2, Suomalaisen Kirjallisuuden Kirjapaino, Helsinki, 1967)

258. Lobb, H., Friend, R. Tactual form discrimination with varying size and duration of exposure. *Psychon. Sci.*, **7**, 415–16 (1967)

259. Lockhart, J. M. Ambient temperature and time estimation. *J. Exptl. Psychol.*, **73**, 286–91 (1967)

260. Luria, S. M. Color-name as a function of stimulus intensity and duration. *Am. J. Psychol.*, **80**, 14–27 (1967)

261. Luria, S., Kinney, A., Weissman, S. Distance estimates with "filled" and "unfilled" space. *Percept. Mot. Skills*, **24**, 1007–10 (1967)

262. Mack, A. The role of movement in perceptual adaptation to a tilted retinal image. *Percept. Psychophys.*, **2**, 65–68 (1967)

263. Malhotra, M. K. Figurale Nachwirkungen. *Psychol. Forsch.*, **30**, 1–104 (1966)

264. Mayzner, M. S., Tresselt, M. E., Adrignolo, A. J., Cohen, A. Further preliminary findings on some effects of very fast sequential input rates on perception. *Psychon. Sci.*, **7**, 281–82 (1967)

265. Mayzner, M. S., Tresselt, M. E., Cohen, A. Preliminary findings on some effects of very fast sequential input rates on perception. *Psychon. Sci.*, **6**, 513–14 (1966)

266. McGrath, J., O'Hanlon, J., Jr., Method for measuring the rate of subjective time. *Percept. Mot. Skills*, **24**, 1235–40 (1967)

267. Mefferd, R. B., Jr., Redding, G. M., Wieland, B. A. Depth perception and its special case, slant in depth, as independent of apparent orientation (perspective) in depth. *Percept. Mot. Skills*, **24**, 679–90 (1967)

268. Mefferd, R. B., Jr., Wieland, B., Cook, T., Sadler, T., Benton, R., Redding, G. Analysis of perspective reversal and associated apparent motion using a perspective-bound move-

ment illusion. *Percept. Mot. Skills,*
22, 835–58 (1966)

269. Meneghini, K. A., Leibowitz, H. W. Effect of stimulus distance and age on shape constancy. *J. Exptl. Psychol.,* **74,** 241–48 (1967)

270. Metzger, W. Das einäugige Tiefsehen. In *Handbuch der Psychologie,* 1. Band, I. Halbband, 556–89 (Thomae, H., Ed., Verlag für Psychologie, Dr. C. Hogrefe, Göttingen, 1179 pp., 1966)

271. Michon, J. Studies on subjective duration. 2. Subjective time measurement during tasks with different information content. *Acta Psychol.,* **24,** 205–19 (1965)

272. Miller, E. F., Graybiel, A. Magnitude of gravitoinertial force, an independent variable in egocentric visual localization of the horizontal. *J. Exptl. Psychol.,* **71,** 452–60 (1966)

273. Minard, J. G., Batcher, J. Disappearance of naturally fixated luminous stimuli and stability of phase sequences: A selective review and related experiment. *Percept. Mot. Skills,* **24,** 747–52 (1967)

274. Moed, H. Constancy and contrast II. *Acta Psychol.,* **24,** 91–166 (1965)

275. Morant, R. B., Aronoff, J. Starting position, adaptation, and visual framework as influencing the perception of verticality. *J. Exptl. Psychol.,* **71,** 684–86 (1966)

276. Mountjoy, P. New illusory effect of the Mueller-Lyer figure. *J. Exptl. Psychol.,* **71,** 119–23 (1966)

277. Moustgaard, I. A phenomenological approach to autokinesis. *Scand. J. Psychol.,* **4,** 17–22 (1963)

278. Munsinger, H., Gummerman, K. Identification of form in patterns of visual noise. *J. Exptl. Psychol.,* **75,** 81–87 (1967)

279. Näätänen, R. Selective attention and evoked potentials. *Ann. Acad. Sci. Fenn.,* Helsinki, **1,** 151 (1967)

280. Natsoulas, T. On the perception of cutaneous figures. *Psychol. Rec.,* **17,** 43–48 (1967)

281. Nesmith, R., Rodwan, A. S. Effect of duration of viewing on form and size judgments. *J. Exptl. Psychol.,* **74,** 26–30 (1967)

282. Novak, S. Effects of free inspection and fixation on the magnitude of the Poggendorff illusion. *Percept. Mot. Skills,* **23,** 663–70 (1966)

283. Nowakowska, M. A quantitative approach to the dynamics of perception. *Gen. Sys.,* **12,** 81–95 (1967)

284. Nurminen, A. M. Evaluation of a technique for measuring subjective similarity. *Scand. J. Psychol.,* **6,** 209–19 (1965)

285. Nyberg, T. The gradients of texture and visual perception of depth. *Rept. Psychol. Inst.,* Univ. Helsinki, **1** (1959)

286. O'Connell, D. C., Weintraub, D. J., Lathrop, R. G., McHale, T. J. Apparent verticality: Psychophysical error versus sensory-tonic theory. *J. Exptl. Psychol.,* **73,** 347–53 (1967)

287. Ogasawara, J. Three formulae for the density-gradient of stimuli in depth perception. *Percept. Mot. Skills,* **23,** 1086 (1966)

288. Olson, R., Orbach, J. Reversibility of the Necker cube: VIII. Parts of the figure contributing to the perception of reversals. *Percept. Mot. Skills,* **22,** 623–29 (1966)

289. Orme, J. Personality, time estimation and time experience. *Acta Psychol.,* **22,** 430–40 (1964)

290. Over, R. Context and movement as factors influencing haptic illusions. *Australian J. Psychol.,* **18,** 262–65 (1966)

291. Over, R. Effect of the angle of tilt of the inspection figure on the magnitude of a kinesthetic aftereffect. *J. Exptl. Psychol.,* **74,** 249–53 (1967)

292. Over, R. Effects of varying the apparent tilt of the inspection figure on a kinaesthetic after-effect. *Quart. J. Exptl. Psychol.,* **19,** 115–24 (1967)

293. Oyama, T., Hsia, Y. Compensatory hue shift in simultaneous color contrast as a function of separation between inducing and test fields. *J. Exptl. Psychol.,* **71,** 405–14 (1966)

294. Panagiotou, M. A., Roberts, W. A. Order of presentation, duration and latency of spiral aftereffect. *Percept. Mot. Skills,* **23,** 1139–46 (1966)

295. Parrish, M., Smith, K. Simultaneous brightness contrast as a function of perceptual set. *Psychon. Sci.,* **7,** 195–96 (1967)

296. Payne, B. The relationship between a measure of organization for visual patterns and their judged complexity. *J. Verbal Learn. Verbal Behav.,* **5,** 338–43 (1966)

297. Pearce, D., Matin, L. The measure-

ment of autokinetic speed. *Can. J. Psychol.*, **20**, 160–72 (1966)

298. Pečjak, V. *Poglavja iz Psihologije.* (Državna Založba Slovenije, Ljubljana, Yugoslavia, 1965)

299. Pick, H. L., Jr., Hay, J. C., Willoughby, R. H. Interocular transfer of adaptation to prismatic distortion. *Percept. Mot. Skills*, **23**, 131–35 (1966)

300. Pickford, R. Colour experiments with modern sources of illumination. *Quart. J. Exptl. Psychol.*, **18**, 96 (1966)

301. Pietarinen, J. The law of categorical judgment and the measurement of color constancy. *Scand. J. Psychol.*, **7**, 197–200 (1966)

302. Pietarinen, J., Virsu, V. Geometric illusions, II. Features of the method of magnitude estimation of length differences. *Scand. J. Psychol.*, **8**, 172–76 (1967)

303. Pollack, R. H. Comment on "Is the figural aftereffect an aftereffect?" *Psychol. Bull.*, **68**, 59–61 (1967)

304. Pressey, A. W. Field dependence and susceptibility to the Poggendorff illusion. *Percept. Mot. Skills*, **24**, 309–10 (1967)

305. Pressey, A. W., Kelm, H. Effects of sleep deprivation on a visual figural aftereffect. *Percept. Mot. Skills*, **23**, 795–800 (1966)

306. Prinz, W. Quantitative Versuche über die Prägnanz von Punktmustern. *Psychol. Forsch.*, **29**, 297–359 (1966)

307. Rachlin, H. C. Scaling subjective velocity, distance, and duration. *Percept. Psychophys.*, **1**, 77–82 (1966)

308. Raymond, B., Glanzer, M. Continuity of exposure length effects in tachistoscopic perception. *Psychon. Sci.*, **7**, 287–88 (1967)

309. Redding, G. M., Mefferd, R. B., Jr., Wieland, B. A. Effect of observer movement on monocular depth perception. *Percept. Mot. Skills*, **24**, 725–26 (1967)

310. Rierdan, J., Wapner, S. Adaptive changes in the relationship between visual and tactual-kinesthetic perception. *Psychon. Sci.*, **7**, 61–62 (1967)

311. Robinson, D. N. Disinhibition of visually masked stimuli. *Science*, **154**, 157–58 (1966)

312. Rock, I. *The Nature of Perceptual Adaptation* (Basic Books, New York, 289 pp., 1966)

313. Rock, I., Harris, C. S. Vision and touch. *Sci. Am.*, **216**, 96–104 (1967)

314. Rommetveit, R. Generation of Words from Stereoscopically Presented Nonword Strings of Letters. (Abstracts of communications of the 18th International Congress of Psychology, **11**, 318, 1966)

315. Royer, F. L. Figural goodness and internal structure in perceptual discrimination. *Percept. Psychophys.*, **1**, 311–14 (1966)

316. Rumar, K. Visible distances in night driving. *Rept. Psych. Dept.*, Univ. Uppsala, 44 (1967)

317. Sarbin, T. R., Chun, K.-T. A logical flaw in an index to suppress response-bias in perceptual defense measures and the application of a proposed improvement. *Australian J. Psychol.*, **19**, 151–57 (1967)

318. Saugstad, P. Effect of food deprivation on perception-cognition. *Psychol. Bull.*, **65**, 80–90 (1966)

319. Saugstad, P., Schioldborg, P. Value and size perception. *Scand. J. Psychol.*, **7**, 102–14 (1966)

320. Schiffman, H. R. Size-estimation of familiar objects under informative and reduced conditions of viewing. *Am. J. Psychol.*, **80**, 229–35 (1967)

321. Schiller, P. H. Forward and backward masking as a function of relative overlap and intensity of test and masking stimuli. *Percept. Psychophys.*, **1**, 161–64 (1966)

322. Schuck, J. R., Leahy, W. R. A comparison of verbal and non-verbal reports of fragmenting visual images. *Percept. Psychophys.*, **1**, 191–92 (1966)

323. Scott, T. R., Lavender, A. D., McWhirt, R. A., Powell, D. A. Directional asymmetry of motion aftereffect. *J. Exptl. Psychol.*, **71**, 806–15 (1966)

324. Segall, M. H., Campbell, D. T., Herskovits, M. J. *The Influence of Culture on Visual Perception* (Bobbs-Merrill, New York, 268 pp., 1966)

325. Seiler, D. A., Zusne, L. Judged complexity of tachistoscopically viewed random shapes. *Percept. Mot. Skills*, **24**, 884–86 (1967)

326. Sekuler, R. W. Choice times and detection with visual backward masking. *Can. J. Psychol.*, **20**, 34–42 (1966)

327. Sekuler, R. W., Bauer, J. A., Jr. Adaptation to prismatic displace-

ments: Hand position and target location. *J. Exptl. Psychol.*, **72,** 207–12 (1966)

328. Sekuler, R., Pantle, A. A model for aftereffects of seen movement. *Vision Res.*, **7,** 427–39 (1967)

329. Sen, A. The effect of set on the two-point tactual threshold. *Quart. J. Exptl. Psychol.*, **19,** 169–74 (1966)

330. Shaffer, O., Wallach, H. Extent-of-motion thresholds under subject-relative and object-relative conditions. *Percept. Psychophys.*, **1,** 447–51 (1966)

331. Shontz, F. C. Estimation of distances on the body. *Percept. Mot. Skills,* **24,** 1131–42 (1967)

332. Singer, G., Day, R. H. Interlimb and interjoint transfer of a kinesthetic spatial aftereffect. *J. Exptl. Psychol.*, **71,** 109–14 (1966)

333. Singer, G., Day, R. H. Spatial adaptation and aftereffect with optically transformed vision: Effects of active and passive responding and the relationship between test and exposure responses. *Ibid.*, 725–31

334. Singer, G., Day, R. H. The effects of spatial judgments on the perceptual aftereffect resulting from prismatically transformed vision. *Australian J. Psychol.*, **18,** 63–70 (1966)

335. Singh, L. Effect of need tension on time perception. *Psychol. Res.*, **1,** 28–32 (1966)

336. Sinha, A. K. P., Sinha, S. N. Mueller-Lyer illusion in subjects high and low in anxiety. *Percept. Mot. Skills,* **24,** 194 (1967)

337. Sjöberg, L. Unidimensional similarity revisited. *Scand. J. Psychol.*, **7,** 115–20 (1966)

338. Smith, A. H. Comparison of the drawing and matching methods for judging shape. *Percept. Mot. Skills,* **23,** 3–15 (1966)

339. Smith, A. H. Perceived slant as a function of stimulus contour and vertical dimensions. *Ibid.*, **24,** 167–73 (1967)

340. Smith, A. H. Perception of shape as a function of order of angles of slant. *Ibid.*, **23,** 971–78 (1966)

341. Smith, A. H. Phenomenal slant as a function of ambiguity of contour perspective. *Ibid.*, 587–94

342. Smith, A. H. Series effect in monocular perception of slant. *Ibid.*, **22,** 295–302 (1966)

343. Smith, G. J., Kragh, U. A serial afterimage experiment in clinical diagnostics. *Scand. J. Psychol.*, **8,** 52–64 (1967)

344. Smith, M. C., Schiller, P. H. Forward and backward masking: A comparison. *Can. J. Psychol.*, **20,** 191–97 (1966)

345. Smith, O. W., Smith, P. C. Response-produced vs. non-response-produced visual stimuli for distance judgments in natural and unnatural units by children and adults. *Percept. Mot. Skills,* **24,** 487–92 (1967)

346. Soudková, M. Funktion der Wiederholung ohne externe Verstärkung bei Verbesserung visueller Urteile: Auf dem Material der Täuschung bei der T-Figur. *Studia Psychol.*, **8,** 117–31 (1966)

347. Soudková, M., Rišková, A. Vlijane vozrasta na pereocenku vertikalnoi linii v T-figure. *Studia Psychol.*, **8,** 204–15 (1966)

348. Spence, D. P. Subliminal perception and perceptual defense: two sides of a single problem. *Behav. Sci.*, **12,** 183–93 (1967)

349. Stager, P. An integration of neurological factors in the spiral aftereffect. *Can. J. Psychol.*, **20,** 400–6 (1966)

350. Stanley, G. Magnitude estimates of distance based on object-size. *Percept. Psychophys.*, **2,** 287–88 (1967)

351. Steedman, W. C. Absolute judgments of size in a restricted visual environment. *Percept. Mot. Skills,* **24,** 731–36 (1967)

352. Stenson, H. H. The physical factor structure of random forms and their judged complexity. *Percept. Psychophys.*, **1,** 303–10 (1966)

353. Sternheim, C. E., Boynton, R. M. Uniqueness of perceived hues investigated with a continuous judgmental technique. *J. Exptl. Psychol.*, **72,** 770–76 (1966)

354. Stevens, J. C. Brightness inhibition re size of surround. *Percept. Psychophys.*, **2,** 189–92 (1967)

355. Stoegbauer, M. K. The relationship of psychometrically determined personality variables to perception of the Ames trapezoidal illusion. *J. Psychol.*, **67,** 90–97 (1967)

356. Streicher, H. W., Pollack, R. H. Backward figural masking as a function of intercontour distance. *Psychon. Sci.*, **7,** 69–70 (1967)

357. Sumi, S. Paths of seen motion and motion aftereffect. *Percept. Mot. Skills,* **23,** 1003–8 (1966)

358. Suzuki, Y., Ueno, H., Tada, H. Effect of sensory deprivation upon perceptual function. *Tohoku Psychol. Folia*, **25**, 24–30 (1966)

359. Sweeney, D. R. Pain reactivity and kinesthetic aftereffect. *Percept. Mot. Skills*, **22**, 763–69 (1966)

360. Takasaki, H. Lightness change of grays induced by change in reflectance of gray background. *J. Opt. Soc. Am.*, **56**, 504–9 (1966)

361. Takasaki, H. Chromatic changes induced by changes in chromaticity of background of constant lightness. *J. Opt. Soc. Am.*, **57**, 93–96 (1967)

362. Tanaka, Y., Uemura, Y., Torii, S. Decrease and increase in test-threshold luminance induced by a contiguous annular field. *Percept. Mot. Skills*, **24**, 1319–26 (1967)

363. Tees, R. C., More, L. K. Identical figures, exposure time and disappearance phenomena under reduced stimulation conditions. *Psychon. Sci.*, **6**, 289–90 (1966)

364. Teller, D. Y., Galanter, E. Brightnesses, luminances and Fechner's paradox. *Percept. Psychophys.*, **2**, 297–300 (1967)

365. Templeton, W. B., Howard, I. P., Lowman, A. E. Passively generated adaptation to prismatic distortion. *Percept. Mot. Skills*, **22**, 140–42 (1966)

366. Thetford, P. E., Klemme, M. E. Arousal and Necker Cube reversals. *Psychol. Rec.*, **17**, 201–8 (1967)

367. Thines, G., Jenart, A. La structure phenomenale des mouvements circulaires: Influence de la distance radiale et de la fixation visuelle sur la perception de la rotation et de la pivotation. *J. Psychol. Norm. Pathol.*, **64**, 9–40 (1967)

368. Thomae, H., Ed. *Handbuch der Psychologie*, 1. Band, Allgemeine Psychologie, 1. Halbband. (Verlag für Psychologie, Dr. C. Hogrefe, Göttingen, 1179 pp., 1966)

369. Thomas, D. R., Lyons, J. The interaction between sensory and tonic factors in the perception of the vertical in pigeons. *Percept. Psychophys.*, **1**, 93–95 (1966)

370. Thor, D., Crawford, L. Time perception during two-week confinement: Influence of age, sex, I.Q. and time of day. *Acta Psychol.*, **22**, 78–84 (1964)

371. Thurmond, J. B., Alluisi, E. A. An extension of the information-deductive analysis of form. *Psychon. Sci.*, **7**, 157–58 (1967)

372. Ueno, H. Particular way of perceiving body in persons who have disease image: From the point of view of body boundary theory. *Tohoku Psychol. Folia*, **25**, 91–96 (1967)

373. Uhr, L. *Pattern Recognition*. (Wiley, New York, 1966)

374. Vatter, O. Die Empfindungen rauh, weich und glatt, ihr adäquater Reiz und seine Messung. *Psychol. Beiträge*, **6**, 51–80 (1961)

375. Vaught, G. M., Augustson, B. Field-dependence and form discrimination in males. *Psychon. Sci.*, **8**, 233–34 (1967)

376. Vernon, M. D. *Experiments in Visual Perception* (Penguin Books, Baltimore, 1966)

377. Virsu, V. Note on the systematic error of estimation as a function of stimulus magnitude. *Scand. J. Psychol.*, **7**, 76–80 (1966)

378. Virsu, V. Contrast and confluxion as components in geometric illusions. *Quart. J. Exptl. Psychol.*, **19**, 198–207 (1967)

379. Virsu, V. Geometric illusions, I. Effect of figural type, instruction, and pre- and intertrial training on magnitude and decrement of illusion. *Scand. J. Psychol.*, **8**, 161–71 (1967)

380. Virsu, V. Geometric illusions as categorization effects: A system of interpretation. *Ann. Acad. Sci. Fenn.*, Helsinki, B 154, **2**, 1–73 (1968)

381. Wallace, G. K. The effect of background on the Zöllner illusion. *Acta Psychol.*, **25**, 373–80 (1966)

382. Warren, R. M. Quantitative judgments of color: The square root rule. *Percept. Psychophys.*, **2**, 448–51 (1967)

383. Warren, R. M., Poulton, E. C. Lightness of grays: Effects of background reflectance. *Percept. Psychophys.*, **1**, 145–48 (1966)

384. Wathen-Dunn, W., Ed. *Models for the Perception of Speech and Visual Form* (M.I.T. Press, Cambridge, 1967)

385. Webster, R. B. Stimulus characteristics and effects of fill, distortion, and noise on pattern perception. *Percept. Mot. Skills*, **23**, 19–33 (1966)

386. Weckroth, J. Studies in colour after-

images. *Ann. Acad. Sci. Fenn.*, Helsinki, **1**, 134 (1964)

387. Weene, P., Held, R. Changes in perceived size of angle as a function of orientation in the frontal plane. *J. Exptl. Psychol.*, **71**, 55–59 (1966)

388. Weintraub, D., Walker, E. *Perception* (Brooks-Cole, Belmont, Calif., 103 pp., 1966)

389. Weisstein, N. Backward masking and models of perceptual processing. *J. Exptl. Psychol.*, **72**, 232–40 (1966)

390. White, B. L. An experimental approach to the effects of experience on early human behavior. In *Minnesota Symposium on Child Psychology*, **1**, 201–25 (Hill, J. P., Ed., Univ. Minnesota Press, Minneapolis, 1967)

391. Whyman, A. D., Moos, R. H. Time perception and anxiety. *Percept. Mot. Skills*, **24**, 567–70 (1967)

392. Wieland, B. A., Mefferd, R. B., Jr. Effect of orientation, inclination, and length of diagonal of Necker cubes on perspective dominance. *Percept. Mot. Skills*, **24**, 139–41 (1967)

393. Wieland, B. A., Mefferd, R. B., Jr. Effects of orientation, inclination and length of diagonal on reversal

rate of Necker cube. *Ibid.*, **23**, 823–26 (1966)

394. Wieland, B. A., Mefferd, R. B., Jr. Individual differences in Necker cube reversal rates and perspective dominance. *Ibid.*, **24**, 923–30 (1967)

395. Wilman, C. W. *Seeing and Perceiving* (Pergamon, New York, 1966)

396. Winnick, W. A., Rosen, B. E. Shape-slant relations under reduction conditions. *Percept. Psychophys.*, **1**, 157–60 (1966)

397. von Wright, J. On qualitative changes in the retention of forms. *Scand. J. Psychol.*, **5**, 65–70 (1964)

398. von Wright, J., Mikkonen, V. Changes in repeated reproduction of weight as a function of adaptation level. *Scand. J. Psychol.*, **5**, 239–48 (1964)

399. Yarbus, A. L. *Eye Movements and Vision* (Plenum, New York, 222 pp., 1967)

400. Yilmaz, H. Perceptual invariance and the psychophysical law. *Percept. Psychophys.*, **2**, 533–38 (1967)

401. Zapparoli, G. C. Perception of simultaneous stroboscopic movements in different directions and the Gestalt theory hypothesis of physiological short-circuiting. *Acta Psychol.*, **26**, 189–201 (1967)

COLOR VISION[1]

135

By H. Ripps[2]

*Department of Ophthalmology, New York University
School of Medicine, New York*

AND

R. A. Weale

*Institute of Ophthalmology
University of London, London, England*

The description of sensory processes involves an understanding of the mechanisms whereby the physical characteristics of a stimulus are transformed into a nervous message, and how this information is represented and modified at every stage in the afferent pathway. With regard to the mechanisms subserving color vision, our understanding of their functional properties continues to be enhanced by subjective studies. However, to identify the physical counterparts of these mechanisms and their mode of action requires contributions from many disciplines—anatomy, biochemistry, and physiology—each of which in recent years has advanced our knowledge of the underlying processes.

The topic of color vision is, therefore, of interest to a variety of students, and all we can hope to accomplish in a relatively brief review is to point to the research areas which are being pursued most actively and direct the reader's attention to papers that are quantitative in nature.

General References

Some of the books dealing with color vision contain much up-to-date information. Wyszecki & Stiles (266) have published a mammoth compendium which offers answers to virtually any question likely to arise in practice. *Vision and Visual Perception*, edited by Graham (94) covers much of color vision theory and experiment and can be recommended to any student of the subject. A symposium on Color Vision, held in London, England, in 1964, under the auspices of the CIBA Foundation, has been edited by de Reuck & Knight (59) and deals with recent research in some detail. Kalmus (119) has written *Diagnosis and Genetics of Defective Colour Vision*, a book that may be recommended more strongly for its genetic aspect than for its basic color physiology. The second edition of Pirenne's *Vision and the Eye* (172) contains three brief chapters on color vision, and Weale's *From Sight to Light*

---

[1] The survey of literature pertaining to this review was concluded in March 1968.

[2] Supported by an Award (5-K3-NB 18, 766) from the National Institute of Neurological Diseases and Blindness, U.S. Public Health Service.

(242) contains a longer chapter which is intended to bring the subject within the grasp of the scientific layman. *Recent Progress in Photobiology* (edited by Bowen) contains several papers on color vision presented at the Fourth International Congress in Photobiology (23), and the proceedings of the Journées Internationales de Couleurs, held in 1965 in Lucerne, Switzerland, have been collated in one issue of *Die Farbe* (179). A splendid collection of sundry lectures, some of which concern color vision, was published by Wright (263) under the title *The Rays are not Coloured*. Bridges gives a lucid account of visual photochemistry in *Comprehensive Biochemistry* edited by Florkin & Stotz (29), and recent review articles by Judd (118), Luria (141), MacNichol (148), Riggs (180, 181), Stiles (213), and Wald (230) provide an excellent survey of theory and research in color vision.

OBJECTIVE STUDIES

Receptors, waveguides, and directional sensitivity.—On morphological grounds, the classical distinction between rods and cones continues to be questioned by Pedler (169), although the concept remains quite useful and studies of directional properties tend to maintain it (10, 252).

Dowling (68) has measured from electron micrographs the dimensions of the foveal cones in rhesus monkey. He finds that whereas the outer segments are indeed rod-like in shape, the inner segments taper gradually from about 2.5 to 3.0 μ at the base to an apical diameter of 1.5 μ. Although Dowling suggests that this may account for funneling of light by cones to increase the apparent photosensitivities of their pigments, funneling is believed to be unnecessary by Weale (243) who finds that rod and cone pigments are approximately equal in this respect.

Funneling and other optical properties associated with receptor shape are frequently invoked to explain the directional sensitivity of the cones (Stiles-Crawford effect) and its absence in rods. But there seems to be no significant difference in shape between foveal cones and extrafoveal rods; the outer segments of both are without taper and "The inner segments of the foveal cones markedly resemble rod inner-segments" (68). That shape may be a factor, however, is supported by Westheimer's (252) demonstration that parafoveal cones, which do have tapered outer segments, have a more pronounced directional sensitivity than those in the fovea.

Snyder and his colleagues (19, 204–207) have ingeniously applied waveguide theory to the problem of cone response but failed to explain why rods do not mediate color vision and why cone density spectra can be measured in a direction perpendicular to the axis of the receptor, e.g., in goldfish (149). Furthermore, much of the theory devolves on the alleged cone taper (204), on which we have commented above.

Spectrophotometry.—In comparison with the previous triennial review period, this has been a meager time for the photochemistry of cone pigments. For reasons which are still obscure, attempts to extract light-sensitive ma-

terial from vertebrate cones have been notably unsuccessful, even when the
pure-cone retinae of grass snake and iguana were used (29). One of the few
exceptions is iodopsin, obtained from the retinae of Gallinaceous birds (52,
231) and exhaustively studied by Yoshizawa & Wald (270).

Cyanopsin, a red-sensitive pigment ($\lambda_{max} = 620$ nm) synthesized previously by combining the protein fraction of chicken iodopsin ($\lambda_{max} = 562$ nm)
with a *cis* isomer of retinal$_2$ (235), was shown by microspectrophotometry to
be present in isolated cones of the tadpole retina (136). After metamorphosis,
however, the retina of the adult frog contains retinal$_1$, and the λ_{max} of its cone
pigment shifts from 620 nm to 570 nm. This interesting experiment again
demonstrates how one visual pigment can be transformed into another
through natural changes in the chemical structure of its prosthetic group [see
also Dartnall & Lythgoe (54)]. It should be emphasized, however, that
equally dramatic alterations in the spectral properties of visual pigments
are effected by differences as yet undefined in the opsin moiety of the pigment. Indeed, the rod and cone pigments of human vision apparently are
formed by joining a single chromophore (11-*cis* retinal$_1$) to a variety of opsins
(36).

Difference spectra measured *in vivo* with a 20' field at the human central
fovea lead to the suggestion that the red-sensitive pigment absorbs maximally at 580 to 590 nm, and evidence for products of bleaching and a blue-
sensitive pigment was obtained (244).

Except for another small sampling from the human parafovea (234),
there have been no recent reports on the microspectrophotometry of single
cone receptors in the primate retina. Such measurements have yet to be
made on foveal cones, and there are still a number of uncertainties concerning the spectral properties of the cone pigments, their *in situ* densities, and
products of bleaching (183), It is clear that the technique is fraught with
difficulties; possible sources of error have been suggested by Ripps & Weale
(183), Enoch (72, 75) and Villermet & Weale (228).

The early receptor potential (ERP).—This very rapid biphasic electrical
response to an intense light flash (34) is still poorly understood, as is true of
all electroretinal potentials, but it appears to result from charge displacements within the lamellae of the outer segments, perhaps on the oriented
visual pigment molecules themselves (9, 31, 47, 99). As such it may provide a
valuable tool for the study of receptor function. However, a recordable ERP
requires the bleaching of large numbers of pigment molecules throughout the
retina. It is not surprising, therefore, that the action spectrum for the ERP
of the all-cone ground squirrel retina (168) does not reveal underlying spectral mechanisms that are detected by behavioral (50) and other electrophysiological (49, 152) methods. What is surprising is that the ERP recorded
from the mixed retina of the frog appears to be generated almost exclusively
by the cone system. Moreover, Kühne's observation regarding the necessity
for the juxtaposition of the retina and pigment epithelium if regeneration of

rhodopsin is to occur is contrasted by measurements on the recovery of the ERP after bleaching, which indicate that the cone pigment(s) in this species regenerate in the isolated retina separated from its pigment epithelium (88).

Intracellular receptor potentials.—An alternative to microspectrophotometry for determining the spectral sensitivities of cone pigments is to record directly the light-evoked electrical responses of individual receptors. Tomita et al. (221), using an ingenious technique for impaling the isolated retina with a micropipette, succeeded in recording from the inner segments of single cones in the carp; response characteristics as well as electrophoretic marking (121) confirmed the recording site. Three spectral response curves were measured, their maxima (462, 529, and 611 nm) in reasonably good agreement with the density spectra of single goldfish cones (137, 149). However, in regard to the relative distribution of cone types, there are gross differences between estimates based on single cell recordings and those culled from microspectrophotometry. Enoch's (73, 74) technique for identifying active receptors histochemically, combined with selective chromatic bleaching, may prove useful in resolving some of these discrepancies.

S-potentials.—The comfortable tripigmental picture that emerged from the researches cited above was rudely shaken almost before the paint had dried when Naka & Rushton (158–160) produced evidence that four cone pigments contribute to the responses recorded from the retinae of tench, a close relative of carp and goldfish. Analysis of S-potentials from color units indicated that these units receive contributions from three cone pigments, the wavelength maxima of which are located at 680 nm, at 540 to 560 nm and in the "blue," respectively; and in the case of units responding only by hyperpolarization (L-units) there is an additional one, maximally sensitive at 620 nm. While the claim of the 680 nm curve to pigment status is buttressed by color mixing data obtained on one element responding well for 45 min, additional evidence for a far-red receptor was obtained in the carp retina by Witkovsky in both S-potential (257) and electroretinographic (258) recordings, although in both instances maximal sensitivity occurred at shorter wavelengths (660 to 665 nm). It is noteworthy that the action spectra of carp ganglion cells (257, 259) show nothing exciting at 680 nm; as Naka & Rushton's data are probably a true bill, the effect of their new "pigment" appears to have vanished before impulses leave the retina.

Although S-potentials have been studied extensively and can be recorded from a large number of vertebrate retinae, little is known of their functional significance. The observation that the polarity of some S-potentials is wavelength dependent (C-units) led to the view that they were responsible, at least in part, for the coding of color information within the retina. Those S-units which give a unidirectional potential (hyperpolarizing) in response to all wavelengths (L-units) were presumed to be involved in signaling luminosity. However, a detailed comparison of S-potential and ganglion cell properties in the same retina (carp) demonstrated that the ganglion cells responded independently of S-potentials for every parameter tested, i.e., wave length, intensity, background field, light-and-dark adaptation, and selective adaptation to colored lights (257). Thus, although C-units may be "looking" at some ongoing opponent-color processing within the retina, it seems that they neither influence nor transmit this information to the neurons responsible for conducting the visual message to the brain. In this respect, S-units behave much like glial cells in the optic nerve of *Necturus* (167) which do not alter the optic nerve discharge either chemically or electrically.

The anatomical basis of S-potentials.—Although a discussion of retinal histology is outside the scope of this review [for a detailed analysis of retinal organization in primates, see Dowling & Boycott (69)], much current interest in the structures intervening between the receptor- and ganglion-cell layers (42, 70, 211, 269) seems to have been aroused by the fact that within this region reside the cells responsible for generating S-potentials. Because of the peculiar properties of these responses (77, 161, 220), it has been suggested that the cells from which they originate are of a special class, intermediate between neuron and glia (77, 195). On the other hand, Dowling and his co-workers (69, 71) are of the opinion that both horizontal and amacrine cells [thought to be the sources of L- and C-responses, respectively (77)] are true interneurons, lacking axons but capable of receiving and transmitting information between those neurons with which their processes make reciprocal synaptic contacts. They suggest further that the amacrine cells, owing to their location, the extent of their processes, and the types of cells they contact, i.e., bipolar, ganglion, and other amacrine cells, are probably involved in mediating peripheral receptive field organization and influencing the responses of color-coded ganglion cells. However, in view of the results cited in the previous section, a good deal more experimental evidence is needed before correlations between structure and function can be established.

The electroretinogram (ERG).—Several investigators (1, 8, 32) have demonstrated the feasibility of recording photopic ERG's from localized regions of the human retina by using bright, steady background illumination to suppress the effects of stray light (27), and summating large numbers of responses in order to extract the extremely weak electroretinal signals from the overriding noise level (12). But despite having summed more than 2800 successive responses to intermittent stimulation, Brindley & Westheimer (32) were able to elicit only a barely detectable ERG from the human fovea, and this differed considerably in waveform from responses of the extrafoveal retina [cf. Brown & Watanabe (35)]. With similar experimental methods, Aiba, Alpern & Maaseidvaag (1) showed that the ERG spectral sensitivity of the central retina agrees reasonably well with subjective measurements of foveal thresholds. However, in view of the foregoing, and the relatively greater short-wavelength sensitivity of the ERG function, it is unlikely that the electrical responses they recorded were derived principally from stimulation of foveal cones.

Granda & Biersdorf (96) have shown that the spectral sensitivity functions for *a*- and *b*-wave responses obtained early in the course of dark adaptation are essentially scotopic, but there is evidence that perhaps two photopic mechanisms are also involved; the contributions of the latter diminish with time in darkness.

A unique method of stimulation involving rapid phase changes in a grating (the pattern consisting of alternate bright and dim stripes of a given wavelength) enabled Johnson, Riggs & Schick (115) to obtain photopic sensitivity functions in substantial agreement with subjective data. When the method was modified to one wherein the alternate bars were of different wavelengths, it was possible to compute a set of trichromatic coefficients (182) that are unlike the conventional concept in that they refer to response (ERG) amplitude ratios rather than stimulus relations (all the stimuli are equiluminant). The technique has clearly demonstrated a system of chromatic discrimination at the retinal level: if the responses in question can be shown to be part of the visual process rather than epiphenomena, color discrimination exists where it would be expected to belong on grounds of economics of transmission lines.

Burkhardt (37) has shown that the ERG spectral sensitivity of the dark-adapted goldfish eye diverges from the extinction curve of its rod pigment. In the light-adapted state, contributions from two photopic mechanisms (neither maximal at 680 nm) can be distinguished. However, since the photopic sensitivity function could not be derived by assuming simple additivity of the underlying cone mechanisms, Burkhardt is of the opinion that neural interaction operates on the trichromatic (receptoral) message in a region distal to that responsible for the ERG [but cf. Riggs, Johnson & Schick (182)].

Tigges, Brooks & Klee (219) find no evidence of scotopic function in the ERG of the diurnal tree shrew. Although selective adaptation was not attempted, the ERG spectral sensitivity function (maximal at about 552 nm) indicates the presence of at least two photopic mechanisms in this species. By contrast, two types of spectral response observed in the lateral eye of *Limulus* (240) are so different in nature that it is hard to see how they can provide a basis for color discrimination.

Using low voltage criteria ($\leq 10\,\mu$V) for threshold determinations, Granda & Stirling (97) obtained triple-humped ERG spectral sensitivity curves for the dark-adapted turtle. But since the sensitivity at the tectum is relatively so much higher in the blue part of the spectrum (98) than that measured with the ERG, they believe there may be a proliferation of afferent channels carrying short-wavelength signals.

Some doubt as to the visual significance of the electroretinogram is raised in a study by Hamasaki & Bridges (102). By exposing the fully dark-adapted shark eye to an intense flash, they induced a state of refractoriness in the ERG such that a second identical flash, delivered as much as 5 sec after the first, failed to evoke a recordable ERG. But during this phase of ERG suppression, little or no reduction was observed in the response of the optic tectum.

Separate rod and cone components can be identified (based on waveform and latency) in responses recorded from the monkey eye with vitreal and intra-retinal electrodes (92). When the two systems are stimulated simultaneously, there is no evidence of significant rod-cone interaction in the ERG, i.e., the resultant waveform represents approximately the algebraic sum of the short-latency photopic potential and the long-latency scotopic potential. Thus, the temporal differences between rod- and cone-potentials are preserved in the electroretinogram and determine their respective times of arrival at the ganglion cell.

Ganglion cell.—Several recent studies emphasize the diversity of ganglion cell responses. Using contiguous stimulus fields (central spots with annular surrounds), Daw (57, 58) finds that the majority of color-coded ganglion cells in the goldfish retina are geared to carry information relating to simultaneous color contrast. Such cells are, for example, preferentially excited by red light in the center and excited also by green light in the periphery; the maximal discharge rate is achieved by the simultaneous presentation of center and surround. Spectral sensitivity measurements on a variety of ganglion-cell types revealed only red-sensitive ($\lambda_{max} \approx 525$ nm) units; the absence of blue-sensitive units is attributed to the paucity of blue-sensitive cones in the goldfish retina (28). Daw's experiments provide an excellent basis for contrast phenomena (151, 222), but whether similar effects can be demonstrated in primates remains to be seen [cf. Wiesel & Hubel (256)].

Interest in the properties of the pure cone retina of the ground squirrel has been maintained: mapping of the retinal receptive fields at the level of the optic nerve revealed "protanopic" characteristics in that green, yellow, or red light elicited the same type of response; i.e., there was never any red-green antagonism (152). However, a unit could be excited by one of these colors and inhibited by blue, and vice versa. Thus, there is electrophysiological as well as behavioral (50) evidence that the ground squirrel can distinguish blue from other colors.

Gouras & Link (93) and Gouras (90, 91) find that although rod and cone signals may converge on the same ganglion cell, the latter cannot transmit both simultaneously. Rather, its response is determined on a first-come, first-served basis. Consequently, after light-adaptation, or when the stimulus exceeds cone threshold, the faster cone response appears to be solely responsible for ganglion-cell excitation.

Central stations.—Records from the superior colliculus of the squirrel monkey obtained simultaneously with ERG's (260) show that blue and red stimuli, "matched for delivered intensity at the cornea," produce very different collicular potentials even though the shapes (but not the amplitudes) of the ERG's are similar. In the absence of sensitivity data, the claim that differential color responses are involved is clearly unsubstantiated.

De Valois and his collaborators (60–62) have continued their pioneer studies of post-synaptic responses in the lateral geniculate body of macaque. Opponent cells, which are excited by some wavelengths and inhibited by others, have been classified (61) into four types: each opponent pair (R–G,

B–Y) has a mirror image that responds in opposite fashion but with the same spectral sensitivity. These cells, which are much more sensitive to wavelength variation than to changes in luminance, appear to be carrying color information. Analysis of opponent-cell responses to wavelength shifts enabled De Valois, Abramov & Mead (62) to compute a wavelength discrimination function which was in qualitative but not quantitative agreement with behavioral results obtained on the macaque.

The spectral sensitivity of non-opponent units, which respond to intensity but not wavelength, follows approximately the CIE photopic function. Since these cells appear to carry information as to brightness, it was hypothesized that in the wavelength region where non-opponent cells are most responsive (i.e., 560 to 580 nm), colors would be less saturated than at the extremes of the spectrum. By determining the ratios of the sensitivities of opponent and non-opponent cells at various wavelengths, it was possible to derive a saturation discrimination function in good agreement with results for human observers (61).

Our knowledge of information processing in the lateral geniculate body of monkey has been advanced in several important respects by Wiesel & Hubel (256). By varying the state of adaptation, the size and color of the stimulus field, and the locus of stimulation, they identified three main cell types, distinguished by the nature of their responses to the various parameters. Some cells are concerned mainly with form, others with color, but the majority are sensitive to both variables. However, the authors were unable to find the type of cell required for signalling color contrast, e.g., one which gives an excitatory response when the center of its receptive field is stimulated by a particular color and a similar response to stimulation of the surround field by the complementary color. But a few complex cells which seem analogous to the color-contrast detectors of the goldfish (58) have been found in the monkey striate cortex (103).

Analysis of lateral geniculate responses to stimulation of the dark-adapted eye shows that few cells receive any input from the rod mechanism even when the stimulus field extends 10° from the fovea (256). In fact, none of the units appears to be connected exclusively to rods; cells of the lateral geniculate receive their input from rods and cones, or cones only. In view of these findings it is hardly surprising that the photopic system dominates the evoked cortical response (see below).

Jones (116) has probed the lateral geniculate body of the nocturnal owl monkey *Aotes* in a vain attempt to locate spectrally opponent cells. However, the spectral sensitivities of non-opponent units and the displacement of their maxima by selective adaptation suggests that they are subserved by more than one spectral mechanism. It is interesting to note in this connection that electrophysiological evidence of photopic function in *Aotes* has been convincingly demonstrated (101, 117), and histological sections of its retina reveal the presence of cone receptors in both central and peripheral regions (78, 101).

The opponent-response pattern so characteristic of wavelength-sensitive units in the primate lateral geniculate body does not appear to be a dominant feature of cells in the visual cortex of the Mangabey monkey (135). Except for a few units which respond in an opponent-color fashion, cortical units representing the central retina exhibit only excitatory "on" responses. Since these are maximally sensitive in the red, green and blue regions of the spectrum, the author hypothesizes that the cortical responses reflect primarily the "on" activity of the various "on-off" geniculate units. But at what stage are the "off" responses suppressed?

It now seems firmly established that evoked potentials, recorded from the scalp overlying the visual cortex, reveal primarily the activity of photopic systems (11, 170, 173). The area-intensity relation, directional properties, and the spectral sensitivity of the human fovea can be determined from analysis of evoked potentials, and these functions agree remarkably well with subjective data obtained with equivalent stimulus conditions (64).

Burkhardt & Riggs (38) have shown that adaptation to various background colors, adjusted for each subject to give equal photopic luminosity, differentially affects the amplitude and latency of cortical responses to intermittent chromatic stimuli. These results and those of Shipley, Jones & Fry (197) suggest that it may soon be possible to determine the spectral sensitivities of mechanisms which contribute to the evoked potentials.

SUBJECTIVE STUDIES

Threshold energies: adaptation and contrast.—A comparison was made of the spectral function of the absolute foveal threshold and that for homochromatic contrast (39). The detection of an incremental flash 32 per cent more intense than the background is relatively harder at the extremes of the spectrum than at 550 nm, and this must mean that the change of criterion from "detecting light" to "detecting additional light" involves a change in effective receptor participation. A consideration of the fluctuations of color appearance near absolute threshold enabled Krauskopf & Srebro (130) to derive spectral functions for two-color mechanisms with maxima at 545 and 578 nm respectively. An extension of the zone theory to include the effects of chromatic adaptation made it possible to show that whereas the green and red fundamental response curves peak at 550 and 595 nm respectively, the λ_{max} for a deuteranomalous observer are 550 and 600 nm; the latter curve shows a shoulder at 550 nm (239). Recovery of anomaloscopic settings following foveal adaptation to red light suggests that protanomaly involves a factor other than dilution of the red pigment; Baker (13) also concludes that adaptation must involve a process other than the accumulation of cone pigment.

Boynton & Das (24) have stressed that the most effective direct visual stimulus is compact from the point of view of space, time and spectral bandwidth, but that the reverse holds for adapting stimuli. Such considerations lead to the question of interaction among chromatic mechanisms, and such interaction has received extensive attention. The most penetrating study was made by Boynton, Ikeda & Stiles (26), who distinguished six types of interaction and found evidence for all of them, although that for probability summation may need reinforcing. The experimental basis for this study is provided by the two-color threshold situation on which there are grafted negative increments in addition to the positive ones, adapting in addition to stimuli, and the use of a low and high level of adaptation. More recent experiments (25) suggest that Stiles' $\pi 4$ and $\pi 5$ mechanisms are compound mechanisms subject to the effects of subliminal integration; as Rushton (189) has identified $\pi 5$ with his erythrolabe these findings hold out interesting prospects for the future. Following Alpern (5), who showed that in the case of metacontrast there is no interaction between rods and cones, Alpern & Rushton (7) found that $\pi 1$, $\pi 4$, and $\pi 5$ act completely independently in this phenomenon. But Richards et al. (178) observed that the spectral sensitivities of inhibiting and inhibited receptors were dissimilar at suprathreshold levels, and when the data of Burkhardt & Whittle (39) are recalled, the results indicate that interaction between different receptor types is manifest under appropriate experimental conditions [cf. also (28)].

Terstiege (217) studied the effects of chromatic adaptation with a monocular color-matching procedure and showed that von Kries' coefficient law fails following substantial photolysis. Like Brindley (30) and Walraven & Bouman (237), he is led to postulate cone pigment densities of 0.8 to 0.9. However, his adapting illuminations, which reached up to 5.4×10^6 td, were such as to cause, in all probability, at least transient damage to the retina (165, 245). Terstiege doubts whether adaptive procedures can be used for the determination of fundamental response curves. Moreover, receptor mechanisms participating in the establishment of Rayleigh matches lead to protanomalous readings when the pigment density is diminished, but to deuteranomalous ones when it is enhanced. If these data can be validated and confirmed, they will usefully extend the aforementioned studies done at lower retinal illuminations.

Akita & Graham (2) measured the change in test wavelength needed to counteract the contrast effect induced by different background colors: clearly the required shift must be in the sense of the inducing color. If two luminance levels are studied, a Bezold-Brücke effect is revealed. The matching of Munsell color samples on chromatic backgrounds, so chosen that only one of Judd's "primary" response mechanisms is altered, gives rise to contrast (216) which manifests a "crispening" of the mechanism. Brown & Ranken (33) studied the properties of the colors induced in a central white area by chromatic surrounds and matched the induced colors binocularly. There is a high correlation between the saturations of inducing and induced colors, an observation confirming Scheibner's (190) expression of Grassmann's third law in set-theoretical terms. Evans (76) fixed a monochromatic inducing field (10°) and a central white (1°) field to a calculated luminance of 100 mL. The eye adapted to these fields for 0.5 to 2 min when maximum color contrast ap-

peared. Then the luminance of the central field was reduced when desaturation of the contrast occurred. Next, its luminance was raised until the desaturation just disappeared. In all cases the original settings were obtained;
whence it follows that in this range the relation between the luminance of the
test field and the desaturation of the induced colors produced therein is
strictly reversible. The retinal location of these effects has been partly eluci-
dated by De Valois & Walraven (63), who studied chromatic contrast binocularly: when one eye was exposed to a high-intensity red stimulus, this eye
would see all wavelengths between 480 and 600 nm as a supersaturated green,
but the other eye saw the region around 500 to 510 nm as completely color-
less. The dilemma of explaining this on the assumption that red and green
signals complement each other, whereas in the ipsilateral case there appears
to be no red signal, was resolved by a comparison of spectral test fields which
were smaller than or equal to the adapting field. The postulate of lateral inhibition leads to the view that color contrast is a retinal phenomenon [cf.
Daw (58)].

A lateral effect also underlies the Mach phenomenon. Matthews (151)
concludes that the bands do not involve an achromatic visual mechanism,
but Van der Horst & Bouman (222) are led to the opposite view. Cavonius
(40) and Cavonius & Schumacher (41) obtained from visual acuity measurements clear evidence to show that there is little, if any, interaction between
wavelength and contrast. This conclusion, clearly at variance with the data
of Thomson (218) and Kelly (122), is to be interpreted in terms of the relatively limited luminance range to which the tests were confined. Walraven
(236) and Miller (153) showed that the Stiles-Crawford effect increases following intense light-adaptation: the recovery from this increase has a half-
time of 30 sec, which leads Walraven to the belief that the underlying element is pigment regeneration. Since he assumes that cone pigments absorb 80
per cent at their λ_{max} and his adapting light was such as to reduce this value
only to some 70 per cent, enormous effects would necessarily be expected
when bleaching is more nearly total [cf. Ripps & Weale (184)].

Vos (229) and Kishto (128) believe that the operation of the Stiles-Crawford effect underlies the well-known color-stereoscopic effect wherein some
colors appear to stand out in front of others.

In experiments involving essentially nonfoveal regions, Weissman (250)
determined the red-green ratios corresponding to the perception of red or
green at retinal eccentricities reaching up to 18° in the upper vertical meri-
dian, luminance providing a parameter within the limits of 0.01 and 0.3 ft-L.
The highest level provides for the stablest conditions. Moreland (154, 155)
has consolidated his study of the blue-arc phenomenon and shown conclusively that cone action can elicit it, but a rod contribution cannot be excluded. The effect is attributed to secondary electrical excitation [cf. also
Alpern & Dudley (6)].

Spatial and temporal effects.—Ruddock (187) studied both wavelength
and intensity discrimination as a function of stimulus subtense and exposure

time. The circular test and comparison fields sandwiched the fixation area and their centers were separated by 40′. As the smallest was 4.5′ and the largest 36′ in diameter, some rods may have been stimulated when light of 490 nm was used (the other test wavelength was 590 nm). Luminance discrimination improved as the test size increased, particularly at long viewing times. The variation of this step with exposure time was complex, rising to a maximum for $t \approx 50$ msec, the rise being attributed to the Broca-Sulzer buildup, whereas the subsequent drop may result from time averaging. Wavelength discrimination $\Delta\lambda$ ($\lambda = 590$ nm) varied inversely with the luminance and with the stimulus area, and more so for $\lambda = 490$ nm. Its temporal function showed a constant level for $t \approx 50$ msec, and a decrease in $\Delta\lambda$ thereafter; its value appears to become independent of stimulus area when $t \approx 2$ sec.

Wright (261) observed that the scaling of color differences is independent of hue and exposure time when the latter exceeds 1 sec. At exposure times of less than 230 msec this was no longer true, but red evoked "a relatively stronger sensation."

Siegel's data (200), expressed in terms of the standard deviation of spectral matching of $\lambda = 575$ nm, are consistent with these results. It is, therefore, not surprising that the appearance of colored stimuli should vary with their exposure time: brief exposures (50 msec) tend to desaturate all except bluish-green stimuli both in the fovea and in the parafovea (123). Again, while the underlying photometry is open to discussion, a study by Luria & Weissman (143) on the visibility of colors in binary stimuli shows the following points: the red-green ratio for the detection of red is constant for exposures between 20 and 300 msec and foveal presentation. It varies inversely with t for 6° off center, but increases with t for seeing green both at the fovea and at 6°. The yellow-blue ratio for seeing yellow behaves like the red-green ratio for red at 6°, but both the foveal and the parafoveal data for blue show the yellow-blue ratio to be minimal at $t > 100$ msec. Luria (142) showed that a Bezold-Brücke phenomenon can be mimicked by varying time instead of luminance and suggests that small-field tritanopia, shown by Wald (232) to be confined to a smaller foveal area than thought correct heretofore, is really a special form of small-energy tritanopia [cf. also (251)].

Temporal factors also enter the problem of summation. Thus Ikeda (107) showed that probability summation can operate for an exposure time of 12.5 msec but ceases when $t = 100$ msec: the breakdown occurs at a value of t varying inversely with the adapting luminance. The amount and quality of color induction naturally varies with the time interval between the onset of the inducing and test stimulus respectively: the saturation of the colors induced by blue and green stimuli is maximal when the eye is first presented with the foveal neutral test area, and if the order is reversed, the apparent brightness is reduced (125).

It is arguable whether ordinary summation can account for the effects observed by Bartley and his collaborators (14, 15, 17) during intermittent stimulation. Working as they do with a frequency of 9.8 c/sec, the actual exposure time varies from 0.0003 to 0.076 sec as the pulse/cycle fraction (P/C) is varied. This barely overlaps the span of the above-mentioned researches (123, 187, 200, 261). Thus, as the P/C is reduced a red stimulus becomes desaturated for all field sizes in the range of 0.75° to 6°. A marked hue shift was reported: intermittency made 650 nm turn even yellowish green (≈ 550 nm). The authors' surprise (17) at this finding is based on the belief that only one cone pigment is activated above 650 nm; this is unlikely (246). However, desaturation is more marked for $\lambda = 500$ nm, particularly at high luminance levels. These studies almost certainly link up also with after-images arising during intermittent stimulation, and Wheeler & LaForce (255) examined the effects of disk rotation, stimulus chromaticity, and luminance on the appearance of the Bidwell effect. They showed it to be much more complex than the usual classroom demonstration would lead one to expect: at some speeds two colors could be observed. When isochromatic rather than complementary sensations were reported, the shift was toward yellow-green; the data are interpreted in terms of opponent-color theory but clearly demand attention to single flash sensations.

McCullough (145) examined a chromatic after-effect observable when one views a vertical black grating on an orange ground and then a similar adjacent horizontal grating on a blue field. If the two gratings are next viewed on a neutral ground, a blue-green after-effect appears on the vertical grating and an orange one on the horizontal one. It would appear that the retinal edge-detectors are capable of chromatic adaptation.

Color matching and colorimetry.—Shirley (198) designed a grating colorimeter in which the bandwidths of the stimuli offer no improvement over the Wright colorimeter: stray light has been noticed at the spectral ends. Wheeler (253) compared Munsell matches for different combinations of tungsten and chromatic light surrounds and found that the validity of the matches was maximal when the luminance of the surround combination was greater than that of the test sample. Friele (84) has pleaded for standardization: it is not enough that stimulus conditions be reproducible—such a little matter as economics demands that standard observing conditions be proposed, agreed upon, and adopted [cf. also (163)].

It is noteworthy that the mere selection of a forced-choice method introduced a learning effect into a study of induced colors produced during Munsell matching; the learning produced a hue shift (254).

Hailman (100) stresses that it is frequency discrimination, not wavelength discrimination, that should form the quantitative basis for spectral hue differences. The need for coordinates of blackbody radiators below 1000°K has prompted the determination of the absolute zero point of the blackbody locus, which was fortunately found (196) to coincide with the red end of the spectrum locus. Friele (85, 86) produced a formula for discrimination with a green primary at $x = -2.6$, $y = 3.6$, which is at variance with the values of $+3.7000$ and -2.6873 respectively, computed by Walraven & Bouman (238) on the basis of an imaginative use of fluctuation theory. Although both hypotheses have been supported admirably, it has been stressed (247) that agreement on the location of the fundamental green stimulus is of crucial importance for our understanding of the trichromatic theory on the one hand and that of objective data on color defects on the other.

Scheibner (191, 192) studied adaptive color shifts and concluded that the hypothesis of fundamental stimuli with invariant spectral shapes cannot be supported: in particular, the red mechanism is more sensitive to chromatic adaptation than are the others. This would imply that chromatic adaptation operates in more than one zone. Ruddock (188) was able to deduce the spectral characteristics of macular pigment from a comparison of foveal and parafoveal color matches and stressed its significance in observations involving a 10° field. Contrary to earlier views, this pigment does not cease absorbing at 500 nm [cf. Stiles & Burch (215)] but absorbs even at 570 nm. Field trials for the supplementary standard observer were published by Wyszecki & Wright (267) and by Das (55). Both studies have revealed discrepancies between predicted data and observations made with zero, artificial daylight, fluorescent and tungsten surrounds. Matteson & Luria (150) repeated Crawford's (48) comparison of determining color mixture function when the requisite desaturant is provided either by one of the primaries or by white, and they confirmed his results.

Sources of error and variability in color measurement were examined theoretically by Nimeroff (164). These are due to spectroradiometric as well as to stimulus uncertainties. The former give rise to ellipses in several instances much larger than those recorded by MacAdam; the latter show a variability one order in magnitude smaller for intra- than for inter-observer values [cf. also (111)]. The discussion is wholly operational and leaves it to further studies to establish causes for the effects examined. Wyszecki (264, 265) discussed the measurement of color differences with initial reference to gray scales. In regard to the application of analytical expressions, he stresses that industry is more inclined to accept empirical line-elements than inductive ones. A multi-dimensional ratio-scaling method wherein the observer judged ratios of color differences by arranging colored tiles in triads led Wright (262) to the view that the colors tested could be represented by points in a two-dimensional Euclidean space, i.e., color differences were related linearly. Friele's development of the analysis of color discrimination data (87) leads to a better approximation to MacAdam's (144) contour diagram.

A series of papers has appeared on the computerization of colorimetry. On the assumption that the reflectance or transmittance of a sample is linearly related to the concentration of the colorant under test, Allen (3, 4) derived a set of equations with coefficients which, when put in matrix form and inverted, can be used not only for the initial formulation of the matching problem but also for iteration to a better solution. Nimeroff (163) used an automatic computer program for a comparison of uncertainty ellipses derived by two methods: (a) from actual observation in color matches of eleven optical filters made on the Donaldson colorimeter; (b) from data based on the standard observer method of spectrophotometric tristimulus colorimetry. As the corresponding ellipses are similar, Nimeroff concluded that those based on the variances and covariances of the spectral stimulus values of the 10°-standard observer system can be used for the estimation of individual chromaticity uncertainty ellipses. Leete & Lytle (134) describe a digital computer technique enabling one to calculate dominant wavelengths: the spectrum locus is divided into 12 sectors, each of which is described by a polynomial of up to the fourth degree (the degree varying inversely with the local radius of curvature), and the computer merely determines the segment wherein the test color is represented. Foster (79) has produced a set of charts which enables one to derive color differences from colorimetric readings in "seconds rather than minutes."

Color naming and scaling: chromatic discrimination.—In a refreshingly elementary paper, Hunter (105, 106) reviews techniques available for the colorimetric study of glossy surfaces, notably those provided by porcelain enamel. Ishak & van Bussel (111) compared various methods used in color assessment in general and concluded that the magnitude estimation method is as reliable as the binocular matching technique and that a method based on memory matches is inferior to both. On the theoretical side, they deny that Munsell value and chroma are linearly related to lightness and saturation, but they maintain that there is a linear relation between Munsell hue and perceived hue. Indow (109) showed by means of saturation measurements done with a red stimulus (dominant $\lambda = 632$ nm) that saturation is a power function of colorimetric purity. A system of color specification based on just noticeable changes in hue was described by Dimmick (65, 66): it is based on the astonishing idea that the wavelength discrimination curve [cf. (100)] can be represented by five straight lines; one of these is defined by two points, and another extrapolated from $\Delta\lambda = 3$ nm to 10 nm. Hunt (104) described an excellent binocular arrangement suitable for the quantitative description of color appearance and demonstrated the remarkable reproducibility of the data for lightness under widely varying conditions. The instrument is of obvious value, e.g., in processing color photographs.

Among a number of interesting papers dealing with metrological problems, we may mention that color naming at longer wavelengths may become more precise if the response "orange" is not admitted to the vocabulary (212), and the accuracy of color naming responses is reduced when forced choice is extended from two to three possibilities (201). Jameson & Hurvich (114) stress that the apparent colors of stimuli perceived in the perifovea are a function of the color of the fixation spot. When constant stimulus presentation is used, the size of the step influences color sensitivity (203), and the fact that random presentation of stimuli is essential is confirmed (202).

The brightness enhancement of spectral color was studied by Wasserman (241), who related it to the opponent-color hypothesis. He finds that wavelengths of 472, 500 and 574 nm give maximum brightness indices in contours relating equal brightness, flash duration, and wavelength. These spectral regions are identified with the so-called unique colors of blue, green and yellow: the attractiveness of this correlation is somewhat sullied by the absence of an enhancement analogue for unique red.

A statistical study of the appearance of movable colored stabilized stimuli 1 min in diameter and 2° off center enabled Krauskopf (129) to show that the retina contains spatially separable classes of color receptors. Working over a larger retinal extent, Verriest & Israel (225) correlated perimetric data obtained with white, blue, green and red targets with the observer's age and sensitivity function. The results include the very important observation (117) that protanopia is not confined to the fovea.

Chromatic adaptation affects color memory along expected lines (112) as might be predicted from the Bezold-Brücke effect. A study of the latter (113) revealed the existence of two groups of observers for "unique green" (176, 177) who differed by as much as 12 nm at a low luminance level (320 td). The conditioning of color perception was attempted by McCullough (146), who occluded her left eye and kept a split red/blue-green filter over her right one for 75 days. No gaze contingent color differences were observed in this heroic study. As the filters were worn effectively in the pupillary plane, this is hardly surprising.

A chromatic study of figural after-effects suggests that hues can generate after-effects in their own right and that these effects may vary, e.g., when orange is replaced with blue. Ratliff (174, 175) confirmed Shurcliff's earlier observation on green blotches and suggests that their nature is similar to that of yellow ones. As this effect requires the presence of a grating, it would be interesting to know whether or not edge-detectors are involved in its perception [cf. (145)].

Turning to the very applied side of this topic, we may note that Blaise & Laffin (21) advocate the use of violet lights in harbor installations and short-range marine distances. This idiosyncrasy from Gaul forms a silhouette against the data of Das (56) who showed that red is the only color name not associated with a blue stimulus 1′ in diameter at low luminance levels (0 to 15 mile-candles); but at 10 to 150 mile-candles even red figured as a name for blue; data on violet are not extant. It has to be admitted, however, that at high luminance levels, blue attracts as much as 50 per cent of the attention attracted by red, and hence scores over green and yellow but drops down the scale at low levels of luminance (193). Underwater visibility of colors was studied in waters of different scattering power, varying from "very murky to clear." Blue, green, gray and black produced generally lower scores than white, red, orange and yellow, and, as expected, harbor water permits relatively higher visibility for long wavelength stimuli (126, 127). The visibility of road traffic signal lights has to be supra-optimal at night to render them adequate during daytime (43), and protanopic drivers require traffic signals some four times as radiant as those suitable for color-normal drivers (44).

COLOR VISION DEFECTS

Wald & Brown (234) and Wald (233) have continued their study of normal and abnormal color vision, determining the test-sensitivities of their retinal mechanisms. Stiles (214) stresses the importance of determining field-sensitivities (which legitimately bear on interpretations of mechanisms in terms of visual-pigment absorption spectra). Wald & Brown failed to find a deuteranope with more than one mechanism sensitive to light of long wavelengths [cf. Kinney (124)], but the "blue" mechanism of protanopes has the famous "red" lobe. They believe that if the normal pigments are based on three different opsins, inheritance of the defects would involve three loci—two on the X chromosome. Evidence is provided supporting the view that tritanopia is based on autosomal dominance (234), but Wald (233) thinks it likely that other modes of inheritance may also be involved. Verriest (223) stresses that the racial variation in the incidence of color defects tolls the death knell to Ladd-Franklin's theory of the development of the chromatic sense.

Richards (176, 177) claims on the basis of the bimodal distribution of unitary green, red-blue additivity, and foveal dark-adaptation curves that color-normal observers are divisible into two classes: the unorthodox class is attributed to their green-sensitive cones innervating the "blue" response mechanism. Color filters cannot improve color vision (138, 139) unless, of course, an apparent defect is due, for example, to a filter resulting from retinal hemorrhage.

Roth (186) damns Farnsworth's 28-hue test as far as congenital defects are concerned, but accepts it for acquired anomalies. The Ishihara plates, while ideal for detection, are useless for the determination of the type of defect, and hence lose heavily to the H-R-R plates and the 15-hue test (46, 132, 140, 224). Two plates for the detection of rod vision (rod-monochromatism) have been produced by Verriest & Seki (226), and they have also reported color tests with orthodox apparatus. The pioneering work of Grey Walter on the effects of intermittent illumination of pseudo-isochromatic charts has been continued by Bartley and his collaborators (16, 162). One cannot question that, important though these interesting studies are, color vision depends on temporal parameters. Any interference with the normal input may modify the response: the interest of this work consists in the fact that intermittency reduces color perception in a characteristic way. Does it do the same for color matches?

The variability in the manifestation of red-green defects was studied by Pickford (171), who believes that changes in the individual's physiological environment (even, e.g., intrauterine stress) can be responsible. This poses an interesting problem for the photochemistry of color vision. The existence of tritanomaly as such is questioned (45) because of the existence in one pedigree of tritanopia and another defect similar to tritanomaly but believed to be incomplete tritanopia on grounds of probability. On the other hand, the red spectral mixture function of one of the incomplete tritanopes militates against the view that only a loss system is involved. Weale (248) drew attention to the difficulties that arise for genetics when color anomalies are treated as states intermediate to those of normality and dichromacies.

Rod-monochromatism can be transmitted as a recessive sex-linked trait (82); it is associated with myopia. Incremental and spectral sensitivities at various luminance levels of adaptation were studied electroretinographically in a rod-monochromat (67) and confirmed the rod-basis of his vision. Studies at even higher levels are needed to determine whether Blackwell & Blackwell's (20) subdivision can be detected and whether products of bleaching of rhodopsin have any visual significance (249).

Electroretinographic and electro-oculographic data on cone-monochromats have been published (133). The flash and flicker amplitudes of the a- and b-waves fall within normal limits, the EOG is normal, and Ikeda & Ripps (108) showed the spectral sensitivity of the b-wave to follow that of protanopia.

The importance of scanning large retinal areas [cf. (227)] has been stressed by Krill & Beutler (131), who measured thresholds for some red light with a 0.25° field on the fovea and up to 15° off center. As the thresholds of carriers were far below those of the protanopes, inactivation of the chromosomal locus in question is unlikely to be responsible for the mode of inheritance. While fine analysis of the retina may yet accommodate the notion of inactivation, it will be hard to secure its statistical significance (18). The inheritance of incomplete rod-monochromatism has been studied (89, 210) and discussed in terms of mosaicism. The fact that color defects are sparser in relatively undeveloped societies was confirmed for Mexico (120).

A case of acquired unilateral tritanopia was found to have but one neutral point (569 nm) and this was associated with a relative loss in sensitivity (95). Other pathological cases involving color defects were studied (80, 81), and it was confirmed that color vision is affected in amblyopia only at low visual acuities (185).

ANIMAL BEHAVIOR STUDIES

It is a pleasure to be able to report that the control of conditions in behavioral experiments designed to test the presence or absence of color vision in animals has greatly improved during the last few years. The study of Sokol & Muntz (208) on the spectral sensitivity of the New Jersey painted turtle suggests that the animal's retinae possess two spectrally different receptors and may, in fact, use them to discriminate hues (98). Similarly, a study of wavelength discrimination (157) in goldfish presupposes an adequate knowledge of the photopic visibility function: this appears to be tripartite and variable by chromatic adaptation (53). The short-wavelength peak appears to be very sensitive to light-adaptation (268): its height varies with the latter. Spectral purity measurements have also been made and subjected to a theoretical treatment based on the opponent-color theory. Ingle (110) has shown that in goldfish interhemispheric transfer of color information may be more effective than that of pattern, although luminance does not appear to have received adequate control.

The tadpole of *Xenopus laevis* has a visibility maximum at 650 to 670 nm (53). An extract of its mini-retina (or a study of individual receptors) might provide a photochemical substrate for Naka & Rushton's (160) deep-red sensitive receptor, but *Xenopus* is visually a very peculiar species and needs more detailed study. A type of wavelength discrimination appears to be involved in the photopositive response of the frog (156). This is explained by Muntz (156) in terms of a number of arbitrary assumptions which unfortunately include the relation between rod and cone thresholds extrapolated from arbitrarily selected human data. The phototropic response of the two-spotted spider mite to the near-ultraviolet and green parts of the spectrum presupposes the activity of two types of receptor (147), but there is no guarantee that these are contained in one and the same pair of eyes; this species possesses two pairs.

Color vision has been demonstrated in the Virginia opossum (83) and is said to be very probable in the rabbit (166). The antelope ground squirrel can distinguish a wavelength of 460 nm from other equiluminant lights in the bracket between 500 and 600 nm (50, 51), and this discrimination is associated with a high spectral sensitivity in that short-wavelength region, much as is observed for the light-adapted human peripheral retina. Boneau et al. (22) claim that pigeons can differentiate between stimuli 1 nm apart almost equally well whether or not they are rewarded.

Operant conditioning techniques enabled Sidley and co-workers (199) to determine the photopic spectral sensitivity of the rhesus monkey. With small test fields (45′ and 2°) flashed on a steady white background (3000 *td*), the resultant curves showed peaks or shoulders in the regions of 450, 530 to 570, and 610 nm. On the other hand, the photopic sensitivity function obtained by Schrier & Blough (194) with their versatile "tracking" technique exhibited none of these features. Their data were in fairly good agreement with the photopic CIE curve for wavelengths ≥ 540 nm, but the monkeys were relatively much more sensitive to shorter wavelength stimuli. Species differences aside, one can hardly expect results obtained in the course of dark adaptation, and with a 4° test field, to correspond with the foveal luminosity function. Spectral sensitivity data for test flashes superimposed on white and colored backgrounds lead Sperling et al. (209) to conclude that increment threshold is determined solely by the underlying spectral mechanism most sensitive to the test wavelength.

212   RIPPS & WEALE

LITERATURE CITED

1. Aiba, T. S., Alpern, M., Maaseidvaag, F. *J. Physiol. (London)*, **189**, 43–62 (1967)
2. Akita, M., Graham, C. H. *Vision Res.*, **6**, 315–23 (1966)
3. Allen, E. *J. Opt. Soc. Am.*, **56**, 1256–59 (1966)
4. Allen E. *Color Eng.*, **4** (4), 24–28 (1966)
5. Alpern, M. *J. Physiol. (London)*, **176**, 462–72 (1965)
6. Alpern, M., Dudley, D. *J. Gen. Physiol.*, **49**, 405–21 (1966)
7. Alpern, M., Rushton, W. A. H. *J. Physiol. (London)*, **176**, 473–82 (1965)
8. Arden, G. B., Bankes, J. L. K. *Brit. J. Ophthalmol.*, **50**, 740 (1966)
9. Arden, G. B., Bridges, C. D. B., Ikeda, H., Siegel, I. M. *Vision Res.*, **8**, 3–24 (1968)
10. Armington, J. C. *J. Opt. Soc. Am.*, **57**, 838–39 (1967)
11. Armington, J. C. In *Clinical Electroretinography* (Suppl. to *Vision Res.*, 225–33, Pergamon, Oxford, 1966)
12. Armington, J. C., Tepas, D. I., Kropfl, W. J., Hengst, W. H. *J. Opt. Soc. Am.*, **51**, 877–86 (1961)
13. Baker, H. D. *J. Opt. Soc. Am.*, **56**, 686–89 (1966)
14. Ball, R. J., Bartley, S. H. *J. Opt. Soc. Am.*, **56**, 695–99 (1966)
15. Ball, R. J., Bartley, S. H. *Am. J. Optom. and Arch. Am. Acad. Optom.*, **44**, 411–18 (1967)
16. Ball, R. J., Bartley, S. H. *Ibid.*, **42**, 573–81 (1965)
17. Bartley, S. H., Ball, R. J. *J. Psychol.*, **64**, 241–47 (1966)
18. Beutler, E. *Cold Spring Harbor Symp. Quant. Biol.*, **30**, 261–71 (1964)
19. Biernson, G., Snyder, A. W. *Electron. Letters* (June 1965)
20. Blackwell, H. R., Blackwell, O. M., *Vision Res.*, **1**, 62–107 (1961)
21. Blaise, P., Laffin, M. *Trans. CIE, Committee 5.1.5* (1967)
22. Boneau, C. A., Holland, M. K., Baker, W. M. *Science*, **149**, 1113–14 (1965)
23. Bowen, E. J., Ed. *Recent Progress in Photobiology* (Proc. Intern. Photobiol. Congr., 4th, Oxford, July 1964; Blackwell Sci. Publ., Oxford, 400 pp., 1965)
24. Boynton, R. M., Das, S. R. *Science*, **154**, 1581–83 (1966)
25. Boynton, R. M., Das, S. R., Gardiner, J. *J. Opt. Soc. Am.*, **56**, 1775–80 (1966)
26. Boynton, R. M., Ikeda, M., Stiles, W. S. *Vision Res.*, **4**, 87–117 (1964)
27. Boynton, R. M., Riggs, L. A. *J. Exptl. Psychol.*, **42**, 217–26 (1951)
28. Boynton, R. M., Scheibner, H., Yates, T., Rinalducci, E. *J. Opt. Soc. Am.*, **55**, 1672–85 (1965)
29. Bridges, C. D. B. In *Comprehensive Biochemistry*, **27**, 31–78 (Florkin, M., Stotz, E. H., Eds., Elsevier, London, 384 pp., 1967)
30. Brindley, G. S. *J. Physiol. (London)*, **122**, 332–50 (1953)
31. Brindley, G. S., Gardner-Medwin, A. R. *J. Physiol. (London)*, **182**, 185–94 (1966)
32. Brindley, G. S., Westheimer, G. *J. Physiol. (London)*, **179**, 518–37 (1965)
33. Brown, J. L., Ranken, H. B. *Vision Res.*, **5**, 443–53 (1965)
34. Brown, K. T., Murakami, M. *Nature (London)*, **201**, 626–28 (1964)
35. Brown, K. T., Watanabe, K. *Nature*, **193**, 958–60 (1962)
36. Brown, P. K., Wald, G. *Nature*, **200**, 37–43 (1963)
37. Burkhardt, D. A. *Vision Res.*, **6**, 517–32 (1966)
38. Burkhardt, D. A., Riggs, L. A. *Vision Res.*, **7**, 453–59 (1967)
39. Burkhardt, D. A., Whittle, P. *J. Opt. Soc. Am.*, **57**, 416–20 (1967)
40. Cavonius, C. R. Eye Res. Found. Bethesda Rept. No. DA-49-193-MD-2839 (Jan. 1967)
41. Cavonius, C. R., Schumacher, A. W. *Science*, **152**, 1276–77 (1966)
42. Cohen, A. I. *J. Anat.*, **99**, 595–610 (1965)
43. Cole, B. L., Brown, B. *J. Australian Road Res. Bd.*, **2**, 21–33 (1966)
44. Cole, B. L., Brown, B. *J. Opt. Soc. Am.*, **56**, 516–22 (1966)
45. Cole, B. L., Henry, G. H., Nathan, J. *Vision Res.*, **6**, 301–13 (1965)
46. Collin, H. B. *Australian J. Opt.* 342–47 (Dec. 1966)
47. Cone, R. A. *Science*, **155**, 1128–31 (1967)
48. Crawford, B. H. *Vision Res.*, **5**, 71–78 (1965)
49. Crescitelli, F. *J. Neurophysiol.*, **25**, 141–51 (1962)
50. Crescitelli, F., Pollack, J. D. *Science*, **150**, 1316–18 (1965)
51. Crescitelli, F., Pollack, J. D. In *Aspects of Comparative Ophthalmology*, 41–55 (Pergamon, Oxford, 1966)

52. Crescitelli, F., Wilson, B. W., Lilyblade, A. L. *Vision Res.*, **4**, 275–80 (1964)
53. Cronly-Dillon, J. R., Muntz, W. R. A. *J. Exptl. Biol.*, **42**, 481–93 (1965)
54. Dartnall, H. J. A., Lythgoe, J. N. In *Colour Vision. Physiology and Experiment Psychology*, 3–21 (deReuck, A. V. S., Knight, J., Eds., J. & A. Churchill Ltd., London, 382 pp., 1965)
55. Das, S. R. *J. Opt. Soc. Am.*, **55**, 1039–1313 (1965)
56. Das, S. R. *Ibid.*, **56**, 789–94 (1966)
57. Daw, N. W. *Color Coded Units of Goldfish Retina* (Doctoral thesis, Johns Hopkins Univ., Baltimore, Md., 1967)
58. Daw, N. W. *Science*, **158**, 942–44 (1967)
59. de Reuck, A. V. S., Knight, J., Eds., *Colour Vision. Physiology and Experimental Psychology* (J. & A. Churchill Ltd., London, 382 pp., 1965)
60. De Valois, R. L. *Cold Spring Harbor Symp. Quant. Biol.*, **30**, 567–79 (1965)
61. De Valois, R. L., Abramov, I., Jacobs, G. H. *J. Opt. Soc. Am.*, **56**, 966–77 (1966)
62. De Valois, R. L., Abramov, I., Mead, W. R. *J. Neurophysiol.*, **30**, 415–33 (1967)
63. De Valois, R. L., Walraven, J. *Science*, **155**, 463–65, (1967)
64. De Voe, R. G., Ripps, H., Vaughan, H. G., Jr. *Vision Res.*, **8**, 135–47 (1968)
65. Dimmick, F. L. *Vision Res.*, **5**, 679–94 (1965)
66. Dimmick, F. L. *Color Engineering*, **4** (1), 20–26 (1966)
67. Dodt, E., VanLith, G. H. M., Schmidt, B. *Vision Res.*, **7**, 231–41 (1967)
68. Dowling, J. E. *Science*, **147**, 57–59 (1965)
69. Dowling, J. E., Boycott, B. B. *Proc. Roy. Soc. (B)*, **166**, 80–111 (1966)
70. Dowling, J. E., Boycott, B. B. *Cold Spring Harbor Symp. Quant. Biol.*, **30**, 393–402 (1965)
71. Dowling, J. E., Brown, J. E., Major, D. *Science*, **153**, 1639–41 (1966)
72. Enoch, J. M. *J. Opt. Soc. Am.*, **56**, 833–35 (1966)
73. Enoch, J. M. *Ibid.*, 116–23
74. Enoch, J. M. *Invest. Ophthalmol.*, **6**, 647–56 (1967)
75. Enoch, J. M., Glismann, L. E. *Invest. Ophthalmol.*, **5**, 208–21 (1966)
76. Evans, R. M. *J. Opt. Soc. Am.*, **57**, 279–81 (1967)
77. Fatechand, R., Svaetichin, G., Negishi, K., Drujan, B. *Vision Res.*, **6**, 271–83 (1966)
78. Ferraz de Oliveira, L., Ripps, H. *Vision Res.*, **8**, 223–28 (1968)
79. Foster, R. S. *Color Eng.*, **4** (1), 17–19, 26 (1966)
80. François, J., Verriest, G. *Pediatric Ophthalmol.*, 59–64 (Oct. 1965)
81. François, J., Verriest, G., Israel, A. *Ann. Oculist.*, **199**, No. 2, 113–54 (1966)
82. François, J., Verriest, G., Matton-Van Leuven, M.Th., De Rouck, A., Manavian, D. *Am. J. Ophthalmol.*, **61**, 1101–8 (1966)
83. Friedman, H. *Nature (London)*, **213**, 835–36 (1967)
84. Friele, L. F. C. *Farbe*, **14**, 555–60 (1965)
85. Friele, L. F. C. *Ibid.*, 302–14
86. Friele, L. F. C. *J. Opt. Soc. Am.*, **55**, 1314–19 (1965)
87. Friele, L. F. C. *Ibid.*, **56**, 259–60 (1966)
88. Goldstein, E. B. *Vision Res.*, **7**, 837–45 (1967)
89. Goodman, G., Ripps, H., Siegel, I. M. *Arch. Ophthalmol.*, **73**, 397–98 (1965)
90. Gouras, P. *Science*, **147**, 1593–94 (1965)
91. Gouras, P. *J. Physiol. (London)*, **192**, 747–60 (1967)
92. Gouras, P. *Ibid.*, **187**, 455–64 (1966)
93. Gouras, P., Link, K. *J. Physiol. (London)*, **184**, 499–510 (1966)
94. Graham, C. H., Ed. *Vision and Visual Perception* (Wiley, New York, 637 pp., 1965)
95. Graham, C. H., Hsia, Y., Stephan, F. F. *Vision Res.*, **7**, 469–79 (1967)
96. Granda, A. M., Biersdorf, W. R. *Vision Res.*, **6**, 507–16 (1966)
97. Granda, A. M., Stirling, C. E. *Vision Res.*, **6**, 143–52 (1966)
98. Granda, A. M., Stirling, C. E. *J. Gen. Physiol.*, **48**, 901–17 (1965)
99. Hagins, W. A., McGaughy, R. E. *Science*, **157**, 813–16 (1967)
100. Hailman, J. P. *J. Opt. Soc. Am.*, **57**, 281–82 (1967)
101. Hamasaki, D. I. *J. Comp. Neurol.*, **130**, 163–74 (1967)
102. Hamasaki, D. I., Bridges, C. D. B. *Vision Res.*, **5**, 483–96 (1965)
103. Hubel, D. H., Wiesel, T. N. *J. Physiol. (London)*, **195**, 215–43 (1968)

214 RIPPS & WEALE

104. Hunt, R. W. G. *J. Opt. Soc. Am.*, **55**, 1540–51 (1965)
105. Hunter, R. S. *Proc. Porcelain Enamel Inst. Forum*, **27**, 18–29 (1965)
106. Hunter, R. S. *SPE Journal*, 51–58 (Feb. 1967)
107. Ikeda, M. *J. Opt. Soc. Am.*, **54**, 89–94 (1964)
108. Ikeda, H., Ripps, H. *Arch. Ophthalmol.*, **75**, 513–17 (1966)
109. Indow, T. *Vision Res.*, **7**, 481–95 (1967)
110. Ingle, D. J. *Science*, **149**, 1000–2 (1965)
111. Ishak, I. G. H., van Bussel, H. J. J. *IPO Ann. Progr. Rept.*, **1**, 63–68 (1966)
112. Jacobs, G. H., Gaylord, H. A. *Vision Res.*, **7**, 645–53 (1967)
113. Jacobs, G. H., Wascher, T. C. *J. Opt. Soc. Am.*, **57**, 1155–56 (1967)
114. Jameson, D., Hurvich, L. M. *Vision Res.*, **7**, 805–9 (1967)
115. Johnson, E. P., Riggs, L. A., Schick, A. M. L. In *Clinical Electroretinography* (Suppl. to *Vision Res.*, 75–91, Pergamon, Oxford, 1966)
116. Jones, A. E. *J. Neurophysiol.* **29**, 125–38 (1966)
117. Jones, A. E., Jacobs, G. H. *Am. J. Physiol.*, **204**, 47–50 (1963)
118. Judd, D. B. *Proc. Natl. Acad. Sci. U.S.*, **55**, 1313–30 (1966)
119. Kalmus, H. *Diagnosis and Genetics of Defective Colour Vision* (Pergamon, Oxford, 114 pp., 1965)
120. Kalmus, H., De Garay, A. L., Rodarte, U., Cobo, L. *Com. Nac. Energia Nucl. Mex.*, No. 181, 134–45 (Dec. 1964)
121. Kaneko, A., Hashimoto, H. *Vision Res.*, **7**, 847–51 (1967)
122. Kelly, D. *J. Opt. Soc. Am.*, **52**, 940–47 (1962)
123. Kinney, J. A. S. *J. Opt. Soc. Am.*, **55**, 738–39 (1965)
124. Kinney, J. A. S. *Ibid.*, **57**, 1149–54 (1967)
125. Kinney, J. A. S. *Vision Res.*, **7**, 299–318 (1967)
126. Kinney, J. A. S., Luria, S. M., Weissman, S., Matteson, H. H. Memo. Rept. No. 65-11, U.S. Naval Submarine Med. Cent., Groton, Conn., Sept. 1965
127. Kinney, J. A. S., Luria, S. M., Weitzman, D. O. *J. Opt. Soc. Am.*, **57**, 802–9 (1967)
128. Kishto, B. N. *Vision Res.*, **5**, 313–29 (1965)
129. Krauskopf, J. *J. Opt. Soc. Am.*, **54**, 1171 (1964)
130. Krauskopf, J., Srebro, R. *Science*, **150**, 1477–79 (1965)
131. Krill, A. E., Beutler, E. *Science*, **149**, 186–88 (1965)
132. Krill, A. E., Bowman, J. E., Schneiderman, A. *Ann. Hum. Genet. London*, **29**, 253–56 (1966)
133. Krill, A. E., Schneiderman, A. In *Clinical Electroretinography* (Suppl. to *Vision Res.*, 351–61, Pergamon, Oxford, 1966)
134. Leete, C. G., Lytle, J. R. *Color Eng.*, **4** (1), 27–30 (1966)
135. Lennox-Buchthal, M. A. *Acta Physiol. Scand.*, **65**, 101–4 (1965)
136. Liebman, P., Entine, G. *Nature*, **216**, 501–3 (1967)
137. Liebman, P. A., Entine, G. *J. Opt. Soc. Am.*, **54**, 1451–59 (1964)
138. Linksz, A. *Am. J. Ophthalmol.*, **60**, 1135 (1965)
139. Linksz, A. *Ibid.*, **61**, 1553–54 (1966)
140. Linksz, A. *Am. J. Ophthalmol.*, **62**, 27–37 (1966)
141. Luria, S. M. *Physics Today*, **19**, 34–41 (1966)
142. Luria, S. M. *Am. J. Physiol.*, **80**, 14–27 (1967)
143. Luria, S. M., Weissman, S. *J. Opt. Soc. Am.*, **55**, 1068–72 (1965)
144. MacAdam, D. *J. Opt. Soc. Am.*, **33**, 18–26 (1943)
145. McCullough, C. *Science*, **149**, 1115–16 (1965)
146. McCullough, C. *Am. J. Psychol.*, **78**, 362–68 (1965)
147. McEnroe, W. D., Dronka, K. *Science*, 782–83 (1966)
148. MacNichol, E. J., Jr. *Proc. Natl. Acad. Sci. U.S.*, **55**, 1331–44 (1966)
149. Marks, W. B. *J. Physiol. (London)*, **178**, 14–32 (1965)
150. Matteson, H. H., Luria, S. M. *J. Opt. Soc. Am.*, **55**, 887–92 (1965)
151. Matthews, M. L. *J. Opt. Soc. Am.*, **57**, 1033–36 (1967)
152. Michael, C. R. *Science*, **152**, 1095–97 (1966)
153. Miller, N. *Am. J. Optom.*, **41**, 599–608 (1964)
154. Moreland, J. D. *Farbe*, **14**, 173–86 (1965)
155. Moreland, J. D. *Vision Res.*, **8**, 99–107 (1968)
156. Muntz, W. R. A. *J. Exptl. Biol.*, **45**, 101–11 (1966)
157. Muntz, W. R. A., Cronly-Dillon, J. R. *Anim. Behav.*, **14**, 351–55 (1966)
158. Naka, K. I., Rushton, W. A. H. *J. Physiol. (London)*, **185**, 536–55 (1966)

9. Naka, K. I., Rushton, W. A. H. *Ibid.*, 556–86

0. Naka, K. I., Rushton, W. A. H. *Ibid.*, 587–99

4. Negishi, K., Svaetichin, G. *Science*, 152, 1621–23 (1966)

2. Nelson, T. M., Bartley, S. H., Mackavey, W. R. *Percept. Motor Skills*, 13, 227–31 (1961)

3. Nimeroff, I. *J. Opt. Soc. Am.*, 56, 230–37 (1966)

4. Nimeroff, I. *Color Eng.*, 4, 24–44 (1967)

5. Noell, W. K., Walker, V. S., Kang, B. S., Berman, S. *Invest. Ophthalmol.*, 5, 450–73 (1966)

6. Nuboer, J. F. W. *Acta Physiol. Pharmacol. Neerl.*, 13, 484–86 (1966)

7. Orkand, R. K., Nicholls, J. G., Kuffler, S. W. *J. Neurophysiol.*, 29, 519–25 (1966)

8. Pak, W. L., Ebrey, T. G. *J. Gen. Physiol.*, 49, 1199–1208 (1966)

9. Pedler, C. M. H. In *Colour Vision. Physiology and Experimental Psychology*, 52–83 (deReuck, A. V. S., Knight, J., Eds., J. & A. Churchill Ltd., London, 382 pp., 1965)

0. Perry, N. W., Jr., Copenhaver, R. M. In *Clinical Electroretinography* (Suppl. to *Vision Res.*, 249–54, Pergamon, Oxford, 1966)

1. Pickford, R. W. *Vision Res.*, 7, 65–77 (1967)

2. Pirenne, M. H. *Vision and the Eye*, 2nd ed. (Chapman & Hall, London, 224 pp., 1967)

3. Potts, A. M., Nagaya, T. *Invest. Ophthalmol.*, 4, 303–9 (1965)

4. Ratliff, F. *J. Opt. Soc. Am.*, 55, 1553–54 (1965)

5. Ratliff, F. *Ibid.*, 56, 409 (1966)

6. Richards, W. *J. Opt. Soc. Am.*, 56, 1451 (1966)

7. Richards, W. *Ibid.*, 57, 1047–55 (1967)

8. Richards, W., Luria, S. M., Matteson, H. H. *Vision Res.*, 7, 1–15 (1967)

9. Richter, M., Ed. Intern. Color Meeting, Lucerne, 1965. *Die Farbe*, 14 & 15, Parts I & II (Musterschmidt, Göttingen, 1966)

0. Riggs, L. A. *Invest. Ophthalmol.*, 6, 6–17 (1967)

1. Riggs, L. A. *Percept. and Psychophys.*, 2, 1–13 (1967)

2. Riggs, L. A., Johnson, E. P., Schick, A. M. L. *J. Opt. Soc. Am.*, 56, 1621–27 (1966)

3. Ripps, H., Weale, R. A. *Nature*, 205, 52–56 (1965)

184. Ripps, H., Weale, R. A. *J. Physiol. (London)*, 173, 57–64 (1964)

185. Roth, A. *Docum. Ophthalmol.*, 20, 631–35 (1966)

186. Roth, M. A. *Bull. Soc. Ophthalmol. France*, 2, 1–8 (1966)

187. Ruddock, K. H. *Farbe*, 14, 215–24 (1965)

188. Ruddock, K. H. *J. Opt. Soc. Am.*, 55, 1180 (1965)

189. Rushton, W. A. H. *J. Physiol. (London)*, 176, 24–37 (1965)

190. Scheibner, H. *Optica Acta*, 13, 205–10 (1966)

191. Scheibner, H. *Farbe*, 12, 6–58 (1963)

192. Scheibner, H. *J. Opt. Soc. Am.*, 56, 938–42 (1966)

193. Scheibner, H., Schneider, H. *Lichttechnik*, 14, 558–61 (1962)

194. Schrier, A. M., Blough, D. S. *J. Comp. Physiol. Psychol.*, 62, 457–58 (1966)

195. Selvin de Testa, A. *Vision Res.*, 6, 51–59 (1966)

196. Shapiro, W. A., Steiglitz, K. *J. Opt. Soc. Am.*, 55, 1555 (1965)

197. Shipley, T., Jones, R. W., Fry, A. *Science*, 150, 1162–64 (1965)

198. Shirley, A. W. *Brit. J. Physiol. Optics*, 23, 254–57 (1966)

199. Sidley, N. A., Sperling, H. G., Bedarf, E. W., Hiss, R. H. *Science*, 150, 1837–39 (1965)

200. Siegel, M. H. *J. Opt. Soc. Am.*, 55, 566–68 (1965)

201. Siegel, M. H. *Psychon. Sci.*, 2, 151–52 (1965)

202. Siegel, M. H. *Rept. Ann. Meeting Opt. Am., San Francisco, FA 11*, 32 (Oct. 1966)

203. Siegel, M. H., Holzman, C. G. *J. Opt. Soc. Am.*, 56, 981–82 (1966)

204. Snyder, A. W. *Electron. Letters* (Sept. 1965)

205. Snyder, A. W. *J. Opt. Soc. Am.*, 56, 705–6 (1966)

206. Snyder, A. W. *IEEE Trans. Antennas Propagation*, AP-13, 821–22 (1965)

207. Snyder, A. W., Kyhl, R. L. *IEEE Trans. Antennas Propagation*, AP-14, 510–11 (1966)

208. Sokol, S., Muntz, W. R. A. *Vision Res.*, 6, 285–92 (1966)

209. Sperling, H. G., Sidley, N. A., Dockens, W. S., Jolliffe, C. L. *J. Opt. Soc. Am.*, 58, 263–68 (1968)

210. Spivey, B. E. *Arch. Ophthalmol.*, 74, 327–33 (1965)

211. Stell, W. K. *Anat. Rec.*, 153, 389–98 (1965)

212. Sternheim, C. E., Boynton, R. M.

216 RIPPS & WEALE

J. Exptl. Psychol., 72, 770-6

(1966)

213. Stiles, W. S. Journal of the Color Group, No. 11, 106-23 (1967)
214. Stiles, W. S. Science, 145, 1016-17 (1964)
215. Stiles, W. S., Burch, J. M. Optica Acta, 6, 1-26 (1959)
216. Takasaki, H. J. Opt. Soc. Am., 57, 93-96 (1967)
217. Terstiege, H. Farbe, 16, 1-120 (1967)
218. Thomson, L. C. J. Physiol. (London), 108, 78-91 (1949)
219. Tigges, J., Brooks, B. A., Klee, M. R. Vision Res., 7, 553-63 (1967)
220. Tomita, T. Cold Spring Harbor Symp. Quant. Biol., 30, 559-66 (1965)
221. Tomita, T., Kaneko, A., Murakami, M., Pautler, E. L. Vision Res., 7, 519-31 (1967)
222. Van der Horst, G., Bouman, M. A. Vision Res., 7, 1027-29 (1967)
223. Verriest, G. Les deficiences de la vision des couleurs. Chim. Peintures, 27, No. 9, 1-12 (1964)
224. Verriest, G., Bozzoni, F. Trans. Soc. Oftalmol. Ital., 49th Congr. Rome, 1965, 23, 1-11
225. Verriest, G., Israel, A. Vision Res., 5, 151-74 (1965)
226. Verriest, G., Seki R. Farbe, 14, 229-39 (1965)
227. Verriest, G., Szmigielski, M. Rev. d'Opt., 45, 293-312 (1966)
228. Villermet, G. M., Weale, R. A. J. Roy. Microscopical Soc., 84, 565-69 (1965)
229. Vos, J. J. Vision Res., 6, 105-7 (1966)
230. Wald, G. Proc. 4th ISCERG Symp., Japan. J. Ophthalmol., 10 (Suppl.), 1-11 (1966)
231. Wald, G. Nature, 140, 455-46 (1937)
232. Wald, G. J. Opt. Soc. Am., 57, 1289-1303 (1967)
233. Wald, G. Proc Natl. Acad. Sci. U.S., 55, 1347-63 (1966)
234. Wald, G., Brown, P. K. Cold Spring Harbor Symp. Quant. Biol., 30, 345-61 (1965)
235. Wald, G., Brown, P. K., Smith, P. H. Science, 118, 505-8 (1953)
236. Walraven, P. L. Nature, 206, 311-12 (1966)
237. Walraven, P. L., Bouman, M. A. J. Opt. Soc. Am., 50, 780-84 (1960)
238. Walraven, P. L., Bouman, M. A. Vision Res., 6, 567-86 (1966)
239. Walraven, P. L., Van Hout, A. M. J., Leebeek, H. J. J. Opt. Soc. Am., 56, 125-27 (1966)
240. Wasserman, G. S. The Physiologist, 9, 314 (1966)

241. Wasserman, G. S. Vision Res., 6, 689-99 (1966)
242. Weale, R. A. From Sight to Light (Oliver & Boyd Ltd., Edinburgh, 135 pp., 1968)
243. Weale, R. A. Photochem. Photobiol., 4, 67-87 (1965)
244. Weale, R. A. Nature, 218, 238-40 (1968)
245. Weale, R. A. Am. J. Ophthalmol., 53, 665-69 (1962)
246. Weale, R. A. Doc. Ophthalmol., 19, 252-86 (1965)
247. Weale, R. A. In Photophysiology, 4 (Academic Press, London, 1968)
248. Weale, R. A. Discovery-Journal of Science, 27, 31 (1966)
249. Weale, R. A. Vision Res., 7, 819-27 (1967)
250. Weissman, S. J. Opt. Soc. Am., 55, 884-87 (1965)
251. Weitzman, D. O., Kinney, J. A. S. J. Opt. Soc. Am., 57, 665-70 (1967)
252. Westheimer, G. J. Physiol. (London), 192, 309-15 (1967)
253. Wheeler, L. J. Opt. Soc. Am., 57, 1036-47 (1967)
254. Wheeler, L. Ibid., 55, 1020-23 (1965)
255. Wheeler, L., LaForce, R. C. J. Opt. Soc. Am., 57, 386-93 (1967)
256. Wiesel, T. N., Hubel, D. H. J. Neurophysiol., 29, 1115-56 (1966)
257. Witkovsky, P. J. Neurophysiol., 30, 546-61 (1967)
258. Witkovsky, P. Vision Res. (In press)
259. Witkovsky, P. Vision Res., 5, 603-14 (1965)
260. Wolin, L. R., Massopust, L. C., Jr., Meder, J. Vision Res., 6, 637-44 (1966)
261. Wright, H. J. Opt. Soc. Am., 56, 1264-65 (1966)
262. Wright, H. Ibid., 55, 1650-55 (1965)
263. Wright, W. D. The Rays are not Colored (Adam Hilger, London, 153 pp., 1967)
264. Wyszecki, G. Farbe, 14, 287-99 (1965)
265. Wyszecki, G. J. Opt. Soc. Am., 55, 1319-24 (1965)
266. Wyszecki, G., Stiles, W. S. Color Science: Concepts and Methods, Quantitative Data and Formulas (John Wiley, New York, 628 pp., 1967)
267. Wyszecki, G., Wright, H. J. Opt. Soc. Am., 55, 1166-74 (1965)
268. Yager, D. Vision Res., 7, 707-27 (1967)
269. Yamada, E., Ishikawa, T. Cold Spring Harbor Symp. Quant. Biol., 30, 383-91 (1965)
270. Yoshizawa, T., Wald, G. Nature, 214, 566-71 (1967)

PERSONALITY[1]

136

By JOSEPH ADELSON

University of Michigan, Ann Arbor, Michigan

The field of personality these days is marked by abundance, diffuseness, and diversity. Abundance: there are roughly 500 citations in this year's literature, and even that is a modest estimate; it does not include some relevant work in such neighboring areas as social, developmental, and clinical psychology; nor does it include that unknown number of papers I have missed. Diffuseness: it is hard to establish clear boundaries between personality and other psychologies. At one time we thought of personality as a matter of enduring dispositions, but in recent years this definition has been under sharp attack. Some writers—this year, Wallace (189) and Mischel (141)—question the generality and consistency of traits and other inner dispositions; they argue that it is more useful to think in terms of response potentials actuated by situations. Whatever the merits of this position— not many, I happen to believe—it does reflect a widespread tendency to include transient states, and their activation, under the rubric of personality. As a result we have a considerable overlap between, for example, social and personality psychology, and it is often a matter of sheer caprice how we classify the many studies which lie within that overlap.

Above all, diversity: Sanford (165) characterizes research in personality as a "disconcerting sprawl." What we have is a loose collation of topics—an achievement literature, an anxiety literature, and so on—each of which more or less goes its own way. One can of course impose some order on this topical array by searching out underlying conceptual unities, but to do so somehow misses the point, for it falsifies the current existential status of the field—*wie es eigentlich ist*. For better or worse, the movement of the field is centrifugal—that is, towards the detailed exploration of empirical domains. The impulse for synthesis, for finding unities, has for the moment been set aside. So, for example, the controversies we have—and there are surprisingly few—rarely center upon either large or substantive issues and usually involve internecine squabbling about this or that measure, method, or technique within a specific domain of research.

The sprawl and diversity in personality can be seen as both a cause and a a consequence of the virtual abandonment of large theoretical ambitions. Daniel Katz, in a valedictory editorial on his stewardship of the *Journal of Personality and Social Psychology* (95), offers his belief that this is the case in social psychology, and it seems to hold equally for personality. "The technology of the field has developed more rapidly than its theory. . . .

---

[1] The survey of literature pertaining to this review was completed in March 1968.

Current work has not generated new ideas and we still reach back and revi* concepts from Allport or Lewin or earlier theoreticians such as Durkhei* Freud, or Weber to meet specific needs." Thus, despite the cant that we co* tinue to preach to our undergraduates to the effect that theory and resear* are bonded, each inspiriting the other—theory generating data, and da* reforming and extending theory—the plain fact is that there are only occ* sional and erratic articulations between the two.

It can be argued that these tendencies—the scatter of research, the l* in theory, the fitful connection between theory and research—merely r* flect the intractability of psychological phenomena to simplistic theoretic formulations and to easy empirical answers. The "simple and sovereig ideas" of the past, to use Sanford's phrase, are not strong enough to carr us very far; and research, for the moment, yields only incomplete and qual fied answers. The argument is, in a sense, comforting since it places the on* for the slow growth of theory and knowledge on the subject matter—i* complexity, its "hardness"; furthermore, the argument comforts because implies that, given time and effort enough, we shall, ultimately, overcom Yet there is some rising conviction that our habits of inquiry and inferenc may be partly to blame.

The dominant style of research emphasizes (a) hypothesis testing, * concert with (b) tight designs which limit both stimulus conditions and t* range of response. As to the first, there is now considerable doubt wheth* hypothesis-testing via the test of significance is a viable strategy given t* quantitatively underdeveloped state of personality theory. Trenchant ana yses of this issue can be found this year in papers by Meehl (127) an Bakan (8).

As to the second, constricted design of the type described constrains t* generation of data. In a stimulating collection of essays on method, Baka (8) argues that in psychology today the experimental mode acts against t* empirical endeavor.

> Most experimentation in the field of psychology falls considerably short of bei* able to be considered really empirical. Consider the ideal of the 'well-designe* experiment.' The usual meaning of 'well-designed' is that the outcomes of t* experiment have been completely anticipated, and that one will not allow t* experience of conducting the experiment to lead one to consider alternatives outsi* of the ones already thought of beforehand.

Our styles of investigation, then, may stifle the discovery of the new an* unexpected and in doing so inhibit the freshening of theory. What we ma* need, as a corrective, is a revival of inductive and naturalistic approache* there are, as we will see, modest but encouraging signs of movement in th direction. As Wyatt (204) points out, psychology, like biology, has legit mate naturalistic concerns, and there is no question that these are no neglected. It is, by the way, a matter of some interest, and of some iron* that most of the theories we lean on are derived from disciplines and schola*

—e.g., psychoanalysis, ethology, Piaget—whose inductive, naturalistic modes of inquiry we neither emulate nor tolerate.

A few words about coverage: Given the abundance and scatter already noted, only a fraction of the available material can be discussed. Since a major function of these reviews is reportorial, an account of what psychologists are up to, I have tried to cover in detail those topics which have attracted the most research attention. This means, regretfully, that mainstream research is more likely to be mentioned than studies which are offbeat or ahead of their time.

THE CRISIS IN METHODOLOGY

Or does that overstate the case? At the least, there are signs of profound disquiet and disaffection about current methodological practices. This year saw two books—both severely critical—on method (8, 67), and there were two others the year before (157, 192); there were two journal symposia and a welter of separate papers—all in all 31 citations bearing on methodology. It is the quality of this criticism, even more than its extent, which makes it noteworthy; in the past, methodological criticism has been largely technical, involving problems of experimental design or statistical strategy. The new criticism is radical in that it strikes to the heart of practice; it challenges the validity of the experimental method itself; and it questions the ethics of contemporary research. To organize our discussion, we can begin with this assertion: The representative study in the field of personality is (1) an experiment in which (2) the experimenter (3) lies to (4) an undergraduate. Let us consider the numbered terms one at a time, in reverse order.

Samples.—Psychology is the study of the college sophomore: a trite observation, a tired joke. By treating it as a joke, as a kind of endearing eccentricity, we seem to have insulated ourselves from an adequate recognition of the problem. Most psychologists, one finds, underestimate the degree to which current research limits itself to undergraduate samples, volunteer or captive. A count of four randomly selected issues of the *Journal of Personality and Social Psychology* in 1967 reveals that (after omitting the small number of papers using children) 90 per cent of the papers published used undergraduates. (The remaining 10 per cent used subjects drawn from equally atypical, usually captive, groups.) A check of the *Journal of Personality* yields the same proportion. Volunteer subjects continue to be employed with considerable frequency, despite mounting evidence this year as in the past (46, 210) that they are markedly different in personality and motivation from nonvolunteers. In an editorial in *Child Development*, Siegel (172) points to the common use of captive subjects in developmental psychology, which has led to the neglect of those age groups (e.g., children 1 to 3 years old) not easily captured. "It appears," she says, "that considerations of availability and convenience govern which children are studied." These considerations obtain equally in personality research, and with far more serious consequences, in that we neglect all but an atypical sampling of late adolescents.

Ethics.—There is widespread and increasing concern about the ethical issues raised by some forms of research in the social sciences. A symposium in *Social Problems* offers several perceptive papers on a number of topics, such as disguised and participant observation (53, 139) and problems of confidentiality (152). In other papers Smith (175) considers problems connected with research on children, and Sykes (181) comments upon a wide variety of ethical issues. Within psychology itself, the focal concern has been deception, its moral and methodological effects. A balanced and sensitive discussion by Kelman (97) surveys the salient issues: those which are ethical, as when the subject is induced into demeaning conduct, or when the debriefing exposes him as having been easily gulled, or worst of all, the insidious "second-order" deceptions, where the ostensible "experimenter" is himself the traduced subject, the total situation breeding an ambience of semi-paranoia akin to what we have in a John Le Carre fiction; and those which are methodological, as when the campus population learns, as it can hardly fail to do, about the common tendency of psychologists to deceive, so that all kinds of unanticipated, unknown expectations enter the experimental situation, the subject aiming to "psych" the experimenter's "psyching" of him, subject and experimenter entangled in a web of mutual suspicion, mutual deception.

So it may be the experimenters who are the most deceived in being self-deceived on the deceiving of their subjects. (And who will debrief them?) As Stricker (178) points out, after offering a useful survey of the extent and topical provenance of studies using deception, most researchers do not search very closely for signs of suspicion in their subjects. It is not a hypothetical matter; a revealing study by Stricker, Messick & Jackson (179) suggests that subjects are far more suspicious than we have suspected them to be. High school students were put through two conformity experiments; a careful scrutiny uncovered the fact that a great many of them suspected the deception elements in the experiment. Suspiciousness is related to sex, ability, and personality; the most skeptical subjects were boys, the more intelligent, and the less docile. Bear in mind that these were high school students, presumably uncontaminated by the climate of suspicion regarding psychologists' intentions, that we find on most university campuses.

Can we find alternatives to deception? Kelman has suggested that role-playing be explored as one possibility, and Greenberg (78) has done so. In a replication of a Schachter study on anxiety and affiliation in relation to birth order, he asked his *S*s to imagine themselves in the experiment, and was able, in general, to repeat Schachter's findings.

Finally, there is a disturbing report by Walster et al. (190) on the effectiveness of debriefing following deception. Deception research has been justified on the grounds that debriefing undoes whatever damage to self-esteem has been induced by the experimental manipulation. The results of this study—the details are too complex to report here—argue that this may not be uniformly so. After a thorough debriefing, the authors report, "Subjects still behaved to some extent as though the debriefing had not taken place." Furthermore, the aftereffects are hard to interpret and predict, and "may depend in part upon the personality traits of the subject."

The experimenter.—The experimenter's intention is to exclude the extraneous, and it is increasingly clear that the extraneous encompasses the experimenter himself, especially his expectations, apprehensions, and wishes. That, in substance, is the message in Rosenthal's perspicacious work on the experimenter effect. That work is too detailed and (hopefully) well known to warrant presentation here. His book (157) is essential reading, as is a lively and at times abrasive book by Friedman (67) dealing with the same topic. An excellent summary of recent work can be found in a paper by Rosenthal (158).

The emphasis in this research has shifted somewhat from the demonstration of experimenter influence to a closer scrutiny of how it operates. In particular, the processes of covert communication are being studied—such variables as posture, gesture, and tone of voice; all these and others, it now seems, may carry the experimenter's expectations to the subject. Another new trend is that work in this vein is now being taken outside the laboratory setting. The influence of teachers' expectations on their students' performance is currently under investigation (159). In a very interesting study, Milmoe et al. (140) demonstrate that the physician's tone of voice, after content has been filtered out, is a postdictor of his success in getting alcoholics to accept treatment.

The experiment.—Given the buffeting about that the experimental method has endured in the last few years—not only the work on the experimenter effect, but also Orne's observations of the "demand characteristics" of the experimental situation (146), which raises questions on the generalizability of findings outside that situation—given these and other doubts, one might suppose that experimentation in personality was on its last legs. To the contrary; it thrives as never before. "It may be crooked, but it's the only game in town." What we may be in for is a period of intellectual dissociation, the right hand studiously ignoring what the left hand is doing. Work on the experimenter effect continues to accumulate—there were, for example, six research papers given at the 1968 meetings of the Midwestern Psychological Association—but there are few signs of any general effort to cope with the challenges that the work presents. Of the hundreds of papers in this year's personality literature, only a handful make any attempt to correct or compensate for experimenter effect. This is discouraging, to say the least, since some of Rosenthal's suggestions for attenuating experimenter effect can be carried out without too much cost and inconvenience.

The disenchantment with the experiment, such as it is, seems to have had the happy effect of spurring an interest in alternative methods of inquiry. In 1966, Webb et al. (192) published *Unobtrusive Measures*, a treasure-trove of ingenious, largely naturalistic research methods. We have this year a superb symposium in *Human Development* on naturalistic methods in psychology. The papers cover a wide range of topics: Raush (153) on clinical methods; Menzel (132) on animal research; Gutmann (80) on cross-cultural studies; Sechrest (169) on social attitudes; Kelly (96) on the ecological approach. There is an excellent general discussion by Willems (199) and a lively commentary by Barker (12).

These papers make it evident that there is no need to think of experimental and naturalistic approaches as opposing each other; rather there is a complex complementarity between them. Some problems can be approached only by naturalistic methods, others only (or more efficiently) by experimentation. The naturalistic approach is less likely to involve a restriction of response range; hence it encourages an open, inductive attitude towards the phenomena being studied. It can also make us aware of contingencies which should be introduced into the experiment. Above all, it is the articulation, or lack of it, between experimental and naturalistic findings which is important. In some instances, as Willems shows, we have learned that we cannot generalize from the laboratory to real life. But in other cases we can, giving us multimethod confirmation, which, as Webb et al. point out, reduces "the possibility of slippage between conceptual definition and operational specification."

Despite the indisputable advantages of naturalistic methods, it remains an open question whether they will be more widely used. They seem to require more ingenuity, which is always in short supply. The ratio of effort to yield is often low and uncertain. Above all, they require far more time and patience and a considerable capacity to delay reward.

We like to pretend that our choice of methods is dictated by scientific considerations alone. In fact, the exigencies of the academic marketplace play an important and perhaps decisive role. The methodological problems we have noted—the nearly exclusive use of undergraduates, the failure to take account of the experimenter effect, the neglect of naturalistic strategies —all these reflect the pressure for quick publication. There is reason to doubt that there will be rapid reforms in methodology until there is some reform of the university.

STUDIES OF MORALITY

After many years of neglect, the study of the moral domain—attitudes and behavior—has revived. If we survey the subject index of the *Annual Review* volumes during the 1960's, we find only occasional references to morality, until 1964, when we begin to see an accumulation of citations. It is not hard to understand why the topic has been moribund. The famous Hartshorne & May studies of character (83) made it fairly clear that—at least in children—moral conduct was considerably influenced by situation, and to pursue a general trait of morality might mean chasing a will-o'-the-wisp. Furthermore, it has been difficult to uncover any simple relationship between moral belief on the one hand and moral conduct on the other. What we have had in the last few years is a more sophisticated search for the variables—ego functions, interpersonal patterns, situational constraints and supports—which determine, or influence, various categories of moral belief and conduct and their interaction. This search has now begun to yield important findings.

Much of the recent research, especially by Kohlberg (105), has pointed to cognitive dimensions, such as intelligence and anticipation, as key determinants of moral conduct. A brilliant study by Grim, Kohlberg, & White (79) uncovers significant relationships between measures of attention—assayed largely by reaction time indexes—and several measures of morality—both teacher ratings and experimental honesty—among first- and sixth-grade children. The authors argue persuasively that attention is the causally prior variable; it is more stable over time and more general over situations than measures of moral conformity. They say that "the temptation to cheat in the ordinary experimental situation is less an arousal of an intense drive than an interesting distracting stimulus. . . . In other words, stable attention seems to promote honesty primarily by leading to a higher threshold to distracting thoughts of the opportunity to cheat." They indicate their argument draws them "near to the older, introspective psychology of the moral will," and point out that William James saw moral will as a function of attentional processes. Finally, they cite some extremely interesting unpublished evidence by Krebs (106), which suggests that the maturity of moral values interacts with attention to determine cheating. Sixth-grade children with autonomous principles of moral judgment do not cheat, even if distractible; those at the conventional level cheat if distractible; those who have not developed to the conventional level tend to cheat whether distractible or not.

Another significant approach has been the study of family climate in relation to variables of moral outlook; it is represented this year in a paper by Hoffman & Saltzstein (87). Working with seventh-grade children, they used a number of devices—projective questionnaires as well as ratings—to appraise the level of moral development. They related these measures to a typology of parent discipline: power assertion, where the parent emphasizes his authority over the child; love withdrawal, in which there are nonphysical expressions of affect; and induction, whereby the parent stresses the consequences of the child's action. The authors' hypotheses were generally borne out, though only for middle-class children; the use of induction by the parents is associated with more advanced moral development in the child, and the use of power with a less advanced level. The authors offer a closely reasoned discussion of the findings and favor an interpretation which stresses the role of empathy as mediating between parent behavior and the child's moral ideology.

There is an accumulating body of research which explores the effect of direct social influence, via observation and modeling, on the induction of good (moral, altruistic, charitable) behavior. Several experiments this year represent the rather wide range of investigations in this vein. In a most ingenious naturalistic study, Bryan & Test (26) examined the effects of altruistic models in evoking helping behavior. They report four separate studies, in each of which an altruistic action by a confederate evoked corresponding behavior among passersby. The most clever of these was a lady-in-distress situation. In both the control and experimental conditions, a young woman stood beside a disabled vehicle on a highway. In the experimental condition, the "subjects" (passing motorists) saw, one-quarter of a mile before reaching the experimental "scene," another young lady having her tire changed by what appeared to be another passing motorist. The experimental condition provoked a significantly greater number of offers to help from the "subjects." Rosenhan & White (156) had children play a game in which they could win gift certificates. Those who observed an adult contributing half his winnings to a charity were more likely to do so, both at the time and on a later occasion when the model was not present. Those who contributed in the model's presence more often did so in his absence; the authors suggest that rehearsal as well as observation educe the phenomenon.

Two experiments are concerned with the training of moral responses. In a carefully designed study, Crowley (38) found that first-graders could be trained to achieve more mature moral judgments, using Piaget's stages as a criterion. The training procedure involved teaching the children to take account of intentionality in making judgments of the naughtiness of story characters. Simple labeling of the correct response was as effective in producing change as labeling plus discussion. The author's interpretation is pleasingly conservative; he does not claim that a higher Piagetan stage is achieved, but rather that "training was effective because it dealt with a relatively specific response." Midlarsky & Bryan (136) found that youngsters were best trained towards altruistic behavior (donating candy) when the experimenter both expressed joy and hugged the subject. Interestingly, neither expressiveness nor hugging alone were more effective than the absence of training in inducing donations.

Does feeling guilty make one more likely to comply? Freedman, Wallington & Bless (65) were able to induce guilt (about lying and about upsetting someone's index cards) and found that the guilty Ss were more likely to agree to volunteer their time for another experiment. This effect is more often found when the S believes he will not meet the person towards whom he feels guilty. The wish to avoid confronting one's "victim" may explain Silverman's contrary results (173); he found that children who had cheated in an experiment were not likely to volunteer more time for a later experiment.

Delinquency and morality.—It has been clear for some time that morality is multiply dimensioned, and it is equally clear that there are many varieties of delinquency. We have long since given up any hope of finding a simple relationship between the two, and research in this area has turned to more subtle questions.

There is an important paper by Ruma & Mosher (162) which combines Freudian and Piagetan approaches to guilt and moral judgment in a study of incarcerated delinquent boys. The stage of moral judgment was assessed along the lines established by Kohlberg. The boys were interviewed about their transgressions and the degree of guilt determined by several measures. There is a positive relationship between intensity of guilt and level of moral development—an important finding, for it suggests that the Piaget-Kohlberg stages can be related to affective states, and it points the way towards a synthesis of psychoanalytic and developmental views on morality and guilt.

The connections between morality and delinquency were approached somewhat differently by Stein et al. (177). They undertook a cluster analysis of a moral values scale given to matched groups of delinquent and nondelinquent adolescent boys. Four dimensions emerged: informing, masculine inadequacy, identity conflict, and aggression. The delinquents were more likely to judge informing as wrong, and less likely to condemn the identity-conflict items. As the authors say, these findings support the position that delinquency involves accepting the values of a deviant subculture.

Probably the best measures we now have for determining antisocial tendencies are those derived from Gough's California Psychological Inventory—a Socialization scale, and a social maturity index. The utility of the measures for assessing delinquency has been demonstrated cross-nationally, indeed in almost a dozen countries. This work has now been extended to Japan (76, 142); both measures distinguish delinquents and nondelinquents in that country. Lefcourt (109) reports a "serendipitous" validity study of the social maturity index. He used it to identify an undergraduate who had destroyed some library materials and to distinguish students who bluffed on an examination and who failed to pick up their term papers.

A test of impulsivity developed by Kipnis (99) also seems to measure, among other things, the presence of irresponsible and antisocial tendencies. He reports that high scoring Ss (male college students and Navy enlisted men)

> overestimated the length of unfilled time, were high on a measurement of sensation seeking, did not accept conventional values relating to the regulation of behavior, stated that there were few activities liable to evoke feelings of embarrassment or anxiety, were easily provoked to aggression, and reported they formed closed and clique-like friendship relations.

In a related study (100) high scorers were found to be more productive when working for high-status than for low-status leaders.

STUDIES OF EFFECTIVENESS

Competence.—The last few years have seen a heightened attention given to studies of personal effectiveness. This growth of interest reflects certain theoretical emphases of the past decade: Robert White's writings on com-

petence (198); the stress on ego autonomy which has developed in psychoanalysis through the work of Hartmann, Rapaport, and Erikson, among
others; and of course the continuing influence of such theorists as Allport
and Maslow. There is also some reason to feel that the new interest in competence involves some backlash against the concentration of psychologists
on narrow realms of behavior, as well as the wish to study socially relevant
conduct. The work to be reported is unified largely by these tendencies.
There is as yet no uniformity of doctrine, nor is there, perhaps blessedly, a
widely used "competence scale" to absorb research unto itself.

An excellent monograph by Ezekiel (55) investigated the sense of the
personal future in relation to success in the Peace Corps. Using these volunteers as subjects involves the investigator's stacking the cards against himself; his subjects are both self-selected and then carefully culled, reducing
considerably the range of competence available for study. Even so, the results are impressive. Ezekiel reports the use of mock autobiographies administered at the time of selection; subjects were asked to depict themselves
in various imagined futures. The autobiographies were coded for the degree
of cognitive differentiation displayed in mapping the future, the extent to
which the life envisioned demanded continuing effort, and the degree to
which the writer pictured himself as the agent actively shaping the future.
These ratings were related to several measures of volunteer performance.
With a variety of predictor and outcome variables available, the results are
not easily summarized, but the general picture is clear: those volunteers who
have well-articulated ideas of themselves in the future, and who represent
themselves in roles demanding effort and autonomy, received high ratings on
almost all criteria of success. The picture that emerges from Q-sort ratings of
interviews is particularly vivid. The highly differentiated volunteers seem
to be more energetic, persistent, and inventive, more self-demanding, more
intellectual in approach, with a well-developed sense of the future and well-
articulated personal identities. Those low on the autobiography ratings
tended to be more dependent on others, more routinized in work, less sure
of themselves, low in energy, less comfortable with natives, more involved
in working out "moratorium" problems.

Somewhat similar findings are reported in a study on a somewhat different problem, the capacity for self-directed change, by Winter, Griffith &
Kolb (201). Graduate students enrolled in a T-group course were asked to
initiate changes in themselves and at the end of the semester were assessed
on the degree to which they had met their goals. High-change Ss showed an
ability to think conditionally about themselves, were aware of the distinction
between a present and a possible self; furthermore, they showed fewer signs
(as did Ezekiel's successful volunteers) of identity-diffusion. In both studies
a well-differentiated sense of the self seems to be related to the achievement
of goals.

Etiology.—It is hard to know whether competence in adults has any relation to the same quality in young children; but if so, we may have some in-

ght into its development through several important studies of effectiveness
n children. Two related researches, by Baumrind (14) and Baumrind &
Black (15), attempted to determine the child-rearing practices associated
with self-reliant, self-controlled, and mature behavior in preschoolers. In the
first study, three patterns of personality were distinguished through teacher
and psychologist ratings. Children judged to be competent, buoyant, and
contented were compared with a group of distrustful and dysphoric youngsters, and with children displaying little self-control and self-reliance. Very
careful assessments of parental behavior and attitudes were done through
home visits, structured observations, and interviews. The parents of the
competent children were "markedly consistent, loving, conscientious, and
secure in handling their children. They respected the child's independent
decisions but demonstrated a remarkable ability to hold a position once they
took a stand. They tended to accompany a directive with a reason." The
parents of dysphoric children were firm but non-nurturant. Essentially they
relied on power, punishment, and unilateral demands. The parents of the
third group, the immature and dependent, seemed to be unsure of themselves, demanded little of them, were lax and at times indulgent, and yet
less intensively involved.

In the second study, all students in a nursery school made up the sample,
rather than selected subtypes; the variables studied and the techniques of
inquiry were much the same, as were the major results:

> . . . Techniques which fostered self-reliance, whether by placing demands on the
> child for self-control and high-level performance or by encouraging independent
> action and decision making, facilitated responsible, independent behavior. Firm
> discipline in the home did not produce conforming or dependent behavior in the
> nursery school. For boys, the opposite was true . . . Firm demanding behavior on
> the part of the parent was not associated in the parent with punitiveness or lack of
> warmth. The opposite was true.

These findings are remarkably close to those reported by Coopersmith
(33) in an extensive and richly detailed study of the nature and sources of
self-esteem. His subjects were middle-class boys 10 to 12 years of age; degree
of self-esteem was assessed by self-report, teacher ratings, and inferences
from projective tests, all of which related highly to each other. Three levels
of self-esteem were studied: those who were high were self-confident, assertive, optimistic, free of anxiety and excessive diffidence; those low were
withdrawn, unsure of themselves, sensitive to criticism, anxious and self-
preoccupied. The middle group seemed to be compliant, conventional, and
conformist, dependent for their sense of self-worth on the opinion of others
and on an adherence to middle-class norms. Those high in self-esteem set
high goals for themselves, both in relation to future vocational goals and in
tests of skill. They participated more vigorously in discussions and were
more likely to disagree with others and to express independent opinions.
The child-rearing patterns reported for this group are closely parallel to

those uncovered for the competent children in the Baumrind studies. Firm limits were set in an atmosphere of warmth, concern, and mutual respect. The parents were open to the child's opinions, ruled by reward as against punishment, provided clear guidance and well-defined codes of conduct. Parents of children low in self-esteem were inconsistent, alternating between extreme permissiveness and harsh punishment.

There is another important study on the possible etiology of effectiveness. The method is longitudinal; the dependent variable is adult psychological health. Using data collected in the Berkeley Guidance Study, Livson & Peskin (116) examined the relationships between personality ratings at four periods in childhood and adolescence (5 to 7, 8 to 10, 11 to 13, and 14 to 16) and assessments of psychological health derived from adult interviews (average age, 31). Ratings from only one period—early adolescence—proved to be effective predictors of adult psychological states, and for both men and women. There is a searching and sophisticated discussion of this finding, one which draws on Helene Deutsch's (43) and Harry Stack Sullivan's (180) observations on the significance of the preadolescent period.

Another study in this area focuses upon sex-role identification in relation to personal adjustment. Rychlak & Legerski (163) argue that cross-sexed parental identification is associated with maladjustment only when it leads the child to adopt a behavioral pattern which does not allow him to meet conventional sex roles. Two studies support this line of reasoning: in one, maladjusted boys showed an identification with a mother perceived as passive rather than dominant; in the other, maladjusted girls were identified with dominant rather than passive fathers.

Self-esteem and self-acceptance.—Much of the work on this topic seemed to me to be more closely related to social (71, 143) or to clinical (25, 184) psychology than to personality per se and will not be reported here. Several studies do seem germane. What they have in common is that they center upon the sources and effects of changes in self-esteem. Marcia (122) has developed an interesting typology of ego-identity statuses. He differentiates four groups: identity achievement (those who have been through identity crises); moratorium (those currently in crisis); foreclosure (those who have avoided crisis); and diffusion (those without commitments). Subjects characterized by high identity status (achievement and moratorium groups) are less vulnerable to false self-esteem data than are the other groups. Rubin (161) finds that sensitivity training increases self-acceptance and produces a decrease in ethnic prejudice; there is a positive relationship between changes in self-acceptance and changes in prejudice. Ludwig & Maehr (119) report changes in self-concept and consequent changes in behavioral preferences following approval or disapproval of their physical performance by a physical development expert; furthermore, the effects of the treatment, though they diminish slowly, are still evident after three weeks.

Achievement.—After at least 20 years of vigorous investigation, there is little slackening of the pace at which achievement motivation and behavior is studied. In part, I suspect, it is because work on these topics has never been seriously deterred by methodological criticism of the n Ach measure. Criticism there has been, and in abundance, and the problem of measurement continues to attract concern, but somehow work on achievement motivation has continued unimpeded. The contrast with authoritarianism is instructive. As Samelson & Yates (164) point out, the widespread panic about acquiescence response set, which now seems to have been overdone, has had the calamitous side effect of inhibiting work on authoritarianism. Another reason—perhaps a more important one—for the continuing vitality of achievement research has been the truly remarkable diversity of contexts in which it has been studied. Students of achievement motivation have been prepared to look out into the world, to examine the phenomenon in relation to historical, economic, sociological, and social-psychological variables. Laboratory research has by no means been neglected—it is in fact the most common medium of inquiry—but there has been a constant reinvigoration of the research through a reciprocity of experimental and naturalistic investigation. A compact summary of the extraordinary range of the achievement literature can be found in a book by Heckhausen (85); it is especially valuable for its summaries of foreign research, most of it unknown in this country.

Careers.—A prime example of imaginative naturalistic research is found in a paper by Andrews (4). He studied the interaction between the dominant values of business firms, their policies of evaluation and reward of personnel, and the motive patterns of their employees. Specifically, he contrasted two Mexican corporations: one was an aggressive, expanding, efficient company and the other a sluggish firm dominated by an authoritarian and apparently capricious owner. Andrews found that the first company was more likely to advance executives high in achievement motivation and not to reward individuals high on n Power. The second company, where power maneuverings were common, advanced executives high on power and failed to reward those high on achievement. Another study of executive need patterns, by Cummin (40), found that successful managers were higher in both n Ach and n Power than unsuccessful ones. Baruch (13) hypothesized that women's n Ach scores would vary with age and family situation, and specifically that returning to work after a period of child-rearing would be associated with a rise in n Ach. The hypothesis is sustained for Radcliffe alumnae; there is a substantial drop in achievement imagery during the child-rearing years compared with the immediate postcollege years, and a considerable rise preceding the return to work. However, the relationship does not hold for women in general, as suggested by the findings from a nation-wide sample; presumably, achievement strivings are more likely to be implicated in the work decisions of well-educated, affluent women. College women with high achievement motivation are much more likely to be pursuing careers after child-rearing than those with low.

Etiology.—The Baruch study suggests, as others have, that achievement motivation may vary over time in response to environmental reinforcement and one's general life situation. Indeed, one can raise a similar question about Andrew's work; to what degree are the variations in achievement and power

level responsive to differences in company patterns of reward? At the me
ment it appears from various sources that achievement level at any give
time represents a combination of fairly stable dispositions and the degre
of current reinforcement, but the matter is far from being settled. Part c
the answer can be provided by longitudinal research, and we now have
study of this kind from Feld (59). For boys studied first in childhood and
then six years later she found a moderate degree of stability ($r = .38$) in th
strength of the achievement motive. A major part of this study concerns th
relationships between maternal attitudes towards independence and achieve
ment (for their sons) and measures of achievement and anxiety; here th
results are rather more complicated. For example, there are generally nega
tive relationships between maternal stress on independence in childhood an
adolescence; the author speculates that mothers who stressed accomplish
ment early now have independent sons and no longer need to emphasize it
while the reverse may be true for mothers who find themselves coping wit
dependent adolescent sons. There is one very strong relationship reported
mothers who early in childhood stress achievement have adolescent son
low in test anxiety.

Davids & Hainsworth (41) compared high-achieving and under-achiev
ing adolescent boys, both groups being of high intelligence. Using the PARI
the authors compared the actual responses of mothers to their sons' percep
tions of them. Differences center upon the factor of maternal control; the
underachievers view their mothers as more controlling than do the high
achievers. Perhaps the most important findings to emerge are the clea
discrepancies between mothers and underachieving sons on control, the sons
seeing the mothers as more controlling than the mothers report themselves
to be; in contrast, high achievers more often agree with their mothers
self-assessments of control. The authors offer some penetrating observations
on the implications of these findings for understanding the impulsivity and
poor self-discipline characteristic of low achievers. Another study on the
connection between maternal attitudes (in this case, as seen by college student Ss) and achievement behavior is reported by Heilbrun, Harrell &
Gillard (86). They find that those who perceived their mothers as "rejecting" (high control, low nurturance) are more sensitive to social nonreaction
in setting aspirations for themselves than those who regard their mothers as
"overprotective" (high nurturance, high control).

Achievement and performance.—There is a wide array of studies here, but
I will report them only briefly. They tend to complex designs and equally
complex results and thus defy summary, let alone comment.

An interesting study by Klinger (102) examined modeling effects on
achievement imagery. Ss exposed only visually (via televised performances)
to achievement-oriented models in interpersonal activity produced higher
levels of achievement fantasy than did those exposed to affiliative or neutra
models. The study is noteworthy for its careful attempt to exclude experimenter effects. In a level of aspiration study, Feather (56) reports that suc-

cess-oriented Ss set higher aspirations and are less responsive to success or failure, but only under conditions of high performance variability. When variability is low, aspiration is determined by cognitive assessments. Another study by Feather (57) examines expectation of success in relation to task difficulty. Two studies, by Wyer (206) and Wyer & Bednar (207), inquire into the effects of task difficulty on perseverance. A very interesting study, also by Wyer (205), discovers, among other things, that college students of low ability and academic accomplishment are high in task conformity, while underachievers are low. Locke (117) argues that affect (satisfaction) is determined by the relationship of outcome to aspiration rather than outcome to expectation, as in McClelland's theory. Hays & Worell (84) suggest an additive relationship between anxiety and achievement in understanding digit symbol performance. Belanger & Sattler (16) did not find motivational pattern to relate to the avoidance of uncertainty. Zander & Forward (208) studied the relationship of achievement style to aspiration in a group setting. Hart (82) found the high Ach Ss did better on a number facility task, though there were no differences between control and competitive conditions. McKeachie et al. (126) were unable to find consistent relationships between n Ach and academic achievement as measured by course grades.

Measurement.—An intriguing and puzzling finding by Alper & Greenberger (3): achievement imagery is more likely to be elicited in college women when parent-child figures in the stimulus pictures are facing each other than when they are averted; furthermore, the finding holds whether the parent figure is father or mother. The nature of the stimulus was also studied for Negro college women in a paper by Cowan & Goldberg (37). In general, achievement imagery is more intensely evoked by male figures, irrespective of race. However, productivity (word count) is affected by race. An analysis and critique of the projective measurement of achievement is offered by Shrable & Stewart (170), while Costello (35) developed two new scales to measure the motive: one a test of achievement, the other on the wish for success.

STUDIES OF CONFLICT

Anxiety.—Anxiety was the most popular single topic in personality this year. Most of the work extends established lines of research; there continues, for example, to be a great deal of interest in the measurement of anxiety and in the correlates of the common anxiety scales; and there is even more research, largely experimental, on the effects of anxiety on performance. A new direction is to be found in studies on the taming of anxiety and fear. What are the processes by which anxiety is dissipated or eliminated? These studies are of some theoretical moment in that they may offer a more compelling rationale than we now have for understanding the behavior therapies.

For the last few years, Epstein & Fenz (50, 61, 62) have been investigating the anxiety reactions of sport parachutists. Now Epstein has written a monograph (49) which summarizes the findings and proposes a general

theory of the arousal and control of anxiety. These studies compare the reactions of novice and experienced parachutists prior to, during, and following
the jump. Three separate methods are used for assessing anxiety: self-ratings,
physiological reactions to a word-association test containing parachute
relevant words, and physiological reactions before, during, and after ascent
in the aircraft. The essential finding is that novice parachutists show a steep
rise in experienced fear and physiological arousal up to the time of the jump;
experienced parachutists show inverted V-shaped curves on all measures.
The experienced subjects peak prior to the jump, then a process of inhibition
occurs through which "anxiety is mastered and turned to adaptive advantage, providing an early warning signal at a low level of arousal."
Furthermore, "novices use drastic defenses tending toward the all-or-none
variety, whereas the defenses of the experienced parachutists are modulated
and involve early inhibitory reactions applied to low intensies of anxiety or
arousal." Longitudinal studies show that the inverted-V pattern is a function
of increased experience; the more experienced the jumper, the earlier the
inhibition process appears. Epstein uses these findings to formulate a unified
theory of anxiety and its mastery, drawing upon such diverse sources as
Pavlov's work on transmarginal inhibition (148), Bond's studies of combat
pilots in World War II (22), and Freud's work on the repetition compulsion
(66). All in all, the monograph and the studies that preceded it are exemplary
in several respects: in the exploitation of a natural situation—real parachutists making real jumps; in utilizing several measures of affect; in studying reactions over an extended period of time; and in the catholicity of
theoretical reference.

The Epstein-Fenz studies place considerable emphasis upon cognitive
processes; parachutists apparently learn to ignore certain cues, to concentrate on others, to ruminate, to plan, and so on. The role of cognition in
handling anxiety is also stressed in an extremely interesting study by Valins
& Ray (186). Subjects were led to believe, through a supposed recording of
their heart beats, that they were not responding physiologically to slides of
snakes, but were reacting to slides of the word "shock" preceding the administration of mild shock. Control Ss heard the same "heart sounds" but were
induced to believe that these were extraneous. The experimental Ss showed
a significantly lesser degree of avoidance behavior when later confronted
with a snake. The authors suggest that their findings provide a challenge to
current desensitization theory, which stresses the incompatibility of fear and
induced muscle relaxation. They point to the role of cognitive desensitization
in that the subject's perception and interpretation of his internal reactions
influence the reduction of fear.

Another important approach to the reduction of anxiety, pioneered by
Bandura, emphasizes the role of symbolic modeling. Several studies confirm
or extend the utility of this work. Bandura & Menlove (9) were able to reduce
(in many cases, undo) the fear of dogs in children by a graduated series of
movies. The study compares single-modeling (one child actor, one dog in
increasingly intimate interaction) with multiple modeling (numerous chil-

dren, numerous dogs of various sizes) and reports that both are successful, but with a clear advantage for multiple modeling. In another modeling investigation, by Geer & Turteltaub (70), fearful Ss (snakes again) observed either a fearful or calm confederate, and as one might expect, became less fearful if they had watched the calm one. The importance of identification with nonfearful exemplars is impressively revealed in a study by DeWolfe (44) of student nurses on a tuberculosis ward. He found a correlation of .50 between the nurses' identification with staff models and the degree of fear decrease. Finally, a study by Leventhal, Watts & Pagano (111) makes it clear that while arousing anxiety may arouse anxiety, it does not necessarily change behavior. Smokers were shown moderately and extremely frightening films on the dangers of smoking. The high-fear movie strengthened the wish to stop smoking but did not produce a change in behavior; instructions on how to stop smoking had no effect on desire but did reduce smoking significantly.

   The measurement and meaning of anxiety.—After all these years, and after literally hundreds of studies on anxiety, there is still no general agreement as to what the commonly used scales are in fact measuring, whether it is drive level, maladjustment, affect, degree of defensiveness, or several of these in some interaction. To some extent the chronically disputatious nature of theory and research on the topic turns on this question, since different investigators have posited rather different meanings of anxiety level. A factor analytic study by Golin et al. (73) aims to clarify some of the issues. The Taylor MA scale, Byrnes' Repression-Sensitization measure, and 14 other scales were given to 226 undergraduates and the factor structure explored. It appears that there is a correlation of .87 between MA and R-S. Furthermore, both scales are "largely determined by two bipolar, orthogonal traits, defensiveness and emotionality." The authors point out that findings for MA have usually been interpreted in terms of drive level, and for R-S in ego-defense theory, yet both measures seem to reflect emotionality and defensiveness; they argue "for improved response-defined measures of drive level and repression-sensitization to clarify the theoretical interpretation of empirical relationships with these scales."

   These findings may help us understand the results of an ingenious study by Kimble & Posnick (98). They constructed a scale by rewriting the items of the Taylor MA scale, retaining the grammatical structure, emotional intensity, and social acceptability of the original items but eliminating anxiety-related content. For example, "My hands and feet are usually warm enough," was transmuted to "My plans and goals are usually clear enough." The correlation between MA and the rewritten scale was .84 in one undergraduate sample and .74 in another. If defensiveness and emotionality underlie MA, these high correlations are quite comprehensible, since the new scale would also seem to tap these traits.

   The importance of separating defensiveness and anxiety is highlighted in a study by Boor & Schill (23), which examined the digit symbol performances of Ss varying on these qualities. They found that the low anxious group performs better, but only when the defensive-low Ss are eliminated from the analysis. About half of the total "low anxious" group consists of Ss who defensively deny anxiety, and the authors suggest that equivocal and contradictory research in the past is probably due to the presence of such Ss. Their work supports similar findings for risk taking by Kogan & Wallach (103).

Almost all of the studies employing the MA or related scales of anxiety have used college student subjects, and several researchers point to the possibility that the measures operate somewhat differently with other samples. Vassiliou, Georgas & Vassiliou (187) gave the Taylor MA scale to a representative sample of urban Greek adults; they found that women score higher than men, that the poorly educated score higher than the well educated. They suggest controlling sex and socioeconomic level when using the scale. In a study relating MA to a mood scale among chronic psychiatric patients, Crumpton, Grayson & Keith-Lee (39) found a positive relation to other measures of anxiety and also to words suggesting apathy and depression; the heightened drive level associated with MA may not operate with a psychiatrically hospitalized sample. Baratz (10) reports that Negro undergraduates scored higher on test anxiety when tested by a white than by a Negro examiner.

These studies do not begin to exhaust the year's literature on the psychometrics of anxiety. New approaches to measurement are presented in several studies (45, 60, 113, 138) and correlational research can be found in others (27, 149, 195).

Anxiety and performance.—A hardy perennial; here are some of the more interesting specimens in this year's harvest. Meisels (130) studied the interaction of anxiety level and degree of stress for various indices of verbal behavior. Some of the results are surprising: although content does reflect anxiety and stress, type-token ratios do not, and both speech-disruption and intrusion ratios, in fact, decrease under high anxiety arousal. There is an intelligent discussion of these somewhat perplexing findings. Ganzer (68) finds that being observed through a one-way screen (more exactly, being told that this is so) inhibits learning of nonsense syllables for high and middle anxious groups, though not for those low. The effect holds only for the first day, however, and is not evident for a relearning task on the second day. Meunier & Rule (135) report that anxious Ss are more conforming than lows on a line-guessing task. The two groups respond differently to lack of feedback: high anxious Ss report confidence ratings which coincide with confidence following failure, low anxious Ss with confidence level following success. Kogan & Wallach (104) continue their work on risk taking. They find that the risky-shift phenomenon (groups being more risk-oriented than individuals prior to group) is more prevalent among groups composed of anxious Ss, and less so among defensive Ss. They conclude that their findings support a responsibility-diffusion theory; groups diffuse responsibility, anxious groups more and defensive groups less. Marlett & Watson (123) find that after continued failure on an avoidance task, the response-latency of anxious Ss increases,

ggesting that failure increases their tendency to avoid the situation. A
udy by Shultz & Hartup (171) does not deal with anxiety directly but uses
e concept of anxiety to interpret the findings derived from a study of per-
rmance under social reinforcement. Procedure is too complex to report
re; essentially Es (both sexes) and Ss (males) represented different degrees
"masculinity-femininity" as assessed by MMPI Mf scores. The most effec-
ve reinforcing agent was a masculine male experimenter; feminine male Ss
d more poorly over time, perhaps because reduction of anxiety reduced
otivation.

Stress.—Although the volume of publication on this topic was low, the
ality of the work was substantial. Two important books appeared. Lazarus
08) has written what will surely be the definitive work on psychological
ress for some years to come. It is thoughtful, remarkably thorough, and
ee of parochialism. A book edited by Appley & Trumbull (6) is a collection
conference papers, and a fine collection, which ranges in coverage from
sychophysiology to anthropology. The conference discussions are included,
d these are less bland and more free-wheeling than is customary on these
casions.

A paper by Opton & Lazarus (145) has a lucid discussion of the problems
volved in relating psychophysiological measures of stress to personality
ariables. Normative (interindividual) measurement often yields weak or
anescent findings, largely because of psychologically irrelevant variations
autonomic response; for example, constitutional differences in response
attern may obscure personality differences. The authors then show how
ese and other problems may be met by ipsative (intra-individual) analyses.
hey report that this approach yielded personality differences in response to
wo different stress situations which a normative analysis did not discern.
paper by Alfert (1) presents a similar finding—idiographic analysis proving
uperior to nomothetic in assessing personality differences associated with
esponse to direct as compared with vicarious threat.

In other experimental studies of stress, Nomikos et al. (144) compared
urprise and suspense in the production of stress reactions. Two versions of a
lm portraying accidents were prepared; the first involved brief anticipation,
he second long anticipation—20 to 30 sec—of an impending accident. Long
nticipation produced higher levels of autonomic disturbance, most of which
ccurred during the period of suspense. Back et al. (7) demonstrated that the
eriod between tasks in an experimental situation can, for some Ss under
ertain conditions, generate physiological stress reactions.

A naturalistic investigation by Vernon, Foley & Schulman (188) explored
he effects of mother-child separation on children's reaction to stressful hos-
ital experiences. When the level of threat was low, as during admissions
rocedures, separation did not appear to be related to the child's response;
when it was high (during the induction of anesthesia), separation did increase
he child's distress.

Defense.—This year has seen several interesting and important studies of the defense processes. There was a revealing investigation by Lipsitt & Strodtbeck (115) on the effect of unconscious sexual identity on decision-making. Their Ss were males categorized into four groups on the basis of conscious and unconscious masculine and feminine orientations. They were asked to reach a decision as to the guilt of a defendent after listening to several tape-recorded versions of a trial hearing for treason; in some versions, the prosecution introduced the issue of the defendant's homosexuality, and in some the judge intervened to raise the issue of moral character. Subjects who were unconsciously masculine were not much influenced in their verdicts by the imputation of homosexuality. The unconsciously feminine-consciously masculine jurors were more likely to find the defendant guilty in those versions where homosexuality was introduced. Unconsciously and consciously feminine Ss showed a kind of backlash, reducing their percentage of guilty decisions when homosexuality was imputed and when the trial judge at the same time made an issue of the defendant's character.

The relation of cognitive controls to defensive and coping processes was studied by Alker (2). The investigation aimed to determine whether coping empathy and defensive projection—a copying-defense pair by the Haan-Kroeber model (81, 107)—are related to cognitive controls, in this case to scanning and category width. The clarity of the findings was somewhat clouded by strong and unexpected sex differences. There was a relationship between scanning and both empathy and projection among female Ss; and, among males, one between cognitive filtering (extensive scanning in tandem with narrow category width) and interpersonal sensitivity. Mendelsohn & Griswold (131) also employed a cognitive framework to interpret their findings on repression and problem solving. Repressors (as determined by MMPI Repression and Denial scores) were less likely to use incidental cues in solving anagrams. Anxiety scores showed a curvilinear relationship to cue utilization; those in the middle range used cues least, contrary to expectation. The paper concludes with an excellent discussion of attention deployment in relation to the repressive defenses. Sex differences were also found in this study, though they were not as strong as those in the Alker research. It is becoming evident, as findings accumulate, that the defensive processes operate rather differently in the sexes, although the precise character and degree of the differences remains obscure.

Two studies of perceptual defense: Schumacher, Wright & Wiesen (167) tested the hypothesis from self-theory that anxiety produces a breakdown in the discrimination between self and milieu. They induced anxiety in female Ss by seating them on what seemed to be an electric chair; these Ss reacted to photographs of themselves, presented tachistoscopically, as though they were threatening stimuli, showing perceptual vigilance at low levels of awareness and defense at higher levels. Lipp et al. (114) found that physically disabled Ss had far more trouble than normals in recognizing tachistoscopically presented slides of physically disabled people. The differences were extreme; it took the disabled group 710 more trials to recognize threat than nonthreat slides, compared to 161 more for the nondisabled group.

Hunter & Goodstein (89) found that Ss high on ego-strength, when asked to defend themselves for ostensibly poor performance, were less defensive and more often used coping responses; those low in ego-strength more often employed rationalization. Kafka & Reiser (91) asked Ss to make drawings of their images and later to recall them. Forgotten images, and those disclaimed as insignificant, had been formed during periods of below-average GSR activity.

Etiology.—Some insight into the etiology of defense preference is offered in two longitudinal studies by Weinstock. Male Ss from the Berkeley Guidance Study were interviewed intensively at the age of 30, and careful ratings of defense and coping mechanisms were obtained by an analysis of interview protocols. In one study (194) the mechanisms were correlated with various measures of childhood (21 to 36 months) and adolescent (11 to 13 years) family climate. The presence of denial and repression in adulthood was correlated with a relaxed, indifferent atmosphere in early childhood, mother and father both seeming to avoid conflict. Regression and doubt were related to a family environment in both childhood and adolescence marked by strain and conflict. Projection was also related to strain, especially in the mother-child interaction in adolescence. The pattern for isolation was particularly interesting—a friendly mother-child relationship early in childhood and a stressful one in adolescence. As to the coping mechanisms, the findings were quite surprising; for example, tolerance of ambiguity and regression in the service of the ego were both related to disciplinary conflicts, parental incompatibility, and paternal instability in adolescence. These findings do not yield easily to interpretation. Weinstock offers the argument that, particularly in childhood, defenses are formed through the parent's modeling; the more mature defenses are responsive to the need to master situational conflicts later in life. The second study (193) using the same data, finds that denial was negatively, and projection and intellectualization positively, correlated with childhood social class, supporting the Miller & Swanson (137) findings of some years ago.

A paper by Thelen (183) also aims to shed some light on the acquisition of defenses. He compared the defense preferences of 17- to 18-year-old boys with those of their mothers and fathers; the measure employed was the Blacky Defense Preference Inventory. The major finding was that when the boys' defense preferences were similar to those of one parent, they were also similar to those of the other; as this suggests, husbands and wives showed similar preferences.

Repression-sensitization.—Over the last few years, Byrne's Repression-Sensitization Scale (R-S) has emerged as the most widely used measure of defensive style. There has been and continues to be considerable controversy as to what it is measuring. We saw earlier in this review that at least one study showed it to be essentially equivalent to the Manifest Anxiety Scale. A related issue is the amount of variance accounted for by social desirability and by acquiescence response set. With some consistency, various investigators using various samples have found correlations of about −.45 between

R-S and measures of social desirability, and somewhat lower positive rela
tionships between R-S and acquiescence. The trend of these results is sup
ported in studies published this year by Feder (58) and by Cosentino & Kah
(34). The prevailing opinion at the moment corresponds to Feder's conclu
sion that R-S ". . . is not merely an equivalent form of the social desirabilit
or acquiescence response set scale, but rather is measuring a rather comple
and currently insufficiently defined dimension."

Some investigators seem to take the validity of R-S for granted, an
having done so, seek to determine the relationship of defensive style to thi
or that dependent variable. The dominant strategy, however, is to attemp
to establish construct validity in the usual pointilliste fashion—that is, b
exploring its relationship to a wide range of other variables, hoping tha
from a mosaic of findings a picture ultimately may be visible. Given th
complexity and insufficient definition of the measure alluded to above, an
given the uncertain status of its validity, this year's research findings ar
extremely difficult to interpret. There is no visible pattern, and negative o
indifferent results, unless they are clearly patterned, are hard to read, sinc
they may reflect either the inadequacy of the measure itself or its inappro
priateness for the specific problem under study. In the latter instance we
may fault the measure when we should perhaps fault the researcher's use o
it.

Kaplan (92) found that repressors were more accurate than sensitizers in
predicting the responses of a neutral target; however, when added informa
tion was given to the judges, neutral Ss increased their accuracy, while both
repressors and sensitizers decreased in accuracy, suggesting that the extreme
groups are more rigid in their judgments of others. Another study by Kaplan
(93) discovered that sensitizers, when acting as interviewers, took a more
active role than either neutrals or repressors and seemed to inhibit the responses of their interviewees. In another interview study Merbaum &
Kazaoka (134) confirm their prediction that sensitizer interviewees more
frequently report negative emotion and repressors positive emotion. Palmer
& Altrocchi (147) found that Rs are more likely to see hostile intent as unconscious. Comparing groups of repressors and sensitizers on problem-solving
tasks, Cohen & Foerst (31) found that repressor groups were in general more
effective; they "developed appropriate problem-solving systems somewhat
earlier, utilized their systems more efficiently, and exhibited significantly
greater leadership continuity."

Yet R and S groups, contrary to prediction, do not respond differently to
success and failure, Cohen & Carrera report (30). Piorkowski (150) studied
the effect of three treatments (distraction, catharsis, and rationalization)
for reducing anxiety following a stress-inducing film, and attempted to
determine whether these methods were differentially effective for R and S
Ss; for the most part, the treatments did not differ in effectiveness, nor were
there R-S differences in response to them. Male sensitizers are more likely
to avoid and repressors to accept aversive stimulation (shock), contrary to

erbaum & Badia's (133) prediction; for women, both R and S *S*s are more
voidant than those in the middle. Bootzin & Stephens (24) did not find
-S differences in perceptual defense. Grebstein (77) discovered no R-S
fferences in response to interpersonal attack.

STUDIES OF AGGRESSION

There was a great deal of research on this topic, in several genres. Much
f the work is experimental; aggression lends itself well to experimental
anipulation. The siting of so many studies in the laboratory may have
roduced a certain bias in the research, in that situational factors become,
ecause of their manipulability, the center of interest. One would like to see
ore research on differences in disposition to aggression and on the interac-
ons between disposition and ambiance; and one would like to see more
udies informed by broad conceptual contexts. The aggression we worry
bout in real life has ideological roots or arises out of domestic ambivalences;
hese and related contexts are poorly represented in current research.

Be that as it may, contemporary experimental work explores situational
ements influencing the stimulation, focusing, and constraint of aggressive
cts. The questions asked are these: Which elements arouse aggression and
etermine the intensity and direction of response? Which elements inhibit
s expression, and what are the mechanisms and effects of inhibition? Once
roused, how is anger reduced and discharged?

Arousal and restraint.—In an extended series of experiments, Berkowitz
as been exploring the range of stimulus cues which influence the expression
f aggression. For example, a study by Berkowitz & LePage (19) shows that
he presence of weapons tends to magnify the aggressive response. Subjects
ho had been shocked by a peer were more likely to counter with a larger
umber of shocks when a rifle and revolver were visible than when they were
ot. Interestingly enough, this effect is found even when the weapons are
ot associated with the target; their mere presence, given arousal, seems to
nhance aggression. Two studies, by Berkowitz & Geen (18), and Geen &
Berkowitz (69) examined the stimulus qualities of the target. Insulted
ubjects, after witnessing an aggressive film, were likely to victimize their
icitimizer when they learned his name was similar to the victim of aggres-
ion in the film. Berkowitz & Buck (17) report that following the injection of
pinephrine, *S*s trained to respond aggressively to certain stimuli were more
ikely to respond to central cues and less to peripheral ones; a focusing of
ggression takes place.

Loew (118) finds that aggression can be stimulated by prior verbal learn-
ng; *S*s trained to choose aggressive words were more likely to administer
hocks in a later phase of the experiment. In competitive situations, Epstein
& Taylor (51) report, the opponent's aggressive intention, as perceived by
he subject, is liable to increase aggressive action towards him and to in-
rease autonomic arousal. Being defeated by him produces frustration and
owers self-esteem but does not seem to increase anger. Defeating the enemy

seems to help one's spirits; you will hold a higher opinion of him for it. In a study of cross-sex effects in aggressive interaction, Taylor & Epstein (182) show that males react to the provocations of their male antagonists but not to females; females also are unaggressive to their own sex but do react strongly to male provocation.

Modeling.—Social learning via modeling is an important influence on the instigation and control of aggression. In a complicated experiment, Wheeler & Smith (197) show that restraint is reduced by witnessing an aggressive model and reinstated by the experimenter's censure of that model. The model's self-censure, however, or censure of the model by another subject, did not reinstate restraints. An interesting side effect: the experimenter's censure increased the subject's sense of depression. In another modeling study, Wheeler & Levine (196) had a confederate (B) aggress against an instigating confederate (A); those Ss who had been led to believe they were dissimilar to B were more likely to aggress against A. Feshbach, Stiles & Bitter (63) discovered that insulted girls, after witnessing the shocking of a "provocateur," showed reinforcement of learning; the uninsulted were negatively reinforced by observing shock. Rosekrans & Hartup (155) found that children who observed adult models damaging toys were later likely to do the same if the model had been praised, and unlikely if she had been punished; models inconsistently reinforced were in the middle in evoking imitative aggression.

Catharsis.—Another direction in aggression research addresses itself to the dissipation of hostility. Pytkowicz, Wagner & Sarason (151) found that among insulted male Ss (females were not aroused by the experimental condition) both daydreaming and TAT fantasy were cathartic in that they decreased hostility towards the self. As predicted, males who daydream frequently show these effects more strongly. This study suggests how complex the phenomena are which are subsumed under such terms as "fantasy," "catharsis," and "aggressive drive," and how bound findings are to specific methods of measurement or induction. In some studies, the arousal of "fantasy" (by films, for example) provokes aggression, in others a different form of "fantasy" reduces it. Furthermore, "aggression" is reduced towards the insulter but apparently increased towards the self.

Humor.—There have been several studies on the relations between humor and aggression. Dworkin & Efran (48) found that previously angered Ss reduced their feeling of hostility and anxiety after listening to humor, and did so whether the humor was hostile or not; the control group which listened to nonhumorous material, showed no reduction. Two researches—by Gollob & Levine (74) and by Singer, Gollob & Levine (174)—focus upon factors determining the inhibition of aggressive humor. The first is a neat test of Freud's hypothesis that tendentious humor depends on the person's remaining "innocent" of the impulses expressed in the joke. Subjects were asked to explain the meanings of cartoons they had earlier rated for humor and to rate their degree of aggressiveness. In a post-test it was found that "the greater the aggression content of the cartoons, the greater decrease in humor ratings between the pre- and post-test sessions." As a matter of fact, the high-aggressive cartoons were rated highest on the pretest and lowest on the post-test, a most impressive demonstration of the effect. In the second study, inhibition of aggression was induced by having the Ss study the gory Goya war etchings (controls viewed benign Goya works), which in turn produced a decreased enjoyment of aggressive humor.

The measurement of aggression.—The relationship between "aggressiveness"—that is, aggressive disposition as measured by psychological tests of one sort or another—and aggressive behavior has not proved to be a simple matter to understand. It is quite clear that both "aggressiveness" and hostile behavior are multi-dimensional; furthermore, other factors, both within the person and in the total situation, mediate the relationship between the two. It is, in short, a thorny problem, and the research reported this year stresses the complexities.

Some studies focus upon the measures employed. Thus, James & Mosher (90) find that a "high pull" thematic stimulus differentiates aggressive from nonaggressive boys (peer ratings), while low pull stimuli do not. Coleman's (32) research also points to the nature of the stimulus; using several measures, he found that only the Rorschach showed a direct relationship to peer-rated aggressiveness, and only one TAT card (18BM) does. Megargee & Cook (129) approached the problem of multidimensionality by using a number of scales derived from the TAT and the Holtzman blots and relating these to 11 different criteria of behavioral aggressiveness in juvenile delinquents; the relations between fantasy and behavior differ depending on scales and criteria employed. Leibowitz (110) tested the notion of a continuum of directness of aggression, using three different measures—behavioral, role-playing, and self-report. The behavioral measure (responses on the Buss Aggression Machine) does not relate to the other two, which do relate to each other. He proposes a model of aggressiveness in which physical and verbal modes are orthogonal. Schaefer & Norman (166) explored the question of whether punishment fantasy mediates between aggressive fantasy and behavior in assessing differences between antisocial and control Ss. Surprisingly, the controls have more aggressive fantasy than the antisocial, but themes of external punishment are more prominent in the latter.

Even that extremeness of aggressive behavior we find in assaultive criminals is not explainable as a direct function of "aggressiveness." In earlier research it had been discovered that assaultive criminals were of two types: some were undercontrolled and simply lash out when provoked; but others (and they are likely to commit the more violent crimes) turn out to be overcontrolled—nice-guy-wouldn't-hurt-a-fly types, in whom tensions build up and suddenly explode. Now Megargee, Cook & Mendelsohn (128) have developed a scale, using MMPI items, for assessing assaultiveness among the overcontrolled. The paper is exemplary for its mixture of both psychometric and clinical sophistication.

Other studies.—There is surprisingly little on the relationship of aggre
sion to other dimensions of behavior, which is a pity. As any clinician c.
attest, the aggressive drives, because of their plasticity and ubiquity, can
seen in many modes and domains, often indirectly or subtly. A good examp
is found in a study by Downing & Rickels (47), who propose that sid
reactions to direct treatment are an indirect way of expressing hostile feelin
for those patients who cannot express themselves directly. The results be
out the hypothesis (although other interpretations are possible, as t'
authors allow) in that side reactors obtain lower pretreatment scores
hostility measures than non-side reactors. The relation of aggression
achievement is investigated by Roth & Puri (160), who find that for ma
youngsters (third through twelfth grade) achievers were more extrapuniti'
(the Rosenzweig test) and underachievers intropunitive and impunitive.

THE COGNITIVE EMPHASIS

Cognitive variables have proved to be extraordinarily useful in the stuc
of personality. We have already had occasion in this chapter to note th.
they are seen to operate in a wide range of domains, being employed to e
plain such diverse phenomena as competence, moral behavior, the reductie
of anxiety, and so on. Yet the very variety of application makes it difficu
to offer a coherent account of work in this area. What we have, as the tit
heading suggests, is an emphasis, a point of view, an orientation, rather tha
a well-articulated set of concepts. The scatter and sprawl which characteriz
the entire field of personality is also found within this rubric.

This section, then, will make no attempt to cover all of the pertiner
literature of the year. We will first look at an array of studies chosen t
illustrate the remarkable range of topics in which the cognitive emphasis
conspicuous. We will then examine the studies of psychological differenti
tion—field dependence-independence—a topic which attracted, this year a
in the past, an unusual amount of research effort.

Esthetics.—Child & Iwao (29) extend earlier findings by Child (28) on th
connection between cognitive independence and openness, on the one hanc
and esthetic sensitivity on the other. The earlier study showed a significan
relationship for college students; they have now essentially replicated th
findings for American high school students and for Japanese college student
The cross-cultural replication is of special interest, and the authors conclud
that "this relation may be found in any society where esthetic values ar
stressed in some generally available part of the cultural tradition."

Humor.—Zigler, Levine & Gould (209) tested and confirmed the hypothe
sis that children appreciate and prefer those cartoons which are at the uppe
limit of their comprehension; in an interesting discussion they examine th
role of cognitive challenge and mastery in the response to humor, drawin
upon the formulations of Freud and White.

Emotionality.—Valins (185) extends the growing body of work on the
role of cognitive processes in the mediation of emotional response. He used a

bogus feedback situation in which male subjects were led to believe that their heart rates were changing in response to certain of a series of slides of semi-nude females. Subjects psychometrically classified as emotional made more use of these cues in developing preferences than did unemotional subjects, supporting the line of reasoning proposed by Schachter and others that differences in the utilization of internal cues, rather than differences in automatic reactivity itself, may be implicated in "emotional response." An interesting side finding in this research is that the low emotional Ss were much less likely to show up for a second appointment (37 per cent to 3 per cent of high emotional Ss), offering some support for the idea that the unemotional are sociopath-like.

The prediction of death.—Riegel, Riegel & Meyer (154) found that among Ss 55 to 64 years of age, those with high rigidity scores had a higher mortality rate.

Drive level.—Two separate studies confirmed the idea that the state of cognitive dissonance acts as a drive to energize behavior. In one research (191) dissonance enhanced task performance on both simple and (counter to expectation) complex tasks; in another (36), dissonance enhanced the emission of dominant responses (verbal habits) at the expense of subordinate responses.

Signal detection.—Antrobus, Coleman & Singer (5) showed that Ss high in daydreaming and thoughtfulness performed differently on a signal-detection task than did Ss low on these measures; the former report more task-irrelevant thoughts but do not show an overall proportion of errors. However, as the task wore on, their accuracy did decrease sharply as compared with the low daydreamers. With reduced novelty, the authors suggest, high day-dreamers tend to turn to inner sources of stimulation, while the lows do not have this alternative available and therefore continue attending to the task.

Time perspective.—Klineberg (101) found that for 10- to 12-year-old children the capacity to delay immediate reward is related "to the degree to which personal future events in general appear to be endowed with a sense of reality, as well as to the degree of everyday preoccupation with future rather than present events." Temporal parameters were also found to be related to punctuality by Blatt & Quinlan (21). Punctual Ss, closely matched on many variables with procrastinators, were found to show greater future time extension in fantasy, to do better on the WAIS Picture Arrangement (a test of anticipation), and to be less preoccupied with death.

Field-dependence-independence.—This is without question the most carefully and thoroughly explored dimension of cognitive style that we have. The background of this work was been rather fully documented in the two previous editions of the *Annual Review*, so I will present only this year's research, and that briefly. Witkin et al. (202) reported important longitudinal results from two groups, one studied from 8 to 13 years of age, the other from 10 to 24 years. The data show a steady increase in field independence until the age of 17, at which point there is a plateau. This study also showed that there is an impressive degree of stability in the extent of field dependence over time, test-retest correlations for the Rod and Frame Test running from .62 to .92 for various periods in a 14-year span. Finally, the various measures of differentiation are substantially correlated at almost all ages surveyed. At the other end of the age spectrum Schwartz & Karp (168) have findings which show a return to field dependence among the elderly, and in a further study Karp (94) reported that among men 60 to 75 years of age, employed males were more field independent than those who are retired. Levinson (112) found that recent arrivals to Skid Row were less field dependent than the long-time homeless. Among male adolescents, Barclay & Cusumano (11) reported, those with fathers absent were more field dependent than those with fathers present; there were no differences between the groups in indices of masculinity or cross-sex identity, and as the authors suggest, the findings are of some importance in understanding the effects of father-absence. In other studies, relationships were reported between field dependence and creative test performance (176), some aspects of locus of control (200), and extroversion (54). Finally, there are two studies which discuss findings in preliterate societies (42, 120). In short, research on this topic continues to show the variety and vitality that have marked it in the past.

The Psychoanalytic Emphasis

David Rapaport's collected works are at last available (72). The collection merits the term "magisterial;" each contribution, from the occasional essay to the monograph in depth, attests to the depth and strength of his thought. We also have a memorial volume prepared by his colleagues and students (88); eight contributions by leading figures in psychoanalytic psychology, and the range of the essays reflects the breadth of Rapaport's intellectual interests. Erikson's new book (52) brings together recent essays, largely on the concept of identity; the inventiveness and subtlety of Erikson's work are fully evident. Mann, Gibbard & Hartman (121) employ the psychoanalytic perspective to capture the complex interactions which evolve in T-groups. Their book succeeds admirably in mixing quantitative methods and naturalistic observation; the methods are here used to illuminate rather than to obscure the dense and shadowed transactions of the group and its leader.

It is good to see that there is some renewed interest in exploring empirically the psychoanalytic character typology. Work on this topic has accumulated very slowly, despite its strong clinical and theoretical base. An imaginative study by Bishop (20) tested the hypothesis that under certain conditions Ss high on anality behave counter to the predictions derived from dissonance theory. She replicated, with some modifications, the Festinger-Carlsmith dissonance experiment (64) and showed that high anal Ss, under conditions of high privation, respond to boring tasks with dislike, and under low privation by increased liking. Another study on anality, by Gordon (75), found that highly anal clinicians "have less confidence in their clinical interpretations, make fewer specific predictions, and find less pathology in their patients than low-anal clinicians."

Studies of orality.—Masling, Weiss & Rothschild (125) reported that *S*s who yield on an Asch-like conformity task have a greater amount of oral dependent imagery on the Rorschach than do non-yielders; furthermore, later-born *S*s are higher on oral dependency than the first-born and only children. Masling, Rabie & Blondheim (124) found that obese *S*s are higher on oral dependency than controls, and Wolowitz (203) reported that peptic ulcer patients scored higher than controls on an inventory measure of oral passivity.

LITERATURE CITED

1. Alfert, E. An idiographic analysis of personality differences between reactors to a vicariously experienced threat and reactors to a direct threat. *J. Exptl. Res. Pers.*, **2**, 200–7 (1967)
2. Alker, H. A. Cognitive controls and the Haan-Kroeber model of ego-functioning. *J. Abnorm. Psychol.*, **72**, 434–40 (1967)
3. Alper, T. G., Greenberger, E. Relationship of picture structure to achievement motivation in college women. *J. Pers. Soc. Psychol.*, **7**, 362–70 (1967)
4. Andrews, J. D. The achievement motive and advancement in two types of organizations. *J. Pers. Soc. Psychol.*, **6**, 163–68 (1967)
5. Antrobus, J. S., Coleman, R., Singer, J. L. Signal-detection performance by subjects differing in predisposition to daydreaming. *J. Consult. Psychol.*, **31**, 487–91 (1967)
6. Appley, M. H., Trumbull, R., Eds. *Psychological Stress* (Appleton-Century-Crofts, New York, 1967)
7. Back, K. W., Wilson, S. R., Bogdonoff, M. D. In-between times and experimental stress. *J. Pers.*, **35**, 456–73 (1967)
8. Bakan, D. *On Method* (Jossey-Bass, San Francisco, 1967)
9. Bandura, A., Menlove, F. L. Factors determining vicarious extinction of avoidance behavior through symbolic modeling. *J. Pers. Soc. Psychol.*, **8**, 99–108 (1967)
10. Baratz, S. S. Effect of race of experimenter, instructions, and comparison population upon level of reported anxiety in Negro subjects. *J. Pers. Soc. Psychol.*, **7**, 194–96 (1967)

11. Barclay, A., Cusumano, D. R. Father absence, cross-sex identity, and field-dependent behavior in male adolescents. *Child Develpm.*, **38**, 243–50 (1967)
12. Barker, R. G. Naturalistic methods in psychological research. *Hum. Develpm.*, **10**, 223–29 (1967)
13. Baruch, R. The achievement motive in women: Implications for career development. *J. Pers. Soc. Psychol.*, **5**, 260–67 (1967)
14. Baumrind, D. Child care practices anteceding three patterns of preschool behavior. *Genet. Psychol. Monogr.*, **75**, 43–88 (1967)
15. Baumrind, D., Black, A. E. Socialization practices associated with dimensions of competence in preschool boys and girls. *Child Develpm.*, **38**, 291–327 (1967)
16. Belanger, R. M., Sattler, J. M. Motive to achieve success and motive to avoid failure as a capacity to tolerate uncertainty in a pain producing situation. *J. Exptl. Res. Pers.*, **2**, 154–59 (1967)
17. Berkowitz, L., Buck, R. W. Impulsive aggression: Reactivity to aggressive cues under emotion arousal. *J. Pers.*, **35**, 415–24 (1967)
18. Berkowitz, L., Geen, R. G. Stimulus qualities of the target of aggression: A further study. *J. Pers. Soc. Psychol.*, **5**, 364–68 (1967)
19. Berkowitz, L., LePage, A. Weapons as aggression-eliciting stimuli. *J. Pers. Soc. Psychol.*, **7**, 202–7 (1967)
20. Bishop, F. V. The anal character: A rebel in the dissonance family. *J. Pers. Soc. Psychol.*, **6**, 23–36 (1967)
21. Blatt, S. J., Quinlan, P. Punctual and procrastinating students: A study

of temporal parameters. *J. Consult. Psychol.*, **31**, 169–74 (1967)

22. Bond, D. D. *The Love and Fear of Flying*. (Intern. Univ. Press, New York, 1952)

23. Boor, M., Schill, T. Digit symbol performance of subjects varying in anxiety and defensiveness. *J. Consult. Psychol.*, **31**, 600–3 (1967)

24. Bootzin, R. R., Stephens, M. W. Individual differences and perceptual defense in the absence of response. *J. Pers. Soc. Psychol.*, **6**, 408–12 (1967)

25. Braun, J. R., Link, J. M. Relation between self-acceptance, food and occupation aversions, and susceptibility to annoyance. *J. Clin. Psychol.*, **23**, 24–26 (1967)

26. Bryan, J. H., Test, M. A. Models and helping: Naturalistic studies in aiding behavior. *J. Pers. Soc. Psychol.*, **6**, 400–7 (1967)

27. Chase, C. I., Sassenrath, J. M. Response bias and test anxiety. *J. Clin. Psychol.*, **23**, 234–36 (1967)

28. Child, I. L. Personality correlates of esthetic judgment in college students. *J. Pers.*, **33**, 476–511 (1965)

29. Child, I. L., Iwao, S. Personality and esthetic sensitivity: Extension of findings to younger age and to different culture. *J. Pers. Soc. Psychol.*, **8**, 308–12 (1968)

30. Cohen, A. M., Carrera, R. N. Changes in the judgments of sensitizers and repressers in response to failure and success evaluations of group performance. *J. Soc. Psychol.*, **72**, 217–21 (1967)

31. Cohen, A. M., Foerst, J. R., Jr. Organizational behaviors and adaptations to organizational change of sensitizer and represser problem-solving groups. *J. Pers. Soc. Psychol.*, **8**, 209–16 (1968)

32. Coleman, J. C. Stimulus factors in the relation between fantasy and behavior. *J. Proj. Tech. Pers. Assess.*, **31**, 68–73 (1967)

33. Coopersmith, S. *Antecedents of Self-Esteem* (W. H. Freeman, New York, 1967)

34. Cosentino, F., Kahn, M. Further normative and comparative data on the Repression-Sensitization and Social Desirability scales. *Psychol. Rept.*, **20**, 959–62 (1967)

35. Costello, C. G. Two scales to measure achievement motivation. *J. Psychol.*, **66**, 231–35 (1967)

36. Cottrell, N. B., Wack, D. L. Energizing effects of cognitive dissonance upon dominant and subordinate responses. *J. Pers. Soc. Psychol.*, **6**, 132–38 (1967)

37. Cowan, G., Goldberg, F. J. Need achievement as a function of the race and sex of figures of selected TAT cards. *J. Pers. Soc. Psychol.*, **5**, 245–49 (1967)

38. Crowley, P. M. Effect of training upon objectivity of moral judgment in grade-school children. *J. Pers. Soc. Psychol.*, **8**, 228–32 (1968)

39. Crumpton, E., Grayson, H. M., Keith-Lee, P. What kinds of anxiety does the Taylor MA measure? *J. Consult. Psychol.*, **31**, 324–26 (1967)

40. Cummin, P. C. TAT correlates of executive performance. *J. Appl. Psychol.*, **51**, 78–81 (1967)

41. Davids, A., Hainsworth, P. K. Maternal attitudes about family life and child rearing as avowed by mothers and perceived by their under-achieving and high-achieving sons. *J. Consult. Psychol.*, **31**, 29–37 (1967)

42. Dawson, J. L. Cultural and physiological influences upon spatial-perceptual processes in West Africa: I. *Intern. J. Psychol.*, **2**, 115–28 (1967)

43. Deutsch, H. *Psychology of Women*, I (Grune & Stratton, New York, 1944)

44. DeWolfe, A. S. Identification and fear decrease. *J. Consult. Psychol.*, **31**, 259–63 (1967)

45. Dildy, L. W., Liberty, P. G., Jr. Investigation of peer-rated anxiety. *Proc. 75th Ann. Conv. Am. Psychol. Assoc.*, **2**, 371–72 (1967)

46. Dohrenwend, B. S., Feldstein, S., Plosky, J. Factors interacting with birth order in self-selection among volunteer subjects. *J. Soc. Psychol.*, **72**, 125–28 (1967)

47. Downing, R. W., Rickels, K. Self-report of hostility and the incidence of side reactions in neurotic outpatients treated with tranquilizing drugs and placebo. *J. Consult. Psychol.*, **31**, 71–76 (1967)

48. Dworkin, E. S., Efran, J. S. The angered: Their susceptibility to varieties of humor. *J. Pers. Soc. Psychol.*, **6**, 233–36 (1967)

49. Epstein, S. Toward a unified theory of anxiety. *Progress in Experimental*

Personality Research, **4** (Maher, B. A., Ed., Academic Press, New York, 1967)

50. Epstein, S., Fenz, W. D. Theory and experiment on the measurement of approach-avoidance conflict. *J. Abnorm. Soc. Psychol.*, **64**, 97–112 (1962)

51. Epstein, S., Taylor, S. P. Instigation to aggression as a function of degree of defeat and perceived aggressive intent of the opponent. *J. Pers.*, **35**, 265–89 (1967)

52. Erikson, E. *Identity: Youth and Crisis* (Norton, New York, 1967)

53. Erikson, K. T. A comment on disguised observation in sociology. *Soc. Probl.*, **14**, 366–73 (1967)

54. Evans, F. J. Field dependence and the Maudsley Personality Inventory. *Percept. Mot. Skills*, **24**, 526 (1967)

55. Ezekiel, R. S. The personal future and Peace Corps competence. *J. Pers. Soc. Psychol. Mongr. Suppl.*, **8**, 1–26 (1968)

56. Feather, N. T. Level of aspiration and performance variability. *J. Pers. Soc. Psychol.*, **6**, 37–46 (1967)

57. Feather, N. T. Valence of outcome and expectation of success in relation to task difficulty and perceived locus of control. *Ibid.*, **7**, 372–86 (1967)

58. Feder, C. Z. Relationship of repression-sensitization to adjustment status, social desirability, and acquiescence response set. *J. Consult. Psychol.*, **31**, 401–6 (1967)

59. Feld, S. C. Longitudinal study of the origins of achievement strivings. *J. Pers. Soc. Psychol.*, **7**, 408–14 (1967)

60. Fenz, W. D. Specificity in somatic responses to anxiety. *Percept. Mot. Skills*, **24**, 1183–90 (1967)

61. Fenz, W. D., Epstein, S. Measurement of approach-avoidance conflict along a stimulus dimension by a thematic apperception test. *J. Pers.*, **30**, 613–32 (1962)

62. Fenz, W. D., Epstein, S. Gradients of physiological arousal of experienced and novice parachutists as a function of an approaching jump. *Psychosom. Med.*, **29**, 33–51 (1967)

63. Feshbach, S., Stiles, W. B., Bitter, E. The reinforcing effect of witnessing aggression. *J. Exptl. Res. Pers.*, **2**, 133–39 (1967)

64. Festinger, L., Carlsmith, J. Cognitive consequences of forced compliance. *J. Abnorm. Soc. Psychol.*, **58**, 203–10 (1959)

65. Freedman, J. L., Wallington, S. A., Bless, E. Compliance with pressure: The effect of guilt. *J. Pers. Soc. Psychol.*, **7**, 117–24 (1967)

66. Freud, S. *Beyond the Pleasure Principle* (Liveright, New York, 1950)

67. Friedman, N. *The Social Nature of Psychological Research: The Psychological Experiment as a Social Interaction* (Basic Books, New York, 1967)

68. Ganzer, V. J. Effects of audience presence and test anxiety on learning and retention in a serial learning situation. *J. Pers. Soc. Psychol.*, **8**, 194–99 (1968)

69. Geen, R. G., Berkowitz, L. Some conditions facilitating the occurrence of aggression after the observation of violence. *J. Pers.*, **35**, 666–76 (1967)

70. Geer, J. H., Turteltaub, A. Fear reduction following observation of a model. *J. Pers. Soc. Psychol.*, **6**, 327–32 (1967)

71. Gergen, K. J., Bauer, R. A. Interactive effects of self-esteem and task difficulty on social conformity. *J. Pers. Soc. Psychol.*, **6**, 16–22 (1967)

72. Gill, M. M., Ed. *The Collected Papers of David Rapaport* (Basic Books, New York, 1967)

73. Golin, S., Herron, E. W., Lakota, R., Reineck, L. Factor analytic study of the manifest anxiety, extraversion, and repression-sensitization scales. *J. Consult. Psychol.*, **31**, 564–69 (1967)

74. Gollob, H. F., Levine, J. Distraction as a factor in the enjoyment of aggressive humor. *J. Pers. Soc. Psychol.*, **5**, 368–72 (1967)

75. Gordon, C. M. Some effects of clinician and patient personality on decision making in a clinical setting. *J. Consult. Psychol.*, **31**, 477–80 (1967)

76. Gough, H. G., DeVos, G., Mizushima, K. Japanese validation of the CPI social maturity index. *Psychol. Rept.*, **22**, 143–46 (1968)

77. Grebstein, L. C. Defensive behavior in an interpersonal situation. *J. Consult. Psychol.*, **31**, 529–35 (1967)

78. Greenberg, M. S. Role playing: An alternative to deception? *J. Pers. Soc. Psychol.*, **7**, 152–57 (1967)

79. Grim, P. F., Kohlberg, L., White, S. H. Some relationships between

conscience and attentional processes. *J. Pers. Soc. Psychol.*, **8**, 239–52 (1968)

80. Gutmann, D. On cross-cultural studies as a naturalistic approach in psychology. *Hum. Develpm.*, **10**, 187–98 (1967)

81. Haan, N. Coping and defense mechanisms related to personality inventories. *J. Consult. Psychol.*, **29**, 373–78 (1965)

82. Hart, J. J. Assessing individual differences in motivation and their effect on performance of number facility. *Psychol. Rept.*, **20**, 55–59 (1967)

83. Hartshorne, H., May, M. A. *Studies in the Nature of Character* (Macmillan, New York, 1928)

84. Hays, L. W., Worell, L. Anxiety drive, anxiety habit, and achievement: A theoretical reformulation in terms of optimal motivation. *J. Personality*, **35**, 145–63 (1967)

85. Heckhausen, H. *The Anatomy of Achievement Motivation* (Academic Press, New York, 1967)

86. Heilbrun, A. B., Jr., Harrell, S. N., Gillard, B. J. Perceived maternal child-rearing patterns and the effects of social nonreaction upon achievement motivation. *Child Develpm.*, **38**, 267–81 (1967)

87. Hoffman, M. L., Saltzstein, H. D. Parent discipline and the child's moral development. *J. Pers. Soc. Psychol.*, **5**, 45–57 (1967)

88. Holt, R. R., Ed. *Motives and Thought* (Intern. Univ. Press, New York, 1967)

89. Hunter, C. G., Goodstein, L. D. Ego strength and types of defensive and coping behavior. *J. Consult. Psychol.*, **31**, 432 (1967)

90. James, P. B., Mosher, D. L. Thematic aggression, hostility-guilt and aggressive behavior. *J. Proj. Tech. Pers. Assess.*, **31**, 61–67 (1967)

91. Kafka, E., Reiser, M. F. Defensive and adaptive ego processes: Their relationship to GSR activity in free imagery experiments. *Arch. Gen. Psychiat.*, **16**, 34–40 (1967)

92. Kaplan, M. F. Repression-sensitization and prediction of self-descriptive behavior: Response versus situational cue variables. *J. Abnorm. Psychol.*, **72**, 354–61 (1967)

93. Kaplan, M. F. Interview interaction of repressors and sensitizers. *J.*

Consult. Psychol., **31**, 513–16 (1967)

94. Karp, S. A. Field dependence and occupational activity in the aged. *Percept. Mot. Skills*, **24**, 603–9 (1967)

95. Katz, D. Editorial, *J. Pers. Soc. Psychol.*, **7**, 341–44 (1967)

96. Kelly, J. G. Naturalistic observations and theory confirmation: An example. *Hum. Develpm.*, **10**, 212–22 (1967)

97. Kelman, H. C. Human use of human subjects. *Psychol. Bull.*, **67**, 1–11 (1967)

98. Kimble, G. A., Posnick, G. M. Anxiety? *J. Pers. Soc. Psychol.*, **7**, 108–10 (1967)

99. Kipnis, D. Studies in character structure. *J. Pers. Soc. Psychol.*, **8**, 217–27 (1968)

100. Kipnis, D., Wagner, C. Character structure and response to leadership power. *J. Exptl. Res. Pers.*, **2**, 16–24 (1967)

101. Klineberg, S. L. Future time perspective and the preference for delayed reward. *J. Pers. Soc. Psychol.*, **8**, 253–57 (1968)

102. Klinger, E. Modeling effects on achievement imagery. *J. Pers. Soc. Psychol.*, **7**, 49–62 (1967)

103. Kogan, N., Wallach, M. A. *Risk-taking* (Holt, Rinehart & Winston, New York, 1964)

104. Kogan, N., Wallach, M. A. Group risk taking as a function of members' anxiety and defensive levels. *J. Pers.*, **35**, 50–63 (1967)

105. Kohlberg, L. Development of moral character and moral ideology. In *Review of Child Development Research*, 1 (Hoffman, M. L., Hoffman, L. W., Eds., Russell Sage Foundation, New York, 1964)

106. Krebs, R. *Relations Between Attention, Moral Judgment and Moral Action* (Doctoral thesis, Univ. Chicago, 1967)

107. Kroeber, T. The coping functions of the ego mechanisms. In *The Study of Lives* (White, R., Ed., Atherton, New York, 1963)

108. Lazarus, R. *Psychological Stress and the Coping Process* (McGraw-Hill, New York, 1966)

109. Lefcourt, H. M. Serendipitous validity study of Gough's social maturity index. *J. Consult. Clin. Psychol.*, **32**, 85–86 (1968)

110. Leibowitz, G. Comparison of self-

report and behavioral techniques of assessing aggression. *J. Consult. Clin. Psychol.*, **32**, 21–25 (1968)

111. Leventhal, H., Watts, J. C., Pagano, F. Effects of fear and instructions on how to cope with danger. *J. Pers. Soc. Psychol.*, **6**, 313–21 (1967)

112. Levinson, B. M. Field dependence in homeless men. *J. Clin. Psychol.*, **23**, 152–54 (1967)

113. Liebert, R. M., Morris, L. W. Cognitive and emotional components of test anxiety: A distinction and some initial data. *Psychol. Rept.*, **20**, 975–78 (1967)

114. Lipp, L., Kolstoc, R., James, W., Randall, H. Denial of disability and internal control of reinforcement: A study using a perceptual defense paradigm. *J. Consult. Clin. Psychol.*, **32**, 72–75 (1968)

115. Lipsitt, P. D., Strodtbeck, F. L. Defensiveness in decision making as a function of sex-role identification. *J. Pers. Soc. Psychol.*, **6**, 10–15 (1967)

116. Livson, N., Peskin, H. Prediction of adult psychological health in a longitudinal study. *J. Abnorm. Psychol.*, **72**, 509–18 (1967)

117. Locke, E. A. Relationship of success and expectation to affect on goal-seeking tasks. *J. Pers. Soc. Psychol.*, **7**, 125–37 (1967)

118. Loew, C. A. Acquisition of a hostile attitude and its relationship to aggressive behavior. *J. Pers. Soc. Psychol.*, **5**, 335–41 (1967)

119. Ludwig, D. J., Maehr, M. L. Changes in self-concept and stated behavioral preferences. *Child Develpm.*, **38**, 453–67 (1967)

120. MacArthur, R. Sex differences in field dependence for the Eskimo: Replication of Berry's findings. *Intern. J. Psychol.*, **2**, 139–40 (1967)

121. Mann, R. D., Gibbard, G., Hartman, J. J. *Interpersonal Styles and Group Development* (John Wiley, New York, 1967)

122. Marcia, J. E. Ego identity status: relationship to change in self-esteem, "general maladjustment," and authoritarianism. *J. Pers.*, **35**, 118–33 (1967)

123. Marlett, N. J., Watson, D. Test anxiety and immediate or delayed feedback in a test-like avoidance task. *J. Pers. Soc. Psychol.*, **8**, 200–3 (1968)

124. Masling, J., Rabie, L., Blondheim, S. H. Obesity, level of aspiration, and Rorschach and TAT measures of oral dependence. *J. Consult. Psychol.*, **31**, 233–39 (1967)

125. Masling, J., Weiss, L., Rothschild, B. Relationships of oral imagery to yielding behavior and birth order. *J. Consult. Clin. Psychol.*, **32**, 89–91 (1968)

126. McKeachie, W. J., Isaacson, R. L., Milholland, J. E., Lin, Y. Student achievement motives, achievement cues, and academic achievement. *J. Consult. Clin. Psychol.*, **32**, 26–29 (1968)

127. Meehl, P. E. Theory testing in psychology and physics: A methodological paradox. *Phil. of Sci.*, **34**, 103–15 (1967)

128. Megargee, E. I., Cook, P. E., Mendelsohn, G. A. Development and validation of an MMPI scale of assaultiveness in overcontrolled individuals. *J. Abnorm. Psychol.*, **72**, 519–28 (1967)

129. Megargee, E. I., Cook, P. E. The relation of TAT and inkblot aggressive content scales with each other and with criteria of overt aggressiveness in juvenile delinquents. *J. Proj. Tech. Pers. Assess.*, **31**, 48–60 (1967)

130. Meisels, M. Test anxiety, stress, and verbal behavior. *J. Consult. Psychol.*, **31**, 577–82 (1967)

131. Mendelsohn, G. A., Griswold, B. B. Anxiety and repression as predictors of the use of incidental cues in problem solving. *J. Pers. Soc. Psychol.*, **6**, 353–59 (1967)

132. Menzel, E. W. Naturalistic and experimental research on primates. *Hum. Develpm.*, **10**, 170–86 (1967)

133. Merbaum, M., Badia, P. Tolerance of repressors and sensitizers to noxious stimulation. *J. Abnorm. Psychol.*, **72**, 349–53 (1967)

134. Merbaum, M., Kazaoka, K. Reports of emotional experience by sensitizers and repressors during an interview transaction. *J. Abnorm. Psychol.*, **72**, 101–5 (1967)

135. Meunier, C., Rule, B. G. Anxiety, confidence and conformity. *J. Pers.*, **35**, 498–504 (1967)

136. Midlarsky, E., Bryan, J. H. Training charity in children. *J. Pers. Soc. Psychol.*, **5**, 408–15 (1967)

137. Miller, D. R., Swanson, G. E. *Inner*

Conflict and Defense (Holt, Rinehart & Winston, New York, 1960)

138. Miller, N. B., Fisher, W. P., Ladd, C. E. Psychometric and rated anxiety. *Psychol. Rept.*, **20**, 707–10 (1967)

139. Mills, T. M. The observer, the experimenter and the group. *Soc. Probl.*, **14**, 373–81 (1967)

140. Milmoe, S., Rosenthal, R., Blane, H. T., Chafetz, M. E., Wolf, I. The doctor's voice: Postdictor of successful referral of alcoholic patients. *J. Abnorm. Psychol.*, **72**, 78–84 (1967)

141. Mischel, W. *Personality and Assessment* (John Wiley, New York, 1968)

142. Mizushima, K., DeVos, G. An application of the California Psychological Inventory in a study of Japanese delinquency. *J. Soc. Psychol.*, **71**, 45–51 (1967)

143. Nisbett, R. E., Gordon, A. Self-esteem and susceptibility to social influence. *J. Pers. Soc. Psychol.*, **5**, 268–76 (1967)

144. Nomikos, M. S., Opton, E., Averill, J. R., Lazarus, R. S. Surprise versus suspense in the production of stress reaction. *J. Pers. Soc. Psychol.*, **8**, 204–8 (1968)

145. Opton, E. M., Lazarus, R. S. Personality determinants of psychophysiological response to stress: A theoretical analysis and an experiment. *J. Pers. Soc. Psychol.*, **6**, 291–303 (1967)

146. Orne, M. T. On the social psychology of the psychological experiment. *Am. Psychol.*, **17**, 776–83 (1962)

147. Palmer, J., Altrocchi, J. Attribution of hostile intent as unconscious. *J. Pers.*, **35**, 164–77 (1967)

148. Pavlov, I. P. *Conditioned Reflexes* (Oxford Univ. Press, London, 1927)

149. Pervin, L. A. Aptitude, anxiety and academic performance: A moderator variable analysis. *Psychol. Rept.*, **20**, 215–21 (1967)

150. Piorkowski, G. K. Anxiety-reducing efficacy of distraction, catharsis, and rationalization in two personality types. *J. Consult. Psychol.*, **31**, 279–85 (1967)

151. Pytkowicz, A. R., Wagner, N. N., Sarason, I. G. An experimental study of the reduction of hostility through fantasy. *J. Pers. Soc. Psychol.*, **5**, 295–303 (1967)

152. Rainwater, L., Pittman, D. J. Ethical problems in studying a politically sensitive and deviant community. *Soc. Probl.*, **14**, 357–66 (1966)

153. Raush, H. L. Naturalistic aspects of the clinical research method. *Hum. Develpm.*, **10**, 155–69 (1967)

154. Riegel, K. F., Riegel, R. M., Meyer, G. A study of the dropout rates in longitudinal research on aging and the prediction of death. *J. Pers. Soc. Psychol.*, **5**, 342–48 (1967)

155. Rosekrans, M. A., Hartup, W. W. Imitative influences of consistent and inconsistent response consequences to a model on aggressive behavior in children. *J. Pers. Soc. Psychol.*, **7**, 429–34 (1967)

156. Rosenhan, D., White, G. M. Observation and rehearsal as determinants of prosocial behavior. *J. Pers. Soc. Psychol.*, **5**, 424–31 (1967)

157. Rosenthal, R. *Experimenter Effects in Behavioral Research* (Appleton-Century-Crofts, New York, 1966)

158. Rosenthal, R. Covert communication in the psychological experiment. *Psychol. Bull.*, **67**, 356–67 (1967)

159. Rosenthal, R., Jacobson, L. Teachers' expectancies: Determinants of pupils' IQ gains. *Psychol. Rept.*, **19**, 115–18 (1966)

160. Roth, R. M., Puri, P. Direction of aggression and the nonachievement syndrome. *J. Counsel. Psychol.*, **14**, 277–81 (1967)

161. Rubin, I. M. Increased self-acceptance: A means of reducing prejudice. *J. Pers. Soc. Psychol.*, **5**, 233–38 (1967)

162. Ruma, E. H., Mosher, D. L. Relationship between moral judgment and guilt in delinquent boys. *J. Abnorm. Psychol.*, **72**, 122–27 (1967)

163. Rychlak, J. P., Legerski, A. T. A sociocultural theory of appropriate sexual role identification and level of personal adjustment. *J. Pers.*, **35**, 31–49 (1967)

164. Samelson, F., Yates, J. F. Acquiescence and the F Scale. *Psychol. Bull.*, **68**, 91–103 (1967)

165. Sanford, N. The field of personality. To appear in *Encyclopedia of the Social Sciences*, Second Edition (1968)

166. Schaefer, J. B., Norman, M. Punishment and aggression in fantasy responses of boys with antisocial

character traits. *J. Pers. Soc. Psychol.*, **6**, 237–40 (1967)

167. Schumacher, A. S., Wright, J. M., Wiesen, A. E. The self as a source of anxiety. *J. Consult. Clin. Psychol.*, **32**, 30–34 (1968)

168. Schwartz, D. W., Karp, S. A. Field dependence in a geriatric population. *Percept. Mot. Skills*, **24**, 495–504 (1967)

169. Sechrest, L. Naturalistic methods in the study of social attitudes. *Hum. Develpm.*, **10**, 199–211 (1967)

170. Shrable, K., Stewart, L. H. Personality correlates of achievement imagery: Theoretical and methodological implications. *Percept. Mot. Skills*, **24**, 1087–98 (1967)

171. Shultz, T. R., Hartup, W. W. Performance under social reinforcement as a function of masculinity-femininity of experimenter and subject. *J. Pers. Soc. Psychol.*, **6**, 337–41 (1967)

172. Siegel, A. E. Editorial. *Child Develpm.*, **30**, 901–8 (1967)

173. Silverman, I. W. Incidence of guilt reactions in children. *J. Pers. Soc. Psychol.*, **7**, 338–40 (1967)

174. Singer, D. L., Gollob, H. F., Levine, J. Mobilization of inhibition and the enjoyment of aggressive humor. *J. Pers.*, **35**, 562–69 (1967)

175. Smith, M. B. Conflicting values affecting behavioral research with children. *Am. Psychol.*, **22**, 377–82 (1967)

176. Spotts, J. V., Mackler, B. Relationships of field-dependent and field-independent cognitive styles to creative test performance. *Percept. Mot. Skills*, **24**, 239–69 (1967)

177. Stein, K. B., Sarbin, T. R., Chu, C., Kulik, J. A. Adolescent morality: Its differentiated structure and relation to delinquent conduct. *Multiv. Behav. Res.*, **2**, 199–210 (1967)

178. Stricker, L. J. The true deceiver. *Psychol. Bull.*, **68**, 13–20 (1967)

179. Stricker, L. J., Messick, S., Jackson, D. N. Suspicion of deception: Implications for conformity research. *J. Pers. Soc. Psychol.*, **5**, 379–89 (1967)

180. Sullivan, H. S. *The Interpersonal Theory of Psychiatry* (Norton, New York, 1953)

181. Sykes, G. M. Feeling our way: A report on a conference on ethical is-.

sues in the social sciences. *Am. Behav. Scientist*, **10**, 8–11 (1967)

182. Taylor, S. P., Epstein, S. Aggression as a function of the interaction of the sex of the aggressor and the sex of the victim. *J. Pers.*, **35**, 474–86 (1967)

183. Thelen, M. H. The relationship of selected variables to intrafamily similarity of defense preferences. *J. Proj. Tech. Pers. Assess.*, **31**, 23–27 (1967)

184. Truax, C. B., Schuldt, W. J., Wargo, D. G. Self-ideal concept congruence and improvement in group psychotherapy. *J. Consult. Clin. Psychol.*, **32**, 47–53 (1968)

185. Valins, S. Emotionality and information concerning internal reactions. *J. Pers. Soc. Psychol.*, **6**, 458–63 (1967)

186. Valins, S., Ray, A. A. Effects of cognitive desensitization on avoidance behavior. *J. Pers. Soc. Psychol.*, **7**, 345–50 (1967)

187. Vassiliou, V., Georgas, J. G., Vassiliou, G. Variations in manifest anxiety due to sex, age, and education. *J. Pers. Soc. Psychol.*, **6**, 194–97 (1967)

188. Vernon, D. T., Foley, J. M., Schulman, J. L. Effect of mother-child separation and birth order on young children's responses to two potentially stressful experiences. *J. Pers. Soc. Psychol.*, **5**, 162–74 (1967)

189. Wallace, J. What units shall we employ? Allport's question revisited. *J. Consult. Psychol.*, **31**, 56–65 (1967)

190. Walster, E., Berscheid, E., Abrahams, D., Aronson, V. Effectiveness of debriefing following deception experiments. *J. Pers. Soc. Psychol.*, **6**, 371–80 (1967)

191. Waterman, C. K., Katkin, E. S. Energizing (dynamogenic) effect of cognitive dissonance on task performance. *J. Pers. Soc. Psychol.*, **6**, 126–31 (1967)

192. Webb, E. J., Campbell, D. T., Schwartz, R. D., Sechrest, L. *Unobtrusive Measures* (Rand-McNally, Chicago, 1966)

193. Weinstock, A. R. Longitudinal study of social class and defense preferences. *J. Consult. Psychol.*, **31**, 539–41 (1967)

194. Weinstock, A. R. Family environment and the development of defense and coping mechanisms. *J. Pers. Soc. Psychol.*, **5**, 67–75 (1967)

195. Weitzner, M., Stallone, F., Smith, G. M. Personality profiles of high, middle, and low MAS subjects. *J. Psychol.*, **65**, 163–68 (1967)

196. Wheeler, L., Levine, L. Observer-model similarity in the contagion of aggression. *Sociometry*, **30**, 41–49 (1967)

197. Wheeler, L., Smith, S. Censure of the model in the contagion of aggression. *J. Pers. Soc. Psychol.*, **6**, 93–98 (1967)

198. White, R. Motivation reconsidered: The concept of competence. *Psychol. Rev.*, **61**, 297–333 (1959)

199. Willems, E. P. Toward an explicit rationale for naturalistic research methods. *Hum. Develpm.*, **10**, 138–54 (1967)

200. Willoughby, R. H. Field-dependence and locus of control. *Percept. Mot. Skills*, **24**, 671–72 (1967)

201. Winter, S. K., Griffith, J. C., Kolb, D. A. Capacity for self-direction. *J. Consult. Clin. Psychol.*, **32**, 35–41 (1968)

202. Witkin, H. A., Goodenough, D. R., Karp, S. A. Stability of cognitive style from childhood to young adulthood. *J. Pers. Soc. Psychol.*, **7**, 291–300 (1967)

203. Wolowitz, H. M. Oral involvement in peptic ulcer. *J. Consult. Psychol.*, **31**, 418–19 (1967)

204. Wyatt, F. How objective is objectivity? *J. Proj. Tech. Pers. Assess.*, **31**, 3–19 (1967)

205. Wyer, R. S., Jr. Behavioral correlates of academic achievement: Conformity under achievement- and affiliation-incentive conditions. *J. Pers. Soc. Psychol.*, **6**, 255–63 (1967)

206. Wyer, R. S., Jr. Effects of task reinforcement, social reinforcement, and task difficulty on perseverance in achievement-related activity. *Ibid.*, **8**, 269–76 (1968)

207. Wyer, R. S., Jr., Bednar, R. Some determinants of perseverance in achievement-related activity. *J. Exptl. Soc. Psychol.*, **3**, 255–56, (1967)

208. Zander, A., Forward, J. Position in group, achievement motivation, and group aspirations. *J. Pers. Soc. Psychol.*, **8**, 282–88 (1968)

209. Zigler, E., Levine, J., Gould, L. Cognitive challenge as a factor in children's humor appreciation. *J. Pers. Soc. Psychol.*, **6**, 332–36 (1967)

210. Zuckerman, M. Schultz, D. P., Hopkins, T. R. Sensation seeking and volunteering for sensory deprivation and hypnosis experiments. *J. Consult. Psychol.*, **31**, 358–63 (1967)

ATTITUDES AND OPINIONS[1]   137

By David O. Sears[2]

University of California, Los Angeles, California

AND

Ronald P. Abeles

Harvard University, Cambridge, Massachusetts

"Attitudes and opinions" are a primary focus of attention throughout social psychology, and indeed throughout all of social science. To make our task manageable we have had to define the boundaries of our attention in terms of those set by the standard journals of social psychology; hence we do not deal with such interesting attitudinal matters as prejudice, mass communications, public opinion, or political socialization. Fortunately, recent and conscientious reviews of these topics are available; several chapters in the revised *Handbook of Social Psychology* deal with such matters, as do Proshansky (190) and Tannenbaum & Greenberg (239). This restriction is in itself scarcely adequate; our perhaps too lengthy bibliography still cites less than half the relevant published material for this 3-year period. We have tried to devote the most space to those issues that have created the most attention, though wherever possible emphasizing issues on which debate has been focused rather than diffuse. This choice unfortunately maximized the probability of reporting confusion rather than clarification; hopefully, student readers will not be discouraged, realizing our sampling has biased the outcome in favor of confusion.

Surveys Of The Attitude Area

The most useful surveys of the area are destined to appear between our writing of this chapter and its appearance in print. Consequently, we have made no serious effort to review them; however, their preprints have circulated widely, and a little advance advertising is not out of order.

The first is the revised edition of the *Handbook of Social Psychology*, edited by Lindzey and Aronson. This is due in 1968, in five volumes. William McGuire's chapter on "nature of attitudes and attitude change" is likely to

[1] Our coverage spans the period from July 1965, where William J. McGuire ended his 1966 *Annual Review* chapter, through May 1968. Our debt to McGuire's example will be evident from the organization and content of this review.

[2] The chapter was prepared while the senior author held a visiting appointment in the Department of Social Relations, Harvard University, whose support is here gratefully acknowledged. We also wish to thank Timothy Brock, Jonathan Freedman, David Kanouse, Howard Leventhal, and Leon Mann for their helpful comments on an earlier draft.

be the standard source in this area for years to come. A little farther afield are chapters by Harding et al. (103) on prejudice and ethnic relations, Sears (214) on political behavior, and Weiss (256) on mass communications. Relevant methodological chapters focus on experimentation (14), attitude measurement (209), and computer simulation (1).

The second has a name so long (*Theories of Cognitive Consistency: A Sourcebook*), so many editors (6), so many chapters (84) and so many authors (68) that the worst fears of its alphabetically-first editor seem almost preordained: that it will come to be known more economically as "TOCCAS" by Abelson et al. (4). If nothing else, it is an anatomical comedown for what in the past had been regarded as the hobgoblin of little minds. Almost all of the chapters deal with theoretical issues rather than new data. Several other volumes of collected papers have appeared, most notably two in the Series, *Advances in Experimental Social Psychology* (24, 25), Feldman's collection (79) on cognitive consistency, and one by the Sherifs (220).

The area is still rather short on texts suitable for undergraduates. The most useful remains Cohen's (60) brief book. Insko's (109) presents clear synopses of the several theories of attitude change, along with abstracts of the most important experimental tests of each. The author justly warns us that the book is slow going as an orthodox undergraduate textbook, but it should receive much use as a more specialized source. Three books of readings devoted specifically to attitudes have appeared (83, 114, 207), as have new editions of the classic *Readings in Social Psychology* and *Group Dynamics*, each with numerous articles on attitude change (56, 191, 233). The new general social psychology text by Jones & Gerard (123) is especially impressive in its intellectual caliber, and its treatment of attitudes and opinions is both extensive and sophisticated. This book, like Brown's (45) (which, however, has little on attitudes), will no doubt be included in many comprehensive examination reading lists, as well as serving the undergraduate course. The forthcoming book by Kiesler, Collins & Miller (137a) may serve the need for an undergraduate text.

The remainder of the review will take up first those problems of persuasion whose origins were, for the most part, in the Yale Attitude Change project, then work growing out of the several consistency theories, and finally those methodological problems of increasing concern.

THE COMMUNICATOR

Credibility and attribution theory.—Communicator credibility has had the reputation of being an uninteresting variable, an unfortunate happenstance in this era of "image politics" (214). Recently it has been revitalized due to a provocative new theoretical approach, Kelley's attribution theory (130), and to several interesting experiments.

Kelley extends Heider's (105) analysis of the phenomenal attribution of causality, proposing that naive observers test the validity of assertions by applying four tests: distinctiveness of the assertion to a particular entity;

consistency of the assertion over time and modalities; and consensus with other observers' views. To be a credible communicator, one's assertion must pass all four tests, thus being attributed to a veridical report about reality rather than to such irrelevant causal factors as personal motives or role demands.

So far, only Jones & Harris's (124) three experiments have sought specifically to determine the conditions under which a stated opinion is attributed to a true attitude. Such attributions were consistently made when the speaker was known to have had free choice about what position he could take, and also to a lesser extent under low choice conditions when his stated position was consistent with that of his reference group (e.g., Southerners' segregationist positions). Confusion was rife when the statement was largely involuntary and the position inconsistent with the speaker's reference group.

Several other experiments fit an attribution analysis: less credibility is attributed to the speaker when he is being ingratiating, self-serving, or even describing physical reality, all presumably because then he is not necessarily expressing his true beliefs. Mills & Jellison (176) found that a speech was more influential, and its communicator regarded as more sincere and impartial, when the speech was presented as having originally been delivered to an audience whose interest it opposed (rather than an audience whose interest it supported). Walster, Aronson & Abrahams (247) found criminals and prosecutors alike were more credible and more persuasive when advocating positions counter to their interests. In a second experiment, an effort to vary the salience of such vested interests failed. Brock (37) found a paint salesman was more persuasive the less expensive was the can of paint he advocated the purchaser buy. And Byrne, Nelson & Reeves (51) found liking for a communicator to be more affected by similarity with his stated opinions when they concerned unverifiable issues than when they concerned verifiable matters. Presumably unverifiable issues, unconstrained by reality considerations, reveal more about true internal attitudes.

A related hypothesis is that attitudinal or experiential similarity should enhance credibility and hence persuasiveness. Berscheid (26) tested this basic hypothesis in two experiments. In the first, a communicator shared the subject's values in one issue domain but was quite dissimilar in another, and was more influential in the former area. In the second, the subject boomeranged from the position of a communicator with values dissimilar to his own, when position and values were in the same issue domain. When they were irrelevant to each other, little change occurred. Mills & Jellison (177a) also found occupational similarity enhanced persuasiveness though it did not affect credibility. And in a clever field experiment, Brock (37) found experiential similarity overrode expertness in determining the sales of a paint salesman.

Forewarning and intent to persuade.—The effects of various advance descriptions of the communicator and communication have been investigated. One kind of description is whether the communication contains new, unfamiliar information or arguments with which the subject is already familiar. Sears & Freedman (216) found that even when the communications were in fact identical, they were more effective when billed as containing new information than when advertised as containing familiar arguments.

Another kind of description is advance warning of the position to be taken in the communication. Freedman & Sears (89) found greater resistance to an attack with longer forewarning of the position to be taken. Apsler & Sears (11) followed this up, hypothesizing that this greater resistance occurs only under conditions of high personal involvement, when the forewarning might help the subject gather his defenses, but that it actually facilitates change under low involvement by cuing the subject to a position he is likely to find persuasive. Their attitude-change data supported the hypothesis, though subsidiary results concerning their involvement manipulation muddied the waters somewhat. Very similar reasoning and results are involved in the finding that delaying identification of a high credibility source until after the message reduces his influence, while delaying a low credibility source's identification enhances his influence (98, 108).

The other advance description often investigated is whether or not the communicator is advertised as intending to persuade the subject. Brock & Becker (42) provided weak support for an earlier finding by Walster & Festinger (246) that a communicator was more effective (at least on involving issues) when overheard than when he was aware of the subject's presence. Rosenblatt & Hicks (205) found that warning of persuasive intent reduced the message's persuasive impact, but the warning used seems likely to have deprecated the message's content as well. Mills (174) tested the further prediction that warnings of persuasive intent actually facilitate change if the subject thinks he is liked by the communicator. His liking/intention interaction was significant and in the predicted direction, but again the subsidiary results suggest that the dynamic of the effect is not well understood. An interesting sidelight is that the "intent" communicator was actually seen as more attractive, though less impartial, than the communicator with no intent to persuade.

Many mechanisms have been proposed for these effects. Source derogation seems to occur in confusing and unsystematic ways (11, 89, 174, 205). Freedman & Sears proposed that forewarning gives subjects time to recruit and rehearse counterarguments, though their data were not very strong on that point. Brock (38) tested directly the hypothesis that discrepancy and intent to persuade both promote the production of counterarguments. He found substantial differences between conditions (though intent to persuade was confounded with source credibility) and significant intracell correlations between the number of arguments produced and attitude change. Rosenblatt (204), for one, seems to have fallen back upon demand characteristics of the experiment as the best explanation. If his evidence is not completely compelling, neither is the current evidence for any competing possibility.

Under some conditions, forewarnings seem to produce anticipatory change. According to McGuire & Millman (166), this occurs when the subject wishes to avoid the embarrassment of changing his mind at the direct behest of the communicator. Thus, Papageorgis (183) expected anticipatory change when the source was advertised as both disreputable and highly effective, but these communicator variations failed. Deaux (67), disconcertingly, found that intent to persuade actually minimized anticipatory change (at least when the subject thought she would not be able to gather more information about the issue). Wicklund, Cooper & Linder (260) present some evidence of anticipatory change, apparently as a form of dissonance reduction, under conditions in which the subject expends much effort in order to hear the communication.

Three specific issues and hypotheses have focused research on discrepancy (the distance between the subject's initial opinion and the communicator's position) and the subject's involvement in his opinion: (a) opinion change is an inverted-U function of discrepancy; (b) the hump of the curve occurs at greater discrepancy with lower levels of involvement (and with greater source credibility); and (c) the exploration of what mechanisms reduce influence at high discrepancy. These hypotheses are widely accepted.

Discrepancy.—Significant curvilinear relationships between discrepancy and opinion change have been found in a variety of settings: Bochner & Insko (30) regarding the hours of sleep required per night; Koslin, Stoops & Loh (143) using the Witkin rod and frame apparatus; Insko, Murashima & Saiyadain (112) in two experiments on numerosity judgments; Brewer & Crano (35) on opinions toward the U.S. space program; and Johnson (121) regarding the subject's self-concept. In some studies, discrepancy has also been found to have a significant positive linear effect upon opinion change across all conditions (30, 70, 121). In a somewhat related finding, Weiss & Steenbock (257) found that persuasion of those initially opposed was actually enhanced when an unpleasant position was spelled out explicitly rather than being left implicit. We could not find any cases in which discrepancy was negatively related to opinion change.

The hump: where and when.—For some years the Sherifs (220, 221) have suggested a simple rule for determining where the hump of the inverted-U occurs: it should be at the point dividing the latitudes of acceptance and rejection. The evidence on this point, however, remains rather weak. Atkins, Deaux & Bieri (20) and Deaux & Bieri (68) found more change within the latitude of acceptance than outside of it, but found no evidence of the predicted interaction with discrepancy variations within each latitude. Whittaker (258) has reanalyzed some earlier experiments from this perspective, but direct evidence on the point is hard to find.

It is equally hard to find solid evidence that lowered involvement or heightened credibility raises the discrepancy level at which the hump occurs. In three separate experiments, the predicted interaction between discrepancy and involvement (or stimulus ambiguity or stability of initial attitude) was obtained, but curiously enough all were either marginal or not significant (70, 112, 143). In three studies, the interaction between discrepancy and source prestige was in the predicted direction (30, 35, 143), but only in one case was the effect significant (30) [nor was a significant interaction presented in the two earlier studies usually cited (16, 85)].

In these studies, the predicted main effects of credibility, discrepancy, and involvement seem to occur consistently and at conventional levels of significance, and the interactions are in the predicted direction but not significant. We are not blind worshippers of the 0.05 level, but perhaps this situation is one to comment upon even so. It may be that experimental social psychologists are using here (and perhaps elsewhere as well) designs too impotent to provide fair tests of their hypotheses (e.g., number of cases too small, manipulations too weak, etc.). More distressing is the possibility that the minimum criterion for a publishable study is a significant predicted main effect (even if uninteresting) and an interesting interaction in the predicted direction (even if not significant).

Mechanisms of resistance.—How do subjects resist influence at high discrepancy? Source derogation is one commonly mentioned possibility, but the evidence seems mixed. Bochner & Insko (30), as in the case of an earlier study by Aronson, Turner & Carlsmith (16), found neither a main effect of discrepancy on source derogation, nor an interaction of discrepancy and source prestige on it, although both studies had obtained the expected decline in opinion change at high discrepancy, especially for low prestige sources. On the other hand, Johnson (121) did obtain a sharp increase in source rejection with greater discrepancy.

Another possibility is that the subject marshals and scans more counterarguments when exposed to a highly discrepant message. Brock (38) indeed found more counterargument production with greater discrepancy, and modest correlations between the number of arguments produced and resistance to change.

It is more likely that the subject simply rejects the position without an elaborate rationale. Bochner & Insko (30) and Feather & Jeffries (78) found sharp increases in disparagement of the communication with greater discrepancy. Most impressive, perhaps, is Waly & Cook's (249) study in which subjects were asked to rate the plausibility of various statements about segregation and integration. The correlation of discrepancy and plausibility was −.84, indicating a clear increase in simple attributions of implausibility with greater discrepancy.

Alternative modes of resolution.—A simple hypothesis implicit in the thinking of most consistency theorists about such matters is that people use a variety of different modes of consistency restoration, and that for purposes of achieving consistency they are all functionally equivalent [see McGuire (162) for an excellent earlier review of these questions]. Several typologies of the various common modes of resolution are available: Aronson & Carlsmith (14) offer the standard dissonance theorist's list (opinion change, source derogation, seeking social support, changing the communicator's opinion); Steiner (232) has presented his list (rejection, conformity, devaluation, and under-recall) in the context of a broader review of responses to interpersonal disagreement; while Kelman & Baron (133) and Sears (215) prefer the simpler distinction of "avoidance" versus "confrontation" of inconsistency.

Most research aimed at determining the conditions for one or another of these has tended toward the situation-specific and descriptive, rather than the situation-free and analytic. Pervin & Yatko (184) surveyed the mechanisms by which smokers handled the problem of smoking and lung cancer and found that they generally questioned the validity of the scientific evidence and underestimated the danger of moderate smoking, but did not do a number of other things they might have done. Steiner (232) has made the most serious effort to develop a general research strategy, although he emphasizes the role of personality rather than situational variables in determining the use of one mode rather than another.

Finally, there is the question of whether or not the several modes of resolution are functionally equivalent alternatives. In Steiner's (232) and Johnson's (121) data they are weakly negatively correlated, but the authors assert that the logic of the functional-alternative argument forbids high negative correlations. Miller & Levy (170) and Bochner & Insko (30) also report negative correlations, this time between source derogation and attitude change. However, proving once again the mortality of attitude research, Pervin & Yatko (184) report only chance relationships between six different methods of reducing dissonance. To date the evidence on functional equivalence is rather shaky, but it is true that it has usually been collected as an afterthought in an experiment designed to find out about something else.

Involvement.—The term "involvement" has come to have a bad reputation in this context, one that it richly deserves. Several different kinds of "involvement" have been noted in the past (85, 220, 268), some but not all (268) of which were hypothesized to reduce opinion change. True to form, several versions have been manipulated here, with almost every possible effect.

Miller (169) found that an omnibus involvement manipulation (varying salience of own position, commitment to it, social support, and production of own arguments) reduced opinion change. Miller & Levy (170) varied emotional arousal (thought to be a central component of involvement) by insulting some subjects and not others on an irrelevant matter. This actually enhanced agreement with a later communication. Apsler & Sears (11) varied what they called personal involvement by proposing a change in educational policy that would affect some subjects and not others, and found involvement did not affect opinion change (though there was a significant interaction with forewarning). To round out the picture, Eagly (70) obtained both results in one study. When the position advocated was a desirable one change was greater under high involvement, but with an undesirable position change was greater under low involvement (at least on one of two measures of change).

Insofar as higher involvement is thought likely to increase the probability of modes of resolution other than opinion change, it is usually expected to increase source derogation. Miller & Levy (170) indeed found it increased source derogation, but Eagly & Manis (71) found involvement had no effect on source derogation, and Apsler & Sears (11) actually found that it decreased derogation, which they attribute to a variant of the *fait accompli* effect. Again, it appears that when involvement decreases influence, it does so mainly by inspiring a blunt and simple rejection of the message. Eagly & Manis (71) found personal relevance of a discrepant message produced significant message derogation but not significant source derogation.

THE COMMUNICATION

Language.—Abelson and his students (3, 95, 128) have conducted a number of novel, fascinating studies into differences in persuasiveness produced by using different language in the communication. He describes it as studying the "semantics of propaganda." In its simplest form it is an effort to determine the types of evidence required to accompany a generic assertion (i.e., an unqualified generalization) to make it persuasive, varying the language of the assertion.

Perhaps the single most interesting finding from this research program is an interaction between verb type and evidence form in producing persuasion. In the inductive evidence form, evidence from a few instances or examples of an assertion is relatively convincing for verbs describing manifest actions with positive affect, such as "have," "buy," "need," or "recommend." It is less convincing for verbs describing negative subjective states, such as "ignore," "hate," or "avoid." For example, one will agree that "Lyndon Johnson appoints Negroes" if he appoints "a few" of them, but in order to agree that he "hates Republicans" he must hate more than just a few of them. Verbs differ in the "implicit quantifiers" (such as "a few," or "many," or "all") commonly understood to accompany them.

The reverse holds for the deductive evidence form, that argues from qualities rather than from instances. Evidence from a few qualities suffices for negative-subjective verbs, but many are required for positive-manifest verbs. Abelson & Kanouse report that "acceptance thresholds for generic assertions are keyed to sentence verbs" (3, p. 185) rather than to nouns used as either subjects or objects. In other words, the verb, not the subject or object, determines how much supporting evidence is required to make the assertion persuasive.

The data are based on four studies using simple subject-verb-object sentence forms (3, 95), and a subsequent study using simple persuasive communications that convincingly replicated the results from the simpler format (128). Theoretical explanations for the effects are still rudimentary, but the area seems likely to become one of considerable interest —not alone for those interested in persuasion, but also for students of naive epistemology and the details of "logical" reasoning.

Mehrabian's ingenious studies (167, 168) on indirect communication of attitudes or affects through variations in the "immediacy" of language also ought to be mentioned here. This work will be interesting to content analysts as well as to those with more general interests in communication.

FEAR AROUSAL

The effects of fear arousal, once thought to be a settled issue, now seem fraught with confusion. The simplest and original empirical question is whether fear arousal in a communication increases or decreases its persuasiveness. The most cited early study, by Janis & Feshbach (117), concluded that fear arousal inhibited change. A lengthy series of experiments by Howard Leventhal now has successfully challenged that early conclusion. He focuses upon three indices of effect: changes in attitude, intentions to change behavior, and actual behavior change.

Of the seven published studies by Leventhal and his colleagues, three concerned smoking and lung cancer (145, 147, 150), three concerned tetanus shots (66, 148, 149), and one dealt with dental caries (146). In all cases, fear arousal was successfully manipulated, as indicated by numerous indices of affect arousal. In the three tetanus studies, fear arousal was positively related to attitude change in terms of raised importance of taking shots. In the smoking and lung cancer studies, greater fear did not produce greater attitude change in terms of believing in the relationship of smoking to lung cancer or the desirability of chest X rays.

Fear arousal generally produced greater intentions to change behavior, though the results were not unequivocal. In two cases the effect was only marginally significant (148, 149); in another it had washed out a week later (150); in another the high fear condition was higher than low fear, but neither was higher than in a control group which received recommendations but no fear arousal (146); and in two others there was no effect (145, 147). In the remaining study (66) the effect was clear, as it was in a study by Chu on the dangers of roundworms to Taiwanese children (57).

With respect to producing changes in health behavior, the pattern again is mixed, but higher fear rarely has been shown to decrease change. Dabbs & Leventhal (66) found high fear more successful than low fear in producing tetanus shot takers, as did Leventhal, Jones & Trembly (148), though the effect was not significant; Leventhal, Singer & Jones (149) obtained no difference. With smoking, the effects were completely mixed. Greater fear arousal decreased X-ray behavior in one case (147), failed to affect the number of subjects trying to stop smoking, but made the attempts more successful (at least in the minority of subjects who could be traced later). The two fear conditions did not differ in the remaining lung cancer studies, though in one case both fear conditions were more successful than was a recommendations-only no-fear control group (145).

These studies also include a great many incidental findings to which this sketchy summary does not do justice. Perhaps most important are the findings in several studies that subjectively reported fear was positively correlated with attitude or behavior change (66, 145-147). Leventhal also tested a number of hypotheses suggesting interactions between fear arousal and other variables: whether the recommendations precede or follow fear arousal [no difference (146)]; whether or not specific instructions are given on how to carry out the behavior [increased shot-taking (148, 149); decreased smoking (150); but decreased attitude change (148)]; and the effectiveness and painfulness of shots [no effects on behavior or intentions to undergo behavior change (66), though Chu (57) found efficacy contributed to acceptance]. Also, such predispositional variables have been investigated as susceptibility to bodily harm (147) or eligibility for possible damage due to smoking history or history of tetanus shots.

Despite the untidiness of these results, it now seems evident, as McGuire (164) has noted, that the original Janis & Feshbach result (117) represents the exception rather than the rule. These recent results seem divided primarily between those indicating that fear facilitates attitude change and behavioral compliance, and those revealing no systematic fear effect. Close on the heels of these numerous experimental studies are three major theoretical reformulations. Leventhal's position has not been spelled out as formally [though see Leventhal (144)], but McGuire (165) and Janis (115) have presented similar models whose bases are inverted U-shaped curves between anxiety or fear arousal and attitude change. A method for scaling fear arousal is badly needed for satisfactory tests of these models.

It might be noted parenthetically that the issue of behavioral concomitants of attitude change has arisen most clearly in the case of fear arousal, though it also preoccupied other researchers (84, 111, 197, 242). As indicated, Leventhal found specific instructions were the strongest determinants of behavioral compliance. Five experiments by Greenwald (99, 100) suggest that one condition in which opinion change is not accompanied by behavior change is when the subject is initially committed to his position. However, the general problem of attitude change unaccompanied by behavior change, and vice versa, still is a neglected issue.

PERSONALITY AND PERSUASIBILITY

The central finding of early work on general (content-free) persuasibility (118) was that its clearest personality correlate was low self-esteem. McGuire (165) has modified this recently by suggesting that self-esteem is positively related to comprehension and negatively related to acceptance; thus the net outcome depends upon the particular circumstances of the experiment. The most direct test of this hypothesis was conducted by Nisbett & Gordon (178), who compared persuasion resulting from simple but implausible unsubstantiated messages, which should produce maximum influence in low self-esteem subjects, with persuasion from complex but plausible substantiated messages, which should produce maximum influence in higher self-esteem subjects. Their results supported this hypothesis. Gollob & Dittes (96) have reported a similar interaction; manipulated self-esteem was positively related to influence on complex issues but negatively related to it on simpler matters. Another such interaction with task difficulty is reported by Gergen & Bauer (94). Sears (213) found aroused social anxiety facilitated opinion change among subjects who had structured the issue in a simple manner around a few central thoughts, but it had no effect on subjects with more complex opinion structures. Wicklund & Brehm (259) find increased agreement with simple assertions under lowered felt competence. These studies thus seem to provide consistent support for McGuire's hypothesis.

Aside from these findings, recent research has not been kind to the general persuasibility area. The other mildly consistent finding is of a negative relationship between the original Janis & Field (118) self-esteem scale, or modifications of it, and persuasibility (70, 94, 227), though the relationship is often weak or even absent (58, 96). Eagly (70) reports an interesting interaction: that high self-esteem subjects are more persuasible when exposed to favorable messages about themselves, whereas low self-esteem subjects are more persuasible with unfavorable messages about themselves.

DISSONANCE THEORY

Most of the substantive debate in the attitude change area has continued to revolve around dissonance theory. Various valuable general statements have been published recently. The current dissonance Establishment view is available in a paper by Aronson (13). The youthful brashness of dissonance theory here is replaced by well-fed middle-aged generosity; Aronson acknowledges much "conceptual fuzziness" about dissonance theory, at least around its fringes, and suggests that research focus upon determining the conditions under which dissonance effects obtain as opposed to those under which other (e.g., incentive or conflict) effects obtain—a far cry from the early days when no behavioral phenomenon was safe from the ravages of the imperialistic dissonance hordes. McGuire (162), in another of his thoughtful overviews of the empirical literature, looks at the consistency theories in general but dissonance in particular. And Abelson (2) has made a conscientious beginning at unraveling the knottiest theoretical tangle in dissonance theory, the problem of determining when, in fact, dissonance can be expected to occur: i.e., when does one cognition psychologically imply another?

Our plan here is to discuss separately the three most active areas of dissonance research: forced compliance, commitment and choice, and selective exposure. First, though, a look at two other developments.

Several experiments have attempted to integrate consistency theories into a more general body of psychological theory and research, tying dissonance phenomena to psychophysical judgments (262), achievement motivation (208), awareness (40), incidental learning (182), and general theories of motivation (63, 80).

There has also been a laudable tendency, harkening back to the earliest days of dissonance theory, to investigate the strength of dissonance predictions in real life. Knox & Inkster (142) conducted interview studies at two race tracks and found bettors considerably more confident their horse would win immediately after betting than they had been immediately beforehand. Kingdon (140), in a look at winners and losers, obtained what he called a "rationalization—congratulation effect." Victorious political candidates attributed the election's outcome to the characteristics of the candidates, while their defeated opponents felt party label was considerably more important. Winners also thought the electorate considerably better informed about campaign issues than did losers. Marlowe, Frager & Nuttall (159) found that losers stuck rigidly to the attitudes that had already cost them money.

Forced Compliance

The most controversial empirical issue surrounding dissonance theory remains its forced compliance prediction: that attitude change following counterattitudinal advocacy is a negative function of the incentive offered for the advocacy. The dissonance position has been most ably articulated by Aronson (12, 13). Two competing theoretical viewpoints have their spokesmen: Janis (116), Elms (74), and Rosenberg (202, 203) favor an incentive formulation, while Bem (21, 22) argues for a radical behaviorism. Amidst much Talmudic debate about what a particular Stanford student of introductory psychology must have been thinking on a sunny afternoon in 1957, empirical work goes on; Collins (61) in particular has conducted numerous careful studies attempting to achieve clarity about the basic empirical facts.

The twenty dollar misunderstanding (cont'd).—Two experiments have yielded clear and compelling results which more or less confirm the dissonance hypothesis. Carlsmith, Collins & Helmreich (55) obtained the "dissonance effect" (attitude change decreased with greater monetary incentive) when subjects advocated a counterattitudinal position face to face, but obtained an "incentive effect" (increased attitude change with greater incentive) after writing an anonymous counterattitudinal essay. And Linder, Cooper & Jones (151) conducted two studies, in each of which the dissonance effect was obtained when the subject was given free choice in whether or not to engage in counterattitudinal behavior, but not under low volition.

Unhappily, these clear results, seemingly focusing upon publicity and freedom of choice (good orthodox dissonance variables) are sailing in what otherwise is a sea of chaos. Most notably, Collins (61) and his colleagues have conducted, at last count, 17 studies in an attempt to obtain the dissonance effect and to define the conditions for its occurrence. Having little success with the first goal, they quite naturally have been unsuccessful with the second. In five experiments, the public-private dimension was manipulated along with financial inducement; in most cases there was a trend toward the incentive effect, and in no case did even the "public" condition yield a dissonance effect. Six subsequent experiments attempted to use the Linder, Cooper & Jones (151) high choice procedure: three experiments to replicate their procedure and results, and three others to supplement the procedure with a public face-to-face confrontation. The outcome appears to have been two incentive effects and one dissonance effect out of the six [see Ashmore et al. (17) for a summary of these studies]. A dissonance effect was finally obtained (106) when subjects' counterattitudinal advocacy was videotaped and not when it was audio-taped anonymously.

This mixture of results, with the accompanying difficulty in obtaining the "dissonance effect," is duplicated in other workers' experiments. Greenbaum (97) found attitude change unaffected by a choice variation; Nuttin (179) obtained a "dissonance effect" when the subjects advocated a consonant position but not when they advocated a dissonant position; and Gerard (92) tested the idea that perceived insufficiency of reward is the critical variable by manipulating expectations of reward, with confusing result. Dissonance predictions were, on the other hand, supported by Powell (188): under conditions of voluntary behavioral compliance, the more credible a source the less was his influence; and Kiesler & De Salvo (136): under conditions of behavioral compliance to a group's wishes, the more attractive the group the less its influence. But significant incentive effects have been obtained at least as often; e.g., in about half of Collins' studies (61) (along with some nonsignificant incentive effects in others), as well as in the anonymous-essay condition in the first of the series (55) and in the low-choice conditions set forth by Linder and associates (151). Bishop (29) obtained an incentive effect for subjects classified as "high anal-retentives" (concerned with parsimony and hoarding) but not for low anals (perhaps the authors of "TOC-CAS" have misplaced cognitive consistency after all).

Another approach has been to look at the mediating processes. This has been a problem for dissonance theorists, since it has proven difficult to measure dissonance reduction in terms other than those of the main dependent variable [here, attitude change, though see Gerard (91) for some useful alternatives]. The incentive theorists assume that higher incentives for counterattitudinal advocacy produce more "biased scanning" of arguments already available to the subject, and invention of new arguments, and thus greater self-persuasion (74, 116, 203). This has the advantage of clarity but the disadvantage of being testable, and indeed the available evidence seems to indicate that higher incentives do not inspire much greater production of arguments supporting the improvisation (55, 151, 201) although there are exceptions (119). Also, the absolute number of arguments produced often seems distressingly small, and their quality seems unrelated to the amount of attitude change produced (97). Elms' point is perhaps well taken that "it is difficult to measure quality of performance meaningfully when the important behavior may occur internally" (74, p. 140), but it strips stimulus-response theorists of some of their previous moral superiority over dissonance theory.

We review this research with the disquieting impression that the dis-

tribution of dissonance, null, and incentive effects obeys a normal curve and
that the internal processes (dissonance reduction and biased scanning) are
not susceptible to any other form of measurement. The most consistent
dissonance effects do center upon the voluntary, public, oral advocacy
(17, 55, 106, 151), though even that has failed in several instances. Hopefully,
as with fear arousal, future research will take us from this quagmire surrounding an obviously oversimplified prediction to the variables that define
the occurrence of one effect rather than another.

   Radical behaviorist critique.—Bem (21, 22) has proposed a radical behaviorist critique of several dissonance experiments. He suggests that the
outcomes derive from subjects' attributions of opinions from the external
circumstances of the experimental situation and not from internal states.
Accordingly, he suggested that "interpersonal observers" should be able to
reproduce the original subjects' responses, given only information about the
experimental situation, without access to the heretofore presumed internal
psychological states experienced by the original subjects. Bem conducted
four "interpersonal replications" of classic dissonance experiments, among
them Cohen's forced compliance study of Yale students' promoting the
New Haven police (33), and indeed obtained results consistent with the
original findings.

   Dissonance enthusiasts, true to their heritage, have quickly risen to this
bait. Jones et al. (127) suggested that the observers' reproductions were
artifactually produced by the observers' inferences of differential subject
self-selection in the original experiments. That is, the observer infers that
a typical subject would be unwilling to comply with the experimenter's
request, and compliance is therefore taken as evidence of unusually favorable initial opinions. If the subject complies for very small rewards, he must
be particularly atypical in his lack of opposition to the behavior. By this
reasoning, if the observers' judgments of differential initial opinions across
conditions were ruled out, they would not reproduce the original subjects'
responses.

   Jones et al. (127) accordingly conducted a series of "interpersonal replications" in the style of Bem's studies but varying the observer's information
about the original subjects' initial opinions. In general, they repeat Bem's
results with his procedure, but consistently fail to do so when the observer
is not allowed to infer initial differences across conditions. They note that
this failure does not discredit Bem's larger point about the individual's
inference of his own opinions from the situation, but claim that Bem's method in these experiments does not support it.

   Emotional role-playing.—Some research has been done to determine
what characteristics of an improvisation make it most effective in changing
attitudes. Janis & Mann (120) present some evidence that emotional role-
playing (e.g., a smoker playing the role of a victim of lung cancer) is more
effective than mere exposure to others' improvisations, even when measured
18 months later (158), and perhaps it is more effective in changing deeply

rooted attitudes than the more standard cognitive counterattitudinal advocacies (157). Empathic ability may contribute to the effectiveness of improvisation (73); so also may the apparent fact that subjects recall their own improvisations better and evaluate them more highly than they do others' improvisations (101). Evidently peace is not guaranteed even when everyone does his own thing.

COMMITMENT AND CHOICE

A second major area of dissonance research has been on post decisional attitude change. Kiesler (134, 137) has most actively pursued the effects of commitment, finding for example, that more commitment (less payment for performing consonant acts) produced more resistance to countercommunications (137). Kiesler, Pallak & Kanouse (138) attempted to manipulate commitment and dissonance orthogonally, but obtained results that were contradictory across items relevant to the two manipulations. They conclude that a "compartmentalization effect" occurred under high commitment. Two other experiments (135, 139) have followed up an earlier observation that conformity is a negative function of attraction to a group when the subject is not committed to continue in the group, but it is a U-shaped function of attraction when he is committed to continue. Similarly, Berscheid, Boye & Darley (27) found that subjects committed to interaction with an unattractive partner subsequently declined the chance to escape; the commitment evidently instigated an enhancement of the attractiveness of the other person.

In none of these experiments was the commitment voluntary, but revisionist dissonance theory (33) has emphasized the role of free choice in producing postdecision dissonance. The determinants of subjective feelings of volition have been discussed by Kelley (130) as attributions of internal causality for one's own behavior. Free choice has been shown to produce greater dissonance in at least two studies besides those mentioned earlier (61, 151). Jones & Brehm (126) find a negative communicator is more persuasive when the subject has chosen voluntarily to expose himself to his message, and Brock (39) finds a volition variation more powerful than a justification variation in producing dissonance reduction (though he confesses the two cannot be compared in any rigorous sense). The picture is clouded, though, by two failures to produce systematic choice effects in what seem to have been well-designed experiments (91, 253). In another good paper on time variations, Watts (254) found that a negative outcome of a decision resulted in dissonance reduction only when the subject perceived a definite possibility of this outcome at the time of the decision.

SELECTIVE EXPOSURE

A third area originally emphasized in dissonance theory is selective exposure. Freedman & Sears (88), reviewing the literature through 1964, concluded there was little evidence that supportive (consonant) information is generally preferred to nonsupportive (dissonant), or that dissonance arousal increases such selectivity. The following is intended to update that review, though the periods covered overlap somewhat.

Preference for supportive information.—Bringing the review up to date gives little reason for altering its first conclusion, that people do not generally seek messages with which they agree or avoid those with which they disagree. Some support was obtained by Brock (36), who found smokers more interested than nonsmokers in information rejecting the link between smoking and lung cancer, but also they were slightly more interested in a message documenting the link. Mills conducted three studies under the guise of a market research survey (171, 172), and found an "approach effect" in one of the three and "avoidance effects" in two of the three. Lowin (153) found Republicans, but not Democrats, preferred consonant information in a mail survey.

On the other hand, no systematic preferences one way or the other were obtained in six experiments (86, 152, 154, 212, 216, 241) nor in the second of Lowin's mail surveys (153). And in two further experiments (87, 210) nonsupportive messages were actually preferred to those supporting the subject's position.

The import of these studies remains a matter of some controversy; Mills (175), for example, feels that selectivity effects are often washed out by other sources of variance but that they exist nonetheless. He cites Heider's observation that "the fact that birds fly does not prove they are not attracted to the earth." As indicated elsewhere (215), our view is that these studies have failed to document any systematic selective exposure effects; the fact that cows walk is scarcely proof that they can also fly.

Selective exposure in real life.—These findings reopen the question of selective exposure in everyday life, a matter once thought closed. Sears & Freedman (217) review earlier field studies of selective exposure and find that they, in general, do not yield as strong and compelling demonstrations of selectivity as has been thought [Katz (129), however, has offered a rebuttal to this view]. More recently, Sears (215) has attempted to reconcile the lack of laboratory evidence of preferences for supportive information with the consistent, albeit weak, field evidence for selective exposure. He emphasizes the unusual availability of supportive information in normal environments, so that even a random choice usually will yield supportive material, and the confounding of supportiveness with other attractive features of the information, such as utility.

Dissonance.—Freedman & Sears also concluded that cognitive dissonance had not been shown to increase selectivity, contrary to the predictions of the several studies on that topic. Rhine (193) has quite properly complained that Festinger's original hypotheses (81) viewed selectivity as a curvilinear function of dissonance, and that most of this research ignored the possibility that the subject should become more receptive to dissonant information at high levels of dissonance. He also notes the difficulty of testing such curvilinear predictions with experiments using just two levels of the independent variable, as has typically been the case in this literature.

More recent studies also have not supported dissonance theory. Lowe & Steiner (152) manipulated both the importance and irrevocability of a decision but found that increased importance actually increased interest in nonsupportive information, while irrevocability did not affect it. Mills conducted three experiments testing the effects of dissonance arousals (171, 172). The difficulty and irrevocability of a decision were each varied in two experiments and the importance of a decision in one experiment. Selectivity was increased by greater choice difficulty in one (172), but the other four variations had no effect. Rhine (194) did find a curvilinear relationship between dissonance arousal and selectivity, though the dissonance manipulation was unorthodox, resting on the unexpectedness of political candidates' policy positions rather than on contradiction with positions to which the subject himself was committed.

Confidence and refutability.—A related hypothesis is that selectivity is primarily manifested by those with little confidence in their opinions, or by those confronted with highly persuasive messages (153). The reasoning has been that nonsupportive information is sought out and rejected when it is seen as unconvincing or when the individual is confident of his opinion; with strong messages or less confident subjects, dissonant information is avoided.

Canon (54) found, as he had expected, that high-confidence subjects preferred dissonant material and low-confidence subjects preferred consonant. Freedman (86), however, repeated Canon's procedure as nearly as possible and found no effect of confidence. Twice Mills (171, 172) varied choice difficulty and hence, presumably, the confidence with which it was made. Choice difficulty had no effect in one study; in the other it increased the seeking of consonant information but did not affect avoidance of dissonant information. Thayer (241) manipulated confidence but found it had no effect upon selectivity. Lowin (154) also manipulated confidence but found this did not affect selectivity. Thus there is little support for the hypothesis in this form.

The corollary hypothesis, dealing with message refutability, has met with more success. In the first of his mail surveys, Lowin found strong consonant messages preferred to strong dissonant messages, and weak dissonant preferred to weak consonant messages. In the other survey there was no such significant effect. In a later experiment (154) he found more selectivity under high credibility than low credibility, as expected. Message refutability is thus the only variable that has so far consistently produced selective exposure, though the failure of the analogous variable, subject confidence, is something of a puzzle.

A somewhat related finding is Ray's (192), that messages advocating minority positions were preferred to those for majority positions on noncontroversial issues; there was no difference on controversial issues. This is perhaps an instance of what McGuire (164) and others have described as "curiosity" or "complexity" motivation, as opposed to "consistency" motivation.

Utility.—Both Canon (54) and Freedman (86) manipulated information utility and found it strongly affected information preferences. Clarke & James (59) found interest in supportive information increased as its utility increased; it was greatest when the subject expected to debate his opinion with someone else and least when no further use of his opinions was expected. Lowe & Steiner (152) found that post-decisional relevant information of all kinds was more interesting to subjects when their decisions were reversible than when they were irreversible.

History of exposure.—A number of studies have moved away from the issues raised by dissonance theory and have begun to investigate the sequencing of exposure choices as a function of previous exposure. Freedman (87) and Sears (210) presented naive subjects with information clearly pointing to a particular evaluation (information about an applicant that made him seem either clearly qualified or clearly unqualified, or evidence about a murder case that clearly suggested either guilt or innocence), then offered further exposure choices. In each case information favoring the opposite evaluation was strongly preferred, especially when new information was expected (210). In another study, exposure to the partisan arguments from one side in a criminal trial led to preferences for exposure to the other side (212). Deaux (67) also found that subjects tended to sample the entire range of information alternatives available to them when given a free choice. Thayer's subjects (241), given a free choice, chose both sides rather than just one or the other, much to the experimenter's consternation.

Two experiments have documented systematic effects of varying the amount of the subject's total prior information. More informed subjects tend to prefer biased, one-sided, negative communications and show less interest in unbiased, two-sided, positive communication (122, 212). Naive subjects generally seem to prefer positive, favorable communications (88, 152).

New theoretical approaches.—These studies have begun to move beyond the earlier excessive interest in selective exposure and the effects of cognitive dissonance. Hopefully, this will lead to more general theories about how people seek information and process it. Some beginning attempts have already been made: e.g., Mills' choice-certainty theory (173, 175, 177), Feather's (76) expectancy-value model of information-seeking behavior, and Ray's (192) expansion on McGuire's immunization theory, with tests of its assumptions about exposure.

Selective attention.—The above studies examine the choice of whether or not to expose oneself to a given communication, prior to any exposure to it. Brock & Balloun (41) have tested for selective attention: i.e., partisan selectivity in the durability and constancy of a subject's exposure to a communication once he has begun it. In their ingenious apparatus, subjects continually had to press a button to keep static out of a message. In four experiments, significant selective attention effects were found on the smoking-lung cancer issue, some evidence for selectivity on Christianity, and almost none on the question of whether or not college males should be draftable. Brock & Fromkin (44) found that subjects expecting to transmit their views attended more to supportive material than did subjects expecting to receive. This resembles the finding of Clarke & James (59) cited above, that selective exposure was greater with transmission-tuning than with reception-tuning.

Selective learning.—Another long-established principle currently under attack is selective learning: i.e., that supportive arguments are learned more readily than nonsupportive. Greenwald & Sakumura (102) conducted three experiments, all of which showed zero-order correlations between the acceptability of a statement and the ease with which it is learned; nor did prior familiarity with a statement facilitate its recall in a learning task. However, more familiar statements were clearly and consistently viewed as more acceptable. This suggests a correlation in nature between familiarity and acceptability that, like *de facto* selectivity, may not be based on the obvious psychological dynamic.

Waly & Cook (250) followed Jones & Kohler (125) in testing a more sophisticated version of the selective learning hypothesis, that plausible supportive and implausible nonsupportive statements are learned most readily. In two separate replications they find no support for the original finding. Several efforts also have been made to demonstrate an analogous principle, that balanced structures are learned more readily than unbalanced structures, but with clear success in only one (266) of four studies (93, 265-267).

Summary.—There seems to be no systematic evidence as yet in favor of a general preference for supportive information, though it remains possible that the relevant experiments have undersampled situations which might produce such a preference. High dissonance or low confidence do not seem to enhance selectivity, though there is some evidence that low message refutability does. There is evidence for selective attention but not for selective learning. Information utility and the past history of exposure seem to have stronger effects than any of these other independent variables, however. It is hard to find any very systematic consistency or curiosity effects, and it may be that this dimension is not very important in determining information reception, though obviously it is quite important in information evaluation.

CONGRUITY THEORY

Tannenbaum in several experiments has further demonstrated the predictive power of congruity theory, another of the consistency theories. This work is reviewed in some detail in his recent summary (237). In perhaps his two clearest studies (236, 238), an initially neutral source was linked either positively or negatively to an initially neutral concept. Then a positive or negative valence was induced upon the concept with an authoritative communication. Consequent changes in source evaluations closely matched congruity theory predictions. In the second study (236), the source was initially linked to two neutral concepts rather than one, and the changes in source evaluations just noted were shown also to determine final attitude regarding this second concept.

Various other studies have represented attempts to determine the limits of pressure toward congruity. Tannenbaum (237) reports two other experiments pitting congruity pressures against the informational value of a communication, and in both cases he found congruity more important. Sears (211) found that congruity predictions held for the influence of single political leaders' positions on opinion formation, but did not hold when two leaders' positions were presented. The nonpreferred leader was found to have considerably more influence in this latter case than would be predicted from congruity theory. The same held when the major political parties were used as sources. A related point is made by Rokeach & Rothman (200); in elaborating their theory of "belief congruence," they suggest that the resultant of two linked cognitive elements is not a simple function of their values as measured in isolation.

Belief similarity and attraction.—A clear implication from congruity theory is that the evaluation of a stimulus person is a positive function of agreement with him about attitude objects. In an extended series of studies, Byrne and his co-workers have tested this notion. Byrne & Nelson (49) document the basic proposition that attraction depends upon the proportion of similar to dissimilar attitudes considering all those presented to the subject, when the subject is given no additional information about the stimulus person. In a variety of other studies, this basic finding has been generalized to other situations and populations; e.g., Byrne & Griffitt (48) obtained the same relationship using children of grades 4 to 8 as subjects, and Byrne *et al.* (52) with such esoteric adult populations as schizophrenics, alcoholics, and Job Corpsmen. Similarity in economic status was found to determine attraction in approximately similar measure (50).

This research program has not been as uniformly successful in determining conditions that affect the relationship between similarity and attraction. Byrne, Nelson & Reeves (51), however, have found that attraction is more contingent on similarity when the attitude statements concern unverifiable matters than when they concern verifiable matters.

Race versus belief.—A more controversial question is whether racial differences or attitudinal differences are more important in determining dislike of, or prejudice against, a stimulus person. Stein, Hardyck & Smith (231) found that when belief and racial similarity of subject to stimulus person were varied orthogonally, both had significant effects upon attraction to the stimulus person, but belief accounted for considerably more of the variance. The greater importance of belief similarity has now been replicated in a variety of cultures over several kinds of subjects and stimulus persons. Stein (230) used gentile, Negro, and Jewish students as subject and object; Smith, Williams & Willis (229) used whites and Negroes as both, in various regions of the USA; Anderson & Côté (6) used French and English-speaking Canadians; Willis & Bulatao (261) used Filipino students; Rokeach & Mezei (199) used whites and Negroes; Triandis, Loh & Levin (244) and Triandis & Davis (243) used college students; and Insko & Robinson (110) used southern white children. In all of these studies, belief similarity more strongly influenced attraction to the stimulus person than did racial or ethnic similarity.

However, this is mitigated seriously by the other consistent finding throughout these studies, that belief similarity is the more important predictor primarily for simple measures of interpersonal attraction or regard, whereas race or ethnicity is the more important (by a substantial amount) for the more intimate forms of interpersonal contact (110, 230, 231, 243, 244, 261). The true influence of belief congruence also seems likely to be exaggerated in these studies by the widespread use of hypothetical stimulus persons and the consequent intrusion of social desirability into subjects' responses. These findings need to be replicated under more realistic conditions.

A third finding that occurs in these data is what Smith, Williams & Willis (229) call a "renegade effect": i.e., belief similarity accounts for more variance in attraction among members of the subject's own racial or ethnic group than it does among members of other groups (110, 229, 261). This finding also is damaging to theories attributing racial prejudice to belief incongruence, since it appears that belief congruence is important mainly within one's own group.

One knotty problem remaining in this area is to scale the dimension along which belief becomes decreasingly important and race increasingly so. Triandis has moved in this direction, using both a "behavioral differential" and factor analysis (243, 244); Insko & Robinson (110) emphasize both intimacy of personal contact and publicity of the contact under conditions of strong institutionalized norms; and it is clear from all studies that marriage and sexual relationships represent an end point of the dimension.

Adding versus averaging.—Another empirical problem that has stimulated much attention is whether averaging models, such as congruity theory, predict stimulus combinations better than do summation or additive models. The two sets of models yield similar predictions when the stimulus elements have different algebraic signs, but they differ when all elements are of like sign. N. H. Anderson (9) has found evidence for the averaging model in several studies, as have others (cf. 31). Some studies have supported summation theories (7). A problem has been that a final response's polarity often seems to be related positively to the number of elements combined—the "set-size effect" (8, 34, 156, 186)—though Anderson (9) feels a modified averaging model can handle this effect. A *post hoc* model offered by Manis, Gleason & Dawes (156) suggests that the final impression is directly proportional to the product of the logarithm of the number of elements and a weighted average of the element values.

Anderson & Jacobson (10) have extended the generality of the averaging model to cases in which the information is differentially reliable. A simple average model was adequate when the subjects were instructed to take all elements into account, but a weighted average model was more accurate when the subjects were allowed or encouraged to discount inconsistent elements.

Balance Theory

Much work has also been done on sources of cognitive bias in the representation of simple social structures of the P-O-X variety. Feather (75), Insko & Schopler (111) and Phillips (185) have presented revisionist theoretical models.

Almost all the empirical studies have presented the subject with hypothetical social situations. A number of dependent variables have been used to establish the existence of a bias toward balance in such situations. Negative affect, feelings of unpleasantness or uneasiness or both were more common with unbalanced structures in several studies (189, 196). Balance predictions also have succeeded for desires to change relationships (196), predictions of what would change over time (47), or actual sentiment changes (15). However, the evidence with regard to the supposed ease of learning balanced structures is more ambiguous, clearly supporting balance theory in but one (266) of several studies (93, 265–267).

The other bias that appears repeatedly is a bias toward positivity, i.e., toward positive relations between people, or even toward positive relations between people and objects. In some studies this emerges as a main effect: in pleasantness ratings (77, 78, 196), expectations about change (47), and learning (265–267). In other cases it interacts with balance, usually in that balance operates as a systematic bias only under conditions of positive P-O relations (93, 189). This combination of consistency and positivity is also a prominent feature of Americans' political opinions (see 214). These interactions seem to be part of a pattern in which interpersonal feelings are treated somewhat differently than attitudes toward nonpersonal objects (47, 93, 189, 266). Reciprocity is another bias that appears in these experiments (47, 240, 266).

Increasingly, attention is being focused upon the conditions for "psychological implication" in the balance as well as the dissonance area (2). Hardyck (104) and Dillehay, Insko & Smith (69) have followed up some earlier work by McGuire and others in this area, and no doubt much more research in this area soon will be seen.

Social Judgment

Judgmental displacements have been analyzed from two main viewpoints: Sherif & Hovland's (221) assimilation-contrast model, which assumes that the individual's own attitude produces actual perceptual distortion, and a variable perspective model (181, 245), which assumes that displacement reflects changes in the language the subject uses to describe his experience. In the latter case, the key variable is the range of stimulus values to which the subject is exposed.

Both theories have received some support. Upshaw (245) and Ostrom (181) varied the range of statements presented to the subjects and found partial support for variable perspective predictions and thus the semantic interpretation. Atkins et al. (20) and Deaux & Bieri (68) found assimilation within the latitude of acceptance and contrast outside of it, as per Sherif & Hovland's position. However, it is not yet clear that such contrasts reflect insensitivity to differences among highly discrepant positions or unpleasant stimuli. Ager & Dawes (5) did, indeed, find subjects making more errors in discriminating among highly discrepant statements, but Irwin, Tripodi & Bieri (113) found subjects differentiating more among negative stimulus persons than positive stimulus persons.

The absolute magnitude of distortions as a function of own-attitude have often not been very great, sometimes not attaining even the .05 level (18, 251), and on other occasions statistically significant but not as much as a single scale point (20, 68, 252). In one study, contrast was enhanced by high ego-involvement, as varied *post hoc* by splitting subjects on self-reported involvement (252); but in another, varied by comparing Negro and white students' judgments of racial statements, involvement seemed to moderate judgment (181). Experimental manipulations of involvement had no significant effects in two studies (19, 251). Even where significant distortion effects have been found, subjects have tended to agree with each other in rank-ordering the stimulus statements (181, 245, 252). Context effects, however, have been quite marked in some studies (18, 72, 155, 181, 245).

METHODOLOGY

As of 1965, the experimental method had won an astonishing victory in social psychology. Everywhere, older methods were in retreat. Since then, however, the experimental method has been under growing and vehement attack on grounds of validity and morality alike. This minor crisis has engaged some of the better minds in the discipline and is a source of no little concern to them (cf. 131, 161, 163, 195). It has also had the less fortunate effect of eliciting a good bit of moral righteousness from some others.

All questions of validity, and a surprising number of the questions of morality, rest finally upon empirical questions. Thus it is encouraging that many such attacks have already been met not by rhetoric but by attempts to assemble the pertinent empirical data. We review these in some detail below. Despite these mature and scientific responses to the growing problems with experimental research, it seems evident that the palmy days of laboratory research are over. There is a good market for alternatives (cf. 255).

Deception.—Ethical concerns arise most frequently with deception experiments, and deception experiments occur most frequently in precisely the areas with which our review is concerned. Stricker's (234) content analysis found that while deception had been used in 19 per cent of the social psychology articles published in 1964, it had been used in 41 per cent of the articles in our areas of opinions, attitude change, dissonance, and conformity. In fact, the latter two areas had the highest rates of all 18 areas surveyed. The subjects' suspicions were also somewhat more likely to be measured and cited in our areas, but scarcely adequately.

The question of validity has been raised over the results obtained from deception experiments; presumably suspicious subjects do not respond normally. Stricker's content analysis found that subject suspicions were rarely measured and cited thoroughly; in a further study (235), he measured some of the characteristics of suspicious subjects and found that they do, in fact, bias the experiment's outcome. Brock & Becker (43) attempted to determine whether or not "debriefing" makes subjects suspicious about, and hence unresponsive to, later manipulations. They varied the amount of debriefing given the subject, and whether or not the later test experiment resembled the debriefed experiment. The main dependent measure in the later test experiment, compliance to a request by the experimenter, was affected only when maximum debriefing was given and the two experiments were quite similar.

The ethical question centers mainly upon the possibility of damage to subjects, though there is a certain amount of concern about social psychology's reputation among students and the general public. Unfortunately, little data is available on this point. Walster et al. (248) used a common manipulation, giving favorable or unfavorable feedback to subjects about their performance in an interview, and then gave what was described as an unusually thorough debriefing. Unhappily, the ego-deflating effects of unfavorable feedback persisted even after debriefing, at least among subjects with strong predispositional fear of rejection. These two studies provide evidence that both careful debriefing and some subject screening are necessary and satisfactory for most purposes. Developing techniques for screening the vulnerable from deception experiments is a considerable challenge for the future.

An alternative method that some experimenters have pursued (cf. 21, 45, 47, 98a, 132, 211, 265) is to use role-playing procedures instead of deception. Our judgment of the utility of this strategy will have to await data indicating whether or not the same results obtain under both sets of conditions. One hope is that such mundane methodological concerns and basic questions of attitude change alike can be addressed in a single experiment. For example, the differences between deception and role-playing procedures may be investigated under the guise of studies of intent-to-persuade (163), or vice versa, and the differences between coerced and volunteer subjects may be analyzed concurrent with research on the effects of choice or forced compliance.

Experimenter biases.—Thorough reviews of the known effects of experimenter bias upon experiment outcome are currently available (141, 206). Social psychologists should find Rosenthal's literature review and research program responsible as well as provocative in terms of further research (206). An interesting sidelight is Sherwood & Nataupsky's (223) finding of meaningful correlations between an investigator's biographical characteristics and his research conclusions regarding racial differences in intelligence. Their report, unfortunately, is too terse about characteristics that failed to correlate with such conclusions.

It is not yet clear how serious a bias has intruded typically into attitude research due to experimenter biases. It is encouraging to note, however, that the use of multiple and blind experimenters, and the explicit testing of experimenter effects, are becoming more common, though not yet routine, in this area. The logical next step is the imposition of what Rosenthal calls "expectancy control groups," explicitly varying the experimenters' expectations about the outcome of the experiment. Cooper et al. (62) have used such a procedure in trying to replicate a dissonance experiment (264) and have found that the expectancies of naive experimenters, when explicitly varied, washed out the dissonance effect.

Demand characteristics.—Orne (180) and Rosenberg (201) have introduced the twin notions of "demand characteristics" of an experimental situation and the subject's "evaluation apprehension" (concern about being evaluated on important personal traits in an experiment). Again encouraging is the growing body of research that attempts to determine empirically rather than rhetorically the character and magnitude of biases these potential artifacts have introduced into experimental research.

Perhaps the broadest claim here is Silverman's (225) suggestion that attitude-change experiments, when defined as "an experiment" to the subject, "demands" change from them. Announcing a given task as an "experiment," Silverman found, did indeed increase attitude change. However, the more serious problem occurs when a demand characteristic interacts with some other variable, thereby affecting not merely the absolute magnitude of change but the direction of difference between two conditions. Here the presence of the artifact must be varied explicitly to determine whether or not the original result is replicable when demand characteristics or evaluation apprehension are ruled out. For example, Silverman & Regula (226) hypothesized that Festinger & Maccoby's (82) finding that distraction facilitates attitude change would hold only when the subjects thought the experimenter was trying to test their powers of concentration. They repeated the study and found that only when distraction was seen as intentional did it promote attitude change; the reverse held when it was supposedly accidental. Sherman (222) conducted a similar analysis of McClintock's (160) earlier study of other-directedness and conformity to antiprejudice appeals. Incidentally, these two papers have some wider usefulness: Sherman offers a useful analysis of the demand characteristics of a typical attitude change experiment; and Silverman & Regula offer a thorough roster of the various perceptions held by their subjects about the experiment's intentions (a welcome relief from the usual speculations, unrestrained by contact with subject thinking, that characterize efforts to figure out, *post hoc*, "how the subject perceived the experiment").

A parallel analysis based on "evaluation apprehension" has led to a more reassuring outcome. Rosenberg (201) had asserted that Cohen's (33) "dissonance effect" in a forced compliance study was artifactually produced by evaluation apprehension. He modified the procedure to eliminate it and obtained the opposite "incentive effect," though, as Aronson (12) has noted, the reversal could just as likely derive from numerous other changes in the procedure. Linder, Cooper & Jones (151) then attempted to show that Rosenberg's findings were not a result of removing evaluation apprehension but were merely an artifact of obtaining a prior commitment from the subject so that he was not free to reject the request to engage in discrepant behavior. They support their point convincingly by first repeating Rosenberg's incentive effect when they duplicate his procedure, and then obtaining the dissonance effect with a minor procedural change freeing the subject's choice.

These efforts seem to reflect the likelihood that recent attacks upon the experimental technique will generally be met by selective replication of earlier findings, using more sensitive controls upon possible artifacts. It currently seems unlikely that more general loss of confidence in earlier research is warranted.

Unobtrusive and indirect attitude measurement.—One consequence of these concerns is a search for attitude measures that are less direct and obtrusive than the standard self-report questionnaire or interview. Webb and his colleagues (255) have made a number of inventive suggestions for nonreactive measures, in a collection that has been widely commended. Many pose difficult ethical problems, however, since by their nature they do not allow for "informed consent." Physiological measures have been tried in several studies, though the jury is still out on their utility (46, 65, 91, 187). White attitudes toward Negroes have been an especially salient focus of interest, since social desirability effects seem so much of a problem with them, and suggestions have ranged far and wide, included seating aggregation (53), conformity (23), and the learning and judging of attitude statements (218, 249, 250). Mehrabian (167) has some ingenious ideas about detecting attitudes and affects from the "immediacy" of free conversation. Convenient reference works should be Woodmansee & Cook's (263) exhaustive attempt to dimensionalize attitudes toward Negroes, and Shaw & Wright's (219) compendium of standard attitude scales.

Finally, we might also note research being done on the effects of prior experimental experience (107), and on the biases introduced by use of volunteer, coerced, and "professional" subjects.

CONCLUSION

We have tried here to emphasize progress made on problems which have been defined as in the "attitude" area of psychology. The problem with this choice is that such a definition finally rests on nothing more sturdy than what self-defined attitude researchers have been doing themselves. We come to the end with the feeling that we have not touched on some of the more interesting work some of these very researchers have been doing, perhaps because some of it has been a little outside the traditional concerns of attitude and opinion research. We thus particularly commend to the reader's attention Brehm's research on reactance (32); Sigall & Aronson's on liking (224); Freedman and co-workers' on obedience (90); the work of Latané and his colleagues on social comparison theory [(143a); see also Singer (228)]; Rokeach's theorizing on the organization of attitudes (198); and the work of several authors on cognitive complexity (28, 64). We also close with the happy awareness of much research currently being conducted, and reports already being informally circulated, that will liven our successor's task.

We also have a nagging need to make a concluding observation about the current "box-score." A superficial reading of current research might well be discouraging, since its results often seem contradictory and inconclusive. What is obvious now is that the simple questions with which attitude change and dissonance research began do not have simple answers. What is needed now is the labor of defining the conditions for one effect as opposed to its opposite: When does fear facilitate change, and when does it inhibit it? When are large incentives most effective, and when are small incentives more useful? Space restrictions have kept us from speculating very much about such matters, but it would seem obvious that this very challenging task must dominate the research of the future. It seems to us that only the cowardly and faint-hearted will become so discouraged at the current complexities and ambiguities in this area that they will choose not to build upon the impressive advances that have been made. In particular, we hope that the spectacular though currently unrealized promise of dissonance theory does not go the way of the brontosaurus. Science should thrive on contradiction, not be discouraged by it.

LITERATURE CITED

1. Abelson, R. Simulation of social behavior. In *Handbook of Social Psychology*, Revised Ed., 2 (Lindzey, G., Aronson, E., Eds., Addison-Wesley, Reading, Mass., 1968)
2. Abelson, R. P. Psychological implication. In *Theories of Cognitive Consistency: A Sourcebook* (See Ref. 4)
3. Abelson, R. P., Kanouse, D. E. Subjective acceptance of verbal generalizations. In *Cognitive Consistency: Motivational Antecedents and Behavioral Consequences*, 173–97 (Feldman, S., Ed., Academic Press, New York, 1966)
4. Abelson, R. P., Aronson, E., McGuire, W. J., Newcomb, T. M., Rosenberg, M. J., Tannenbaum, P. H., Eds., *Theories of Cognitive Consistency: A Sourcebook* (Rand McNally, Chicago, 1968)
5. Ager, J. W., Dawes, R. M. The effect of judges' attitudes on judgment. *J. Pers. Soc. Psychol.*, 1, 533–38 (1965)
6. Anderson, C. C., Côté, A. D. J. Belief dissonance as a source of disaffection between ethnic groups. *J. Pers. Soc. Psychol.*, 4, 447–53 (1966)
7. Anderson, L. R., Fishbein, M. Prediction of attitude from the number, strength, and evaluative aspect of beliefs about the attitude object: A comparison of summation and congruity theories. *J. Pers. Soc. Psychol.*, 2, 437–43 (1965)
8. Anderson, N. H. Averaging model

analysis of set-size effect in impression formation. *J. Exptl. Psychol.*, **75**, 158–65 (1967)

9. Anderson, N. H. A simple model for information integration. In *Theories of Cognitive Consistency: A Sourcebook* (See Ref. 4)

10. Anderson, N. H., Jacobson, A. Effect of stimulus inconsistency and discounting instructions in personality impression formation. *J. Pers. Soc. Psychol.*, **2**, 531–39 (1965)

11. Apsler, R., Sears, D. O. Warning, personal involvement, and attitude change. *J. Pers. Soc. Psychol.*, **9**, 162–66 (1968)

12. Aronson, E. The psychology of insufficient justification: An analysis of some conflicting data. In *Cognitive Consistency*, 109–33 (See Ref. 79)

13. Aronson, E. Dissonance theory: Progress and problems. In *Theories of Cognitive Consistency: A Source book* (See Ref. 4)

14. Aronson, E., Carlsmith, J. M. Experimentation in social psychology. In *Handbook of Social Psychology* (See Ref. 1)

15. Aronson, E., Cope, V. My enemy's enemy is my friend. *J. Pers. Soc. Psychol.*, **8**, 8–12 (1968)

16. Aronson, E., Turner, J. A., Carlsmith, J. M. Communicator credibility and communication discrepancy as determinants of opinion change. *J. Abnorm. Soc. Psychol.*, **67**, 31-36 (1963)

17. Ashmore, R. D., Collins, B. E., Hornbeck, F. W., Whitney, R. E. Studies in forced compliance. XIII. In search of a dissonance producing forced compliance paradigm. (Mimeo, U.C.L.A., 1968)

18. Atkins, A. L. Own attitude and discriminability in relation to anchoring effects in judgment. *J. Pers. Soc. Psychol.*, **4**, 497–507 (1966)

19. Atkins, A. L., Bieri, J. *Differential Effects of Two Types of Involvement upon Changes in Latitude of Acceptance* (Presented at Eastern Psychol. Assoc., Boston, 1967)

20. Atkins, A. L., Deaux, K. K., Bieri, J. Latitude of acceptance and attitude change: Empirical evidence for a reformulation. *J. Pers. Soc. Psychol.*, **6**, 47–54 (1967)

21. Bem, D. J. An experimental analysis of self-persuasion. *J. Exptl. Soc. Psychol.*, **1**, 199–218 (1965)

22. Bem, D. J. Self-perception: An alternative interpretation of cognitive dissonance phenomena. *Psychol. Rev.*, **74**, 183–200 (1967)

23. Berg, K. R. Ethnic attitudes and agreement with a Negro person. *J. Pers. Soc. Psychol.*, **4**, 215–20 (1966)

24. Berkowitz, L., Ed. *Advances in Experimental Social Psychology*, 2 (Academic Press, New York, 1965)

25. Berkowitz, L., *Ibid.*, **3** (1967)

26. Berscheid, E. Opinion change and communicator-communicatee similarity and dissimilarity. *J. Pers. Soc. Psychol.*, **4**, 670–80 (1966)

27. Berscheid, E., Boye, D., Darley, J. M. Effect of forced association upon voluntary choice to associate. *J. Pers. Soc. Psychol.*, **8**, 13–19 (1968)

28. Bieri, J., Atkins, A. L., Briar, S., Leaman, R. L., Miller, H., Tripodi, T. *Clinical and Social Judgment: The Discrimination of Behavioral Information* (Wiley, New York, 1966)

29. Bishop, F. V. The anal character: A rebel in the dissonance family. *J. Pers. Soc. Psychol.*, **6**, 23–36 (1967)

30. Bochner, S., Insko, C. A. Communicator discrepancy, source credibility, and opinion change. *J. Pers. Soc. Psychol.*, **4**, 614–21 (1966)

31. Bossart, P., Di Vesta, F. J. Effects of context, frequency, and order of presentation of evaluative assertions on impression formation. *J. Pers. Soc. Psychol.*, **4**, 538–44 (1966)

32. Brehm, J. W. *A Theory of Psychological Reactance* (Academic Press, New York, 1966)

33. Brehm, J. W., Cohen, A. R. *Explorations in Cognitive Dissonance* (Wiley, New York, 1962)

34. Brewer, M. B. Averaging versus summation in composite ratings of complex social stimuli. *J. Pers. Soc. Psychol.*, **8**, 20–26 (1968)

35. Brewer, M. B., Crano, W. D. Attitude change as a function of discrepancy and source of influence. *J. Soc. Psychol.*. (In press)

36. Brock, T. C. Commitment to exposure as a determinant of information receptivity. *J. Pers. Soc. Psychol.*, **2**, 10–19 (1965)

37. Brock, T. C. Communicator-recipient similarity and decision change. *Ibid.*, **1**, 650–54 (1965)

38. Brock, T. C. Communication discrepancy and intent to persuade as determinants of counterargument production. *J. Exptl. Soc. Psychol.*, **3**, 296–309 (1967)

39. Brock, T. C. Relative efficacy of

volition and justification in arousing dissonance. *J. Pers.*, **36**, 49–66 (1966)

40. Brock, T. C. Dissonance without awareness. In *Theories of Cognitive Consistency: A Source book (See Ref. 4)*

41. Brock, T. C., Balloun, J. L. Behavioral receptivity to dissonant information. *J. Pers. Soc. Psychol.*, **6**, 413–28 (1967)

42. Brock, T. C., Becker, L. A. Ineffectiveness of "overheard" counterpropaganda. *J. Pers. Soc. Psychol.*, **2**, 654–60 (1965)

43. Brock, T. C., Becker, L. A. "Debriefing" and susceptibility to subsequent experimental manipulations. *J. Exptl. Soc. Psychol.*, **2**, 314–23 (1966)

44. Brock, T. C., Fromkin, H. L. Cognitive tuning set and behavioral receptivity to discrepant information. *J. Pers.*, **36**, 108–25 (1968)

45. Brown, R. *Social Psychology* (Free Press, New York, 1965)

46. Buckhout, R. Changes in heart rate accompanying attitude change. *J. Pers. Soc. Psychol.*, **4**, 695–99 (1966)

47. Burnstein, E. Sources of cognitive bias in the representation of simple social structures: Balance, minimal change, positivity, reciprocity, and the respondent's own attitude. *J. Pers. Soc. Psychol.*, **7**, 36–48 (1967)

48. Byrne, D., Griffitt, W. A developmental investigation of the law of attraction. *J. Pers. Soc. Psychol.*, **4**, 699–702 (1966)

49. Byrne, D., Nelson, D. Attraction as a linear function of proportion of positive reinforcements. *J. Pers. Soc. Psychol.*, **1**, 659–63 (1965)

50. Byrne, D., Clore, G. L., Jr., Worchel, P. Effect of economic similarity-dissimilarity on interpersonal attraction. *J. Pers. Soc. Psychol.*, **4**, 220–24 (1966)

51. Byrne, D., Nelson, D., Reeves, K. Effects of consensual validation and invalidation on attraction as a function of verifiability. *J. Exptl. Soc. Psychol.*, **2**, 98–107 (1966)

52. Byrne, D., Griffitt, W., Hudgins, W., Reeves, K. Attitude similarity-dissimilarity and attraction: Generality beyond the college sophomore. *J. Soc. Psychol.* (In press)

53. Campbell, D. T., Kruskal, W. H., Wallace, W. P. Seating aggregation as an index of attitude. *Sociometry*, **29**, 1–15 (1966)

54. Canon, L. Self-confidence and selective exposure to information. In *Conflict, Decision, and Dissonance* (Festinger, L., Ed., Stanford University Press, Stanford, Calif., 1964)

55. Carlsmith, J. M., Collins, B. E., Helmreich, R. L. Studies in forced compliance. I. The effect of pressure for compliance on attitude change produced by face-to-face role playing and anonymous essay writing. *J. Pers. Soc. Psychol.*, **4**, 1–13 (1966)

56. Cartwright, D., Zander, A., Eds. *Group Dynamics*, 3rd. ed. (Harper & Row, New York, 1968)

57. Chu, G. C. Fear arousal, efficacy, and imminency. *J. Pers. Soc. Psychol.*, **4**, 517–24 (1966)

58. Chu, G. C. Culture, personality, and persuasibility. *Sociometry*, **29**, 169–74 (1966)

59. Clarke, P., James, J. The effects of situation, attitude intensity and personality on information-seeking. *Sociometry*, **30**, 235–45 (1967)

60. Cohen, A. R. *Attitude Change and Social Influence* (Basic Books, New York, 1964)

61. Collins, B. E. The effect of monetary inducements on the amount of attitude change induced by forced compliance. In *Role Playing, Reward, and Attitude Change* (Elms, A., Ed., Van Nostrand, Princeton, 1969)

62. Cooper, J., Eisenberg, L., Robert, J., Dohrenwend, B. S. The effect of experimenter expectancy and preparatory effort on belief in the probable occurrence of future events. *J. Soc. Psychol.*, **71**, 221–26 (1967)

63. Cottrell, N. B., Wack, D. L. Energizing effects of cognitive dissonance upon dominant and subordinate responses. *J. Pers. Soc. Psychol.*, **6**, 132–38 (1967)

64. Crockett, W. H. Cognitive complexity and impression formation. In *Progr. Exptl. Pers. Res.*, **2**, 47–90 (1965)

65. Cronkhite, G. Autonomic correlates of dissonance and attitude change. *Speech Monogr.*, **33**, 392–99 (1966)

66. Dabbs, J. M., Jr., Leventhal, H. Effects of varying the recommendations in a fear-arousing communication. *J. Pers. Soc. Psychol.*, **4**, 525–31 (1966)

67. Deaux, K. K. Variations in warning, information preference, and antic-

ipatory attitude change. *J. Pers. Soc. Psychol.*, **9**, 157–61 (1968)

68. Deaux, K. K., Bieri, J. Latitude of acceptance in judgments of masculinity-femininity. *J. Pers.*, **35**, 109–17 (1967)

69. Dillehay, R. C., Insko, C. A., Smith, M. B. Logical consistency and attitude change. *J. Pers. Soc. Psychol.*, **3**, 646–54 (1966)

70. Eagly, A. H. Involvement as a determinant of response to favorable and unfavorable information. *J. Pers. Soc. Psychol., Monogr. No.* **643**, Part 2, 1–15 (Nov. 1967)

71. Eagly, A. H., Manis, M. Evaluation of message and communicator as a function of involvement. *J. Pers. Soc. Psychol.*, **3**, 483–85 (1966)

72. Edrich, H., Selltiz, C., Cook, S. W. The effects of context and of raters' attitudes on judgments of favorableness of statements about a social group. *J. Soc. Psychol.*, **70**, 11–22 (1966)

73. Elms, A. C. Influence of fantasy ability on attitude change through role playing. *J. Pers. Soc. Psychol.*, **4**, 36–43 (1966)

74. Elms, A. C. Role playing, incentive, and dissonance. *Psychol. Bull.*, **68**, 132–48 (1967)

75. Feather, N. T. A structural balance approach to the analysis of communication effects. In *Advances in Experimental Social Psychology*, **3**, 100–65 (See Ref. 25)

76. Feather, N. T. An expectancy-value model of information-seeking behavior. *Psychol. Rev.*, **74**, 342–60 (1967)

77. Feather, N. T., Armstrong, D. C. Effects of variations in source attitude, receiver attitude, and communication stand on reactions to source and content of communications. *J. Pers.*, **35**, 435–55 (1967)

78. Feather, N. T., Jeffries, D. G. Balancing and extremity effects in reactions of receiver to source and content of communications. *J. Pers.*,**35**, 194–213 (1967)

79. Feldman, S., Ed. *Cognitive Consistency: Motivational Antecedents and Behavioral Consequences* (Academic Press, New York, 1966)

80. Feldman, S. Motivational aspects of attitudinal elements and their place in cognitive interaction. *Ibid.*, 75–108

81. Festinger, L. *A Theory of Cognitive Dissonance* (Row, Peterson, Evanston, Ill., 1957)

82. Festinger, L., Maccoby, N. On resistance to persuasive communications. *J. Abnorm. Soc. Psychol.*, **68**, 359–66 (1964)

83. Fishbein, M., Ed. *Readings in Attitude Theory and Measurement* (Wiley, New York, 1967)

84. Fishbein, M. Attitude and the prediction of behavior. *Ibid.*, 477-92

85. Freedman, J. L. Involvement, discrepancy, and change. *J. Abnorm. Soc. Psychol.*, **69**, 290–95 (1964)

86. Freedman, J. L. Confidence, utility, and selective exposure: A partial replication. *J. Pers. Soc. Psychol.*, **2**, 778–80 (1965)

87. Freedman, J. L. Preference for dissonant information. *Ibid.*, 287–89

88. Freedman, J. L., Sears, D. O. Selective exposure. In *Advan. Exptl. Soc. Psychol.*, **2**, 58–97 (1965) (See Ref. 24)

89. Freedman, J. L., Sears, D. O. Warning, distraction and resistance to influence. *J. Pers. Soc. Psychol.*, **1**, 262–66 (1965)

90. Freedman, J. L., Wallington, S. A., Bless, E. Compliance without pressure: The effect of guilt. *J. Pers. Soc. Psychol.*, **7**, 117–24 (1967)

91. Gerard, H. B. Choice difficulty, dissonance, and the decision sequence. *J. Pers.*, **35**, 91–108 (1967)

92. Gerard, H. B. Compliance, expectation of reward, and opinion change. *J. Pers. Soc. Psychol.*, **6**, 360–64 (1967)

93. Gerard, H. B., Fleischer, L. Recall and pleasantness of balanced and unbalanced cognitive structures. *J. Pers. Soc. Psychol.*, **7**, 332–37 (1967)

94. Gergen, K. J., Bauer, R. A. Interactive effects of self-esteem and task difficulty on social conformity. *J. Pers. Soc. Psychol.*, **6**, 16–22 (1967)

95. Gilson, C., Abelson, R. P. The subjective use of inductive evidence. *J. Pers. Soc. Psychol.*, **2**, 301–10 (1965)

96. Gollob, H. F., Dittes, J. E. Effects of manipulated self-esteem on persuasibility depending on threat and complexity of communication. *J. Pers. Soc. Psychol.*, **2**, 195–201 (1965)

97. Greenbaum, C. W. Effect of situational and personality variables on improvisation and attitude change. *J. Pers. Soc. Psychol.*, **4**, 260–69 (1966)

98. Greenberg, B. S., Miller, G. R. The effects of low credible sources on message acceptance. *Speech Monogr.*, **33**, 127–36 (1966)

98a. Greenberg, M. S. Role playing: An alternative to deception? *J. Pers. Soc. Psychol.*, **7**, 152–57 (1967)

99. Greenwald, A. G. Effects of prior commitment on behavior change after a persuasive communication. *Publ. Opin. Quart.*, **29**, 595–601 (1965)

100. Greenwald, A. G. Behavior change following a persuasive communication. *J. Pers.*, **33**, 370–91 (1965)

101. Greenwald, A. G., Albert, R. D. Acceptance and recall of improvised arguments. *J. Pers. Soc. Psychol.*, **8**, 31–34 (1968)

102. Greenwald, A. G., Sakumura, J. S. Attitude and selective learning: Where are the phenomena of yesteryear? *J. Pers. Soc. Psychol.*, **7**, 387–97 (1967)

103. Harding, J., Proshansky, H., Chein, I., Kutner, B. Prejudice and ethnic relations. In *Handbook of Social Psychology*, **5** (See Ref. 1)

104. Hardyck, J. A. Consistency, relevance, and resistance to change. *J. Exptl. Soc. Psychol.*, **2**, 27–41 (1966)

105. Heider, F. *Psychology of Interpersonal Relations* (Wiley, New York, 1958)

106. Helmreich, R., Collins, B. E. Studies in forced compliance: Commitment and magnitude of inducement to comply as determinants of opinion change. *J. Pers. Soc. Psychol.*, **10**, 75–81 (1968)

107. Holmes, D. S. Amount of experience in experiments as a determinant of performance in later experiments. *J. Pers. Soc. Psychol.*, **7**, 403–7 (1967)

108. Husek, T. R. Persuasive impacts of early, late, or no mention of a negative source. *J. Pers. Soc. Psychol.*, **2**, 125–28 (1965)

109. Insko, C. A. *Theories of Attitude Change* (Appleton-Century-Crofts, New York, 1967)

110. Insko, C. A., Robinson, J. E. Belief similarity versus race as determinants or reactions to Negroes by southern white adolescents: A further test of Rokeach's theory. *J. Pers. Soc. Psychol.*, **7**, 216–21 (1967)

111. Insko, C. A., Schopler, J. Triadic consistency: A statement of affective-cognitive-conative consistency. *Psychol. Rev.*, **74**, 361–76 (1967)

112. Insko, C. A., Murashima, F., Saiyadain, M. Communicator discrepancy, stimulus ambiguity, and influence. *J. Pers.*, **34**, 262–74 (1966)

113. Irwin, M., Tripodi, T., Bieri, J. Affective stimulus value and cognitive complexity. *J. Pers. Soc. Psychol.*, **3**, 135–44 (1967)

114. Jahoda, M., Warren, N., Eds. *Attitudes* (Penguin Books, Baltimore, 1966)

115. Janis, I. L. Effects of fear arousal on attitude change: Recent developments in theory and experimental research. In *Advan. Exptl. Soc. Psychol.*, **3**, 166–224 (1967) (See Ref. 24)

116. Janis, I. L. Attitude change via role playing. In *Theories of Cognitive Consistency: A Sourcebook* (See Ref. 4)

117. Janis, I. L., Feshbach, S. Effects of fear-arousing communications. *J. Abnorm. Soc. Psychol.*, **48**, 78–92 (1953)

118. Janis, I. L., Field, P. B. Sex differences and personality factors related to persuasibility. In *Personality and Persuasibility*, 55–68 (Hovland, C. I., Janis, I. L., Eds., Yale Univ. Press, New Haven, Conn., 1959)

119. Janis, I. L., Gilmore, J. B. The influence of incentive conditions on the success of role playing in modifying attitudes. *J. Pers. Soc. Psychol.*, **1**, 17–27 (1965)

120. Janis, I. L., Mann, L. Effectiveness of emotional role-playing in modifying smoking habits and attitudes. *J. Exptl. Res. Pers.* **1**, 84–90 (1965)

121. Johnson, H. H. Some effects of discrepancy level on responses to negative information about one's self. *Sociometry*, **29**, 52–66 (1966)

122. Johnson, P. B. Exposure preference (Senior honors thesis, Psychol. Dept., Univ. California, Los Angeles, Calif., 1967)

123. Jones, E. E., Gerard, H. B. *Foundations of Social Psychology* (Wiley, New York, 1967)

124. Jones, E. E., Harris, V. A. The attribution of attitudes. *J. Exptl. Soc. Psychol.*, **3**, 1–24 (1967)

125. Jones, E. E., Kohler, R. The effects of plausibility on the learning of controversial statements. *J. Abnorm. Soc. Psychol.*, **57**, 315–20 (1958)

126. Jones, R. A., Brehm, J. W. Attitudinal effects of communicator attractiveness when one chooses to listen. *J. Pers. Soc. Psychol.*, **6**, 64–70 (1967)

127. Jones, R. A., Linder, D. E., Kiesler, C. A., Zanna, M., Brehm, J. W. Internal states or external stimuli: Observers' attitude judgments and the dissonance theory-self-persua-

sion controversy. *J. Exptl. Soc. Psychol.*, **4**, 247–69 (1968)

128. Kanouse, D. E., Abelson, R. P. Language variables affecting the persuasiveness of simple communications. *J. Pers. Soc. Psychol.*, **7**, 158–63 (1967)

129. Katz, E. On reopening the question of selectivity for exposure to mass communication. In *Theories of Cognitive Consistency: A Sourcebook* (See Ref. 4)

130. Kelley, H. H. Attribution theory in social psychology. In *Nebraska Symposium on Motivation*, 192–238 (Levine, D., Ed., Univ. Nebraska Press, Lincoln, 1967)

131. Kelley, H. H. *The Development of Social Psychology in the U.S.A.: A Trend Report* (Presented to Social Science Research Council's Committee on Transnational Social Psychology, Vienna, 1967)

132. Kelman, H. C. Human use of human subjects: The problem of deception in social psychological experiments. *Psychol. Bull.*, **67**, 1–11 (1967)

133. Kelman, H. C., Baron, R. M. Determinants of modes of resolving inconsistency dilemmas: A functional analysis. In *Theories of Cognitive Consistency: A Sourcebook* (See Ref. 4)

134. Kiesler, C. A. Commitment. *Theories of Cognitive Consistency: A Sourcebook* (See Ref. 4)

135. Kiesler, C. A., Corbin, L. H. Commitment, attraction and conformity. *J. Pers. Soc. Psychol.*, **2**, 890–95 (1965)

136. Kiesler, C. A., De Salvo, J. The group as an influencing agent in a forced compliance paradigm. *J. Exptl. Soc. Psychol.*, **3**, 160–71 (1967)

137. Kiesler, C. A., Sakumura, J. A test of a model for commitment. *J. Pers. Soc. Psychol.*, **3**, 349–53 (1966)

137a. Kiesler, C. A., Collins, B. E., Miller, N. *Attitude Change: A Critical Analysis of Theoretical Approaches* (Wiley, New York, in press)

138. Kiesler, C. A., Pallak, M. S., Kanouse, D. E. Interactive effects of commitment and dissonance. *J. Pers. Soc. Psychol.*, **8**, 331–38 (1968)

139. Kiesler, C. A., Zanna, M., De Salvo, J. Deviation and conformity: Opinion change as a function of commitment, attraction, and presence of a deviate. *J. Pers. Soc. Psychol.*, **3**, 458–67 (1966)

140. Kingdon, J. W. Politicians' beliefs about voters. *Am. Polit. Sci. Rev.*, **61**, 137–45 (1967)

141. Kintz, B. L., Delprato, D. J., Mettee, D. R., Persons, C. E., Schappe, R. H. The experimenter effect. *Psychol. Bull.*, **63**, 223–32 (1965)

142. Knox, R. E., Inkster, J. A. Postdecision dissonance at post time. *J. Pers. Soc. Psychol.*, **8**, 319–23 (1968)

143. Koslin, B. L., Stoops, J. W., Loh, W. D. Source characteristics and communication discrepancy as determinants of attitude change and conformity. *J. Exptl. Soc. Psychol.*, **3**, 230–42 (1967)

143a. Latané, B. Studies in social comparision. *J. Exptl. Soc. Psychol.*, Suppl. 1 (1966)

144. Leventhal, H. Experimental studies in anti-smoking communications. In *Smoking, Health, and Behavior* (Borgatta, E., Evans, R., Eds., Aldine, Chicago, in press)

145. Leventhal, H., Niles, P. A field experiment on fear-arousal with data on the validity of questionnaire measures. *J. Pers.*, **32**, 459–79 (1964)

146. Leventhal, H., Singer, R. P. Affect arousal and positioning of recommendations in persuasive communications. *J. Pers. Soc. Psychol.*, **4**, 137–46 (1966)

147. Leventhal, H., Watts, J. C. Sources of resistance to fear-arousing communications on smoking and lung cancer. *J. Pers.*, **34**, 155–75 (1966)

148. Leventhal, H., Jones, S., Trembly, G. Sex differences in attitude and behavior change under conditions of fear and specific instructions. *J. Exptl. Soc. Psychol.*, **2**, 387–99 (1966)

149. Leventhal, H., Singer, R., Jones, S. Effects of fear and specificity of recommendation upon attitudes and behavior. *J. Pers. Soc. Psychol.*, **2**, 20–29 (1965)

150. Leventhal, H., Watts, J. C., Pagano, F. Effects of fear and instructions on how to cope with danger. *J. Pers. Soc. Psychol.*, **6**, 313–21 (1967)

151. Linder, D. E., Cooper, J., Jones, E. E. Decision freedom as a determinant of the role of incentive magnitude in attitude change. *J. Pers. Soc. Psychol.*, **6**, 245–54 (1967)

152. Lowe, R. H., Steiner, I. D. Some effects of the reversibility and consequences of decisions on postdecision information preferences. *J. Pers. Soc. Psychol.*, **8**, 172–79 (1968)

153. Lowin, A. Approach and avoidance: Alternate modes of selective ex-

posure to information. *J. Pers. Soc. Psychol.*, **6**, 1–9 (1967)

154. Lowin, A. *On the Choice Between Supportive and Non-supportive Information* (Presented at Am. Psychol. Assoc. Conv., Washington, D. C., 1967)

155. Manis, M. Context effects in communication. *J. Pers. Soc. Psychol.*, **5**, 326–34 (1967)

156. Manis, M., Gleason, T. C., Dawes, R. M. The evaluation of complex social stimuli. *J. Pers. Soc. Psychol.*, **3**, 404–19 (1966)

157. Mann, L. The effects of emotional role playing on desire to modify smoking habits. *J. Exptl. Soc. Psychol.*, **3**, 334–48 (1967)

158. Mann, L., Janis, I. L. A followup study on the long-term effects of emotional role playing. *J. Pers. Soc. Psychol.*, **8**, 339–42 (1968)

159. Marlowe, D., Frager, R., Nuttall, R. L. Commitment to action taking as a consequence of cognitive dissonance. *J. Pers. Soc. Psychol.*, **2**, 864–68 (1965)

160. McClintock, C. G. Personality syndromes and attitude change. *J. Pers.*, **26**, 479–93 (1958)

161. McGuire, W. J. Some impending reorientations in social psychology: Some thoughts provoked by Kenneth Ring. *J. Exptl. Soc. Psychol.*, **3**, 124–39 (1967)

162. McGuire, W. J. The current status of cognitive consistency theories. In *Cognitive Consistency*, 1–46 (See ref. 3)

163. McGuire, W. J. Suspiciousness of experimenter's intent as an artifact in research. In *Artifact in Social Research* (Rosenthal, R., Rosnow, R., Eds., Academic Press, New York, in press)

164. McGuire, W. J. The nature of attitudes and attitude change. In *Handbook of Social Psychology*, **3** (See Ref. 1)

165. McGuire, W. J. Personality and susceptibility to social influence. In *Handbook of Personality Theory and Research* (Borgatta, E. F., Lambert, W. W., Eds., Rand-McNally, Chicago, 1968)

166. McGuire, W. J., Millman, S. Anticipatory belief lowering following forewarning of a persuasive attack. *J. Pers. Soc. Psychol.*, **2**, 471–79 (1965)

167. Mehrabian, A. Immediacy: An indicator of attitudes in linguistic communication. *J. Pers.*, **34**, 26–34 (1966)

168. Mehrabian, A. The effect of context on judgments of speaker attitude. *Ibid.*, **36**, 21–32 (1968)

169. Miller, N. Involvement and dogmatism as inhibitors of attitude change. *J. Exptl. Soc. Psychol.*, **1**, 121–32 (1965)

170. Miller, N., Levy, B. H. Defaming and agreeing with the communicator as a function of emotional arousal, communication extremity, and evaluative set. *Sociometry*, **30**, 158–75 (1967)

171. Mills, J. Avoidance of dissonant information. *J. Pers. Soc. Psychol.*, **2**, 589–93 (1965)

172. Mills, J. Effect of certainty about a decision upon postdecision exposure to consonant and dissonant information. *Ibid.*, 749–52

173. Mills, J. The effect of certainty on exposure to information prior to commitment. *J. Exptl. Soc. Psychol.*, **1**, 348–55 (1965)

174. Mills, J. Opinion change as a function of the communicator's desire to influence and liking for the audience. *Ibid.*, **2**, 152–59 (1966)

175. Mills, J. Interest in supporting and discrepant information. In *Theories of Cognitive Consistency: A Sourcebook* (See Ref. 4)

176. Mills, J., Jellison, J. M. Effect on opinion change of how desirable the communication is to the audience the communicator addressed. *J. Pers. Soc. Psychol.*, **6**, 98–101 (1967)

177. Mills, J., Jellison, J. M. Avoidance of discrepant information prior to commitment. *Ibid.*, **8**, 59–62 (1968)

177a. Mills, J., Jellison, J. M. Effect on opinion change of similarity between communicator and the audience he addressed. *J. Pers. Soc. Psychol.*, **9**, 153–56 (1968)

178. Nisbett, R. E. Gordon, A. Self-esteem and susceptibility to social influence. *J. Pers. Soc. Psychol.*, **5**, 268–76 (1967)

179. Nuttin, J. M., Jr. Attitude change after rewarded dissonant and consonant "forced compliance." *Intern. J. Psychol.*, **1**, 39–57 (1966)

180. Orne, M. T. On the social psychology of the psychological experiment: With particular reference to demand characteristics and their implications. *Am. Psychol.*, **17**, 776–83 (1962)

181. Ostrom, T. M. Perspective as an intervening construct in the judgment of attitude statements. *J. Pers. Soc. Psychol.*, **3**, 135–44 (1966)

182. Pallak, M. S., Brock, T. C., Kiesler,

C. A. Dissonance arousal and task performance in an incidental verbal learning paradigm. *J. Pers. Soc. Psychol.*, **7**, 11–20 (1967)

183. Pagageorgis, D. Anticipation of exposure to persuasive messages and belief change. *J. Pers. Soc. Psychol.*, **5**, 490–96 (1967)

184 Pervin, L. A., Yatko, R. J. Cigarette smoking and alternative methods of reducing dissonance. *J. Pers. Soc. Psychol.*, **2**, 30–36 (1965)

185. Phillips, J. L., A model for cognitive balance. *Psychol. Rev.*, **74**, 481–95 (1967)

186. Podell, J. E., Amster, H. The evaluative concept of a person as a function of the number of stimulus traits. *J. Pers. Soc. Psychol.*, **4**, 333–36 (1966)

187. Porier, G. W., Lott, A. J. Galvanic skin responses and prejudice. *J. Pers. Soc. Psychol.*, **5**, 253–59 (1967)

188. Powell, F. A. Source credibility and behavioral compliance as determinants of attitude change. *J. Pers. Soc. Psychol.*, **2**, 669–76 (1965)

189. Price, K. O., Harburg, E., Newcomb, T. M. Psychological balance in situations of negative interpersonal attitudes. *J. Pers. Soc. Psychol.*, **3**, 265–70 (1966)

190. Proshansky, H. M. The development of intergroup attitudes. In *Review of Child Development Research*, **2**, 311–71 (Hoffman, L. W., Hoffman, M. L., Eds., Russell Sage Foundation, New York, 1966)

191. Proshansky, H., Seidenberg, B., Eds. *Basic Studies in Social Psychology* (Holt, Rinehart & Winston, New York, 1965)

192. Ray, M. L. *The Effect of Choice, Controversy, and Selectivity on the Effectiveness of Various Defenses to Persuasion* (Doctoral thesis, Northwestern Univ., Evanston, Ill., 1967)

193. Rhine, R. J. Some problems in dissonance theory research on information selectivity. *Psychol. Bull.*, **68**, 21–28 (1967)

194. Rhine, R. J. The 1964 presidential election and curves of information seeking and avoiding. *J. Pers. Soc. Psychol.*, **5**, 416–23 (1967)

195. Ring, K. Experimental social psychology: Some sober questions about some frivolous values. *J. Exptl. Soc. Psychol.*, **3**, 113–23 (1967)

196. Rodrigues, A. Effects of balance, positivity, and agreement in triadic social relations. *J. Pers. Soc. Psy-chol.*, **5**, 472–76 (1967)

197. Rokeach, M. Attitude change and behavioral change. *Publ. Opin. Quart.*, **30**, 529–50 (1966)

198. Rokeach, M. A theory of organization and change within value-attitude systems. *J. Soc. Issues*, **24**, 13–33 (1968)

199. Rokeach, M., Mezei, L. Race and shared belief as factors in social choice. *Science*, **151**, 167–72 (1966)

200. Rokeach, M., Rothman, G. The principle of belief congruence and the congruity principle as models of cognitive interaction. *Psychol. Rev.*, **72**, 128–42 (1965)

201. Rosenberg, M. J. When dissonance fails: On eliminating evaluation apprehension from attitude measurement. *J. Pers. Soc. Psychol.*, **1**, 28–42 (1965)

202. Rosenberg, M. J. Some limits of dissonance: Toward a differentiated view of counter-attitudinal performance. In *Cognitive Consistency*, 135–70 (See Ref. 79)

203. Rosenberg, M. J. Counterattitudinal behavior and attitude change. In *Theories of Cognitive Consistency: A Sourcebook* (See Ref. 4)

204. Rosenblatt, P. C. *Alternative Explanations of Warning Effects* (Presented at Western Psychol. Assoc., San Diego, Calif., 1968)

205. Rosenblatt, P. C., Hicks, J. M. Pretesting, forewarning, and persuasion (Presented at Midwestern Psychol. Assoc. Meeting, Chicago, 1966)

206. Rosenthal, R. *Experimenter effects in Behavioral Research* (Appleton-Century-Crofts, New York, 1966)

207. Rosnow, R. L., Robinson, E. J., Eds. *Experiments in Persuasion* (Academic Press, New York, 1967)

208. Schlachet, P. J. The effect of dissonance arousal on the recall of failure stimuli. *J. Pers.*, **33**, 443–61 (1965)

209. Scott, J. P. Attitude measurement. In *Handbook of Social Psychology*, **2** (See Ref. 1)

210. Sears, D. O. Biased indoctrination and selectivity of exposure to new information. *Sociometry*, **28**, 363–76 (1965)

211. Sears, D. O. Effects of the assassination of President Kennedy on political partisanship. In Greenberg, B. S., Parker, E. B., Eds., *The Kennedy Assassination and the American Public*, 305–26. Stanford Univ. Press, Stanford, Calif., (1965)

212. Sears, D. O. Opinion formation and information preferences in an adversary situation. *J. Exptl. Soc. Psychol.*, 2, 130–42 (1966)
213. Sears, D. O. Social anxiety, opinion structure, and opinion change. *J. Pers. Soc. Psychol.*, 7, 142–51 (1967)
214. Sears, D. O. Political behavior. In *Handbook of Social Psychology*, 5 (See Ref. 1)
215. Sears, D. O. The paradox of de facto selective exposure without preferences for supportive information. In *Theories of Cognitive Consistency: A Sourcebook* (See Ref. 4)
216. Sears, D. O., Freedman, J. L. The effects of expected familiarity with arguments upon opinion change and selective exposure. *J. Pers. Soc. Psychol.*, 2, 420–26 (1965)
217. Sears, D. O., Freedman, J. L. Selective exposure to information: A critical review. *Publ. Opin. Quart.*, 31, 194–213 (1967)
218. Selltiz, C., Edrich, H., Cook, S. W. Ratings of favorableness of statements about a social group as an indicator of attitude toward the group. *J. Pers. Soc. Psychol.*, 2, 408–15 (1965)
219. Shaw, M. E., Wright, J. M. *Scales for the Measurement of Attitudes* (McGraw-Hill, New York, 1967)
220. Sherif, C. W., Sherif, M., Eds., *Attitudes, Ego-Involvement, and Change* (Wiley, New York, 1967)
221. Sherif, M., Hovland, C. I. *Social Judgment* (Yale Univ. Press, New Haven, Conn., 1961)
222. Sherman, S. R. Demand characteristics in an experiment on attitude change. *Sociometry*, 30, 246–61 (1967)
223. Sherwood, J. J., Nataupsky, M. Predicting the conclusions of Negro-white intelligence research from biographical characteristics of the investigator. *J. Pers. Soc. Psychol.*, 8, 53–58 (1968)
224. Sigall, H., Aronson, E. Opinion change and the gain-loss model of interpersonal attraction. *J. Exptl. Soc. Psychol.*, 3, 178–88 (1967)
225. Silverman, I. Role-related behavior of subjects in laboratory studies of attitude change. *J. Pers. Soc. Psychol.*, 8, 343–48 (1968)
226. Silverman, I., Regula, C. Evaluation apprehension, demand characteristics, and the effects of distraction on persuasibility. *J. Soc. Psychol.* (In press)
227. Silverman, I., Ford, L. H., Jr., Morganti, J. B. Interrelated effects of

social desirability, sex, self-esteem, and complexity of argument on persuasibility. *J. Pers.*, 34, 555–68 (1966)
228. Singer, J. E. Social comparison: Progress and issues. *J. Exptl. Soc. Psychol., Suppl.*, 1, 103–10 (1966)
229. Smith, C. R., Williams, L., Willis, R. H. Race, sex, and belief as determinants of friendship acceptance. *J. Pers. Soc. Psychol.*, 5, 127–37 (1967)
230. Stein, D. D. The influence of belief systems on interpersonal preference: A validation study of Rokeach's theory of prejudice. *Psychol. Monogr.*, 80, No. 616, 1–29 (1966)
231. Stein, D. D., Hardyck, J. A., Smith, M. B. Race and belief: An open and shut case. *J. Pers. Soc. Psychol.*, 1, 281–89 (1965)
232. Steiner, I. D. Personality and the resolution of interpersonal disagreements. *Progr. Exptl. Pers. Res.*, 3, 195–239 (1966)
233. Steiner, I. D., Fishbein, M., Eds., *Current Studies in Social Psychology* (Holt, Rinehart & Winston, New York, 1965)
234. Stricker, L. J. The true deceiver. *Psychol. Bull.*, 68, 13–20 (1967)
235. Stricker, L. J., Messick, S., Jackson, D. N. Suspicion of deception: Implications for conformity research. *J. Pers. Soc. Psychol.*, 5, 379–89 (1967)
236. Tannenbaum, P. H. Mediated generalization of attitude change via the principle of congruity. *J. Pers. Soc. Psychol.*, 3, 493–99 (1966)
237. Tannenbaum, P. H. The congruity principle revisited: Studies in the reduction, induction and generalization of persuasion. In *Advances in Experimental Social Psychology*, 3, 272–320 (See Ref. 25)
238. Tannenbaum, P. H., Gengel, R. W. Generalization of attitude change through congruity principle relationships. *J. Pers. Soc. Psychol.*, 3, 299–304 (1966)
239. Tannenbaum, P. H., Greenberg, B. S. Mass communication. *Ann. Rev. Psychol.*, 19, 351–86 (1968)
240. Taylor, H. F. Balance and change in the two-person group. *Sociometry*, 30, 262–79 (1967)
241. Thayer, S. Confidence and postjudgment exposure to consonant and dissonant information in a free-choice situation. *J. Soc. Psychol.* (In press, 1968)
242. Tittle, C. R., Hill, R. J. Attitude

288 SEARS & ABELES

measurement and prediction of behavior: An evaluation of conditions and measurement techniques. *Sociometry*, **30**, 199–213 (1967)
243. Triandis, H. C., Davis, E. E. Race and belief as determinants of behavioral intentions. *J. Pers. Soc. Psychol.*, **2**, 715–25 (1965)
244. Triandis, H. C., Loh, W. D., Levin, L. A. Race, status, quality of spoken English, and opinions about civil rights as determinants of interpersonal attitudes. *J. Pers. Soc. Psychol.*, **3**, 468–72 (1966)
245. Upshaw, H. The effect of variable perspectives on judgments of opinion statements for Thurstone Scales: Equal-appearing intervals. *J. Pers. Soc. Psychol.*, **2**, 60–69 (1965)
246. Walster, E., Festinger, L. The effectiveness of "overheard" persuasive communications. *J. Abnorm. Soc. Psychol.*, **65**, 395–402 (1962)
247. Walster, E., Aronson, E., Abrahams, D. On increasing the persuasiveness of a low prestige communicator. *J. Exptl. Soc. Psychol.*, **2**, 325–42 (1966)
248. Walster, E., Berscheid, E., Abrahams, D., Aronson, V. Effectiveness of debriefing following deception experiments. *J. Pers. Soc. Psychol.*, **6**, 371–80 (1967)
249. Waly, P., Cook, S. W. Effect of attitude on judgments of plausibility. *J. Pers. Soc. Psychol.*, **2**, 745–49 (1965)
250. Waly, P., Cook, S. W. Attitude as a determinant of learning and memory: A failure to confirm. *Ibid.*, **4**, 280–288 (1966)
251. Ward, C. D. Ego involvement and the absolute judgment of attitude statements. *J. Pers. Soc. Psychol.*, **2**, 202–8 (1965)
252. Ward, C. D. Attitude and involvement in the absolute judgment of attitude statements. *Ibid.*, **4**, 465–76 (1966)
253. Watts, W. A. Cognitive reorganization following a disconfirmed expectancy. *J. Pers. Soc. Psychol.*, **2**, 231–41 (1965)
254. Watts, W. A. Commitment under conditions of risk. *Ibid.*, **3**, 507–15 (1966)
255. Webb, E. J., Campbell, D. T., Schwartz, R. D., Sechrest, L. *Unobtrusive Measures: Nonreactive Research in the Social Sciences* (Rand-McNally, Chicago, 1966)
256. Weiss, W. Effects of mass media of communication. In *Handbook of Social Psychology*, **5** (See Ref. 1)
257. Weiss, W., Steenbock, S. The influence on communication effectiveness of explicitly urging action and policy consequences. *J. Exptl. Soc. Psychol.*, **1**, 396–406 (1965)
258. Whittaker, J. O. Resolution of the communication discrepancy issue in attitude change. In *Attitude, Ego-Involvement, and Change*, 159–77 (See Ref. 221)
259. Wicklund, R. A., Brehm, J. W. Attitude change as a function of felt competence and threat to attitudinal freedom. *J. Exptl. Soc. Psychol.*, **4**, 64–75 (1968)
260. Wicklund, R. A., Cooper, J., Linder, D. E. Effects of expected effort on attitude change prior to exposure. *Exptl. Soc. Psychol.*, **3**, 416–28 (1967)
261. Willis, R. H., Bulatao, R. A. Belief and ethnicity as determinants of friendship and marriage acceptance in the Philippines (Presented at Am. Psychol. Assoc. Conv., Washington, D. C., 1967)
262. Wilson, P. R., Russell, P. N. Modification of psychophysical judgments as a method of reducing dissonance. *J. Pers. Soc. Psychol.*, **3**, 710–12 (1966)
263. Woodmansee, J. J., Cook, S. W. Dimensions of verbal racial attitudes: Their identification and measurement. *J. Pers. Soc. Psychol.*, **7**, 240–50 (1967)
264. Yaryan, R. B., Festinger, L. Preparatory action and belief in the probable occurrence of future events. *J. Abnorm. Soc. Psychol.*, **63**, 603–6 (1961)
265. Zajonc, R. B., Burnstein, E. The learning of balanced and unbalanced social structures. *J. Pers.*, **33**, 153–63 (1965)
266. Zajonc, R. B., Burnstein, E. Structural balance, reciprocity, and positivity as sources of cognitive bias. *J. Pers.*, **33**, 570–83 (1965)
267. Zajonc, R. B., Sherman, S. J. Structural balance and the induction of relations. *J. Pers.*, **35**, 635–50 (1967)
268. Zimbardo, P. G. Involvement and communication discrepancy as determinants of opinion conformity. *J. Abnorm. Soc. Psychol.*, **60**, 86–94 (1960)

ELECTRICAL STIMULATION OF THE BRAIN IN BEHAVIORAL CONTEXT[1,2]

138

BY ROBERT W. DOTY[3]

Center for Brain Research, University of Rochester, Rochester, New York

Electrical change is a fundamental feature of the flow of information between and within neurons. As a consequence, functions of the brain are exceedingly sensitive to imposed electrical fluctuations which pass effectively through the surfaces of neurons. The centennial of two major advances in the utilization of this fact is just now being celebrated: first, the use of electrical stimulation in unanesthetized mammals through electrodes implanted in the brain stem, initiated by Simonoff (192) in 1866; and second, the discovery by Fritsch & Hitzig (62) in 1870 that the cerebral cortex is electrically excitable. Simonoff's technique saw little further use until Hess (85) began his now renowned studies on the hypothalamus in the late 1920's, but Fritsch & Hitzig's contribution was immediately fruitful.

The peculiarly serendipitous nature of this discovery is often overlooked. Hitzig was led to his famous experiments by the observation that when he applied electrical current across the head with electrodes in the temporal area, the subject's eyes moved (87, 88). Since this occurred also in the blind, he reasoned that it was a directly elicited movement rather than the result of efforts to follow the whirling visual field consequent to the induced vertigo (87). Had the function and electrical sensitivity of the vestibular system been understood at the time, Hitzig would have been led to explore the inner ear rather than the cerebral cortex for the origin of these eye movements, but it was also in 1870 that Goltz (72) published his paper that ultimately led to the elucidation of labyrinthine function [see (33) for review]. Would that all experiments begun rationally, but in error from inadequate knowledge, turned out so well!

J. R. Ewald, who followed Goltz at Strasbourg, not only contributed many of the decisive experiments on the vestibular system, but also introduced a technique for electrical stimulation of the cerebral cortex in unanesthetized dogs by using implanted electrode assemblies made from buttons of ivory. Perhaps because the latter experiments were published (202)

[1] The survey of literature pertaining to this review was concluded in May 1968.

[2] The following abbreviations will be used frequently in this chapter: CR (conditioned response); CS (conditioned stimulus); UR (unconditioned response); US (unconditioned stimulus).

[3] Preparation of this review was assisted by Grant NB03606 from the National Institute of Neurological Diseases and Blindness, National Institutes of Health, U. S. Public Health Service.

only in summary by an American postdoctoral fellow in his laboratory, they have never received the emphasis they deserve. Talbert & Ewald (202) showed that in the unanesthetized mammal, electrical stimulation any place in the cerebral cortex can give rise to movement. This has been confirmed extensively (40, 92, 122) but remains overshadowed by the fact that movements from the motor cortex often have the much lower threshold and are always more repeatable. Another important discovery was also made in Ewald's laboratory. Baer (8) showed in chronically prepared dogs that by pairing stimulation of the visual cortex, for instance, with stimulation of motor cortex, subsequent stimulation of the visual cortex could by itself produce the same movements as had stimulation of the motor cortex. This direct demonstration of the mutability of cortical effects was greatly extended almost 30 years later by Loucks (124–126) in Gantt's laboratory. Loucks achieved a permanent alteration in the consequences of cortical excitation when he used appropriate repetition and pairing with other stimuli.

This aspect of Loucks' experiments showed first that electrical stimulation could be used directly to study the manner in which changes in organization arise in the brain as a consequence of experience; and second, that in certain instances of significantly diverse past histories, different effects may be expected from stimulating the same anatomical region in different individuals. The most dramatic examples of such individualization of effect are found in human subjects in which personal memories (9, 156) or speech sounds (186) are called forth by the electrical stimulus. It is not certain whether similar findings are present for animals, although the rather diffuse representation of such synergies as feeding (166, 168, 171, 222) or vocalization (99, 169), when sampled by exploring electrical stimulation in different individuals, strongly suggests this possibility. This is not to say that no anatomical focus exists common to all individuals for these activities, but rather that the vagaries of individual experience or inheritance or both make it possible also to elicit similar responses by excitation at loci unique for given individuals.

It is well known that the result of stimulation at the same central locus may vary depending upon environmental setting (e.g., 81, 89, 93, 113, 120, 166, 168, 212), satiation (54, 75, 130, 153, 217, 222), hormone level (21, 83, 153), simple repetition (40, 48, 70, 209), or previous activity (81, 142, 149, 212). Stimulation at some points yields a constant response throughout hundreds of repetitions; such points include sensorimotor cortex for movement in cats, dogs, or macaques (29, 40, 46, 48), and the mesencephalic reticular formation for alerting (209). On the contrary, repeating stimulation three to ten times at most cortical points, or at some loci in the caudate nucleus or amygdala (209), or even the tectal area or mesencephalic reticular formation in rats (70) leads to disappearance of the response. Such loss of responsiveness has some of the characteristics of habituation for the alerting response (209), but this is probably not true for the decrementing movements elicited by near-threshold cortical stimuli. In both cases after loss of the response to stimulation on one side, initial stimulation of the corresponding point in the other hemisphere yields a response of undiminished vigor. In other words, the decrement is highly specific to the stimulated pathway. Yet it is difficult to believe the unresponsive state is due to fatigue since it can be relatively permanent (40), and many systems respond indefinitely without change (29, 46). Certainly it is not tissue damage, as the same point for which the inherent response has disappeared can be stimulated to elicit a conditioned response (CR) with unchanged threshold over many months (40, 48, 148). Cursory observations indicate that when the corpus callosum is severed, the inherent responses elicited by cortical stimulation in macaques become much more persistent (Doty, unpublished). It is thus possible that a major factor normally leading to disappearance of these responses is active suppression by the unstimulated area of the other hemisphere.

Such suppression is common for noncongruent natural stimuli in the visual system. A particularly relevant example is found in the work of Ewert (54) on toads. A toad with only one eye is very slow in attacking prey since the normal visual signal for attack is conveyed via binocular fixation. Similarly, unilateral electrical stimulation of the intact toad's optic tectum seldom produces an attack response because the contralateral retino-tectal system conveys the information that "there is no object present." If, however, prey is presented to one eye, the other having been removed and its optic tectum stimulated electrically, the attack proceeds with normal celerity, while failing with either stimulus, electrical or visual, alone. Since a lesion in one optic tectum facilitates prey-catching behavior controlled by the other, it must be inferred that each tectum inhibits the other in this regard (54). A comparable situation seems to exist in macaques where stimulation of area 18 (and possibly areas 17 and 19) can produce prey-catching behavior if the corpus callosum and anterior commissure are cut, but so far it has not been observed in full form with intact animals. In both intact and "split-brain" monkeys the eyes converge and fixate upon a point in space within arm's reach when this area is stimulated, and the eyes then slowly track downward. Split-brain animals at this point may then make rapid capturing movements (with either hand for unilateral stimulation!) exactly as macaques make in catching insects. They then carefully examine the hand to assay success of the endeavor, or convey the hand to the mouth and attempt to ingest the hallucinated "bug" (44). For the intact animals the hallucination is probably less compelling because of "contradictory information" emanating from the nonstimulated hemisphere, just as with Ewert's toads. The general subjective nature of the monkey's experience can be inferred from the report of a human epileptic patient who performed the identical movements when the region of area 18 was stimulated in his brain. When asked what he was endeavoring to catch, he replied, "that butterfly" (!), which was one of his epileptic auras (58).

Stereotypic behavior or sensation elicited by electrical stimuli.—From the above it is apparent that electrical stimulation of the brain can elicit behaviors and sensations of great neural complexity. While it is seldom stated, and there is no direct evidence to prove it, current neurophysiological knowledge makes it essentially axiomatic that the neural organization responsible for such complex outcome lies remote to the neurons stimulated. This principle or axiom follows from the fact that any coordinated movement involving spatiotemporal sequencing of action in motoneuronal pools requires equally precise phasing of excitatory and inhibitory control, as does most sensory experience. It is impossible to achieve this by electrical stimulation. The current cannot impose upon neurons the spatiotemporally coded and integrated output they normally achieve; it can only drive them in bizarre and nonsensical synchrony. Thus any subtle, highly integrated neural effects resulting from the stimulation must ensue only because the neural systems downstream (or, possibly, to a slight degree upstream) receiving the nonsense signal are able to transform it into an effective neural code. Were the stimulation inserted into the midst of neurons required to organize a complex action, it could only interfere with, not produce, this action.

In these terms then, coordinated movements elicited by stimulation of the precentral "motor" cortex must be organized either by surrounding cortex not directly stimulated or by spinal and extrapyramidal systems upon which the stimulated neurons project. Evidence for this comes from the fact that the same synergy can be elicited from more than one cortical locus, e.g., hand and arm flexed up toward opening mouth, elicited either from rhinal fissure (29) or precentral gyrus (36). This strongly suggests that both stimulated cortical systems are afferent to a subcortical neural mechanism whose output yields this pattern of response. In similar vein, stimulation of the dominant hemisphere in man never yields speech but only interference with speech processes from a very extensive area (157). Stimulation of the rostral thalamus, on the other hand, particularly in the dominant hemisphere where it is likely to be afferent to speech mechanisms, can yield phrases such as "Now one goes home," "Thank you," or "I see something, I hear something, now I say thou to thee" (186). The phrases are different in each patient, reproducible upon repeated stimulation; they are uttered without his control and usually without his recollection of having spoken and are accompanied by various motor automatisms [(186) and personal communication from Professor Schaltenbrand]. No one could imagine that such speech was organized by the stimulation. Rather, the stimulation must engage systems afferent to the transforming mechanism, just as do peripherally applied electrical stimuli which can evoke such intricate actions as scratching (191) or swallowing (35, 45) provided they possess the appropriate spatiotemporal pattern to pass through the afferent portal to the command systems.

It is of great interest that in the relatively simple nervous system of nudibranchs a single pulse applied to a single neuron can trigger a complex behavioral sequence enduring several seconds (219). Likewise in the crayfish, stimulation of a single cell can produce a coordinated output among several motoneurons, and each interneuron controls a different output (105).

Since it is probable that a single impulse in a single human touch receptor can be perceived (82), similar sensitivity must be expected in responses of the mammalian brain, but probably only in special circumstances. Perhaps the greatest sensitivity so far observed is in a macaque able to make a lever-pressing CR upon application of a single 0.02-mA, 0.5-msec pulse in the area of the postcentral gyrus representing the fingers (Doty, unpublished). Measurements (199) suggest that such a pulse should stimulate only a few dozen neurons at most.

Stimulation in the nervous system of insects produces a variety of stereo-typed behaviors (e.g., 91), and here too the same behavior can be elicited from different areas. Both normal and abnormal songs depending upon stimulus location can be induced in crickets. For locomotion, respiratory movements, feeding, or cleaning, the stimulus frequency in crickets is relatively unimportant, but, for singing, the temporal patterning of the stimulus is critical (91), much as it is with elicitation of deglutition by stimulation of peripheral nerves in mammals (35, 36, 45).

Feeding behavior has been elicited in fish by electrical stimulation of the olfactory paths (78), and feeding-attack movements from stimulation of the mesencephalic tegmentum (57). The prey-capturing behavior elicited in toads by stimulation of the optic tectum (53) has been discussed above. It is surprising that in the bullfrog the postural effects from stimulation of the optic tectum are able to overcome those from concurrent stimulation of the cerebellum (73). Both "release" and "warning" vocalizations in frogs (187) and hissing in alligators (74) can be elicited by stimulation of the mesencephalon. This system for vocalization can be similarly entered at this level in birds (13, 14, 144), cats (100, 104), and squirrel monkeys (135), and is part of an aggressive-defensive pattern of behavior. In wild ducks a variety of attack or escape patterns can be elicited, often accompained by vocalization, upon stimulation in the archistriatum (the homologue of the mammalian amygdala) and in the septal area [(159); see (14) for review of effects of electrical stimulation in birds].

Stimulation of the amygdala produces a variety of responses, among them sniffing, alerting and orienting, chewing, licking and swallowing, and strong aggressive-defensive behavior. So far, the system has resisted efforts to assign clear anatomical substrates to these various functions (3, 208). Progress has been reported in separating a path for flight in the dorsal hypothalamus from that for aggressive behavior in the ventral hypothalamus (173), although this is somewhat contrary to earlier reports and to the variation in the response depending upon external conditions (15, 93). Several types of vocalization (aggressive, fearful, social calling, etc.) can be elicited by stimulation throughout the limbic system in squirrel monkeys (99) and macaques (169). Besides overlapping areas yielding aggressive-fearful responses, the vocalization areas also interdigitate with those from which penile or clitoral erection can be obtained (129, 134, 170), The expression of these evoked responses, either vocal or sexual, has not yet been studied in a social situation. Elicited mating responses can, however, be obtained in opossums but only if another opossum or furry object is present (168). In other words, response is not always a simple automatism that can be called forth *in vacuo*, but instead may require environmental feedback. This also holds true for many other behaviors evoked by hypothalamic stimulation in opossums, rats, cats, or monkeys (84, 120, 166, 171, 212, 222). The interest of ethologists in this area of experimentation is obviously justified (15).

Stimulation of the antero-mesial thalamus at 7 to 30/sec in cats produces an "arrest reaction" (94, 176, 177). Upon stimulation, all ongoing behavior such as eating or walking ceases and a fixed posture is maintained. Reflexes are undisturbed, but affective response to painful stimuli is absent. With cessation of stimulation the animal returns almost immediately to its previous activities.

A similar effect can be obtained also in cats by stimulating the caudate nucleus (2, 18, 25, 117, 136). The arrest is maintained as long as the stimulus lasts (up to 30 min) and is thus more effective than the anterior thalamic stimulation which does not "hold" the animals indefinitely (94). It is not clear whether this reflects a greater effectiveness of caudatal over thalamic stimulation or merely the use of bilateral stimulation for the caudate nucleus (18, 136) versus unilateral stimulation for the thalamus (94). The effects are highly similar for stimulation of either structure yet survive for one following destruction of the other (24). However, destruction of either motor cortex or pallidal outflow, including the entopeduncular nucleus, leads to loss of the effect for caudatal stimulation, but lesions limited to globus pallidus and ansa lenticularis do not (25).

Typical arrest reactions can be obtained for stimulation of the caudate nucleus in macaques (30) and man (213). The human subjects have amnesia for the period of stimulation. Although they may speak inappropriately, smile, or laugh during the stimulation, appropriate speech, like other voluntary movement, is brought to a halt.

A much more subtle form of arrest is sometimes seen with stimulation of the basolateral amygdala. With very low intensities which give no overt responses, hungry cats immediately stop eating or performing lever-presses to obtain food (60). Both eating (222) and stalking of prey (95) can be elicited in cats by stimulation of the same points in the lateral hypothalamus among fibers of the ansa lenticularis. Cats that normally ignore rats can be made to stalk and kill them when this region is stimulated (49). Such elicited attack, however, is completely inhibited if the amygdala is stimulated at low intensities concurrent with the hypothalamic stimulation (49). Since stimulation elsewhere in the amygdala, at higher currents, often produces fearlike behavior, it might be expected that the inhibition of behavior associated with feeding results simply from imposed fear. Unfortunately, the motivational properties, if any, of the amygdalar stimulation was not determined in any of these experiments. Nevertheless, fear does not seem relevant since weak stimulation of the basolateral amygdala has a dramatically calming effect on dogs making CRs to avoid either foot-shock or stimulation of the hypothalamus (59). In this instance the stimulation does not inhibit the CRs but greatly reduces the random, intertrial presses which so characteristically reflect the animal's "anxiety"—yet the same stimulation also yields prompt cessation of eating. Stimulation of what seems to be the same system in the amygdala of rats inhibits their self-stimulation of the septal area (103).

With cats, bilateral stimulation in the ventral portion of the diagonal band of Broca at frequencies of 5 to 250/sec also arrests ongoing activity, but then the animal falls asleep within 5 to 180 sec if the stimulation continues (196). Thus, the effect here is distinctly different from that with the caudate nucleus or dorsomedial thalamus. Prolonged stimulation of almost every place in the brain has been reported to put cats to sleep if frequencies of 3 to 8/sec are used, but since laboratory cats normally sleep about 17 hr out of 24 (198), the significance of such findings is difficult to judge. However, such objections do not apply to the sleep produced by stimulation of the basal forebrain since it is obtained after a very short latency and with a wide range of frequencies.

Motivation.—Some of the stereotypes described above are mere motor automatisms lacking in significant relation to motivational systems. This is particularly true for those elicited via neocortex (31, 32, 39, 46), but also may be true for those elicited from the caudate nucleus (39, 149) and probably other brain stem sites, if negative findings were to be emphasized [see, e.g., charts in (218)]. On the other hand, stimulation at most sites in the limbic system has the still mysterious ability to organize motor activity in any fashion required to produce more of the stimulation or to avoid it, as the case may be. It is regrettable that these motivational aspects of the stimulation tend to be studied separately from the sterotyped, inherent responses elicited by it.

Of course, often there is no consistent correlation between the evoked inherent movements and the sign of the motivational effect. In fact, the outward appearance of the animal can be strangely at variance with the motivational response it displays. Thus, cats stimulating their posterior hypothalamus for 0.5 sec per lever-press at rates up to 1500/hr look as though they are severely frightened, i.e., there is pupillary dilatation, piloerection, escape of urine, and abrupt darting movements (39, 218). That these animals are on the verge of extreme fear is readily demonstrated by changing the duration of the burst of stimuli from 0.5 to 1.0 sec. Lever-pressing ceases immediately (39, 164, 218), and the animal shows great hesitation about ever pressing the lever again. Such external appearance of fearful or aggressive behavior is a very common accompaniment of self-stimulation at other loci in cats (39) but apparently not of goats (158). The same phenomenon probably occurs in rats that will self-stimulate through electrodes in the periaqueductal gray (28). The stimulation is accompanied by squealing and other signs of pain and fright, and it seems very likely that were the stimulus train prolonged beyond 0.5 sec, an aversive effect would ensue. Similarly, the pigeon will peck a key up to 300 times in 10 min to receive stimulation in the laterodorsal tegmental nucleus just beneath the posterior commissure (75). Stimulation at this locus produced aggressive signs and actual attack upon a normally dominant companion bird if present.

From the foregoing it is possible to discern, however dimly, a startling and heretofore unsuspected principle of neural organization. Certain patterns of activity within systems responsible for fearful or aggressive behavior, rather than being aversive are perversely gratifying. This is clearly recognized in the sociology of man, but its unexpected appearance as a basic element of neural organization accessible to study by the methods of electrophysiology should prompt further interest in the effort to understand the

TABLE I

SPECIES COMPARISON OF POINTS IN LIMBIC SYSTEM TESTED FOR SELF-STIMULATION

Behavior	Rat	Rabbit	Cat	Cat
Percentage of points where stimulus sought	28	27	15	18
Percentage of points where stimulus avoided	35	36	70	54
Percentage of points neutral	18	22	6	28
Percentage of points ambivalent	19	15	9	—
Total points tested	96	109	125	70
Reference	154	16	218	38, 39, 149

nature and to control the consequences of this feral inheritance. In this connection it may be of interest that neutral (149) or even initially rewarding (142) stimulation can, with training, be altered to yield aversive effects; or that rats can be trained to attack one another in order to receive rewarding central stimulation (194).

A converse lack of correlation between external signs and chosen behavior was seen with stimulation of the preoptic area beneath the anterior commissure in one macaque. This led to penile erection and, ultimately, ejaculation (170). From such signs a high level of self-stimulation might be expected; yet self-stimulation by the usual criteria was not obtained, and the animal would curtail externally applied stimuli with a latency of about 2 sec. Self-stimulation to the point of ejaculation occurred, but it took only 76 presses spread over 25 min (170).

Table I emphasizes the fact that stimulation of points primarily in the limbic system (including midbrain and hypothalamus) is more often sought by rats and rabbits and avoided by cats. The areas sampled in these studies are similar, and while there are certain differences in detail, all probably represent a rather random sample within these areas. The evaluations of the nonpositive points in the rabbit were made entirely on the basis of external appearances and may thus be unreliable (see above). The aversive points in the rat were specified on the basis of active avoidance, whereas those for the cat were determined by coupling the central stimulation with lever-pressing for food. If the cat when satiated continues pressing indefinitely at a rapid rate while food is withheld, the stimulation is considered to be rewarding in itself; while if the hungry animal stops pressing even though food is given, the effect is judged to be aversive (149). For most areas this is probably an excellent method, but it obviously might yield spurious indications of aversiveness should the stimulation produce arrest responses (117) or interfere with appetite as described above for the amygdala (49, 60). Despite these technical problems it seems likely that Table I reflects a genuine species difference. It cannot be held merely that significant loci are less likely to be struck in large brains since it is apparent (Table I) that the percentage of motivationally effective points is highest in cats. A contradictory study (152) on the cat can be dismissed because of glaring shortcomings. The authors failed to find any aversive points despite a method which, though peculiar and inadequate on other grounds, should have revealed them. Perhaps the failure is linked to the confused state of the animals from too much stimulation at too many points with 0.8-mm diameter electrode shafts moved acutely through the brain, since several of the animals displayed some degree of hemianopsia (152).

Self-stimulation was found for four electrode placements in the optic tectum of the goldfish, but other tectal points were aversive as were some in the telencephalon [(11) and personal communication from E. Boyd)]. Chicks, 5 to 14 days old, will peck a key up to 260 times in 10 min to deliver stimuli to the rostral end of the medial forebrain bundle at the anterior commissure (5). The chicks give peeping calls of approach while thay are self-stimulating. Similar self-stimulation is obtained from this same general region in the paleostriatum of the pigeon (75, 130) and also in the neostriatum (130). The self-stimulation is absent in some cases if the bird has been fed; yet prolonged stimulation at such loci produce no feeding or drinking behavior but only agonistic signs plus a single coo when the stimulus ceases (75).

In cats, self-stimulation can be produced for the anterior thalamic nuclei (from which arrest reactions can be evoked) but not from centrum medianum and the pretectal area of the posterior thalamus (76). A puzzling situation exists in the hippocampus of the rat for which moderate self-stimulation is obtained from electrodes in cornu Ammonis (sometimes erroneously termed "hippocampal gyrus" in the paper), whereas stimulation in gyrus dentatus depresses the background level of pressing (210). In an inadequate test for aversiveness, no difference was found between these two areas (210), nor did any difference among hippocampal sites for self-stimulation appear in a subsequent study using similar techniques on rats (200).

For certain placements in rats and cats it is apparent that the animal can detect the stimulation at much lower intensities than required for self-stimulation (22, 149, 215). It can thus be inferred for these loci that the self-stimulation effect requires either extensive occupation of systems engaged by the more excitable fibers (i.e., recruitment with increasing intensity), or that the higher intensity is required to engage less excitable fibers, or both. It is not known whether this inference is valid for all loci, but it probably is a safe and an important assumption that it is.

A high correlation has been reported between self-stimulation at loci in the lateral hypothalamus and the elicitation of eating or drinking by stimulation through the same electrodes in satiated animals. This seems paradoxical; why should an animal choose, in effect, to make itself hungry? Actually, the initial reports were unconvincing that it did. Half-second trains of stimuli were used for self-stimulation while much longer trains were used for elicitation of feeding behavior and, as noted above and elsewhere [e.g., (10)], changing the train duration from 0.5 to 1.0 sec can completely reverse the motivational properties of the stimulation. Recent reports (27, 137, 141, 143), however, show unequivocally that rats will self-stimulate with the same stimulus trains that induce them to eat or drink, and under some conditions the self-stimulation occurs only if the food or water is available. On the other hand, some animals will choose self-stimulation of the lateral hypothalamus instead of food, even when they are starving (51, 178, 193). If it is true that such electrically elicited hunger is its own reward, it should have motivational properties reflecting the hunger as well as the reward aspect. This has indeed been found to be true [see (55), (221) for review].

A similar relation occurs between male sexual activity evoked in rats by posterior hypothalamic stimulation and self-stimulation from the same point (21, 83). In other words, either form of stimulation evokes sexual responses, and when stimulated, the rat will learn and perform maneuvers to gain access to receptive females (21). It is of great interest and import that male sexual behavior can be evoked from females by stimulation of the medial preoptic area in opossums (168), but the motivational properties of such stimulation have not been determined.

As mentioned above, stimulation of the same locus has been shown capable of eliciting both stalking attack and eating (95), and under the drive of such electrical stimulation normally nonhunting cats will solve problems to gain access to rats which can be attacked (167). Problem solving likewise has been reported for gaining access to wood to gnaw upon during hypothalamic stimulation (166). The specific or inherent nature of such electrically elicited "drives," however, is now open to serious question since it develops that they can be changed with surprising ease (212). If in the presence of wood, food, and water, a rat always gnaws, eats, or drinks when the lateral hypothalamus is stimulated, the "drive" would seem to be specific. Yet when the animal is deprived of the chosen object during stimulation, it comes to accept a substitute, and the substitute then is preferred even when the original is reintroduced (212).

Masserman's contention (133) that the behavioral patterns of fear or aggression evoked by hypothalamic stimulation lack motivational consequences now has been amply disproven. Cats and monkeys usually learn to avoid such stimulation equally as well as pain from peripheral stimulation

(26, 31, 32, 110, 145, 165, 172, 195); indeed, almost any place in the nervous system yielding such behavioral patterns can be used. Similarly, water-satiated goats will perform CRs to obtain water when the hypothalamic area which elicits drinking is stimulated (4). Conditioning of the patterns of fear behavior also can be obtained using an auditory CS (175), as can changes in heart rate using stimulation of the septum for which self-stimulation occurs (132). There are, however, a sufficient number of negative instances to suggest that further facts must be learned. For instance, some cats can learn to escape from hypothalamic stimulation but not to avoid it (163), thus suggesting that the stimulation can interfere with learning. Stimulus-driven feeding also has been reported for pigeons, yet it could not be used as motivation for the animal to seek food (81). Finally, it is not yet clear whether animals will learn when their only motivation is a brief bout of the same stimuli for which the animal had previously displayed self-stimulation (19). A possibly serious technical flaw in the latter experiment is the administration of the reward by the experimenter rather than the animal, i.e., the inter-train interval is probably very critical in many instances for the rewarding effect.

Space precludes discussion of the difficult and largely unsolved problem of what elaboration is required within the nervous system to obtain the motivational effects, but some aspects of the problem have been reviewed (211). Other recent reviews (63, 71, 153) overlap the present one, but each has a different perspective and must therefore be consulted to gain full coverage of the extensive literature on the phenomena of self-stimulation.

Learning without motivation.—Electrical stimulation of the brain has played a major role in defining and elucidating the question as to whether learning requires motivational support or can proceed instead merely as a consequence of appropriate temporal concatenation of stimuli. Much of the experimental approach also has involved sensory-sensory preconditioning, but this aspect will not be reviewed here. The work of Loucks (124, 125) forms the major point of origin for the concept that motivation is essential to learning. With careful and thorough training, Loucks was unable to form CRs to an auditory CS using stimulation of the motor cortex as the US. With this paradigm, the limb movements elicited by the US never appeared to the CS alone; but movements were readily established when each CS-US combination was immediately followed by presentation of food (125). From these consistent results, Loucks drew the fully justified conclusion that simple Pavlovian pairing was not enough to establish CRs; there must be an added factor of motivation. Loucks' work had wide influence on western thinking, but possibly because knowledge of it arrived in Eastern Europe just at the outbreak of the war (see 112), it seems to have had so little impact there that the problem usually goes unrecognized.

The basic result of being able to "instrumentalize" a movement elicited directly by cortical stimulation if it is followed by food (i.e., the animal begins making the movement spontaneously to obtain the food) was observed independently by Konorski & Lubinska (112). Oddly enough, it was subsequently found that the experiment failed if the hindlimb movements used were evoked by stimulation of motor cortex but succeeded for similar movements with stimulation of somatosensory cortex (203). Either cortical area was adequate with foreleg movements.

However, where Loucks had failed by using elicited movement as the US and UR, Kriayev (115) in a cursory report independently claimed success after only five to six pairings of tone and stimulation of motor cortex. Conditioned responses were formed with equal rapidity by Brogden & Gantt (12) using stimulation of the cerebellum as US. Beginning in Kupalov's laboratory in Leningrad in 1951, and initially without knowledge of Loucks' failure, Giurgea (67, 69) proved unequivocally that stimulation of the motor cortex could be used as the US, at the same time using stimulation at other cortical loci as the CS. In other words, merely by persistent pairing over several days, Giurgea was able to make permanent the changes in excitability described in 1905 by Baer (8) whereby stimulation in "visual" cortex could elicit the same movements, though with less vigor and consistency, as did stimulation of the "motor" cortex.

Giurgea's observations have been amply confirmed and extended (39, 46, 138, 151, 204, 214). The phenomenon has been observed in dogs, cats, and macaques and has been produced using radio-transmitted stimulation to freely moving dogs (138). Stimulating the "arm area" of precentral cortex in squirrel monkeys (first stimulating one hemisphere followed immediately by the other), it has been possible after hundreds of pairings to establish a stereotyped movement such that stimulation of the first hemisphere and movement of the one arm leads to movement of the other arm despite omission of the second stimulus (Fentress, unpublished). Vascular or meningeal afferents are not involved since Giurgea's experiment is successful following trigeminal neurotomy (69, 160); and when meningeal pain from the stimulation is present, it interferes with the phenomenon (138). The motivational effects from subcortical stimulation may likewise interfere with the appearance or form of motor CRs evolved when the stimulation is used as US. Nevertheless, there is extensive evidence that the movements, or even autonomic effects, evoked as URs by stimulation in thalamus, hypothalamus, amygdala, field of Forel, septal area, or mesencephalic reticular formation, appear as CRs in a variety of conditioning procedures (1, 7, 39, 46, 132, 175, 190, 223, 224, 226). The CS can be applied to the visual cortex of one hemisphere and the US to the motor cortex of the other, and CRs can be obtained in intact dogs (68) or following section of the corpus callosum (69).

Two questions remain: first, why did Loucks obtain negative results; second, is any motivation involved in forming CRs by Giurgea's procedure? The most likely answer to the first question is that Loucks used short intertrial intervals (30 to 60 sec) and massed trials. It is, however, also possible that the animals chosen were too restless, excitable, or inhibited. In other words, the experiment is more likely to succeed with some types of dog than with others. Different conditionability according to temperament applies particularly to macaques, but also to cats, complete failures being obtained with animals that constantly fidget or fight restraint, as most of them do. Failure might also be expected were presentations given each time with the animal in a different starting position, or while it was moving, etc.

The evidence for the absence of motivational effects from stimulation of motor or sensory neocortex is very strong. Perhaps foremost are the negative experiments of Loucks; for it is difficult to argue in the vein that if the procedure fails, there is no motivation, but if it succeeds, there must be motivation. This is the well-recognized logical trap of circular reasoning. Loucks showed conclusively that when motivation was present, so also was conditioning; and the conclusion still stands that, under his conditions, when motivation is absent, as when stimulation of motor cortex serves as US, conditioning is also absent. Changing the intertrial interval and obtaining successful conditioning can scarcely be held to have changed the putative motivation, since the US remains the same. Certainly all are agreed that, given the opportunity, an animal neither seeks nor avoids stimulation of most neocortical areas (31, 32, 39, 46, 153). Thus, aside from a slight initial curiosity or orienting, no motivational effects have been attributed to neocortical stimulation even when it evokes abrupt and forceful movement.

This leaves as the final argument the possibility that the motivation for making the CR is to effect some postural adjustment which lessens the disturbance of equilibrium by the UR. A recent clever and well-performed series of experiments purports to show that this is likely to be the case (214). In effect, it was shown that dogs prefer a determinate to an indeterminate future, since they choose to be warned when their motor cortex will be stimulated rather than to be surprised. This says that the warning is rewarding, but need it say that the movement is aversive?

Actually, a much better evaluation of the hypothesis of postural adjustment is made simply by observing the animal's performance. There is rarely any evidence of postural preparation for the UR as part of the CR. Particularly with the sitting macaque (46) with a forearm UR, but also with some of the dogs resting their weight on the leg cuffs, no postural adjustment is required to maintain balance. The CR almost invariably terminates 1 or 2 sec prior to the UR, does not alter the vigor of the UR, and not infrequently the animal is caught off balance by the UR. Finally, it is commonly observed that dogs may make the CRs with the leg opposite that in which the UR occurs (39, 46, 68, 214), scarcely an expedient adjustment for coping with the claimed aversiveness of the forthcoming movement. Ultimately, of course, it may be possible to answer the question decisively by using only electrical indices of conditioning, and indeed this has to some degree already been done by Bureš and his colleagues (20, 65; see below).

In one monkey where stimulation of visual cortex elicited an arm flexion after being paired for many days with stimulation of motor cortex, 0,55 mA was the minimal effective current. When stimulation of the same point in visual cortex served as a signal for shock-avoidance, the same arm moved with only 0.2 mA (46). Thus, motivation greatly augmented the effectiveness of the cortical stimulation.

More important, however, if the foregoing interpretation is correct, is the fact that a fundamental change in the consequences of excitation of visual cortex is effected initially without motivational support. If the neurologically obscure phenomena of motivation are truly absent from such effects, the way is open for understanding learning in terms of relatively simple neural events which probably are common to most species. Without doubt the most significant (and most consistently ignored) clue as to what these events may be is the "temporal paradox" of conditioning (37, 43). The paradox arises because it is the antecedent stimulus, the CS, whose effectiveness is altered, rather than that of the subsequent stimulus, the US. In all classical neurophysiological studies, the conditioning, antecedent stimulus has been found to change the response to subsequently presented test stimuli, as in multisynaptic post-tetanic potentiation (220), but not vice versa. This is easy to understand, but how can the alteration in effectiveness of the antecedent stimulus be achieved retrospectively, as occurs in Pavlovian conditioning, without resort to the complexities of motivation?

It is proposed (43) that this is accomplished through the uptake of material which improves the effectiveness of synaptic transmission of initially ineffective axon terminals. The source of the augmenting material could be either axon terminals that are effective (i.e., those activated by the US) or cells that are discharged by the US and upon which the ineffective axons impinge. Release of the augmenting material would occur only briefly following discharge of the "donor" cell or terminal. If the initially ineffective terminals could receive the augmenting material only within a brief period after their discharge, both the "temporal paradox" and the temporal requirements for conditioning (e.g., virtual absence of backward conditioning) would be explained. The hypothesis states, in other words, that there is a chemical feedback from the discharged (probably postsnyaptic) unit, accessible only to synaptic terminals that have also discharged in the immediate past. Thus, synaptic action that is successful is chemically reinforced in a manner that strengthens the synaptic bond or augments its effectiveness. The hypothesis also predicts that only certain types of neurons (possibly in mammals the stellate cells in neocortex, or reticular neurons in the brain stem) would be able to serve in this capacity: (a) in receiving connections from both CS and US systems; (b) in having effective output for behavior; and (c) in offering the opportunity for permanent augmentation of synaptic effectiveness.

Space here precludes detailed elaboration of this hypothesis. Its generality, however, is worth noting. Motivation being dispensable according to the above interpretation, the hypothesis is relevant to all Pavlovian conditioning; and since there is extensive overlap of the phenomena of Pavlovian and instrumental conditioning (161), much of the latter may be subsumed as well. It applies with equal success to the first purely neurophysiological paradigm of the Giurgea experiment, the specific heterosynaptic facilitation of unidentified neurons in *Aplysia* [(102); see (101) for review]. Finally, it can explain many of the otherwise puzzling results of Bureš and his colleagues (20, 65). They found that if an antecedent stimulus, which might or might not affect a given neuron, were consistently followed by effective electrical stimulation of that individual neuron, in roughly 10 per cent of the cells of neocortex, hippocampus, thalamus, or mesencephalic reticular formation a change in the response of that cell to the antecedent stimulus could be observed. Thus, alterations in excitability, often resembling those of conditioning and produced by procedures formally comparable to conditioning, can be achieved by manipulation confined essentially to single neurons. Certainly "motivation" cannot be called upon to explain these changes, but then neither has the possibility been explored that such changes in response can be made permanent. Since inhibitory as well as excitatory effects can be enhanced by these procedures (20, 65), the hypothesis of release of "synaptic augmentors" consequent to neuronal discharge may have to be modified to include as well some form of feedback transaction associated with inhibitory postsynaptic potentials and their underlying membrane phenomena.

It is perhaps significant that when stimulation of the mesencephalic reticular formation was used as US (90), a much higher proportion of neurons (43 per cent), mostly from midline thalamus, showed changes in firing pattern to the CS (electrical stimulation of the lateral geniculate nucleus) than was the case with the local US employed by Bureš et al (20, 65). The mesencephalic stimulation, of course, might be expected to have strong motivational effects.[4]

Many other phenomena associated with learning and habituation, and amenable to electrophysiological analysis, have been well reviewed recently (101, 205).

Central stimulation as signal for the performance of learned acts.—With the apparent exception of the cerebellum (34), it is possible to use excitation any place in the brain as a CS in chickens, cats, rats, rabbits, guinea pigs, dogs, or monkeys (17, 22, 38, 40, 48, 50, 61, 66, 97, 109, 114, 117, 127, 140, 146–150, 155, 174, 179, 183, 200, 207). This means that the stimulated ele-

[4] Repeated, intense stimulation of the motivational systems in the brain stem of unanesthetized, immobilized animals incapable of conveying to the investigator any indication of the behavioral consequences of such stimulation can be a ruthless procedure. In experiments where such stimulation is required, ethical considerations should prompt the investigator either to gauge the behavioral intensity of the effect prior to immobilization (i.e., using permanently implanted electrodes) or to offer some evidence (e.g., duration of EEG arousal reaction) that the animal is not repeatedly experiencing the extremely severe pain or discomfort that such central stimulation can produce. Editors should demand that in the reporting of experiments of this type the authors indicate their awareness of this problem and the manner in which they coped with it.

ments at any neocortical locus, in basal ganglia, thalamus, hypothalamus, hippocampus, or mesencephalon, ultimately have access to all the effector systems that control behavior. This is not wholly unexpected, but it poses interesting problems: First, why should stimulation at so many loci in the human brain be subjectively silent? Second, what subjective effects, if any, might accompany responses from human subjects once they were trained to respond to stimulation of initially silent points? Of course, should it develop that it is impossible to effect such alterations in responsiveness in man as compared to animals, the first clear neurophysiological difference between the brain of man and animals would have been discovered! It is unfortunate that either the interests of the neuropsychiatrist or the exigencies of the clinical situation, or both, so far have left this fascinating question untouched.

From data on thresholds in neocortex of macaques (40) it is clear that the most excitable elements of the brain are capable of serving as the substrate for such conditional stimuli. These are probably the larger pyramidal cells and their axons, although effects from collaterals of large corticipetal fibers cannot be excluded. However, since there are no significant differences in excitability of any of the various cortical areas (e.g., area 17, 4 or 9) insofar as ability to elicit CRs is concerned, the effective elements must be common to all areas. Technical factors have a strong influence on thresholds. For instance, in tests at 126 points in various neocortical areas (Doty, unpublished) using platinum-iridium electrodes (128), 0.2-mm diameter with 1 mm tip separation inserted into the cortex and 0.5-msec rectangular pulses (50/sec), the threshold averaged 0.11 mA (range 0.02 to 0.4). Thresholds were approximately double this when stimulation was applied through surface rather than intracortical electrodes (40). More interesting is the fact that it not infrequently requires intensities several times the ultimate threshold to achieve the first CRs (40, 48, 61, 114).

Once an animal is trained using stimulation at 50/sec, it may fail to respond when the frequency is lowered below 15 to 20/sec [(96, 114, 150) and Doty, unpublished]. This is not always the case since many animals continue responding with no particular hesitation as stimulus frequencies are rapidly lowered to 2/sec (40, 61). There is moderate failure of cats and perhaps macaques trained at 3/sec to generalize to frequencies of 30 to 300/sec (150, 188). Related phenomena are reported for human subjects in whom direct cortical responses or cortical responses to stimulation of the ventral posterolateral nucleus of the thalamus can be elicited in somatosensory cortex at 2/sec without subjective accompaniment, even using stimuli 20 times greater than the subjective threshold at 60/sec (121). On the other hand, the thresholds for these evoked potentials in man (121) or in the piriform cortex in cats for stimulation of the lateral olfactory tract (61), when averaging techniques are used, are very close to the threshold for detection (by report or performance of a CR, respectively) when stimulation at 30 to 60/sec is used.

Stimulation of group I proprioceptive, muscle-afferent fibers in cats is as ineffective as a CS at 100/sec as it is at 4/sec, even though the latter elicits a high-amplitude response in sensorimotor cortex (201). This clear demonstration that muscle spindle afferents lack access to the systems subserving conditioned reflexes [and to conscious processes in man (64)], strengthens evidence of similar nature for the cerebellum (34). Although cutaneous and other inputs reach the cerebellum, it is unquestionable dominated by the proprioceptive systems. Stimulation of the dentate or fastigial nuclei or of neocerebellar cortex is ineffective as a CS in cats at intensities of excitation which evoke potentials in sensorimotor cortex (34). If the intensity is increased to the point where movement is also elicited, the cat can learn to make CRs to this stimulation (34). A major problem here, however, may be that the threshold for movement is very near the threshold for stimulation of the most excitable elements, as it is in area 4 of macaques (40), so that further reduction yields currents which would be ineffective in any system. Still, unquestionably there seems to be something unique about the cerebellar systems in this regard. The threshold for evoked potentials in somatosensory cortex is nearly the same as that for action as a CS when the ventral posterolateral nucleus of the thalamus is stimulated at 4/sec, but very large cortical potentials must be evoked with 4/sec stimulation of the ventrolateral nucleus of the thalamus or the dentate nucleus before the excitation is effective as a CS [personal communication from J. E. Swett; also see (201)].

One other instance has been claimed in which cortical potentials can be evoked by stimuli which remain relatively ineffective as CS. This is for stimulation of the medial thalamus in cats at 7/sec, eliciting recruiting responses in neocortex (6, 184). Certain shortcomings in the design of these experiments led to a re-examination of the question using as CS thalamic stimulation which elicited recruiting responses in squirrel monkeys (155). No convincing evidence was found that the recruiting responses disturbed conditioning. Nevertheless, further study is needed since it now appears that the areas yielding behavioral arrest and those yielding recruiting responses are not necessarily congruent in the thalamus (177). Stimulation of the caudate nucleus of cats at 3/sec can be used as a CS even though this initially can elicit spindle bursts in neocortex and behavioral inhibition (18). Even more dramatic is the fact that stimulation of the basal forebrain can be used as a CS and the cats actually fall asleep to this stimulation during the course of training to make shock-avoidance CRs (148).

With stimulation of the optic nerve in the cat at 1/sec, large potentials are evoked in visual cortex, but they display no certain alteration when a CR is or is not made in response to this stimulation (96). Changes in the evoked potentials appear to be correlated to some degree with attentive processes (96). These are nonspecific since in macaques with stimulation of optic radiation the response in visual cortex undergoes abrupt, dramatic, and highly similar changes for either a photic or auditory CS (162). Similar nonspecific effects are probably present for the alterations in potentials evoked in sensorimotor cortex of cats by 7/sec stimulation of the ventrolateral nucleus as it becomes effective as a CS for food reward CR (185). No controls were undertaken to check this possibility that the changed potentials reflect merely a general shift in the level of arousal.

Specific changes in potentials evoked by a centrally applied CS as it becomes effective in eliciting CRs have, however, been found. Most ingenious and convincing by its inherent controls is the demonstration that for symmetrical placements on each suprasylvian gyrus of the cat the interhemispheric extracallosal response is enhanced only when elicited by stimuli at the point used effectively as CS (181). Transcallosal responses remain unchanged, as does the extracallosal response if the cortex is only stimulated repeatedly but not used for the CS. The alterations appear to be permanent and are recorded during chloralose anesthesia (181). Other changes unequivocally related to use of the central stimulus as CS have been reported for stimulation of the lateral geniculate body and mesencephalic reticular formation in cats (98, 119). Particularly interesting here is the very great enhancement of a potential evoked in the amygdala to stimulation of the lateral geniculate body when it serves as CS for shock-avoidance CR.

Generalization and discrimination.—As noted above, stimulation at the same locus with different frequencies may or may not be equally as effective in eliciting CRs as is the original frequency. This phenomenon, and the presence of frequency specific versus nonspecific circuitry which it implies, has not been adequately studied.

Stimulation at points other than the initial one to which the animal has been trained is without immediate effect in eliciting CRs unless the initial and test points lie within the same functional system (40, 42, 44, 119, 127, 146, 150, 188, 200). Because negative results are easy to obtain, such tests for stimulus generalization are meaningless unless inherent responses are evoked by the test stimulus or it is subsequently shown that the animal can be trained to respond to stimulation at the point tested. Most remarkable is the nearly total equivalence obtained between points in area 17 of macaques (40, 42, 44, 188, 189). Following training to make CRs either to avoid shock or to obtain food for stimulation at one locus in area 17, the monkeys make immediate and unhesitant CRs (without reinforcement) when stimulated anyplace else in area 17 of either hemisphere. In such cases CRs are also made about 50 per cent of the time to stimulation of area 18, and never to stimulation of area 19 (Doty, unpublished). The failure to find such generalization between electrodes in area 17 and those at the boundary between areas 17 and 18 or 29 in rats (80) may reflect a situation similar to that with area 19 in macaques. The extraordinary degree of generalization for the striate cortex of macaques suggests the presence of some special mechanism to achieve this unity, for it is not found within areas 4 or 2 unless the electrodes lie within the same region of body representation, e.g., generalization fails between electrodes in area 4 eliciting cheek versus hand movements, or between area 4 and 2 where both electrodes elicit hand movements. Similarly, generalization is absent between dorsomedial versus ventrolateral portions of prelunate area 19 (Doty, unpublished).

Generalization also has been found between ipsilateral regions of prepiriform cortex and lateral olfactory tract, but not to comparable contralateral areas even though stimulation of the latter evokes orienting responses indistinguishable from those elicited from the initial point (61). Generalization is also almost entirely absent between either ipsilateral or contralateral loci in the hippocampus of cats (109). There is, of course, some possibility that the stimulation in these limbic areas might elicit local seizure activity, but as noted above for self-stimulation in the hippocampus of rats (210), slight differences in electrode placement are significant. When the hippocampal and septal placements both are capable of yielding self-stimulation, there is considerable generalization between them in producing a conditioned emotional response (200). Following training of cats to press or withold pressing of a lever for milk upon stimulation of the caudate nucleus or ventrolateral nucleus of the thalamus, they make the same CR for stimulation at other loci in the same structure either ipsilaterally or contralaterally (17). Generalization also occurs to stimulation of optic radiation or visual cortex in cats and macaques when the lateral geniculate body is the initial point (40, 119). The same is true for stimulation in the "auditory radiation" for test at auditory cortex (146), or for two points in the medial lemniscus (150), or for testing in either direction between basal forebrain and mesencephalic reticular formation (148).

Expectations are sometimes expressed or implied that qualities of a peripherally presented stimulus will be evoked or imitated by a central electrical stimulus. In view of the elaboration of natural sensory input into spatiotemporal patterns of excitation and inhibition of extreme complexity, such expectations are at best unrealistic except possibly for a crude distinction of e.g., auditory versus visual quality, or for the judgment "few" versus "many" at stimulus frequencies of 1 to 10/sec. Generalization has been reported between clicks at 100/sec and stimulation of the inferior colliculus at the same frequency for a shock-avoidance CR in cats (146). It seems likely here, however, that the central test stimulus was inherently aversive and released the response just as does stimulation of nucleus centrum medianum or the posterior hypothalamus in such circumstances (77, 113). This interpretation is reinforced by the fact that in the same experiments stimulation of the cochlear nucleus was ineffective (146). Nevertheless, generalization in the reverse sense between central stimulation (inferior colliculus or "auditory radiation") and test stimulation of clicks, was obtained and would be difficult to explain on the foregoing basis unless the clicks were startlingly loud.

Comparable experiments on the visual system, testing with stimulation of optic tract, lateral geniculate body, or visual cortex after initial training to photic stimulation in cats and macaques, have been consistently negative (40, 47, 96, 119, 139, 188, 189,). In fact, macaques even fail to generalize between 6/sec flashes and steady light (188). The finding is thus unexpected that rats generalize to stimulation of visual cortex in a shock-avoidance situation, or to visual cortex and especially to the optic chiasm in a food-reward setting, after initial training to steady light as CS (107, 108). It seems likely that random intertrial pressing, especially in response to onset of extinction procedures, may have influenced the outcome in this case, although this is not obvious in the data reported.

Results with transfer of training, in which reinforcement is given for the test stimulation, are much more difficult to interpret than is stimulus generalization in the absence of reinforcement. They are meaningless on macaques, since once they are trained some of these animals can transfer to a new CS after only one or two reinforcements. With cats, where learning is less rapid, significant data can be obtained, since it not infrequently takes as many trials for them to learn to a second point of test stimulation as it did to the first two points of initial training (47). Nevertheless, in transfer tests that show significant savings, the factor of stimulus generalization is confounded with that of training and learning (119, 150). It is probably the latter which accounts for much of the unexpectedly high level of transfer between certain heterotopic cortical areas or between tonal and photic CS (47).

Since the data for generalization suggest that there is little similarity of effect for stimulation of most parts of the brain, it should be relatively easy to establish discrimination between stimulation at each of two points. This has been true for rabbits, using stimulation of the septal area and ventral nucleus of the thalamus, visual cortex and hippocampus, etc. (97), or between the hippocampus or mesencephalic reticular formation and the homotopic area in the other hemisphere (114). The same is true for various neocortical points in cats (48) and macaques (40). More difficult and significant is spatial differentiation of points which the animal initially apparently perceives as equivalent, i.e., those for which stimulus generalization is present. Cats are able to respond differentially to stimulation of points in the caudate nucleus <1 mm apart (174). However, it is not certain whether this is a spatial or merely an intensive discrimination since tests were not made with different frequencies and intensities of stimulation. Such tests however, have, been made for the neocortex in macaques. Surprisingly, the location of stimulation can be discriminated equally well within all the cortical areas tested, perhaps because no tests have yet approached the limits of capability in this regard. In any event, well-trained animals have been able to perform correctly over 90 per cent of the time for electrodes <1 to 3 mm apart in area 17 (three cases), area 18 (two cases), area 19 (two cases), area 9 medial to sulcus principalis (three cases), and area 20 (one case) (40, 41, 44). In these experiments the frequency and intensity of stimulation were both randomly varied—frequency 2 to 100/sec, and intensity over a four to tenfold range of current. When the current was too high, discrimination failed, probably because of increasing commonality in the population of excited neurons.

Macaques can also discriminate 2/sec versus 10/sec stimulation over a wide range of randomly varied intensities at the same central locus. Again, any cortical area seems to be capable of serving for such discrimination. It is, of course, essential to prove that the discrimination is independent of stimulus intensity since it is obvious, especially in the frequency range of 10 to 100/sec, that the animal initially makes the discrimination of the basis of total neural effect (i.e., intensity) rather than on the basis of stimulus frequency. Failure to consider this intensive factor makes it unlikely that frequency discrimination per se actually occurred in experiments on chickens, rats, and cats (98, 119, 127, 216), in which differentiation was achieved between stimulation at different frequencies.

Pathways by which the centrally applied CS is effective.—With electrical excitation of area 17 serving as CS, a macaque is able to respond about 30 msec sooner than it can to a photic CS (139). The 30 msec is the latency for the appearance of the earliest potential at area 17 evoked by the photic stimulus. About 70 msec after the signal enters area 17, pyramidal cells in area 4 begin discharging to produce the CR (52). One of the major problems of neuroscience is to define what happens in that intervening 70 msec. The first essential step in the solution is to find where the critical events occur, and to this end the electrically applied CS provides a most useful tool.

Just as with the organization of electrically elicited motor stereotypes, it is apparent that the engram lies at least one synapse downstream to the applied stimulus. Thus, in human cases where cortical stimulation elicits specific memories, extirpation of the stimulated area does not affect recall of this memory (156). Likewise, in cats, radical extirpation of the cortex utilized for the CS does not change the capacity of other cortical areas to elicit the CR when stimulated for the first time (47). It would, however, be worth repeating the latter experiment in macaques where stimulus generalization rather than transfer of training could be tested. Extirpation of frontal cortex produces a several-fold increase in threshold for excitation of thalamic and mesencephalic reticular systems to serve effectively as CS (148). Extirpation of other areas is without effect in this case, and the frontal ablation does not alter thresholds for elicitation of CRs by stimulation in thalamic sensory "relay" nuclei. A single electroconvulsive seizure, on the other hand, changes thresholds for elicitation of CRs from all subcortical loci for several days (147). It is not yet clear whether the results with ablation signify that the frontal cortex provides an essential link in the elaboration of the CS from the reticular systems or whether the latter merely receive important background support from frontal areas. Recently, however, it has been shown that the mesencephalic reticular formation becomes electrically silent when deprived of peripheral and ipsilateral forebrain inputs (225).

Surgical limitation of pathways from the marginal gyrus in cats shows that elaboration of a CS applied here normally proceeds via subcortical projection rather than through intracortical channels (181). Similar results apparently have been obtained for the chicken, although no anatomical details are available (127). Anatomical evidence is also lacking to support the contradictory claim that the intracortical pathways are the more important (111). It is of interest that stimulation of undercut cortex, for which all exit paths must be tangential, ultimately can be effective as a CS, and it now appears that the electrical stimulation alone produces permanent changes in the excitability of this partially isolated cortex (182).

Interhemispheric stimulus generalization or transfer affords certain unique opportunities for tracing mnemonically significant pathways. As happens with frustrating frequency (118), here too, by multiple available pathways, the engram eludes efforts to isolate it. Thus, generalization occurs between caudate nuclei in the two hemispheres despite midline section of corpus callosum and much of the thalamus (174). The anterior commissure, however, was intact in these experiments (Buchwald, personal communication). Transfer of training also occurs readily using the ectosylvian "auditory" cortex for the CS in cats with section of most of the callosum (47). Here the anterior commissure is unlikely to be significant in the transfer, and experiments with macaques so far have shown poor or no interhemispheric generalization between superior temporal gyri when the commissure is intact and callosum fully severed (Doty, unpublished). Either the anterior commissure (42, 44) or splenium (Doty, unpublished) is sufficient for generalization between one area 17 and the other in macaques, not only for elicitation of a CR, but for discrimination as well on the basis of locus or frequency. If both anterior commissure and callosum (including, of course, the psalterium) are severed, there is no interhemispheric transfer of any kind in macaques despite preservation of bilateral inherent reactions such as control of either hand by stimulation of one hemisphere (e.g., in the "butterfly response" discussed earlier), but also in making CRs. Thus, in this case the interesting changes in excitability of extracallosal pathways described for cats (180) must be either absent or irrelevant.

In any event, the question can be asked as to whether the splenial path serves to lay down an engram in the contralateral hemisphere or whether it merely provides access from the tested hemisphere to an engram which remains in the trained hemisphere. The first macaque tested has provided an apparently definitive answer (Negrão & Doty, unpublished). The anterior commissure and rostral callosum were severed and a snare placed around the splenium. After the bone flap had knit, the animal was trained to stimulation of right area 17 and routinely made CRs by licking a lever on his left for food reward. One test stimulation in left area 17 elicited an unhesitant CR, showing the snare had not blocked splenial transmission. The snare was then pulled, severing the splenium without disturbing the electrodes. Conditional responses were then no longer evoked by stimulation of left area 17, while they continued without change for stimulation of right area 17. Thus the splenial connection appears to serve as an access path to the engram, which remains in the initially trained hemisphere.

Augmentation of or interference with learned performance.—Space precludes adequate discussion of this topic, but the following references will provide access to most of the relevant literature or to recent developments (23, 79, 86, 98, 106, 116, 123, 131, 197, 206). Unless resulting from motivational effects, it is difficult to see how gross electrical intrusion into the highly organized patterns of brain activity could improve performance, yet sometimes this does appear to be the case (23, 123, 131, 197). Interference is much easier to understand, but if the process is localizable as well as reversible, it provides a useful analytical tool (79, 86, 106). Electrical interference can be used also to block or garble the flow or processing of afferent information and thus identify critical times or components in sensory systems (56, 98, 206).

Conclusions.—Electrical stimulation has been used extensively to study the functional fabric of the nervous system. From these efforts, as reviewed above, several major facts and concepts are emerging with varying degrees of clarity and certainty.

(*a*) Movement is an inherent response to stimulation at essentially all loci, cortical or subcortical, in the brains of freely behaving animals.

(*b*) With unilateral stimulation, the contralateral homotopic system probably exerts a suppressive effect upon the abnormally elicited response.

(*c*) A perverse aspect of the neural systems that organize fearful or aggressive behavior is that momentary excitation of these systems can be highly rewarding.

(*d*) There is considerable latitude for variation as a consequence of past experience so that stimulation of the same anatomical location in different individuals may give different effects. Perhaps the most extreme examples are the elicitation of different memories or speech phrases in human subjects or the conditioned responses elicited in animals after training to stimulation at almost any selected locus.

(*e*) A system that is uniquely refractory to use as the substrate for a conditional stimulus includes the group IA spindle afferents, cerebellum, dentate nucleus, and ventrolateral nucleus of the thalamus. The cerebellum at least can serve as substrate for an unconditional stimulus.

(*f*) Equally intriguing, but probably not related, is the problem of the extensive areas of human cortex apparently silent to electrical stimulation.

(*g*) Using central stimulation, conditioned reflexes can be formed without motivation. This shows the essential feature of conditioning to be the temporal relation between the stimuli. Neurophysiologically this relation is paradoxical. An hypothesis is proposed to explain this paradox, suggesting that conditioning occurs via augmentation of successful synapses by chemical feedback from the discharged neuron.

(*h*) By training an animal with pathways that are intact and that are known to be essential for interhemispheric stimulus generalization (between areas 17 in macaques) and then severing these paths, it can be shown that the engram is not available in the tested hemisphere but remains in the trained hemisphere.

LITERATURE CITED

1. Affanni, J., Marchiafava, P. L., Zernicki, B. *Arch. Ital. Biol.*, **100**, 305–10 (1962)
2. Akert, K., Andersson, B. Experimenteller Beitrag zur Physiologie des Nucleus caudatus. *Acta Physiol. Scand.*, **22**, 281–98 (1951)
3. Allikmets, L. Kh. Behavioral reactions to electrical stimulation of amygdala in cats. *Neurosci. Translations*, **1**, 119–27 (1967–68)
4. Andersson, B., Wyrwicka, W. The elicitation of a drinking motor conditioned reaction by electrical stimulation of the hypothalamic "drinking area" in the goat. *Acta Physiol. Scand.*, **41**, 194–98 (1957)
5. Andrew, R. J. Intracranial self-stimulation in the chick. *Nature*, **213**, 847–48 (1967)
6. Ángyán, L., Grastyán, E., Sakhiulina, G. T. Avoidance conditioning to stimulation of the recruiting system used as a conditioned stimulus. *Fed. Proc. Transl. Suppl.*, **23**, T264–67 (1964)
7. Arias, L. P., Ross, N., Piñeyrúa, M. Stimulation of the nonspecific thalamic nuclei in relation to conditioning. *Exptl. Neurol.*, **16**, 93–103 (1966)
8. Baer, A. Über gleichzeitige elektrische Reizung zweier Grosshirnstellen am ungehemmten Hunde. *Pflüger's Arch. Ges. Physiol.*, **106**, 523–67 (1905)
9. Baldwin, M. Electrical stimulation of the mesial temporal region. In *Electrical Studies on the Unanesthetized Brain*, 159–76 (Ramey, E. R., O'Doherty, D. S., Eds., Hoeber, New York, 423 pp., 1960)
10. Bower, G. H., Miller, N. E. Rewarding and punishing effects from stimulating the same place in the rat's brain. *J. Comp. Psysiol. Psychol.*, **51**, 669–74 (1958)
11. Boyd, E. S., Gardner, L. C. Positive and negative reinforcement from intracranial stimulation of a teleost. *Science*, **136**, (May 1962)
12. Brogden, W. J., Gantt, W. H. Intraneural conditioning—cerebellar conditioned reflexes. *Arch. Neurol. Psychiat.*, **48**, 437–55 (1942)
13. Brown, J. L. Vocalization evoked from the optic lobe of a songbird. *Science*, **149**, 1002–3 (1965)
14. Brown, J. L. The control of avian vocalization by the central nervous system. In *Studies on Bird Song* (Hinde, R. A., Ed., Cambridge Univ. Press, Cambridge, 1969)
15. Brown, J. L., Hunsperger, R. W. Neuroethology and the motivation of agonistic behaviour. *Animal Behav.*, **11**, 439–48 (1963)
16. Bruner, A. Self-stimulation in the rabbit: An anatomical map of stimulation effects. *J. Comp. Neurol.*, **131**, 615–30 (1967)
17. Buchwald, N. A., Romero-Sierra, C., Hull, C. D., Wakefield, C. Learned and unlearned responses to stimulation of the same subcortical site. *Exptl. Neurol.*, **17**, 451–65 (1967)
18. Buchwald, N. A., Wyers, E. J., Lauprecht, C. W., Heuser, G. The "caudate-spindle" IV. A behavioral index of caudate-induced inhibition. *Electroencephalog. Clin. Neurophysiol.*, **13**, 531–37 (1961)
19. Bull, J. Failure of apparently rewarding electrical brain stimulation to serve as a reinforcer for T-maze learning. *Psychol. Rec.*, **18**, 81–88 (1968)
20. Bureš, J., Burešová, O. Plastic changes of unit activity based on reinforcing properties of extracellular stimulation of single neurons. *J. Neurophysiol.*, **30**, 98–113 (1967)
21. Caggiula, A. R., Hoebel, B. G. "Copulation-reward site" in the posterior hypothalamus. *Science*, **153**, 1284–85 (1966)
22. Campbell, J. F., Jr. *A Comparison of Thresholds for the Detection of Subcortical Electrical Current and for Self-Stimulation* (Doctoral thesis, Univ. Virginia, 60 pp., 1964)
23. Cardo, B. Effets de la stimulation du noyau parafasciculaire thalamique sur l'acquisition d'un conditionnement d'évitement chez le rat. *Physiol. Behav.*, **2**, 245–48 (1967)
24. Cherkes, V. A., Mironchik, K. V. Functional relationships between dorsomedial nucleus of the thalamus and the corpus striatum as exemplified by inhibitory reactions. *Fed. Proc. Transl. Suppl.*, **25**, T10–14 (1966)
25. Cherkes, V. A., Mironchik, K. V. Functional discrimination between caudate nucleus and other forebrain structures in cats. *Neurosci. Translations*, **1**, 341–49 (1967–68)
26. Cohen, B. D., Brown, G. W., Brown, M. L. Avoidance learning moti-

vated by hypothalamic stimulation. *J. Exptl. Psychol.*, **53**, 228–33 (1957)

27. Coons, E. E., Cruce, J. A. F. Lateral hypothalamus: Food current intensity in maintaining self-stimulation of hunger. *Science*, **159**, 1117–19 (1968)

28. Cooper, R. M., Taylor, L. H. Thalamic reticular system and central grey: Self-stimulation. *Science*, **156**, 102–3 (1967)

29. Delgado, J. M. R. Prolonged stimulation of brain in awake monkeys. *J. Neurophysiol.*, **22**, 458–75 (1959)

30. Delgado, J. M. R. Free behavior and brain stimulation. *Intern. Rev. Neurobiol.*, **6**, 349–449 (1964)

31. Delgado, J. M. R., Roberts, W. W., Miller, N. E. Learning motivated by electrical stimulation of the brain. *Am. J. Physiol.*, **179**, 587–93 (1954)

32. Delgado. J. M. R., Rosvold, H. E., Looney, E. Evoking conditioned fear by electrical stimulation of subcortical structures in the monkey brain. *J. Comp. Physiol. Psychol.*, **49**, 373–80 (1956)

33. Dohlman, G. Experimentelle Untersuchungen über die Galvanische Vestibularisreaktion. *Acta Oto-Laryngol. Suppl.*, **8**, 48 pp. (1929)

34. Donhoffer, H. The role of the cerebellum in the instrumental conditional reflex. *Acta Physiol. Acad. Sci. Hung.*, **29**, 247–51 (1966)

35. Doty, R. W. Influence of stimulus pattern on reflex deglutition. *Am. J. Physiol.*, **166**, 142–58 (1951)

36. Doty, R. W. Neural hierarchies and behavior. In *The Central Nervous System and Behavior. Trans. Third Conference*, 414–21 (Brazier, M. A. B., Ed., Josiah Macy Jr. Foundation, New York, 475 pp., 1960)

37. Doty, R. W. General discussion. In *Brain Mechanisms and Learning*, 659 (Fessard, A., Gerard, R. W., Konorski, J., Eds., Blackwell Sci. Publ., London, 702 pp., 1961)

38. Doty, R. W. The role of subcortical structures in conditioned reflexes. *Ann. N. Y. Acad. Sci.*, **92**, 939–45 (1961)

39. Doty, R. W. Conditioned reflexes formed and evoked by brain stimulation. In *Electrical Stimulation of the Brain*, 397–412 (Sheer, D. E., Ed., Univ. Texas Press, Houston, 641 pp., 1961)

40. Doty, R. W. Conditioned reflexes

elicited by electrical stimulation of the brain in macaques. *J. Neurophysiol.*, **28**, 623–40 (1965)

41. Doty, R. W. Ability of macaques to discriminate locus of electrical stimuli applied to neocortex. *Abst. Communications 23rd Intern. Physiol. Congress*, p. 458 (1965)

42. Doty, R. W. Interhemispheric transfer of conditioned reflexes established to electrical stimulation of neocortex. *Physiologist*, **9**, 170 (1966)

43. Doty, R. W. The nerve impulse and synaptic transmission. In *Comprehensive Textbook of Psychiatry*, 110–11 (Freedman, A. M., Kaplan, H. I., Eds., Williams & Wilkins, Baltimore, 1666 pp., 1967)

44. Doty, R. W. On butterflies in the brain. In *Current Problems in Electrophysiology of the Central Nervous System*, 96–103 (Rusinov, V. S. Ed., Science Press Moscow, 368 pp., 1967) (Russian)

45. Doty, R. W. Neural organization of deglutition. In *Handbook of Physiology. Sect. 6, Alimentary Canal*, **4**, 1861–1902 (Code, C. F., Heidel, W., Eds., Am. Physiol. Soc., Washington, D.C., 1968)

46. Doty, R. W., Giurgea, C. Conditioned reflexes established by coupling electrical excitation of two cortical areas. In *Brain Mechanisms and Learning*, 133–51 (Fessard, A., Gerard, R. W., Konorski, J., Eds., Blackwell Scient. Publ. Ltd., London, 702 pp., 1961)

47. Doty, R. W., Rutledge, L. T., Jr. "Generalization" between cortically and peripherally applied stimuli eliciting conditioned reflexes. *J. Neurophysiol.*, **22**, 428–35 (1959)

48. Doty, R. W., Rutledge, L. T., Jr., Larsen, R. M. Conditioned reflexes established to electrical stimulation of cat cerebral cortex. *J. Neurophysiol.*, **19**, 401–15 (1956)

49. Egger, M. D., Flynn, J. P. Effects of electrical stimulation of the amygdala on hypothalamically elicited attack behavior in cats. *J. Neurophysiol.*, **26**, 705–20 (1963)

50. Ellen, P., Powell, E. W. Conditioning of septum and hippocampus. *Exptl. Neurol.*, **16**, 162–71 (1966)

51. Endröczi, E., Lissák, K. Behavioral reactions evoked by electrical stimulation in the medial forebrain bundle region. *Physiol. Behav.*, **1**, 223–27 (1966)

52. Evarts, E. V. Pyramidal tract activity associated with a conditioned hand movement in the monkey. *J. Neurophysiol.*, **29**, 1011–27 (1966)
53. Ewert, J. P. Aktivierung der Verhaltensfolge beim Beutefang der Erdkröte (*Bufo bufo L.*) durch elektrische Mittelhirnreizung. *Z. Vergleich. Physiol.*, **54**, 455–81 (1967)
54. Ewert, J. P. Untersuchungen über die Anteile zentralnervöser Aktione an der taxisspezifischen Ermüdung beim Beutefang der Erdkröte (*Bufo bufo L.*) *Z. Vergleich. Physiol.*, **57**, 263–98 (1967)
55. Fantl, L., Schuckman, H. Lateral hypothalamus and hunger: Responses to a secondary reinforcer with and without electrical stimulation. *Physiol. Behav.*, **2**, 355–57 (1967)
56. Fentress, J. C., Doty, R. W. Protracted tetanization of the optic tract in squirrel monkeys. *Fed. Proc.*, **25**, 573 (1966)
57. Fiedler, K. Versuche zur Neuroethologie von Lippfischen und Sonnenbarschen. *Zoologischer Anzeiger. Suppl.*, **28**, 569–80 (1965)
58. Foerster, O. Sensible corticale Felder. In *Handbuch der Neurologie, Bd. 6*, 358–448 (Bumke, O., Foerster, O., Eds., Springer, Berlin, 1153 pp., 1936)
59. Fonberg, E. The inhibitory role of amygdala stimulation. *Acta Biol. Exptl.* (Warsaw), **23**, 171–80 (1963)
60. Fonberg, E., Delgado, J. M. R. Avoidance and alimentary reactions during amygdala stimulation. *J. Neurophysiol.*, **24**, 651–64 (1961)
61. Freeman, W. J. Comparison of thresholds for behavioral and electrical responses to cortical electrical stimulation in cats. *Exptl. Neurol.*, **6**, 315–31 (1962)
62. Fritsch, G., Hitzig, E. Ueber die elektrische Erregbarkeit des Grosshirns. *Arch. Anat. Physiol.*, **37**, 300–32 (1870)
63. Gallistel, C. R. Electrical self-stimulation and its theoretical implications. *Psychol. Bull.*, **61**, 23–34 (1964)
64. Gelfan, S., Carter, S. Muscle sense in man. *Exptl. Neurol.*, **18**, 469–73 (1967)
65. Gerbrandt, L. K., Skrebitsky, V. G., Burešová, O., Bureš, J. Plastic changes of unit activity induced by tactile stimuli followed by electrical stimulation of single hippocampal and reticular neurons. *Neuropsychologia*, **6**, 3–10 (1968)
66. Gerken, G. M. Detection by the guinea pig of acoustic stimulation and of electrical stimulation of the brain. *Percept. Psychophys.*, **1**, 137–41 (1966)
67. Giurgea, C. Elaboration of conditioned reflexes by direct excitation of the cerebral cortex. OTS 64-11118, IPST Cat No. 1211, National Library of Medicine, U.S.P.H.S. Bethesda, Md., 131 pp., 1964 (Translated from Romanian, published by Academiei R. P. R., Bucuresti, 1953)
68. Giurgea, C., Raiciulescu, N. New data on conditioned reflexes elaborated by direct stimulation of the cerebral cortex. OTS 64-11117, IPST Cat No. 1212, National Library of Medicine, U.S.P.H.S., Bethesda, Md., 7 pp, 1964 (Translated from Romanian: *Rev. Fiziol. Normala Patol.*, **4**, 218–25 (1957)
69. Giurgea, C., Raiciulescu, N. Étude électroencéphalographique du réflexe conditionnel a l'exictation électrique corticale directe. *Int. Cong. Neurol. Sci.*, *1st*, **3**, 156–76 (1957)
70. Glickman, S. E., Feldman, S. M. Habituation of the arousal response to direct stimulation of the brainstem. *Electroencephalog. Clin. Neurophysiol.*, **13**, 703–9 (1961)
71. Glickman, S. E., Schiff, B. B. A biological theory of reinforcement. *Psychol. Rev.*, **74**, 81–109 (1967)
72. Goltz, F. Ueber die physiologische Bedeutung der Bogengänge des Ohrlabyrinths. *Pflüger's Arch. Ges. Physiol.*, **3**, 172–92 (1870)
73. Goodman, D. C. Cerebellar stimulation in the unanesthetized bullfrog. *J. Comp. Neurol.*, **110**, 321–35 (1958)
74. Goodman, D. C., Simpson, J. T., Jr. Cerebellar stimulation in the unrestrained and unanesthetized alligator. *J. Comp. Neurol.*, **114**, 127–35 (1960)
75. Goodman, I. J., Brown, J. L. Stimulation of positively and negatively reinforcing sites in the avian brain. *Life Sciences*, **5**, 693–704 (1966)
76. Grastyán, E., Ángyán, L. The organization of motivation at the thalamic level of the cat. *Physiol. Behav.*, **2**, 5–13 (1967)
77. Grastyán, E., Lissák, K., Kékesi, F.

Facilitation and inhibition of conditioned alimentary and defensive reflexes by stimulation of the hypothalamus and reticular formation. *Acta Physiol. Acad. Sci., Hung.*, 9, 133–51 (1956)

78. Grimm, R. J. Feeding behavior and electrical stimulation of the brain of *Carassius auratus. Science*, 131, 162–63 (1960)

79. Gross, C. G. Aspects of the delayed alternation deficit produced by electrical stimulation in monkeys. *Psychon. Sci.*, 3, 501–2 (1965)

80. Grosser, G. S., Harrison, J. M. Behavioral interaction between stimulated cortical points. *J. Comp. Physiol. Psychol.*, 53, 229–33 (1960)

81. Harwood, D., Vowles, D. M. Defensive behaviour and the after effects of brain stimulation in the ring dove (*Streptopelia risoria*). *Neuropsychologia*, 5, 345–66 (1967)

82. Hensel, H., Boman, K. K. A. Afferent impulses in cutaneous sensory nerves in human subjects. *J. Neurophysiol.*, 23, 564–78 (1960)

83. Herberg, L. J. Seminal ejaculation following positively reinforcing electrical stimulation of the rat hypothalamus. *J. Comp. Physiol. Psychol.*, 56, 679–85 (1963)

84. Herberg, L. J., Blundell, J. E. Lateral hypothalamus: Hoarding behavior elicited by electrical stimulation. *Science*, 155, 349–50 (1967)

85. Hess, W. R. Hirnreizversuche über den Mechanismus des Schlafes. *Arch. Psychiatrie*, 86, 287–92 (1928)

86. Hirano, T. Effects of hippocampal electrical stimulation on memory consolidation. *Psychologia*, 9, 63–75 (1966)

87. Hitzig, E. Physiologisches und therapeutisches über einige elektrische Reizmethoden. *Berlin klin. Wschr.*, 7, 137–38 (1870)

88. Hitzig, E. Ueber die beim Galvanisöiren des Kopfes entstehenden Störungen der Muskelinnervation und der Vorstellungen vom Verhalten im Raume. *Arch. Anat. Physiol.*, 38, 716–70 (1871)

89. von Holst, E., von Saint Paul, U., Vom wirkungsgefüge der Triebe. *Naturwissenschaften*, 18, 409–22 (1960) Translated in *Animal Behaviour*, 11, 1–20 (1963)

90. Hori, Y., Toyohara, I., Yoshii, N. Conditioning of unitary activity by intracerebral stimulation in cats. *Physiol. Behav.*, 2, 255–59 (1967)

91. Huber, F. Central control of movements and behavior of invertebrates. In *Invertebrate Nervous Systems*, 333–51 (Wiersma, C. A. G., Ed., Univ. Chicago Press, 370 pp., 1967)

92. Hughes, J. R. Studies on the supracallosal mesial cortex of unanesthetized, conscious mammals. I: Cat. movements elicited by electrical stimulation. *Electroencephalog. Clin. Neurophysiol.*, 11, 447–58 (1959)

93. Hunsperger, R. W. Affektreaktionen auf elektrische Reizung im Hirnstamm der Katze. *Helv. Physiol. Acta*, 14, 70–92 (1956)

94. Hunter, J., Jasper, H. H. Effects of thalamic stimulation in unanesthetized animals. *Electroencephalog. Clin. Neurophysiol.*, 1, 305–24 (1949)

95. Hutchinson, R. R., Renfrew, J. W. Stalking attack and eating behaviors elicited from the same sites in the hypothalamus. *J. Comp. Physiol. Psychol.*, 61, 360–67 (1966)

96. Ikeda, T. Fluctuation of optic evoked potentials during conditioned avoidance behavior in cats: Effects of attention and distraction on primary evoked potentials. *Acta Psychiat. Neurol. Japan*, 21, 19–30 (1967)

97. Iordanis, K. A. Differentiation of conditioned reflexes elaborated to electrical stimulation of various cerebral structures in rabbits. *Zh. Vyzssh. Nerv. Deiat. Pavlov*, 14, 77–85 (1964) (Russian)

98. John, E. R. *Mechanisms of Memory* (Academic Press, New York, 468 pp., 1967)

99. Jürgens, U., Maurus, M., Ploog, D., Winter, P. Vocalization in the squirrel monkey (*Saimiri sciureus*) elicited by brain stimulation. *Exptl. Brain Res.*, 4, 114–17 (1967)

100. Kanai, T., Wang, S. C. Localization of the central vocalization mechanism in the brain stem of the cat. *Exptl. Neurol.*, 6, 426–34 (1962)

101. Kandel, E. R., Spencer, W. A. Cellular neurophysiological approaches in the study of learning. *Physiol. Rev.*, 48, 65–134 (1968)

102. Kandel, E. R., Tauc, L. Heterosynaptic facilitation in neurones of the abdominal ganglion of *Aplysia depilans. J. Physiol.*, 181, 1–27 (1965)

103. Kant, K. J., Thomas, G. J. Effects of lesions or stimulation in amygdala

on septal self-stimulation. *Fed. Proc.*, **27**, 277 (1968)

104. Kelly, A. H., Beaton, L. E., Magoun, H. W. Midbrain mechanism for facio-vocal activity. *J. Neurophysiol.*, **9**, 181–89 (1946)

105. Kennedy, D., Evoy, W. H., Hanawalt, J. T. Release of coordinated behavior in crayfish by single central neurons. *Science*, **154**, 917–19 (1966)

106. Kesner, R. P., Doty, R. W. Amnesia produced in cats by local seizure activity initiated from the amygdala. *Exptl. Neurol.*, **21**, 58–68 (1968)

107. Kitai, S. T. Substitution of intracranial electrical stimulation for photic stimulation during extinction procedure. *Nature*, **207**, 222 (1965)

108. Kitai, S. T. Generalization between photic and electrical stimulation to the visual system. *J. Comp. Physiol. Psychol.*, **61**, 319–24 (1966)

109. Knight, J. M. *Stimulus Generalization in the Hippocampus of the Cat.* (Doctoral thesis, Univ. Utah, 39 pp., 1964)

110. Knott, P. D., Clayton, K. N. Durable secondary reinforcement using brain stimulation as the primary reinforcer. *J. Comp. Physiol. Psychol.*, **61**, 151–53 (1966)

111. Kogan, A. B. On the structure of the closing mechanism of the conditioned reflex. *Zh. Vyzssh. Nerv. Deiat. Pavlov*, **11**, 651–59 (1961) (Russian)

112. Konorski, J., Lubińska, L. Sur un procédé nouveau d'élaboration et réflexes conditionnels du II type et sur les changements d'excitabilité du centre cortical moteur au cours de l'apprentissage. *Acta Biol. Exptl.*, **13**, 143–52 (1939)

113. Kopa, J., Szabó, I., Grastyán, E. A dual behavioural effect from stimulating the same thalamic point with identical stimulus parameters in different conditional reflex situations. *Acta Physiol. Acad. Sci. Hung.*, **21**, 207–14 (1962)

114. Korányi, L., Endröczi, E., Lissák, K., Homoki, I. Functional characteristics of conditioned reflex activity evoked by electrical stimulation of the hippocampus and mesencephalic reticular formation. *Acta Physiol. Acad. Sci. Hung.*, **32**, 69–79 (1967)

115. Kriayev, V. Ya. *Priroda*, No. 4, Russian (1938)

116. Kuraev, G. A. Inhibitory influence of neostriatum on conditioned-reflex activity in macaques. *Neurosci. Transl.*, **1**, 458–60 (1968)

117. Lagutina, N. I., Rozhanskii, N. A. Location of subcortical feeding centers. *Fiziol. Zh. SSSR*, **35**, 587–93 (1949) (Russian)

118. Lashley, K. S. In search of the engram. In *Physiological Mechanisms in Animal Behaviour. Symp. Soc. Exptl. Biol. IV*, 454–82 (Academic Press, New York, 482 pp., 1950)

119. Leiman, A. L. *Electrophysiological Studies of Conditioned Responses Established to Central Electrical Stimulation* (Doctoral thesis, Univ. Rochester, 200 pp., 1962)

120. Levison, P. K., Flynn, J. P. The objects attacked by cats during stimulation of the hypothalamus. *Animal Behav.*, **13**, 217–20 (1965)

121. Libet, B., Alberts, W. W., Wright, E. W., Jr., Feinstein, B. Responses of human somatosensory cortex to stimuli below threshold for conscious sensation. *Science*, **158**, 1597–1600 (1967)

122. Lilly, J. C. Correlations between neurophysiological activity in the cortex and short-term behavior in the monkey. In *Biological and Biochemical Bases of Behavior*, 83–100 (Harlow, H. F., Woolsey, C. N., Eds., Univ. Wisconsin Press, Madison, 476 pp., 1958)

123. Lippold, O. C. J., Redfearn, J. W. T. Mental changes resulting from the passage of small direct currents through the human brain. *Brit. J. Psychiat.*, **110**, 768–72 (1964)

124. Loucks, R. B. Preliminary report of a technique for stimulation or destruction of tissues beneath the integument and the establishing of conditioned reactions with faradization of the cerebral cortex. *J. Comp. Psychol.*, **16**, 439–44 (1933)

125. Loucks, R. B. The experimental delimitation of neural structures essential for learning: The attempt to condition striped muscle responses with faradization of the sigmoid gyri. *J. Psychol.*, **1**, 5–44 (1935–36)

126. Loucks, R. B. Studies of neural structures essential for learning. II. The conditioning of salivary and striped muscle responses to faradization of cortical sensory elements, and the action of sleep upon such mechanisms. *J. Comp. Psychol.*, **25**, 315–32 (1938)

127. Loucks, R. B. Methods of isolating stimulation effects with implanted barriers. In *Electrical Stimulation of the Brain*, 145–54 (Sheer, D. E., Ed., Univ. Texas Press, Austin, 641 pp., 1961)

128. Loucks, R. B., Weinberg, H., Smith, M. The erosion of electrodes by small currents. *Electroencephalog. Clin. Neurophysiol.*, 11, 823–26 (1959)

129. MacLean, P. D., Ploog, D. W. Cerebral representation of penile erection. *J. Neurophysiol.*, 25, 29–55 (1962)

130. Macphail, E. M. Self-stimulation in pigeons: The problem of "priming." *Psychon. Sci.*, 5, 7–8 (1966)

131. Mahut, H. Effects of subcortical electrical stimulation on discrimination learning in cats. *J. Comp. Physiol. Psychol.*, 58, 390–95 (1964)

132. Malmo, R. B. Classical and instrumental conditioning with septal stimulation as reinforcement. *J. Comp. Physiol. Psychol.*, 60, 1–8 (1965)

133. Masserman, J. H. Is the hypothalamus a centre of emotion? *Psychosomat. Med.*, 3, 1–25 (1941)

134. Maurus, M., Mitra, J., Ploog, D. W. Cerebral representation of the clitoris in ovariectomized squirrel monkeys. *Exptl. Neurol.*, 13, 283–88 (1965)

135. McGlone, R. E., Richmond, W. H., Bosma, J. F. A physiological model for investigation of the fundamental frequency of phonation. *Folia Phoniat.*, 18, 109–16 (1966)

136. McLennan, H., Emmons, P. R., Plummer, P. M. Some behavioral effects of stimulation of the caudate nucleus in unrestrained cats. *Can. J. Physiol. Pharmacol.*, 42, 329–39 (1964)

137. Mendelson, J. Lateral hypothalamic stimulation in satiated rats: The rewarding effects of self-induced drinking. *Science*, 157, 1077–79 (1967)

138. Michel, J. Über die Ausbildung bedingter motorischer Reaktionen durch Kombination eines Tonreizes mit drahtloser elektrischer Hirnreizung bei völlig freibeweglichen Hunden. *Acta Biol. Med. Ger.*, 14, 291–309 (1965)

139. Miller, J. M., Glickstein, M. Neural circuits involved in visuomotor reaction time in monkeys. *J. Neurophysiol.*, 30, 399–414 (1967)

140. Mogenson, G. J. Avoidance responses to rewarding brain stimulation: Replication and extension. *J.. Comp. Physiol. Psychol.*, 58, 465–67 (1964)

141. Mogenson, G. J., Morgan, C. W. Effects of induced drinking on self-stimulation of the lateral hypothalamus. *Exptl. Brain Res.*, 3, 111–16 (1967)

142. Mogenson, G. J., Morrison, M. J. Avoidance responses to "reward" stimulation of the brain. *J. Comp. Physiol. Psychol.*, 55, 691–94 (1962)

143. Mogenson, G. J., Stevenson, J. A. F. Drinking and self-stimulation with electrical stimulation of the lateral hypothalamus. *Physiol. Behav.*, 1, 251–54 (1966)

144. Murphey, R. K., Phillips, R. E. Central patterning of a vocalization in fowl. *Nature*, 216, 1125–26 (1967)

145. Nakao, H. Emotional behavior produced by hypothalamic stimulation. *Am. J. Physiol.*, 194, 411–18 (1958)

146. Nieder, P. C., Neff, W. D. Auditory information from subcortical electrical stimulation in cats. *Science*, 133, 1010–11 (1961)

147. Nielson, H. C. Evidence that electroconvulsive shock alters memory retrieval rather than memory consolidation. *Exptl. Neurol.*, 20, 3–20 (1968)

148. Nielson, H. C., Davis, K. B. Effect of frontal ablation upon conditioned responses. *J. Comp. Physiol. Psychol.*, 61, 380–87 (1966)

149. Nielson, H. C., Doty, R. W., Rutledge, L. T., Jr. Motivational and perceptual aspects of subcortical stimulation in cats. *Am. J. Physiol.*, 194, 427–32 (1958)

150. Nielson, H. C., Knight, J. M., Porter, P. B. Subcortical conditioning, generalization, and transfer. *J. Comp. Physiol. Psychol.*, 55, 168–73 (1962)

151. Nikolaeva, N. I. Changes in the excitability of various regions of the cerebral cortex in the presence of the formation of motor conditioned reflexes. *Sechenov Physiol. J. USSR*, 41, 19–24 (1955) (Russian)

152. O'Donohue, N. F., Hagamen, W. D. A map of the cat brain for regions producing self-stimulation and unilateral inattention. *Brain Res.*, 5, 289–305 (1967)

153. Olds, J. Hypothalamic substrates of

reward. *Physiol. Rev.*, **42**, 554–604
(1962)

154. Olds, M. E., Olds. J. Approach-avoidance analysis of rat diencephalon.
J. Comp. Neurol., **120**, 259–95
(1963)

155. Pecci-Saavedra, J., Doty, R. W.,
Hunt, H. B. Conditioned reflexes
elicited in squirrel monkeys by
stimuli producing recruiting responses. *Electroencephalog. Clin.
Neurophysiol.*, **19**, 492–500 (1965)

156. Penfield, W., Perot, P. The brain's
record of auditory and visual experience—A final summary and
discussion. *Brain*, **86**, 595–696
(1963)

157. Penfield, W., Roberts, L. *Speech and
Brain Mechanisms* (Princeton
Univ. Press, Princeton, 286 pp.,
1959)

158. Persson, N. Self-stimulation in the
goat. *Acta Physiol. Scand.*, **55**,
276–85 (1962)

159. Phillips, R. E. "Wildness" in the
Mallard duck: Effects of brain
lesions and stimulation on "escape
behavior" and reproduction. *J.
Comp. Neurol.*, **122**, 139–55 (1964)

160. Raiciulescu, N., Giurgea, C., Savescu,
C. Reflex conditionat la excitarea
directa a cortexului cerebral dupa
distrugerea ganglionului lui Gasser.
Rev. Fiziol. Normala Patol., **3**, 304–
8 (1956)

161. Rescorla, R. A., Solomon, R. L. Two-
process learning theory: Relationships between Pavlovian conditioning and instrumental learning.
Psychol. Rev., **74**, 151–82 (1967)

162. Ricci, G. F., Valassi, F., Zamparo, L.
Electrophysiological study of visual
cortical mechanisms activated during avoidance conditioning trials in
macaques. *Arch. Ital. Biol.*, **105**,
413–35 (1967)

163. Roberts, W. W. Rapid escape learning without avoidance learning
motivated by hypothalamic stimulation in cats. *J. Comp. Physiol.
Psychol.*, **51**, 391–99 (1958)

164. Roberts, W. W. Both rewarding and
punishing effects from stimulation
of posterior hypothalamus of cat
with same electrodes at same intensity. *J. Comp. Physiol. Psychol.*,
51, 400–7 (1958)

165. Roberts, W. W. Fear-like behavior
elicited from dorsomedial thalamus
of cat. *J. Comp. Physiol. Psychol.*,
55, 191–97 (1962)

166. Roberts, W. W., Carey, R. J. Rewarding effect of performance of
gnawing aroused by hypothalamic
stimulation in the rat. *J. Comp.
Physiol. Psychol.*, **59**, 317–24 (1965)

167. Roberts, W. W., Kiess, H. O. Motivational properties of hypothalamic
aggression in cats. *J. Comp. Physiol. Psychol.*, **58**, 187–93 (1964)

168. Roberts, W. W., Steinberg, M. L.,
Means, L. W. Hypothalamic mechanisms for sexual, aggressive, and
other motivational behaviors in
the opossum, *Didelphis Virginiana.
J. Comp. Physiol. Psychol.*, **64**, 1–15
(1967)

169. Robinson, B. W. Vocalization evoked
from forebrain in *Macaca mulatta.
Physiol. Behav.*, **2**, 345–54 (1967)

170. Robinson, B. W., Mishkin, M. Ejaculation evoked by stimulation of the
preoptic area in monkey. *Physiol.
Behav.*, **1**, 269–72 (1966)

171. Robinson, B. W., Mishkin, M. Alimentary responses to forebrain
stimulation in monkeys. *Exptl.
Brain Res.*, **4**, 330–66 (1968)

172. Romaniuk, A. The formation of defensive conditioned reflexes by direct stimulation of the hypothalmaic
"flight-points" in cats. *Acta Biol.
Exptl. (Warsaw)*, **24**, 145–51 (1964)

173. Romaniuk, A. Representation of aggression and flight reactions in the
hypothalamus of the cat. *Ibid.*, **25**,
177–86 (1965)

174. Romero-Sierra, C., Buchwald, N. A.,
Wakefield, C., Hull, C. D. Two
point discrimination of subcortical
electrical stimulation. *Nature*, **214**,
837–38 (1967)

175. Ross, N., Piñeyrúa, M., Prieto, S.,
Arias, L. P., Stirner, A., Galeano, C.
Conditioning of midbrain behavioral responses. *Exptl. Neurol.*, **11**,
263–76 (1965)

176. Rougeul, A. Inhibition de l'activité
motrice par stimulation centrale
chez l'animal libre. *Acualités Neurophysiol.*, **6**, 183–200 (1965)

177. Rougeul, A., Perret, C., Buser, P. Effects comportementaux et électrographiques de stimulations électriques du thalamus chez le chat
libre. *Electroencephalog. Clin. Neurophysiol.*, **23**, 410–28 (1967)

178. Routtenberg, A., Lindy, J. Effects of
the availability of rewarding septal
and hypothalamic stimulation on
bar pressing for food under conditions of deprivation. *J. Comp.
Physiol. Psychol.*, **60**, 158–61 (1965)

179. Rüdiger, W., Grastyan, E., Madarasz,

I. Über die Beziehungen von Effekten der elecktrischen Reizung der kortikalen Hörsphäre zur bedingt-reflektorischen Tätigkeit beim Hunde. *Acta Physiol. Acad. Sci. Hung.*, **9**, 163–72 (1956)

180. Rutledge, L. T. Facilitation: Electrical response enhanced by conditional excitation of cerebral cortex. *Science*, **148**, 1246–48 (1965)

181. Rutledge, L. T., Doty, R. W. Surgical interference with pathways mediating responses conditioned to cortical stimulation. *Exptl. Neurol.*, **6**, 478–91 (1962)

182. Rutledge, L. T., Ranck, J. B., Jr., Duncan, J. A. Prevention of supersensitivity in partially isolated cerebral cortex. *Electroencephalog. Clin. Neurophysiol.*, **23**, 256–62 (1967)

183. Sadowski, B. Electric stimulation of the caudate nucleus as a stimulus for conditional defense reflex in rabbits. *Bull. Acad. Polon. Sci.*, **8**, 369–72 (1960)

184. Sakhiulina, G. T., Merzhanova, G. K. The recruiting response mechanism used as a conditional stimulus for the elaboration of the defensive conditioned reflex. *Electroencephalog. Clin. Neurophysiol.*, **17**, 497–505 (1964)

185. Sakhiulina, G. T., Merzhanova, G. Kh., Serdyuchenko, V. M. Conditioned reflexes formed to stimulation of the ventrolateral nucleus of the thalamus. *Zh. Vyssh. Nerv. Deiat.*, **16**, 729–30 (1966) (Russian)

186. Schaltenbrand, G. The effects of stereotactic electrical stimulation in the depth of the brain. *Brain*, **88**, 835–40 (1965)

187. Schmidt, R. S. Central mechanisms of frog calling. *Behaviour*, **26**, 251–85 (1966)

188. Schuckman, H. Area and stimulus specificity in the transfer of responses conditioned to intracranial stimulation: a replication. *Psychol. Rept.*, **18**, 639–44 (1966)

189. Schuckman, H., Battersby, W. S. Frequency specific mechanisms in learning. II. Discriminatory conditioning induced by intracranial stimulation. *J. Neurophysiol.*, **29**, 31–43 (1966)

190. Segundo, J. P., Roig, J. A., Sommer-Smith, J. A. Conditioning of reticular formation stimulation effects. *Electroencephalog. Clin. Neurophysiol.*, **11**, 471–84 (1959)

191. Sherrington, C. S. Observations on the scratch-reflex in the spinal dog. *J. Physiol. (London)*, **34**, 1–50 (1906)

192. Simonoff, L. N. Die Hemmungsmechanismen der Säugethiere experimentell bewiesen. *Arch. Anat. Physiol., Leipzig*, **33**, 545–64 (1866)

193. Spies, G. Food versus intracranial self-stimulation reinforcement in food-deprived rats. *J. Comp. Physiol. Psychol.*, **60**, 153–57 (1965)

194. Stachnik, T. J., Ulrich, R. E., Mabry, J. H. Reinforcement of aggression through intracranial stimulation. *Psychon. Sci.*, **5**, 101–2 (1966)

195. Stein, L. Facilitation of avoidance behavior by positive brain stimulation. *J. Comp. Physiol. Psychol.*, **60** 9–19 (1965)

196. Sterman, M. B., Clemente, C. D. Forebrain inhibitory mechanisms: sleep patterns induced by basal forebrain stimulation in the behaving cat. *Exptl. Neurol.*, **6**, 103–17 (1962)

197. Sterman, M. B., Fairchild, M. D. Modification of locomotor performance by reticular formation and basal forebrain stimulation in the cat: evidence for reciprocal systems. *Brain Res.*, **2**, 205–17 (1966)

198. Sterman, M. B., Knauss, T., Lehmann, D., Clemente, C. D. Circadian sleep and waking patterns in the laboratory cat. *Electroencephalog. Clin. Neurophysiol.*, **19**, 509–17 (1965)

199. Stoney, S. D., Jr., Thompson, W. D., Asanuma, H. Direct excitation of pyramidal tract (PT) cells by intracortical microstimulation. *Fed. Proc.*, **27**, 387 (1968)

200. Stutz, R. M. Stimulus generalization within the limbic system. *J. Comp. Physiol. Psychol.*, **65**, 79–82 (1968)

201. Swett, J. E., Bourassa, C. M. Comparison of sensory discrimination thresholds with muscle and cutaneous nerve volleys in the cat. *J. Neurophysiol.*, **30**, 530–45 (1967)

202. Talbert, G. A. Ueber Rindenreizung am freilaufenden Hunde nach J. R. Ewald. *Arch. Anat. Physiol., Leipzig (Physiol. Abstr.)*, **24**, 195–208 (1900)

203. Tarnecki, R. The formation of instrumental conditioned reflexes by direct stimulation of sensori-motor cortex in cats. *Acta Biol. Exptl. (Warsaw)* **22**, 35–45 (1962)

204. Tchilingaryan, L. I. Changes in ex-

citability of the motor area of the cerebral cortex during extinction of a conditioned reflex elaborated to direct electric stimulation of that area. In *Central and Peripheral Mechanisms of Motor Functions*, 167–75 (Gutmann, E., Hnik, P., Eds., Czechoslovak Acad. Sci., Prague, 1963)

205. Thompson, R. F., Spencer, W. A. Habituation: A model phenomenon for the study of neuronal substrates of behavior. *Psychol. Rev.*, **173**, 16–43 (1966)

206. Thorn, F. *The Physiological Mechanisms Underlying Visual Detection in the Cat* (Doctoral thesis, Univ. Rochester, 215 pp. plus 59 pp. appendix, 1967)

207. Tuge, H., Kanayama, Y., Chang, H. Y. Food motor conditioned reflex and electrical stimulation of the brain stem reticular formations. *Japan. J. Physiol.*, **12**, 1–16 (1962)

208. Ursin, H., Kaada, B. R. Functional localization within the amygdaloid complex in the cat. *Electroencephalog. Clin. Neurophysiol.*, **12**, 1–20 (1960)

209. Ursin, H., Wester, K., Ursin, R. Habituation to electrical stimulation of the brain in unanesthetized cats. *Electroencephalog. Clin. Neurophysiol.*, **23**, 41–49 (1967)

210. Ursin, R., Ursin, H., Olds, J. Self-stimulation of hippocampus in rats. *J. Comp. Physiol. Psychol.*, **61**, 353–59 (1966)

211. Valenstein, E. S. The anatomical locus of reinforcement. *Progr. Physiol. Psychol.*, **1**, 149–90 (1966)

212. Valenstein, E. S., Cox, V. C., Kakolewski, J. W. Modification of motivated behavior elicited by electrical stimulation of the hypothalamus. *Science*, **159**, 1119–21 (1968)

213. Van Buren, J. M. Evidence regarding a more precise localization of the posterior frontal-caudate arrest response in man. *J. Neurosurg. Suppl.*, 2nd Symposium on Parkinson's Disease, 416–17 (Nashold, B. S., Huber, W. V., Eds., 1966)

214. Wagner, A. R., Thomas, E., Norton, T. Conditioning with electrical stimulation of motor cortex: Evidence of a possible source of motivation. *J. Comp. Physiol. Psychol.*, **64**, 191–99 (1967)

215. Ward, H. P. Stimulus factors in septal self-stimulation. *Am. J. Physiol.*, **196**, 779–82 (1959)

216. Weinberg, H. Temporal discrimination of cortical stimulation. *Physiol. Behav.*, **3**, 297–300 (1968)

217. Wilkinson, H. A., Peele, T. L. Modification of intracranial self-stimulation by hunger satiety. *Am. J. Physiol.*, **203**, 537–40 (1962)

218. Wilkinson, H. A., Peele, T. L. Intracranial self-stimulation in cats. *J. Comp. Neurol.*, **121**, 425–40 (1963)

219. Willows, A. O. D. Behavioral acts elicited by stimulation of single, identifiable brain cells. *Science*, **157**, 570–74 (1967)

220. Wilson, V. J. Post-tetanic potentiation of polysynaptic reflexes of the spinal cord. *J. Gen. Physiol.*, **39**, 197–206 (1955)

221. Wyrwicka, W. Conditioned behavioral analysis of feeding mechanisms. In *Handbook of Physiology, Section 6: Alimentary Canal, Vol. I*, 63–78 (Code, C. F., Heidel, W., Eds., Am. Physiol. Soc., 459 pp., 1967)

222. Wyrwicka, W., Doty, R. W. Feeding induced in cats by electrical stimulation of the brain stem. *Exptl. Brain Res.*, **1**, 152–60 (1966)

223. Yoshii, N., Yamaguchi, Y. Studies on 'memory tracer' with conditioning technique I. Conditioning by electrical stimulation of the brain stem in the dog. *Med. J. Osaka Univ.*, **13**, 1–19 (1962)

224. Yoshii, N., Yamaguchi, Y. Conditioning of seizure discharges with electrical stimulation of the limbic structures in cats. *Folia Psychiat. Neurol. Jap.*, **17**, 276–86 (1963)

225. Zernicki, B., Doty, R. W., Santibanez, G. Isolated midbrain in cats. (Submitted to *Electroencephalog. Clin. Neurophysiol.*)

226. Zernicki, B., Osetowska, E. Conditioning and differentiation in the chronic midpontine pretrigeminal cat. *Acta Biol. Exptl. (Warsaw)*, **23**, 25–32 (1963)

NEUROPSYCHOLOGICAL BASES OF SCHIZOPHRENIA[1,2]

139

By Allan F. Mirsky[3]

*Division of Psychiatry, Boston University School of Medicine,
Boston, Massachusetts*

Introduction

The original intent of this review was to survey research concerned broadly with the study of the physiological bases of abnormal behavior. A MEDLARS[1] search of relevant literature in this general area for the period encompassing June 1964 through 1967 uncovered in excess of 800 papers. This attests to the efficiency of the MEDLARS retrieval system and to the proliferation of biologically oriented studies in mental disease. In their survey of experimental (primarily behavioral) studies of schizophrenia, Schooler & Feldman (82) have abstracted nearly 1000 references for the years 1950 to 1965. It became obvious that it would be necessary to limit the scope of the survey, and the present title reflects the decision that was made. Many of the studies that are not reviewed here are concerned with a variety of endocrinological, hematological, dietary, anatomical, and general physiological variables that have been related in some fashion to disordered behavior. Some of these may well prove to be significant in the future. Nevertheless, the question of disordered CNS function in mental disease, and particularly in schizophrenia, has received special attention in recent years, and the studies to be presented seem to provide a surprisingly consistent and coherent body of research. Consequently, it was decided to concentrate in depth on research concerned directly with CNS variables in schizophrenia, referring where necessary to earlier studies in the interest of completeness. An occasional study appearing after 1967 was included if it appeared particularly relevant in some section, but coverage from about mid-1967 on is incomplete.

An area of investigation within schizophrenia that may be concerned

[1] The survey of literature reviewed here covers primarily the period from 1964 to the end of 1967. Thanks are due to Miss Margaret MacClymont for her assistance and to Mrs. Marcia Ford of the Francis A. Countway Library of Medicine of Harvard University for her help in facilitating and conducting the MEDLARS search of the literature.

[2] The following abbreviations will be used: ARAS (ascending reticular activating system); CNS (central nervous system); EEG (electroencephalogram); REM (rapid eye movements).

[3] Research Scientist Awardee 1 KO 5 MH 14915 of the National Institute of Mental Health. The preparation of this work was supported by Grant MH 12568 from the National Institute of Mental Health.

directly with the CNS involves the possible disordered nature of various neural transmitter substances such as the catecholamines (serotonin, epinephrine, norepinephrine, dopamine and other biogenic amines) and other metabolic and serological factors. Although this material properly falls within the purview of this survey, it has been extensively reviewed recently by a number of authors (45, 67, 74, 96, 105) and it therefore seemed unnecessary to duplicate their scholarship here. A reasonably conservative summary would appear to be that although there are a number of promising leads, there is still insufficient evidence to demonstrate unequivocally any single biochemical factor in schizophrenia.

With respect to altered brain function in schizophrenia, it was perhaps inevitable that research would focus on the possible relevance of disturbance in the ARAS. Disturbed, clouded or impaired attention is frequently cited as a characteristic of schizophrenic behavior (14), and the classic studies of Bremer (7), Moruzzi & Magoun (66), Lindsley, Bowden & Magoun (57), Jasper (40), and others have provided convincing evidence of the role of thalamic, midbrain and brain-stem portions of the ARAS in the behavioral functions of arousal, attention and consciousness. Aside from this realistic justification for focusing on the ARAS, however, it is a fact that almost every major advance in biological thought has been examined by some researchers for possible relevance to schizophrenia and the other psychoses. The research on endocrine glands (and particularly the pituitary-adrenal axis) during the early decades of the twentieth century raised the possibility of over or undersecretion of important hormones and led to such drastic therapeutic measures as gonadectomy (3) or adrenalectomy (77). Later, research on the role of the frontal lobes and affective behavior led to the lobotomizing of many thousands of schizophrenic patients (32). As research on the CNS (specifically, the limbic system) correlates of emotion progressed (78), there were other targets provided for the psychosurgeon: the orbital cortex of the frontal lobes (83), the cingulate gyrus, the anterior thalamus, the amygdala (15) and the hippocampus (84). Studies of central transmitter substances (noted above) have led to research on the possible pathogenic role of their hyper- and hypofunction in schizophrenia. During the past 10 years there has been a concentration of effort more or less directly related to the ARAS in schizophrenia. The risk of producing permanent somnolence or paralysis probably has deterred the development of the direct neurosurgical approach to the ARAS in this disease.

Much of the research described above has led, and probably will continue to lead to more useful information about specific biological and CNS systems than about schizophrenia; this is an acceptable outcome but one that is hopefully not inevitable. With this *caveat*, the position to be developed later in the review can be viewed with the appropriately skeptical frame of mind.

Before proceeding to the literature review, it is well to discuss a number of factors which concern clinical research in general and the schizophrenia research to be cited below, in particular. A recurrent question has to do with diagnostic categories. The designation of a patient group as schizophrenic, while still common, is becoming less acceptable. Clearly, there are so many forms of deviant behavior falling within this classification that two investigators with apparently differing results may be talking about completely different populations. While it is true that the reliability of psychiatric diagnostic labels may be poor, this is not an acceptable reason for failing to describe the patient population as carefully and fully as possible. The description should not be limited to age, sex, and length of hospitalization, but must include the behavioral and pharmacological state of the patient at the time of testing. The researchers from the Soviet Union are usually extremely careful to specify the subgroup of the schizophrenias which is being studied; the labels may not correspond with those used in the West (i.e., "grafted schizophrenia," "weak-flowing paranoid") but the descriptions of symptomatology appear reasonably clear and coherent.

The specification of pharmacological factors is important since they may alter or interact with the experimental measure, manipulation, or treatment being employed (particularly in EEG studies); further, past drug (or other somatic) therapies may alter the outcome of intercurrent research due to such factors as tolerance, sensitization, etc. It is possible to create enzymatic changes in the liver (59) on the basis of treatment with one compound which may modify the subsequent neuropsychopharmacological response to a variety of other compounds on a long term basis. Cochin & Kornetsky (16) have demonstrated recently that it is possible to detect effects of a single dose of morphine in the rat more than 6 months later. It is becoming more and more difficult to obtain for neuropsychopharmacological studies schizophrenic subjects who have not had extensive courses of treatment with antipsychotic (usually phenothiazine) medication. Factors such as these argue for the usefulness and relevancy of animal experimentation to model symptoms and central states in the psychoses; only in controlled animal studies can the necessary precision and rigor be obtained in research.

These considerations are of particular relevance in view of the fact that the major portion of the research on schizophrenia to be reviewed below (in excess of 50 studies) involves the EEG, which is a sensitive index of drug action. Many of these involve qualitative or clinical evaluations of the EEG in schizophrenics as compared with other diagnostic groups, others involve various quantitative methods of reducing EEG data, and some use pharmacological methods to activate the CNS. Sleep and sensory-evoked potential studies are also performed with some frequency; these, together with the other EEG research, comprise the first of the four main sections of this chapter.

Although the question of organic brain disease often enters the discussion of EEG results, there is a body of studies in which schizophrenia and well-recognized organicity are compared directly. These and other papers which deal directly with neuropathology, neurosurgery or CNS effects of serological factors make up the second main section.

The third section discusses developmental and autistic processes, and the last concerns psychological or behavioral studies conducted more or less simultaneously with drug treatment or EEG or other physiological measurements.

EEG Studies

Schizophrenic and control populations compared.—Early work by Davis & Davis (17), Liberson (55), and others reported that schizophrenics were more likely to show a "choppy" record and that their resting rhythms tended more towards the faster end of the frequency spectrum. No particular pathological EEG pattern emerged in these studies as pathognomonic of the disease. Later, in studies of large numbers of schizophrenics in comparison with other psychopathological groups, Hill (37) concluded that the former were indeed more likely to show abnormal paroxysmal patterns, including symmetrical fast and slow waves, bilateral spikes, and fast (4 to 6 cps) spike and wave bursts, as well as clear-cut temporal lobe spikes. Beek et al. (2) found no differences in alpha between 114 chronic schizophrenics and 87 controls of the same age and sex. Nor were differences seen in pathological EEG signs. Cases with epilepsy and those who had drugs or electroconvulsive shock therapy in the 3 years prior to the study were excluded. The more recent work of Tucker et al. (97), however, tends to confirm the Hill result; in a survey of 95 psychiatric patients with abnormal EEGs and 45 with normal EEGs, the former were much more likely to have been diagnosed as schizophrenic. No particular abnormal EEG pattern predominated. Those with abnormal EEGs were also much more likely to show aggressive outbursts, irritability, and other types of disturbed or psychotic behavior. Bruck & McNeal (9) warn that the EEGs of schizophrenics are more likely to show artifacts of movement, tremor, and restlessness, and they caution that the fast transients that are produced by movement might distort the genuine electrographic patterns.

Some resolution of the differing results of various investigators may be provided by the work of two Soviet researchers. Korchinskaia[4] (48) compared two schizophrenic groups. In the first, the disease is seen as episodic, occurring later in life, and is less malignant; it tends to include paranoid and periodically recurring states. The second type tends to be present in earliest childhood and is more enduring and malignant. The first type is characterized by focal abnormality in the EEG, but with alpha activity clearly present and relatively normal (blocking) response to light stimulation. The (malignant) type shows little or no alpha, diffuse slow rhythms, and poor response to light stimulation. Thus the more pathological, long-term disease state is accompanied by more pathological EEG patterns. The similarity of relation between the first and second types and the reactive versus process dimension is notable. A related EEG-clinical correlation is described by

---

[4] From the French summary; no translation was available.

Feigenberg (22). Patients diagnosed as nuclear and nuclear early (the diseases are of long duration and are characterized by blunting, negativism, hebephrenic processes, and stupor) differ from those described as paranoid, weak-flowing paranoid, and circular (there is some degree of depersonalization, delirium, delusions, and acute affective symptoms). The former types show dominant alpha, weak response to light, and relatively few paroxysmal signs. The latter show less alpha, better response to light, and somewhat higher amounts of paroxysmal pathology. Patients described as "paranoial" fall in between the two types. Feigenberg notes that the first (nuclear) type is less responsive to chlorpromazine, because the ARAS is already weakened. The drug is more effective in the second type (paranoid, etc.) where the ARAS is overactive and there are active symptoms like delirium and hallucinations. There seems to be close agreement in the characterizations of the less malignant types by Korchinskaia and Feigenberg, but there appear, possibly, to be two distinct types of malignant schizophrenia. In the Korchinskaia study patients show little or no alpha, whereas in Feigenberg's survey alpha predominates. Both agree, however, that the alpha is unresponsive to light and that there is less focal paroxysmal activity in the disease forms which are of long standing.

When viewed in the perspective of the Soviet research, the study by Salamon & Post (81) would seem to have been conducted on patients with the nuclear or more pathological form of schizophrenia. A group of 20 patients showed shorter alpha blockade to a light stimulus than 20 matched controls. The comparison to the Soviet studies is not certain, however, since neither Korchinskaia nor Feigenberg provided a normal group. Thus it is not known whether or not their patients with good response to light might have also been somewhat impaired in comparison with normal controls. In any event, the impaired alpha-responsiveness to light of some groups of schizophrenic patients is clearly established and confirms the earlier research by Blum (4, 5).

Quantitative EEG analysis.—The automatic quantitative analysis of EEG possesses certain advantages over visual inspection and interpretation: small changes or differences which are difficult or impossible to detect by the naked eye can be readily quantified; large masses of data may be processed quickly; the data so obtained may be more easily subjected to statistical evaluation. Methods range from total integrated energy (more properly, voltage) through base-line crossing, frequency analysis, and analysis of slope changes (convertible into amplitude measures). Although still more sophisticated techniques are available (cross- and auto-correlation; power-density spectra, etc.), the studies to be reviewed below made use only of the simpler techniques. As used they possess the disadvantage that generally only one EEG placement is sampled (the experienced reader of EEGs can scan 12 to 16 channels) and that complex pattern changes (i.e., spike and wave, phase reversals of a spike potential, and other multichannel phenomena) are not recognized and get ground up in the pot with all the other signals. Nevertheless, certain of these techniques have been applied with apparent profit to the study of CNS function in schizophrenia.

The group of workers which includes Goldstein, Pfeiffer, Sugerman, Burdick, and associates (10, 30, 75) has explored extensively the technique of Mean Energy Content [later corrected (10) to Mean Integrated Voltage]. In several replication studies, employing the Drohocki integrator, it was found that schizophrenics do not show voltages different from that of controls but that they are simply less variable. Amphetamine and LSD can reduce the variability of the normal EEG to the point where it resembles the schizophrenic. The interpretation offered (32) is that this characteristic of the schizophrenic is due to sustained hyperarousal. In one study (10) it was found that normal groups show an increase in variability as a function of increasing voltage; in pathological groups, on the other hand (especially, in catatonics), the slope of increase of variability with voltage is less steep. Marjerrison, Krause & Keogh (60), using an EEG voltage-integration technique similar to the Drohocki, have essentially confirmed the work of the Goldstein-Pfeiffer group. Not only were their schizophrenic patients less variable than controls, but the presence of phenothiazine medication did not seem to alter the result.

Because of the nature of the Drohocki integrator and similar devices which form the cornerstone of these workers' technique, no statement can be made about altered frequency characteristics in this disease. However, other researchers have examined frequency characteristics directly. Fink, Itil & Clyde (24) showed that schizophrenics (mean age 22.9) showed more delta and theta (0 to 3.5 and 3.6 to 7.5 cps, respectively) and less beta-2 (20 to 26.6 cps) than a group of depressives (mean age 43.5). Because the EEG differences could be interpreted as being due to the age difference, the results of this study are equivocal. However, Volavka, Matousek & Roubicek (103) obtained a result which may rescue the Fink, Itil & Clyde data from oblivion. By use of an automatic frequency analyzer, they found higher alpha and theta activity in both younger and older schizophrenics. According to their results young schizophrenics as well as normals showed enhanced amounts of low-frequency activity; this is apparently outgrown in the normals but not in the schizophrenic group, raising the question of a defect in maturation. Hence, the data of Fink, Itil & Clyde may in fact be orthogonal to age differences.

The final study in this group is by Bruck (8). In contrast to the results of other workers, Bruck reports on the basis of a laborious hand-analysis of EEG that schizophrenics have lower occipital voltages than controls and show greater frontal-occipital synchrony as well. However, so many comparisons were made in this study that the possibility of a purely chance finding cannot be excluded. The study needs replication, but the methods appear so difficult that it seems unlikely that anyone but Bruck will attempt it.

Drug activation of the EEG.—Work in this area has taken several directions: exploration of the EEG effects of compounds which have antipsychotic effects or the reverse (i.e., study of the effect of compounds with hallucinogenic action); the description of drugs which have "normalizing" effects on the pathological EEG found in some schizophrenics; the description of drugs which activate or augment pathological features of the EEG in schizophrenia, which may or may not be present in baseline, nondrug tracings. The general goal, explicitly stated by some of the researchers (39), is to use the EEG as an additional, sensitive index of the central state of the patient so as to be able to prescribe the appropriate medication or combination of medications.

Soviet workers have been intent on normalizing the EEG in schizophrenia. Kostandov[5] (51) reports that small doses of chlorpromazine restore normal responsiveness to acoustic and verbal stimuli both in the EEG and in vegetative systems. The patients were described as apathic-aboulic. The results of a related study raise questions about the permanence of this effect. Libus & Dusek (56) indicate that the EEG effects of phenothiazines studied in 86 schizophrenics, including slowing of the frequency and increased voltage, gradually diminish and the EEG may return entirely to the predrug state. Gamburg & Denisova[5] (26) describe favorable effects on selected pathological elements in the EEG with atropine, adrenalin, and other adrenergic hormones. Acetylcholine, on the other hand, may provoke pathological patterns. The results are interpreted as due to the action of the compounds on adrenergic or cholinergic brain systems. Kamenskaia & Aleksandrovskii[5] (44), working with 32 schizophrenics treated with haloperidol, indicate that the drug tends both to speed up slow EEGs and to slow down fast ones. Both of these effects are seen as directly or indirectly damping the activity of the ARAS. The drug is ineffective in simple schizophrenia (roughly comparable to nuclear), the authors aver, because of the fact that activity there is already lowered.

In contrast to the Russian research, other investigators have used a wide variety of compounds to activate or provoke abnormal activity in the EEG of schizophrenics. The presumption is that these studies may provide additional information of diagnostic value or may say something useful about the brain defect in the disease. Monroe and collaborators (64, 65) have some evidence that the effect seen following oral administration of alpha-chloralose (i.e., bifrontal paroxysmal slow bursts in the EEG) is somewhat more pronounced in schizophrenics than in normals. This action of the drug is reportedly enhanced by phenothiazines and blocked to some extent by chlordiazepoxide. Some confirmatory evidence for the antagonistic action of phenothiazines and chlordiazepoxide on the EEG of schizophrenics is provided by the study of Ulett and collaborators (98). In a balanced design experiment, it was seen that chlordiazepoxide lowered the theta activity in the EEG that was elicited by thioridazine, tetrabenazine, or fluphenazine. In addition, this drug enhances beta activity and decreases alpha activity and voltage generally. In a brief note, hyoscine (99) is said to have sharpened focal slowing in

---

[5] From the French summary.

two schizophrenics and to have produced genuine spikes. The most dramatic report of activation, however, is provided by Goldman (29). By a series of two or three successive intravenous injections of 100 mg. of sodium pentothal, it is possible to elicit high voltage theta activity in the EEG specifically of schizophrenics. The differences between schizophrenics and controls were highly significant. The few exceptions are ascribed to inadequacies in the present classification system. Although this study was based on a large number of cases (i.e., 140), the potential importance of these controversial findings requires that it be replicated by other investigators, using airtight controls with respect to independence of the EEG and psychiatric information.

The final two studies are concerned with the EEG effects of the hallucinogenic compound ditran in schizophrenics: Wilson & Hughes (106) describe a general increase in frequency, with low voltage beta replacing alpha as hallucinations develop. Often, however, these were seen in the absence of marked EEG change, suggesting the independence of these electrographic and behavioral signs. This is underscored, the authors feel, by the observation that atropine, which induces high voltage slow EEG activity, may also induce hallucinations. A more optimistic view of EEG-behavioral correlations is taken by Itil (39). Using the automatic frequency analysis system previously referred to (24), it was seen that low and high doses of ditran had distinct effects. While low doses decrease alpha and augment beta, high doses increase theta and delta and induce 8 to 14 cps spindles as well. All patients (24 chronic schizophrenics; 4 psychopathic controls) who showed at least 10 per cent change in the three frequency bands (i.e., delta-theta, alpha, beta) under the drug showed behavioral change as well. Some success in reversing both kinds of effects was reported for various compounds with anticholinergic action, including prostigmin and chlorpromazine. Itil looks to the day when automatic analysis of the EEG can provide a titer of the amount of excessive inhibitory activity (slow waves) or excitatory activity (fast waves) and allow a precise prescription of the medication appropriate to a particular case.

Sleep studies.—In a monograph concerned with the "D-state" (the dreaming or REM phase of sleep), Hartmann (34) notes that the presence of schizophrenia does not necessarily alter D-time; however, mania may lower it and painful stress and depression may raise it. The D-state is also notoriously sensitive to drugs, stress, etc. It may be that some symptoms of psychosis are due to acute D-deprivation because a person becoming ill usually sleeps poorly and is generally sleep deprived. Other investigators (23, 70, 71) confirm that while it may be more variable, the onset and duration of REM-sleep, both in adult and childhood schizophrenia, does not differ from that seen in controls. Lester & Ewards (54) were concerned more specifically with the fast activity (18 to 26 cps) seen during REM sleep. Both visual and automatic analysis of the sleeping EEG revealed that schizophrenics showed more fast activity than controls during REM; some increase was seen in the awake, resting, and drowsy stages, as well. This work is based on analysis of a precentral-frontal placement in 40 patients and about the same number of controls.

Several reports concur in the conclusion that characteristics of sleep other than Stage I REM differentiate schizophrenics from controls. Kornetsky (49) found that schizophrenic patients sleep less than normal controls; chlorpromazine did not alter this difference although 200 mg of secobarbital reduced it to a nonsignificant level. Caldwell & Domino (11) confirmed the shorter duration of sleep in schizophrenics and found also that 10 of their 25 patients exibited complete absence of Stage IV (high voltage, slow wave) sleep. Both these investigators and Feinberg, Koresko & Gottlieb (23) found that schizophrenics require longer to to fall asleep than controls. In a study referred to in a prior section, Beek et al. (2) noted the more infrequent occurrence of sleep in schizophrenics than in normals during EEG examinations.

None of the studies discussed above made particular reference to sleep differences among schizophrenic subgroups. However, in a study by Struve & Becka (95), it was seen that the "b-mitten" pattern described earlier was present in 8 of 11 reactive schizophrenics and in only one of ten process schizophrenics. This finding emphasizes the usefulness of this classificatory system in EEG research in schizophrenia; however, the fact that secobarbital (presumably up to 190 mg.) may have been necessary to induce sleep suggests that some interaction between drug and patient variables may be responsible for the phenomenon. Also, the question is raised of the similarity between this result and the marked bifrontal theta activity reported by Goldman (29) with pentothal.

Sensory evoked responses.—In recent years electronic devices have become available which permit the extraction of evoked responses to sensory stimuli from the "noise" of scalp EEG. This has stimulated considerable research on sensory function in man, particularly in states of altered consciousness. Shagass & Schwartz were among the pioneers in applying this technique to psychiatric patients. A method used by them in several studies has involved comparing in various groups the averaged evoked response to two stimuli, separated by a period of 15 to 70 msec or longer. This so-called recovery function provides some electrographic index of the capacity of the subject's brain to respond in separate and distinct fashion to the two signals. Various sensory modalities have been studied by these investigators, and the work described below, which is typical of their research, involved somatosensory (87) and visual (88) stimuli.

Generally, the sensory system in schizophrenics, psychotic depressives, and personality disorders does not recover from the effects of the first stimulus within a period of 200 msec. Consequently, the evoked response to the second stimulus of the pair is blunted and difficult to see in the averaged record. Thus, the "recovery cycle" to pairs of light flashes was complete within 200 msec in 15 of 19 controls, but in only 45 of 78 patients. These effects are not obtained in dysthymic patients. Another difference between normal and patient subjects lies in the fact that the former are more likely to show a rhythmic oscillatory pattern ("ringing") in their averaged record than are patients (16 of 19 controls versus 60 of 78 patients). The intensity-amplitude of evoked response gradient to graded levels of shock to the ulnar nerve at the wrist was compared in various groups (87). Normal subjects and dysthymic patients show a less steep gradient than other patient groups, including schizophrenics. Drugs such as LSD, amobarbital, and methedrine are without apparent effect on the gradient. A significant feature of this altered recovery cycle is that it may return to the normal state when the patient is in clinical remission.

Results similar to those obtained by Shagass & Schwartz with visual paired flashes are reported by Speck, Dim & Mercer (92). In this study the impairment was characterized by a reduced response to the pair as compared to the single flash in patients; quantification of this single/pair relationship differentiated them significantly from normal controls. Ringing was also noted, but this was more a function of the presence of alpha activity in the EEG than of diagnostic group [see also (88)]. Depressive patients were also seen to show a somewhat longer latency to light flashes than schizophrenics and controls, who did not differ. Generally, the schizophrenic group was more variable than the other groups studied and some could not be differentiated from normals. This was not found to be related to diagnostic subgroup.

Another approach to the averaged sensory-evoked response technique in psychiatric patients is provided by Callaway and associates (12, 13). This technique involves the presentation of two tones, one at 600 Hz, the other at 1000 Hz. When given no instructions to respond differentially to the tones, normal persons ignore the difference, both behaviorally and electrophysiologically. Comparison of averaged responses to the two tones by means of a correlation based on similar points in time in the two curves yields an r of 0.95. Patient groups, including schizophrenics, show far lower correlations, behaving (so far as their evoked responses are concerned) like normals instructed to attend to the difference. In a series of studies employing this method, it has been found that paranoid schizophrenics resemble normals more than they resemble other schizophrenics, and that the process-reactive dimension is irrelevant to the phenomenon (13). Other studies have related the low correlation to specific symptomatology; thus, it occurs in association with disordered fragmented thinking, high anxiety, and incoherent delusional talk. It is not seen in the chronic, withdrawn, blunted patients, or in those with well-ordered delusional systems (41, 42). Callaway (12) has noted that the finding is unrelated to drugs, age, sex, or hospitalization, but that the correlation may be reduced under some circumstances in normal subjects when the procedure becomes monotonous and irritating and produces variable evoked responses. As is the case with the altered recovery cycle described by Shagass & Schwartz, the lowered two-tone correlation approaches normal values as the disordered and disconnected thinking subsides. This may accompany either clinical recovery or greater withdrawal; however, the phenomenon is said to reflect the current state of psychological functioning of the patient rather than some underlying permanent trait.

Many of the studies reviewed in this section have examined the amplitude of the evoked response to single stimuli in schizophrenic versus normal persons as an index of CNS function or attentiveness. The results are so variable from study to study, however, as to suggest that there is no consistent relation between amplitude and diagnostic category.

Schizophrenia and Organic Brain Disease

The question of the possible organic etiology of the major psychoses has always interested alienists, even prior to Kraeplin and Bleuler. Indeed, the stimulus for many of the EEG studies reported in the first section of this review can be thought of generally as a search for objective CNS indicators of the schizophrenic process. In that sense, the division between the EEG studies and those of the present section is artificial and represents a relatively arbitrary classification. However, the work to be considered below is concerned in a more direct sense with the comparison between schizophrenia and objective CNS disease, and many of the studies involve actual study or manipulation of the brain or both.

Schizophrenia and epilepsy.—The relation between these two entities is a curious one; had it not been for the belief (mistaken, to be sure!) of Sakel and Meduna that the two diseases could not coexist within one person, the convulsive therapy which is effective for certain major psychopathological symptoms would never have been developed. Countering this point of view is that stemming from the finding by Gibbs & Gibbs, and reported in their prestigious *Atlas of Electroencephalography* (28); they noted that 40 to 50 per cent of patients with temporal lobe abnormalities exhibited some form of personality disorder, whereas only 10 per cent of cases with other cerebral abnormalities had such problems. Several studies have attempted to substantiate this relationship but without success, i.e., no difference could be detected between objective indicators of personality and psychopathology in temporal lobe versus diffuse unlocalized epileptics [See (63), for example]. Nevertheless, the possibility that additional study might reveal a relationship between some forms of schizophrenia and some epileptic phenomena continues to motivate research.

Two papers, one by Chapman (14) and the other by Slater, Beard & Glithero (89), illustrate some recent thinking in this area. Chapman provides a clinical comparison of the disturbance of consciousness seen in schizophrenia (generalized) and three forms of epilepsy: petit mal, grand mal and psychomotor. Although no epileptic subtype is completely identical with his idealized, archetypical description of a schizophrenic fugue, psychomotor epilepsy seems to possess the greatest similarity to it. As is well known, this form of epilepsy is usually associated with focal temporal lobe disorder.

Slater, Beard & Glithero raise the question of how psychosis can result from epilepsy in seizure patients with schizophrenic-like behavior. They conclude from their studies of such cases that the two diseases occur in the same individual far too often to be due to chance alone; moreover, the psychotic behavior is probably not an epileptic "equivalent" but is more likely to result some years later from stresses to the brain induced by the continuous fits. This is supported by evidence of brain pathology as provided by procedures such as pneumoencephalography. They are cautious in their conclusions but suggest that nuclear schizophrenias might in fact be organic psychoses.

A case study by Sagarra (80) illustrates the will-o'-the-wisp nature of the problem. A patient was treated for several years with shock and other organic therapies for schizophrenia with paranoid features. Although he received some benefit, remissions were temporary. After belated EEG studies revealed focal bifrontal (not temporal) theta activity under hyperventilation, he was started on a course of hydantoin therapy. There was a profound and sustained recovery. Was this patient a cryptic epileptic, or does schizophrenia respond favorably to anticonvulsant drugs? If it does, does this necessarily implicate disordered brain function in the etiology of the disease?

Studies by Small, Stevens & Milstein (91) and Small, Small & Surphilis (90) have been concerned with emotional factors in temporal lobe epilepsy. In the first of these, "emotional activation" of the EEG was attempted by reading affect-laden messages to 44 epileptic patients. EEG activation of the disorder was seen in 12 cases, but no difference was observed between those with temporal and nontemporal foci. Eight of the 12 cases had been rated schizophrenic or schizoid. In another investigation, 7 out of a population of 70 newly hospitalized schizophrenics were identified as having temporal lobe foci (15 cases had other types of EEG abnormalities). These 7 were matched on a number of variables with 7 cases with normal EEGs. Those with temporal foci were rated as more hostile and paranoid; the controls were more agitated and catatonic.

Greenberg & Pollack (31) were interested specifically in the clinical correlate of the 14 and 6/sec positive spiking pattern in EEG. There are conflicting claims that this is related to aggressive, psychopathic behavior. Nine cases who exhibited this in a sleep EEG were matched with 9 cases who did not; all were drawn from a pool of 60 consecutive admissions to a psychiatric hospital. The $14 = $ and $= 6$/sec group had more pathological ratings on aggressiveness and suicidal tendencies, among other attributes. This suggested to the authors that the $14 = $ and $= 6$/sec pattern might be more highly correlated with psychiatric disturbance in some groups than in others.

Pathological and neurosurgical studies.—The test of any theory of the organic etiology of schizophrenia ultimately requires the demonstration of clear-cut changes in brain tissue. Objective evidence of this sort is often difficult to obtain and more difficult to evaluate. Patients who show particularly striking symptomatology from the point of view of localization of function may outlive the investigator; or they may be so aged at the time of death that it is not possible to disentangle the presumed schizopathology from more diffuse, generalized changes which may be due to age, to the effect of massive series of electroconvulsive shock therapy, or to the slings and arrows of decades of institutional life. The EEG and other neurological diagnostic procedures (skull films, air encephalography, angiography, studies of cerebrospinal fluid, radioactive tracer scans, echoencephalography) can provide additional information about the living brain. However, these methods may also reflect injury or damage which is not specific to the disease per se. A further difficulty lies in the fact that the pathological changes associated with schizophrenia may be of the nature of subtle biochemical-metabolic "lesions" which even careful histological studies may not detect.

Despite these problems, it would appear essential to conduct intensive brain studies both pre- and postmortem so as to help anchor the rapidly accumulating EEG literature in schizophrenia. If large enough series are studied, especially with patients of varying age at the time of death, then some of the errors of sampling aged institutional populations may be reduced.

Only two neuropathological studies[6] were encountered in the period covered by this summary and both concerned single cases. In the first there was a coincidence of seizure and schizophrenic behavior. Kury & Cobb (52), referring in their work to the prior study by Slater, Beard & Glithero (89), describe pathological changes in the brain of a 75-year-old epileptic schizophrenic woman who had been hospitalized periodically over a long time interval. Her history included many episodes suggestive of traumatic and infectious injury. She was characterized as confused, demented, aggressive, and in poor contact. There was considerable enlargement of the lateral ventricle in the left hemisphere, complete destruction of the left hippocampus, distorted and shrunken temporal cortex, as well as evidence of arteriosclerotic changes. Borreguero & Iñiguez de Onzoño (6) describe a younger case who had had serial EEGs and pneumonencephalograms in the years preceding his death at age 30. His psychosis, which had strong hebephrenic and catatonic components, was said to date back to his seventeenth year. The EEG was notable for bilateral temporal and frontal slow waves, while the air studies revealed a ventricular system that was abnormally large and gradually increasing in size. This hydrocephalic state was particularly notable on the right lateral ventricle. Detailed gross and fine pathological studies are reported; most prominent were the ventricular alterations and changes in the rostral forebrain. There was evidence of cell loss and change in the frontal cortex, the head of the caudate and in the medialis dorsalis nucleus of the thalamus. No changes were noted in temporal or occipital cortex, amygdala, mammillary bodies or the corpus callosum. Other studies on larger series of cases are referred to which also implicate cell changes in the medialis dorsalis. Cellular alterations are said to be much more prominent in catatonic than in paranoid patients; they are not seen in control cases. This discursive paper reviews other recent (primarily German) histopathological studies of brain

[6] A third study of Khaime (46) was available only as an abstract in English. It is a brief paper (five pages) describing pathological-anatomical material from the brains of 200 schizophrenics. Organic disease was seen in 60 cases and in 38 of these it was said to have modified the symptomatology. Various kinds of damage and disease processes are reported, including abscesses, tumors, thromboses and arteriosclerosis.

changes in schizophrenia and discusses as well some of the possible artifacts introduced by fixing, embedding, etc.

The question arises as to whether or not other investigators have implicated the frontal-caudate-medial thalamus system in schizophrenia. Earlier studies by Sem-Jacobsen and co-workers (85, 86), involving the implantation of multiple depth electrodes in the brains of schizophrenics, seem to provide some confirming evidence. Although many of the cases had normal scalp recordings, paroxysmal high voltage slow activity was regularly seen in the medial orbital frontal surface and in other regions of the depths of the frontal lobes. Such slow wave activity was also seen in temporal, parietal and hypothalamic regions and seemed more prominent during acute psychotic episodes. In the studies by Heath (35, 36) with implanted electrodes in schizophrenics there are similar observations excepting that the abnormal EEG activity is described as spiking in the septal region. This is not seen in epileptics or in cases with Parkinsonism. This research tends to implicate the septal-fornical-hippocampal (i.e., limbic) system in the pathogenesis of schizophrenia rather than a frontal system, and Heath has speculated that defective appreciation of pleasure is at the basis of the schizophrenic process. This inference depends heavily on the results of self-stimulation studies in rats. Chitanondh (15) has reported some success from neurosurgical ablation of a limbic area. Several patients with olfactory hallucinations were reported to have been benefited by a unilateral stereotaxic lesion in the corticomedial region of the amygdala (i.e., part of the so-called olfactory brain).

CNS effects of schizophrenic serum.—Although consideration of serological differences between schizophrenic and nonschizophrenic persons is not within the scope of this review, we shall include some studies of the effects of administered serum on CNS activity of recipient animals, since inferences were made to brain functions of the donor patients. Stenhouse et al. (94) attempted to reproduce the finding, previously reported, that topical application of schizophrenic serum to rat cortex increased the amplitude of somatosensory evoked potentials. They failed. In a following note in the same journal issue, German et al. (27), authors of the inital observation, admitted that they also were unable to reproduce their original work if the identity of the donor subject was unknown. Two Russian scientists, Faivishevskii & Nemtsov, apparently have found a more reliable method. This technique involves the injection of blood serum via an intracerebral cannula into the third ventricle of chronic cat preparations. Serum from nuclear schizophrenics produces a long lasting slowing of the EEG and a diminution of the large negative component of the visual evoked potential. Changes of the same magnitude or direction are not seen with serum from periodic or paranoid schizophrenics or from normal persons (20).[7] In a further study (68)[7] these workers report on the multiple, dissociable components of the blood serum responsible for the CNS effects. That factor which is responsible for the EEG effect in periodic serum (presumably a lesser effect than that seen in nuclear cases) is

[7] From the French summary.

unchanged after being maintained for 10 hr at the temperature of melting ice. The factor responsible for the evoked potential changes is destroyed under these conditions. The third paper from these researchers (69) provides more detail about the procedure, including the control measures and the time course of the effect (21 to 30 min). The slowing of EEG and the enhancement of the initial negative phase over the somatosensory and visual cortices is interpreted as a direct inhibitory effect on the ARAS; the authors caution, however, that a direct effect on cortex cannot be ruled out.

Direct current effects on the brain.—Lippold & Redfearn (58) and Redfearn, Lippold & Costain (76) describe a rather novel procedure for the amelioration of mood. Small currents are applied over the eyebrows, using the leg as an indifferent electrode. Subjects have the currents passed for many hours by means of a 15V battery they carry with them. Positive dc (range 100 to 300 μA) induces an elevation of mood and alertness, wheareas negative dc produces silence and withdrawal. Thirteen of 29 depressed patients treated with positive dc showed marked improvement. On the basis of some rat experiments, the authors report that the effect of the procedure is to induce a fourfold increase in firing of neurons. The neurons presumed to be responsible for the ameliorative effects are those of the ARAS acting on the cortex.

DEVELOPMENTAL AND AUTISTIC PROCESSES

Only a small number of studies fall into this category; however, the importance of the area suggests that the number should increase in the future. Two of the investigations involve autistic children, but the two papers offer markedly different EEG characterizations. In the study by Hutt et al. (38), austistic children are described as having a flat (low voltage fast) EEG with no dominant rhythms. Only one of the ten children showed alpha activity with eyes closed. Some telemetric studies with two of these children suggested that the flat EEG was a function of situations which evoked stereotyped behavior. The desynchronized record was not seen in sleep, which was described as normal. The inference was drawn that the hyperaroused condition of the ARAS, which was responsible for the flat EEG, was present only in the waking state. It is true, however, that sleep was not studied in great detail with these subjects. In contrast with these findings, White, DeMyer & DeMyer (104) report a variety of pathological, epileptiform patterns in their sample of 58 autistic children. A frequent finding was polyspike-and-wave patterns, as well as focal slowing and focal spikes. These patterns were also seen frequently among 44 chronic, undifferentiated schizophrenic children and among 37 with behavior disorders. Only one abnormal record was seen in 10 neurotic and 13 normal children. Three papers from Soviet researchers will be described briefly.[8] Deglin (18) addresses the problem of the fragmental, poorly generalized form which characterized catatonic syndromes and particularly the stupor in children. The retarded development

---

[8] The paper by Deglin (18) was available only in the form of a French summary; the other two papers (19, 102), only as English summaries.

of inhibitory processes in the CNS is said to form the basis of the stupor. Another paper by this author (19) concerns the significance of slow waves in the EEG in childhood and adolescent schizophrenia. This work, based on the study of over 500 psychotic children, is said to delineate three types of slow activity: that correlated with the pathology (i.e., presumably associated with stupor); that associated with stimulus effects; that slow wave activity which is strictly related to immaturity. Using EEG and clinical data, Vishnevskaya (102) characterized 52 adolescents suffering from schizophrenia. In 10 of them, organic factors were clearly evident in the etiology; in 30, the disease had a prepubertal onset and worsened at puberty; in 12, the illness began in puberty. Unfavorable prognoses include early manifestation of automatisms and delusions, hebephrenic behavior, impulsiveness, and emotional dullness. EEG data are said to indicate the stability and irreversibility of the process.

Neuropsychology, Psychopharmacology, and Psychophysiology

No theory that implicates a specific brain area or bodily system in schizophrenia can be completely convincing without evidence of a direct relationship between behavioral and physiological variables. Inferences drawn exclusively from EEG data, from the presumed central effects of drugs, from measures of peripheral autonomic function, or even from correlations among these may be erroneous. Thus, there are conditions under which the EEG recorded from the scalp may be misleading with respect to the degree to which it mirrors a behavioral state. These conditions include the administration of some centrally acting drugs, and the effects of certain subcortical brain lesions. Data obtained with precisely these methods are often used to provide evidence of the link between a specific behavior and its psysiological *Anlage*. While the dissociation between behavior and EEG has often been exaggerated (62), it is nevertheless true that recordings from the scalp may be vastly different from those done at the cortical surface or from underlying deeper structures (1). Centrally acting drugs may exert differing effects depending on the dose and the time after administration. Peripheral autonomic measures may show great lability and are influenced by baseline values in an individual. Consequently, investigations in which specific behaviors were measured, particularly when done in conjunction with physiological recordings, provide data essential for testing theories about arousal, hyperarousal, sustained vigilance, and the like. After all, these terms are inferences from behavior and are not appropriately applied to physiological measures.

Despite these cautionary notes, it is nevertheless the case that the results of behavioral studies accord well with the more purely physiological ones. A certain proportion of schizophrenic patients seem to merit the designation of hyperaroused when examined with procedures and under conditions used to study sustained attention. Orzack & Kornetsky (72) compared a population of chronic schizophrenics, alcoholics, and normals (matched for age and educational achievement) on their performance of two tasks: the Continuous Performance Test (CPT), designed by Rosvold et al. (79) for investigating sustained visual attention, and the Digit Symbol Substitution Test (DSST), which provided a measure of cognitive ability. In comparison to the normal subjects, the alcoholics showed a selective deficit on the DSST, whereas the schizophrenics were significantly impaired only on the CPT. This poor mean performance was due to 7 of the 16 schizophrenic subjects; the scores of the other nine fell within the normal range. No difference could be discerned between the two groups with respect to subdiagnosis, sex, or length of hospitalization. The deficits seen in the two clinical groups were attributed, in the case of the alcoholics, to cortical impairment, and in the case of the schizophrenics, to defect in the ARAS.

The basis of these attributions stems largely from a theoretical paper by Mirsky & Kornetsky (61) in which it was suggested, on the basis of neuropharmacological, neurophysiological, and behavioral data, that the CPT and DSST are dependent upon different brain systems. The CPT, which is preferentially impaired by chlorpromazine, sleep deprivation, and petit mal epilepsy, was said to be dependent primarily upon intact functioning of the brain areas which include the ARAS. The DSST, which is particularly sensitive to the barbiturates, LSD, and cortical lesions, was viewed as requiring intact cortical functioning. The dichotomy which was drawn was a relative one and deemed to be useful to order research data and to suggest additional experiments.

Further consideration of this dichotomy, with particular reference to schizophrenia, is provided in a paper by Kornetsky & Mirsky (50). The following observations led to the position developed in this paper: Schizophrenics are less affected than are normals by chlorpromazine on both behavioral and cardiovascular measures, and they sleep less than normals after ingestion of this drug (49); the reduced impairment is seen most clearly in behavioral tasks requiring sustained attention. Low doses of barbiturates, on the other hand, seem to affect normal and schizophrenic persons equally. By way of contrast, certain conditions seem to elicit greater deficit on attention tasks in schizophrenics; thus, schizophrenics matched against normals and hospitalized neurotics on the CPT show significantly greater impairment following a distracting visual or auditory stimulus condition then either of the other groups (93). Similarly, schizophrenics matched with normal subjects on a simple reaction time task fail to show improvement with a foreperiod of 2 or 4 sec and may become significantly more impaired (21).

An attempt to resolve these contradictions was provided by recourse to an inverted U function relating arousal or activation level and performance. According to this model, reproduced in Figure 1, the maximum performance of which a person is capable is attained with medium levels of activation; under or overactivation elicits poorer performance. The basal activation level is assumed to be higher in schizophrenics than in normal persons; thus, chlorpromazine, which reduces activation an equal amount in the two groups, will produce less deficit in schizophrenics than in normals.[9] Further, condi-

[9] Additional studies of the effect of phenothiazines on the CPT in schizophrenics were performed by Latz & Kornetsky (53) and by Orzack, Kornetsky & Freeman (73).

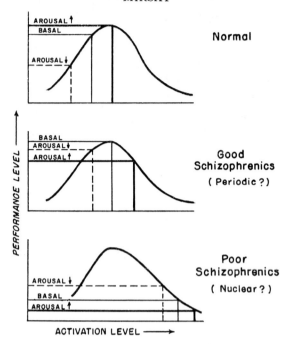

Three hypothetical inverted U models corresponding to normal, "good" and "poor" schizophrenic groups. Agents which decrease arousal, such as chlorpromazine, may have differing behavioral effects depending on the basal level. Similarly, the effect of increasing arousal level (via environmental stimulation or stress) can differ among the groups. For further discussion related to this, see Table I and text concerning it. The outcome of experiments should help determine the curve parameters such as degree of kurtosis. For the sake of simplicity, the same roughly Gaussian curve is assumed to underlie the performance-activation relation in the three groups. This need not be the case, nor is it necessary that objectively similar modifiers of arousal produce equal movement along the activation abscissa in all groups.

tions which produce an increment in arousal may result in improvement among normals and decrement among schizophrenics; the latter are concieved as having moved "over the hump" onto the descending limb of the continuum. Although the inverted U hypothesis seems to accord well with the data which led to it, there are certain difficulties. The schizophrenic patients who showed less impairment with chlorpromazine were not the same groups of individuals who failed to improve or worsened in performance under arousing conditions. The latter group may have been much less deteriorated and better preserved than the former and may represent a somewhat different population. Moreover, the effects of prior or intercurrent phenothiazine medication is unknown and difficult to assess. Certainly, the previous pharmacological histories of any unselected group of normal and psychotic persons is likely to be grossly dissimilar. The investigations which led to the formulation should be repeated, if possible, with patients not previously maintained on tranquilizer medications, and conditions which augment and diminish activation level should be applied to the same subjects. Notwithstanding these problems in interpretation, the work of other investigators affords some confirmation, on a behavioral level, for the concept of hyperarousal in at least some schizophrenic persons. Gromoll (33) used EEG measures, whereas Venables & Wing (101) and Venables (100) used skin conductance and two-flash discrimination threshold. With the exception of patients who have marked coherent delusions without concomitant incoherence of speech, there is a high correlation between degree of withdrawal (and presumably degree of illness) and intensity of arousal.

Conclusion

In lieu of a summary of the more than 100 studies referred to in this survey, what will be attempted is a preliminary, tentative, theoretical integration of the work which leads, hopefully, to a number of useful suggestions for additional research. This integration will focus on aspects of the problem with which workers in the field of schizophrenia, and in the area of the major psychoses generally, have been struggling: the diversity and variability of the phenomenon, the relation to brain damage, and the issue of hyperarousal.

Regarding the question of diversity, some of the Soviet workers have proposed rather elaborate schemas for classifying the schizophrenias; these do not in every case correspond immediately to the diagnostic categories used in the West. The Soviet studies often lack the kind of detail, specificity, and controls that are demanded in the West; however, the descriptions seem thoughtful and painstakingly derived and undoubtedly bespeak long years of clinical experience. Although the specific labels may be unfamiliar there seems to be considerable descriptive overlap among the many polarities that have been described for schizophrenia, such as nuclear versus periodic; chronic, blunted, demented, catatonic versus episodic and paranoial; process versus reactive. On the one hand, in the case of nuclear schizophrenia the disease process is described as beginning early in life, is associated with profound symptoms of dementia, blunting, stupor, and withdrawal, and the prognosis is extremely poor. On the other hand, periodic schizophrenia occurs relatively late in adolescent life, tends to be characterized be periodic episodes of florid, "productive" symptomatology including assaultiveness, depersonalization, delusions, and paranoid thinking. Each of these major categorizations may possibly be subdivided even further; the Soviet authors, in particular, argue for this.

The first type of patient (nuclear-chronic) generally tends to give the impression of an individual with a badly made brain. Grossly slow EEGs and abnormal insensitivity to stimulation are characteristic of this group, and some studies that have been done on the pathological anatomy of patients of this type (6) suggest greater evidence of objective brain damage than in paranoid patients. In the case of the second type (periodic-paranoial), the available evidence does not demonstrate a grossly abnormal EEG. If indeed there is a long-standing organic lesion in this group, it may be one that is un-detectable with ordinary scalp recordings (2) and may be apparent only with automatic frequency analyses of the EEG (24, 103) or with the activation procedures employing alpha-chloralose (64, 65) or pentothal (29). The ex-istence of a normal EEG, at least so far as rough qualitative inspection is concerned, is well documented in cases of prolonged coma due to pontomes-encephalic hemorrhage. The inference can be drawn that the EEG may have shown evidence initially of pathology but that it may have recovered. [See discussion of this evidence in (62).] The objection may be raised that both an abnormal and a normal EEG is used to bolster the argument for brain pathology and that such evidence thereby loses its force. However, the data of activation procedures and of automatic frequency analysis support the inference of altered CNS function as does the profoundly altered behavior! With respect to the periodic-paranoial group, there may be more evidence of a nearly normal EEG and response to sensory stimulation, but the incidence of focal electrographic abnormality may be more prominent among these subjects.

The case that is being made, therefore, is for two basically distinct types of brain pathology in schizophrenia: In the chronic, nuclear cases, it is one of long standing that may be associated, in particular, with diffuse frontal lobe damage including destruction of tissue in ventral and orbital frontal areas and associated subcortical structures such as the medialis dorsalis of the thalamus and the head of the caudate nucleus (6). This is the group de-scribed as stuporous, blunted, and withdrawn. In the episodic, paranoial group, on the other hand, the damage may preferentially be found in the septal, hippocampal, and temporal lobe areas (35, 36), although frontal dam-age may occur as well (85, 86). This latter population is more likely to be characterized as having personality difficulties (28) and to be described as aggressive and assaultive or fragmented and bizarre.

The question also arises as to how to deal, in this context, with the consid-erable evidence of hyperarousal or hyperactivation among schizophrenics. To essay an answer to this question, to summarize much of the material that has been reviewed, and to add a few daring leaps over areas that are sparsely populated with data points, a schematization of the schizophrenias, with heavy emphasis on neuropsychological speculation, is offered in Table I.

Some comments on the table are in order. The tabular entries are sup-ported by varying amounts of substantiating data; the numbers below the row headings refer to literature cited. The rows below Diagnostic Label entitled Fundamental Lesion or Damage, Additional Cortical Damage, and Development are quite speculative; the last named of these is the most con-troversial of all. Although a loose trichotomy is being proposed here, it should be clear that there are probably many gradations and subcategories, pre-sumably corresponding to locus and extent of damage, the age at which damage is incurred, specific life stresses, and the like.

The notion that hyperarousal is characteristic of all schizophrenics seems defensible; it is supported by studies of physiological (10, 30, 33, 60, 75, 100,

TABLE I

TENTATIVE NEUROPSYCHOLOGICAL SCHEMATIZATION OF THE SCHIZOPHRENIAS

DIAGNOSTIC LABEL (22, 48)	Nuclear, chronic; process (?)	Periodic, episodic, paranoial; reactive (?)		Paranoid
Fundamental lesion or damage (10, 21, 30, 33, 49, 60, 75, 93, 100, 101)	*Hyperfunction of central mesodiencephalic core—structural (?) functional (?)*			
Additional cortical damage (6, 29, 35, 36, 65, 85, 86)	Widespread loss in frontal systems (temporal as well?)	Frontal or temporal or both?		Minimal absent?
Onset (22, 48, 52, 80, 89)	Early—childhood or adolescence	Late adolescence, early adulthood		
		May follow head trauma Life stress Late sequela of epilepsy		Life stress?
Development (18, 20, 22, 38, 48, 68, 69, 104)	Initial hyperfunction of ARAS; poor inhibitory control by cortex—leads to massive permanent overdamp (How?) to control sensory inflow—Humoral factors (?)	Defective, fragile but partial control of overstimulation		Tight, rigid control of overstimulation (usually adequate cortical mechanisms)
		Periodic florid "productive" symptoms		
Symptoms (22, 28, 48, 90, 91)	Blunting, withdrawn catatonic, affectless, stupor	Disconnected, Fragmented, Delusional Thought. Frontal (?)	Hostile, Aggressive, Assaultive, Destructive. Temporal (?)	Paranoid systems
EEG Studies (17, 22, 24, 29, 37, 48, 54, 65)	Abnormal slow; Poor response to stimuli may be "recovered" & fast normal	Normal background but fast; Focally abnormal drug activated foci		Normal background but fast
Evoked potential studies—Recovery cycle & 2-tone correlation (12, 13, 41, 42, 87, 88, 92)	Normal	Pathological during active symptom period		Normal
Sleep (2, 11, 23, 49)	*Poor, disturbed, absence or reduction of Stage IV*			
Behavior on attention-type tests (21, 50, 72, 73, 93)	Poor	Variable; if good, falls with arousal		Good, but falls with arousal (?)
Response to phenothiazines (22, 25)	Poor	Good		Poor (?)

101) as well as psychological variables (21, 49, 93) and bolstered by results of drug investigations (50, 73). This is in accord with the position taken by Fish (25). The assumption is made, therefore, that all schizophrenia begins with a basic fault in the ARAS, which may be of some obscure, as yet unidentified, biochemical nature. The functional outcome of this depends upon the mechanisms remaining to cope with the overintense barrage of stimuli emanating from the ARAS. If there is extensive damage to the cortical mantle as well, and in particular to the inhibitory frontal and temporal corticofugal systems (presumed to be the case in nuclear schizophrenia), then the organism may be unable to adapt in any sense to the environment. Alternatively, the defect in the ARAS may be such that the hyperarousal is greatest in this group. The earliest manifestation of this is as infantile, autistic schizophrenia. The fast EEGs (38) or grossly abnormal records (104) may represent differing stages of adaptation in a severely damaged organism. When hyperarousal effects supervene, and this would have to be an earlier developmental stage, then the desynchronized EEG would prevail. Evidence of focal or diffusely abnormal EEGs might represent the fragmented, unsuccessful efforts at inhibitory action by a damaged cortex. The cortical "failure" might be compounded by the lack of maturity in the brain systems of a child. Something akin to this is described in the less profound, less sustained catatonia seen in children (18). Possibly, if the cortical damage is not too extensive, there may be sufficient control of the ascending excitation so that this patient might graduate to the periodic, episodic category.

At some point in the history of the children who fail to achieve some adaptation (possibly because their damaged frontal or temporal lobes possess epileptogenic foci which serve only to further activate subcortical systems) a profound damping effect takes place, possibly by means of a major reorganization in the titer of neurohumors within the brain. These children, as they grow, then would become eventually the chronic blunted, stuporous, withdrawn, catatonic, backward cases. The introduction of the humoral factor seems required to account for the somniferous serum effects described for nuclear schizophrenics (20); these effects are not described for periodic paranoial cases, so the presumption is that the neurohumoral adjustment does not play a role. The EEG studies in adulthood of these nuclear cases may show many pathological signs or it may be that of the "recovered" normal. In the latter case, drug activation (29, 65) may elicit signs of pathology, as may studies of alpha blocking to sensory stimuli (4, 5, 22, 48). The endogenous damping down of excitation in this group results in diminished effectiveness of chlorpromazine (22, 25), poor attentive test performance (i.e., among those that are even testable), and a normal appearance in the recovery cycle or two-tone correlation evoked potential investigations. Abnormal functioning on these procedures apparently requires the presence of active, uncontrolled excitement (hyperarousal) seen only in the periodic patients at the time of exacerbation of their symptomatology.

Let us note some additional points of description of the periodic etiology: The overexcitation from the ARAS may be less in these cases, or the amount of cortical damage may be less or both. The onset of symptoms may thus be delayed until the stressful life period occasioned by adolescence. In some individuals the symptoms may arise after a head trauma damages the cortical inhibitory controls or as a late sequela of epilepsy (89). In this latter instance, the schizophrenia may develop gradually as the cortical control areas become progressively more epileptogenic and deteriorated. Since there is some possibility for relatively normal development and adaptation to the environment, the symptomatology of the periodic group, while varied and multiform, would differ from that of the nuclear group. In cases with frontal damage, the fragmented, delusional, disconnected thought disorders may predominate. In patients with temporal lobe damage, the hostile, aggressive, assaultive symptomatology may predominate (90). Both kinds of symptoms might be present. These cases may respond favorably to phenothiazines or to hydantoins (80); the treatment of choice might combine the two. Parenthetically, note that the question of the diagnostic conundrum of schizophrenia versus epilepsy has been finessed. Instead, there is an individual in whom the nature of the brain damage leads to a particular set of neurological signs and a behavioral syndrome which is a function of the damage to his brain. Even when the periodic patient is in good remission, the fragile nature of his control over the ARAS is illustrated by the worsening performance on attention tasks when distraction or arousal (in effect, a stress) is introduced. Drug activation procedures may also reveal epileptiform abnormalities in the EEG.

Least is known regarding the paranoid case, which is also schematized in Table I. Since most neurological, anatomical, and serological studies fail to reveal abnormality in this group, it must be assumed that cortical damage is minimal or absent and that only the hypothetical ARAS lesion is present. Despite the adequacy of cortical controls, the underlying pathology is nevertheless reflected in the necessity of rigid, tight paranoid thought systems. The underlying hyperaroused state is kept so tightly in check that phenothiazines may provide no benefit; it is not clear whether arousal-stress would produce impaired attentiveness. A final bit of meta-speculation: Jouvet (43) and Koella (47) have described the effect of lesions in the raphé nuclei of brainstem upon sleep in the cat. Unlike the effects of lesions in the nearby locus coeruleus (abolition of REM sleep), destruction of the raphé group may virtually eliminate or substantially reduce Stage IV sleep. The raphé group also are specialized in that they are active serotinin-secreting cells. In view of the altered sleep patterns in schizophrenia, these data might reinforce the presumptive evidence of disturbance or lesion within the brainstem. The question also arises as to whether the active principle in the serum of nuclear schizophrenics might be related in some fashion to serotonin, norepinephrine, or another catechol amine (45).

Aside from any value that Table I may have in summarizing a complex and confusing area of research into a complex and confusing table, it may serve to generate some experiments that would be profitable to perform. Thus, it might be worthwhile to apply rigorous batteries of neuropsychological tests to schizophrenics, particularly of the periodic, paranoial group, in order to substantiate or infirm the notion of specific damage to frontal or temporal cortical areas or both. The results of such procedures might be used to predict the outcome of EEG (especially drug-activated) examinations in such patients. It is not clear how the concept of the inverted U can accomodate to this heterogenous classification, but some ideas as to how this might be done are presented in Figure 1. Patients who do poorly on tests such as the CPT might improve with chlorpromazine; those who do well might perform more poorly under the drug (50) but show less decrement than normal controls. This prediction assumes that these groups occupy different places on the arousal continuum.

No clear therapeutic recommendations stem from this presentation of data and speculation; even if some of the presumptions about etiology and sites of damage prove to be accurate, there is no necessary relation between identifying the source of a disease process and being able, at least initially, to provide any useful remedy. However, the area of schizophrenia will remain a source of intense research interest, undoubtedly, for some time to come. As was the case with the other major theoretical approaches to the disease, the outcome may teach us more about the ARAS and the brain than about schizophrenia. However, the bulk of the evidence reviewed here indicates that to study the one is to learn about the other.

LITERATURE CITED

1. Ajmone-Marsan, C., Van Buren, J. Epileptiform activity in cortical and subcortical structures in temporal lobe of man. In *Temporal Lobe Epilepsy*, 18–108 (Baldwin, M., Bailey, P., Eds., Charles C Thomas, Springfield, Ill., 581 pp., 1958)
2. Beek, H. H., van Bork, J. J., Herngreen, H., Van Der Most Van Spijk, D. Considerations on electroencephalography in schizophrenics with reference to a survey in 25 Dutch mental hospitals. *Psychiat. Neurol. Neurochirurgia*, 67, 95–101 (1964)
3. Bleuler, E. *Dementia Praecox or the Group of Schizophrenias* (Translated by Zinbin, J., International Universities Press, New York, 548 pp., 1950)
4. Blum, R. H. Photic stimulation, imagery and alpha rhythm. *J. Ment. Sci.*, 102, 160–67 (1956)
5. Blum, R. H. Alpha-rhythm responsiveness in normal, schizophrenic, and brain-damaged persons. *Science*, 126, 749–50 (1957)
6. Borreguero, A. D., Iñiguez de Onzoño, A. Estudio clinico, electro-pneumoencefalográfico seriado y anatompathológico de un caso de esquizo-

frenia. *Arch. de Neurobiol. (Madrid)*, 28, 414–39 (1965)
7. Bremer, F. Cerveau isolé et physiologie du sommeil. *Compt. Rend. Soc. Biol.*, 118, 1235–41 (1936)
8. Bruck, M. A. Synchrony and voltage in the EEG of schizophrenics. *Arch. Gen. Psychiat.*, 10, 454–68 (1964)
9. Bruck, M. A., McNeal, B. F. Artifacts in the EEG of schizophrenic patients. *Am. J. Psychiat.*, 121, 265–66 (1964)
10. Burdick, J. A., Sugerman, A. A., Goldstein, L. The application of regression analysis to quantitative electroencephalography in man. *Psychophysiology*, 3, 249–54 (1967)
11. Caldwell, D. F., Domino, E. F. Electroencephalographic and eye movement patterns during sleep in chronic schizophrenic patients. *Electroencephalog. Clin. Neurophysiol.*, 22, 414–20 (1967)
12. Callaway, E. Averaged evoked responses in psychiatry. *J. Nerv. Ment. Dis.*, 143, 80–91 (1966)
13. Callaway, E., Jones, R. T., Layne, R. S. Evoked responses and segmental set of schizophrenia. *Arch. Gen. Psychiat.*, 12, 83–89 (1965)

BASES OF SCHIZOPHRENIA 345

14. Chapman, J. The early symptoms of schizophrenia. *Brit. J. Psychiat.*, **112**, 225–51 (1966)
15. Chitanondh, H. Stereotaxic amygdalotomy in the treatment of olfactory seizures and psychiatric disorders with olfactory hallucination. *Confinia Neurol.*, **27**, 181–96 (1966)
16. Cochin, J., Kornetsky, C. Development and loss of tolerance to morphine in the rat after single and multiple injections. *J. Pharmacol. Exptl. Therap.*, **145**, 1–10 (1964)
17. Davis, P. A., Davis, H. The electroencephalograms of psychotic patients. *Am. J. Psychiat.*, **95**, 1007–25 (1939)
18. Deglin, V. I. A. Study of the development ontogenetic aspect of the catatonic syndrome in schizophrenia (based on clinical and electroencephalic data). *Zh. Nevropatol. i Psikhiatrii*, **65**, 1066–72 (1965)
19. Deglin, V. I. A. The significance of slow waves in EEG in childhood and adolescent schizophrenia. In *Problemy Psikhvnevrologii Detskogo Vozrasta*, 163–71 (Fedotov, D. D., Ed., Ministerstvo Zdravookhraneniya RSFSR, Moscow, 532 pp., 1964)
20. Faivishevskii, V. A., Nemtsov, A. V. Effect of the blood serum of patients with schizophrenia on the electrical activity of the brain of experimental animals. II. Study of the blood serum of patients with the nuclear forms of schizophrenia. *Zh. Nevropatol. i Psikhiatrii*, **65**, 247–50 (1965)
21. Fedio, P., Mirsky, A. F., Smith, W. J., Parry, D. Reaction time and EEG activation in normal and schizophrenic subjects. *Electroencephalog. Clin. Neurophysiol.*, **13**, 923–26 (1961)
22. Feigenberg, I. M. Comparative electroencephalographic characteristics of various clinical groups of schizophrenia patients. *Zh. Nevropatol. i Psikhiatrii*, **64**, 567–74 (1964)
23. Feinberg, I., Koresko, R. L., Gottlieb, F. Further observations on electrophysiological sleep patterns in schizophrenia. *Comprehen. Psychiat.*, **6**, 21–24 (1965)
24. Fink, M., Itil, T., Clyde, D. The classification of psychoses by quantitative EEG measures. *Recent Advan. Biol. Psychiat.*, **8**, 305–12 (1965)

25. Fish, F. The unitary psychosis–a neurophysiological method. *Confinia Psychiat.*, **6**, 156–70 (1963)
26. Gamburg, A. L., Denisova, A. M. The effect of certain pharmacological preparations on the cerebral bioelectrical activity in schizophrenia. *Zh. Nevropatol. i Psikhiatrii*, **64**, 116–24 (1964)
27. German, G. A., Antebi, R. N., Dear, E. M. A., McCance, C. A further study of the effects of serum from schizophrenics on evoked cortical potentials in rats. *Brit. J. Psychiat.*, **111**, 345–47 (1965)
28. Gibbs, F., Gibbs, E. *Atlas of Electroencephalography*, 2nd ed. (Addison-Wesley, Reading, Mass., 2 vols., 1951)
29. Goldman, D. Electroencephalographic manifestations associated with psychotic illness: Pentothal activation technique and pharmacologic interrelationships. *Comprehen. Psychiat.*, **5**, 80–92 (1964)
30. Goldstein, L., Sugerman, A. A., Stolberg, H. Electro-cerebral activity in schizophrenic and non-psychotic subjects: Quantitative EEG amplitude analysis. *Electroencephalog. Clin. Neurophysiol.*, **19**, 350–61 (1965)
31. Greenberg, I. M., Pollack, M. Clinical correlates of 14 and 6/sec positive spiking in schizophrenic patients. *Electroencephalog. Clin. Neurophysiol.*, **20**, 197–200 (1966)
32. Greenblatt, M. Psychosurgery. In *Comprehensive Textbook of Psychiatry*, 1291–95 (Freedman, A. M., Kaplan, H. I., Eds., Williams & Wilkins, Baltimore, 1666 pp., 1967)
33. Gromoll, H. F. *The Process-Reactive Dimension of Schizophrenia in Relation to Cortical Activation and Arousal* (Doctoral thesis, Univ. Illinois, Urbana, Ill., 1961)
34. Hartmann, E. The D-state and mental illness. In *The Biology of Dreaming* (Boston State Hosp. Monogr. Ser. No. 2, Kugelmass, I. N., Ed., Charles C Thomas, Springfield, Ill., 206 pp., 1967)
35. Heath, R. G. Developments toward new physiologic treatments in psychiatry. *J. Neuropsychiat.*, **5**, 318–31 (1964)
36. Heath, R. G. Factors altering brain function and behavior in schizophrenia. In *Recent Research on Schizophrenia*, 178–98 (Solomon, P., Glueck, B., Jr., Eds., Psychiat. Res. Rept. No. 19, The Am.

Psychiat. Assoc., Washington, D.C., 205 pp., 1964)

37. Hill, D. Electroencephalogram in schizophrenia. In *Schizophrenia: Somatic Aspects*, 33–51 (Richter, D., Ed., Pergamon Press, London, 181 pp., 1957)

38. Hutt, S. J., Hutt, C., Lee, D., Ounsted, C. A behavioral and electroencephalographic study of autistic children. *J. Psychiat. Res.*, **3**, 181–97 (1965)

39. Itil, T. M. Quantitative EEG changes induced by anticholinergic drugs and their behavioral correlates in man (panel discussion). *Recent Advan. Biol. Psychiat.*, **8**, 151–73 (1965)

40. Jasper, H. H. Recent advances in our understanding of ascending activities of the reticular system. In *Henry Ford Hospital Symposium on Reticular Formation of the Brain*, 319–31 (Jasper, H. H., Proctor, L. D., Knighton, W. G., Noshay, W. G., Costello, R. T., Eds., Little, Brown, Boston, 766 pp., 1958)

41. Jones, R. T., Blacker, K. H., Callaway, E. Perceptual dysfunction in schizophrenia: Clinical and auditory evoked response findings. *Am. J. Psychiat.*, **123**, 639–45 (1966)

42. Jones, R. T., Blacker, K. H., Callaway, E., Layne, R. S. The auditory evoked response as a diagnostic and prognostic measure in schizophrenia. *Am. J. Psychiat.*, **122**, 33–41 (1965–1966)

43. Jouvet, M. The pharmacology of sleep. In *Proc. 6th Ann. Meeting Am. Coll. Neuropsychopharmacol.* (In press)

44. Kamenskaia, V. M., Aleksandrovskii, I. U. A. Clinico-electroencephalographic study of the effect of haloperidol on schizophrenics. *Zh. Nevropatol. i Psikhiatrii*, **64**, 896–902 (1964)

45. Kety, S. S. Current biochemical approaches to schizophrenia. *New Engl. J. Med.*, **276**, 325–31 (1967)

46. Khaime, T. B. Organic pathologies of the brain in schizophrenia. *Zh. Nevropatol. i Psikhiatrii*, **67**, 113–18 (1967)

47. Koella, W. Discussion of M. Jouvet's paper "The pharmacology of sleep". In *Proc. 6th Ann. Meeting Am. Coll. Neuropsychopharmacol.* (In press)

48. Korchinskaia, E. I. Comparative electroencephalographic characteristics of patients with pfropf-schizophrenia and patients with noncomplicated malignant schizophrenia. *Zh. Nevropatol. i Psikhiatrii*, **65**, 263–67 (1965)

49. Kornetsky, C. Attention dysfunction and drugs in schizophrenia. In *Neuro-psycho-pharmacology. Proc. 5th Intern. Congr. Collegium Internationale Neuro-psycho-pharmacologicum*, 948–54 (Brell, H., Ed., Excerpta Medica Found., Amsterdam, 1277 pp., 1967)

50. Kornetsky, C., Mirsky, A. F. On certain psychopharmacological and physiological differences between schizophrenic and normal persons. *Psychopharmacologia*, **8**, 309–18 (1966)

51. Kostandov, E. A. Changes in the cortex-subcortical relationships under the influence of chlorpromazine. *Zh. Vysshei Nervnoi Deyatel' nosti im I. P. Pavlov*, **14**, 397–405 (1964)

52. Kury, G., Cobb, S. Epileptic Dementia resembling schizophrenia: Clinico-pathological report of a case. *J. Nerv. Ment. Dis.*, **138**, 340–47 (1964)

53. Latz, A., Kornetsky, C. A comparison of the effects of benzquinamide with those of chlorpromazine and secobarbital on a number of performance tests in chronic schizophrenics. *Pharmacologist*, **5**, 233 (1964)

54. Lester, B. K., Edwards, R. J. EEG fast activity in schizophrenic and control subjects. *Intern. J. Neuropsychiat.*, **2**, 143–56 (1966)

55. Liberson, W. T. Functional electroencephalography in mental disorders. *Dis. Nervous Sys.*, **5**, 357–64 (1944)

56. Libus, J., Dusek, K. Electroencephalographic patterns in schizophrenia treated with ataractics. *Activtas Nervosa Super.*, **7**, 255 (1965)

57. Lindsley, D. B., Bowden, J. W., Magoun, H. W. Effect upon the EEG of acute injury to the brain stem activating system. *Electroencephalog. Clin. Neurophysiol.*, **1**, 475–86 (1949)

58. Lippold, O. C. J., Redfearn, J. W. T. Mental changes resulting from the passage of small direct currents through the human brain. *Brit. J. Psychiat.*, **110**, 768–72 (1964)

59. Mannering, G. J. Significance of stimulation and inhibition of drug metabolism in pharmacologic test-

ing. In *Pharmacological Testing Methods* (Berger, A., Ed., Marcel Dekker, New York, in press)

60. Marjerrison, G., Krause, A. E., Keogh, R. P. Variability of the EEG in schizophrenia: Quantitative analysis with a modulus voltage integrator. *Electroencephalog. Clin. Neurophysiol.*, 24, 35–41 (1968)

61. Mirsky, A. F., Kornetsky, C. On the dissimilar effects of drugs on the digit symbol substitution and continuous performance tests. *Psychopharmacologia*, 5, 161–77 (1964)

62. Mirsky, A. F., Pragay, E. B. The relation of EEG and performance in altered states of consciousness. In *Sleep and Altered States of Consciousness*, 514–34 (Kety, S. S., Evarts, E. V., Williams, H. L., Eds., Williams & Wilkins, Baltimore, 591 pp., 1967)

63. Mirsky, A. F., Primac, D., Ajmone-Marsan, C., Rosvold, H. E., Stevens, J. A comparison of the psychological test performance of patients with focal and nonfocal epilepsy. *Exptl. Neurol.*, 2, 75–89 (1960)

64. Monroe, R. R., Kramer, M. D., Goulding, R., Wise, S. EEG activation of patients receiving phenothiazines and chlordiazepoxide. *J. Nerv. Ment. Dis.*, 141, 100–7 (1965)

65. Monroe, R. R., Mickle, W. A. Alpha chloralose-activated electroencephalograms in psychiatric patients. *J. Nerv. Ment. Dis.*, 144, 59–68 (1967)

66. Moruzzi, G., Magoun, H. W. Brain stem reticular formation and activation of the EEG. *Electroencephalog. Clin. Neurophysiol.*, 1, 455–73 (1949)

67. Musil, J., Skalickova, O. Biochemical aspects of schizophrenia. *Cesk. Psychiat.*, 63, 264–73 (1967)

68. Nemtsov, A. V., Faivishevskii, V. A. The action of blood serum from schizophrenic patients on the electric activity of the brain in experimental animals. III. On the multiple components of the active factor in the blood serum of patients with periodic schizophrenia. *Zh. Nevropatol. i Psikhiatrii*, 65, 1197–1200 (1965)

69. Nemtsov, A. V., Faivishevskii, V. A. Effect of blood serum from patients with schizophrenia on cerebral electrical activity of experimental animals. I. Investigation of serum from patients in acute stage. *Fed-eration Proc. (Transl. Suppl.)*, 24, 450–54 (1965)

70. Onheiber, P., White, P. T., DeMyer, M. K., Ottinger, D. R. Sleep and dream patterns of child schizophrenics. *Arch. Gen. Psychiat.*, 12, 568–71 (1965)

71. Ornitz, E. M., Ritvo, E. R., Walter, R. D. Dreaming sleep in autistic twins. *Arch. Gen. Psychiat.*, 12, 77–79 (1965)

72. Orzack, M. H., Kornetsky, C. Attention dysfunction in chronic schizophrenia. *Arch. Gen. Psychiat.*, 14, 323–26 (1966)

73. Orzack, M. H., Kornetsky, C., Freeman, H. The effects of daily administration of carphenazine on attention in the schizophrenic patient. *Psychopharmacologia*, 11, 31–38 (1967)

74. Osmond, H., Hoffner, A. A comprehensive theory of schizophrenia. *Intern. J. Neuropsychiat.*, 2, 302–9 (1966)

75. Pfeiffer, C. C., Goldstein, L., Murphree, H. B., Sugerman, A. A. Time-series, frequency analysis, and electrogenesis of the EEGs of normals and psychotics before and after drugs. *Am. J. Psychiat.*, 121, 1147–55 (1965)

76. Redfearn, J. W. T., Lippold, O. C. J., Costain, R. A preliminary account of the clinical effects of polarizing the brain in certain psychiatric disorders. *Brit. J. Psychiat.*, 110, 773–85 (1964)

77. Redlich, F. C., Freedman, D. X. *The Theory and Practice of Psychiatry* (Basic Books, New York, 880 pp., 1966)

78. Roberts, D. R. Schizophrenia and the brain. *J. Neuropsychiat.*, 5, 71–79 (1963)

79. Rosvold, H. E., Mirsky, A. F., Sarason, I., Bransome, E. D., Jr., Beck, L. H. A continuous performance test of brain damage. *J. Consult. Psychol.*, 20, 343–50 (1956)

80. Sagarra, J. S. Schizophrenia and temporal epilepsy in neuropsychiatric practice. *Arch. de Neurobiol. (Madrid)*, 28, 580–89 (1965)

81. Salamon, I., Post, J. Alpha blocking and schizophrenia. I. Methodology and initial studies. *Arch. Gen. Psychiat.*, 13, 367–74 (1965)

82. Schooler, C., Feldman, S. E. *Experimental Studies of Schizophrenia* (Psychonomic Press, Goleta, Calif., 260 pp., 1967)

83. Scoville, W. B. Late results of orbital undercutting. Report of 76 patients undergoing quantitative selective lobotomies. *Am. J. Psychiat.*, **117**, 525–32 (1960)

84. Scoville, W. B., Milner, B. Loss of recent memory after bilateral hippocampal lesion. *J. Neurol. Neurosurg. Psychiat.*, **20**, 11–21 (1957)

85. Sem-Jacobsen, C. W., Petersen, M. C., Dodge, H. W., Jr., Lazarte, J. A., Holman, C. B. Electroencephalographic rhythms from the depths of the parietal, occipital and temporal lobes in man. *Electroencephlog. Clin. Neurophysiol.*, **8**, 263–78 (1956)

86. Sem-Jacobsen, C. W., Petersen, M. C., Lazarte, J. A., Dodge, H. W., Jr., Holman, C. B. Electroencephalographic rhythms from the depths of the frontal lobe in 60 psychotic patients. *Electroencephalog. Clin. Neurophysiol.*, **7**, 193–210 (1955)

87. Shagass, C., Schwartz, M. Evoked potential studies in psychiatric patients. *Ann. N. Y. Acad. Sci.*, **112**, 526–42 (1964)

88. Shagass, C., Schwartz, M. Visual cerebral evoked response characteristics in a psychiatric population. *Am. J. Psychiat.*, **121**, 979–87 (1965)

89. Slater, E., Beard, A. W., Glithero, E. Schizophrenia-like psychoses of epilepsy. *Intern. J. Psychiat.*, **1**, 6–30 (1965)

90. Small, J. G., Small, I. F., Surphilis, W. R. Temporal EEG abnormalities in acute schizophrenia. *Am. J. Psychiat.*, **121**, 262–64 (1964/1965)

91. Small, J. G., Stevens, J. R., Milstein, V. Electro-clinical correlates of emotional activation of the electroencephalogram. *J. Nerv. Ment. Dis.*, **138**, 146–55 (1964)

92. Speck, L. B., Dim, B., Mercer, M. Visual evoked responses of psychiatric patients. *Arch. Gen. Psychiat.*, **15**, 59–63 (1966)

93. Stammeyer, E. C. The Effects of Distraction of Performance in Schizophrenic, Psychoneurotic, and Normal Individuals (Doctoral dissertation, The Catholic Univ. of Am. Press, Washington, D.C., 1961)

94. Stenhouse, D., Antebi, R., Dear, E. M. A., Herrington, R. N., McCance, C. Effect of serum from schizophrenics on evoked cortical potentials in the rat. *Brit. J. Psychiat.*, **111**, 339–44 (1965)

95. Struve, F. A., Becka, D. R. The rela-

tive incidence of the B-mitten EEG pattern in process and reactive schizophrenia. *Electroencephalog. Clin. Neurophysiol.*, **24**, 80–82 (1968)

96. Throne, M. L., Gowdey, C. W. A critical review of endogenous psychotoxins as a cause of schizophrenia. *Can. Psychiat. Assoc. J.*, **12**, 159–74 (1967)

97. Tucker, G. J., Detre, T., Harrow, M., Glaser, G. H. Behavior and symptoms of psychiatric patients and the electroencephalogram. *Arch. Gen. Psychiat.*, **12**, 278–86 (1965)

98. Ulett, G. A., Bowers, C. A., Heusler, A. F., Quick, R., Word, T., Word, V. A study of the behavior and EEG patterns of patients receiving tranquilizers with and without the addition of chlordiazepoxide. *J. Neuropsychiat.*, **5**, 558–65 (1964)

99. Vas, C. J., Exley, K. A., Parsonage, M. J. An appraisal of hyoscine as an EEG activating agent. *Electroencephalog. Clin. Neurophysiol.*, **22**, 373–77 (1967)

100. Venables, P. H. Input dysfunction in schizophrenia. *Progr. Exptl. Pers. Res.*, **1**, 1–47 (1964)

101. Venables, P. H., Wing, J. K. Level of arousal and the subclassification of schizophrenia. *Arch. Gen. Psychiat.*, **7**, 114–19 (1962)

102. Vishnevskaya, A. A. Clinical and EEG data in schizophrenia running a protracted course with remissions in adolescents. In *Problemy Psikhvnevrologii Detskogo Vozrasta*, 151–62 (Fedotov, D. D., Ed., Ministerstvo Zdravookhraneniya RSFSR, Moscow, 532 pp., 1964)

103. Volavka, J., Matousek, M., Roubicek, J. EEG frequency analysis in schizophrenia. An attempt to reconsider the role of age. *Acta Psychiat. Scand.*, **42**, 237–45 (1966)

104. White, P. T., DeMyer, W., DeMyer, M. EEG abnormalities in early childhood schizophrenia: A double-blind study of psychiatrically disturbed and normal children during promazine sedation. *Am. J. Psychiat.*, **120**, 950–58 (1963/1964)

105. Wiener, H. External chemical messengers, III. Mind and body in schizophrenia. *N. Y. State J. Med.*, **67**, 1287–310 (1967)

106. Wilson, W. P., Hughes, J. L. Observations on the effects of JB-329 (ditran) on the electroencephalogram of man. *J. Neurospychiat.*, **5**, 310–15 (1964)

HUMAN ABILITIES[1]

140

By Edwin A. Fleishman

American Institutes for Research, Washington, D. C.

and C. J. Bartlett

University of Maryland and American Institutes for Research, Washington, D. C.

Until 1965 reviews of research covering the field of human abilities in the *Annual Review of Psychology* appeared under the title of "Individual Differences." The present review is only the second under the more restrictive heading of "Human Abilities," the first having been written by Ferguson (52) in 1965. The present review covers roughly the 4 years since Ferguson's review, from early 1964 to April 1968.

Although the field of Human Abilities helps delimit an area of Individual Differences, it is still much too broad to cover in all its aspects within the present page allotment, especially in coverage of a 4-year period. Part of the problem is definitional, since the term "human ability" is often used to encompass a variety of human performances and achievements. We shall deal with the definitional problem shortly.

Following the tradition established by Ferguson, this review excludes the literature specifically concerned with methodologies such as factor analyses and psychological test theory. Factor analysis is one of several multivariate statistical methods with applications in many different areas of psychology. Similarly, work on such topics as scaling, the logic of measurement, and new statistical methods have application beyond the human ability area. We will deal with such studies here only in the context of substantive information about the nature of human abilities or the factors affecting them. Similarly, we will not provide a survey of new tests or new test applications, or even new data on old tests, topics more appropriate for Buros' *Mental Measurement Yearbook* (21), the sixth edition of which was published in 1964. This includes the large amount of work which continues to be produced on such widely used tests as the Wechsler and Binet measures of intelligence. For a major review of research with the Wechsler Adult Scale from 1960 to 1965, see Guertin et al. (80).

We have chosen to exclude also the vast and growing literature on mental retardation and mental disease. It is hoped these topics will receive the attention they deserve in other *Annual Review* chapters. Finally, with the increased support for research in educational settings in recent years there

[1] This review was facilitated, in part, by Contract #F-44620-67-C-0116 with the Advanced Research Projects Agency for "The Development and Verification of a Taxonomy of Human Performance." The writers are greatly indebted to Susan B. Silverman for extensive assistance throughout the preparation of this review.

has been a sharp increase in publications on school achievements and factors affecting achievement in specific skill areas. As in the case of all the other areas excluded, we have reviewed the articles in these areas but will reference here only those studies which help illuminate more general issues of human ability.

The general theme of this review is to consider human abilities as general traits or capacities within individuals on which performance in a variety of specific tasks depend.

Theoretical and Conceptual Issues

Elsewhere, Fleishman (58–60) has discussed some conceptual issues regarding the term "ability" and the place of this construct in general psychological theory. Abilities are seen as representing a class of "mediating processes," identified through combinations of experimental and correlational research, in terms of score consistencies among separate performances. An ability is postulated to account for observed consistencies in performance, obtained after variations in stimuli and response requirements. The distinction is made between ability and skill (achievement), the former being more general to performance across different tasks, and the latter referring to level of proficiency attained on a specific task. Such proficiency (skill) may depend on one or a combination of abilities. The role of learning and maturation in the development of abilities, the relation of abilities to transfer of learning, and abilities as learning parameters are discussed in these and earlier papers. Abilities are viewed as relatively stable attributes, probably a result of phenomena such as overlearning, and are seen as exerting their influence through differential transfer in subsequent learning of different tasks. These formulations, and the experimental data, are in line with Ferguson's (50, 51) earlier theoretical development. Elsewhere, Fleishman (59, 66) has suggested that the ability-skill paradigm proposed is consistent with an information-processing model of human learning in which abilities represent capacities for processing different kinds of information (e.g., spatial, proprioceptive, verbal). The paradigm seems useful in conceptualizing the systematic changes in correlations which the author and others have obtained between ability measures and performance at different stages of learning more complex skills (56, 66).

A major treatment of the nature of intelligence, and a review of alternative theories of intelligence, has been provided by Guilford's article (81) and his latest book (82). The book makes a major attempt to integrate his structure of intellect model with traditional psychological problems in the areas of perception, learning, retention, problem solving, and creative thinking. Guilford continues to follow through the implications of his matrix model, in which intellectual abilities are classified along three dimensions: kind of operation performed (cognition, memory, divergent and covergent production, evaluation); kind of content on which the operations are performed (figural, symbolic, semantic, behavioral); and kind of product resulting from the operations on the content (units, classes, relations, systems, transformations, implications). The model leads to the continued search and identification of new factors within categories and cells of the three-dimensional matrix.

The proliferation of factors has been criticized (see e.g., 134), but the argument will not be settled until the various factors have been shown to have meaning and utility beyond the factor analytic context. Perhaps a more general model is required. Fleishman (61, 62) has called for the development of a taxonomy of human abilities which will link laboratory and "real world" tasks and will allow more dependable generalizations of experimental data. Guttman (85) has proposed a facet model of logically derived dimensions which is at once similar, but simpler, than Guilford's matrix model. However, Guttman's has not yet been fully developed.

Cattell's theory of fluid and crystallized intelligence (27, 103) generated some empirical work during this period. "Crystallized intelligence" (Gc) is postulated as more highly involved in cognitive tasks in which skilled habits have become "crystallized" as the result of earlier learning. "Fluid intelligence" (Gf) is more involved in tasks requiring adaptation to new situations, where crystallized skills, developed from prior learning, are of no great advantage. Fluid intelligence is thought to be more hereditary, whereas crystallized intelligence depends more on environmental factors. Fluid intelligence is thought to level off at 14 or 15 years, whereas crystallized intelligence may increase to 25 or 30 or beyond. Extrapolations from the theory allow postulations about the effects of general brain damage (greater effect on fluid intelligence) and cultural variables, etc. Within the constraints of the factor analytic methodology employed, these two kinds of intelligence are seen as represented by second order factors derived from clusters of primary general factors within each category. Studies during this period designed to explore implications of the theory have been reported by Cattell (29), Horn (100), Horn & Bramble (101) and Horn & Cattell (102–104).

Humphreys (107) was critical of the earlier Cattell (29) study, especially in terms of methodology, and reanalyzed the original data as well as the Horn-Cattell (103) data. The general conclusion, however, even in Humphreys' reanalysis, is that the evidence pointed to two broad patterns of the kind referred to in the Gf-Gc theory. Humphreys points out, however, that in many respects the Gf-Gc theory is congruent with heirarchical-group factor theories put forth by investigators such as Vernon (187) and Burt (22).

Like Cattell's theory, the theoretical developments stemming from the work of Piaget (153) and his followers ascribes a central role to both environment and developmental influences. However, despite the volume of references to Piaget's work, mainly in foreign journals, his work has had relatively little impact on the psychometrically oriented study of abilities. The work often seems unclear to American differential psychologists because it appears as anecdotal, clinical, and generally methodologically loose. Piaget's theory does not recognize individual differences and hence is difficult to incorporate into traditional approaches. His view is that understanding how individuals acquire and use knowledge is the key to understanding intelligence; his research aims, to a great extent, at discovering the logical laws governing thought. Knowledge is developed early in life through organized innate sensorimotor action sequences (schemata). The individual's knowledge (cognitive structure) is generated from the functioning of these few hereditary schemata, which change by modification to become largely acquired schemata. The two important ways of schema building are assimilation and accommodation. A mass of observational data has been accumulated based on observations and comparisons of children's performances at different ages on tasks involving number, quantity, time, movement, velocity, spatial relations, reasoning, etc.

Ferguson (52) in his earlier review chapter questioned whether the work of Piaget and his followers can be brought usefully into any clear relation with the more psychometric research discipline. Guilford (82) has made an important attempt to come to grips with Piaget's ideas (one of the few American psychologists to do so), and he is able to draw parallels with his own structure of intellect model. Gyr, Brown & Cafagna (86) have tested experimentally some implications of Piaget for identifying cognitive styles of development; but Ranzi & Tampieri (155) are critical of the adequacy of the theory for explaining the genesis of cognitive structures.

Wesman (190) discusses the nature of intelligence as representing summations of learning experiences of the individual. He decries the search for the structure of intelligence and prefers to think of intelligence as unstructured; that is, differentially comprised in every individual—the sum total of his learning experiences at a given moment in time. Such structure as we perceive is structure we have imposed. The problem becomes one of sampling these previous learnings relevant to the particular learnings we wish to predict. In some cases we may wish to use homogeneous domains such as verbal, numerical, and spatial abilities; in other cases we may want to sample from a wider variety of learnings and apply labels such as "intelligence." The utility criterion is also used by Wesman to distinguish between aptitude and achievement, which he says cannot be distinguished on the basis of test content.

Critical examination of the concepts of intelligence and ability have been presented in foreign jounals by Oleron (144), Hofstatter (97) Meili (138), and Rican (157), and Leites (127) has reviewed the views of Teplov on individual differences and abilities.

Organization of Abilities

Factor analytic studies continue to be the predominant form of empirical investigation in describing ability interrelations and in defining ability dimensions. Some of these are in fairly specialized new areas, such as ability to spell (1), auditory signal detection abilities (91), oral communication (137), and mathematical ability (188). The literature still has its share of poorly designed or undesigned shotgun studies which do not yield much useful information. Programmatic efforts are becoming even more rare.

The most prolific program continues to be that of Guilford and his associates who take their cues from the structure of intellect model and conclude that the model continues to lead fruitfully to yet other undiscovered differentiable intellectual abilities. Thus, Hoepfner, Nihira & Guilford (96) found evidence for the distinction between symbolic and semantic evaluation and between these and other factors in the model; Hoepfner, Guilford & Merrifield (95) conducted a large scale analysis of 54 measures specifically designed to clarify the status of six hypothesized abilities of symbolic evaluations. The latter area appears especially critical to "mathematical thinking." Guilford & Hoepfner (83) replicated factors in the divergent-production abilities area with ninth-grade students. Several studies in the area of memory (179) helped define the kinds of stimulus materials and processes which best define separate memory functions; memory factors seem quite distinct from cognition and evaluation abilities. The picture in this area is less than clear, but methodological problems in the study of memory are not unique to factor analytic studies. However, Guilford (82) makes an important effort to reconcile the structure of intellect model with recent experimental data on short and long term memory. A useful report from this program summarizes and defines the structure of intellect factors thus far established and lists the marker tests recommended to represent each factor (83).

Another important review is provided by Merrifield (139), who reviewed trends in the measurement of special abilities. He foresees continued active development of orthogonally depicted measures of separate abilities, probably, within the plan of the structure of intellect, with greater attention to issues of validity.

Fleishman (55, 56, 58, 59) continues his programmatic efforts in defining the areas of perceptual-motor abilities. A major publication during this period was the book, *The Structure and Measurement of Physical Fitness* (55), summarizing his work in the area of physical proficiency measurement. The area of physical fitness measurement is reviewed and hypotheses generated based on earlier factor analytic and correlational studies. After a critical analysis of 100 commonly used tests, two large-scale factor analytic studies, including established and experimental tests, were designed to clarify the distinctions among hypothesized factors and to investigate their role in a variety of physical performances. Nine primary factors were identified and labeled: Static Strength, Explosive Strength, Dynamic Strength, Trunk Strength, Extent Flexibility, Dynamic Flexibility, Gross Body Coordination, Equilibrium, and Stamina. The *Basic Fitness Tests* were developed as a battery to measure the indicated factors and an *Examiner's Manual* (54) prepared. The book presents a theoretical model of human strength consistent with both the factor analytic results and a physiological-mechanical model of muscle systems. Also presented are developmental curves and national norms for tests of the various factors.

A major review of the organization and definition of spatial abilities and their educational and social significance was provided by Smith (166).

Some light on the structure of human abilities during the high-school years is provided by Project TALENT, a large-scale cross-sectional and longitudinal study of over 400,000 high-school students, carried out by the American Institutes for Research (e.g., 34, 53). These students were given a comprehensive 2-day battery of tests in 1960 and are now being followed up on a long-term basis. Several factor analyses, based on varying segments of this vast body of data, have been carried out by Shaycoft (160) and Cureton (39). The factor patterns were surprisingly similar for boys and girls. One of the few differences was that for the girls there were two English factors encompassing the grade 9 to 12 range, instead of just one such factor. Another difference is that the math factor accounts for substantially more variance in the case of the boys than for the girls. A few other sex differences in factor pattern were found, but they are either trivial or have obvious explanations based on known sex differences in interests and behavior patterns.

A very large number of test-specific factors were found representing reliable overlapping variance for corresponding grade 9 and grade 12 variables. This was taken as evidence that it is a serious mistake to assume when a factor analysis is based on data obtained at only one point in time that just the common factors are important. Patterns of abilities have involved a substantial number of stable components that don't overlap the usual "common factors" at all.

Cooley (33) applied mulivariate techniques to the grade 9 TALENT data and the corresponding grade 12 retest data to study interactions among interests, abilities, and career plans. He found that when shifts of interests occur, shifts of abilities tend to follow. He also found evidence for the converse relationship: shifts of abilities are followed by shifts of interest.

The Project TALENT data found relative constancy in factor patterns of abilities during the adolescent years. This stability seems to be characteristic of the findings for earlier and later years as well. For example, Quereshi (154) provides an encouraging study of the invariance of certain ability factors, for 7 independent samples of 100 children each, with respect to (a) consistency of factors for a fixed set of variables, across samples; and (b) consistency for a fixed sample, from one set of variabled to another. With respect to changes in factor structure with age, some clarity may be emerging with respect to the "ability differentiation hypothesis": that there is a fractionating down of general ability into a number of specialized abilities with increasing age. In general, little support was found for this hypothesis during this period. Thus, Osborne & Lindsey (146) find more stability than change across preschool, grade 1, and grade 3 levels, and Weiner (189) has found stability in the proportion of common variance accounted for by a general factor across seven different age groups ranging from early adolescence to 54 years of age. Hundal (108) has reported invariance of factor pattern of abilities from grades 9 through 11.

During this period, a number of factor analytic studies were carried out on special groups of handicapped or subnormal groups. Thus, Juurmaa (119) summarizes findings of the organization of abilities among blind and deaf groups, and Dingman & Meyers (43) summarize the role of factor analysis in mental retardation research. Other relevant studies with mental retardates are those of Belmont, Birch & Belmont (13, Smith 168), and Kebbon (121).

The concept of creativity and its relation to intelligence continues to generate interest. Evidence has been accumulated to support the concept of a threshold of intelligence in relating creative ability to achievement, as well as in the relationship between creative ability and intelligence. Yamamoto (191) classified highly creative secondary school students into three groups of intelligence, finding that the high and middle IQ groups were superior in achievement to the low IQ groups, yet he found no significant difference between the high and middle groups. In another study, Yamamoto (192) finds that the correlation between IQ and creative ability shows a consistent decline as level of IQ increases. Further evidence of the threshold of ability concept is offered by Yamamoto & Chimbidis (193), where a correlation with intelligence was .5 for children with IQ scores below 120, but only .2 for children with IQ above 120. Similar findings are reported by Hasan & Butcher (92) with Scottish children. It seems clear that creative ability is not likely to be high if intelligence levels are in the average range or below; however, high IQ does not assure high creative ability. A major review of his program on creativity has been provided by Taylor (177).

HUMAN ABILITY, LEARNING, AND TRAINING

During the past few years, some provocative lines of inquiry have opened up on the relation between human abilities and learning. The important book, *Learning and Individual Differences*, edited by Gagné (74), indicates that experimental psychologists at last are becoming aware of the need to consider individual differences as more than troublesome error variance. The chapters by Anderson (8), Fleishman (59, 60), Jensen (114), and Zeaman & House (195) are perhaps the most relevant to the class of individual difference variables called human abilities.

The general misconception of defining intelligence as the "ability to learn" dies hard, but the evidence against this notion continues to accumulate [(e.g., Duncanson (46), Carver (25), Harootunian (89), Guilford (82) and Zeaman & House (195)]. The evidence comes from several sources: (a) factor analyses have shown that intelligence is not a unitary ability; (b) correlations between IQ and gain (however measured) resulting from training are often quite low; (c) improvement in one task is often uncorrelated with improvement in other tasks. Under special conditions, intelligence may be correlated with rate of learning, but this is not a necessary relationship. Level of achievement after learning or at different stages of learning is more predictable from ability measures than is rate of learning [see e.g., Fleishman (63)].

The problems of adapting instruction to individual differences in human abilities are effectively reviewed by Cronbach (37). Cronbach & Gleser (38) have shown that aptitude information is not useful in adapting instruction unless the aptitude and treatment interact—more specifically, unless the regression line relating aptitude to payoff under one treatment crosses the regression line for the competing treatment. The aptitude measure that validly predicts success for both treatments may have no value in deciding what treatment to give. This implies that general ability is likely to be a poor basis for differentiating instruction.

Some work on ability-training method interaction has been carried out during this period. Early in work on programmed learning it was thought that linear small-step programs would succeed with everyone. Stolurow (170) reports that learning from a set of irregularly sequenced exercises correlated with general ability, but when the same exercises were formed into a well-sequenced program the correlation vanished. The sequence, Stolurow says, does for the poorer students what the good ones can do for themselves. Stolurow (171) reviewed studies showing interactions between abilities and techniques employed in self-instructional programs. The evidence suggests that programs featuring knowledge of results, overt responding, and immediate feedback make a difference for low ability students, but that high ability students do just as well in programs without these features. Anderson (8) reviews some additional studies and issues related to the interpretation and practical utility results showing aptitude-training condition interactions. Taylor & Fox (178), using learning tasks based on Gagné's categories of learning (73), in a series of significant studies also found significant interactions between different training methods and ability levels. However, this depended on the category of learning task. These workers stratified on a general ability measure and worked with low aptitude airmen. Had they used differential ability measures related to each task category, they might have obtained more interactions.

One of the difficulties in studies of this kind is the problem of confounding method and subject matter content so that it is not possible to determine whether reported interactions are with learner abilities and training methods or between learner abilities and course content. This is illustrated in a study by Bush and co-workers (24). Important reports dealing with questions of learner abilities and instructional methods are those of Briggs (17), Briggs and associates (18), and Tallmadge (175). Clearly, more studies relating training methods and human abilities need to be carried out, and it is likely that such studies will increase in the years ahead.

Fleishman (58, 59) has summarized his programmatic work, investigating relations between ability reference tests and performances at different stages of learning more complex tasks, utilizing combinations of experimental, correlational and factor analytic methods. These studies, with a wide variety of perceptual-motor tasks, indicate that (a) the particular combinations of abilities contributing to performance change as practice continues; (b) these changes are progressive and systematic and eventually become stabilized; and, at least in perceptual motor tasks, (c) the contribution of "non motor" abilities (e.g., verbal, spatial) which may play a role in early learning, decreases systematically with practice, relative to motor abilities; and (d) there is also an increase in a factor specific to the task itself. Later studies in this series have attempted to define more clearly the variables accounting for variance at advanced levels of proficiency after training. During the period under review, these general findings have been replicated by Kohfeld (124); extended to concept learning tasks by Bunderson (19), Manley (136), and by Dunham, Guilford & Hoepfner (47); and extended to verbal tasks by Fredericksen (70). Earlier, Fleishman & Fruchter (64) had demonstrated the same phenomena with an auditory-perceptual task (learning Morse Code), and Games (75) had found such changes for repeated memory span tasks.

Some alternative explanations have been offered for these results. Corballis (35) has suggested that changes in factor structure of performance measures over time, such as those represented in these studies, may be artifactual. Both he and Jones (117) observe that a matrix of intercorrelations between practice trials on some tasks may be fitted by a simplex. Corballis argues that it may be reasonable to assume that the factor loadings of a task remain constant from trial to trial but that the individual's factor scores change [a possibility also noted earlier by Humphreys (106)], and that this notion is compatible with the view that practice is a stochastic process. However, Corballis also observed that when criterion factors (defined independently of the practice matrix) are correlated with trial scores, the resulting change in correlations with practice can provide "fairly convincing evidence for genuine change in factor loadings with practice" [see (35), p. 404]. Jones (117), following through the implications of the simplical model, prefers to interpret the observed intertask and intratask correlation patterns as representing "learning as a process of simplification" in which the abilities necessary to the acquisition of skill in a given task become progressively fewer in number with practice. Fleishman (58) concurs on the general increase in specificity with practice, but argues that the factor analytic model is more heuristic in allowing for a better definition of the sources of variance at early and late stages of practice. His subsequent work (e.g., 56, 66) has identified additional abilities predictive of advanced levels of perceptual-motor learning.

Fredericksen (70), in a landmark study, prefers to interpret the changes in factorial composition with practice as reflecting changes in "strategies" employed in early learning which may be quite different from those employed later in learning. The consideration of strategies as mediating responses to the task situation may be important eventually in predicting changes in the factorial composition of a learning task with practice. This view is consistent with the "information processing" model of human abilities described by Fleishman (63).

Some earlier criticisms of the Fleishman series by Jones (118), who prefers a simplical model, and by Bechtoldt (12), who prefers a multiple regression model centered on the use of reference and practice task measures in the same matrix in the early Fleishman series. However, the same basic findings have been obtained with a variety of alternative factor analytic designs and experimental methods [see e.g., Fleishman (56)]. These included establishing the factor structure of reference measures separately and then projecting factor loadings of practice trials onto the reference factors, cross-sectional comparative factor analysis rather than longitudinal analysis, multiple regression analysis, and utilizing straight experimental procedures, where the subject's pretask abilities become major treatment variables whose interactions with learning trials can be investigated (66). The latter procedures appear most useful where the ability variables and measures are already well defined. Fruchter & Fleishman (72) reviewed some of these issues in the analysis of correlational learning data.

Other trends during this period included (a) the use of more sophisticated methods of analysis in relating abilities and learning; (b) the adoption of a more analytical framework of measurement for dealing with human performance measurement; and (c) the extension of studies of human abilities to other learning phenomena, such as transfer, reminiscence, interference and inhibition. The failure to find relationships between ability measures and learning performance may be due in part to the nature of the learning measures used. Bunderson (19) and Duncanson (46) used a variation of Tucker's (182) procedure for determining parameters of generalized learning curves. Bunderson found temporal changes in the contribution of abilities to scores in a concept learning task and Duncanson was able to identify three factors common to ability and such learning measures on concept formation, paired associate and rate memory tasks. He also found three factors specific to the learning measures, but in no case was a single "ability to learn" factor identified across learning tasks.

Ferguson (51), earlier, offered a theory of transfer and abilities which is strongly supported by the evidence on the changing factorial structure of learning tasks. The transfer function, symbolizing transfer from ability x to task y, takes the form $y = f(x, t_y)$; i.e., performance on y is a function of practice on y and level of ability on x (where t_y represents the amount of practice on y). The notion provides a link between learning and ability. Bunderson's (19) study, following up this notion, actually determined such transfer functions from several abilities to a concept learning task. An important implication of the notion of transfer and ability is that it enables one to consider the state of the organism as an important determiner within a theory of learning.

Fredericksen (70), in a complex experimental-correlational design, related ability and learning measures to test the theory that cognitive strategies, which are a function of task characteristics, and organism state (abilities) provide a mechanism of transfer from abilities to learning performance. The notion is that some abilities may function through the use of particular strategies. Thus, "associational fluency" may operate through choice of strategy involving the formation of associations, where "verbal closure" may be related to a strategy involving finding some structure in a list of words which facilitates recall. The consideration of strategies as mediators implies that transfer occurs from abilities to performance in the restructured learning task—restructured by the individual through his choice of strategy. An individual's being high or low in a particular ability may influence his performance by increasing or decreasing the probability that he will select specific strategies or by influencing, through positive transfer, his performance using these strategies. Fredericksen obtains considerable support for these hypotheses and these results help integrate Ferguson's transfer notions, the results of Fleishman's program on changing factor structure of tasks with practice, and much experimental data on verbal learning.

Fredericksen's results also support the plea by Jensen (111, 114) that by including procedural variables in factor analytical studies of human abilities we are more apt to discover more basic and pervasive genotypes of individual differences. In this connection, Fleishman (63) investigated relations between a range of ability measures and transfer, learning rate, and performance level measures, when a procedural variation was introduced in the learning of a perceptual-motor task (a change in display-control relations). The study showed that learning rates were not predictable from a subject's pretask abilities, but performance and independent transfer measures were predictable from abilities. Another procedural variable investigated was performance during a massed versus distributed practice schedule. Results showed that the same abilities predicted performance on the massed trial as was true on the distributed trials, but that prediction of performance during the trial following massed practice fell off dramatically. Apparently recovery from continuous practice following rest depends on different abilities.

Jensen (110, 112), has studied extensively other transfer and interference effects. Neither Fleishman nor Jensen could identify a general susceptibility to interference factor, as originally hypothesized by Don Lewis in the 1950's. Jensen's results tend to support three kinds of interference factors: one involving principally retroactive inhibition, one involving proactive inhibition, and one involving interference due to response competition. Fleishman (57) studied part-whole task learning in relation to ability concepts, and Fleishman & Fruchter (65) have studied changes in part-whole task relations as a function of practice and ability variables.

Tucker continues to make landmark contributions in mathematical-statistical methods required for the complex multivariate designs needed to investigate abilities and learning. Particularly significant during this period is his work on three-mode factor analysis (184) and new cluster analysis techniques (183). The former allows consideration, within a single multivariate analysis, of data classified by individuals, abilities measured, and occasion of measurement. The latter work opens up the possibility of studying the structure of individual differences of within-individual relations between variables. If clusters of individuals can be identified, theories of learning might be constructed such that special cases would be applicable for each cluster of individuals. These special case learning theories might fit the learning behavior of individuals better than a learning theory that ignored individual differences.

ABILITIES, TASK REQUIREMENTS, AND LABORATORY MEASUREMENT

Aside from the work on learning and abilities previously described, research attempting to integrate ability variables into the general framework of experimental psychology continue to be rare, but there are some hopeful signs.

Elsewhere, Fleishman (61, 62) describes a study attempting to relate ability variables to changes in task difficulty represented by systematic alterations of control-display relations in a perceptual-motor task. Subjects received a battery of reference ability measures and then performed on the criterion task under eight different degrees of display rotation. The factor analysis of criterion and reference measures showed systematic changes in ability requirements as a function of display rotation and consequent task difficulty. For example, as display rotation increased, loadings on perceptual speed, the primary factor measured in the 0° rotation position, dropped systematically, and two factors, spatial orientation and response orientation, increased systematically. Subsequent studies in this series have examined relations with ability variables of such task variables as stimulus-response compatibility, type of feedback provided, and predictability-nonpredictability of stimulus information. These studies would appear to open one way for laboratory based studies developing principles relating task dimensions to ability requirements, using combinations of experimental and correlational methods.

Following a similar paradigm, Lemke, Klausmeier & Harris (128) investigated the relation between selected cognitive abilities (e.g., perceptual speed, deduction, memory span) to performance on concept-attainment and information-processing tasks. They found that the abilities of general reasoning, induction, and verbal comprehension were related to the three concept-attainment and information-processing factors identified and that these two types of tasks represented relatively distinct activities. In a more comprehensive study, Manley (136) was able to identify three distinct concept formation factors in commonly used laboratory concept formation tasks and was able to define these in terms of reference ability test measures.

Locke, Zavala & Fleishman (130) studied the requirements of the complex task of helicopter piloting. Through a factor analysis of correlations among performances on 261 specific tasks, grouped into 18 maneuvers, they were able to identify common factors which seemed related to ability factors previously identified in laboratory research on perceptual-motor abilities.

An area receiving increased concern during this period was that of laboratory task development, which might allow more dependable generalization of treatment variable effects to real work tasks or to other laboratory tasks. The specification of task variables in terms of such general categories as verbal versus motor, cognitive versus non cognitive, just is not sufficient. On the other hand, highly specific descriptions such as represented by the task analysts are not adequate either. Do we need high fidelity simulations [e.g., Grodsky (78)], or are tasks representative of more general categories able to lead us out of the woods? Here is the challenge for psychologists concerned with human abilities who have heretofore worked in a psychometric tradition separate from these experimental concerns. Alluisi (3) has developed a standardized battery of laboratory tasks covering such categories as vigilance process, short-term memory, communication, procedural functions, intellectual, and motor functions. The tasks have a great deal of face validity for various operator jobs. They have been used in studies of confinement (30), long-term performance (4), and effects of infectious disease (5, 181). The nine categories implicit in Gagné's categories of learning (73) represented a basis for such task development, and Taylor & Fox (178) developed a battery based on this system for use in investigating differential effects of training methods. However, our knowledge of the interrelations among human performance would argue for greater specificity and diversity of functions within categories as broad as those offered by Alluisi or Gagné. Baker, Elkin, Van Cott & Fleishman (9) have developed tasks around factor analytically developed categories for study of drugs and other treatment variables. And Parker, Reilly, Dillon, Andrews & Fleishman (150) have developed a console for use in the space environment, which purports to measure separate perceptual-motor abilities identified in earlier studies. Whether or not these approaches will turn out to be useful in generalizing treatment effects remains to be seen.

Also relevant to the problem of choice of tasks to sample human abilities in skills research are the tasks described by Pearson (152) and by Passey & McLaurin (151). Chiles (30) provides an especially useful rationale for the test battery by him and by Alluisi in studies of the effects of stressful environments. Particularly helpful are the specifications of criteria for task selection and a discussion of performance interactions.

EFFECTS OF ENVIRONMENTS

Schneider & Bartlett (158) have contrasted the traditional role of the differential psychologists who have concentrated efforts on a search for ability measures which can be used to account for performance, with the experimental and social psychologists who have concentrated on environmental variables which influence or control performance. Studying the organismic ability measures and the environmental measures separately has not achieved a satisfactory explanation of human performance. Schneider & Bartlett have urged a combination of the differential and environmental approaches where not only are both domains taken into account, but the in-

teractions between ability and environmental variables are considered. Performance is a function of ability and situation, but different patterns of
ability may be required, depending on the situation. Furthermore, the nature
of ability may be differentially determined as a function of environment variables. Schneider & Bartlett have proposed a design for study of the interaction between individual difference measures and organizational climate.

Also relevant to this area are studies which have investigated the effect
of unusual environments on the ability to perform. Problems of space flight
and anticipated requirements for individuals to function in unusual environments (e.g., undersea) have stimulated increased concern for effects on
human abilities. Thus, Graybiel et al. (77) studied the effects of a rotating
environment (10 rpm) such as might be found in an orbiting space craft
over a period of 12 days. Functions assessed included static strength (dy-
namometer), reaction time, speed of arm movement, time estimation, memory span, verbal comprehension, numerical facility, and vigilance. The main
effects were the decrements in static strength on days 11 and 12 and a
slight drop in memory span and numerical facility. Alluisi, Chiles & Hall
(4) studied the effects of sleep loss on six performance tasks during 12-day
confinements, under different work-rest schedules. Performance was worse
on the 4 hr work–2 hr rest schedule compared with a 4–4 schedule, but
specific losses depended on the task and time-sharing requirements. Using
a similar battery of tasks, Alluisi, Thurmond & Coates (5) are investigating
the effects of man's incapacitations due to selected infectious diseases (e.g.,
tularemia). Decrements were most evident in what they call active tasks
(arithmetic computation and target identifications) relative to passive
tasks (e.g., monitoring), but recovery to baseline was less complete in these
latter tasks following treatment. There is a wide range of individual differences, however.

Evans (49) and Carver & Winsmann (26) have utilized Fleishman's
Basic Fitness Tests and other component ability measures to investigate
possible ability decrements under conditions of high altitude. Thus, Carver
found that an abrupt change to 13,000 ft did not affect dynamic, explosive,
or static strength or extent flexibility or cognitive functioning but did affect
stamina as measured by the 600 yard run-walk. Fox (68) recently has reviewed the effects of cold on different human capacities; Bowan, Anderson
& Promisel (16), Miller et al. (140), Zavala (194), and Parker (149) have
discussed problems of measuring human abilities in the underwater environment. Harris & Shoenberger (90) have found that decrements in performance
as a function of frequency of vibrations tended to follow the general shape
of the physiological tolerance curves, and Halcomb & Kirk (87) report a
decrement in ability to perform related to positive air ionization. An even
more exotic environment was studied by Shavelson & Seminara (159), who
found a simulation of lunar gravity (one-sixth g) resulted in a 25 per cent
decrement in performance on manual dexterity tasks, and impairment was
even greater (up to 150 per cent) when the subjects wore pressurized suits.

The Effects of Drugs

There has been an increasing interest in the effects of psychopharmacological agents and compounds upon human abilities. However, sophistication in experimental design and measurement techniques in human experimentation have lagged. Considerable reliance is still placed on clinical or physiological evidence, with not enough attention to development of standardized performance indices. Physiological and behavioral drug effects are not perfectly related. Compounds that apparently act by different physiological mechanisms may yield the same effects on human capabilities, and drugs assumed to act on the same physiological mechanisms may have different effects on specific human performances. The absence of an adequate taxonomy of pharamacological agents is a major limitation. What is needed is a methodology by means of which a profile of behavioral toxicity may be determined in much the same way as blood and urine analysis reveal physiological toxicity.

The problem of generalizing results of drug effects to different tasks is related to the problem of task standardization and to the careful definition of ability measures. Experimenters tend to ignore this, and the laboratory measures are frequently matters of experimenter convenience. There remains also the problem of generalization from laboratory tasks to real-world jobs and tasks. These problems have been reviewed elsewhere by Fleishman (61, 62) and Elkin, Fleishman, and associates (48). Baker et al. (9) describe a program which attempts to evaluate the reliability and sensitivity of sensory, cognitive, perceptual-motor, and physical performance measures based initially on factor analytic categories of human abilities for inclusion in a standardized battery for use in drug research. Results point up the need for designs to take into account the marked individual differences in effects of the same dosage of the same drug, and some solutions have been proposed (9). However, it has been possible to demonstrate differential effects of drugs between factor categories in absolute magnitude of effects, time to reach maximum effect, and duration of recovery period.

The drug Cylert (magnesium pemoline) has produced considerable interest as a possible enhancer of performance and learning. Cylert, a mixture of 5-phenyl 2-imino 4-oxazolidinone and magnesium hydroxide, has been found to produce mild CNS stimulation. Behavioral effects suggesting enhancement of performance for treated subjects have been reported in several animal and clinical studies. It has been suggested that the agent may aid in offsetting fatigue, inducing greater levels of alertness, and possibly be an aid to learning and memory, with little, if any, effect on the cardiovascular system.

A number of single low-dose studies with normal human subjects did not show improvements in the performance of treated subjects. For example, Burns and associates (20) could find no improvements in a complex learning task under small doses (6.25, 12.5, and 25 mg) of Cylert. Similarly, Smith

(167) could find no facilitative effects with doses of 25 and 37.5 mg and, in fact, he has suggested possible deterioration of performance under the larger dose for verbal and motor learning. Talland & McGuire (172), using a 25 mg dose, found no improvement in learning a push-button maze, a difficult narrative text, or a series of figure drawings. Rate of forgetting of the text over periods of 75 min and 1 week was unaffected, but they found some evidence for fewer trials to relearn the maze and for better retention of it over a week period.

Perhaps the most comprehensive study of Cylert, using human subjects and well-defined measures of separate abilities in the psychomotor and physical proficency areas, was carried out by Baker, Geist & Fleishman (10). Dosages of 25, 50, and 100 mg were used, and performance tests included measures of control precision, finger and manual dexerity, arm-hand steadiness, multilimb coordination, static strength, dynamic flexibility, dynamic strength, and balance. A repeated measure design was used in which tests were administered on a fixed schedule throughout the day. A major methodological finding was that the most reliable and sensitive measure of change was an adaptation of the Manning-DuBois residual gain score (45), which partials out effects of initial pretreatment differences. A major variable investigated was the effect of continuous work versus rest on the results. Would the drug tend to offset fatigue effects? The general impression gained is that for the active group the action of the drug was delayed and less pronounced. Facilitation of performance was found for 100 mg on several psychomotor tasks, with 50 mg showing similar patterns to a lesser degree. Doses of 50 to 100 mg were effective only with arm-hand steadiness. Physical proficiency is only slightly influenced by Cylert; but this was mainly for dynamic strength for active subjects. Poor balance resulted for resting subjects. A dose of 25 mg was generally ineffective, and this result may account for the inconclusive results of earlier studies. This study underscores the need for more analytical performance measures of separate abilities, the need to take into account wide individual differences in responses to drug effects, and the need for designs allowing statements of interactions among drug dosage, subject states, environmental conditioning, specific ability measures, and time frame.

Two additional studies were carried out on the effects of drugs on learning and memory. Talland and co-workers (173) showed some effects of tricyanoaminopropene (TRIAP) with 3 doses of 600 mg a day over a 2-week period for senile patients. The treatment was not found effective in restoring lost learning abilities. Osborn et al. (145) administered thiopental and found a loss of memory for events discussed while under sedation, where measures of letter pairs and picture recognition were used. Loss was correlated with concentration of thiopental in the blood at the time the material was learned. Subjects could recall material learned prior to sedation.

The tremendous interest in LSD in recent years, surprisingly, has not generated much definitive knowledge about its effects on human abilities.

Anecdotal and clinical evidence still predominates, and myth is still difficult to separate from data. Those engaged in clinical use of LSD in psychotherapy and treatment of mental disorders continue to operate with some evangelical fervor. Experiments do not allow the separation of environmental, organismic, and drug effects. Perhaps more than with any other drug, it is clear that the subject's predrug emotional history is a major factor in determining the LSD's subsequent effect, although there is still insufficient basis for predicting the direction of these effects.

Honingfeld (98, 99), using a 200 g injection of LSD-25, found that (as measured by Cloze analyses) intelligibility of verbal behavior was impaired, with the peak effect about 2 hr after injection; this contrasted with the effect of 300 μg of epinephrine which enhanced intelligibility. Using a smaller dosage (100 μg), Goldberger (76) still found significant impairment with LSD-25 on 8 of 9 cognitive tests utilized. McGlothin, Cohen & McGlothlin (133) found less conclusive results using measures of fluency, flexibility, and originality using a post-LSD test one week later. Using less standardized measures, Langs (126) found that LSD produced a constricting effect on recall, and Harman et al. (88) found some evidence for a facilitating effect of "creative-problem solving," particularly in the "illumination" phase. However, the methodology of the latter study left much to be desired, since the drug effects could not really be separated from certain group and social interaction effects. Claridge & Hume (31) found some evidence for disassociation of perceptual and autonomic functions after LSD. Finally, Ray & Bivens (156) investigated level of training of performance in relation to drug effects but found only inconclusive results. The general trend for the better designed studies with LSD is for decrement in most performances as a result of the drug.

A CNS drug which is difficult to categorize is scopolamine which may produce psychogenic effects similar to LSD if given in larger doses. Baker et al. (9), Elkin et al. (48), and Fleishman (62) report a series of studies relating scopolamine to performance on a carefully chosen battery of psychomotor, physical proficiency, sensori-perceptual and cognitive abilities developed from factor analysis research. The effects over time of injection of 12 μg/kg were investigated. Performance on ability tests, in general, was poorest from 2 to 4 hr after drug administration. Near visual acuity was most severely affected, while static strength, reaction time, and accuracy of time estimation were only slightly affected. Forty-five minutes after drug administration, manual dexterity and balance were more severely affected than near visual acuity. Differences between abilities existed in rate of recovery to normal performance. The differential effect according to ability was a primary finding. The research also demonstrated the wide individual differences which existed in response to a given dosage and the need to utilize experimental designs which take this into account in generalizing these effects. Another study (116) with a smaller dose of scopolamine, using a single task (mirror tracing), was inconclusive.

Forney, Hughes & Greatbatch (67) and Hughes, Forney & Richards (105) found alcohol produced a decrement in motor abilities as measured by pursuit motor, as well as in performance on verbal and numerical facility tests, when blood alchohol concentrations measured less than 50 mg per 100 ml of blood. In the latter study, an interesting feature of practical consequence was their investigation of possible additive effects of alcohol with two tranquilizers, chlordiazepam and diazepam. The tranquilizers, in the dosage given, did not produce any decrements in the motor, verbal, and numerical tasks used, nor were there additive effects. Two other studies with depressant compounds included one by Talland & Quarton (174) with pentobarbital, in which they found intravenous doses of the drug slowed responses on three types of perceptual-motor performances as well as reaction time. The authors interpret their results as due to a delay in monitoring the areas required for response. Of practical interest is a study on the effects of 200 mg phenobarbital on 7 sensorimotor and perceptual tasks over a 6-day period (69). Decrement on sensorimotor and perceptual tasks were found, but subjects' subjective ratings of their own performance showed no corresponding decrement.

A considerable number of studies investigated the class of CNS stimulants of amphetamine and related drugs. Thus, dexamphetamine was found by Frankenhauser & Post (69) to improve performance on sensorimotor and perceptual tests, and, in contrast to their findings with depressants, there was close agreement between objective improvement and subjective ratings of improvement. Lovingood and co-workers (131), using 15 mg of amphetamine, found significantly improved performance on strength, psychomotor, and mental tests, although this dose also produced increased heart rate. In contrast, they found caffein (500 mg) produced no increment in these same measures. Talland & Quarton (174), using intravenous injections of methamphetamine, found no effect on reaction time but did get an increase in speed with which repetitive motor activities were performed. With the lesser 10 mg dose, Mackworth (135) investigated the effect on a vigilance task (detection of a brief pause in movement of a clock hand, where three pauses per minute occur). She found that initial level of vigilance was inaffected, but the decrement in performance that normally occurs over time was reduced, and the facilitating effects of the drug with a "knowledge-of-results" condition were additive. This latter finding was underscored in the review by Cole (32), who calls for guidelines paying increased attention to the specific conditions under which given dosages are related to given performance change. In general then, these studies with dosages of 15 mg of amphetamine tend to show some positive effects although they depend somewhat on the ability. Dosages below this level yield negligible or no effects on abilities. Evidence during the period of this review generally supports earlier findings that such drugs can delay fatigue-induced performance decrement.

Of general interest is the review by Freeman (71) on the effects of drugs on learning of children, and the discussion of Berry, Gelder & Summerfield (14) on the value of cummunication models for research on drug effects on human abilities. The latter interpret the effects of CNS depressants in terms of effects on input and short-term memory processes rather than on motor components of tasks. Finally, a study by Janke & Ritzmann (109) has methodological implications for evaluation batteries in that they found the factorial composition of tests under the influence of an hypnotic agent (Medomin) was different than for a placebo group. However, their analysis was done with too limited a number of finger and manual dexterity tests. More studies on this methodological problem need to be made.

AGE AND SEX DIFFERENCES

Does ability increase with age, decrease with age, or remain constant? Recent work in the area of relating the aging process to ability would indicate that the answer to this question is "yes." To which part the "yes" applies is dependent on a number of factors, including the nature of the ability studied and the research method.

The research literature continues to be filled with cross-cultural studies showing the effect of increasing age on abilities [e.g., Craik (36); Kleemeier & Jones (123); Thumin & Boernke (180); Davis & Obrist (40); Noble, Baker & Jones (143); Taub (176)]. Some difficulties in evaluating such research have been pointed out by a number of authors. Munnichs (141) mentions problems involving cooperation of older subjects in testing, the appropriateness of tests designed for younger people, the change in culture, and the unanswered question of the nature of an appropriate criterion of intelligence for the aged.

Cross-sectional studies have shown a clear decrease in tested general intelligence with increased age. Hirt (94) conducted a study of change in differential aptitudes as measured by the GATB and found a significant quadratic relationship for the General, Verbal, Numerical, and Spatial subtests, with the greatest age decrement being in spatial. He studied a wide range of ages, including a group past 70. The decline in the 70-year-old group appears to have been the primary contributing factor in the quadratic effect. Tested ability must decline with severe biological deterioration, and the inclusion of very old age groups would seem to assure a large enough group of persons with severe enough physical problems to lower significantly the mean test scores in this advanced age group.

As Tyler (185) points out, cross-sectional and longitudinal studies of age-ability relationships have led to contradictory results. Owens (148) has completed a second follow-up of a group tested while in their first year in college in 1919, retested in 1950, and now retested again in 1961. In the first follow-up (147), a significant increase in Army Alpha scores was noted at age 50 in comparison to the original testing. The last ten years from 50 to 60 showed relative constancy in test performance. Owens showed that the increment in ability from 1919 to 1961 could be explained in terms of cultural change rather than individual differences. His data indicated that examination of only the cross-sectional data could result in the conclusion of an increment, while a proper conclusion from both sets of data would be that there is no consistent change in general ability with age. If the past studies which have studied the relationship of aging and abilities only cross-sectionally or only longitudinally can be compared to the blind men's descriptions of the elephant, Owens' study should open some eyes. Owen's results may not generalize to the whole population since his group was restricted to college-trained persons, many of whom entered the teaching profession. Nevertheless, his study has methodological implications which cannot be ignored in studying the effects of age on ability.

The interpretation of the differences in ability as a function of age may vary as a result of the ability studied. General ability can be shown to increase when studied longitudinally and to decrease when studied cross-sectionally. The most valid conclusion may be that it remains relatively constant. Furthermore, Weiner (189) has shown that the factorial concentration of the general factor on the GATB remains constant across seven different age groups varying from 14 to 54 years. The study of only the general factor may be misleading, however. Horn & Cattell (104) have found that when the general factor is broken down into "fluid intelligence" and "crystallized intelligence," fluid intelligence decreases with age while crystallized intelligence shows a systematic increase. The study offers support for Cattell's theory and also gives an explanation of the finding of intelligence constancy with age when only a single general intelligence is studied. Although this was a cross-sectional study, further support for this theory was noted by Owens' (148) longitudinal results when the Army Alpha was scored for reasoning, numerical, and verbal abilities. From testing at age 50 to 60, a small decrement was noted in reasoning and numerical ability while an increment was found for verbal ability. When scored for only general intelligence, these abilities canceled each other out, resulting in a conclusion that ability remains constant. Of particular relevance is the book by Birren (15) on the *Psychology of Aging*.

In a carefully controlled experimental study, Noble, Baker & Jones (143), following up their earlier work on age and sex parameters in psychomotor and human selective learning, found age and sex to be critical parameters. Six hundred male and female subjects in 30 groups between ages 8 and 87 received 320 trials on a discrimination reaction apparatus. Confirming and extending the classicel age-performance data, acquisition speeds followed differential trends for both age and sex while overall proficiency was a nonmonotonic function of age. Males performed faster than females; the maximum level for females was at 16 and for males at 20, followed by a nonparalled decline into the age group in the 70's. Noble proposes the multiplicative law $R = f$ [T (no. of practice trials) x A (age) x S (sex)] for a discrimination-reaction task learning. More experimental data like Noble's obviously are needed to assess properly the role of age, sex, and other individual difference phenomena on general laws of learning.

Fleishman (54, 55) has provided developmental data (ages 12 to 18) on sex differences in abilities in the physical proficiency area. On his Basic Fitness Tests, administered to 20,000 high school youth across the U.S., most of the curves for boys show a linear increase in such abilities as Dynamic Strength, Explosive Strength, Stamina, and Coordination, with some differences in the critical age at which the curves level off for different abilities. Balance shows no change with age, and static strength shows a linear trend right through age 18. Dynamic Flexibility shows a decrease in ability to age 16. In contrast to boys, curves for girls reflect definite developmental stages during which there is no improvement, and even a decrease in ability. This was interpreted in terms of sex differences in maturational and interest patterns. In general, there is no overlap in curves for boys and girls, except for Extent Flexibility (girls get less flexible, with the cross-over point at age 15!).

A major review of sex differences in intellectual functioning has been completed by Maccoby (132); therefore, we will not review the individual studies here. The major conclusions are that with regard to general ability girls tend to score higher in preschool years but boys catch up and surpass girls during the high school years. Girls show superior test performance throughout school on tests of verbal ability. Numerical ability tends to be about the same for both sexes in grammar school, with boys consistently out-performing girls by the time they reach high school. Spatial ability shows a marked superiority for boys, which begins during the early school years and continues on through the later school years. Analytical ability or "field independence" shows a similar pattern to spatial ability with regard to sex differences. Maccoby summarizes the possible causes of the various sex differences in abilities. These include differences in the developmental time table, sex-typed interests, opportunities to learn because of differential environment for boys and girls, and identification and modeling after the same sex parent.

Differences in space perception have been found to be among the most clear-cut sex differences. Sherman (161) notes that sex differences found in analytical ability may be a function of the dependence on spatial ability of measures of analytical ability, and she points out a need to control for spatial factors before any conclusion can be made about an independent construct of spatial ability. Furthermore, the differences in numerical ability also may be related to differential spatial abilities required in geometric and mathematical problem solving.

HEREDITY

A review of the contributions of twin research to psychology has been completed by Vandenberg (186), indicating a strong interest by psychologists in hereditary behavior. Using an F test for the Holzinger heritability index, he reports a significant hereditary factor for four PMA subtests: Number, Verbal, Space, and Word Fluency. Jensen (113) developed a new formula for estimating heritability which yields a better estimate of the proportion of total variance due to heredity. Using this index he has reanalyzed results from a number of studies and concludes that about 80 per cent of variance in ability can be accounted for by heredity and 12 per cent by systematic environmental variance (within families). He concludes that current IQ tests reflect innate intellectual potential and that biological inheritance is far more important than social psychological environment.

One study of particular interest was reported by Burt (23) who compared ability measures of identical twins reared apart. Burt studied 53 pairs of twins who were reared in environments that were slightly negatively correlated when rated on socioeconomic status. Growing up in dissimilar environments, these separated twins were correlated on intelligence (.77 on a group test and .86 on a modified Stanford-Binet). This compares to a correlation for unrelated children reared together of .28 and .25.

Although the inheritance of intellectual ability is recognized, behavior geneticists such as Dolzhausky (44) and Hirsch (93) feel that correlational approaches to estimating percentages of heritability may lead to an overestimate and that there is a need for the identification and behavior-genetic analysis of phenotypic dimensions of human variations.

Skeels (163) reports a follow-up of his study originally reported in 1939 (164), which indicated that the mentally retarded children who received special attention and were placed for adoption in good homes had become self-sufficient and normal children. The contrast group who remained institutionalized tended to be less self-sufficient, either remaining institutionalized or holding menial jobs. Jensen (115) has criticized the already heavily criticized study at length, indicating that it was not necessarily contradictory of a hereditary theory of intelligence. The simplest explanation is that these children may have inherited normal intelligence which was temporarily depressed by extreme cultural deprivation. Even if we were to accept Jensen's estimate that 20 per cent of intelligence may be due to environment, a wide range in IQ scores is still possible for a few extreme cases.

CULTURAL AND ETHNIC DIFFERENCES

Since the last review, over 100 research studies which have a direct bearing on cultural and ethnic differences in ability have been identified from the literature. By far the largest proportion of this research has been related to the measurement of abilities of Negroes and has been summarized recently by Shuey (162). Much of this increased activity can be attributed to an increased public awareness of differential test performance by persons from various cultural and ethnic groups and its relationship to equal employment and educational opportunity. The inclusion of cultural differences and ethnic differences in ability under one subheading follows from the unresolved controversy over the genetic or environmental origin of the differences. Jensen (115) recognizes the effect of extreme cultural deprivation on ability but feels that there is considerable evidence that biological inheritance factors may contribute to ethnic differences in ability. He urges further research on the heredity-environment uncertainty concerning racial differences in intelligence and educability and questions the more popular interpretation that differences are not innate but result from different cultural values and opportunities.

Dolzhausky (44) has criticized the conclusions from twin studies that one-half or more of the inter-racial variance in IQ must be genetic. Nevertheless he indicates that genetic components of these differences may indeed exist, and it should be a challenge to find out. Furthemore, he feels that heritability of such traits is fairly low and that concentration of efforts needs to be in a study of the environmental variance.

Evidence for the environmental influence of the culturally disadvantaged is presented by Deutsch (41), Deutsch & Brown (42), and Nisbet & Entwistle (142). In finding that intelligence test scores tend to decrease as disadvantaged children become older, there is support for a cumulative deficit hypothesis regarding the continued effect of cultural deprivation on intelligence.

An unusual study examining cultural differences in abilities was reported by Gross (79). The study involved a comparison of two groups which by many standards would be expected to have comparable abilities. Both groups were from the same general neighborhood in Brooklyn, all children and their mothers were native born, English was the language of the home, none possessed physical or mental handicaps, all went to private religious schools, and all were of the same Jewish ethnic background. Although both groups were of middle class socioeconomic status, they differed in their cultural origin; one group whose origin was Ashkenazic Europe scored considerably higher on several ability measures than the other whose origin was Sephardic-Arabia. The cultural difference was not based on economic status, but rather on how this economic status was achieved. The higher ability children evolved in a background where status was achieved by money. The cultural values rather than the socioeconomic status appeared to be the determiner of ability.

Lesser, Fifer & Clark (129) have reported a study comparing the patterns of abilities for four different racial groups: Chinese, Jewish, Negro, and Puerto Rican, all living in New York City. Middle and lower class groups were also compared for all four ethnic groups. Of particular interest was the fact that each ethnic group had a distinct profile of abilities which was different from each of the other groups. Although the level of performance was consistently higher for the middle class, the shape of the profile was almost identical to those of the racially similar groups from the lower class. Whether this can be attributed to inheritance or cultural history cannot be determined, but the pattern of abilities seems to be determined by racial heritage. Stodolsky & Lesser (169) have replicated these findings for middle and lower class children of Chinese and Negro descent, living in Boston.

A number of years ago much was made of the superiority of European youth over American youth in physical fitness. Later, Fleishman (55) pointed out that this depended on the ability measured. Confirmation comes from a comparative study by Tenora & Snapka (179a) using the nine standardized Fleishman Basic Fitness Tests, with 18 to 19-year-old youths in Czechoslovakia. The investigation showed Czech youth to be clearly superior in tests of Static Strength and Stamina and U.S. boys to be superior in Explosive Strength and Balance. Smaller differences in favor of the Czechs were in four of the remaining tests.

Several investigators have examined the effect of race of the examiner and testing conditions on the differential ability test scores between Negroes and whites (2, 122, 165). Although the race of the examiner tends to have an effect and also tends to interact with testing conditions, the differences were not always clearly significant. Katz, Epps & Axelson (120) found that instructions to Negro subjects as to whether they were to be compared to local Negro norms or national white college norms affected test scores. The Negro students tended to score higher when they were compared to their own college norms. This threatened comparison may offer a partial explanation of the effect of the race of the examiner on test scores. Additional explanations may include better compatability in language for communicating instructions or even examiner bias towards subjects of like race.

The major concern about the differential test performance of different racial groups has been whether tests may be an agent of inadvertant discrimination in denying minority group persons equal employment and educational opportunity. As Guion (84) has pointed out, differentiation in testing is not necessarily unfair as long as the test is validly predicting success on some criterion. Just because an ability measure is related to cultural or ethnic variables does not mean we should eliminate it. Anastasi (7) has indicated that criteria themselves are correlated with cultural conditions, and the elimination of cultural bias in tests could also eliminate validity.

Bartlett & O'Leary (11) have suggested a need for research on differential validation of tests for various subcultural groups. Tests which have been constructed for use with middle-class white populations may take on different meanings when applied to lower-class minority groups. A solution to discrimination in testing may lie in using race or socioeconomic status as a moderator variable in prediction where different regression lines may be identified for various subgroups. Bartlett & O'Leary identify 11 different situations where differential prediction might be helpful in avoiding inadvertant discrimination through testing. Further support is given this viewpoint by Krug (125), who has indicated a need to validate tests separately on as many different subgroups as possible. Krug states that it is unethical to utilize a test unless it has been validated on a similar group for which it is to be used.

Psychological testing must initiate research to explore further the problem of racial differences in tests and prediction. Procedures which are not in line with the most modern and sophisticated test practices and which indicate differential performance for different ethnic groups have even come under fire in a recent court decision. As reported in the Washington Report (6) of the American Psychological Association, Judge J. Skelly Wright indicated that the use of IQ or other tests can be unconstitutional in denying opportunities. This judgment was based in part on the fact that many norms developed on white middle class children are being improperly applied to poor and Negro students. Unless we can improve our utilization of the most sophisticated methods for dealing with differential meaning of test results on minority group populations, psychological testing of ability for applied use may be endangered.

CONCLUDING REMARKS

While it is impossible to summarize fairly, wisely, and comprehensively the literature trends of 4 years in as broad a field as human ability, some developments seem especially worthy of note. There does appear to be some significant movement toward integration of what Cronbach in 1957 called the "two disciplines of psychology"—differential and experimental psychology. In particular, increasing attention is being given to the relations between individual differences and learning. The linkage of variables in these two areas within a common conceptual framework would seem necessary in order to assess the moderating effects of individual variation on more general principles of learning. The incorporation of ability and other individual difference variables in learning research and theory appears to be required in order to define more explicitly the individual parameters within which one might expect principles of learning to be applicable. It is encouraging to see these attempts in such diverse areas as perceptual-motor and verbal learning and concept attainment. However, while there is evidence that some experimentalists are moving toward some common ground, most of the methodological and conceptual development still comes from psychometrically oriented differential psychologists.

During this period we had more data but less resolution of critical questions regarding a theory of human abilities and their organization. Most of our information still rests on factor analytic methods. There is a need for additional methods, but there are some encouraging developments in increased sophistication in combinations of multivariate experimental and correlational designs. In this connection, the *Handbook of Multivariate Experimental Psychology*, edited by Cattell (28), is a major contribution.

There appears to be increased concern for problems of task standardization for use in laboratory research. The attempt needs to be made to organize experimental data on such treatment variables as environments, stressors, and drug effects, and perhaps some model of human abilities may provide a way to do it.

The current educational and social ferment has brought to the fore in fresh perspective culture, race, sex, age, and the relation of educational method to issues of ability development and ability measurement. These issues provide new challenges for research on human abilities in the years ahead.

LITERATURE CITED

1. Allen, D., Anger, J. A factor analytic study of the ability to spell. *Educ. Psychol. Measmt.*, **25**, 153–61 (1965)
2. Allen, S. A., Dubanoski, R. A., Stevenson, H. W. Children's performance as a function of race of E, race of S, and type of verbal reinforcement. *J. Exptl. Child Psychol.*, **4**, 248–56 (1966)
3. Alluisi, E. A. Methodology in the use of synthetic tasks to assess complex performance. *Human Factors*, **9**, 375–84 (1967)
4. Alluisi, E. A., Chiles, W. D., Hall, T. J. Combined effects of sleep loss and demanding work-rest schedules on crew performance (Aerospace Med. Res. Lab., Ohio, 1964)
5. Alluisi, E. A., Thurmond, J. B., Coates, G. D. Behavioral effects of infectious diseases: Respiratory pasteurella talarensis in man (Univ. Louisville, Ky., 1967)
6. American Psychological Association, Washington Reports, III (1967)
7. Anastasi, A. Some implications of cultural factors for test construction. In *Testing Problems in Perspective* (Anastasi, A., Ed., Am. Council on Educ., Washington, D. C., 1966)
8. Anderson, R. C. Individual differences and problem solving. In *Learning and Individual Differences*, 66–89 (Gagné, R. M., Ed., Merrill, Columbus, Ohio, 1967)
9. Baker, W. J., Elkin, E. H., Van Cott, H. P., Fleishman, E. A. Effects of drugs on human performance: The development of analytical methods and tests of basic human abilities (Am. Inst. Res., Washington, D.C., 1966)
10. Baker, W. J., Geist, A. M., Fleishman, E. A. Effects of Cylert (magnesium pemoline) on physiological, physical proficiency and psychomotor performance measures (Am. Inst. Res., Washington, D.C., 1967)
11. Bartlett, C. J., O'Leary, B. S. A differential prediction model to moderate the effects of heterogeneous groups in personnel selection and classification. *Personnel Psychol.*, **22** (1969)
12. Bechtoldt, H. P. Factor analysis and the investigation of hypotheses. *Percept. Mot. Skills*, **14**, 319–42 (1962)
13. Belmont, I., Birch, H. G., Belmont, Lillian. The organization of intelligence test performance in educable mentally subnormal children. *Am. J. Ment. Defic.*, **71**, 969–76 (1967)
14. Berry, C., Gelder, M. G., Summerfield, A. Experimental analysis of drug effects on human performance using information theory concepts. *Brit. J. Physiol.*, **56**, 255–65 (1965)
15. Birren, J. E. *The Psychology of Aging* (Prentice-Hall, Englewood Cliffs, N. J., 1964)
16. Bowen, H. M., Anderson, B., Promisel, D. Studies of divers' performance during the SEALAB II project. *Human Factors*, **8**, 183–99 (1966)
17. Briggs, L. J. *Sequencing of Instruction in Relation to Competence* (Am. Inst. Res., Pittsburgh, Pa., 1968)
18. Briggs, L. J., Campeau, P., Gagné, R. M., May, M. A. *Instructional Media: A Procedure for the Design of Multi-Media Instruction, a Critical Review of Research, and Suggestions for Future Research* (Am. Inst. Res., Palo Alto, Calif., 1965)
19. Bunderson, R. V. Transfer functions and learning curves: The use of ability constructs in the study of human learning (Educ. Testing Serv., Princeton, N. J., 1964)
20. Burns, J. T., House, R. F., Fensch, F. C., Miller, J. G., Effects of magnesium pemoline and dextroamphetamine on human learning. *Science*, **155**, 849–51 (1967)
21. Buros, O. K., Ed. *The Sixth Mental Measurement Yearbook* (Gryphon, N.J., 1964)
22. Burt, C. The evidence for the concept of intelligence. *Brit. J. Educ. Psychol.*, **25**, 158–77 (1955)
23. Burt, C. The genetic determination of differences in intelligence: A study of monozygotic twins reared together and apart. *Brit. J. Psychol.*, **57**, 137–53 (1966)
24. Bush, W. J., Gregg, D. K., Smith,

E. A., McBride, C. B. Some interactions between individual differences and modes of instuction (Aerospace Med. Res. Labs. Wright-Patterson AFB, 1965)

25. Carver, R. P. The relation of intelligence to the ability to learn (Washington Univ. Dept. Psychol. Tech. Rept., 12, 1966)

26. Carver, R. P., Winsmann, F. R. Effect of high elevation upon physical proficiency, cognitive functioning and subjective symptomatology. *Percept. Mot. Skills*, **26**, 223–30 (1968)

27. Cattell, R. B. Theory of fluid and crystallized intelligence: A critical experiment. *J. Educ. Psychol.*, **54**, 1–22 (1963)

28. Cattell, R. B., Ed. *Handbook of Multivariate Experimental Psychology* (Rand McNally, Chicago, Ill., 1966)

29. Cattell, R. B. Theory of fluid and crystallized general intelligence checked at the 5–6 year level. *Brit. J. Educ. Psychol.*, **37**, 209–24 (1967)

30. Chiles, W. D. Assessment of the performance effects of the stresses of space flight (Aerospace Med. Res. Labs., Ohio, 1966)

31. Claridge, G. S., Hume, W. I. Comparison of effects of dexamphetamine and LSD-25 on perceptual and autonomic function. *Percept. Mot. Skills*, **23**, 456–58 (1966)

32. Cole, S. O. Experimental effects of amphetamine: a review. *Psychol. Bull.* **68**, 81–90 (1967)

33. Cooley, W. W. Interactions among interests, abilities, and career plans. *J. Appl. Psychol.*, **51**, 1–16 (1967)

34. Cooley, W. W., Lohnes, P. R. Predicting the development of young adults (Am. Inst. Res., Palo Alto, Calif., 1968)

35. Corballis, M. C. Practice and the simplex. *Psychol. Rev.*, **72**, 399–406 (1965)

36. Craik, F. I. The nature of the age decrement in performance on dichotic listening tasks. *Quart J. Exptl. Psychol.*, **17**, 227–40 (1965)

37. Cronbach, L. J. How can instruction be adapted to individual differences? In *Learning and Individual Differences*, 23–39 (Gagné, R. M., Ed., Merrill, Columbus, Ohio, 1967)

38. Cronbach, L. J., Gleser, G. C. *Psychological Tests and Personnel De-cisions*, 2nd Ed. (Univ. Illinois Press, Urbana, Ill., 1965)

39. Cureton, E. E. A factor analysis of Project TALENT tests and four other test batteries (Project TALENT Office, Am. Inst. Res., Palo Alto, Calif., 1968)

40. Davis, S. H., Obrist, W. D. Age differences in learning and retention of verbal material. *Cornell J. Soc. Relat.*, **1**, 95–103 (1966)

41. Deutsch, M. The role of social class in language development. *Am. J. Orthopsychiatry*, **35**, 78–88 (1965)

42. Deutsch, M., Brown, B. Social influences in Negro-white intelligence differences. *J. Soc. Issues*, **20**, 24–35 (1964)

43. Dingman, H. F., Meyers, C. E. The structure of intellect in the mental retardate. *Intern. Rev. Res. Ment. Retard.*, **1**, 55–76 (1966)

44. Dolzhausky, T. Of flies and men. *Am. Psychol.*, **22**, 41–48 (1967)

45. DuBois, P. H. The design of correlational studies in training. In *Training Research and Education*, 63–86 (Glaser, R., Ed., Wiley, N.Y., 596 pp., 1965)

46. Duncanson, J. P. Intelligence and the ability to learn (Educ. Testing Serv., Princeton, N. J., 1964)

47. Dunham, J. L., Guilford, J. P., Hoepfner, R. Abilities pertaining to classes and the learning of concepts (Univ. Southern California, 38 pp., 1966)

48. Elkin, E. H., Fleishman, E. A., Van Cott, H. P., Horowitz, H., Freedle, R. O. Effects of drugs on human performance—Phase I: Research concepts, test development, and preliminary studies (Am. Inst. Res., Washington, D.C., 1965)

49. Evans, W. O. Performance on a skilled task after physical work or in a high altitude environment. *Percept. Mot. Skills.*, **22**, 371–80 (1966)

50. Ferguson, G. A. On learning and human ability. *Can. J. Psychol.*, **8**, 95–112 (1954)

51. Ferguson, G. A. On transfer and the abilities of man. *Ibid.*, **10**, 121–31 (1956)

52. Ferguson, G. A. Human abilities. *Ann. Rev. Psychol.*, **16**, 39–62 (1965)

53. Flanagan, J. C., Davis, F. B., Daile J. T., Shaycoft, Marion F., Orr, D. B., Goldberg, L., Neyman, C. A. The American high-school stu-

dent (Am. Inst. Res., Pittsburgh, Pa., 1964)

54. Fleishman, E. A. *Examiner's Manual for the Basic Fitness Tests* (Prentice-Hall, Englewood Cliffs, N. J., 1964)

55. Fleishman, E. A. *The Structure and Measurement of Physical Fitness* (Prentice-Hall, Englewood Cliffs, N.J., 1964)

56. Fleishman, E. A. The description and prediction of perceptual-motor skill learning. In *Training Research and Education*, 137–76 (Glaser, R., Ed., Wiley, N. Y., 596 pp., 1965)

57. Fleishman, E. A. The prediction of total task performance from prior practice on task components. *Human Factors*, 7, 18–27 (1965)

58. Fleishman, E. A. Human abilities and the acquisition of skill. In *Acquisition of Skill* (Bilodeau, E. A., Ed., Academic Press, N. Y., 539 pp., 1966)

59. Fleishman, E. A. Individual differences and motor learning. In *Learning and Individual Differences*, 165–92 (Gagné, R. M., Ed., Merrill, Columbus, Ohio, 265 pp., 1967)

60. Fleishman, E. A. Human abilities and learning. *Ibid.*, 58–66

61. Fleishman, E. A. Development of a behavior taxonomy for describing human tasks: A correlational-experimental approach. *J. Appl. Psychol.*, 51, 1–10 (1967)

62. Fleishman, E. A. Performance assessment based on an empirically derived task taxonomy. *Human Factors*, 9, 349–66 (1967)

63. Fleishman, E. A. Prediction of transfer and other learning phenomena from ability and personality measures (Am. Inst. Res., Washington, D.C., 1968)

64. Fleishman, E. A., Fruchter, B. Factor structure and predictability of successive stages of learning Morse code. *J. Appl. Psychol.*, 44, 96–101 (1960)

65. Fleishman, E. A., Fruchter, B. Component and total task relations at different stages of learning a complex tracking task. *Percept. Mot. Skills*, 20, 1305–11 (1965)

66. Fleishman, E. A., Rich, S. Role of kinesthetic and spatial-visual abilities in perceptual-motor learning. *J. Exptl. Psychol.*, 66, 6–11 (1963)

67. Forney, R. B., Hughes, F. W., Greatbatch, W. H. Measurement of attentive motor performance. *Percept. Mot. Skills*, 19, 151–54 (1964)

68. Fox, W. F. Human performance in the cold. *Human Factors*, 9, 203–20 (1967)

69. Frankenhaueser, M., Post, B. Objective and subjective performance as influenced by drug-induced variations in activation level. *Scand. J. Psychol.*, 7, 168–78 (1966)

70. Fredericksen, C. H., Abilities, transfer, and information retrieval in verbal learning (Univ. Illinois, Urbana, Ill., 1967)

71. Freeman, R. D. Drug effects on learning in children: A Selective review of the past thirty years. *J. Spec. Educ.*, 1, 17–44 (1966)

72. Fruchter, B., Fleishman, E. A. A simplical design for the analysis of correlational learning data. *Multivariate Behav. Res.*, 2, 83–88 (1967)

73. Gagné, R. M. *The Conditions of Learning* (Holt, Rinehart & Winston, N. Y., 1965)

74. Gagné, R. M., Ed. *Learning and Individual Differences* (Merrill, Columbus, Ohio, 1967)

75. Games, P. A. A factorial analysis of verbal learning tasks. *J. Exptl. Psychol.*, 63, 1–11 (1962)

76. Goldberger, L. Cognitive test performance under LSD-25, placebo and isolation. *J. Nerv. Ment. Dis.*, 142, 4–9 (1966)

77. Graybiel, A., Kennedy, R. S., Knoblock, E. C., Guedry, F. E., Mertz, W., McLeod, M. E., Colehour, J. K., Miller, E. F., Fregly, A. R. Effects of exposure to a rotating environment (10 RPM) on four aviators for a period of twelve days. *Aerospace Med.*, 36, 733–54 (1965)

78. Grodsky, M. A. The use of full scale mission simulation for the assessment of complex operator performance. *Human Factors*, 9, 341–48 (1967)

79. Gross, M. *Learning readiness in two Jewish groups: a study in cultural deprivation* (Center for Urban Educ., N. Y., 1967)

80. Guertin, W. H., Ladd, C. E., Frank, G. H., Rabin, A. I., Heister, D. S., Research with the Wechsler intelligence scale for aults: 1960–1965. *Psychol. Bull.*, 66, 385–409 (1966)

81. Guilford, J. P. Intelligence: 1965 model. *Am. Psychol.*, 21, 20–25 (1966)

82. Guilford, J. P. *The Nature of Human Intelligence* (McGraw-Hill, N. Y., 538 pp., 1967)

83. Guilford, J. P., Hoepfner, R. Structure-of-intellect factors and their tests (Psychol. Lab., Univ. Southern California, 1966)

84. Guion, R. M. *Personnel Testing* (McGraw-Hill, N. Y., 1965)

85. Guttman, L. The structure of interrelations among intelligence tests. In *Invitational Conference of Testing Problems*, 25–36 (Harris, C. W., Ed., Educ. Testing Serv., Princeton, N. J., 1965)

86. Gyr, J. W., Brown, J. S., Cafagna, A. C. Quasi-formal models of inductive behavior and their relation to Piaget's theory of cognitive stages. *Psychol. Rev.*, **74**, 272–89 (1967)

87. Halcomb, C. G., Kirk, R. E. Effects of air ionization upon the performance of a vigilance task. *J. Eng. Psychol.*, **4**, 120–26 (1965)

88. Harman, W. W., McKim, R. H., Mogar, R. E. Psychedelic agents in creative problem-solving: A pilot study. *Psychol. Rept.*, **19**, 211–27 (1966)

89. Harootunian, B. Intelligence and the ability to learn. *J. Educ. Res.*, **59**, 211–14 (1966)

90. Harris, C. S., Shoenberger, R. W. Effects of frequency of vibration on human performance. *J. Eng. Psychol.*, **5**, 1–15 (1966)

91. Harris, J. D. A factor analytic study of three signal detection abilities. *J. Speech Hearing Res.*, **7**, 71–78 (1964)

92. Hasan, P., Butcher, H. J. Creativity and intelligence: A partial replication with Scottish children of Getzels' and Jackson's study. *Brit. J. Psychol.*, **57**, 129–35 (1966)

93. Hirsch, J. Behavior-genetic or "experimental" analysis: The challenge of science versus the lure of technology. *Am. Psychol.*, **22**, 118–30 (1967)

94. Hirt, M. L. Aptitude changes as a function of age. *Pers. Guid. J.*, **43**, 174–76 (1964)

95. Hoepfner, R., Guilford, J. P., Merrifield, P. R. A factor analysis of the symbolic-evaluation abilities: Studies of aptitudes of high-level personnel. (Psychol. Lab., Univ. California, 1964)

96. Hoepfner, R., Nihira, K., Guilford, J. P. Intellectual abilities of symbolic and semantic judgment. *Psychol. Monogr.*, **80**, 47 pp. (1966)

97. Hofstaetter, P. R. Zum Begriff der Intelligenz. *Psychol. Rdsch.*, **17**, 229–48 (1966)

98. Honingfeld, G. Temporal effects of LSD-25 and epinephrine on verbal behavior. *Newsletter for Res. in Psychol.*, **6**, 15–17 (1964)

99. Honingfeld, G. Temporal effects of LSD-25 and epinephrine on verbal behavior. *J. Abnorm. Psychol.*, **70**, 303–6 (1965)

100. Horn, J. L. Short-period changes in human abilities (Denver Res. Inst., Denver, Colo., 1966)

101. Horn, J. L., Bramble, W. J. Second-order ability structure revealed in rights and wrongs scores. *J. Educ. Psychol.*, **58**, 115–22 (1967)

102. Horn, J. L., Cattell, R. B. Age differences in primary mental abilities. *J. Geront.*, **21**, 210–20 (1966)

103. Horn, J. L., Cattell, R. B. Refinement and test of the theory of fluid and crystallized intelligence. *J. Educ. Psychol.*, **57**, 253–70 (1966)

104. Horn, J. L., Cattell, R. B. Age differences in fluid and crystallized intelligence. *Acta Psychol.*, **26**, 107–29 (1967)

105. Hughes, F. W., Forney, R. B., Richards, A. B. Comparative effect in human subjects of chlordiazepoxide, diazepam, and placebo on mental and physical performance. *Clin. Pharmacol. Therap.*, **6**, 139–45 (1965)

106. Humphreys, L. G. Investigations of the simplex. *Psychometrika*, **25**, 313–23 (1960)

107. Humphreys, L. G. Critique of Cattell's "Theory of fluid and crystallized intelligence: a critical experiment." *J. Educ. Psychol.*, **58**, 120–36 (1967)

108. Hundal, P. S. Organisation of mental abilities at successive grade levels. *Indian J. Psychol.*, **41**, 65–72 (1966)

109. Janke, W., Ritzmann, H. Research on the influence of pharmacological dosage to simple psychomotor performance. *Arch. Ges. Psychol.*, **116**, 33–57 (1964)

110. Jensen, A. R. *Individual Differences in Learning: Interference Factor* (Univ. California, Berkeley, Calif., 1964)

111. Jensen, A. R. Individual differences in concept learning. In *Analysis of Concept Learning* (Klausmeier, H. J., Harris, C. W., Academic Press, N. Y., 272 pp., 1966)

112. Jensen, A. R. The measurement of reactive inhibition in humans. *J. Gen. Psychol.*, **75**, 85–93 (1966)
113. Jensen, A. R. Estimation of the limits of heritability of traits by comparison of monozygotic and dizygotic twins. *Proc. Natl. Acad. Sci.*, **58**, 149–56 (1967)
114. Jensen, A. R. Varieties of individual differences in learning. In *Learning and Individual Differences*, 117–35 (Gagné, R. M., Merrill, Columbus, Ohio, 265 pp., 1967)
115. Jensen, A. R. The culturally disadvantaged and the heredity-environment uncertainty. In *The Culturally Disadvantaged Child* (Hellmuth, J., Ed., Special Child Publ., Seattle, Wash., 1968)
116. Johnson, C., Wendt, G. R. Chemical studies of behavior: VII. Mirror tracing after dramamine and scopolamine. *J. Psychol.*, **57**, 87 (1964)
117. Jones, M. Individual differences. In *Acquisition of Skill*, 109–46 (Bilodeau, E. A., Ed., Academic Press, N. Y., 539 pp., 1966)
118. Jones, M. R. Practice as a process of simplification. *Psychol. Rev.*, **69**, 224–94 (1962)
119. Juurmaa, J. The ability structure of the blind and the deaf: Final report. *Am. Fedn. for the Blind, Res. Bull.*, 109–21 (1967)
120. Katz, I., Epps, E. G., Axelson, L. J. Effect upon negro digit-symbol performance of anticipated comparison with whites and with other negroes. *J. Abnorm. Soc. Psychol.*, **69**, 77–83 (1964)
121. Kebbon, L. The structure of abilities at lower levels of intelligence (Skand. Test Forlaget AB, Stockholm, Sweden, 112 pp., 1965)
122. Kennedy, W. A., Vega, M. Negro children's performance on a discrimination task as a function of examiner race and verbal incentive. *J. Pers. Soc. Psychol.*, **2**, 839–43 (1965)
123. Kleemeier, R. W., Jones, A. W. Psychomotor differences between three age groups of older men. *Bull. Assoc. Intern. Psychol. Appl.*, **15**, 48–53 (1966)
124. Kohfeld, D. L. The prediction of perceptual-motor learning from independent verbal and motor measures. *Psychon. Sci.*, **4**, 413–14 (1966)
125. Krug, R. E. The industrial psychologist: Selection and equal employment opportunity (a symposium): V. Some suggested approaches for test development and measurement. *Personnel Psychol.*, **19**, 24–34 (1966)
126. Langs, R. J. Stability of earliest memories under LSD-25 and placebo. *J. Nerv. Ment. Dis.*, **144**, 171–84 (1967)
127. Leites, N. S. The problem of abilities in the writings of B. M. Teplov. *Vop. Psikhol.*, **5**, 39–48 (1966)
128. Lemke, E. A., Klausmeier, H. J., Harris, C. W. Relationship of selected cognitive abilities to concept attainment and information processing. *J. Educ. Psychol.*, **58**, 27–35 (1967)
129. Lesser, G. S., Fifer, G., Clark, D. H. Mental abilities of children from different social-class and cultural groups. *Monogr. Soc. Res. Child Devel.*, **30**, 1–115 (1965)
130. Locke, E. A., Zavala, A., Fleishman, E. A. Studies of helicopter pilot performance: the analysis of task dimensions. *Human Factors*, **7**, 285–302 (1965)
131. Lovingood, B. W., Blyth, C. S., Peacock, W. H., Lindsay, R. B. Effects of d-amphetamine sulfate, caffeine, and high temperature on human performance. *Res. Quart.*, **38**, 64–71 (1967)
132. Maccoby, E. E. *The Development of Sex Differences* (Stanford Univ. Press, Palo Alto, Calif., 1966)
133. McGlothlin, W. H., Cohen, S., McGlothlin, Marcella S. Short-term effects of LSD on anxiety, attitudes and performance. *J. Nerv. Ment. Dis.*, **139**, 266–73 (1964)
134. McNemar, Q. Lost: our intelligence. Why? *Am. Psychol.*, **19**, 871–82 (1964)
135. Mackworth, J. F. Effect of amphetamine on the detectability of signals in a vigilance task. *Can. J. Psychol.*, **19**, 104–10 (1965)
136. Manley, M. B. A factor analytic study of three types of concept attainment tasks (Educ. Testing Serv., Princeton, N. J., 1965)
137. Marge, M. A factor analysis of oral communication skills in older children. *J. Speech Hearing Res.*, **7**, 31–46 (1964)
138. Meili, R. Intelligence interpreted by factor analysis. *Schweiz. Z. Psychol. Anwend.*, **23**, 135–55 (1964)
139. Merrifield, P. R. Trends in the mea-

surement of special abilities. *Rev. Educ. Res.*, **35**, 25–33 (1965)
140. Miller, J. W., Radloff, R., Bowen, H. M., Helmreich, R. L. Sealab II. Human behavior program. In *Project Sealab report—An Experimental 45-Day Undersea Saturation Dive at 205 Feet* (Pauli, D. C., Clapper, G. P., Eds., ONR Rept. ACR-124, 1967)
141. Munnichs, J. M. Some problems of research about the intelligence of the aged. *Gawein*, **13**, 268–79 (1965)
142. Nisbet, J. D., Entwistle, N. J. Intelligence and family size. *Brit. J. Educ. Psychol.*, **37**, 188–93 (1967)
143. Noble, C. E., Baker, B. C., Jones, T. A. Age and sex parameters in psychomotor learning. *Percept. Mot. Skills*, **19**, 935–45 (1964)
144. Oleron, P. *Intellectual Activities* (Presses Universitaires de France, 163 pp., 1964)
145. Osborn, A. G., Bunker, J. P., Cooper, L. M. Effects of thiopental sedation on learning and memory. *Science*, **157**, 574–76 (1967)
146. Osborne, R. T., Lindsey, J. M. A longitudinal investigation of change in the factorial composition of intelligence with age in young school children. *J. Gen. Psychol.*, **110**, 49–58 (1967)
147. Owens, W. A. Age and mental abilities: A longitudinal study. *Gen. Psychol. Monogr.*, **48**, 3–54 (1953)
148. Owens, W. A. Age and mental abilities: A second adult follow-up. *J. Educ. Psychol.*, **57**, 311–25 (1966)
149. Parker, J. F. The identification of performance dimensions through factor analysis. *Human Factors*, **9**, 367–73 (1967)
150. Parker, J. F., Reilly, R. E., Dillon, R. F., Andrews, T. G., Fleishman, E. A. Development of tests for measurement of primary perceptual-motor performance (Biotechnology, Inc., Arlington, Va., 1965)
151. Passey, G. E., McLaurin, W. A. Perceptual-psychomotor tests in aircrew selection: Historical review and advanced concepts (USAF PRL Tech. Rept., 236 pp., 1966)
152. Pearson, R. G. Performance tasks for operator-skills research. *Off. Aviation Med. Rept.*, 13 pp., 1966.
153. Piaget, J., Inhelder, B. *The Early Growth of Logic in the Child* (Harper & Row, N. Y., 1964)
154. Quereshi, M. Y. The invariance of certain ability factors. *Educ. Psy-*

chol. *Measmt.*, **27**, 803–10 (1967)
155. Ranzi, A., Tampieri, P. Factors in the development of thinking: Equilibration and learning. *Riv. Psicol. Soc. Arch. Ital. Psicol. Gen. Lav.*, **33**, 399–430 (1966)
156. Ray, O. S., Bivens, L. W. Performance as a function of drug, dose, and level of training. *Psychopharmacologia*, **10**, 103–9 (1966)
157. Říčan, P. K základním pojmum theorie schopnosti. *Cesk. Psychol.*, **9**, 243–50 (1965)
158. Schneider, B., Bartlett, C. J. Individual differences and organizational climate I: The research plan and questionnaire development. *Personnel Psychol.*, **21**, (1968)
159. Shavelson, R. J., Seminara, J. L. Effect of lunar gravity on man's performance of basic maintenance tasks. *J. Appl. Psychol.*, **52**, 177–83 (1968)
160. Shaycoft, M. F. The high school years: Growth in cognitive skills. (*Am. Inst. Res., Pittsburgh, Pa.*, 1967)
161. Sherman, J. A. Problem of sex differences in space perception and aspects of intellectual functioning. *Psychol. Rev.*, **74**, 290–99 (1967)
162. Shuey, Audrey M. *The Testing of Negro Intelligence* (2nd Ed.) (Soc. Sci. Press, N. Y., 1968)
163. Skeels, H. M. Adult stature of children with contrasting early life experience: A follow up study. *Child Develpm. Monogr.*, **31**, 111 pp. (1966)
164. Skeels, H. M., Dye, H. B. A study of the effects of differential stimulation on mentally retarded children. *Proc. Am. Assoc. Ment. Defic.*, **44**, 114–36 (1939)
165. Smith, H. W., May, W. T. Influence of the examiner on the ITPA scores of negro children. *Psychol. Rept.*, **20**, 499–402 (1967)
166. Smith, I. M. *Spatial Ability: Its Educational and Social Significance* (Knapp, San Diego, Calif., 1965)
167. Smith, R. G. Magnesium pemoline: Lack of facilitation in human learning, memory, and performance tests. *Science*, **155**, 603–5 (1967)
168. Smith, R. M. Creative thinking abilities of educable mentally handicapped children in the regular grades. *Am. J. Ment. Defic.*, **71**, 571–75 (1967)
169. Stodolsky, S. S., Lesser, G. Learning patterns in the disadvantaged.

Harvard Educ. Rev., **37**, 546–93 (1967)

170. Stolurow, L. M. Social impact of programmed instruction: Aptitudes and abilities revisited. In *Educational Technology*, 348–55 (De-Ceddo, J. P., Ed., Holt, Rinehart & Winston, N. Y., 1964)

171. Stolurow, L. M. Programmed instruction and teaching machines. In *The Impact of New Media on Education and Society* (Rossi, P. H., Biddle, B. J., Eds., Aldine, Chicago, Ill., 1965)

172. Talland, G. A., McGuire, M. T. Tests of learning and memory with cylert. *Psychopharmacologia*, **10**, 445–51 (1967)

173. Talland, G. A., Mendelson, J. H., Koz, G., Aaron, R. Experimental studies of tricyanoaminopropene on the memory and learning capacities of geriatric patients. *J. Psychol. Res.*, **3**, 171–79 (1965)

174. Talland, G. A., Quarton, G. C., Methamphetamine and pentobarbital effects on human motor performance. *Psychopharmacologia*, **8**, 241–50 (1965)

175. Tallmadge, G. K. Relationships between training methods and learner characteristics. *J. Educ. Psychol.*, **59**, 32–36 (1968)

176. Taub, H. A. Paired associates learning as a function of age, rate and instruction. *J. Gen. Psychol.*, **111**, 41–46 (1967)

177. Taylor, C. W. *Creativity: Progress and Potential* (McGraw-Hill, N. Y., 1964)

178. Taylor, J. E., Fox, W. L. Differential approaches to training (HumRRO, Monterey, Calif., 1967)

179. Tenopyr, Mary L., Guilford, J. P., Hoepfner, R. A factor analysis of symbolic memory abilities: Studies of the aptitudes of high-level personnel. *Rept. Psychol. Lab., Univ. Southern California*, 31 pp. (1966)

179a. Tenora, V., Šnapka, J. Sledvvaní těllsné výkonnosti pomocí Fleishmanova Testu. *Tevr. Praxe Tele. Vych.*, **15**, 178–84 (1967)

180. Thumin, F. J., Boernke, C. Miller Analogies Test performance as related to age, sex, and academic field. *Psychol. Rept.*, **19**, 751–54, (1966)

181. Thurmond, J. B., Alluisi, E. A. Behavioral effects of infectious diseases: Third annual progress report (Univ. Louisville, Ky., 1967)

182. Tucker, L. R. Determination of generalized learning curves by factor analysis (Educ. Testing Serv., Princeton, N. J., 1960)

183. Tucker, L. R. Cluster analysis and the search for structure underlying individual differences in psychological phenomena (Univ. Illinois, Urbana, Ill., 1967)

184. Tucker, L. R. Three-mode factor analysis of Parker-Fleishman complex tracking behavior data. *Multivariate Behav. Res.*, **2**, 139–51 (1967)

185. Tyler, L. *The Psychology of Human Differences* (3rd Ed.) (Appleton-Century-Crofts, N. Y., 1965)

186. Vandenberg, S. G. Contributions of twin research to psychology. *Psychol. Bull.*, **66**, 327–52 (1966)

187. Vernon, P. E. *The Structure of Human Abilities* (2nd Ed.) (Methuen, London, 1961)

188. Very, P. S. Differential factor structures in mathematical ability. *Gen. Psychol. Monogr.*, **75**, 169–207 (1967)

189. Weiner, M. Organization of mental abilities from ages 14 to 54. *Educ. Psychol. Measmt.*, **24**, 573–87 (1964)

190. Wesman, A. G. Aptitude, intelligence, and achievement. *Psicol. Educ.*, **1**, 42–48 (1964)

191. Yamamoto, K. Threshold of intelligence in academic achievement. *J. Exptl. Educ.*, **32**, 401–5 (1964)

192. Yamamoto, K. Effects of restriction of range and test unreliability on correlation between measures of intelligence and creative thinking. *Brit. J. Educ. Psychol.*, **35**, 300–5 (1965)

193. Yamamoto, K., Chimbidis, M. E. Achievement: intelligence and creative thinking in fifth grade children: A correlational study. *Merrill-Palmer Quart.*, **12**, 233–41 (1966)

194. Zavala, A. The definition and measurement of cognitive abilities in unusual environments (Am. Inst. Res., Washington, D. C., 1967)

195. Zeaman, D., House, B. J. The relation of IQ and learning. In *Learning and Individual Differences*, 192–213 (Gagné, R. M., Ed., Merrill, Columbus, Ohio, 265 pp., 1967)

INSTRUCTIONAL PSYCHOLOGY[1,2]

141

By ROBERT M. GAGNÉ AND WILLIAM D. ROHWER, JR.

University of California, Berkeley, California

Much of the work designed to investigate the phenomena of human learning may be thought of as having its ultimate applicability in the design of effective conditions for instruction. This is true whether these conditions are conceived as being arranged by an instructor, by some form of teaching machine or training device, by a set of materials like a book or film, or by the learner himself. In some general sense, therefore, it would be truly difficult to distinguish the psychology of instruction from the psychology of learning. In this first review bearing such a title, we have attempted to limit attention to studies of those variables and conditions that appear to have a fairly direct applicability to the design of instruction.

Remoteness of applicability to instruction, we note with some regret, characterizes many studies of human learning, retention, and transfer, appearing in the most prestigious of psychological journals. The findings of many studies of human learning presently cannot be applied directly to instructional design for two major reasons: (*a*) the conditions under which the learning is investigated, such as withholding knowledge of learning goals from the subject and the requiring of repetition of responses, are often unrepresentative of conditions under which most human learning occurs; and (*b*) the tasks set for the learner (e.g., the verbatim reproduction of verbal responses, the guessing of stimulus attributes chosen by the experimenter, among many others) appear to cover a range from the merely peculiar to the downright esoteric. This is not to imply that such studies do not further an understanding of the learning process. However, it would seem that extensive theory development centering upon learning tasks and learning conditions will be required before one will be able to apply such knowledge to the design of instruction for representative human tasks.

Within the limitation of the criterion of direct applicability to instruction, our review of studies of human learning, retention, and transfer has been fairly broad. We have sought relevant reports in psychological journals and books of general orientation, as well as in those devoted more specifically

[1] The survey of literature pertaining to this review was concluded in April 1968.

[2] The preparation of this paper has been supported in part by funds made available under a contract with the U. S. Office of Education (Contract No. OEC 4-7-062949-3066), and under a contract with the U. S. Office of Economic Opportunity (Contract No. OEO 2404).

to educational studies. We have included only recent investigations covering the last 4 years. The review of educational psychology by Anderson (7), dealing as it does with variables in instruction, has provided many suggestions about lines of investigation. Although we have tried to avoid covering the same ground, many of the topics treated in his article may be considered to be brought up to date by the present review.

EVENTS OF INSTRUCTION

The organization of this review is derived from a consideration of the events which take place in instruction, as described by Gagné (62, 63). These are the distinguishable conditions, external to the learner, each of which may be arranged independently by an instructor or an instructional designer, and each of which may be considered as accomplishing a different subordinate purpose of the "single-lesson" instructional process. Each of these events may be varied in its characteristics, and it is these characteristics which we conceive to be the focus of interest of research in instructional psychology.

According to this model, the manager of instruction may manipulate the following sets of conditions, evidence related to each of which is considered in our review:

(a) employ techniques to gain and maintain the attention of the learner; (b) establish within the learner certain preconditions for learning by giving pretraining, by providing verbal directions, by stimulating recall; (c) present the stimuli directly involved in learning as actual objects and events, printed materials, or pictures, among other forms; (d) aid the learning process by methods of prompting and guiding, often in the form of verbal communications; (e) specify the conditions for responding as in the contrast between overt and covert responses; (f) employ methods to provide feedback to the learner concerning the correctness or incorrectness of his performance at various stages of learning; (g) establish conditions to promote retention, including such factors as repetition and rehearsal; (h) use techniques which enhance the transfer of learning to subsequent learning tasks or other performances.

GENERAL WORKS

Some important works have appeared in recent years which provide a general background to the area of instructional psychology. Besides the previously mentioned article by Anderson (7), there is a series of reports pertaining to audio-visual instruction sponsored by the U. S. Office of Education that deal with several categories of variables involved in the design of instruction using media. Three of these are by May (114–116) and a fourth by Briggs (24). A fifth report by John B. Carroll is expected, but unfortunately was not ready in time for this review. The series contains much of value for the instructional researcher, although it has not been widely distributed. Still another review in the audio-visual area is by Chu & Schramm (32), dealing with factors which influence the effectiveness of instruction by tele-vision and film. Of considerable general interest is Atkinson's (10) article describing the characteristics of several modes of computer-assisted instruc-tion and some recent findings obtained from their use in teaching elementary reading.

Besides the various general treatments of instructional psychology in textbooks of educational psychology, several individual volumes have par-ticular importance for providing general background to research issues in the field. Discovery learning is the subject of a volume by Shulman & Keislar (169). A text edited by Siegel (171) presents several theoretical ap-proaches to instruction. Skinner (175) has assembled some of his most penetrating speeches and papers into an integrated book on the technology of teaching. A book edited by Gagné (64) contains the views of learning in-vestigators on the relations of individual differences to learning variables. Adams (1) deals with empirical data and theory in the field of human mem-ory.

Gaining and Maintaining Attention

Attention is a term that has many meanings in psychological research. Some of them appear to be directly relevant to instruction; while others are at most indirectly related, e.g., "looking behavior," alertness, vigilance. The meanings of attention which appear to be of highest relevance to instruction may be formulated somewhat as follows: (a) What factors in the instructional situation bring about the establishment of an attentional set? (b) What factors in instruction operate to maintain an attentional set? (c) What con-ditions operate to overcome the effects of distracting stimuli on the mainten-ance of an attentional set?

Establishing an attentional set.—Certain pre-existing dispositions or capacities may affect the establishment of attention. Semmel & Williams (166) compared the performance of normal, borderline, and retarded chil-dren of 10 to 11 years in learning to anticipate the order of common objects shown in projected drawings, each with a different background color. In-tentional learning was best with normals, least good for retardates. Incidental learning for background colors was poorest for retardates when number of exposures was made equal. Suchman & Trabasso (179) showed that the learning of concepts of object-categories was facilitated when a preferred dimension (color or form) was relevant to the category, but was retarded when the preferred dimension was irrelevant. A study by Levonian (101) relates retention of information to arousal increment, measured by galvanic skin response, in high-school students who watched a traffic safety film. The author points out the relation of these findings to the orienting reflex, as dis-cussed by Maltzman (104).

Several studies relate the arousal of attention to certain motivating conditions, particularly curiosity. Thus Berlyne (19) reports the effectiveness of a guessing condition over that of no guessing in a task in which high-school students were asked to remember the authors of 28 prose quotations. Retention was better in the guessing condition and also better for delayed versus immediate telling of answers. These results are interpreted to support the notion of epistemic curiosity, dependent on conceptual conflict, as a factor in attention. Paradowski (133) showed illustrations of strange looking animals contrasted with familiar animals to different groups of college students, who were to learn the verbal information presented with each picture. Recall of both intentional and incidental background items was better with the strange looking animals, suggesting the action of some curiosity-like motivation. A study by Crandall (40) investigated the attentional effects of familiar and unfamiliar words. Attention was measured by frequency of alternations of eye fixations during prolonged viewing of word pairs. The familiar words produced higher rates of alternation and also a greater number of fixations away from the words.

Other kinds of motivation appear to be involved in such studies as those of Parker & Nunnally (134), who showed the effect of penny rewards on children's "time of looking" at nonsense syllables presented in a spin-wheel game. Still another type may have had some effect in Coats & Smidchens' (34) finding that sizeable differences in immediate recall of lecture material resulted when the lecture was delivered with much animation, eye contact, etc., as compared with the amount recalled when the lecture was read.

For students who have learned to respond to them, instructions can be effective in arousing attention. Amster (6) used the task of reproducing flags of various colors and designs in kindergarten and fourth and fifth grade children to study the effects of intentional and incidental learning instructions. Kindergarten learners, it was found, improved with practice under the intentional set to a greater degree than under the incidental set. The presence of irrelevant features depressed learning more for the kindergarterners than for the older group. Johnson (83) studied the effects of prompting on the learning of university students, using a programmed videotape concerned with student classroom behavior. Prompting was found to be effective, as shown by post-tests, in focussing students' attention on relevant aspects of the pictures. Other kinds of prompting have been studied. Anderson & Faust (8) gave each of two groups of learners a training sequence containing 16 English-Russian word pairs, presented in programmed booklets. In one form the response terms in the copying frames were underlined; in the other they were not. Significantly better performance was obtained in the no-underline condition. The authors interpret this finding to mean that underlining encourages inadequate inspection behavior. An interesting contrast is provided by the study of Simon & Jackson (174), who employed a task of concept identification requiring subjects to classify upper- and lower-case letters into groups 1 and 2. In one condition a dot appeared over the relevant dimension of the stimulus; in a second condition the dot was over the irrelevant dimension; in a third condition no dot was used. The relevant-dot treatment produced the fewest errors, the irrelevant-dot the most. These results are interpreted as showing the effect of an "observation stimulus" in increasing the probability of an observing response and thus facilitating learning. Considering these last two studies together, one would need to conclude that an extra stimulus (a dot or an underline) may under some conditions aid the establishment of attention and under other conditions hinder it. May's (114) discussion of cue identifiers and emphasizers also is relevant to this question.

The idea of attention as an observing response occurs prominently in the work of Zeaman & House (203), and this contrasts with the view of the Kendlers (90) that the act of attending has as its outcome some form of mediational or coding response. Kendler & Kendler (91) provide an informative review of these two theoretical positions, with evidence to support the mediational view. Wolff (198) presents a review of concept-shift and discrimination-reversal learning, with particular attention to these two contrasting theories, as well as to the perceptual-differentiation hypothesis [Tighe & Tighe (184)]. Evidence is cited which supports the idea that dimensional observing responses are essential to the solution of concept-shift tasks. In his review of several varieties of perceptual tasks, Egeth (52), in contrast, interprets various lines of evidence to show that subjects employ adaptive mediational processes in processing sensory input. Many studies have been designed to illuminate this very important though thorny theoretical question. It may be noted that the issue is primarily one of the basic nature of attention, and as such is not directly concerned with the question of how a set for attention becomes established.

Maintaining attentional sets.—In his discussion of the relation of attention to instruction, Skinner (175, pp. 105–6; 121–23) points out that capturing attention is less important to instruction than is teaching the student to continue to look at and listen to the relevant stimuli. He conceives the latter problem as one of shifting stimulus control so that originally uninteresting things become interesting after they have been read or listened to. In addition, contingencies of reinforcement may be used to establish attention as a form of "precurrent self-management behavior."

Rothkopf's work (151), showing that general (as opposed to specific) effects on "inspection behavior" can result from the insertion of questions following segments of text, as opposed to specific effects of questions presented before the segments, appears to have opened many possibilities for research, as Anderson (7) points out. The technique of inserting questions is generally interpreted as bringing about the maintenance of an attentional set, and this is of considerable importance to instructional psychology. Rothkopf & Bisbicos (153) found that questions inserted following passages of printed text brought about selective facilitation; that is, retention was improved selectively depending on whether the questions pertained to a term or name, or to an English word or technical word. General improvement (i.e., nonspecific to question type) in retention was also shown. The presence of questions was found to increase inspection time initially; however, this effect diminished as study of the text proceeded. On this latter point, Rothkopf (152) conducted a study to determine the effect of repeated presentations of meaningful passages, which college students read up to four times. The proportion of correct responses on a post-test, using the Cloze procedure, increased with number of exposures up to two and leveled off thereafter. Inspection time went steadily downward with increased repetitions, suggesting that inspection behavior was subject to extinction.

Other studies confirm and elaborate Rothkopf's findings. Frase (60) had college students read a biographical passage with interspersed questions. The questions were inserted before the text segment or after the segment and were relevant or incidental to the post-test questions. In addition, one condition provided knowledge of correctness but another did not. For relevant questions both positions had a positive effect, as did knowledge of results. For incidental questions only the placement after the text segments had a facilitating effect. A second Frase study (61) concerned itself with the variables of question position (before or after text segments) and frequency of question occurrence (every paragraph versus every other). The results indicate that after-questions produced greater retention, even from the beginning of the passage, and more markedly with more frequent occurrence. The effect of questions, the author says, is to maintain previously established inspection skills in reading. Still another study of a confirming nature is by Bruning (26), who had college students study a 1500-word passage divided into six sections, each followed by from three to seven test-review items. A strong facilitating effect on retained information was found for both test-relevant and test-irrelevant items. Increased inspection time, more active reading behavior, and increased self-prompting are among the effects the author believes to account for improvement in learning resulting from inserted questions.

Duration of attention and the effects of distraction.—To the elementary school teacher, the problem of attention is often seen as one of bringing about an increased time span during which the child can maintain an attentional set, or even a more gross "focus" to his behavior, in the face of distracting stimulation from the external environment and from his own body. This, of course, is not at all the classical psychological meaning of "span of attention," but it is most often what the phrase means to the teacher.

Samuels (157) found that pictures used with reading texts retarded reading acquisition in young children, presumably because they distract attention. A developmental study of sustained attention was conducted by Grim (70), who compared the effects of irregularly varied preparatory intervals on the reaction time of first graders, sixth graders, and adults. The preparatory intervals varied from 3 to 20 sec. Galvanic skin response and digital vasoconstriction were also measured. Reaction times were found to increase for children but not for adults as the preparatory interval increased, indicating age differences in the sustaining of attention, presumably because of differences in distractibility. Hagen (73) had children in grades one, three, five, and seven perform a task requiring observation of pictures of well-known objects, followed by identification of the location (on a card) of pictures previously shown. For distraction, a melody of high-pitched piano notes was used, interspersed with occasional low notes in response to which the subject had to tap the table at which he sat. Performance on the task was found to improve steadily with age. Incidental learning, involving the matching of animals with paired household objects, did not change significantly with age, except for the fact that distraction reduced the scores of seventh graders. In a study by Eagle & Ortoff (50) subjects were asked to memorize 26 words under two different conditions: (a) with focal attention, and (b) while performing a distracting task. The distracted group showed more recognition errors which could be classified as having acoustic similarity, suggesting that under these conditions words were frequently stored in this auditory manner, rather than being more adequately encoded.

Summary statement.—Concerning the problems of establishing and maintaining attentional sets and protecting them from distractions, it is good to be able to note that some work is going on, even though as yet it has barely scratched the surface. Promising directions in the establishment of attentional sets appear to lie in the investigation of motivational and instructional variables and their interactive effects. As for maintaining attention, the application of techniques employing reinforcement contingencies seems to hold much promise, as indicated, for example, by the work of Hewett (77). More experimental studies are needed. The insertion of questions, or "test-like events," into texts to be studied is a technique that suggests a variety of experimental problems which as yet are unexplored: kinds of questions, frequencies of questions, amounts of questioning. Not much work has been done on the effects of distractions on attention. We need to know not only what these effects are but also how various kinds of distractors operate, and particularly what means can be effective in overcoming their influence.

DIRECTING AND PREPARING THE LEARNER

The topic of directions and other learning preparations, including the sub-topic of pretraining, overlaps both conceptually and, in fact, with another topic of major importance to be treated later, namely, transfer. Nevertheless, some distinction can be made. The present discussion will be concerned with those instructional activities that are directed toward improving performance on a specific task, usually within a narrowly defined and circumscribed setting rather than with activities designed to foster successful performance on a variety of related tasks. Accordingly, relevant research will be reviewed under three category labels: verbal directions, pretraining, and recall of relevant past learning.

Verbal directions.—In virtually all cases the onset of any learning task is preceded by some form of verbal directions or instructions. As a minimum, learners are given a description of the events that will follow, of the general procedures that will ensue, and of the kind of activity they are expected to engage in. These forms of verbal instruction, i.e., matters of procedural description, will be of little concern here; not because they are irrelevant to the objective of preparing the learner, but because little, if any, systematic research has been reported as to the effects on subsequent performance of variations in such instructions.

Verbal directions that go beyond these minimum forms, however, have attracted some research attention recently. On a digit cancellation task, for example [Jones (84)], one group was instructed to mark four of eight specific digits, while the other group was instructed to mark all digits except the remaining four. The group receiving the "except" instructions made more errors and was characterized by longer latencies of response than the other group, suggesting that negative directions should not be used when equivalent positive instructions are available. One of the most provocative of the studies on verbal directions was reported by King & Russell (96). Groups of undergraduates were asked to memorize a 200-word story about drug addiction. Prior to the presentation of the story, one group was instructed to remember it word for word and not its main ideas, whereas the other group was instructed to remember the main ideas and not to remember the story word for word. Retention was measured in a variety of ways, including indices of both verbatim and main-idea recall. Although there were no significant differences on measures of recall of main ideas, the group instructed not to engage in verbatim memorization recalled more of the letters, words, and sentences from the original passage than the group explicitly instructed to do so. Should this finding survive replication with less sophisticated populations, with alternatively worded instructions, and with a variety of prose materials, it would suggest that the activity of storing main ideas for recall entails the storage of verbatim information as well.

Another possible implication of the King-Russell results is that effective verbatim memorization begins with a kind of learning that, despite its appearance, is not at all rote in its underlying processes. A substantial amount of evidence in support of this supposition is now available. Post-criterion interviews, taken at the completion of paired-associate learning, reveal that subjects engaged in considerable covert activity during performance on presumably rote tasks [Bugelski (27); Martin, Boersma & Cox (110); Martin, Cox & Boersma (111); Montague, Adams & Kiess (121); Montague & Wearing (122)]. These activities vary in character from simple rehearsal to the construction of complex grammatical contexts; they will be referred to here as elaborative activities.

Bower (23) reports that specific elaboration directions, prior to paired-associate learning, exert a marked facilitative influence on the retention of multiple lists. College students were instructed to form an image involving the two members of each pair. After the successive presentation of five lists of noun pairs, the group given elaboration instructions responded correctly to 81 per cent of the 100 stimulus nouns, whereas a control condition produced only 50 per cent correct responses. Yuille & Paivio (202) report that directions to construct imagery elaboration, as well as directions to construct verbal elaboration, facilitate paired-associate learning in college students as compared with instructions to simply repeat each pair as it is presented. Finally, Milgram (119) has shown that instructions to use sentence elaboration promote faster learning in both normal children and in retardates than standard instructions. Even though the measure of performance in all of these paired-associate studies was the verbatim recall of noun pairs, the directions given the experimental groups invariably emphasized the importance of non-rote activities. Such directions clearly facilitate learning on paired-associate tasks, but it remains to be determined whether or not they can exert similar effects on the learning of school-subject materials.

Pretraining.—Experimental studies that can be construed as investigations of the effects of pretraining on performance are numerous indeed. Many of these, however, can be reviewed more appropriately in connection with the topic of transfer. A number of the investigations reported by those engaged in research on verbal learning processes offer suggestions about the importance of pretraining for learning. Studies of associative mediation, for example, clearly demonstrate that prior learning can affect new learning. Nikkel & Palermo (124) observed that natural language associates, estimated from children's association norms, can either facilitate or interfere with new paired-associate learning, depending upon the paradigm used. Palermo (132) also reports mediated facilitation for children when paradigms selected to take advantage of prior backward associations are used. Similarly, Cramer (39) reports facilitation for adults in a variety of mediation paradigms when normative associations are considered in designing the paired-associate lists.

Such facilitation as is observed in studies of associative mediation seems to depend upon whether or not subjects are aware of the interlist relationships in the paradigm. Richardson (142) reports slightly faster learning for subjects apprised of the relationship between the lists. A more telling study has been reported by Lee & Jensen (100), in which one group was informed about the interlist relationships while the other was not; all subjects were interviewed at the conclusion of learning. More facilitation was observed in the informed than in the uninformed condition; but more importantly, when subjects in the uninformed conditions were categorized with respect to their reported awareness of the interlist relations, facilitation was observed only for those who did admit discovering the mediating relationship.

Mediation paradigms, of course, are not the only form of pretraining investigated by those concerned with verbal learning. With regard to the the traditional topics of learning-to-learn and warm-up, Schwenn & Postman (162) found that the former kind of practice exerts a greater positive effect on subsequent learning than the latter. Keppel (93) reported that performance on terminal, two-list, paired-associate transfer tasks is facilitated by pretraining on any one of a variety of other two-list transfer tasks. Again, it must be said that these findings are suggestive for instruction but limited, at present, in their generalizability. It should be emphasized also that the amount of time consumed by the combination of pretraining and criterion learning, whether in mediation, warm-up, or learning-to-learn paradigms, is often greater than that consumed by a control condition on the criterion task alone when no time is spent in pretraining activities.

Along a somewhat different line, Mandler & Stephens (106) report replicating with second-, fourth-, sixth-, and eighth-grade girls a finding originally obtained with college-age subjects [Mandler & Pearlstone (105)]. The terminal task was that of recalling a stimulus list of 15 high-frequency words. Prior to recall, one group of subjects was required to sort repeatedly the stimulus items into categories of their own choosing until a stable categorization was achieved. In the other condition, subjects were constrained to use the categories chosen by yoked subjects in the free condition. Subsequent stimulus recall was superior for those allowed to use their own basis for categorization. Such results suggest that students, even as young as those in second-grade classes, impose structure upon presented materials and that, within the limits of these investigations, self-imposed structures facilitate learning more than presented structures.

Recall of relevant past learning.—In considering means for preparing a student to derive maximum benefit from an instructional sequence, it is important to stimulate the recall of previous learning that can facilitate his present efforts. Unfortunately, however, among the studies reviewed, very little of relevance to this important problem was detected. Apart from the obvious method of complete review of relevant past learning, only the following studies add to our knowledge of methods for stimulating relevant recall.

A study of free-recall learning reported by Earhard (51) suggests that a single cue can function to rearouse previous learning if the number of items attached to that cue is not too large.

A series of studies of associative priming suggests that the prior presentation of words to be evoked in a subsequent word-association task increases the probability that they will be emitted to previously unpresented stimulus words [Clifton (33); Cramer (38); Segal (164)]. Beyond the basic priming phenomenon, and of more direct relevance to instruction, Dominowski & Ekstrand (47) found that anagram solving is facilitated by the prior presentation of the solution words or of their associates. A study by Johnson (81) shows the direct applicability of the priming method to instruction. A group of high-school seniors who had completed a mechanics unit in a physics course were presented with the task of solving ten physics problems. Half of the students were given a 2-min word association pretest in which the stimulus words named concepts necessary for the solution of the subsequent problems. A significantly larger number of problem solutions were attained by the group given the prior association test than by the unprimed group.

Summary statement.—With regard to the topic of verbal directions, reported findings suggest that: the phrasing of instructions appears to affect learning efficiency; under some as yet unspecified conditions, learner behavior is opposite to that suggested in verbal directions; and learning can be facilitated by instructions to elaborate materials presented. Apart from transfer conditions, the facilitative effects of pretraining appear so small that their utility is doubtful. Thus far, priming is alone among methods of demonstrable use in stimulating relevant recall. In all cases, much additional research is needed, especially with tasks designed to mirror those commonly involved in instruction.

PRESENTING STIMULI

In planning instruction, consideration must be given to the effects on learning of variations in the stimulus materials presented. Research relevant to these effects will be reviewed in connection with the following subtopics: characteristics of the stimuli, mode of presentation of the stimuli, and contexts in which stimuli are presented.

Stimulus characteristics.—In connection with many learning tasks, the instructor has the option of presenting materials in the form of objects, pictures, or words. Several recent studies suggest that given such an option, the stimulus type of choice is either objects or pictures rather than words. In one study [Rohwer, et al. (148)] of paired-associate learning in third- and sixth-grade children, it was found that pictorial materials produced roughly twice as many correct responses as printed names of the objects depicted. In both conditions, the stimulus and response nouns were read aloud as the visual materials were presented. In a related paired-associate experiment, Dilley & Paivio (45) discovered a differential picture-word effect for stimulus and response terms among nursery school, kindergarten, and first-grade children. It is important to note that in contrast to the study by Rohwer et al., the presentation of the pictorial materials in the present experiment was not accompanied by the names of the objects depicted. The results showed that, in the stimulus position, pictorial materials produced more efficient learning than word materials, whereas in the response position, word materials were superior. In order to clarify the discrepancies between this and the previous experiment, a complete factorial design is needed to examine, separately for stimulus and response positions, the effects of pictorial and printed-word stimuli on the learning of aurally presented word materials. Results confirming those of Dilley & Paivio (45) have been reported by Cole et al. (35). Stimulus members of paired-associate lists presented pictorially were associated with faster learning than stimulus members presented as words. The superiority of the pictures was greater for third- than for fifth-grade children. Finally, in a free-recall learning task, undergraduates were observed to recall more object than word stimuli [Scott (163)].

Studies of materials within the verbal domain indicate that learning efficiency varies as a function of the characteristics of words themselves. In an experiment reported by Paivio & Yuille (131), the learning of a 16-pair list of concrete nouns was easier for fourth-, sixth-, and eighth-grade children than the learning of a list of abstract nouns. The positive effect of concreteness was generally more pronounced for stimulus than for response members of pairs. A similar finding resulted when adults were asked to learn a list of adjective-noun or noun-adjective pairs [Kusyszyn & Paivio (98)]. Paivio, Smythe & Yuille (130) also have found that the rated imagery of nouns exerts a positive effect on paired-associate learning (more so on the stimulus than on the response side) when meaningfulness is held constant, whereas meaningfulness exerts a negative effect when rated imagery is held constant.

Tasks requiring the memorization or the comprehension of sentence materials are related to some instructional tasks. Recent research in this area has been concerned principally with the effects of sentence (stimulus) structure on performance. In two studies of comprehension, understanding was measured by a verification task in which subjects are asked to judge the congruence between a sentence and a related pictorial depiction of the sentence referents. Gough (69) reports that it is easier to verify: active than passive sentences; affirmative than negative sentences; and true than false sentences. Slobin (176) found these same variables important in determining response latency in a verification task. Similarly, sentence retention has been shown to be a direct function of structural, that is, syntactic, complexity [Epstein (56); Martin & Roberts (113)].

The degree of structure inherent in visual displays also seems to affect performance proficiency in learning tasks. Reynolds (140, 141) asked subjects to learn a set of factual statements in sentence form. In the experimental condition prior to sentence learning, subjects were shown a map drawing in which pictorial items were labeled with words presented later in the sentences to be learned. That is to say, the factual statements were illustrated in the map drawing. In one control condition, subjects were exposed to the same map except that it was presented successively, that is, in parts rather than simultaneously, while in the other control condition no previous exposure to the map drawing was provided. Significant facilitation of sentence learning was observed for the experimental condition.

Stimulus characteristics also have been shown to be of importance in concept learning tasks. Elkind, Van Doorninck & Schwarz (55), for example, performed an experiment in which the task was to attain either the concept of a character, or of a setting, or of an activity, all of which were presented pictorially. Alternate grade levels from kindergarten to grade 6 were sampled, and performance was found to increase with age. Evidence is reported in support of the inference that setting and activity concepts are especially difficult for kindergarten-age children. Clearly, the effects of variations in the content of concepts to be learned may be of considerable importance for instructional design.

Mode of presentation.—Although it is of extraordinary relevance for instruction, the problem of variations in the relative efficacy of aural and visual channels of presenting stimuli has received little additional attention since the previously mentioned reviews of Anderson (7) and May (115). The results of investigations which have been reported recently emphasize the need for further clarifying research. That is to say, the relative efficacy of auditory and visual channels appears to depend upon subject characteristics (especially age) as well as on task and stimulus characteristics. A variable of considerable interest, namely, stage of learning and its possible interaction with mode of presentation, has been left entirely unexplored during the period under review.

To understand the complexity of this problem area, consider the results of the following studies. In an experiment on concept formation [Haygood (74)], concept instances were presented to college students in an aural and in a visual mode simultaneously. Four different kinds of concepts having two dimensional solutions were used. The two relevant dimensions were: both aural; both visual and aural—information in the two modes was completely redundant; or divided such that one dimension was visual and the other aural. Performance across the first three conditions did not differ significantly, but the cross-modal concept was more difficult than the other three. Cooper & Gaeth (36) have reported a study of paired-associate learning in which the interaction of mode (aural versus visual) with meaningfulness revealed no mode difference for high-meaningful material (words), whereas the visual mode was superior for low-meaningful material (trigrams). The study was performed with fourth-, fifth-, sixth-, tenth-, and twelfth-grade subjects, and a developmental interaction was significant such that the aural mode was better for younger and the visual mode was better for older subjects.

Presentation context.—Some of the most substantial effects reported in connection with the topic of stimulus presentation have been observed in connection with variations in the context of presentation. The relevance of this matter for instruction is obvious, but the specific implications are not. The situation is much like that noted in connection with the topic of modes of presentation, that is, the relationships between independent variables and performance are complex. As will be seen shortly, the problem of drawing implications for instruction is made more difficult by the fact that some of the most clarifying experimental analyses of context effects have been made with learning tasks that are not broadly representative of those usually found in instructional settings.

In general, the presentation of nonverbal stimulus materials in a context such that each stimulus is given a verbal label facilitates learning involving those materials. The specific effect of labeling, however, may be either positive or negative depending on characteristics of the labels themselves. Chan & Travers (31) have reported an illustrative study in which the task was that of recognizing previously seen silhouette figures when later presented in the company of distractors. Each silhouette was accompanied by either a meaningful-word or a nonsense-word label presented either aurally or visually. Performance was significantly better in the meaningful-label condition than in the no-label condition, which in turn was superior to the nonsense-label condition.

Three studies indicate that kindergarten children have a much weaker propensity for engaging in spontaneous labeling and rehearsal behavior than do first-grade and other older children. This same result was obtained in all three experiments, each of which used a recall task [Corsini, Pick & Flavell (37); Keeney, Cannizzo & Flavell (86); Flavell, Beach & Chinsky (58)]. Clearly, labeling is an important operant capability, and the fact that it cannot be counted upon routinely in kindergarten subjects suggests that instruction must be designed specifically to elicit it in such children.

In connection with the topic of pretraining, it was noted that the instruction to elaborate noun pairs into sentences facilitates paired-associate learning. In a series of studies, this form of elaboration has been analyzed experimentally by manipulating features of the grammatical contexts in which noun pairs are presented. The results of these experiments indicate that word-string contexts facilitate the learning of constituent noun pairs but only under rather specific conditions [Rapier (137); Rohwer (143, 144); Rohwer & Levin (145); Rohwer & Lynch (146, 147); Rohwer, Lynch, Levin & Suzuki (148, 149); Rohwer, Lynch, Suzuki & Levin (150); Suzuki & Rohwer (181)]. Aspects of grammatical contexts are potent variables in paired-associate learning, but the important question remains as to their effects on types of learning that more nearly approximate the paradigms that underlie the acquisition of school subjects.

Reese (138) also observed that noun-pair learning is facilitated by sentence contexts in an experiment designed to examine the effect of a pictorial analogue of grammatical contexts. The stimulus and response members of paired associates were presented verbally (nouns) and visually (pictures) to all subjects. For half the subjects, however, an interaction involving the pair members was described verbally (CAT carrying an UMBRELLA), while for the other half it was not so described. Furthermore, for half the subjects in each of these groups, the described interaction was depicted visually, while for the other half, only the paired members, not the interactions, were depicted visually. Both verbal and visual contexts depicting interactions facilitated learning for the subjects sampled (age range: 3 to 8 years). Milgram (120) has more recently reported a replication of this experiment with essentially the same results. In a similar experiment, Rohwer et al. (149, 150) report congruent findings when the visual analogues of grammatical contexts are achieved by means of movie film.

Summary statement.—Considerable evidence has now been amassed indicating that when there is a choice of method for presenting equivalent information, the following results prevail: pictorial materials are superior to verbal; concrete verbal materials are preferable to abstract verbal; and grammatically structured are better than unstructured materials. In contrast, the conditions that might dictate choices among various available modes of presenting stimuli are almost entirely undetermined thus far. Finally, stimulus context appears to be one of the most potent of the variables determining the effects of materials presented, although tasks other than traditional laboratory ones remain to be investigated.

PROMPTING AND LEARNING GUIDANCE

When the learner is confronted with the stimulus situation to which he must react by learning, he may also be provided with various kinds of extra stimulation having the function of "prompting" a correct response, and in a more general sense, "guiding" his performance along lines which avoid extreme errors. As learning continues, this extra guidance may be removed, or in the language of the instructional programmer, the prompting stimuli may be "faded" and ultimately "vanished." Learning guidance is an important instructional technique which is applicable to a considerable variety of learning tasks.

In discrimination learning.—Some new studies of prompting and fading in discrimination learning have been influenced by the work of Terrace (182), who found it possible to establish discriminations without the occurrence of errors by progressively narrowing the differences between two stimuli to be discriminated. This technique differs from the more traditional one of discrimination training, in which errors originally are allowed to occur but are not reinforced or sometimes corrected. Sidman & Stoddard (170) used fading procedures with retarded children, beginning with an easy discrimination of bright versus dark, continuing through form versus no form, to circle versus ellipse. This program was found to be more effective than one using reinforcement for correct responses and nonreinforcement for incorrect responses; seven of ten children learned by means of the fading procedure, while only one of nine learned with the reinforcement-extinction method. Incidentally, an important distinction is made between this kind of procedure as "stimulus shaping" and the somewhat more familiar "response shaping" of motor acts. Touchette (185) also used the fading technique to bring about discrimination of the position of a black square in a larger field by gradually reducing the size of the black area. Learning and retention in retarded boys were superior in the group taught by the method of "graduated stimulus change" to those taught by the reinforcement-extinction method. For the learning of discriminations by retarded children, as well as by normal young children, this method appears to hold much promise.

In programmed instruction.—A review of recent literature on response prompting and response confirmation is provided by Aiken & Law (3), who conclude that prompting usually is shown to be as effective as confirmation in studies of verbal learning and signal monitoring, but this is not always the case in discrimination learning (of the sort which uses the error and correction method rather than stimulus fading).

In concept learning.—Johnson & Stratton (80) compared the effectiveness of five different methods of learning abstract concepts, including defining, sentence completion, classifying instances, synonyms, and a mixed method. The methods were found to be about equally effective, and transfer from learning by one method to performance on another was 100 per cent. Various kinds of prompts have been shown to facilitate the learning of concepts by children. Gollin, Saravo & Salten (68) found that the use of four non-odd stimuli, as opposed to two, aided the establishment of oddity-problem solving by kindergarten children, but not that of preschool or second-grade children. Norman & Rieber (125) showed that added color cues were effective prompts for the learning of single- and double-alternation tasks in children 6 to 11 years of age. Reese (139) found that verbal prompts facilitated learning and transposition in preschool children learning to choose a "medium" (not big or little) stimulus object.

In this area, the prompting variable continues to be of great interest. Faust & Anderson (57) found that prompting sentences worked better when embedded in a context of other sentences than when presented in copying frames. In this situation, they believe, the incidental sentences help to insure that the learner notices the stimulus before making his response. Anderson, Faust & Roderick (9) compared a heavily prompted version of an instructional program with a standard version and found that students made higher achievement scores with the latter version. Overprompting can lead to a reduction in learning effectiveness. The study of Seidel & Rotberg (165) also found that a high degree of prompting led to reduced effectiveness of performance on criterion tasks in writing computer programs. Merrill & Stolurow (118) showed that a hierarchically arranged summary, given before the program, increased the number of correct responses during both learning and testing and did not add to the total time required.

In rule learning.—Studies of learning guidance in the learning of rule-governed behavior are of various sorts. Bandura & Harris (11) found that second-grade children could learn to generate passive sentences most readily when verbal models were combined with procedures designed to increase distinctiveness of sentence types. In contrast, procedures emphasizing attention and the use of reinforcement were relatively ineffective. Haygood & Stevenson (75) found that college students' learning of conjunctive, disjunctive, and conditional rules was unaffected by the presence of irrelevant dimensions. It should be noted that rule learning, with prior identification of relevant attributes, is carefully distinguished in this study from concept attainment. Scandura, Woodward & Lee (161) found that the degree of generality of the rule used in instruction tended strongly to determine the degree of generality of the rules discovered during the playing of the mathematical game of NIM. In a classroom study, Lamb (99) found that verbal instructions encouraging rapid work or accurate work, given to second- and third-grade classes, had no effect on achievement on a reading test.

A study of particular significance in learning guidance was made by Guthrie (72), who compared methods designated as Rule-Example, Example-Rule, Example, and Control (No-Training), in the learning and transfer of rules for solving cryptograms. While retention of the rules acquired usually was greater for the Rule-Example group, transfer scores were clearly superior in the Example-Rule and Example groups. The author's interpretation is that the example methods evoke searching, or exploratory behavior, which carries over to the transfer task. In view of the many studies which have preceded it [cf. Shulman & Keislar (169)], it is good to have this suggestion of a fairly definite kind of mediating behavior in learning by discovery. A test of discovery methods of teaching under classroom conditions was conducted by Worthen (200), with results indicating superiority of these methods in promoting retention and transfer.

Summary statement.—Prompting and learning guidance take many forms and are applicable to many varieties of learning. Generally, these techniques appear to make possible the acquisition of behaviors which are intermediate to the criterion behavior desired and thus, through "transfer," to facilitate the acquisition of that criterion behavior. In discrimination learning via stimulus fading, the intermediate behavior gradually may be changed by small increments. In concept learning, prompting may operate by increasing the distinctiveness of dimensional cues. In rule learning, guidance can provide verbal cues which speed the acquisition of rule-governed behavior by limiting symbolic exploration. A number of studies remind us, though, that too much guidance or overprompting may narrow the limits of what is learned beyond what is most desirable for learning transfer.

CONDITIONS OF RESPONDING

Other conditions which may be specified in the conduct of instruction are those pertaining to the learner's responding. Obviously, he may be required to make overt responses or not to make them; the timing and frequency of (overt) responding may be set at one value or another; and the frequency and consequences of error responses may be systematically varied.

Overt responding.—Since Anderson's (7) review of the topic, only a few studies have appeared which contrast the effectiveness of overt responding with other forms in programmed instruction. Crist (41) compared overt and covert responding in sixth graders learning from a programmed text and found no differences in achievement, although covert responding took less time. Williams (196) used: (*a*) constructed responses, (*b*) multiple-choice responses, and (*c*) a combination, with sixth graders who learned from a linear program and were tested via constructed responses. Results show a relation between response mode used in training and performance on the same mode used in testing; otherwise, no advantage was shown for a varied format during learning. Seidel & Rotberg (165) compared instructional programs on computer-program writing of varieties which required the student to (*a*) write the rules, (*b*) write the names of the rules in conjunction with the programs, and (*c*) write only the programs. The latter two conditions were found superior to the first, as measured by criterion performance in writing programs. In a concept-attainment task, Byers & Davidson (28) found that requiring subjects to make overt hypotheses facilitated concept acquisition.

Errors.—Continuing study of the "blackout technique," obliterating all material in an instructional program which can be eliminated without affecting error rate, is evidenced in a study by Kemp & Holland (89). The technique was applied to 12 sets of materials used in previous studies of overt versus covert responding. The lowest blackout ratios were found in those programs which previously demonstrated an advantage for overt responding, and the highest in programs which yielded no response-mode differences. When answers are truly dependent on the content, overt responding seems to have an advantage.

Related studies.—Certain studies in the verbal learning area may be considered to have some relevance to the problem of responding conditions in school-type learning. For example, Carmean & Weir (29) found that verbalizations of the correct stimulus after each response facilitated the learning of two-choice discriminations in adults; verbalizing the stimulus responded to, or the incorrect stimulus, had no effect; and verbalizing stimuli at random had an interfering effect. Keppel (94) considered evidence regarding the extinction-recovery hypothesis in accounting for superior retention of verbal pairs learned under distributed practice. He concluded that the evidence runs contrary to this hypothesis and that learners under distributed practice seem to exercise a selection process to acquire stable and strong associations. Tulving (188) studied the effects of recall tests in promoting retention and concluded that these affect recall to about the same extent as do events occuring in the "input" phase of retention. Recall of individual items was found to be quite labile, even when the total amount of recall was stable, favoring the view of a limited-capacity retrieval system.

Summary statement.—On the whole, the mode of responding does not appear to be a factor of remarkable importance to instruction, although overt responding may be shown to be effective under some conditions. Many questions about the frequency and spacing of responses remain unanswered, and these would appear to be variables of potentially high significance to the learning and remembering of school subjects. Evidence from verbal learning studies particularly suggests a need for investigations of spaced recall in the retention of meaningful materials.

PROVIDING FEEDBACK

The nature of feedback provided in the course of learning can vary widely; furthermore, it can vary both with respect to its informational properties and with respect to its incentive properties. Each of these kinds of variation has been shown to affect performance, but the precise form of the effect depends, in part, on predispositions of the learner. Some instructionally relevant studies of individual differences in these predispositions have appeared during the period under review. In a study of discrimination learning reported by Bisett & Rieber (20), for example, the incentive conditions were defined in every case in terms of the child's own preference among a set of reinforcers (e.g., paper clip, penny, etc.). The high-incentive condition produced significantly more correct responses than the low-incentive condition.

Allen (4) has reported a study concerned with feedback predispositions as a function of age (kindergarten versus fifth grade), task (sorting, drawing, puzzle), and feedback type (praise, criticism, silence). The dependent variables were, principally, persistence (amount of time spent before quitting the task), and, secondarily, rate of response. The results were comparable for both measures. For the younger subjects, praise was more effective in all three tasks than either criticism or silence. For older subjects, however, praise and silence were equally effective in the easier tasks (sorting and drawing), while criticism was more effective in the more difficult task (puzzle).

During the review period, three studies have appeared that cast considerable doubt on the widely-disseminated assertion that Negro and other lower-class children are less responsive to symbolic and social reinforcers than are white, middle-class children. In a complex factorial design, Allen, Dubanoski & Stevenson (5) examined changes from base rate of response in a simple marble-dropping task as a function of age and race of the subject (grades 1 to 2 versus 4 to 6; Negro versus white); race of experimenter (Negro versus white); and type of feedback (praise, criticism, silence). All subjects were drawn from schools serving low socioeconomic areas. These results indicated that no main effect was associated with type of reinforcement but several interactions were significant. In the control (silence) condition, increase from the base rate of responding was greater when experimenters and subjects were of the same race. In the criticism conditions, response rate of older subjects increased more than that of younger subjects. In the praise conditions, the response rate of Negro subjects increased from the base, while that of white subjects decreased; and, in general, Negro experimenters were associated with greater rate increases than white experimenters. In a related study of discrimination learning in lower-and middle-class preschool children, Spence & Dunton (178) manipulated the variables of feedback direction (reward, punishment, combined) and feedback type ("right" versus "wrong," and candy versus a sound). The results revealed that the candy-reward condition was inferior to other combinations for both groups. The "right"-reward condition was also an inferior one, especially so for the lower-class children. Finally, a study by Marshall (109), using a discrimination learning task, suggests that the critical feedback dimension for middle-class children is material-symbolic, whereas for lower-class children it is immediate-delayed. It is obvious at this point that considerable additional research is needed to clarify the relationships among learner predispositions, feedback direction, feedback type, and the temporal locus of feedback delivery.

An interesting study by Sullivan, Baker & Schutz (180) suggests that variations in feedback schedules may be more important in determining performance during initial learning than in determining the final amount learned. A self-instructional program was administered to adults in one of two feedback conditions. Subjects in the no-feedback condition made significantly more correct responses on mastery items within the program than subjects given feedback. On a 100-item criterion test, however, there was no significant difference between the two groups. With regard to its instructional implications, this finding needs to be examined as a function of age, for it seems likely that the capacity for adequate performance in the absence of external feedback should increase with increasing experience. Even for adults, however, the provision of feedback can be quite important, as a study by Johnson (83) indicates. The experiment was concerned with the ability of prospective teachers to make accurate observations of specific pupil behaviors. Twenty-one videotaped scenes of teacher-pupil interactions were presented as a training device. On a test of observation skill in connection with posttraining scenes, the immediate feedback group was superior to the no-feedback group, which differed little from an untrained control.

Another line of research concerned with feedback variables, namely, studies of vicarious reinforcement, is of considerable presumptive relevance for instruction. At least until the classroom method of organizing students for school learning is supplanted, it is important to discover methods for delivering feedback that do not necessitate the direct receipt of feedback by each individual student. Two studies with children suggest that the efficacy of vicarious reinforcement may vary with age in such a way that younger children derive more benefit from it than older ones. The task in an experiment reported by Barnwell & Sechrest (12) was simply that of playing with one of two construction toys. In the first-grade sample, vicarious reinforcement, both positive and negative, had the same effect as direct reinforcement; that is, observers repeated praised-model choices and did not repeat criticized-model choices. Among third-grade children, however, no differential effects of vicarious praise and criticism were detected; these subjects simply chose whichever task the model had previously selected, regardless of the consequences. In a similar study [Kelly (88)], a simple motor task was used and the dependent measure was response rate. The rates obtained were highest in both the direct- and vicarious-criticism conditions, lower in the direct- and vicarious-praise conditions, and lowest in the no-feedback condition. The effects of vicarious learning were studied by Kanfer & Duerfeldt (85) in connection with a paired-associate task involving nonsense-syllable materials. When subjects were exposed to the performance of a model early in their learning, the effects were the same as those of direct learning experience. When the exposure was delayed until late in the subjects own learning, it was detrimental to performance. These effects obtained whether the model received positive or negative feedback. Thus, the implication is that the efficacy of vicarious experience in connection with learning depends upon the stage of learning during which it is provided.

In a study of teacher-pupil roles as a feedback system, students were set the task of learning 60 German-English word pairs [Myers, Travers & Sanford (123)]. The results indicated that performance was best among subjects assigned to the pupil role, worst among subjects assigned to the teacher role, and at a median level among subjects in the control condition. This result deserves empirical extension to other tasks and materials in view of the rather widely accepted belief that one of the best ways to learn is to teach.

Summary statement.—A characteristic of recent research is that it reveals clearly the highly variable nature of feedback effects. Moreover, the research indicates that the sources of this variance are to be found in learner characteristics, type of feedback, timing of feedback, direction of feedback, and type of task. Growing interest in the problem of vicarious reinforcement eventually should provide important information about the uses of feedback in group instructional situations.

Promoting Retention

One of the first questions that occurs in any consideration of retention concerns the means to be used in measuring the amount retained. Keppel (95) has provided an excellent discussion of this matter, and it can be bypassed here except for mention of two studies that have appeared recently. The first [Shepard (167)] is important for the perspective it provides on the question of how much material human beings are capable of retaining. The answer provided is that, depending upon the material to be retained and the method used for measuring retention, a very great deal of information indeed can be retained. The subjects were shown a series of some 600 stimuli selected randomly from a still larger original population. Afterwards, the percentage of stimuli correctly recognized varied with the type of stimulus to which the subject was exposed: 90 per cent for single words, 88 per cent for sentences, and 98 per cent for pictures. In another experiment, Bruce & Cofer (25) compared three methods of measuring acquisition and retention of a list containing 28 CVC trigrams (free recall versus recognition with 28 distractors versus recognition with 70 distractors). Acquisition was most rapid in the short-recognition condition, less rapid in the long-recognition condition, and least rapid in the free-recall condition. On the retention test, groups that had learned by a free-recall method performed better than groups using either of the other two methods, suggesting that retention is better promoted by recall than by recognition learning. As to the specific effects of methods for testing retention, however, both kinds of recognition produced higher scores than did free recall.

One component of the foregoing results must be qualified, namely, that pertaining to the superiority of the free-recall method for promoting retention. The qualification does not call the results themselves into question; rather it raises the issue of whether the three acquisition groups had attained the same degree of learning at the end of the acquisition trials. If not, then the conclusion that free recall is a superior method for the purpose of retention must be viewed with considerable doubt. Underwood (189, 190) has provided a full discussion of the issues involved, along with a method for equating different conditions of acquisition for degree of original learning. The implications of this argument for instruction are profound indeed, for when degree of original learning is equated, other variables seem virtually irrelevant in determining the amount retained. For example, it has been shown already that learning ability [Underwood (189)], intralist similarity

[Underwood & Richardson (193)], meaningfulness [Underwood & Richardson (192)], and associative strength [Underwood & Keppel (191)]—all factors that exert great influence on learning efficiency—are of no consequence for retention, provided that degree of original learning has been equated.

If this phenomenon proves to be of as great a degree of general validity as now seems to be the case, then the concern of instructional psychology with simple retention comes down to this: what are the methods necessary for insuring a high degree of original learning; and what are the methods necessary for achieving that state as efficiently as possible? Presently available answers to these questions have, of course, been given already in other sections of this review, sections concerned with conditions that affect acquisition. Consider an example. It will be recalled that grammatical context has been shown to exert a considerable influence on the speed of acquisition in paired-associate learning. Olton (127) recently conducted an experiment designed to examine the effects of grammatical context on the retention of paired associates. As expected, learning was more rapid in a sentence condition than in a control condition, but different numbers of trials were afforded the two groups in accord with the method suggested by Underwood for equating degree of original learning. Retention was measured one week later. The results were clear: even when the original sentence frames were re-presented immediately prior to the retention trial, there were virtually no differences between the sentence and control conditions in the numbers of pairs retained.

In view of the pervasive import of the phenomena attached to degree of original learning, it is well to keep in mind that effects on retention reported in many studies are probably more accurately attributable to variables that affect acquisition rather than retention. Two major exceptions to this must be underlined: (a) the effects of variations in activities that intervene between acquisition and retention, viz., retroactive effects; and, possibly, (b) the effects of motivational variables. A comprehensive review of studies in the area of motivation and retention is now available [Weiner (195)].

An experiment by Montague, Adams & Kiess (121) suggests that elaborative activities can facilitate the retention of paired associates. As each pair was presented, the subject responded with whatever kind of elaboration occurred to him, if any. Rentention of pairs that had been elaborated during acquisition, and for which the elaboration was still reportable 24 hrs later, was significantly greater than for other pairs.

Two studies have been reported concerning the effects of distributed practice on recall. In one on short-term memory [Borkowski (22)], four-pair lists were presented and recall was assessed after a delay of 9, 15, or 45 sec. The distributed practice condition was superior to the massed practice condition at both the 15 and 45-sec retention intervals. In a study having considerably more direct applicability to instruction, Rothkopf & Coke (154) also observed that distributed practice was superior to massed practice in promoting retention. All subjects read a passage of prose material regarding a fictional primitive tribe. Eight of the sentences in the passage were repeated once each, either in immediate succession or after other intervening material from the passage. Delayed repetition of the sentences resulted in better retention than immediate repetition even when the repeated versions were different in phrasing from the originals.

Delay of feedback during acquisition can also promote better retention. In a study of learning of bigrams by a paired-associate method, Lintz & Brackbill (102) found that delay-feedback conditions were associated with higher recall one week later than immediate-feedback conditions. Using a factorial design, Sassenrath & Yonge (159) investigated the effects of feedback delay, feedback cue, and retention set on recall. During the original session, all subjects were administered a 60-item multiple-choice test. The only significant difference that emerged on an immediate retention test was the superiority of the stem over the no-stem feedback-cue conditions. After a 5-day interval, however, all three factors were associated with significant differences such that the delayed-feedback, stem, and retention-set conditions were superior to the immediate-feedback, no-stem, and no-set conditions, respectively. This last experiment is of obvious relevance to instruction, suggesting the desirability of a number of additional studies to assess the generality of the effects obtained.

Consider next a group of studies concerned with the effects of interpolated learning on the retention of previously learned material, that is, studies of retroactive inhibition. The relevant instructional question is: What conditions can be used to minimize the effects of retroactive inhibition on recall?

Two reported studies reveal that retroactive inhibition varies as a function of learning method. In a study by Shuell & Keppel (168), the amount of retention loss was less for conditions in which different methods of learning were employed on the two lists than in conditions where the methods of learning were identical. In an experiment reported by Goggin (67), list-one recall was better with low than with high degrees of second-list learning, and better with a prompting than with an anticipation method of learning. Adams & Montague (2) have reported an experiment suggesting that elaboration of paired adjectives during first-list learning reduces the susceptibility of the pairs to retroactive inhibition from a subsequently learned list. Information as to whether individual pairs were elaborated was obtained by questionnaire after first-list learning, after second-list learning, and after first-list recall. First-list recall was positively related to the use of elaboration during first-list learning but independent of elaboration during second-list learning. The results of the experiment suggest that elaboration not only promotes more efficient learning but also better retention after intervening learning.

Before taking leave of the topic of conditions that promote retention, mention should be made of a relevant line of research that probably has more direct applicability to instructional concerns than any of the experiments mentioned thus far. This is the series of experiments reported by Rothkopf and others concerning the effect on retention of test-like events, interspersed throughout instructional prose [Bruning (26); Frase (60, 61);

Rothkopf (151, 152); Rothkopf & Bisbicos (153)]. Since these studies have been reviewed in connection with the topic of attention, they are simply noted here for their relevance to the problem of promoting retention.

Summary statement.—Two features of the work reviewed in the present section are auspicious for the development of a psychology of instruction. The first lies in a perceptible increase in the research attention given to conditions that facilitate retention and to conditions that decrease the deleterious effects of interference. The second feature of importance concerns the pervasive effects on retention of degree of original learning and the implication of this, that work on conditions that facilitate acquisition will eventuate in better retention as well.

CONDITIONS AFFECTING TRANSFER

It is generally agreed that the promotion of positive transfer of learning is one of the most important purposes of instruction. It may even be argued that criteria of learning and of retention derive their relevance to instruction from the consideration that they are intermediate criteria which must be met if transfer of learning to new situations and tasks is to occur. As will be apparent in the studies to be reviewed, the investigator typically has one or another criterion of transfer in mind, and sometimes both: (*a*) the degree to which instruction in one task will facilitate the learning of another; and (*b*) the degree to which the learning of a given task will generalize to performances of the same general class of task in different contexts. Gagné (62, p. 231) has distinguished these two questions in terms of the categories of vertical transfer and lateral transfer.

Many of the recent studies of transfer, insofar as they deal with the vertical type, may be considered primarily relevant to the question of instructional sequence. While sequence is not itself a variable which can be described in a unitary sense, it obviously becomes a part of the conditions of instruction whenever the learner is required to progress from one learning task to another, as is frequently the case in educational and training settings. The particular question of interest to the designer of instruction becomes: What kind of prior learning contributes to (i.e., transfers positively to) the learning of a given class of performance? It may be noted that Gagné's (62, p. 60) hypothesis proposes that certain kinds of learning are necessary prerequisites to other kinds. Studies of transfer of prior learning are frequently consistent with this hypothesis, although few are confirming in a crucial sense.

Verbal sequences.—Most investigators of human learning apparently would agree with the general statement that paired-associate and serial learning require a multi-process theory [cf. Battig (13, pp. 158–164)]. In effect, such a theory states that several different forms of prior learning transfer positively to the learning of verbal lists, including particularly stimulus-term discrimination, response-term discrimination, response learning, and stimulus coding, among others. A few notable examples contributing evidence to this notion are studies by Duncan (49); Mandler & Pearlstone (105); Martin (112); Postman & Stark (136); and Shuell & Keppel (168).

Concept learning.—Quite a number of recent studies are concerned with identifying the particular kind of prior learning which is necessary for children to perform transposition and reversal-shift tasks. The first class presumably demonstrates the attainment of concepts such as "the larger," "the brighter," etc., whereas the latter is employed to show the learning of the concept "reverse" or "opposite." Marsh & Sherman (108) used transposition problems with two groups of children, of ages three and four to five, and elicited overt verbalization during performance of the tasks. Verbalization was found to be effective in controlling the amount of correct transposition in older children, but not in the younger. Beaty & Weir (14) studied performance on the intermediate-size transposition problem and found transfer to be greater when the prior training included sets of stimuli which bounded the stimulus dimension, as opposed to sets which were adjacent at the small end of the continuum. Caron (30) investigated far-transposition of the concept "medium-size" in children in the 3 to 4-year age range. He attributes the transfer effects of prior learning to the establishment of attentional responses rather than to labeling.

The effects of prior learning of discriminations on reversal-shift learning is of importance to those who hold a differentiation theory of discrimination learning [cf. Gibson & Gibson (66)]. Tighe (183) showed that pretraining of first-grade children in discrimination of the objects later used in shift tasks facilitated reversal shifts but did not affect nonreversal shifts. The pretrained groups, the author says, improved in their ability to utilize the distinguishing features later essential to reversal. Smiley & Weir (177) trained one group of kindergarten children in discrimination of a dimension previously found to be dominant, and another group on the nondominant dimension. Rate of learning was found related to dimensional dominance, as was also the performance on reversal and nonreversal tasks. Johnson & White (82) gave discrimination training within the dimensions of size or brightness to 6-year-old children, then tested reversal shift performance. Discrimination within the dimensions was not found to transfer to reversal problems, suggesting that discrimination among dimensions rather than within is the kind of prior learning essential for transfer.

Some investigators have attempted to study the effects of variables in prior discrimination learning which favor the establishment of mediational processes and their use in the reversal task [cf. Kendler & Kendler (91)]. Trabasso, Deutsch & Gelman (186) found differences in the attainment of reversals in 4-year-olds when the discrimination training was on patterns as compared to objects. Reversals were slower than other shifts in the first case and faster in the second case. The authors conclude that although attentional responses were learned and transferred, thay did not facilitate reversal shifts. Eimas (53) showed that reversal learning was retarded in young children by prior discrimination learning which included two irrelevant dimensions, whereas nonreversal learning was retarded by overtraining. In a second study, Eimas (54) tested the effects of overtraining in discrimination learning and found reversal shifts to be facilitated by the overtraining, whereas nonreversal shifting was impaired. Heal (76) also found reversal shifts to be facilitated by overtraining and others to be slowed. In general, these studies support the notion that reversal learning involves a mediational process that is not involved in other kinds of shifts. The effect of verbalizations on reversal shift learning was studied by Silverman (173) in two groups of children, aged 3 to 4 and 7 to 8. When verbal labels were used to name the dimensions relevant in the final task, positive transfer was found to the reversal performance in both age groups. Verbalizations of the discrimination problems by nursery school children was found by Blank (21) to lead to more rapid solutions when only partial training was provided, but not to facilitate reversals as much as did a full course of training. Other evidence of the effects of verbalization may be found in a study by Wolff (199), whose results showed that labeling of stimulus classes exhibited positive transfer to a concept-learning task.

Odom (126) presented children of three age groups with pictures of heads and bodies of common animals, to which they were to respond differentially and could learn concepts of "headness" and "bodiness." Transfer tests showed the effects of prior concept learning in 5-year-olds, as well as in the older groups. In acquiring concepts, Saltz & Sigel (155) point out, children may make errors of "overdiscrimination." Younger children made many more errors than did 7 to 9-year-olds in answering the question, "Is this the same boy or a different boy?" when recognizing different pictures of the same boy. Dukes & Bevan (48) tested the effect of stimulus variation in training to achieve concepts of people shown in pictures. In one condition, the same photograph of each person was repeatedly presented; in the other, four different photographs were used. When testing was done on the pictures used in training, repeated practice was the superior method; when identification of new poses had to be made, the variation treatment showed the greater advantage.

Reading and language.—Still another set of studies in the category of concept learning and its prerequisites relates to reading instruction. Marchbanks & Levin's (107) study showed that children recognized words on the basis of individual letter cues, with the first letter being the most salient. Wintz & Bellerose (197) gave first-and second-grade children training in the correct sound of a phoneme cluster, /sr/, and found that children trained on pronunciation of unfamiliar words performed better than those trained on familiar ones. This finding was confirmed in a related study by McNeil & Stone (117). In a study by Samuels (156), it was found that the learning of word pairs prior to reading training on the same word pairs transferred positively to recognizing the second word from each pair. Samuels & Jeffrey

(158) had kindergarten children learn to pronounce words composed of two letters from an artificial alphabet, in three lists differing in discriminability, as determined by number of common elements. Learning rate was found to increase with ease of discrimination. Jeffrey & Samuels (78) found that letter-trained groups of children showed greater transfer than word-trained, when the transfer task was composed of new words. Mace (103) made a comparison of three different instructional sequences in beginning French with elementary school children. In one treatment, speaking lessons preceded listening lessons; in another, this sequence was reversed; in a third, speaking and listening were presented concurrently. On a listening comprehension post-test, the speaking-first groups outperformed the listening-first, suggesting the importance of vocal response discrimination as prior learning to acquiring concepts of language sounds. Keislar, Stern & Mace (87) carried out an additional study of this sequence, including a control for the effect of "recency" between the listening training and the listening comprehension testing. Results showed markedly superior performance in the groups given speaking training first, and maintenance of these effects over 3 months.

Rule learning in children.—In investigating transfer from prior learning to rule-governed behavior, much interest continues to center on conservation tasks of the sort studied by Piaget and his associates. Generally, transfer is found to be relatively specific. For example, Beilin (15) trained kindergarten children on conservation tasks of length and number, using several methods, and found no transfer to a task involving conservation of area. In another Beilin study (16), training on infralogical techniques (translocation of areas, counting squares) was given to first and second-graders and found to be insufficient by itself for transfer without training involving feedback on the area conservation task. Beilin, Kagan & Rabinowitz (17) used both perceptual and verbal training preceding the task of water-level representation in second-graders. Perceptual training was found more effective, but transfer was limited to jars of the same form. Wallach, Wall & Anderson (194) found that reversibility training was effective, while addition and subtraction were ineffective, as prior learnings for number conservation. A different kind of "conservation" pertaining to the meanings of defined concepts such as father, mother, doctor, etc., was studied by Sigel, Saltz & Roskind (172), who found that the degree of irrelevant stimulation that can be tolerated in conserving these concepts increases with age in the range 5 to 8. Their evidence suggests that defined concepts are originally subject to "over-discrimination."

In this area, the study of Kingsley & Hall (97) is of particular interest because of its attempt to make a specific analysis of a hierarchy of subordinate skills in conservation tasks and then to train each of the missing ones in individual children. The results indicate considerable transfer to the tasks of weight and length conservation and some from weight conservation to that of substance. Gagné (65) proposed that transfer to conservation tasks can be understood in terms of subordinate prior learnings, and that such transfer may be expected to be relatively specific, until the cumulative effects of a number of specific skills make possible broader generalizability. Another study pertaining to transfer of subordinate skills is by Bem (18), who gave a small number of children of 3 to 4 years the task of pressing switches the correct number of times to turn off one to five lights on a panel. Subordinate skills were identified and trained, and the ultimate performance was virtually perfect for all subjects. Still another study involving integration of subordinate rules was carried out by Kendler, Kendler & Carrick (92) on kindergartners and third graders. Learning verbal labels for the objects involved in the original rules (a marble, a ball-bearing) facilitated problem solution for kindergartners, but had either no effect or an interfering effect for the third-graders.

Rule using and problem solving in adults.—A variety of studies of rule-governed behavior, sometimes achieved by problem solving, have been carried out to explore the effects of prior learning on transfer. Johnson (79) reviews evidence concerning the solution of anagrams, which has shown this to be a multi-stage process dependent on several subordinate skills. A review of problem solving by Davis (42) distinguishes those tasks which depend heavily upon associations formed by trial and error within the experiment and those which require the problem to be solved by covert testing and rejection of alternatives. A study by Davis, Train & Manske (44), and another by Davis (43) demonstrated the effectiveness in transfer of previously learned verbal rules, and contrasted these effects with those obtained by prior trial and error learning, in the solution of switch-light problems. Overing & Travers (128, 129) carried out two studies on learning to hit an underwater target. Transfer to the task was improved by prior training with irrelevant information, by establishing a set to attend to relevant features, and by verbalizing rules prior to their application. When subjects were trained in a situation containing much irrelevant visual information, they showed no differences in transfer when given the problem with large or small amounts of irrelevant information; whereas, subjects trained with little irrelevant information showed reduced transfer in the more complex context.

The relative specificity of transfer of previously learned rules is also shown in the study of Di Vesta & Walls (46), who investigated the solution of the Maier two-string problem by college students given different kinds of "pre-utilization" training. Yonge (201) also found specific transfer to this task from pre-utilization training, as well as evidence of a primacy effect. Concrete prior training in games involving mathematical groups and combinatorial topology was found by Scandura & Wells (160) to be more effective for transfer than prior learning from printed passages. Grotelueschen & Sjogren (71) found that prior learning from verbal materials to a task of supplying symbols for numbers in base 4 yielded transfer effects in the order: (a) principles of number bases; (b) base 7 number system; (c) base 10 number system; and (d) history of measurement. Tuckman et al. (187) found transfer effectiveness for both search strategies and problem-solving skills learned during practice in adding number matrices to problems some of which could be solved by short-cut solutions. When criterion problems were fairly dissimilar to practice problems, subjects having search experiences did more searching, but were less successful in finding solutions than those having greater amounts of practice. Foss (59) investigated the learning of rules in a miniature linguistic system and their application to linguistic items not previously encountered. Evidence was obtained that the subjects learned systematic relations among the units of the system and were able to apply them without error.

A highly systematic study of the effects of eight different scrambled versus linear arrangements of three instructional programs was conducted by Payne, Krathwohl & Gordon (135). No effect of sequential arrangement was found, although all scrambled forms had higher error rates. It is noteworthy that the authors account for the effects of scrambling by inferring that learners treat the scrambled program as a "large-step" program, mentally sorting out the items as relevant to the problem at hand and inductively building the knowledge they need. This interpretation reaffirms an important distinction between sequence of presentation and sequence of learning events in transfer.

Summary statement.—There can be little doubt that the problem of identifying and measuring the effects of prior learning on the learning of subsequent tasks (i.e., vertical transfer) commands the attention of investigators with a variety of specific interests. The facts of transfer, as they emerge from these studies, give much support to the notion that the learning of particular classes of tasks depends (in a positive transfer sense) on the prior learning of other particular classes of performance. Learning verbal associates typically receives much positive transfer from prior discrimination learning, stimulus coding, and response intergration; concept learning from prior learning on dimension discrimination; rule learning from prior concept learning; and problem solving from prior learning of relevant rules. The implication of such generalizations for the design of instruction seems clearly to be that specification of efficient instruction must include consideration of the sequence of learning events.

Much of the evidence on transfer from prior learning, including particularly the findings of studies of Piaget-derived conservation tasks, emphasizes the relatively specific nature of transfer. Training on various kinds and combinations of subordinate skills has frequently been shown to transfer positively to tasks having content similar to that used in training, but not to transfer more broadly in the sense which may be implied by "being able to conserve." Piaget's view of the reason for such evidence presumably would be that the child has not attained the requisite stage of cognitive development. An opposing view is that the child has not learned a sufficient number and variety of specific conservation-type skills to make broad transfer possible.

Turning to the question of the conditions which promote breadth of

lateral transfer, we note that this is in current research a less popular problem. The variables which are identified as affecting breadth of transfer
include: (a) verbalizing the learned rules; (b) using sufficient variety of
examples in concept and rule learning; and (c) including in the learning
situation a context of irrelevant stimuli. The effects of the factor of variety
are particularly emphasized in studies of "overdiscrimination," among
others. None of these variables is a newly discovered one. Yet additional
evidence of their effectiveness in facilitating breadth of transfer is valuable,
particularly when they can be so directly applied in the design of instruction.

LITERATURE CITED

1. Adams, J. A. *Human Memory* (Mc-Graw-Hill, New York, 326 pp., 1967)
2. Adams, J. A., Montague, W. E. Retroactive inhibition and natural language mediation. *J. Verbal Learn. Verbal Behav.*, 6, 528–35 (1967)
3. Aiken, E. G., Law, A. W. Response prompting and response confirmation: A review of recent literature. *Psychol. Bull.*, 68, 330–41 (1967)
4. Allen, S. A. The effects of verbal reinforcement on children's performance as a function of type of task. *J. Exptl. Child Psychol.*, 3, 57–73 (1966)
5. Allen, S. A. Dubanoski, R. A., Stevenson, H. W. Children's performance as a function of race of *E*, race of *S*, and type of verbal reinforcement. *J. Exptl. Child Psychol.*, 4, 248–56 (1966)
6. Amster, H. Effect of instructional set and variety of instances on children's learning. *J. Educ. Psychol.*, 57, 74–85 (1966)
7. Anderson, R. C. Educational psychology. *Ann. Rev. Psychol.*, 18, 103–64 (1967)
8. Anderson, R. C., Faust, G. W. The effects of strong formal prompts in programmed instruction. *Am. Educ. Res. J.*, 4, 345–52 (1967)
9. Anderson, R. C., Faust, G. W., Roderick, M. C. "Overprompting" in programmed instruction. *J. Educ. Psychol.*, 59, 88–93 (1968)
10. Atkinson, R. C. Computerized instruction and the learning process. *Am. Psychologist*, 23, 225–39 (1968)
11. Bandura, A., Harris, M. B. Modification of syntactic style. *J. Exptl. Child Psychol.*, 4, 341–52 (1966)
12. Barnwell, A., Sechrest, L. Vicarious reinforcement in children at two age levels. *J. Educ. Psychol.*, 56, 100–6 (1965)
13. Battig, W. F. Paired-associate learning. In *Verbal Behavior and General Behavior Theory*, 149–71 (Dixon, T. R., Horton, D. L., Eds., Prentice-Hall, Englewood Cliffs, N. J., 596 pp., 1968)
14. Beaty, W. E., Weir, M. W. Children's performance on the intermediate-size transposition problem as a function of two different training procedures. *J. Exptl. Child Psychol.*, 4, 332–40 (1966)

15. Beilin, H. Learning and operational convergence in logical thought development. *J. Exptl. Child Psychol.*, 2, 317–39 (1965)
16. Beilin, H. Feedback and infralogical strategies in invariant area conceptualization. *Ibid.*, 3, 267–78 (1966)
17. Beilin, H., Kagan, J., Rabinowitz, R. Effects of verbal and perceptual training on water level representation. *Child Develpm.*, 37, 317–30 (1966)
18. Bem, S. L. Verbal self-control: The establishment of effective self-instruction. *J. Exptl. Psychol.*, 74, 485–91 (1967)
19. Berlyne, D. E. Conditions of prequestioning and retention of meaningful material. *J. Educ. Psychol.*, 57, 128–32 (1966)
20. Bisett, B. M., Rieber, M. The effects of age and incentive value on discrimination learning. *J. Exptl. Child Psychol.*, 3, 199–206 (1966)
21. Blank, M. The effects of training and verbalization on reversal and extradimensional learning. *J. Exptl. Child Psychol.*, 4, 50–57 (1966)
22. Borkowski, J. G. Distributed practice in short-term memory. *J. Verbal Learn. Verbal Behav.*, 6, 66–72 (1967)
23. Bower, G. H. *Mental Imagery and Memory*. (Paper presented at several psychology departments, 1967)
24. Briggs, L. J. *Sequencing of Instruction in Relation to Hierarchies of Competence*. (Am. Inst. of Res., Palo Alto, Calif., 103 pp. Final Report, USOE Contract OEC-1-7-071070-3771, 1967)
25. Bruce, D., Cofer, C. N. An examination of recognition and free recall as measures of acquisition and long-term retention. *J. Exptl. Psychol.*, 75, 283–89 (1967)
26. Bruning, R. H. Effects of review and testlike events within the learning of prose materials. *J. Educ. Psychol.*, 59, 16–19 (1968)
27. Bugelski, B. R. Presentation time, total time, and mediation in paired-associate learning. *J. Exptl. Psychol.*, 63, 409–12 (1962)
28. Byers, J. L., Davidson, R. E. The role of hypothesizing in the facilitation of concept attainment. *J. Verbal*

Learn. Verbal Behav., **6**, 595–600 (1967)

29. Carmean, S. L., Weir, M. W. Effects of verbalizations on discrimination learning and retention. *J. Verbal Learn. Verbal Behav.*, **6**, 545–50 (1967)

30. Caron, A. J. Far transposition of intermediate-size in preverbal children. *J. Exptl. Child Psychol.*, **3**, 296–311 (1966)

31. Chan, A., Travers, R. M. W. The effect on retention of labeling visual displays. *Am. Educ. Res. J.*, **3**, 55–67 (1966)

32. Chu, G. C., Schramm, W. *Learning from Television: What the Research Says.* (Inst. for Commun. Res., Stanford Univ., 213 pp. Final Report, USOE Contract 2EFC-708-94, 1967)

33. Clifton, C., Jr. Some determinants of the effectiveness of priming word associates. *J. Verbal Learn. Verbal Behav.*, **5**, 167–71 (1966)

34. Coats, W. D., Smidchens, U. Audience recall as a function of speaker dynamism. *J. Educ. Psychol.*, **57**, 189–91 (1966)

35. Cole, M., Sharp, D. W., Glick, J., Kessen, W. Conceptual and mnemonic factors in paired-associate learning. *J. Exptl. Child Psychol.*, **6**, 120–30 (1968)

36. Cooper, J. C., Jr., Gaeth, J. H. Interaction of modality with age and with meaningfulness in verbal learning. *J. Educ. Psychol.*, **58**, 41–44 (1967)

37. Corsini, D. A., Pick, A. D., Flavell, J. H. Production deficiency of nonverbal mediators in young children. *Child Develpm.*, **39**, 53–58 (1968)

38. Cramer, P. Mediated priming of associative responses: The effect of time lapse and interpolated activity. *J. Verbal Learn. Verbal Behav.*, **5**, 163–66 (1966)

39. Cramer, P. Mediated transfer via natural language association. *Ibid.*, **6**, 512–19 (1967)

40. Crandall, J. E. Satiation of interest in words as a function of their familiarity. *J. Verbal Learn. Verbal Behav.*, **6**, 398–402 (1967)

41. Crist, R. L. Overt versus covert responding and retention by sixth-grade students. *J. Educ. Psychol.*, **57**, 99–101 (1966)

42. Davis, G. A. Current status of research and theory in human prob-lem solving. *Psychol. Bull.*, **66**, 36–54 (1966)

43. Davis, G. A. Detrimental effects of distraction, additional response alternatives, and longer response chains in solving switch-light problems. *J. Exptl. Psychol.*, **73**, 45–55 (1967)

44. Davis, G. A., Train, A. J., Manske, M. E. Trial and error versus "insightful" problem solving: Effects of distraction, additional response alternatives, and longer response chains. *J. Exptl. Psychol.*, **76**, 337–40 (1968)

45. Dilley, M. G., Paivio, A. Pictures and words as stimulus and response items in paired-associate learning of young children. *Research Bulletin #63* (Dept. Psychol., Univ. Western Ontario, London, Canada, Nov. 1967) (In press, *J. Exptl. Child Psychol.*)

46. Di Vesta, F. J., Walls, R. T. Transfer of object-function in problem solving. *Am. Educ. Res. J.*, **4**, 207–16 (1967)

47. Dominowski, R. L., Ekstrand, B. R. Direct and associative priming in anagram solving. *J. Exptl. Psychol.*, **74**, 84–86 (1967)

48. Dukes, W. F., Bevan, W. Stimulus variation and repetition in the acquisition of naming responses. *J. Exptl. Psychol.*, **74**, 178–81 (1967)

49. Duncan, C. P. Transfer and mediation in verbal concept learning. *J. Verbal Learn. Verbal Behav.*, **6**, 590–94 (1967)

50. Eagle, M., Ortoff, E. The effect of level of attention upon "phonetic" recognition errors. *J. Verbal Learn. Verbal Behav.*, **6**, 226–31 (1967)

51. Earhard, M. Cued recall and free recall as a function of the number of items per cue. *J. Verbal Learn. Verbal Behav.*, **6**, 257–63 (1967)

52. Egeth, H. Selective attention. *Psychol. Bull.*, **67**, 41–57 (1967)

53. Eimas, P. D. Effects of overtraining, irrelevant stimuli, and training task on reversal discrimination learning in children. *J. Exptl. Child Psychol.*, **3**, 315–23 (1966)

54. Eimas, P. D. Effects of overtraining and age on intradimensional and extradimensional shifts in children. *Ibid.*, 348–55

55. Elkind, D., Van Doorninck, W., Schwarz, C. Perceptual activity and concept attainment. *Child Develpm.*, **38**, 1153–61 (1967)

56. Epstein, W. Some conditions of the influence of syntactical structure on learning: Grammatical transformation, learning instructions, and "chunking." *J. Verbal Learn. Verbal Behav.*, 6, 415–19 (1967)

57. Faust, G. W., Anderson, R. C. Effects of incidental material in a programmed Russian vocabulary lesson. *J. Educ. Psychol.*, 58, 3–10 (1967)

58. Flavell, J. H., Beach, D. R., Chinsky, J. M. Spontaneous verbal rehearsal in a memory task as a function of age. *Child Develpm.*, 37, 283–99 (1966)

59. Foss, D. J. An analysis of learning in a miniature linguistic system. *J. Exptl. Psychol.*, 76, 450–59 (1968)

60. Frase, L. T. Learning from prose material: Length of passage, knowledge of results, and position of questions. *J. Educ. Psychol.*, 58, 266–72 (1967)

61. Frase, L. T. Some data concerning the mathemagenic hypothesis. *Am. Educ. Res. J.*, 5, 181–90 (1968)

62. Gagné, R. M. *The Conditions of Learning* (Holt, Rinehart & Winston, 308 pp., 1965)

63. Gagné, R. M. Instruction and the conditions of learning. In *Instruction, Some Contemporary Viewpoints*, 291–313 (Siegel, L., Ed., Chandler, San Francisco, 376 pp., 1967)

64. Gagné, R. M., Ed. *Learning and Individual Differences* (Charles E. Merrill Books, Columbus, Ohio, 265 pp., 1967)

65. Gagné, R. M. Contributions of learning to human development. *Psychol. Rev.*, 75, 177–91 (1968)

66. Gibson, J. J., Gibson, E. J. Perceptual learning: Differentiation or enrichment? *Psychol. Rev.*, 62, 32–41 (1955)

67. Goggin, J. First-list recall as a function of second-list learning method. *J. Verbal Learn. Verbal Behav.*, 6, 423–27 (1967)

68. Gollin, E. S., Saravo, A., Salten, C. Perceptual distinctiveness and oddity-problem solving in children. *J. Exptl. Child. Psychol.*, 5, 586–96 (1967)

69. Gough, P. B. Grammatical transformations and speed of understanding. *J. Verbal Learn. Verbal Behav.*, 4, 107–11 (1965)

70. Grim, P. F. A sustained attention comparison of children and adults using reaction time set and the GSR. *J. Exptl. Child Psychol.*, 5, 26–38 (1967)

71. Grotelueschen, A., Sjogren, D. O. Effects of differentially structured introductory materials and learning tasks on learning and transfer. *Am. Educ. Res. J.*, 5, 191–202 (1968)

72. Guthrie, J. T. Expository instruction versus a discovery method. *J. Educ. Psychol.*, 58, 45–49 (1967)

73. Hagen, J. W. The effect of distraction on selective attention. *Child Develpm.*, 38, 685–94 (1967)

74. Haygood, D. H. Audio-visual concept formation. *J. Educ. Psychol.*, 56, 126–32 (1965)

75. Haygood, R. C., Stevenson, M. Effects of number of irrelevant dimensions in nonconjunctive concept learning. *J. Exptl. Psychol.*, 74, 302–4 (1967)

76. Heal, L. W. The role of cue value, cue novelty, and overtraining in the discrimination shift performance of retardates and normal children of comparable discrimination ability. *J. Exptl. Child. Psychol.*, 4, 126–42 (1966)

77. Hewett, F. Educational engineering with emotionally disturbed children. *Exceptional Children*, 33, 459–67 (1967)

78. Jeffrey, W. E., Samuels, S. J. Effect of method of reading training on initial learning and transfer. *J. Verbal Learn. Verbal Behav.*, 6, 354–58 (1967)

79. Johnson, D. M. Solution of anagrams. *Psychol. Bull.*, 66, 371–84 (1966)

80. Johnson, D. M., Stratton, R. P. Evaluation of five methods of teaching concepts. *J. Educ. Psychol.*, 57, 48–53 (1966)

81. Johnson, P. E. Word relatedness and problem solving in high-school physics. *J. Educ. Psychol.*, 56, 217–24 (1965)

82. Johnson, P. J., White, R. M., Jr. Concept of dimensionality and reversal shift performance in children. *J. Exptl. Child Psychol.*, 5, 223–27 (1967)

83. Johnson, R. B. The effects of prompting, practice and feedback in programmed videotape. *Am. Educ. Res. J.*, 5, 73–80 (1968)

84. Jones, S. The effect of a negative qualifier in an instruction. *J. Verbal Learn. Verbal Behav.*, 5, 497–501 (1966)

85. Kanfer, F. H., Duerfeldt, P. H. Learner competence, model com-

petence, and number of observation trials in vicarious learning. *J. Educ. Psychol.*, **58**, 153–57 (1967)

86. Keeney, T. J., Cannizzo, S. R., Flavell, J. H. Spontaneous and induced verbal rehearsal in a recall task. *Child Develpm.*, **38**, 953–66 (1967)

87. Keislar, E. R., Stern, C., Mace, L. Sequence of listening training in beginning French: A replication experiment. *Am. Educ. Res. J.*, **3**, 169–78 (1966)

88. Kelly, R. Comparison of the effects of positive and negative vicarious reinforcement in an operant learning task. *J. Educ. Psychol.*, **57**, 307–10 (1966)

89. Kemp, F. D., Holland, J. G. Blackout ratio and overt responses in programmed instruction. *J. Educ. Psychol.*, **57**, 109–14 (1966)

90. Kendler, H. H., Kendler, T. S. Vertical and horizontal processes in problem solving. *Psychol. Rev.*, **69**, 1–16 (1962)

91. Kendler, H. H., Kendler, T. S. Selective attention versus mediation: Some comments on Mackintosh's analyses of two-stage models of discrimination learning. *Psychol. Bull.*, **66**, 282–88 (1966)

92. Kendler, T. S., Kendler, H. H., Carrick, M. A. Verbal labels and inferential problem solution of children. *Child Develpm.*, **37**, 749–64 (1966)

93. Keppel, G. Association by contiguity: Role of response availability. *J. Exptl. Psychol.*, **71**, 624–28 (1966)

94. Keppel, G. A reconsideration of the extinction-recovery theory. *J. Verbal Learn. Verbal Behav.*, **6**, 476–86 (1967)

95. Keppel, G. Verbal learning and memory. *Ann. Rev. Psychol.*, **19**, 169–93 (1968)

96. King, D. J., Russell, G. W. A comparison of rote and meaningful learning of connected meaningful material. *J. Verbal Learn. Verbal Behav.*, **5**, 478–83 (1966)

97. Kingsley, R. C., Hall, V. C. Training conservation through the use of learning sets. *Child Develpm.*, **38**, 1111–26 (1967)

98. Kusyszyn, I., Paivio, A. Transition probability, word order, and noun abstractness in the learning of adjective-noun paired associates. *J. Exptl. Psychol.*, **71**, 800–5 (1966)

99. Lamb, G. S. Teacher verbal cues and pupil performance on a group reading test. *J. Educ. Psychol.*, **58**, 332–36 (1967)

100. Lee, S. S., Jensen, A. R. The effect of awareness of three-stage mediated association. *J. Verbal Learn. Verbal Behav.* (In press)

101. Levonian, E. Retention of information in relation to arousal during continuously-presented material. *Am. Educ. Res. J.*, **4**, 103–16 (1967)

102. Lintz, L. M., Brackbill, Y. Effects of reinforcement delay during learning on the retention of verbal material in adults. *J. Exptl. Psychol.*, **71**, 194–99 (1966)

103. Mace, L. Sequence of vocal response-differentiation training and auditory stimulus-discrimination training in beginning French. *J. Educ. Psychol.*, **57**, 102–8 (1966)

104. Maltzman, I. Individual differences in "attention": The orienting reflex. In *Learning and Individual Differences*, 94–112 (Gagné, R. M., Ed., Merrill, Columbus, Ohio, 265 pp., 1967)

105. Mandler, G., Pearlstone, Z. Free and constrained concept learning and subsequent recall. *J. Verbal Learn. Verbal Behav.*, **5**, 126–31 (1966)

106. Mandler, G., Stephens, D. The development of free and constrained conceptualization and subsequent verbal memory. *J. Exptl. Child Psychol.*, **5**, 86–93 (1967)

107. Marchbanks, G., Levin, H. Cues by which children recognize words. *J. Educ. Psychol.*, **56**, 57–61 (1965)

108. Marsh, G., Sherman, M. Verbal mediation of transposition as a function of age level. *J. Exptl. Child Psychol.*, **4**, 90–98 (1966)

109. Marshall, H. H. *Learning as a function of task interest, reinforcement, and social class variables* (Doctoral thesis, Univ. Calif., Berkeley, Calif., 1967)

110. Martin, C. J., Boersma, F. J., Cox, D. L. A classification of associative strategies in paired-associate learning. *Psychonomic Sci.*, **3**, 455–56 (1965)

111. Martin, C. J., Cox, D. L., Boersma, F. J. The role of associative strategies in the acquisition of paired-associate material: An alternative approach to meaningfulness. *Psychonomic Sci.*, **3**, 463–64 (1965)

112. Martin, E. Stimulus recognition in aural paired-associate learning. *J.*

Verbal Learn. Verbal Behav., **6**, 272–76 (1967)

113. Martin, E., Roberts, K. H. Grammatical factors in sentence retention. *J. Verbal Learn. Verbal Behav.*, **5**, 211–18 (1966)

114. May, M. A. *Enhancements and simplifications of motivational and stimulus variables in audiovisual instructional materials.* (U. S. Dept. of Health, Education and Welfare, Washington, D.C., 109 pp. Final Report, USOE Contract OE-5-16-006, 1965)

115. May, M. A. *Word-picture relationships in audio-visual presentations. Ibid.*, 115 pp.

116. May, M. A. *The role of student response in learning from the new educational media. Ibid.*, 149 pp.

117. McNeil, J. D., Stone, J. Note on teaching children to hear separate sounds in spoken words. *J. Educ. Psychol.*, **56**, 13–15 (1965)

118. Merrill, M. D., Stolurow, L. M. Hierarchical preview versus problem oriented review in learning an imaginary science. *Am. Educ. Res. J.*, **4**, 251–62 (1966)

119. Milgram, N. A. Retention of mediation set in paired-associate learning of normal children and retardates. *J. Exptl. Child Psychol.*, **5**, 341–49 (1967)

120. Milgram, N. A. Verbal context versus visual compound in paired-associate learning by children. *J. Exptl. Child Psychol.*, **5**, 597–603 (1967)

121. Montague, W. E., Adams, J. A., Kiess, H. O. Forgetting and natural language mediation. *J. Exptl. Psychol.*, **72**, 829–33 (1966)

122. Montague, W. E., Wearing, A. J. The complexity of natural language mediators and its relation to paired-associate learning. *Psychonomic Sci.*, **7**, 135–36 (1967)

123. Myers, K. E., Travers, R. M. W., Sanford, M. E. Learning and reinforcement in student pairs. *J. Educ. Psychol.*, **56**, 67–72 (1965)

124. Nikkel, N., Palermo, D. S. Effects of mediated associations in paired-associate learning of children. *J. Exptl. Child Psychol.*, **2**, 92–102 (1965)

125. Norman, C., Rieber, M. Facilitation of concept formation in children by the use of color cues. *J. Exptl. Psychol.*, **76**, 460–63 (1968)

126. Odom, R. D. Concept identification and utilization among children of different ages. *J. Exptl. Child Psychol.*, **4**, 309–16 (1966)

127. Olton, R. M. The effect of a mnemonic upon the retention of paired-associate verbal material. *J. Verbal Learn. Verbal Behav.* (In press)

128. Overing, R. L. R., Travers, R. M. W. Effect upon transfer of variations in training conditions. *J. Educ. Psychol.*, **57**, 179–88 (1966)

129. Overing, R. L. R., Travers, R. M. W. Variation in the amount of irrelevant cues in training and test conditions and the effect upon transfer. *Ibid.*, **58**, 62–68 (1967)

130. Paivio, A., Smythe, P. C., Yuille, J. C. Imagery versus meaningfulness of nouns in paired-associate learning. *Research Bulletin #68* (Dept. Psychol., Univ. Western Ontario, London, Canada, Jan. 1968)

131. Paivio, A., Yuille, J. C. Word abstractness and meaningfulness and paired-associate learning in children. *J. Exptl. Child Psychol.*, **5**, 81–89 (1966)

132. Palermo, D. S. Mediated association in the paired-associate learning of children using heterogeneous and homogeneous lists. *J. Exptl. Psychol.*, **71**, 711–17 (1966)

133. Paradowski, W. Effect of curiosity on incidental learning. *J. Educ. Psychol.*, **58**, 50–55 (1967)

134. Parker, R. K., Nunnally, J. C. Association of neutral objects with rewards: Effects of reward schedules on reward expectancy, verbal evaluation, and selective attention. *J. Exptl. Child Psychol.*, **3**, 324–32 (1966)

135. Payne, D. A., Krathwohl, D. R., Gordon, J. The effect of sequence on programmed instruction. *Am. Educ. Res. J.*, **4**, 125–32 (1967)

136. Postman, L., Stark, K. Studies of learning to learn. IV. Transfer from serial to paired-associate learning. *J. Verbal Learn. Verbal Behav.*, **6**, 339–53 (1967)

137. Rapier, J. L. Learning abilities of normal and retarded children as a function of social class. *J. Educ. Psychol.*, **59**, 102–10 (1968)

138. Reese, H. W. Imagery in paired-associate learning in children. *J. Exptl. Child Psychol.*, **2**, 290–96 (1965)

139. Reese, H. W. Verbal effects in the intermediate-size transposition problem. *Ibid.*, **3**, 123–30 (1966)

140. Reynolds, J. H. Cognitive transfer in verbal learning. *J. Educ. Psychol.*, **57**, 382–88 (1966)

141. Reynolds, J. H. Cognitive transfer in verbal learning: II. Transfer effects after prefamiliarization with integrated versus partially integrated verbal-perceptual structures. *Ibid.*, **59**, 133–38 (1968)

142. Richardson, J. Facilitation of mediated transfer by instructions, B-C training, and presentation of the mediating response. *J. Verbal Learn. Verbal Behav.*, **4**, 59–67 (1966)

143. Rohwer, W. D., Jr. Constraint, syntax, and meaning in paired-associate learning. *J. Verbal Learn. Verbal Behav.*, **5**, 541–47 (1966)

144. Rohwer, W. D., Jr. *Social class differences in the role of linguistic structures in paired-associate learning: Elaboration and learning proficiency.* (U. S. Dept. of Health, Education and Welfare, Washington, D.C., 106 pp. Final Report, USOE Basic Research Project 5-0605, Contract OE6-10-273, Nov. 1967)

145. Rohwer, W. D., Jr., Levin, J. R. Action, meaning and stimulus selection in paired-associate learning. *J. Verbal Learn. Verbal Behav.*, **7**, 137–41 (1968)

146. Rohwer, W. D., Jr., Lynch, S. Semantic constraint in paired-associate learning. *J. Educ. Psychol.*, **57**, 271–78 (1966)

147. Rohwer, W. D., Jr., Lynch, S. Form class and intralist similarity in paired-associate learning. *J. Verbal Learn. Verbal Behav.*, **6**, 551–54 (1967)

148. Rohwer, W. D., Jr., Lynch, S., Levin, J. R., Suzuki, N. Pictorial and verbal factors in the efficient learning of paired associates. *J. Educ. Psychol.*, **58**, 278–84 (1967)

149. Rohwer, W. D., Jr., Lynch, S., Levin, J. R., Suzuki, N. Grade level, school strata, and learning efficiency. *Ibid.*, **59**, 26–31 (1968)

150. Rohwer, W. D., Jr., Lynch, S., Suzuki, N., Levin, J. R. Verbal and pictorial facilitation of paired-associate learning. *J. Exptl. Child Psychol.*, **5**, 294–302 (1967)

151. Rothkopf, E. Z. Learning from written instructive material: An exploration of the control of inspection behavior by test-like events. *Am. Educ. Res. J.*, **3**, 241–50 (1966)

152. Rothkopf, E. Z. Textual constraint as function of repeated inspection. *J. Educ. Psychol.*, **59**, 20–25 (1968)

153. Rothkopf, E. Z., Bisbicos, E. E. Selective facilitative effects of interspersed questions on learning from written materials. *J. Educ. Psychol.*, **58**, 56–61 (1967)

154. Rothkopf, E. Z., Coke, E. U. Variations in phrasing, repetition intervals, and the recall of sentence material. *J. Verbal Learn. Verbal Behav.*, **5**, 86–91 (1966)

155. Saltz, E., Sigel, I. E. Concept overdiscrimination in children. *J. Exptl. Psychol.*, **73**, 1–8 (1967)

156. Samuels, S. J. Effect of experimentally learned word associations on the acquisition of reading responses. *J. Educ. Psychol.*, **57**, 159–63 (1966)

157. Samuels, S. J. Attentional process in reading: The effect of pictures on the acquisition of reading responses. *Ibid.*, **58**, 337–42 (1967)

158. Samuels, S. J., Jeffrey, W. E. Discriminability of words, and letter cues used in learning to read. *J. Educ. Psychol.*, **57**, 337–40 (1966)

159. Sassenrath, J. M., Yonge, G. D. Delayed information feedback, feedback cues, retention set, and delayed retention. *J. Educ. Psychol.*, **59**, 60–73 (1968)

160. Scandura, J. M., Wells, J. N. Advance organizers in learning abstract mathematics. *Am. Educ. Res. J.*, **4**, 295–301 (1967)

161. Scandura, J. M., Woodward, E., Lee, F. Rule generality and consistency in mathematics learning. *Am. Educ. Res. J.*, **4**, 303–19 (1967)

162. Schwenn, E., Postman, L. Studies of learning to learn. V. Gains in performance as a function of warm-up and associative practice. *J. Verbal Learn. Verbal Behav.*, **6**, 565–73 (1967)

163. Scott, K. G. Clustering with perceptual and symbolic stimuli in free recall. *J. Verbal Learn. Verbal Behav.*, **6**, 864–66 (1967)

164. Segal, S. J. The priming of association test responses: Generalizing the phenomenon. *J. Verbal Learn. Verbal Behav.*, **6**, 216–21 (1967)

165. Seidel, R. J., Rotberg, I. C. Effects of written verbalization and timing of information on problem solving in programmed learning. *J. Educ. Psychol.*, **57**, 151–58 (1966)

166. Semmel, M. I., Williams, J. Intentional and incidental learning in

normal, borderline, and retarded children. *Am. Educ. Res. J.*, **5**, 233–38 (1968)

167. Shepard, R. N. Recognition memory for words, sentences, and pictures. *J. Verbal Learn. Verbal Behav.*, **6**, 156–63 (1967)

168. Shuell, T. J., Keppel, G. A further test of the chaining hypothesis of serial learning. *J. Verbal Learn. Verbal Behav.*, **6**, 439–45 (1967)

169. Shulman, L. S., Keislar, E. R., Eds. *Learning by Discovery: A Critical Appraisal* (Rand-McNally, Chicago, 224 pp., 1966)

170. Sidman, M., Stoddard, L. T. The effectiveness of fading in programming a simultaneous form discrimination for retarded children. *J. Exptl. Anal. Behav.*, **10**, 3–15 (1967)

171. Siegel, L. *Instruction, Some Contemporary Viewpoints* (Chandler, San Francisco, 376 pp., 1967)

172. Sigel, I. E., Saltz, E., Roskind, W. Variables determining concept conservation in children. *J. Exptl. Psychol.*, **74**, 471–75 (1967)

173. Silverman, I. W. Effect of verbalization on reversal shifts in children: Additional data. *J. Exptl. Child Psychol.*, **4**, 1–8 (1966)

174. Simon, S. H., Jackson, B. Effect of a relevant versus irrelevant observation stimulus on concept-identification learning. *J. Exptl. Psychol.*, **76**, 125–28 (1968)

175. Skinner, B. F. *The Technology of Teaching* (Appleton-Century-Crofts, New York, 271 pp., 1968)

176. Slobin, D. I. Grammatical transformations and sentence comprehension in childhood and adulthood. *J. Verbal Learn. Verbal Behav.*, **5**, 219–27 (1966)

177. Smiley, S. S., Weir, M. W. Role of dimensional dominance in reversal and non-reversal shift behavior. *J. Exptl. Child Psychol.*, **4**, 296–307 (1966)

178. Spence, J. T., Dunton, M. C. The influence of verbal and nonverbal reinforcement combinations in the discrimination learning of middle and lower class preschool children. *Child Develpm.*, **38**, 1177–86 (1967)

179. Suchman, R. G., Trabasso, T. Stimulus preference and cue function in young children's concept attainment. *J. Exptl. Child Psychol.*, **3**, 188–98 (1966)

180. Sullivan, H. J., Baker, R. L., Schutz, R. E. Effect of intrinsic and ex-

trinsic reinforcement contingencies on learner performance. *J. Educ. Psychol.*, **58**, 165–69 (1967)

181. Suzuki, N., Rohwer, W. D., Jr. Verbal facilitation of paired-associate learning: Type of grammatical unit vs. connective form class. *J. Verbal Learn. Verbal Behav.*, **7**, 577–83 (1968)

182. Terrace, H. S. Errorless transfer of discrimination across two continua. *J. Exptl. Anal. Behav.*, **6**, 223–32 (1963)

183. Tighe, L. S. Effect of perceptual pretaining on reversal and nonreversal shifts. *J. Exptl. Psychol.*, **70**, 379–85 (1965)

184. Tighe, L. S., Tighe, T. J. Discrimination learning: Two views in historical perspective. *Psychol. Bull.*, **66**, 353–70 (1966)

185. Touchette, P. E. The effects of graduated stimulus change on the acquisition of a simple discrimination in severely retarded boys. *J. Exptl. Anal. Behav.*, **11**, 39–48 (1968)

186. Trabasso, T., Deutsch, J. A., Gelman, R. Attention in discrimination learning of young children. *J. Exptl. Child Psychol.*, **4**, 9–19 (1966)

187. Tuckman, B. W., Henkelman, J., O'Shaughnessy, G. P., Cole, M. B. Induction and transfer of search sets. *J. Educ. Psychol.*, **59**, 59–68 (1968)

188. Tulving, E. The effects of presentation and recall of material in free-recall learning. *J. Verbal Learn. Verbal Behav.*, **6**, 175–84 (1967)

189. Underwood, B. J. Speed of learning and amount retained: A consideration of methodology. *Psychol. Bull.*, **51**, 276–82 (1954)

190. Underwood, B. J. Degree of learning and the measurement of forgetting. *J. Verbal Learn. Verbal Behav.*, **3**, 112–29 (1964)

191. Underwood, B. J., Keppel, G. The effect of degree of learning and letter-sequence interference on retention. *Psychol. Monogr.*, **77**, 16 pp. (4) (1963)

192. Underwood, B. J., Richardson, J. The influence of meaningfulness, intra-list similarity, and serial position on retention. *J. Exptl. Psychol.*, **52**, 119–26 (1956)

193. Underwood, B. J., Richardson, J. Studies of distributed practice: XVIII. The influence of meaningfulness and intra-list similarity of

serial nonsense lists. *Ibid.*, **56,** 213–18 (1958)

194. Wallach, L., Wall, A. J., Anderson, L. Number conservation: The roles of reversibility, addition-subtraction, and misleading perceptual cues. *Child Develpm.*, **38,** 425–42 (1967)

195. Weiner, B. Effects of motivation on the availability and retrieval of memory traces. *Psychol. Bull.*, **65,** 24–37 (1966)

196. Williams, J. P. Combining response modes in programmed instruction. *J. Educ. Psychol.*, **57,** 215–19 (1966)

197. Wintz, H., Bellerose, B. Phoneme-cluster learning as a function of instructional method and age. *J. Verbal Learn. Verbal Behav.*, **4,** 98–102 (1965)

198. Wolff, J. L. Concept-shift and discrimination-reversal learning in humans. *Psychol. Bull.*, **68,** 369–408 (1967)

199. Wolff, J. L. Effects of verbalization and pretraining on concept attainment by children in two mediation categories. *J. Educ. Psychol.*, **58,** 19–26 (1967)

200. Worthen, B. R. Discovery and expository task presentation in elementary mathematics. *J. Educ. Psychol. Monogr. Suppl.*, **59,** (1, part 2), 13 pp. (1968)

201. Yonge, G. D. Structure of experience and functional fixedness. *J. Educ. Psychol.*, **57,** 115–20 (1966)

202. Yuille, J. C., Paivio, A. Imagery and verbal mediation instructions in paired-associate learning. *Research Bulletin #69* (Dept. Psychol., Univ. Western Ontario, London, Canada, Jan. 1968. (A shorter version is in press, *J. Exptl. Psychol.*)

203. Zeaman, D., House, B. J. The role of attention in retardate discrimination learning. In *Handbook in Mental Deficiency: Psychological Theory and Research*, 159–223 (Ellis, N. R. Ed., McGraw-Hill, New York, 722 pp., 1963)

PERSONNEL SELECTION[1]

By William A. Owens[2]

The University of Georgia, Athens, Georgia

AND

Donald O. Jewell[2]

Georgia State College, Atlanta, Georgia

142

Social Contexts

Personnel selection literature is not produced in social isolation. It manifests reactions for, or against, prevailing social, cultural, and professional attitudes pertinent to selection issues. The reviewers feel that much of the significance of current writings and research in selection would be lost if the context within which it appeared were not examined. Naturally, a rather broad brush must be used to paint the setting, but hopefully a bit of the tenor of the times, as we perceive it, will be conveyed.

Maximal manpower utilization.—The philosophy that every individual who is capable of work should be placed in a job which demands full and efficient use of his talents can be seen as a rising directional force, exerting increasing pressures on the personnel psychologist to employ methods consistent with this view. Certainly the present selection-rejection model, as Wallace (137) refers to it, does not fit comfortably into this philosophical context. The strength of this classic model lies in its provision for probabilistic demonstration that applicant A is more likely to succeed in a specific job than applicant B. The model fails, however, to provide information about the skills and abilities of either the selected or rejected applicants as they relate to jobs with different requirements. The selection-rejection model is designed to meet the immediate needs of industry in the most efficient (profitwise) way possible. The needs of the individual and of society are secondary, arguments to the contrary notwithstanding.

The model which fits the maximum manpower utilization philosophy is the classification model. Adhering to it, the evaluation of an applicant is akin to the one which occurs in vocational guidance—subject (S) is directed into a job most suited to his particular vocational strengths and weaknesses.

---

[1] This review selectively covers the literature from May 1, 1966 through December 31, 1967; earlier and later references are included only where they seem to provide continuity.

[2] The writers gratefully acknowledge the assistance of the following graduate students who helped them to explore the literature and to divest themselves of some of their customary professorial vagaries: J. B. Bryson; Rebecca B. Bryson; E. S. Ruda; P. R. Pinto; D. E. Pryor; B. D. Smart; and D. A. Wood.

There is little doubt that this model would theoretically provide the fullest utilization of available manpower if, as Wallace (137) has suggested, classification could be done at the national level. Wallace conceives of a national data bank with information on the entire labor force. Organizations would submit job specifications, and applicants most closely meeting the requirements would be referred to them. Such a system, however, is many years away. At present none but the very largest of firms can realistically contemplate the adoption of the classification model. Not only is the diversity of jobs within a given organization limited, but present training programs are not equipped to meet the demands such a system would impose. Nor are most management people ready to accept the idea of hiring everyone who walks in the door.

There are, however, some very real and immediate manpower problems facing industrial organizations for which the traditional selection-rejection model provides no adequate solutions. The most pressing of these is the shortage of qualified personnel to fill positions at the technical, professional, and managerial levels. It is difficult to use the traditional method when one has fewer applicants than jobs. At the lower end of the labor market continuum, a different kind of problem exists. For the available unskilled and semiskilled jobs there is an oversupply of applicants. Technology is partially responsible for this condition. Automation displaces persons on low level jobs and increases the number of higher level jobs to be filled. Few of the displaced workers can qualify for the newly created jobs, and they become part of an oversupplied unskilled-semiskilled labor force. Herein lies the source of another problem. As the size of this low-level unemployed group grows, both government and industry feel a responsibility to utilize this relatively unused manpower resource. Government must deal with unemployment and industry with a shortage of qualified workers. In addition, there is the humanitarian philosophy founded on the premise that because a person is a human being he deserves the opportunity to realize his talents in activities of his choice—including work. Despite difficulties with its implementation, some approximation to the classification model seems to be the only reasonable way to deal with both a lopsided labor force and a compelling philosophy. There is evidence that a responsive movement has already begun. Multiple-selection models are a practical compromise which many organizations have already adopted. This is the first step; others will follow. If maximum manpower utilization is to be approximated, other considerations aside, the classification approach must be adopted.

Fair employment.—The Fair Employment philosophy, if it can be so called, is maximal manpower utilization viewed from an individual frame of reference; i.e., it represents the conviction that an individual should have the opportunity to fully utilize his resources.

In the opinion of the reviewers, past inadequacies in personnel appraisal have contributed two major obstacles to the attainment of the Fair Employment goal—underemployment and overemployment. An individual is underemployed when he is locked into an employment situation not requiring full use of his resources. This category includes both the all too obvious "unemployed" and the all too inconspicuous workers who would like to be, and could be, more productive. The overemployed individual finds his job demands beyond his capabilities. Both problems are the result of either under- or overestimation of an individual's potential contribution in an employment situation.

One source of erroneous estimation is bias. To paraphrase Cleary & Hilton (30)—a selection method is biased if the predictors involved do not relate to the criteria in the same way for all subgroups of an applicant population. The need to identify the variables relating to bias among subgroups such as the handicapped, women, the aged, and the culturally different is of tremendous importance. While progress has been made, there is evidence that much is yet to be learned. The excellent presentation by Wallace, Kissinger & Reynolds (136) on testing minority group applicants presents convincing evidence of the existence of bias against such groups, especially Negroes. It discusses the possible sources of bias and suggests guidelines to be used to prevent its occurrence. In the same vein, Ewen & Kirkpatrick (46) found that moderating a prediction equation by race often improved validity. By contrast, the studies of Tenopyr (127), Cleary (29), and Stanley & Porter (117) are interesting to note. In general, they found no bias against Negroes in their predictions of performance. Of perhaps greater interest is Tenopyr's (127) summary of studies which seems to demonstrate that "culture fair" (i.e., nonverbal) tests actually increase mean differences between majority and minority groups.

After struggling through the literature concerning bias, the reviewers feel a need to step back for perspective. As long as research findings are interpreted as for or against minority groups, little progress will be made. In attempting to define superiority or deny inferiority, the issue becomes clouded. If the individual is to be placed in a situation where he will be maximally successful, the variables related to prediction must be known. Inferiority and superiority are totally relative questions and are neither useful nor defensible when applied as generalizations. In the present context, the fact that differences may exist—individually, racially, or culturally—can and should be viewed as information helpful in a placement situation. A study by Hall (65) lends perspective in that he notes several abilities possessed to a greater degree by Negroes, Indians, and Eskimos than by the middle class white.

The plight of the overemployed is every bit as crucial, both for the individual and for industry, as that of the underemployed. Overprediction of performance has doomed the individual to failure or, at best, frustration and mediocrity. Overemployment can occur when initial selection standards are lowered, when selection and promotion techniques overpredict, and when "natural selection" goes one step too far. The costs of overemployment must be enormous, but because they are so difficult to document they are largely ignored. If all individuals are to be "fairly" employed, the upper limits of performance for the average and above average workers should be as thoroughly investigated as the limits of the "below average" applicant.

Invasion of privacy.—The issue of the invasion of privacy in personnel selection is still far from being settled. The thoughtful and insightful writings of Ash (5, 6), Bennett (16), Conrad (32), and Lovell (85) aid in an understanding of the problem. There is an urgent need for the psychological profession to take steps to establish strict guidelines before the federal government passes laws restricting the use of selection devices. The Ervin bill (S. 1035) is a case in point. The testing provisions of this bill would effectively prevent, in the selection of federal employees, any group administration of tests involving questions about family relationships, religious beliefs, or attitudes and conduct relating to sexual matters. If passed, this bill could establish precedents which would extend far beyond the selection of federal employees. Without doubt the applicant has interests which should receive consideration. On the other hand, bills like the Ervin bill could progressively restrict item content, decrease inventory validity, and ultimately operate to the detriment of society. The balance is a delicate one.

The reviewers feel that the invasion of privacy crisis which exists in selection testing today can be traced to a lack of a real understanding of psychological testing and its purposes on the part of the American public. As Newman (91, p. 696) points out:

> Over the years, psychology as an organized profession has paid little attention to the problem of how psychological theories, methods, and findings are understood, appreciated and utilized by the American public. . . . Thus in the case of testing, while the antitest movement developed more and more strength, organized psychology took few steps to correct or modify the situation.

It is conceivable that the objections to certain types of tests are largely a function of the context in which they are used. Few people object to the use of personality tests in the clinical or counseling setting. They are confident that their welfare is foremost in the minds of the examiners and that information revealed through testing will be used to their benefit. The selection situation is not perceived in this light. Applicants see it as a competition in which tests may, because of their nature, reveal information which will act to their detriment. An applicant may feel he is being forced to "testify against himself."

If this assumption is accurate, it is easy to see how the selection-rejection model and the lack of public understanding of tests set up a situation almost certain to elicit negative feelings toward testing. An individual applies for a position he desires; he is tested and rejected. Perhaps he has read antitest literature (Gross, Black, Hoffman, etc.) which condemns testing. Almost certainly he has read nothing in its favor. Rather than blame himself, he blames the tests, particularly the seemingly non-work-relevant personality inventories, for his failure to get the job. The problem can be seen as only partly rational. Educating the public is essential, but education should be geared to the changing of attitudes and sets as well as to the transmitting of facts. Newman (91) suggests establishing a department of public affairs in the American Psychological Association to handle this task.

A recent study germane to the above discussion is worth mentioning. Tesser & Leidy (129) obtained "attitude toward testing" data from 12,000 high school students. As they point out, the subjects knew little about testing and had had little exposure to certain types of tests, particularly in the selection context. Their attitudes were found to be generally favorable—70 per cent did not feel that personality tests invaded their privacy, and 59 per cent believed that employers are justified in using them for selection. It appears that negative attitudes may not yet have developed at this level and that high schools are a likely place to start the testing education process.

One of the few studies involving an actual attempt to determine the kinds of questionnaire items to which Ss will object, or on which they will fake, is that of Larsen, Swarthout & Wickert (74). Employing autobiographical items as a vehicle, and both behavioral criteria and ratings, they found that self-rating or evaluation items were both objectionable and fakeable and that items dealing with family relationships were the former but not the latter. More such studies are needed.

RECRUITMENT

The recruitment of applicants, by affecting the selection ratio, influences the validity of selection procedures. Although the matter is incidental to their main purpose, Alf & Dorfman (4) illustrate the use of this relationship by showing that if one knows the failure rate on a job and the validity of a selection device or devices, he can vary the recruiting expenditure to attain an optimal selection ratio. However, psychologists seem thus far to have paid recruitment relatively scant attention.

Possible explanations of this neglect are tenuous, but one may be that recruitment lies in a small hinterland, adjacent to both industrial and consumer psychology, where the former has the greater concern and the latter the more appropriate methodologies. Perloff (96) depicts these overlapping concerns nicely when he says: "Whether the individual is being wooed as a consumer or as a recruit he is still being sought, and is in the happy situation of having to select from among several apparently attractive options."

A little-known study by Carson (28) is of considerable relevance to this viewpoint, since it essentially regards the college student in the employment interview as a consumer of job opportunities. In substance, carefully devised and pretested questionnaires were mailed to 2000 college seniors majoring in various fields of engineering and business administration at four major midwestern universities. Of the 1210 students (61 per cent) who responded, three-fourths had already participated in at least three employment interviews and were in this sense qualified and interested judges of both interview characteristics and employment needs. The obtained results suggest that (*a*) the most important factor influencing interviewee registration is the reputation of the company as an "industry leader"; (*b*) among topics discussed, "job for which applicant is being considered" is rated most important and "specific company projects" as least; (*c*) the usefulness of summer experience as a recruiting device is a function of its relevance to the students' academic training; (*d*) "interesting work" and "opportunity for advancement" are the most highly rated job characteristics; and (*e*) company ads in popular magazines are the medium through which the largest number had obtained company information. All in all, the Carson study is a reasonable prototype of those concerned with the college recruit's needs, interests, and perceptions of organizations.

Korman (72) has further investigated this area and found that *S*s high in self-esteem are more likely to search for the relevance of job requirements to self-perceived characteristics. Similarly, Vroom (134) has reported that the attractiveness of an organization varies with the extent to which membership in it is seen as instrumental to the attainment of personal goals.

Conversely, Carroll (27) has investigated the organizations' perceptions of the recruit. He attempted to empirically relate student characteristics obtained from placement data sheets to popularity in the job market. His criteria of the latter were number of job offers received, number of visit offers received, two derived ratios, and a combination of these, all obtained via a postcard survey. He found ranking on appearance related to three criteria, marital status to one, and office experience to two. The results appear to be somewhat atypical in that grades and extracurricular activities are unrelated to the criteria and appearance is strongly related. While the generality of these results may be limited by methodological considerations, the paradigm is sound.

Several writers have commented on the present or potential size of the applicant pool for industry. Torpey (131) feels that a shortage of counseling personnel is shrinking the potential supply of scientific and technical talent. Encouragingly, however, Roberts & Nichols (102) report on a source of financial support for outstanding Negro students, which, if multiplied, would help increasing numbers of Negroes to enter the job market at a relatively high level.

Of growing concern to the industrial community, Baumhart & Fitzpatrick (14) cite the Harris poll as indicating some perceived aversions to a business career; and Ryans & Hise (105) note that even among M.B.A.'s committed to such a career the "traditional" concern for primarily financial rewards is not prominent.

Recruiting pressures are greater at higher job levels and much of the literature relates to college recruiting. Comparable principles apply at all levels, however; and what is needed by both prospective employer and employee is current and accurate information coupled with some mutual understanding of desires, capabilities, expectations, and potential sources of satisfaction. More research seems called for in this area.

EXPERIENCE, SETS, AND TESTING CONDITIONS

In discussing the role of experience, sets, and testing conditions as partial determiners of test scores, it is convenient to turn to Cronbach's dichotomy and to regard tests and questionnaires as measures of either maximum performance or typical performance. A recent survey by Fiske (50) indicates that in a probability sampling of adults over 75 per cent evaluated tests as good for assessing abilities and likes versus dislikes, whereas only about one half felt that they were good for appraising a *S*'s social relations or personal problems. Clearly the esoteric dichotomy has a base in general perception.

Maximum performance measures.—To turn first, then, to maximum performance measures, two recent articles suggest a tendency of scores on cognitive tests to relate inversely to measures of anxiety. Within a group given negative feedback on a prior assembly task, Walker, Neilsen & Nicolay (135) obtained negative correlations of 0.42 and 0.45 between two anxiety measures and the Object Assembly subtest of the WAIS. Similarly, Carrier & Jewell (26), in the third of a series of studies, related predicted final examination scores generated by a regression equation employing three anxiety measures and their three cross products to actual final examination scores in Introductory Psychology. Correlations of 0.32 for males and 0.52 for females were obtained. Ultimate causal inferences are not easily made from studies of this type, but it seems clear that individual differences in anxiety were confounding individual differences in ability or achievement in both instances. Another kind of confounding occurs if some *S*s have had prior exposure to, or experience with, a test and others have not.

The Equal Employment Opportunities Commission's (EEOC) *Guidelines on Employment Testing Procedures* (45) specifically encourage employers to provide for the retesting of "failure candidates" who have undertaken some self-improvement since initial testing. If this is done, it is clear that the issue of making an appropriate adjustment in retest scores will arise. In a series of studies, Droege (41) and Showler & Droege (112) have estimated the magnitude of the required correction for each of the subtests of the GATB and for each of eight retest intervals from 1 day to 3 years. It is to be regretted that similar data are not available for more tests in frequent use.

Changes in external testing conditions are of as great concern as changes within the subject. Thus, Kirchner (70) reports lower means and larger variances on a typing test for *S*s tested in a group situation than for those tested individually. The same pattern existed for both speed and errors, and the author concludes that "it is better to test subjects individually whether the setting is industrial or otherwise."

Typical performance measures.—Turning to the area of typical performance measures, where basic assumptions are both less robust and less frequently fulfilled, it is relevant to recall that Fiske's (50) subjects evaluated interest measures roughly equivalently with ability measures, and more highly than personality measures. Accordingly, it is intriguing to note that two recent studies of interest do imply considerable stability and freedom from bias. Stephenson, Smith & Rimland (119) employed a substantial sample and noted that scores on the Strong Vocational Interest Blank do not differ significantly for NROTC applicants tested at home and for those tested at recruiting stations. Stephenson (118) also noted that the Strong contains only six regionally biased items and that if a subject selected the typical far western response to each he would increase his raw scores on one-quarter to one-third of the scales only a point or two. He concluded that this amount of bias has no practical significance.

The literature regarding the relationship between experience, sets, and testing conditions and personality measures is seen as having two facets. On the one hand it speaks to basic assumptions, methodological issues, or appropriate uses of personality tests; on the other hand it concerns itself with the probable nature and magnitude of specific influences on such measures. In the former category we may place Lovell's (85) very cogent argument that it is not the content of personality questionnaires but the way they are used that is wrong. It is his contention that the personnel function and the client function must be carefully discriminated, and that personality measures are simply not appropriately applied in the former context. The primary point of the Fiske (50) survey falls in the same category. It is that "Ss manifest a wide variety of reactions to tests and to being tested"; and that Ss who approach tests differently will score differently because of it. Campbell et al. (23) propose that response to a specific interest item is a function of both the S's perception of the constellation of items to which the given item belongs and of its attraction. Their stress on perception of the item is significant, since individual differences here may be a large and confounding influence. As illustration, Brand (20) reports a negative relationship between higher levels of reading difficulty and item validity. By implication our personality questionnaires could profitably be screened for items and wordings which fail to convey similar meanings to all potential Ss.

A number of writers have suggested or implied that subject reactions to personality inventories are rather generally unfavorable. Winkler & Mathews (141), on the other hand, report that only 13 per cent to 34 per cent of their sample of 77 male and 75 female industrial employees found the nine most offensive items of the GAMIN and STDCR inventories objectionable. Unhappily, generalizations should be made with caution since their Ss were volunteers.

In four studies major attention has been devoted to the effects of instructions or sets on noncognitive test performance. Bartlett & Doorley (12), with an interest in the problem of faking, administered 24 forced-choice items to 30 students in Introductory Psychology. Six weeks later they broke the class into three subsamples and retested them. One subset was instructed to answer honestly, a second was provided with a reason to fake, and the third was instructed to do so. In general, the mean score of the last group differed significantly from the other two which did not differ themselves. However, test-retest reliabilities of 0.87, 0.50 and 0.35 respectively, indicate that differential shifts in score were nearly as common in group two as in group three. A nice point is made: namely, that of those Ss who can fake not all will; and when a subject has a reason to fake, one does not know whether or not he has done so.

Gomez & Braun (59), employing the Eysenck Personality Inventory, also investigated faking. They found that an instruction to fake decreased the Neuroticism (N) score and increased the Extraversion (E) and Lie (L) scores. Interestingly enough, however, an instruction to fake but to conceal it resulted in comparable changes on N and E, but in a significantly smaller increment in the L score. Thus, validation or suppressor scores themselves can be faked, and independently of other scores. In a third study of faking, Wiggins (139) employed the MMPI as his test vehicle and the usual retest design. Feeling that Ss who fake must be able to estimate either the social desirability of an item or the consensus response to it (communality), he gave instructions to do each on administrations both before the standard and after it. Communality estimates, in either order, had no effect; but social desirability appraisals, on a prestandard administration, were followed by more accurate faking. Order effects could not entirely account for the finding or the communality instruction should also have been effective. The importance of some awareness of the social desirability of a response prior to making it is documented and re-emphasized. Invoking a quite different set, Bloxom (17) administered a personality questionnaire with both anger-arousing and neutral instructions and found that his college Ss endorsed more negative self-statements with the former. Several less parsimonious constructions can be placed on the data, or it may simply be that authoritarian and threatening instructions to respond carefully are still effective with some college students.

A concluding study by Lebovits & Ostfeld (77) involved administration of the MMPI to 1852 industrially employed males. When scores were examined by level of education, it was observed that the K scores, representing amount of defensiveness, were lower for Ss with less education. Since K scores are correlated with scores on other scales, profiles for the more and less educated were quite different. The authors recommend that educational status needs control when groups are compared. An unhappy aside is that the more valid responses are obtained from the less educated where the marginal utility of a man is smaller.

In summary, it seems that scores on noncognitive measures are particularly susceptible to influence by prior experience, sets, and testing conditions. Thus, in this context as in others, the burden is still upon those who would employ such measures in business and industry.

CRITERIA

Methods and types.—A discussion of criteria may be appropriately begun with a comment on Lawler's (75) clear and convincing study of the multitrait-multirater approach to appraising managerial job performance. In essence, the argument is that one should rate a small number of critical characteristics like ability and effort; that correlations between ratings for a given trait, across judges, should be significantly different from zero; and that a logical pattern of trait-rater matrix relationships should exist in which one of three requirements is that a trait have higher correlations across judges than across both traits and judges. The author also points out how off-quadrant cases in comparisons among subordinates ratings, self-ratings, peer ratings, and superiors ratings may be diagnostic of age, seniority, time in position, and satisfaction. If a criticism is to be offered, it would have to be only a question as to the feasibility of collecting peer, subordinate, and self-ratings in an administrative or predictive context. Pym & Auld (98) do suggest self-ratings as a measure of employee satisfactoriness, but advise sagacity and the selection of circumstances in their utilization—a sentiment the writers can only echo.

Along quite a different line, Mackenzie (86) reports on the development of a functional job knowledge test for dental students which is to serve as a criterion of both knowledge and the ability to apply it. This device discriminates groups as predicted and seems potentially useful. In still a different dimension, Patten (95) recounts the construction of scalograms, based on a configuration of plant data, which suggest characteristics potentially useful in ranking the positions of managers of plants of various sizes. Complementing some human relations trends in the United States, Velehradsky (133) argues that a justifiable method of employee evaluation should constitute but one facet of a comprehensive, naturalistic, and complex system for working with people.

Strengths and limitations.—Against a backdrop of theoretical discussion, Lennerlof (78) describes the development of a supervisory criterion instrument constructed for the measurement of the reactions of subordinates. Encouragingly, when this device was administered at two separate plants and the results factor analyzed, there was generally good agreement in outcomes, and minor divergences appeared to be related to company differences in production and administration. In a different vein, MacKinney (87) discusses a variety of evidence which he interprets to be indicative of a systematic change in job performance over time. By implication, some inadequacy of criteria and failures in prediction may have resulted from our rather customary disregard of such changes. Prien (97) also speaks for the dynamic nature of criteria and suggests that some job functions will wax and wane in importance with shifts in organizational goals and objectives. Jobs involving abstract functions and intangible outcomes are held to be most susceptible.

Although his central concern is with efficient manpower utilization, Wilson (140), by implication, feels that the so-called criterion problem lies more in the area of job design than in that of criterion methodology. He argues that jobs in the Royal Navy have been composed of psychologically heterogeneous elements; a fact which has complicated their performance, their evaluation, and their differential prediction. His contention is for the reorganization and "purifying" of job activities, a task on which he reports some progress in the Navy setting.

Dimensions or components.—Since an overall rating is so often the only criterion either employed or available, two studies which dissect such criteria seem noteworthy. In the first of these, Pallett & Hoyt (94) related behavioral characteristics to judged success in general business activities. Subjects were 230 University of Iowa graduates who had been out of college for five to ten years and who were rated by their supervisors on two overall characteristics (rate of progress and potential) and on 23 specific behavioral scales. A critical finding was that eight of the ratings of specific behaviors, including such variables as Persuasiveness, Identification with the business world, and Leadership, contributed significantly to a multiple correlation of 0.77 with the sum of progress and potential ratings. As the authors recognize, it would have been ideal to have the behavioral ratings made earlier and by different judges; however, the specification of characteristics related to general business success is of real interest. With a similar basic paradigm, Fallis (47) obtained ratings on 26 behavioral dimensions of salesman performance from 110 sales managers. The design was complex, but a central outcome was that six factors yielded good prediction of the average evaluations of salesman performance in a cross-validation group. These dimensions were willingness to learn, Cooperation with other employees, Sales planning and organizing, Drive and dedication to the job, Ability as a trainer, and Ability to learn and remember. The specification of behavioral criterion dimensions of overall performance is of clear importance. In a quite different domain, Fine (48) proposes a three-dimensional skill analysis of the world of human performance. His dimensions are adaptive, functional, and specific-content skills, and he conceives of jobs as differing only in the pattern of those required. The argument has rational appeal, but compelling data are apparently not yet available.

Obviously, much of the criterion research conducted during the review period has been devoted to managerial performance or other tasks in which functions are difficult to define and outcomes difficult to evaluate. In part, this reflects an increasing concern for the shortage of qualified applicants for higher level jobs and the need to develop more accurate management selection methods to tap a larger applicant population.

Space limitations make it impossible to review here all of the classical prediction studies undertaken during the current review period. In an effort to affect a compromise between a large body of literature and necessary brevity, the writers present in Table I a summary of those studies which seemed best to meet the criterion of general interest. Many good situation-specific studies have, of necessity, been omitted.[3]

Several of the studies listed require a further comment. Streufert, Castore & Kliger (120) had subjects involved in a simulated international conflict situation repeatedly rate themselves and other participants on Stogdill's leadership characteristics. A measure of conceptual complexity was found to be highly related to leadership ratings; e.g., complex leaders were rated higher on "Tolerance for Uncertainty," "Assumption of Leadership Role," "Consideration," and "Predictive Accuracy." Simple leaders were rated higher on "Initiation of Structure," "Production Emphasis," and "Demands Reconciliation."

Greenshields & Platt's (62) study employing the Drivometer provides an outstanding example of the direction in which work sample testing needs to go. Rather than yielding a global performance measure, the Drivometer provides quantitative data on many critical behaviors and events in the overall task. When installed, the Drivometer records driver control actions, vehicle motions, and traffic events. The authors found significant differences on these variables between groups of high accident versus low accident drivers, and between high-violator versus beginning drivers. Hopefully, this paradigm can be applied to other selection problems.

In the ever popular area of management performance prediction, four studies are particularly worth noting. The relationship between scores on SCORES, an instrument developed by The American Institute for Research (AIR), and a supervisory success type of criterion was determined in a study by Flanagan & Krug (51). Using *a priori* weights based on test profiles, individuals were assigned to criterion categories. Predicted versus actual assignments were compared and correlations between *a priori* weighted scores and the criterion were computed. All findings were highly significant and, if they can be replicated, SCORES promises to be a potentially useful device for selecting management personnel. In a study with similar intent, Tenopyr & Ruch (128) compared the validities of a number of leadership scales relative to success in production management. Their finding singled

---

[3] Our complete bibliography may be obtained, on request, from Dr. Jewell.

out the Leadership Evaluation and Development Scale (LEADS) as the best ($r = .36$) of four predictors of salary, corrected for age and length of service. LEADS was also found to be the best predictor of ratings on performance in the employee relations area. The authors conclude that LEADS taps meaningful dimensions of supervisory performance not measured by the other predictors examined.

In a study of the labor-relations field, Tenopyr (126, p. 10) related six psychometric measures and four biodata type items to eight criteria of success. Her findings suggest that "in developing an efficient and practical selection program for labor-relations representatives probably only Verbal Comprehension, LEADS, and the experiences tapped by biodata should be considered. Variables concerned with temperament should probably be subjected to further research, particularly with respect to the possibility of curvilinear relations with criteria."

Grant, Katkovsky & Bray (61), in one of the articles generated by their work in the Bell Systems Assessment Centers, state strongly that there is little doubt that the projectives they employed do yield valid information regarding managerial motivation. They base this contention on the facts that (a) projective data seemed to play a very important role in determining assessment staff ratings which, in turn, proved to be effective predictors of management performance; and (b) several of the projective variables, especially those pertaining to leadership and achievement motivation, were related to salary and management progress. The projective devices employed were the Rotter Incomplete Sentences Blank, the Management Incomplete Sentences Test, and six TAT cards. Projective tests have not yet been interred.

One type of predictor that is just now beginning to show its true potential is biographical data. Scott & Johnson (111) determined that 19 biographical items could effectively predict tenure among unskilled employees ($r = .45$ in a cross-validation group). A factor analysis indicated that "convenience" and "family responsibility" accounted for most of the explained variance in the tenure criterion.

Owens' (92) approach to the prediction of creativity recognizes the importance of a comprehensive, closed-system type of analysis. He selected predictors which would permit an examination of the relationships between cognitive, noncognitive, and job environment variables, their interactions, and their criterion relationships. Validities, some of them longitudinal or predictive, were moderate; and the design, though somewhat complex, seems true to life.

New Models and Methods

Trends are not always easy to document, but in the present instance at least one trend seems undeniable. Researchers have addressed themselves to the issue of test validation with increased sophistication and with refined

TABLE I

Some Representative Classical Selection Studies

Author	Predictors	Criteria	Subjects	General Findings
Barrett et al. (10)	Job concept interview	Employee attitudes and performance	Clerks and secretaries	Attitudes were predictable, performance was not
Campbell & Johansson (24)	SVIB Academic Achievement Scale	Occupational choice and performance	College students	Ss followed over a maximum of 3 yrs; occupational choice predicted better than performance
Carlson (25)	Selection interview	Interview decisions	Insurance company managers	Interview reliability and selection decisions vary as a function of several external factors
Cline et al. (31)	Biodata	Rated creativity	Scientists	Low but significant validities
Cooper & Payne (33)	Eysenck Personality Inventory	Work performance and absenteeism	Employees	Extraversion correlated negatively with length of service and positively with unexcused absences
Cummin (34)	TAT, 4 cards	Management success	Engineers, supervisors and top management	Needs for achievement and power were related to success
Droege (42)	Age-adjusted and unadjusted GATB scale scores	Occupational success	Workers in various jobs	Differences in validities for age-adjusted and unadjusted scores tended to be small
Flanagan & Krug (51)	SCORES battery profiles	Supervisory vs. nonsupervisory position: high vs. low rate of advancement	Engineers (60)	Scores related significantly to both criteria
Gambaro & Schell (53)	Porteus maze test and ratings of personnel effectiveness	Rated employability	Educationally handicapped adolescents	Combined predictors provided good prediction, but screened out 30% who were successful
Ghiselli (57)	Personnel interview	Survival with the company for a 3-yr. period	Stock broker applicants	The biserial correlation between the criterion and interview ratings was .35
Gordon (60)	Clinical, psychometric work-sample, brief assessment	Board selection decisions	Peace Corps applicants	Validities ranged from .37 to .41. Clinical and psychometric methods were uncorrelated and all methods about equally effective
Grant et al. (61)	Rotter Incomplete Sentence Blank, Management Incomplete Sentences Test, and Thematic Apperception Test	Assessment-center staff evaluations, progress in management	Managerial applicants	Projectives weighted strongly in evaluations, and related to progress in management
Greenshields & Platt (62)	Drivometer	Driving histories	Range of high-to-low accident drivers	Measurements revealed significant differences between samples; accuracy of individual prediction about?2 in 3

TABLE I (*Continued*)

Author	Predictors	Criteria	Subjects	General Findings
Howell (67)	Personality inventories and other measures	Personal effectiveness	Physicians	Significant relationships found on a variety of measures
Howell et al. (68)	Programmer Aptitude Tests, Federal Service Entrance Examination	Work sample of programming	Civil Service Employees	This type of criterion appeared quite predictable
Levy (79)	Biodata (preappointment factors)	Police failures	Policemen (4500)	Successful group was older, less educated, more highly trained and more stable, both in residence and work history
Nagatsuka (89)	Discriminative reaction multiple performance test	Accident frequency	Bus drivers	Test performance discriminates between accident-nonaccident drivers
Nash (90)	SVIB	Managerial effectiveness	Managers (168)	57-item key predicts managerial effectiveness
Owens (92)	Cognitive (longitudinal), situational, biodata	Complex, judgmentally weighted creativity measures	Research &development engineers (457)	All classes of predictors effective; overall R about 0.40
Reynolds (99)	Sociometric ratings	Leadership behavior	AF cadets	Early sociometric ratings predicted leadership
Schuh (109, 110)	Biographic items and Wonderlic Personnel Test	Tenure	Salesmen	Failed to predict
Scott & Johnson (111)	Biographical items	Tenure	Unskilled employees	Empirically weighted application blank as effective as multiple R techniques
Skawran et al. (115)	Fault-finding Test of Mechanical Aptitude	On-the-job effectiveness	Mechanical job applicants	Correlated .28 with criterion
Streufert et al. (120)	Conceptual complexity	Leadership style	College students	Complexity and leader behavior were highly related
Taylor & Ellison (124)	Biographical inventory	Scientific performance	High school and college students	Comparable items predicted creativity in scientists and students
Tenopyr (126)	Leadership Evaluation and Development Scale, Verbal Comprehension Test, Logical Reasoning, a general reasoning test, et al.	Ratings and salary	Labor-relations personnel	LEADS, verbal comprehension and experience predicted best
Tenopyr & Ruch (128)	LEADS, Leadership Opinion Questionnaire	Present salary rating	Production managers	LEADS predicted best, r=.36
Zdep & Weaver (143)	Graphoanalysis	Commissions	Life insurance salesmen	Failed to predict success, may predict failure

and often highly analytical approaches. Ghiselli's classic review, *The Measurement of Occupational Aptitude*, highlighted the problem by indicating our failure to enhance the general magnitudes of validities reported by Hull in his *Aptitude Testing* of 1928. Dunnette's (43) revision of Guetzkow and Forehand has provided an appropriate analytical model, and both he (44) and Ghiselli (55) have suggested new methodologies which others have recognized and exploited.

New models.—In view of the priority of their efforts, it seems appropriate to make initial reference to a recent investigation by each of these researchers Accordingly, a nicely conceived study by Hobert & Dunnette (66) contains a report on "The development of moderator variables to enhance the prediction of managerial effectiveness." Basically, two moderator scales were empirically developed to identify and eliminate the "off-quadrant" cases. This elimination resulted in improved prediction and reduced criterion overlap for the remainder of the sample. With clarity and analytical similarity, Ghiselli & Sanders (58) have demonstrated that the usual assumption of homoscedasticity is sometimes in error and that it is possible to develop a moderator capable of differentiating two subsets of Ss displaying opposite patterns of heteroscedasticity. An important implication for sequential testing is that good prediction may be achieved, by different routes, for Ss with differing patterns of predictor versus moderator scores.

An important conception in the Dunnette model (43) is that prediction may be differential for various subsets of Ss. Thus, it is pertinent to note that a number of investigators have been concerned with the methodology or with the utilization of subgrouping. In an unusually thorough study, Schoenfeldt (108) established that comparable subgroups can be identified across samples, and that hierarchical procedures result in a structuring very similar to the one derived from a factoring of the intersubject cross-products matrix. Similarly, Lorr & Radhakrishnan (84), Ball & Hall (9), and Guertin (63) have all commented constructively on methods of subgrouping.

Following the development of models and methods, there have been a substantial number of studies utilizing and applying them. Klein et al. (71), employing hierarchical grouping, established four subsets of Ss based upon their responses to five moderator variable items. In cross-validation they found prediction superior to that in the total group in one subset, comparable to it in a second subset, and inferior to it in the remaining two. It is of interest to note that the moderators were not effective as predictors, and that a paradigm is provided for the simultaneous use of multiple item moderators. Tesser, Starry & Chaney (130) administered an extensive biodata form to 220 British scientists, factored the results, and applied hierarchical grouping to the factor scores. Distinct subgroups did emerge, but the authors encountered the problem of "the vanishing n" when they attempted within-groups item analysis and cross-validation. Taylor (125), with a sample of 444 male managerial-level employees of a large oil company, obtained his primary subgroups in a comparable fashion, applied a minimum distance classifier to generate comparable subsets in a cross-validation sample, and then examined the simple affinity of subgroup membership for type of work. His findings include one showing that 84 per cent of his salesmen came from three subgroups in the validation sample and 81 per cent from the parallel subgroups in the cross-validation sample. Such results would seem to denote a preferred method which should be investigated further.

Single and multiple moderator variable designs have also been employed in a number of other investigations. Race has been the single moderator in several such studies: one of an automated office situation by Ruda & Albright (104); one concerned with predicting success in machine shop training by Tenopyr (127); one relating to an evaluation of the problem of selective admission to nursing school by Ewen & Kirkpatrick (46); and one involving a series of industrial personnel selection studies by Acker (1). Differential validities have been the rule, although the magnitudes and directions of differences have varied from study to study.

Apart from race, Dawis et al. (40) found that satisfaction moderated the relationship between ability test scores and job performance for male and female assemblers. Similarly, Stricker (121) observed that compulsivity measures served to moderate the prediction of college grades for students in engineering but not for those in liberal arts, an illustration of the specificity of moderators. In a particularly searching study, Baker (8) applied a biodata predictor to a sample of 965 managerial, technical, and marketing employees of a large oil company. He factored his biodata form and employed the factor scores as predictors of both salary level and potential salary level; he also tested each factor for moderator effects by splitting its distribution into high and low halves to determine if prediction were better for Ss in the one than in the other. Pursuing the matter one step further, he selected his two best moderators and observed their combined effects within the cells of a fourfold table. In part, he observed in cross-validation that the moderator approach had an inconclusive effect upon overall prediction, although it did enhance it within particular subgroups.

It must be noted that the new look at prediction is a differential look. Correlations in some segments of the sample are increased and those in other segments are constant or decreased; the total may remain essentially unchanged. Moderators tend to be specific and to require large Ns for their development. Methods of subgrouping, although they do have inferential utility, are numerous and plagued with a variety of inexactitudes and uncertainties. If the subgrouping is accomplished to enhance prediction within subsets, restriction in range, relative stability of betas, and similar methodological problems arise; one must also hope that the subgroup within which prediction is enhanced is the one of interest and concern. Some of these problems are lost if attention is given only to the simple fact of subgroup membership and to the differential affinities of subsets for criteria. In any event, the analytical search for enhanced differential validities is clearly a promising move in the right direction. Given some of the indicated problems, however, the form it may ultimately assume is only beginning to emerge.

Before leaving the topic of models it seems worth noting that Sines (114) has criticized the direction of inference in the usual paradigm of empirical test validation. His contention is that an argument from real life behavior to test behavior is not the inverse of an argument from the latter to the former, which he regards as preferable. Happily, Lieberman (80) has shown the logical equivalence of the two strategies by essentially noting that one cannot meaningfully comment upon three cells of a fourfold table (i.e., behavior-nonbehavior versus test response-nonresponse) while ignoring the fourth. Given their equivalence, a choice between the two strategies must depend upon the goals and hypotheses of the investigator.

Measurement methods.—As though in recognition of the frequent need for its control, several studies of the social desirability (S.D.) variable have appeared in the recent measurement literature. Simon (113) notes that a simple question concerning the favorability or unfavorability of a statement yields results which correlate 0.94 and 0.95 with the methods of Edwards and Kogan, respectively. Instructions to Ss could be explained more fully, but the method seems a simpler equivalent of conventional methods. Bloxom (18) observes that variability in response to items of neutral S.D. is positively related to the Edwards type of S.D. and negatively related to the Marlow-Crowne "lie" type. Thus, if response variability suggests carefulness, the most careful Ss would be those low on Edwards "self-esteem" and high on Marlow-Crowne "need for social approval." In a third study, Boe et al. (19) performed both Q and R types of factor analyses on a matrix composed of the S.D. ratings of 700 MMPI items by 112 Ss. They found a large general S.D. factor in the former but none in the latter. Clearly, people agree quite well in their judgments of S.D., but items are not meaningfully united along this dimension.

Still in the context of measurement methods, two articles seem noteworthy in that they deal with potentially new types of tests or procedures in testing. Of these, the one with largest implications is by Bayroff & Seeley (15). They compared conventional verbal and arithmetic reasoning subtests of the Air Force Qualification Test with programmed, branching tests in the same areas. The latter were constructed by presenting Ss with a harder item following a success and an easier one following a failure. The possible range of scores after eight items was 16 points, based on the difficulty of the last item answered. Thus, although the branching tests contained 36 items, no given S completed more than eight. Spearman-Brown estimates indicated that conventional tests would need approximately twice as many items to achieve comparable reliability (0.76 for verbal and 0.73 for numerical). A possible, though unlikely, source of bias may reside in the fact that the branching tests were individually administered, whereas the conventional tests were not; a more realistic problem would seem to concern the feasibility of utilizing measures requiring individual administration in the military or other large group situations. At any event, since the branching procedure resembles the finding of a limen and departs dramatically from those presently employed, its possible implications for theory and practice are impressive.

An interesting sort of proposal for a new selection device comes from Barrett (11), who suggests that a measure of the candidates' performance style would be useful as an indicant of his potential compatibility with the requirements of the job and the expectations of his supervisor. The utility of this notion would seem to rest on a demonstration that significant dimensions of performance style on an unfamiliar job can be reliably measured "at the gate."

Classification methods.—Recognizing that an approach to full employment means a shift away from selection and toward classification, it seems important to make at least brief reference to the latter topic. As might be anticipated, both the Army's Behavioral Science Research Laboratory and the Navy's Personnel Research Activity have been able to devote themselves to the pure case with substantial success. Swanson & Dow (123), for example, have described and are apparently implementing, a computer-assisted classification system for the assignment of Navy recruits to schools. The program is designed to maximize the sum of selection test scores for individual schools. As compared with conventional methods, its use results in raising the average school selector test score and in filling quotas when eligible recruits are in short supply. In a followup on the computerization of enlisted classification, Rimland (101) devoted himself to possible criteria, Alf (2) to training cost minimization, and Swanson (122) to avoiding short term quota fluctuations. Overall, the program seems to be well conceived and to offer numerous advantages.

Referring to matters of methodology, Darlington & Stauffer (37) applied decision theory to the problem of evaluating tests or items used to categorize people, and Alf & Dorfman (4) present an analytic method for optimizing the classification of Ss into two subgroups based upon the locating of a cutting score so as to maximize the expected value of the decision procedure. Noteworthy is an article by Sorenson (116) proposing the assignment of personnel to "criterion activities" so that some function is optimized. One begins with a binary classification matrix Ψ, in which columns equal jobs and rows equal persons. The author has then developed a matrix operation which transforms predictor data to a matrix L approximating Ψ. He also presents a computer program for computation and evaluation of the matrix transformation. The method is independent of the number of Ss to be assigned, and resulted in a nearly optimum allocation which satisfied approximate quota restrictions.

Two years ago this review could not have been written without a fairly lengthly comment on Dawes & Meehl's proposal for mixed group validation of diagnostic signs (39). Since then, Linn (82) has offered a careful criticism and evaluation, and Alf & Abrahams (3) have presented an example demonstrating that the method can lead to results which are mathematically inconsistent. At very least, endorsement must be suspended.

Statistical methods.—Among a group of articles which are statistically oriented about test validity and validation, the following should be mentioned. Darlington & Bishop (36) devoted themselves to the issue of how to select items in order to maximize test validity. Briefly put, they found that beyond a small pool of most valid items, an optimum increment is provided by methods which add several moderately valid but relatively unique items at a time. Woodbury & Novick (142) provide a method for determining those test lengths which will optimize the validity of a battery that must be administered in a fixed total time; and Bashaw (13) sets forth a potentially very useful formula for estimating the correlation of predicted with actual criterion scores in a cross-validation sample given the betas in the validation sample, plus the validity coefficients and intercorrelations of the predictors in the cross-validation sample.

Concerned with the relative efficiency of test selection methods in cross-validation and on generated data, Schine (107) found the Wherry-Gaylord method with integer weights optimal for small numbers of cases and large numbers of predictors (50 and 12); for larger numbers of cases (200) he found the Wherry Test Selection method best. In a somewhat parallel fashion, Curtis (35) compared correlational decision theory and functional utility approaches to estimating the value of selection tests. Overall results obtained from both decision theory and functional utility methods were more favorable to the value of tests than those derived from the correlational method. Darlington & Stauffer (38) also employed decision theory to derive a formula for setting cut points on a test used to distinguish two criterion groups; and Genkin & Bodov (54) propose a new statistical algorithm for discriminating "good" and "poor" occupational risks based on sequential analysis of a test battery.

In the context of obtaining estimates of validity, Linn (83) has addressed himself to range restriction problems in the use of self-selected groups. Since the explicit selection variable is often both unknown and unknowable, he provides an example illustrating the effect of substituting an implicit selection variable for it in the standard correction formula. The substitution results in an undercorrection if implicit and explicit variables are highly correlated, or an overcorrection if they are not. In terms of summarizing and presenting validity data, Wesman (138) provides both illustrations of, and instructions for, developing the double entry expectancy table.

At a very fundamental level of statistical summarization, Bakan (7) has voiced a scopeful criticism of the test of significance in psychological research. In part, he notes that a probability value provides neither an estimate of magnitude nor automaticity of inference, and he feels that the Bayesian approach has much to recommend it.

Computer utilization.—Two computer innovations of direct relevance to the present section seem noteworthy. First, Richards (100) has recently indicated through a rigorous simulation that computers can, at least in principle, construct a verbal comprehension test; and Finney (49) has shown that computers can be programmed to both interpret test results and to compose psychological reports. Thus, it is possible to conceive of the automation of the entire testing program, in industry or elsewhere.

Integrative approaches.—The present section may be concluded by commenting on several studies directed at the integration of methods or findings. Accordingly, Fleishman (52) has capably devoted himself to the "development of a behavior taxonomy for describing human tasks." His concern is with the unifying dimensions underlying skilled behavior, and the real goals are to be able to generalize from the simulator in the laboratory to the task in the real world, and from one task to another. Starting with such knowns as his 11 psychomotor factors, for example, Fleishman (52) proceeds across both correlational and experimental studies by a process of progressive abstraction and generalization to the revised definition of basic dimensions. In terms of integrating some data, simplifying some problems, and standardizing tasks his approach seems to offer real promise.

In a revisitation of the issue of statistical versus clinical prediction, Sawyer (106) offers both a helpful redefinition and a very informative summary. He first points out that prediction is only the latter phase of a process of which the former phase is measurement. He then examines both phases of both methods across 45 studies and concludes in favor of both statistical measurement and statistical prediction. It is, in fact, implied that the clinician is more likely to contribute through observation than through integration. Sawyer himself suggests that the comparisons are confounded by many uncontrolled differences across studies.

Finally, in some opposition to both the contemporary findings of Sawyer (106) and to the classical earlier findings of Kelly and Fiske, is a scopeful and provocative study by Bray & Grant (21) entitled "The assessment center in the measurement of potential for business management." Basically, this report contains evidence on the character and longitudinal validity of personnel assessments of 1956 produced in the context of the Bell Systems' Management Progress Study. Subjects were 207 college graduate employees and 148 noncollege graduates advanced into management who originally spent three and one-half days at the Assessment Center devoted to interviews, situational tests, projective devices, paper and pencil tests and questionnaires, a Q-sort, and an autobiographical essay. A largely professional assessment staff summarized the results in 25 ratings plus one overall rating. The procedures were sensibly focused and standardized, and the rating evaluations yielded readily to factorial interpretation. Situtional test

results weighed heavily in the variance of staff judgments, and prediction of
this difficult criterion was very good. Of 55 men who advanced into middle
management, 43 had been predicted to do so; conversely, of 73 men who
had not advanced beyond the first level of management, 69 had been
correctly predicted. The present writers are inclined to stress the very great
importance of predictor-criterion congruence in interpreting these results.
The criterion is heavily interpretive and judgmental; if the predictor is
also, it is an unmixed asset in this context. Indeed, the latter may well be
the former in microcosm and at an earlier point in time.

Book Reviews and Literature Summaries

During this review period several noteworthy books, summaries, and
literature reviews pertinent to personnel selection have been published.
Dunnette's (44) *Personnel Selection and Placement* is an excellent exposition
of the logical and methodological steps involved in developing systematic
selection programs. The author argues convincingly that sound personnel
decisions require evidence about the individuality of people, the special
requirements of jobs, and the interactions between the two; he also presents
a model for implementing this approach.

McKenna (88) has produced a thoroughly practical, readable, and worthwhile programmed text on personnel selection. It is meant to be an introduction to the field, and it achieves its goal. No previous exposure to either
selection procedures or psychological concepts is presumed.

In one of his most recent books, Ghiselli (56) summarizes and evaluates
test validities for a second time. Primary attention is directed to the validities of occupational aptitude tests, and the coverage is thorough, incisive,
and useful, as might be expected. Individuals planning aptitude testing
programs for industrial situations will find this book a welcome resource. As
a comprehensive treatment of the subject, Guion's (64) *Personnel Testing* is
pretty much in a class by itself. He deals with the problems, the tests, and
the methods in a way professionals will appreciate. Lawshe & Balma (76)
have updated their earlier book and revised it to include more difficult
material. Although it is still written for the businessman, it conceivably
could be used as an introductory text.

As part of an article of greater scope, Sawyer (106) presents an admittedly selective but excellent review of predictive validity studies which
employed a variety of clinical and statistical measurement and prediction
methods. He compares the utility of clinical and statistical approaches.

The Life Insurance Agency Management Association (LIAMA, 81) researchers have published an overview of their findings in the areas of Recruiting, Selection, Training, and Supervision. The research is good, and the
outcomes should be of interest to professional and practitioner alike.

Korman (73), after an extensive survey of the literature on the prediction to management performance, reaches three conclusions—two expected

and one unexpected. The expected: research has made little or no contribution to leadership theory, and increases in the effectiveness of prediction will not be made until more knowledge of leader behavior is available. The unexpected: judgmental predictions seem to be superior to actuarial predictions. The latter conclusion is at variance with Sawyer's findings but may be a function of predictor-criterion parallelism.

Kinslinger (69) has traced the role of projective techniques in personnel selection since 1940. With the possible exception of the Tomkins-Horn Picture Arrangement Test, the author concludes that the utility of most projective techniques for personnel selection is questionable.

Owens & Henry (93) review both the biographical data literature and the methods employed in constructing biographical item keys for selection purposes. They present a most compelling rationale for the utility of biodata in the personnel selection context.

Researchers in and for the armed forces have produced a number of extremely useful publications. Examples are: the abstracts of U. S. APRO research publications (Brown, 22); Psychological Research in National Defense Today (Uhlaner, 132); and a review of the literature on the predictability of employee tenure by Schuh (110).

Peripheral, but none the less relevant, is Ronan & Prien's (103) critical summary of the research literature dealing with job performance behavior and the problems of criterion measurement and evaluation. Their guides for future research are well worth noting.

Trends

The assessment of trends in personnel selection, in the absence of some fixed referent, becomes an exercise in the projection of opinions. The writers offer theirs in the hope that a recent immersion in the literature has somehow saturated them with atypical validity.

1. It appears that responsible and ethical testing will be done with increasing consideration for the rights, sensibilities, needs, and prior opportunities of the testee.

2. Given many pressures for full employment, the role of the psychologist will less often involve classical selection and will more often involve multiple selection or even, infrequently, classification.

3. In view of the tremendous competition for high-level personnel, it seems that the professional concerned with personnel selection must become increasingly involved with facilitating college recruiting. In this context, the graduate may be viewed as a consumer of job opportunities whose needs, desires, tastes, and preferences must be identified and accommodated.

4. Based upon evidence of the limitations of the classical selection model, increasingly analytical approaches to text validation will continue to unfold, guided and directed by the implications of new models and by the feasibility of new methods—both quantitative and substantive.

5. Accompanying evidence from the broader field of measurement, there will be an increasing sensitivity to the impact of experience, sets, and testing conditions on test and questionnaire performance. As one aspect of this there will be a continuing shift away from the acceptance of concurrent validation and towards the requirement of predictive validation, a trend which will impinge most heavily on typical behavior measures.

6. In the absence of other feasible criteria of performance on somewhat unstructured jobs, such as managerial, rating procedures of increasing sophistication and complexity will be utilized.

7. Where jobs, like sales and managerial jobs, involve judgmental criteria of performance, predictors involving a judgmental component will be increasingly utilized. The assessment center is illustrative.

8. The selection interview will be subjected to intensive and extensive study with respect to its validity and reliability, and new interviewing methods and guidelines will emerge.

9. The awareness of personnel selection as a systems function will increase, and changes in research will reflect this change in perspective.

LITERATURE CITED

1. Acker, S. R., *The effect of moderator variables on the assessment of intelligence* (Corporate Personnel Dept., Olin Mathieson Chemical Corp., New York, 1966)
2. Alf, E. F., Jr. *Studies in the computerization of enlisted classification*, SRM 67-10 (U.S. Naval Personnel Res. Activity, San Diego, Calif., 1966)
3. Alf, E. F., Jr., Abrahams, N. M. *Psychol. Bull.*, **67**, 443–44 (1967)
4. Alf, E. F., Jr., Dorfman, D. D. *Psychometrika*, **32**, 115–23 (1967)
5. Ash, P. *Am. Psychol.*, **21**, 797–803 (1966)
6. Ash, P. *Personnel*, **44**, 8–17 (1967)
7. Bakan, D. *Psychol. Bull.*, **66**, 423–37 (1966)
8. Baker, B. L. *The Use of Biographical Factors to Moderate Prediction and Predict Salary Level* (Doctoral thesis, Purdue Univ., Lafayette, Ind., 1967)
9. Ball, G. H., Hall, D. J. *Behav. Sci.*, **12**, 153–55 (1967)
10. Barrett, G. V., Svetlik, B., Prien, E. P. *J. Appl. Psychol.*, **51**, 233–35 (1967)
11. Barrett, R. S. *Personnel Psychol.*, **19**, 375–87 (1966)
12. Bartlett, C. J., Doorley, R. *Personnel Psychol.*, **20**, 281–88 (1967)
13. Bashaw, W. L. *J. Exptl. Educ.*, **34**, 69–70 (1966)
14. Baumhart, R. C., Fitzpatrick, G. D. *Personnel*, **44**, 30–36 (1967)
15. Bayroff, A. G., Seeley, L. C. *An exploratory study of branching tests*, Tech. Res. Note *188* (U. S. Army Behav. Sci. Res. Lab., Milit. Selection Res. Div., 1967)
16. Bennett, C. C. *Am. Psychol.*, **22**, 371–76 (1967)
17. Bloxom, B. *Effects of anger-arousing instructions on personality questionnaire performance*, RB-67-17 (Educ. Testing Serv., Princeton, N. J., 1967)
18. Bloxom, B. *Social desirability as a predictor of behavior on neutral social desirability items*, RB-67-26 (Educ. Testing Serv., Princeton, N. J., 1967)
19. Boe, E. E., Gocka, E. F., Kogan, W. S. *Multivariate Behav. Res.*, **1**, 287–92 (1966)
20. Brand, J. S. *Readability and validity of items in tests of job proficiency*, Tech. Res. Study No. 25 (U. S. Army Enlisted Evaluation Center, 12 pp., 1966)
21. Bray, D. W., Grant, D. L. *Psychol. Monogr.*, **18**, 1–27 (1966)
22. Brown, Emma E., *Abstracts of U. S. APRO Research Publications*: FY 1966, APRO Tech. Res. Note *177* (U. S. Army Personnel Res. Office, Washington, D.C., 50 pp., 1966)

23. Campbell, D. P., Borgen, F. H., Eastes, Suzanne H., Johansson, C. B., Peterson, R. A. *A set of basic interest scales for the Strong Vocational Interest Blank for Men* (Center for Interest Measmt. Res., Student Counsel. Bur., Univ. Minnesota, Minneapolis, Minn., 1967)

24. Campbell, D. P., Johansson, C. B. *J. Counsel. Psychol.*, **13**, 416–24 (1966)

25. Carlson, R. E. *Personnel Psychol.*, **20**, 259–79 (1967)

26. Carrier, N. A., Jewell, D. O. *J. Educ. Psychol.*, **57**, 23–26 (1966)

27. Carroll, S. J., Jr. *J. Appl. Psychol.*, **59**, 421–23 (1966)

28. Carson, R. L. *Findings of the American Oil Recruitment Survey, No. 13*, 99–104 (Am Oil Co., Chicago, Ill., 123 pp., 1965)

29. Cleary, A. *Test bias: validity of the scholastic aptitude test for Negro and white students in integrated colleges, RB-66-31* (Educ. Testing Serv., Princeton, N. J., 1966)

30. Cleary, A., Hilton, T. L. *An investigation of item bias, RB-66-17* (Educ. Testing Serv., Princeton, N. J., 1966)

31. Cline, V. B., Tucker, M. F., Anderson, D. R. *Psychol. Rept.*, **19**, 951–54 (1966)

32. Conrad, H. S. *Am. Psychol.*, **22**, 356–59 (1967)

33. Cooper, R., Payne, R. *Personnel Psychol.*, **20**, 45–57 (1967)

34. Cummin, P. C. *J. Appl. Psychol.*, **51**, 78–81 (1967)

35. Curtis, E. W. The application of decision theory and scaling methods to selection test evaluation. *Dissert. Abstr.*, **26**, 4794 (1966)

36. Darlington, R. B., Bishop, C. H. *J. Appl. Psychol.*, **50**, 322–30 (1966)

37. Darlington, R. B., Stauffer, G. F. *J. Appl. Psychol.*, **50**, 125–29 (1966)

38. Darlington, R. B., Stauffer, G. F. *Ibid.*, 229–31

39. Dawes, R. M., Meehl, P. E. *Psychol. Bull.*, **66**, 63–67 (1966)

40. Dawis, R. V., Betz, E., Lofquist, L. H., Weiss, D. J. *Proc. 75th Ann. Am. Psychol. Assoc. Conv.*, **2**, 269–70 (1967)

41. Droege, R. C. *J. Appl. Psychol.*, **50**, 306–10 (1966)

42. Droege, R. C. *Ibid*, **51**, 181–86 (1967)

43. Dunnette, M. D. *J. Appl. Psychol.*, **47**, 317–23 (1963)

44. Dunnette, M. D. *Personnel Selection and Placement* (Wadsworth Publ., Belmont, Calif., 239 pp., 1966)

45. Equal Employment Opportunity Commission, *Guidelines on employment testing procedures* (EEOC, Washington, D. C., 1966)

46. Ewen, R. B., Kirkpatrick, J. J. *Selection of Minority Groups: Predictive and Moderated Validities for Samples of Nursing Students* (Presented at Am. Psychol. Assoc. Conv., Washington, D. C., 1967)

47. Fallis, R. F. The determination, weighting, and cross-validation of criterion dimensions of salesman's performance. *Dissert. Abstr.*, **27**, 2523–24 (1967)

48. Fine, S. A. *Proc. 75th Ann. Am. Psychol. Assoc. Conv.*, **2**, 365–66 (1967)

49. Finney, J. C. *Behav. Sci.*, **12**, 142–52 (1967)

50. Fiske, D. W. *Am. Psychol.*, **22**, 287–96 (1967)

51. Flanagan, J. C., Krug, R. E. *Personnel Admin.*, **27**, 3–5, 36–39 (1964)

52. Fleishman, E. A. *J. Appl. Psychol.*, **51**, 1–10 (1967)

53. Gambaro, S., Schell, R. *Educ. Psychol. Measmt.*, **26**, 1021–29 (1966)

54. Genkin, A. A., Bodov., V. A. *Voprosy Psikhol.*, **13**, 92–105 (1967)

55. Ghiselli, E. E. *Educ. Psychol. Measmt.*, **20**, 3–8 (1960)

56. Ghiselli, E. E. *The Validity of Occupational Aptitude Tests* (Wiley, New York, 155 pp., 1966)

57. Ghiselli, E. E. *Personnel Psychol.*, **19**, 389–94 (1966)

58. Ghiselli, E. E., Sanders, E. P. *J. Educ. Psychol. Measmt.*, **27**, 581–90 (1967)

59. Gomez, B. J., Braun, J. J. *Psychol. Rept.*, **20**, 192 (1967)

60. Gordon, L. V. *J. Appl. Psychol.*, **51**, 111–19 (1967)

61. Grant, D. L., Katkovsky, W., Bray, D. W. *J. Appl. Psychol.*, **51**, 226–32 (1967)

62. Greenshields, B. D., Platt, F. N. *J. Appl. Psychol.*, **51**, 205–10 (1967)

63. Guertin, W. H. *Educ. Psychol. Measmt.*, **26**, 151–65 (1966)

64. Guion, R. M. *Personnel Testing* (McGraw-Hill, New York, 585 pp., 1965)

65. Hall, E. T. *Emplyt. Serv. Rev.*, **4** (1967)

66. Hobert, R., Dunnette, M. D. *J. Appl. Psychol.*, **19**, 389–94 (1966)

67. Howell, Margaret A. *J. Appl. Psychol.*, **50**, 451–59 (1966)

68. Howell, M. A., Vincent, J. W., Gay, R. A. *Psychol. Rept.*, **20**, 1251–56 (1967)

69. Kinslinger, H. J. *Psychol. Bull.*, **66**, 134–49 (1966)

70. Kirchner, W. K. *J. Appl. Psychol.*, **50**, 373–74 (1966)

71. Klein, S. P., Rock, D. A., Evans, F. R. *The use of multiple predictors in academic prediction, RB-67-50* (Educ. Testing Serv., Princeton, N. J., 1967)

72. Korman, A. K. *J. Appl. Psychol.*, **50**, 479–86 (1966)

73. Korman, A. K. *The prediction of managerial performance: A review* (Univ. Oregon, Eugene, Ore., mimeo rept., 1967)

74. Larsen, R. H., Swarthout, D. M., Wickert, F. R. *Objectionability and Fakeability of Biographical Inventory Items* (Presented at Midwestern Psychol. Assoc., Chicago, Ill., 1967)

75. Lawler, E. E., III. *J. Appl. Psychol.*, **61**, 369–81 (1967)

76. Lawshe, C. H., Balma, M. J. *Principles of Personnel Testing* (McGraw-Hill, New York, 427 pp., 1966)

77. Lebovits, B. Z., Ostfeld, A. M. *J. Pers. Soc. Psychol.*, **6**, 381–90 (1967)

78. Lennerlof, L. *Supervisory Criteria, Rept. No. 44* (Swedish Council for Personnel Admin., Stockholm, 155 pp., 1966)

79. Levy, R. J. *J. Criminal Law, Criminol. Police Sci.*, **58**, 265–76 (1967)

80. Lieberman, L. R. *Psychol. Rev.*, **73**, 262–64 (1966)

81. Life Insurance Agency Mgmt. Assoc. *LIAMA Research in perspective series: Recruiting, selection training and supervision* (LIAMA, Hartford, Conn., 102 pp., 1966)

82. Linn, R. L., *Psychol. Bull.*, **67**, 378 (1967)

83. Linn, R. L. *Ibid*, **68**, 69–73 (1968)

84. Lorr, M., Radhakrishnan, B. K. *Educ. Psychol. Measmt.*, **27**, 47–53 (1967)

85. Lovell, V. R. *Am. Psychol.*, **22**, 383–93 (1967)

86. Mackenzie, R. S. The development and evaluation of a criterion measure of functional job-knowledge. *Dissert. Abstr.*, **27**, 2896 (1967)

87. MacKinney, A. C. *Org. Behav. Hum. Perf.*, **2**, 56–72 (1967)

88. McKenna, F. S. *Personnel selection* (Educ. Methods, Inc., Chicago, Ill., 118 pp., 1967)

89. Nagatsuka, Y. *Tohoku Psychol. Folia*, **25**, 81–90 (1967)

90. Nash, A. N. *J. Appl. Psychol.*, **50**, 250–54 (1966)

91. Newman, S. H. *Psychol. Rept.*, **19**, 695–701 (1966)

92. Owens, W. A. *The predictive validity of certain measures of creativity in machine design, NONR-1100(22) /NR196-031* (Eng. Psychol. Branch, Off. Naval Res., Washington, D. C., 1968)

93. Owens, W. A., Henry, E. R. *Biographical data in industrial psychology: A review and evaluation* (Creativity Res. Inst., Richardson Found., Greensboro, N. C., 20 pp., 1966)

94. Pallett, J. E., Hoyt, D. P. *J. Appl. Psychol.*, **51**, 174–80 (1967)

95. Patten, T. H. *Personnel Admin.*, **29**, 17–26 (1966)

96. Perloff, R. *A suggested relationship between consumer psychology and personnel recruiting* (Purdue Univ., Lafayette, Ind., mimeo rept., March 1968)

97. Prien, E. P. *J. Appl. Psychol.*, **50**, 501–4 (1966)

98. Pym, D. L. A., Auld, H. D. *Occup. Psychol.*, **39**, 103–13 (1965)

99. Reynolds, H. H. *Psychol. Rept.*, **19**, 35–30 (1966)

100. Richards, J. M., Jr. *J. Appl. Psychol.*, **51**, 211–15 (1967)

101. Rimland, B. *Studies of the computerization of enlisted classification, SRM 67-10*, 1–5 (U. S. Naval Personnel Res. Activity, San Diego, Calif., 16 pp., 1966)

102. Roberts, R. J., Nichols, R. C. *Participants in the National Achievement Scholarship Program for Negroes* (Natl. Merit Scholarship Corp., Evanston, Ill., 45 pp., 1966)

103. Ronan, W. W., Prien, E. P. *Toward a criterion theory: A review and analysis of research and opinion* (Creativity Res. Inst., Richardson Found., Greensboro, N. C., 108 pp., 1966)

104. Ruda, E. S., Albright, L. E. *Personnel Psychol.*, **21**, 31–41 (1968)

105. Ryans, J. R., Hise, R. T. *Personnel J.*, **46**, 444–47 (1967)

106. Sawyer, J. *Psychol. Bull.*, **66**, 178–200 (1966)

107. Schine, L. C. *Educ. Psychol. Measmt.*, **26**, 833–46 (1966)

108. Schoenfeldt, L. F. *The Grouping of Subjects into Homogeneous Subsets— A Comparison and Evaluation of*

Two Divergent Approaches (Doctoral thesis, Purdue Univ., Lafayette, Ind., 1966)

109. Schuh, A. J. *Personnel Psychol.*, **20**, 59–64 (1967)

110. Schuh, A. J. *Ibid*, 133–53

111. Scott, R. D., Johnson, R. W. *J. Appl. Psychol.*, **51**, 393–95 (1967)

112. Showler, W. K., Droege, R. C. *Proc. 75th Ann. Am. Psychol. Assoc. Conv.*, **2**, 263–64 (1967)

113. Simon, W. B. *Educ. Psychol. Measmt.*, **27**, 135–37 (1967)

114. Sines, J. O. *Psychol. Rev.*, **71**, 517–23 (1964)

115. Skawran, P. R., van der Reis, P., Moore, M. *Psychol. Afr.*, **11**, 157–81 (1967)

116. Sorenson, R. C. Development and evaluation of a matrix transformation useful in personnel classification. *Dissert. Abstr.*, **27**, 296 (1966)

117. Stanley, J. C., Porter, A. C. *J. Educ. Measmt.*, **4**, 199–217 (1967)

118. Stephenson, R. R. *Geographical differences in responses to a test of vocational interests, SRR 66-10* (U. S. Naval Personnel Res. Activity, San Diego, Calif., 1966)

119. Stephenson, R. R., Smith, L. H., Rimland, B. *A comparison of responses to a vocational interest test taken under standard conditions at recruiting stations and responses to the same test taken as a self-administered test at home, SRM 65-3* (U. S. Naval Personnel Res. Activity, San Diego, Calif., May 1965)

120. Streufert, S., Castore, C. H., Kliger, S. C. *Leadership in negotiations and the complexity of conceptual structure, Tech. Rept. 3* (Office Naval Res. Group Psychol. Branch, Contract No. N00014-67-0115-0002, Project No. RR 006-08-02, Washington, D. C., July 1967)

121. Stricker, L. J. *J. Appl. Psychol.*, **50**, 331–35 (1966)

122. Swanson, L. *Studies in the computerization of enlisted classification, SRM 67-10*, 11–16 (U. S. Naval Personnel Res. Activity, San Diego, Calif., 16 pp., 1966)

123. Swanson, L., Dow, A. N. *Project compass: A computer assisted classification system for Navy enlisted men, SRR 66-6* (U. S. Naval Personnel Res. Activity, San Diego, Calif., 1965)

124. Taylor, C. W., Ellison, R. L. *Science*, **155**, 1075–80 (1967)

125. Taylor, L. R. *A Quasi-actuarial Approach to Assessment* (Doctoral thesis, Purdue Univ., Lafayette, Ind., 1968)

126. Tenopyr, Mary L. *Characteristics of Men Successful in the Labor-Relations Field* (Presented at Am. Psychol. Assoc., New York, 1966)

127. Tenopyr, Mary L. *Race and Socioeconomic Status as Moderators in Predicting Machine-shop Training Success* (Presented in Selection of Minority and Disadvantaged Personnel Symp., Am. Psychol. Assoc., Washington, D. C., 1967)

128. Tenopyr, Mary L., Ruch, W. W. *The Comparative Validity of Selected Leadership Scales Relative to Success in Production Management* (Presented at Am. Psychol. Assoc., Chicago, Ill., 1965)

129. Tesser, A., Leidy, T. R. *Psychological Testing Through the Looking-glass of Youth* (Presented at Midwestern Psychol. Assoc., Chicago, Ill., 1967)

130. Tesser, A., Starry, A. R., Chaney, F. B. *Proc. 75th Ann. Am. Psychol. Assoc. Conv.*, **2**, 261–62 (1967)

131. Torpey, W. G. *Personnel J.*, **45**, 489–93 (1966)

132. Uhlaner, J. E. *Psychological research in national defense today, Tech. Rep. S-1* (U. S. Army Behav. Sci. Res. Lab., Washington, D. C., 1967)

133. Velehradsky, A. *Psychol. Ekonomicke Praxi*, 3–4, 1–9 (1966)

134. Vroom, V. H. *Org. Behav. Hum. Perf.*, **1**, 212–25 (1966)

135. Walker, R. E., Neilsen, M., Nicolay, R. C. *J. Clin. Psychol.*, **21**, 400–4 (1965)

136. Wallace, Phyliss, Kissinger, Beverly, Reynolds, Betty. *Testing of minority group applicants for employment, RR 1966-7* (Off. Res. and Rept., Equal Emplymt. Oppor. Comm., Washington, D. C., 1966)

137. Wallace, S. R. *Adventure in Humanity* (Presented at Am. Compensation Assoc., Pittsburgh, 1967)

138. Wesman, A. G. *Test Serv. Bull.*, 56 (1966)

139. Wiggins, J. S., *Educ. Psychol. Measmt.*, **26**, 329–41 (1966)

140. Wilson, N. A. B. *Occup. Psychol.*, **40**, 179–93 (1966)

141. Winkler, R. C., Mathews, T. W. *Per-*

sonnel *J.*, **46,** 490–92; 501; 515 (1967)

142. Woodbury, M. A., Novick, M. R. *Maximizing the validity of a test battery as a function of relative*
lengths for a fixed total testing time, *RB-67-3* (Educ. Testing Serv., Princeton, N. J., 1967)

143. Zdep, S. M., Weaver, H. B. *J. Appl. Psychol.*, **51,** 295–99 (1967)

SCALING[1,2]

By Joseph L. Zinnes

Department of Psychology, Indiana University, Bloomington, Indiana

Unlike the previous review of scaling by Ekman & Sjöberg (35), the theme of this review is that scaling theory should be a theory of choice. Ekman & Sjöberg are critical of the concept of a choice experiment because such experiments are difficult to define precisely or conceptualize uniquely, but the same can be said for learning experiments. The advantage in using the concept of choice is that it avoids having to ask unanswerable questions —such as, what is measured by a scaling theory?—or having to make untenable assumptions—for example, that subjects are measuring instruments capable of being activated at any level of measurement by appropriate instructions. Instead, the scaling theorist asks the same kind of questions that the learning theorist asks: How can he account for a certain domain of data, choice data in the case of the scaling theorist and learning data in the case of the learning theorist, using a model that is not too unsightly or too unwieldy? In case it is not completely obvious, a set of learning data consist of responses that change significantly over time and a set of choice data consists of responses that do not. There is, of course, an in between ground where both the static choice theory and the dynamic learning theory come into play.

Because of this conceptualization of scaling theory, major emphasis is given in this review to the question of whether a particular model gives a good account of a set of data or at least a better account than existing models. Unfortunately, too many of the papers considered in this review do not take this question seriously enough to carry out reasonable tests of the model being proposed. Many of the experimental tests can only be described as weak and sloppy. Part of the difficulty can be found in the often repeated plea that optimal tasks are too difficult to perform or that they do not exist. For these writers, the computer revolution, described so well by Green (48), does not yet exist. To quote Green: "Today there is no need to find ways of simplifying calculations so that they may be done by desk calculators. Nor is there any excuse for avoiding procedures solely on the basis of computational difficulty" (48 p. 437). Along with Green's example of the centroid method of factor analysis, many other examples of thoroughly anachronistic procedures could be mentioned that routinely occur in the papers reviewed here.

[1] The survey of literature pertaining to this review covers the period principally from April 1964 to April 1968.

[2] Preparation of this chapter was facilitated by grant MH 08975-04 from the National Institute of Mental Health. The author gratefully acknowledges the help of Clifford B. Gillman in surveying the literature and abstracting the references.

Another aspect of the computer revolution referred to by Green has relevance here. Green emphasizes the importance and potentiality of the algorithmic methods over the purely analytical methods. Many of the theoretical papers here seem to be painfully attempting to solve estimations and other problems by analytical means when algorithmic ones would be completely straightforward and would free the authors to pursue more worthwhile goals.

The space limitations imposed on this review require omitting many topics and papers that really should be included.

NEW BOOKS

Perhaps the most important theoretical texts to appear recently are those by Bock & Jones (15) and by Pfanzagl (107). The book by Bock & Jones can be considered as the logical successor to Torgerson's book, though it does not cover all the topics treated by Torgerson, such as multidimensional scaling. However, the careful way in which all the scaling models are developed and the detailed treatment of all statistical questions raised in connection with testing these models, including the sampling characteristic of relevant statistics, make the Bock & Jones book indispensable. Its limitations are that it concentrates on the Thurstonian models to the exclusion of others, and that it tends to emphasize estimation procedures based on linear approximations of the scaling model rather than procedures that directly apply to the original model. Pfanzagl's (107) book is an absolutely first-rate work having great clarity, precision, and readability. It covers mainly the algebraic models and discusses in detail many of the questions fundamental to the logic of measurement. It should raise the level of discourse in this area a considerable number of jnds.

A number of other important books also have appeared recently. Coombs (21) has published the result of his extensive research program using nonmetric models. The important features of Coombs' book are its strong emphasis on treating individual differences within the model, its emphasis on the possibility of alternative single and multidimensional models for treating the same set of data, its systematization of a broad class of choice models, and its introduction and distinction of preferential choice models from other choice models. Lord & Novick's (79) book is concerned with test theory, but it covers a number of scaling-related topics, such as the chapters contributed by Birnbaum on the logistic distribution, in greater depth than is normally encountered. Lazarsfeld & Henry (73) describe all the latent structure models conceivable—there is even a sinister sounding latent Markov chain model—and the statistical aspects of the models are treated more thoroughly than had been done previously. This book is physically the most attractive book in this collection; the graphs and tables are very attractive, and other aspects of the book are also done exceedingly well.

Frederiksen & Gulliksen's (40) collection of papers contains a good biography of Thurstone by Adkins and a complete bibliography of Thurstone's writing. The third volume of the *Handbook of Mathematical Psychology* has appeared, and it contains an important and highly readable review article by Luce & Suppes (91). Although the title of the review suggests a somewhat limited area, it actually covers a wide variety of topics, including the algebraic theories such as the conjoint measurement model, the relationship and properties of probabilistic choice theories, the application of learning concepts, and experimental tests of the probabilistic choice models. Some elementary or graduate texts covering scaling topics also have appeared recently (43, 58, 104), and two classical hard-to-obtain books have been re-issued recently, one by a certain G. Fechner (39) in an English translation, and the other, the World War II classic by Stouffer et al. (141).

Mention also should be made of a major treatise on measurement by A. Weitzenhoffer that probably will not be published for a while, but that will be worth waiting for. It contains a tremendous amount of material, especially the older literature that is virtually unknown to psychologists. It should become the best historical reference available.

PAIR-COMPARISON THEORIES AND EXPERIMENTS

Choice theory and the Thurstone model.—Although the choice model generated a great deal of interest among psychologists following publication of Luce's monograph (81), not a great deal of experimental work has been done with it. (The term "choice" model describes nothing whatever that is unique to this model, but because so many people evidently have had a hand in some aspect of this model, it seems more convenient and safer to use this neutral term.) There is no really good explanation for this neglect; possible reasons are the feeling on the part of some that the results are not strikingly different from the traditional Thurstone analysis, or the view of Ekman & Sjöberg (35) that the choice model deals with data on a macro-level since its assumptions do not say how a single response is determined. If these are the reasons why the choice theory has not received the theoretical and experimental attention that it deserves, then this may be changed by some current papers, along with some older, less well-known, theoretical papers. In some recent papers (17, 146), and in some older papers (74, 122), the choice model is derived from assumptions about the discriminal process. Furthermore, these papers, along with some others to be mentioned, show clearly that the choice model and the Thurstone Case-5 model are theoretically as different as night and day; it is only their practical implications that are so similar, but this fact need not be any more significant to scaling theorists than, say, the practical implications of Newtonian and relativistic mechanics are to theoretical physicists.

Lehmann (74) and Savage (122) have shown that the choice model for pair-comparison judgments can be derived by assuming that the discriminal processes have distribution functions that are equal to each other except for the value of an exponent. This exponent in each case gives the scale parameter of each stimulus. Bradley (17) shows how this result may be generalized to random variables that are correlated. The important thing about these results is that they postulate the same decision rule that is used in the Thurstone model, but they involve a fundamentally different class of distribution functions. In the Thurstone Case-5 model the distributions differ from each other by their first moments only (or in Case 3, by their first two moments only), while in these papers the distributions will tend to differ from each other by all their moments.

Thompson & Singh (146), in an absolutely first-rate theoretical paper, also derive the Thurstone and the choice models from fundamentally different assumptions. They show that the Thurstone model follows from the assumption that the discriminal process is the result of the sum of a large number of independent signals or sensations, while the choice model follows from the assumption that the discriminal process results from the maximum of a large number of independent signals. They also show that it does not make any difference whether the signals are summed, averaged, or even if the median value is considered, for in all cases the Thurstone Case-5 type of model results. Their derivation requires making certain assumptions about the limits to which certain parameters go when the number of signals increases indefinitely.

In addition to these theoretical differences between the Thurstone and the choice models, Burke & Zinnes (19) show that, in principle, their empirical implications are enormously different as well. Their principal theorem shows that it is possible for the Thurstone Case-5 theory to predict that a subject will be indifferent between two stimuli when, under the identical conditions, the choice model predicts that he will prefer one stimulus over the other with a probability equal to 1.0. They also show for pair-comparison judgments of three stimuli that only a very trivial class of choice probabilities will satisy precisely both the choice and Thurstone model. It may be noted that this class of choice probabilities is also satisfied by any model that postulates a monotonic function between the probabilities and scale values. These theoretical papers should dispel the notion that the Thurstone and choice models are trivially different from each other or that, in any sense, one theory is more molecular or more macro than the other.

Bradley (17) also discusses triple comparisons and compares the choice model for triple comparisons with one described by Pendergrass & Bradley (106). Both of these papers show that each model for triple comparisons satisfies certain conditional probabilities that are not satisfied by the other and, even more importantly, that it is not possible to develop a model that will satisfy all these intuitively desirable conditional probabilities simultaneously. Other properties of the choice model are discussed by Marley (94).

The most thorough test of the choice model, with bias parameters added, has been done by Shipley & Luce (131). From their study of weights presented in pairs and in triples, they conclude that the model gives a good account of their data because there are no systematic deviations of observed points from the predicted points, and the clustering of the observed points around the predicted line is relatively tight. They reach this conclusion despite their finding that more than half the chi-squares, calculated separately for each subject and for each condition, are statistically significant, and therefore that the clustering of the observed points around the predicted line is not close enough to be consistent with the model. Actually it should be stated that Shipley & Luce discount the goodness-of-fit chi-square test as a means for evaluating the model because it shows only that the model failed to capture all that is present in the data, and this probably is too much to ask of any model. Their preference for evaluating a model is to determine whether there are systematic deviations from the line of perfect prediction, but such results can be accomplished easily by estimating a large enough number of parameters and using a theory that is not too pathological. A more useful approach to supplement the chi-square goodness-of-fit test would be to compare the results of several models that have about the same number of free parameters. It would have been desirable, for example, for Shipley & Luce to apply the Thurstone Case-5 model to their data and compare the results of that analysis with the one based on the choice analysis.

Shipley & Luce also emphasize the parameter invariance properties of a model, and they conclude here that the stimulus parameters have the desired invariance because the different estimates of the stimulus parameters based on different conditions do not differ from each other by more than about 10 per cent, which they say is about the variability to be expected. However, these parameter invariance tests seem weaker than they need be. A better procedure would be to use likelihood ratio tests based on separate estimates of the parameters for each condition and single estimates of the parameters across conditions.

Other tests of the choice model for tasks containing a different number of stimuli have been carried out by Hodge (59) and by Rosenberg & Cohen (113). Both studies find experimental support for the choice model, although the analysis in each case consists solely of plotting predicted proportions against observed proportions or correlating these two quantities. Hodge claims that a satisfactory test is not available. Neither paper compares the choice theory with the Thurstone Case-5 theory. Experimental comparison of the choice and Thurstone Case-5 theories have been reported by Hohle (60) and by Burke & Zinnes (19). Hohle's study contained maximum likelihood estimates of the choice and Thurstone parameters for six different sets of data, some of which were obtained from the literature, and in every case the chi-squares based on these estimates were greater for the Thurstone model than for the choice model. The opposite finding was obtained by Burke & Zinnes in a re-analysis of three sets of data. Their analyses were based on only a small subset of the data matrix that was available in each case, because they thought that would permit finer discrimination between the two models than is normally possible. However, this procedure raises some statistical questions that were not thoroughly dealt with by Burke & Zinnes.

New pair-comparison models.—An analysis of variance approach for linear models of pair-comparison judgments has been developed by Bechtel (11, 12). The linear model that Bechtel postulates would be applicable to pair-comparison judgments in which the subject gives a numerical rating for his preference of one stimulus over the other stimulus, or to pair-comparison judgments in which the numerical response of the subject indicates his utility for the combined pair of stimuli. Making normal distribution assumptions for the error terms, Bechtel works out the usual kinds of tests for analysis of variance. He also considers tests for the invariance of the scale parameters across different conditions or between different subjects. The linear model used by Bechtel is probably not too different from the Thurstone Case-3 model when the probabilities are not too extreme, although Bechtel makes no attempt to compare his model with the Thurstone one.

Sutcliffe's (145) model relates the square of the distance between pairs of stimuli to the relative incidence of error by an exponential function, and he shows that his model is not equivalent to a Thurstone model. Eisler (26) makes use of set theoretical ideas and imperfectly nested sets to derive a pair-comparison model that has the choice model as a special case. Using some data based on pair comparisons and others on magnitude estimation judgments and estimating one of the parameter values from the magnitude estimation judgments, he finds that for two of his three subjects his model seems to do better than the Thurstone or the choice model. Greenberg's approach (51) for analyzing pair-comparison preference judgments consists of first determining the order of the stimuli on the scale and then, using the choice probabilities, determining the order of the midpoints between pairs of stimuli. After this has been accomplished, he recommends using one of the numerical methods for obtaining a set of "interval scale values." Greenberg's test of his model consists of its ability to predict the subjects' first choices, though no attempt is made to show whether the first choice would not be predicted by any other model.

Greenberg (52) also considers a modification of the pair comparison task that permits the subject to say "same" as well as to choose one of the two stimuli in a pair. The theoretical model considered is a natural generalization of the Thurstone pair-comparison model. The subject is assumed to say "same" when the differences between the two stimulus random variables does not exceed some constant. When it does, the subject chooses the stimulus associated with the larger value. Greenberg's estimation procedure for the stimulus parameters follows very closely the Mosteller approach, because he says that a true least-squares estimate of the threshold parameter would be quite difficult. No other model is considered by Greenberg for his modified pair-comparison task. Maximum likelihood estimates of the parameters in this model, along with a number of other closely related models, were carried out by Zinnes & Kurtz (158) in their experimental study of the same-different judgment.

LOGIC OF MEASUREMENT

Current writing on measurement theory continues to reflect some interest in three basic issues: the necessary conditions for fundamental measurement (that which does not require a prior measurement); the definition of scale types; and the implications of scale types for statistical analyses. These three issues are discussed separately in the three sections following. It is probably not too optimistic to say that the most recent work in this area departs from the older literature in two basic ways: First of all the level of discourse has been elevated immensely. The older psychological literature on measurement theory was never noted for its precise statements or rigorous proofs. No doubt much of the heat that has been generated over the years has been due to the inherently vague treatments presented. The careful work now being done should lower the level of heat and make possible wider consensus on specific points. The exciting thing about the more recent papers is the way in which they build and expand on each other. A second feature of the current papers is their emphasis on more specific and perhaps more manageable problems. Possibly this stems from greater consensus on the broader questions of measurement. Much of this work is now centered around developing alternative algebraic models or axiom systems that are necessary or, in some cases, sufficient to establish the existence of certain kinds of numerical assignments. The encouraging thing about this kind of work is that it is not bogged down by a reverence for any particular axiom system. Some of this work is described in the next major section following.

One word of caution should be given to the experimentalist looking for a new measurement technique. Many of these papers do not have as yet any immediate obvious experimental implication. In this respect, then, they are disappointing. However, the long-term results of this work are bound to be beneficial in at least clearing the air of extraneous noises and possibly even in eliminating pointless lines of research. Eventually, the experimental implications will doubtlessly be more specific and more profound.

Definition of fundamental and derived measurement.—There continue to be some adherents (36, 46, 118) to the familiar position, attributed to N. R. Campbell, that fundamental measurement requires the existence of a physical addition operation, or to use Luce & Tukey's term (92), a concatenation operation. Goude (46) seems to accept the Campbell position, but then he says that magnitude estimation is probably a fundamental ratio scale, provided one assumes that observers use numbers in agreement with the axioms and theorems of mathematics. Evidence for this conclusion is presumably provided by his finding that the experimental results for magnitude estimation are in agreement with those obtained by the "addition method." Since Goude also finds Thurstone's pair-comparison theory to agree with the addition method, he concludes that pair comparisons also give fundamental measurement (at the interval level). These experiments are based on measuring subjective weight, angle, two ability factors, and reaction strength. In each case, Goude is able to define an appropriate physical addition operation.

Ross (118) distinguishes between ordinal and additive measurement theory, as did Campbell, and between physical and psychological measurement theory, which Campbell did not. The physical and psychological theories turn out to be equivalent to each other, the difference being in the interpretation of some of the primitive terms in the psychological theory. The additive theory differs from the ordinal theory by the introduction of the physical addition operation. Although Ross's assumptions for the ordinal theory are typical of those that have been stated by the Campbellians, they turn out not to be sufficient to guarantee the existence of the desired numerical assignment. This and other deficient conclusions in Ross are discussed by Eisler (28) and Zinnes (157). Besides requiring physical addition, Ellis (36) asserts that fundamental measurement requires the existence of procedures for determining equality and also the existence of a sufficiently large number of objects to be measured.

The position developed by Suppes & Zinnes (144), which follows from Scott & Suppes (125), minimizes the importance of the physical addition operation. Neither this operation nor any other is assumed to be necessary for fundamental measurement at any level of measurement. Fundamental measurement is there defined as a homomorphic mapping of an empirical system into a numerical system. The statement that such a homomorphic mapping exists between particular empirical and numerical systems or class of systems is called a representation theorem. This definition of fundamental measurement leads to the conclusions (a) that the empirical systems containing a physical addition operation do not have any special properties that would justify calling them fundamental; and (b) that the representation theorem is not uniquely determined by a given empirical system.

The first conclusion is justified by Suppes & Zinnes (144) with examples of empirical systems not containing the physical addition operation that lead to interval and ratio scales. The second conclusion follows from the fact that it is possible to map a given emprical system into different numerical systems that contain different numerical relations. Even the so-called physical addition operation can be mapped into either the arithmetical operation of addition or the arithmetical operation of multiplication. Nor do these two interpretations of the physical addition operation exhaust the possibilities. There are an unlimited number of numerical interpretations for each empirical system, and each interpretation leads to a different representation theorem. In most cases, the representation theorem selected is probably based on convenience or tradition.

This point of view of fundamental measurement is consistent with the treatments by Pfanzagl (107); Rozeboom (119); Adams, Fagot & Robinson

(4); Luce & Tukey (92); and Luce (89). There are, however, important technical refinements and extensions in each. Pfanzagl, for example, defines the representation theorem in terms of a homomorphism of an irreducible empirical system into a k-dimensional numerical system. The assumption of an irreducible system implies that the homomorphism is one to one. Any empirical system easily can be made irreducible by partitioning the elements (objects) into equivalent classes, so that this is not an important restriction. However, the use of irreducible empirical systems at the start does simplify the statement and proofs of many theorems. Luce (89) would restrict the term "fundamental measurement" to those empirical systems containing relations that, at the very least, order the objects according to some attribute.

Some important reservations about the "representational" theory of measurement are expressed by Adams (3). It is not always the case, according to Adams, that mathematical operations are made to correspond to empirical relations. No one, he says, has succeeded in saying what operations and relations among times are made to correspond to operations and relations among numbers in time measurement. Also, some empirical laws that are supposed to be satisfied for measurement to be carried out are, in fact, false. His approach would emphasize the role of measurement in application rather than in research.

The concept and properties of derived measurement described by Suppes & Zinnes (144) are completely analogous to the fundamental case. The non-uniqueness property of the representation theorem for the fundamental case also applies to the derived case. This property of the representation theorem is illustrated by examples of a number of different representation theorems for several pair-comparison theories, including the Thurstone Case 5 theory.

One of the representations of the Thurstone Case-5 theory has been called Case 6 by Goude (46) and Eisler[3] (27). Case 6 assumes that the discriminal processes are log-normally distributed and that the subject's decision rule is based on the ratio of scale values. Eisler (27) points out that Case 5 and Case 6 also differ by having different Weber functions. Eisler cites some references to show that although Case 5 is indistinguishable from Case 6, scaling theorists have tended to regard a given set of data as supporting or refuting the specific Case-5 assumptions. It is amusing to note that the common practice of comparing scaling models by comparing their scale values would suggest erroneously that Case 5 and Case 6 are not equivalent.

Scale types.—Scale types were originally (135) distinguished by the existence of different empirical operations. Thus an interval scale required the existence of an operation for determining equality of intervals, for determining greater or less, and for determining equality. This type of

---

[3] Note added in proof: The term "Case 6" was evidently first used by S. S. Stevens in a 1959 review paper in *Contemporary Psychology.*

definition continues to be used by some writers, but without complete agreement as to which operations are required for which scales. Goude (46) says that interval scales require an interpretation for equality, for less than and for the addition of differences between numbers. Nunnally (104) requires that the objects be rank ordered with respect to some attribute and that information exist on how far apart the objects are from one another but not on the absolute magnitude of the attributes for the objects. For ratio scales it is also necessary to determine the distance from a "rational origin." This definition of interval and ratio scales may not accurately reflect Nunnally's position, because at a later point in his discussion he labels the preceding as "the fundamentalist" point of view, which, among other things, assumes that each measure has some real characteristics that permit its proper classification. In the subsequent discussion, Nunnally suggests that scale types are determined by an analysis of a scaling model, by convention, or by what will produce the simplest forms of relationships with other variables.

Ross is severely critical of the Stevens system of scales; only the ordinal scale, he says, fulfills the basic demands of a philosophy of measurement.

The definition of scale types by Suppes & Zinnes (144) is stated in terms of the uniqueness properties of the numerical assignments, rather than in terms of the existence of any particular set of empirical operations or interpretations. If the numerical assignment specified in the representation theorem for the fundamental or the derived case is unique up to a positive linear transformation, then the measurement is an interval scale. The fact that the numerical assignment is non-unique means simply, in the fundamental case, that more than one function will map the empirical system homomorphically into the numerical system specified in the representation theorem.

The non-uniqueness characteristics of the numerical assignments for both the fundamental and the derived case are specified in the "uniqueness theorem," which therefore specifies the scale types obtained from a particular representation theorem. From the standpoint of this definition of scale type, it follows that the scale type or uniqueness theorem depends on which representation theorem is selected for a given empirical system. A number of examples are given by Suppes & Zinnes (144) to show how the uniqueness theorem changes for a fixed empirical system when the representation theorem changes for that system.

The non-uniqueness aspects of these two theorems have traditionally been a source of confusion. Evidently it has been easy to avoid distinguishing between the non-uniqueness of the representation theorem and the non-uniqueness specified in the uniqueness theorem. For the fundamental case, the first refers to the class of numerical assignments that map homomorphically into different numerical systems, while the second refers to the class of numerical assignments that map into the same numerical system. This difference is important because in the former case, a change from one numerical assignment to another, that is, a change from one representation theorem to another, requires a corresponding change in the numerical interpretation of the empirical relation. In the latter case, no change in the interpretation of the physical operations is required in changing from one numerical system to another.

The criticism of scale types given by Ellis (36) apparently is based on failure to distinguish between the different uniqueness aspects of these two theorems. Ellis criticizes the classification of the centigrade and fahrenheit scales as interval scales because to show that they are interval scales, he argues, one must show that the purposes of these scales could not be served by a scale which is nonlinear with respect to either. For similar reasons, Ellis (36) also concludes that even the common scales of mass, length, etc. appear to be ordinal rather than ratio scales.

Since, according to this view, the scale type is not uniquely determined by the empirical system, attempts to obtain interval or ratio scales cannot meaningfully be described as attempts to find equal units of measurement or as attempts to find a true zero point. Units that are equal for one possible uniqueness theorem can be highly unequal for another possible uniqueness theorem. Similarly, the zero point of a ratio scale can be changed easily by changing the representation theorem.

There are some technical differences in the definition of scale types given in three recent papers (4, 107, 119). Adams, Fagot & Robinson (4) define scale type in terms of the class of permissible transformation of the numerical assignment, rather than in terms of the uniqueness of the numerical assignment. For most purposes, the two definitions are equivalent. Pfanzagl (107) occasionally adds additional restrictions to the definitions of certain scales. For the ordinal scale, the homomorphic mapping is required to satisfy certain continuity conditions.

In a paper on inexact measurement, Adams (2) attempts to deal with one of the severe limitations of the usual types of scales. These scales generally assume or imply perfectly exact measurement. In his paper he modifies this assumption by avoiding the use of the equality relation as a primitive empirical relation. It is unrealistic to assume, he says, that it is possible to determine by observation that an object weighs exactly 2 pounds and not 2 pounds plus some infinitesimal quantity. By assuming that the numerical assignment exists with a given constant jnd, he determines the upper and lower bounds on the accuracy obtainable in the measurement of any object in a given set. One limitation of Adams' approach to the problem of inexact measurement is that the existence of the numerical assignment with a fixed jnd is not derived from empirical assumptions.

Permissible statistics.—Which statistical or mathematical operations can be performed with which scale type? Stevens (135) originally listed a number of statistics that were appropriate to each scale type. The criterion for appropriateness of a statistic for a particular scale type was stated to be its invariance under the permissible transformations defined by the scale type, that is, the transformations described in the uniqueness theorem. This criterion evidently was not intended to imply that the value of the statistic be absolutely invariant, that is, that it not change at all under the permissible transformations. This notion of absolute invariance would explain some of the examples given by Stevens (135), such as the correlation coefficient and percentile scores but it would not explain others. The median and the mean are listed as appropriate to the ordinal and interval scale, respectively, although both change when either a monotonic or linear transformation is performed on the sample. The median is appropriate for ordinal scales, according to Stevens' explanation (135), because the object that stands at the median of a distribution maintains its position after a monotonic transformation. Similarly, the mean is appropriate for an interval scale but not for an ordinal scale, because an item located at the mean remains at the mean under a linear transformation but not under a monotonic transformation. However, as pointed out by Adams, Fagot & Robinson (4), neither this notion of relative invariance nor the one of absolute invariance would explain why the standard deviation is listed as permissible for an interval scale. Its value changes under a linear transformation, and an object in a sample whose value is equal to that of the standard deviation would not take on the new value of the standard deviation after a linear transformation has been performed.

Ellis' (36) treatment of the question of permissible statistics follows directly from Stevens' criterion of relative invariance. He considers the implication of this criterion for a number of possible measures of central tendency. He concludes that the arithmetical mean is the only measure of central tendency that is permissible for an interval scale, although it turns out that a large number of central tendency measures are appropriate for a ratio scale. Ellis also attempts to generalize this criterion by considering cases in which the physical addition operation exists or in which another operation exists that has some arithmetical interpretation.

The question of the appropriateness of a statistic has often been treated as part of the problem of determining which mathematical operations are permissible with which types of scales. However, such an approach nearly always leads to disaster by confusing the permissible operations defined in the uniqueness theorem with the operations that are used to calculate the value of the statistic. Nunnally (104) says that the permissible mathematical operations for each type of scale relate to the circumstances under which invariance of the scale properties is obtained. He then concludes that for an interval scale multiplication and division are permissible only with respect to the intervals themselves; on the other hand, addition and subtraction are permissible with scale values as well as with the intervals of an interval scale. Immediately following this conclusion, the reader is given the contradictory piece of information that an interval scale is invariant under linear transformations of the scale values. In contrast to an interval scale, the ratio scale, according to Nunnally, is susceptible to all the fundamental operations of algebra, while the ordinal scale is susceptible to none.

Historically, there is another very familiar approach to this problem. In Hays' (58) elementary text on measurement, the reader is told that the ability to find physical parallels to the arithmetic operations permits a scientist to perform the purely symbolic and mechanical operations of mathematics and to deduce the results of the parallel physical operation. In the case of fundamental measurement, such physical parallels exist for each arithmetic operation on numbers. After being told how important physical addition is, the reader is then told that for psychological measurement there exist no clear cut parallels between such mathematical operations as addition and experimental psychological procedures, so that psychological measurement theory is more incomplete and more disorganized than physical measurement theory.

Ross (118) and Goude (46) do not treat this topic of permissible statistics in their monographs on measurement. Suppes & Zinnes (144) treat the question of permissible statistics as part of the problem of determining when numerical statements, such as equations or inequalities containing fundamental and derived variables, are meaningful. Using the concept of empirical meaningfulness given earlier by Suppes (142), they define a meaningful numerical statement to be one whose truth value does not change when permissible transformations are made in any of the fundamental or derived numerical assignments it contains. Meaningful numerical statements are, therefore, experimentally verifiable in the sense that their validity can be determined unambiguously, even though there are inherent ambiguities in the values of the numerical variables contained in the statement. It may be noted that this definition of meaningfulness does not require any kind of parallelism between empirical and arithmetical operations.

This notion of meaningfulness leads to the conclusion that a particular statistic cannot be regarded a priori as appropriate or inappropriate for a given scale type. One needs to know what numerical statements are to be made about this statistic. If a particular numerical statement containing a given statistic is meaningful, then the statistic, according to one's point of view, would be appropriate in that context; otherwise the statistic would not be appropriate, although it may be appropriate in another context. There are instances, for example, when the mean would be an appropriate statistic for an ordinal scale and other instances in which it would not be appropriate for an interval scale.

This notion of the relativeness of permissible statistics has been developed further. Pfanzagl (107) treats the concept of a numerical statement as a relation defined over the set of scale values for a given collection of objects. Pfanzagl shows that a meaningful relation on the scale values implies a unique relation over the objects in the set, and for this reason, he emphasizes, meaningful relations are statements about reality. Some fundamental properties of meaningful relations are proven by Pfanzagl. Adams, Fagot & Robinson (4, 112) put the matter this way: The criterion of appropriateness for a statement about a statistical operation is that the statement be empirically mean-

ingful, which they define in about the same way as the meaningfulness concept is defined by Suppes & Zinnes (144). They also conclude that the use of
inappropriate statistics leads to statements that will not be empirically
meaningful, which in turn means either that the statement is semantically
meaningless or that it is empirically insignificant.

Those who have refused to let scale types influence their statistical behavior probably will continue to be unmoved even by these elegant threats
of semantical meaninglessness. There is some justification for their stubborn
behavior, because some of the basic issues they have put forth have not yet
been answered in a thoroughly clean way. None of the above papers gives a
really satisfactory treatment of Lord's football number parable (78). In the
last section of their paper, Adams, Fagot & Robinson (4) argue that Lord's
example is irrelevant because the set of permissible transformations is not
clearly defined. This conclusion is unfortunate and surprising, because the
example could hardly be more explicit on all relevant details, including how
the numbers are assigned to each player.

Luce (89) indirectly attempts to cope with the football number type of
problem by distinguishing between statistical hypotheses that say something
about the scale and those that do not. In the former case, the hypothesis
must be invariant over permissible transformations, but in the latter case it
need not be. The latter case presumably applies to the football example.

Another type of problem that has yet to be dealt with in a serious way
is given in Burke's most recent statement of his position (18). In Burke's
problem, which deserves to be placed in the same league with the Lord
problem, four children are asked to determine the length of two courses by
counting the number of steps it takes to walk around each course. Although
the children's measure of distance is clearly not linearly related to the actual
distance, Burke nevertheless recommends testing the null hypothesis that the
two courses are of the same length by using a t-test (not a nonparametric
test). Burke's use of a t-test is undoubtedly correct, but it has yet to receive a
sound justification. Luce's distinction between the two types of hypotheses
does not seem to be appropriate here. Nor is Burke's statement that statistical problems should be solved with statistical theorems (measurement
models are irrelevant) completely sufficient.

One of the issues raised by Burke's example has to do with the robustness
of a statistical test. Some discussion of the application of the F test to ordinal
data is given in (4), but the analysis there seems weak because it avoids any
treatment of the robustness aspects of the statistic.

Other limitations to the notion of meaningful statements and the relativeness of permissible statistics described above are given by Adams (3). He
gives the example "Ernest Adams weighs 190 pounds," which he says is not
invariant; however, if such statements were excluded on the grounds that
they are not meaningful, Adams says that all data would be banished from
science. Similarly, it would also seem strange to tell an experimentalist that

he cannot report the mean of his interval scale measurements until he specifies what statements he intends to make with these means.

Luce (84) treats a problem that has some bearing on the class of meaningful statements. If the independent and dependent variables have certain scale types, then what is the class of equations involving these variables that are meaningful? In an earlier paper (80) Luce considered the two-variable problem. Later (84) he treats the n variable case. Luce's results depend on restricting oneself to the class of equations in which permissible transformations in the independent variables are absorbed by appropriate permissible transformations in the independent variable. The alternative and more common procedure is to let dimensional constants absorb all changes in the independent and the dependent variables.

CONJOINT MEASUREMENT

With the rise in concern for the logic of measurement, there has been a concomitant increase in the development of algebraic models. The model that has generated the greatest interest is the conjoint measurement system introduced by Luce & Tukey (92). The basic idea of the Luce-Tukey model is that by considering simultaneously the contribution of two factors it is possible to measure each factor separately. Of course, there is nothing startlingly new in this idea of measuring factors simultaneously; it is the essence of all multidimensional and factor analytical methods. The feature of the conjoint measurement axioms, and of the algebraic models in general, is that these assumptions are stated entirely in terms of the observable properties or constraints on data. Multidimensional models, on the other hand, are stated either in terms of nonobservable quantities or, what amounts to the same thing, in terms of a particular numerical representation. It should be emphasized at the start, however, that there is nothing inherently more fundamental in one approach over the other. In fact, most of the multidimensional models, and for that matter the single dimensional ones as well, can be written easily in a form that would satisfy the definition of fundamental measurement given by Supples & Zinnes (144).

Unlike the usual Campbellian axioms, or the axioms for extensive measurement, the four conjoint measurement axioms do not explicitly contain the concatenation operation. These axioms postulate only a single observable binary relation on the objects, or more precisely, on the ordered pair of factors. Axiom 1 assumes that the observable binary relation weakly orders the objects; axiom 2, the solvability axiom, assumes that the objects are sufficiently dense and unbounded so that, to use the example of momentum, it is possible to match the momentum of any two objects by changing the velocity component of either object or by changing the mass component of either object; axiom 3, the cancellation axiom, is most easily thought of as another form of transitivity; and axiom 4 is one version of the familiar archimedian axiom. Luce & Tukey show that these four axioms are sufficient, though not necessary, to establish a particularly simple representation theorem, one in which the effects of the two factors appear in a simple additive way. The uniqueness theorem is important here, to, because the level of measurement obtained is surprisingly high. The numerical assignment of each factor is determined up to a linear transformation.

Luce & Tukey (92) discuss the relationship between their axioms and a number of older, closely related systems. One of these, an axiom system given by Suppes & Winet (143), incorporates versions of all four Luce & Tukey axioms, and their representation and uniqueness theorems are also quite similar to that of Luce & Turkey's. The principal difference between these two axiom systems lies in the use of one additional axiom by Suppes & Winet and in their definition of the basic set over which the relations are defined. Suppes & Winet define the basic empirical relations over a single set of objects or elements, while Luce & Tukey define them over a cartesian product of two sets. The Suppes & Winet representation theorem, therefore, contains only a single numerical function, while the Luce & Tukey representation theorem contains two numerical functions, one for each factor. The additional axiom used by Suppes & Winet essentially assumes that an object exists at the midpoint between each pair of objects. This axiom seems to take the place of the two-factor aspects of the Luce & Tukey axioms. However, since both the Luce & Tukey and the Suppes & Winet results are so similar, it should be clear that the multidimensional aspect of conjoint measurement is not a critical factor in arriving at interval scale measurement.

Because of the similarity of conjoint measurement with analysis of variance, comparisons between these two approaches are inevitable. Luce & Tukey point out that a significant interaction term in analysis of variance possibly may be eliminated by monotonic transformations of the data, but the analysis of variance procedure does not tell how to do this. The transformations that are used occasionally in analysis of variance are used primarily for the purpose of equalizing variances. As an alternative to analysis of variance, Luce & Tukey seem to suggest testing the conjoint measurement axioms. But since the conjoint measurement axioms are only sufficient for establishing a simple additive representation, rather than being both necessary and sufficient, rejection of these axioms does not inevitably imply that an additive representation does not exist. In this sense, the Luce-Tukey axioms have the same limitations as analysis of variance.

Recent papers by Scott (124) and Adams[4] (2) have been directed at the problem of determining the conditions that are both necessary and sufficient for a simple additive representation to exist. Their results are important

---

[4] Note added in proof: The results of Scott and Adams were arrived at independently by A. Tversky in the technical report *Finite Additive Structures*. Michigan Math. Psychol. Program MMPP 64-6 (Dept. Psychol., Univ. Michigan, Ann Arbor, Mich., 1964).

theoretically, but not too useful experimentally, because they involve an infinite set of conditions. Tversky (152) has generalized this work to include any polynomial representation and to include infinite sets of objects, but his results have the same experimental limitations. And according to Scott & Suppes (125), it never will be possible to express these conditions in a simple form (that is, by a universal sentence).

Testing the conjoint measurement axioms has its problems, too. Since these axioms require the existence of an infinite number of objects (or attribute values), the axioms cannot be tested literally in detail. Some inductive approach is necessary. With finite sets of objects, the axioms can be tested in detail, but the uniqueness theorem (and the solvability axiom) then no longer applies. More serious difficulties in testing the conjoint measurement axioms arise from the deterministic nature of these axioms. Because of this property of these axioms, no set of data can be expected to satisfy the axioms precisely. But how close must the experimental observations come? Unlike analysis of variance, there are no well-developed statistical procedures for conjoint measurement; nor are any likely until probabilistic assumptions are explicitly introduced into the model.

There have been a number of theoretical developments and extensions of the Luce-Tukey axioms. Krantz (66) gives an alternative, simpler proof of the conjoint measurement representation and uniqueness theorems. He starts out with: (a) the same basic product set corresponding to the two factors; (b) an equivalence relation defined over this set; (c) a solvability axiom; and (d) a cancellation axiom defined in terms of this equivalence relation. The solvability and cancellation axioms are very much like Luce & Tukey's. A concatenation operation is then defined (not assumed) over the equivalence classes determined by the equivalence relation. The resulting structure is shown to be a commutative group. By assuming the existence of an order relation over the basic equivalence classes, and by assuming further that the resulting system is an archimedian-simply-ordered group, the Luce-Tukey theorems drop out immediately. The reason the Luce-Tukey results come off so easily this way is because the brunt of the proof is absorbed by known theorems about archimedian simply-ordered groups.

Those looking for an introduction to the conjoint measurement model should start with the first part of Krantz's paper. The notation and proofs are simpler than those of Luce & Tukey, and the theorems build up in a logical way. Some may feel cheated when important aspects of the proof of the principal theorem are taken over by external theorems, but the alternative approach tends to produce tedious proofs that make it easy for the reader to lose sight of the forest for the trees.

In the last part of Krantz's paper, an n-dimensional version of conjoint measurement is developed. Luce (88) also treats the n-dimensional case but uses a weaker cancellation axiom. In this same paper, Luce also weakens the solvability axiom. The Luce-Tukey (92) version of this axiom assumes that the values of each factor are unbounded; but Luce (88) postulates upper and lower bounds for the factors and then has to supply an additional axiom to obtain the same representation and uniqueness theorems.

Roskies (114) considers the multiplicative form of conjoint measurement. Here the joint effect of the two factors is represented by their product instead of by their sum. Of course, the two versions are completely equivalent, provided only positive valued functions are used in the multiplicative representation. In this case, the additive and multiplicative versions are just two of the possible representation theorems for the conjoint measurement axioms. However, Roskies considers the case in which negative valued functions are permitted in the multiplicative representation. For this case, the conjoint measurement axioms need to be weakened, and Roskies does this mainly by modifying the cancellation axiom. Gioia (45) has shown that one of Roskies axioms is implied by the other four. Luce (86), incidentally, makes use of the multiplicative version of conjoint measurement in his study of the relationship between conjoint measurement and extensive or Campbellian measurement when both can be applied to the same domain. By making one new assumption concerning this relationship, he shows that the multiplicative form of conjoint measurement is a power function of the additive form of extensive measurement.

MULTIDIMENSIONAL MODELS

Nothing startlingly new has happened with the nonmetric models since Shepard (127) and Kruskal (68, 69) developed their numerical algorithms. Similar approaches have been developed by Guttman and Lingoes (76, 77) and by Torgerson and Mueser [referred to in (147)]. The expected avalanche of articles using these methods is just beginning; cited here is a small sampling of papers using the Shepard-Kruskal algorithms (53, 54, 75, 100, 101, 121, 133). The kinds of stimuli treated in this sample of papers include solution mixtures (53, 64, 121), musical intervals (75), and random forms (133). Noneuclidean solutions were found by Gregson (53, 54) and Gregson & Russell (121) and, using somewhat different analyses, were also obtained by Cross (22) in an experiment involving generalization and discrimination.

Important theoretical work, as usual, has been done by Shepard (129). Shepard carried out some Monte Carlo studies for the purpose of determining to what extent an increase in the number of points increases the accuracy of the numerical solution in two different types of analyses: proximity analysis and nonmetric factor analysis. In the former case, Shepard carried out a number of Monte Carlo runs for each set containing different numbers of stimuli and for each set he determined the minimum correlation and the root-mean-square correlation between the original distance and the reconstructed distance. On the basis of these correlations, Shepard concludes that for all practical purposes essentially perfect agreement is reached at 15 or more points and that for these intermediate values of n, a purely ordinal scale of proximity entails, with overwhelming probability, an essentially ratio scale of distance. Similar conclusions are reached for the case of non-metric factor analysis.

Shepard's use of the correlation coefficient as a measure of accuracy here seems unfortunate. While the correlation coefficient is a useful index when two variables are only crudely related, it is practically useless when the variables agree on the ordering of the stimuli. This property of the correlation coefficient is amply demonstrated by Abelson & Tukey (1). Since Shepard assumes no error in his Monte Carlo runs, his final solution will order the distances in precisely the same way as the original distances. A more useful measure of accuracy would be the smallest per cent accuracy that can be expected in the measurement of each distance or the largest error that can be expected (with the distance suitably normalized). Such a measure of accuracy is used by Benzecri (14)—cited by Shepard—who shows that, under certain distribution assumptions concerning the location of the stimuli, the accuracy can be made arbitrarily large with enough points. But how many points it takes to achieve a given level of accuracy is not implied by these results, nor by Shepard's results.

Shepard (129) has a long discussion on the features of the nonmetric methods, although most of the features he describes are characteristic of the the metric methods as well. The heart of the difference is probably in what Shepard calls the "strong and controversial assumptions" that are made in the metric methods. However, while historically there are a number of good reasons why psychologists have wished to avoid certain kinds of assumptions, the fear of strong assumptions, which in practice mean probabilistic assumptions, should not make one lose sight of what is, after all, the purpose of any scaling (or psychological) theory: to account for a broad class of psychological data, using relatively few parameters that have to be estimated from data. But how do you determine whether the nonmetric model gives a good account of a given set of data? This is not so easy to determine for the same reason that the algebraic models are so difficult to test. The measure of stress or goodness-of-fit in the Kruskal model is deceptive and difficult to interpret because it has no obvious relation to the number of parameters that are estimated and the number of stimuli that are used. Consider what typically happens when a Shepard-Kruskal type of solution is compared with a solution based on a probabilistic model—such as that of Shepard (126) and Luce (83)—and both types use the same set of data, say the data from McGuire (102). Shepard has claimed (127) that the solutions obtained by these two different approaches are negligibly different from each other, yet if goodness-of-fit tests of the probabilistic model based on likelihood ratio tests are carried out, it turns out that the chi-squares obtained are statistically significant. In other words, the variabilility in the McGuire data cannot be accounted for on the basis of the Shepard-Luce model; but if the nonmetric solution corresponds so closely to the probabilistic one, what then should one conclude about the goodness-of-fit properties of the non-metric solution?

One approach, of course, is to add probabilistic assumptions to the Shepard-Kruskal model, but this brings you to the metric models—which is not a bad place to be. The real weakness all along of the probabilistic (metric) models has been the difficulty of obtaining good estimates of the parameters and reasonable tests of the model. However, today these aspects of the probabilistic models need present no problem whatever.

Shepard (128) has started another direction of multidimensional work, or at least he has brought into focus issues that have remained dormant for some time. Shepard makes the distinction between unitary and analyzable stimuli and shows that for the latter type of stimulus, subjects may attend or respond at any given moment to only one of the relevant dimensions. This distinction between two types of stimuli is similar to the distinctions now being made by a number of writers. Torgerson (147) makes the distinction between multiattribute and multidimensional models and shows that the choice depends on the stimulus context and the cognitive strategy of the subjects. Torgerson argues that the multidimensional models may be valuable even when the distance (multidimensional) type of model is, strictly speaking, not appropriate, because they may help show up the underlying structure. In speaking of structures, Torgerson says that they should remain invariant despite variations in experimental procedure, stimulus context, etc. However, this seems to be too severe a restriction to demand even of a multidimensional theory, since there are many other elegant ways for a theory to treat experimental variations without keeping any particular set of parameters constant.

Handel (56) distinguishes between separable dimensions and nonseparable dimensions in his study of classification and similarity judgments. He concludes that for some stimuli the dimension structure is used; for others, the distance properties are used; and for still another set of stimuli, the property that is used depends on the particular task. Similar conclusions are reached by Imai & Garner (61) in their study of visual stimuli. They found that similarity judgments depended on the attribute structure rather than the metric structure of the stimuli. A distinction between homogeneous and heterogeneous stimuli is made by Kunnapas (70) and Kunnapas, Malhammar & Svenson (71), who showed that the relationship found previously between ratio and similarity estimations for homogeneous stimuli (30) does not hold for heterogeneous stimuli. They admit, however, that the distinction between these two types of stimuli is not always easy to make.

Probably the most important theoretical papers in the multidimensional domain are those of Beals, Krantz & Tversky (10) and Krantz (67). These papers are important because they represent the beginning of an attempt to determine what empirical properties need to be satisfied by a set of data to guarantee the existence of given multidimensional representations. In the first part of the paper by Beals, Krantz & Tversky, it is assumed that the empirical observations consist of an ordering of all pairs of stimuli with respect to their similarity. In their first theorem they indicate six properties of this ordering that permit it to be represented by a metric with additive segments, a metric that is a slight generalization of the usual metric space. The most important property required by this theorem is stated in terms of concentric isosimilarity surfaces, but such surfaces are probably very difficult to work with empirically. The six properties given in this first theorem evidently are not necessary conditions, because it is easy to give examples of theories, such as the Thurstone Case-3 theory, that would not generate data consistent with all six properties, but which are, nevertheless, represented by a metric with additive segments.

In the next part of this paper it is assumed that a specific dimensional representation exists for a set of stimuli—that is, the components of each stimulus is assumed known—and also that a numerical dissimilarity measure on pairs of stimuli exists. Under what conditions can this dissimilarity measure play the role of a distance function in what they call an additive-difference model, a model that is somewhat more general than a Minkowski metric? The second theorem stated gives five properties that guarantee the existence of the additive-difference model. In both of these theorems the properties are stated as sufficient conditions only, but the previous discussion in each case suggests that the properties are also necessary. Unfortunately, the proofs of these theorems are not given and in some cases are contained only in unpublished papers.

In the third section of their paper, Beals, Krantz & Tversky attempt to combine the results of the two previous sections to determine the conditions that generate a metric with additive segments and satisfy the additive-difference model as well. However, the theorem stated is not as successful as the previous ones because the properties described are not sufficient to guarantee the desired result, although by using one more assumption they are able to show that the additive-difference model and the metric with additive segments assumption implies and is implied by the Minkowski metric. The results of these last two theorems depend on knowing in advance the dimensionality of the stimulus space and the nominal scale values of the stimuli on each dimension. Eventually, one may hope that similar theorems can be expressed in terms of conditions that are both necessary and sufficient, without the above restrictions.

Krantz's (67) paper concentrates on triads in which the subject chooses one of two stimuli that is more similar to a standard stimulus. Assuming at the outset that similarity measures exist and that the difference between appropriate similarity measures determines the choice probabilities for the triadic judgments, Krantz raises the question of what additional constraints need to be met by the observed judgments in order to insure that the function relating the similarity measures to the choice probabilities has the properties of a metric, or what Krantz calls a pseudo-metric. The principal theorem does, in fact, give the additional assumptions that are needed to guarantee this result, and these additional assumptions are stated principally in terms of the observed choice probabilities. Two of the assumptions, how-

ever, would probably be difficult to work with since they involve finding
finite sequences of stimuli that satisfy certain properties. However, these
theoretical results are important first steps in determining the empirical
implications of a metric space.

The experimental part of Krantz's paper consists of indirect attempts
to verify the assumption of "simple scalability" for triads, which is similar
to the assumption stated previously for the relationship between the choice
probabilities and the similarity measures. Krantz's tests are indirect because
they are based first on fitting a specific model that satisfies simple scalability,
and then showing not only that the goodness-of-fit chi-squares are too large
but that the discrepancies between predicted and observed probabilities are
in the direction of a model that does not satisfy simple scalability. Since
these results are obtained within the context of a specific scaling model,
Krantz's vigorous rejection of simple scalability seems too strong, although,
to be sure, in the long run simple scalability can be regarded only as a first
order approximation.

Ross (116) presents a much-needed discussion of a Tucker-Messick (151)
multidimensional model that allows for subject differences. The basic idea
of the Tucker-Messick model is to determine a limited number of points of
view, each of which is represented by a complete set of interpoint distances,
and then to characterize each subject's responses by weights that determine
his way of combining the distances from each point of view. Ross shows that
by changing the subject's weights, a two-dimensional configuration can be
made to look like a three-dimensional configuration, or even worse, the
distances can be made to look nonmetric. These remarks by Ross illustrate
the need to determine more fully the properties of new models before they
are put into circulation. At the very least, they should be tried out on a
variety of hypothetical data, including those that are consistent with the
model and those that are not.

POWER VERSUS LOGARITHMIC FUNCTIONS

The number of papers purporting to show that the correct psychophysical law is a power law or a logarithmic law is probably increasing exponen-
tially. The standard experimental defense of the power law continues to be
either the magnitude estimation experiment or the cross modality experiment. Log-log plots of the magnitude estimation data or similar data against
the physical parameters look linear in a large number of papers (24, 32, 41,
57, 62, 99, 105, 111, 132, 134, 139), and in some cases (31, 34, 93, 120) these
plots are based on individual data. Similar results are obtained in many cross
modality experiments (57, 105, 137, 138), some of which are also based on
individual subjects. However, the linearity properties in these papers are not
found universally (90, 108). The extent of the statistical analysis in nearly all
of these papers, even in those papers where the variability of the points seems
fairly large, consists of at most a least-squares fit of straight lines to data
points (41, 55, 57), or correlations between observed and predicted points,

neither of which establishes very much about the ability of the power function to account for the observed points or its ability relative to the log function.

Some of the nonlinearity can be accounted for by the addition of constant terms to the power function [for example, (98)], but even here there is no agreement on where or how these constant terms should be added (37, 38, 57, 93, 99, 140). Procedures for estimating these additive constants are discussed by Mashhour (96), who gives a graphical and iterative approach—though both procedures probably could be adapted for digital computer—and Fagot (37), who gives maximum likelihood estimates under various simplified conditions.

The question of the value or the stability of the slopes in these log-log plots is a more delicate matter. A great number of papers show that the exponent varies under a wide variety of experimental conditions or manipulations (9, 13, 62, 63, 96, 97, 98, 99, 134, 137, 140), that it is especially influenced by the range of the stimuli (63, 109, 110), and that there are large differences in the exponents between subjects (31, 34, 93, 120). Stevens (136) concludes on the basis of such results that the slope of the line in the cross modality experiment is accurately predicted from the exponent in a magnitude estimation experiment and that the range of exponents obtained is sufficiently close to conclude that evidence is converging. Mashhour & Hosman (98) arrive at the opposite conclusion, that a large percentage of the slopes are significantly different from those predicted and that the empirical outcomes do not support the validity of the power law even as a first approximation.

Apart from these purely empirical questions, there are a number of theoretical or semantical issues. Stevens (137) objects to the statement by Ekman & Sjöberg (35) that the power law is verified only by direct magnitude or ratio estimation methods, but the evidence he cites—linearity of the log-log plots in the cross modality experiments and transitivity among the slopes such that any two can be used to predict a third—are consistent with the log function as well, a fact pointed out by many (for example, 148, 149). On the other hand, Rosner (115) seems to find it an advantage for the power law to be confirmed by direct data, because he argues that no direct data exist that support the log law. Not so, says Treisman (148), because categorical data and others are no less direct than the ratio or magnitude estimation data.

The terms "direct" and "indirect" judgments are being used far more frequently these days, and this seems unfortunate. The distinction between the direct and indirect tasks appears to be based on whether the subjects are required to make a numerical response or not. However, there appears to be no important sense in which numerical responses are more direct than non-numerical responses; if anything, numerical responses are more indirect because they are more complex, depending not only on perceptual processes, but on the subject's use and familiarity with numbers as well. Ultimately, a theory of numerical responses will have to be more complex than a theory of non-numerical responses, because it will have much more to explain.

Other cases on behalf of the power function have been presented by Yilmaz (156), who derives the power function from two assumptions that are supposed to rule out the log function, and by Eisler (28), who appeals mainly to criteria of simplicity and communicability.

Perhaps it is too much to hope for, but there seems to be a microscopic trend toward accepting the idea that a complete duality or equivalence exists between power and log functions. For the non-numerical tasks, it appears inescapable to this writer that the choice of a log and power function is a choice between two equivalent representation theorems, neither of which has any better or stronger implications than the other. For this reason, statements to the effect that there are no exceptions as yet to the principle that equal stimulus ratios produce equal sensation ratios (136) are safe statements to make, because they are completely ambiguous without a specification of the representation theorem intended.

For the numerical responses, the situation is analogous but a little deceptive because here it looks as though a choice of representation theorems is not as arbitrary; some representation theorems seem to involve transformations of the observed data or the introduction of hidden processes. But even with numerical responses, the complete duality between the power and log functions is preserved. If it is necessary to introduce a log transformation of magnitude estimation data to account for those data by a log function—by assuming, for example, that the subjects' use of numbers in that particular experiment is logarithmically related to its subjective value, as Ekman (29, 33) and Treisman (148, 150) have done—then it is equally true that an exponential transformation of categorical data would be necessary to account for those data from the power function principle. Even more specifically, if the power function predicts the cross modality slope from the magnitude estimation data, then the same prediction can be obtained from the log function interpretation of the magnitude estimation data. Stevens (136) seems to be doubtful on this point, but it is the case that a log transformation of the magnitude estimation data does not introduce any new arbitrary parameters or change the number that are uniquely determined by those data. It also follows that categorical data will predict the slope in the cross modality experiment from either a log or power function interpretation. However, here it is necessary to insure either that the categorical response is on a difference scale (that is, that it is unique up to an additive constant) or that the units of the two scales have been made comparable by, for example, equating the size of the two scales or by equating the standard deviations of the two scales.

It is comforting to note that Stevens (136, 138) gradually seems to be accepting the point of view that there is nothing particularly unique or direct about the magnitude estimation task, because he now refers to the magnitude estimation task as a matching task, involving the matching of numbers to some other physical variable. It is only a hop, skip, and a jump from here to disposing of the problem of the psychophysical law in the first place and replacing it with the more meaningful study of the cross modality experiment, or even better, with the study of all choice experiments.

The log-power controversy may yet be settled in still another way. Fagot (37) notes that the power function can be made to look like a log function by taking small valued exponents. This suggests that the log function is a special case of a power function and, therefore, that the power function can fit anything the log function can fit, but not conversely. This result seems correct, but puzzling because the basic properties of these two functions are so different.

Important emphasis should be given to the theoretical and empirical paper by Luce & Mo (90) on magnitude estimation, because it is one of the few attempts to take magnitude estimation data seriously enough to try to account for all of its properties. Their theory, consisting of a continuous analogue of the choice theory for recognition experiments, does not fit their data particularly well, but it is a start in the right direction. Another very different theoretical approach to magnitude estimation is the multidimensional, vector model of Ross & DiLollo (117), which predicts how the magnitude estimation judgment is influenced by a number of experimental variables. However, so far their predictions are mainly qualitative, because they have not as yet worked out procedures for estimating the parameters for individual subjects.

Eisler (25) has shown how his "general psychophysical differential equation" can be used to derive the relationship between two scales, such as magnitude estimation and category scales, from a knowledge of the Weber functions of both continua. Mashhour (95) has questioned the arbitrariness of Eisler's assumption and the accuracy of his prediction, although Eisler (28) has reaffirmed his faith in these predictions by reanalyzing the data questioned by Mashhour. One of the difficulties in deciding on the accuracy of Eisler's differential equation is that his analysis does not carefully distinguish between the discrepancies due to inaccurate Weber functions and those due to the inappropriateness of his equation.

Comparisons have been made recently between magnitude estimation and the scale values obtained from a pair-comparison task (72), but as indicated by Eisler (28), these comparisons are heavily influenced by the more or less arbitrary representation theorems selected for the pair-comparison data and also by the pair-comparison theory selected in the first place.

DETECTION

A few new things have happened in the detection domain that should have broad implications for all choice experiments. A number of new theories having relatively simple assumptions have been proposed for the detection experiment, and learning assumptions have been incorporated into many of these detection models. The learning assumptions are important, not only because they help to account for more of the fine-grain properties of data, those that ordinarily would be dismissed as error, but in addition they make explicit the relationship between some of the detection parameters and various experimental variables. They also help to unite two broad areas of psychology, choice and learning.

Two of the simplest and most attractive theories for detection experiments are the two-state model by Luce (82, 83, 85) and the three-state model by Atkinson (5, 6). To keep matters clear, it is necessary to distinguish the two-state model of Luce from another detection model that he has derived from the choice model (83). An important feature of both the Luce and Atkinson models is that they allow different response biases or tendencies to occur when the subject is in different states. The observed response then depends jointly on the state the subject is in on a given trial and on the response bias parameters associated with that state.

Further discussion and experimental tests of the Luce two-state model are presented by Wickelgren (153, 154). A generalization of this model to detection tasks in which the stimulus is presented at random times is given by Green & Luce [(49); see also (87)]. Experimental tests of the Atkinson three-state model are reported by Atkinson and associates (7, 64). Tests of the Luce choice model were conducted by Yellott & Curnow (155). Simultaneous treatment of the detection and recognition experiment has also been considered using the Luce two-state model (103) and using the choice model (83, 130).

The learning models that have been used in connection with these detection models assume that the response bias parameters change from trial to trial, but under the usual experimental conditions, eventually they reach some stationary state. In the "state-sensitive" model (5, 6, 8, 82, 83, 123) the trial-by-trial parameter changes are assumed to depend both on the response that is reinforced and on the state that the subject is in on each trial. In the "state-insensitive" model (20, 85), the learning is influenced only by the reinforced response. Oddly enough, the asymptotic properties of these two kinds of learning models are identical and can be discriminated only by an analysis of the sequential statistics and the pre-asymptotic data.

Generally, these learning models have utilized some version of the linear learning models, though in the earlier papers of Atkinson (5) a version of the stimulus sampling model was used. However, these two classes of models are also similar in many respects. Other learning models or modifications of the above model are discussed by Friedman and co-workers (42) and by Kinchla and associates (65). The interesting thing about these linear models, when used with either the two- or three-state detection models, is that the asymptotic formulae obtained are identical to those obtained from the choice model. This means that the response bias parameter in the choice model can be viewed as the end result of a stochastic process. It also means that the dependency of the response bias parameters on the a priori probability (and on the learning rate parameters) is made explicit, and in some experiments, when the a priori probabilities are manipulated, the learning model may offer a parameter free prediction of the asymptotic values of the response bias parameters. Most of the references cited above also use the linear model to account for various trial-by-trial sequential aspects of the detection or recognition data.

The Tanner-Swets detection theory has been covered thoroughly in the recent text by Green & Swets (50), but one still looks in vain for any serious statistical test of this model. There is little basis for this complacency, because in nearly all instances when some of the old detection data cited in Green & Swets' book have been reanalyzed by this writer's students (in class projects using maximum likelihood estimation methods and likelihood ratio tests), the chi-squares for the Tanner-Swets model generally have been significantly large. Scaling theorists probably will be surprised also to learn from Green & Swets that the Thurstone theory is not enjoying a great deal of popularity among psychophysicists at the present time. Their extensive criticism of the Thurstone model is surprising because it shares so much in common with the Tanner-Swets model.

Estimation and goodness-of-fit tests for the Tanner-Swets model, or equivalently for the Thurstone pair-comparison model, have been described by Dorfman & Alf (23), Gourevitch & Galanter (47), and by Hohle (60), whose paper was discussed earlier. Gourevitch and Galanter's approach to the estimation question, which is used by Galanter & Holman (44), seems to require an unnecessary number of simplifying assumptions, while Dorfman & Alf's approach uses a straightforward application of the Newton-Raphson method to solve the nonlinear maximum likelihood equations. The application of the Newton-Raphson method here probably is more complicated than necessary, because it requires calculating the first and second derivatives of the likelihood function. A number of other numerical procedures suitable for a digital computer make this calculation unnecessary and even, on occasion, faster (16).

Overview

Words and phrases, like theories, have a way of surviving long after they are useful or have been supplanted by better ones. In the interest of speeding up progress, here are some phrases that need rapid extinction, at least as used in the psychological scaling literature: substantive theory, law of comparative judgment, the theory of signal detection, latent, manifest, fallible data, method of pair comparison, rational equation, scaling method, direct or indirect scaling method, and the psychophysical law.

LITERATURE CITED

1. Abelson, R. R., Tukey, J. W. Efficient utilization of non-numerical information in quantitative analysis: General theory and the case of simple order. *Ann. Math. Stat.*, **34**, 1347–69 (1963)

2. Adams, E. W. Elements of a theory of inexact measurement. *Phil. Sci.*, **32**, 205–28 (1965)

3. Adams, E. W. *On the Nature and Purpose of Measurement. Measurement Theory and Mathematical*

Models Technical Report No. 4
(Dept. Psychol., Univ. Oregon,
Eugene, Ore., 1966)

4. Adams, E. W., Fagot, R. F., Robinson, R. E. A theory of appropriate
statistics. Psychometrika, 30, 99–
127 (1965)

5. Atkinson, R. C. A variable sensitivity
theory of signal detection. Psychol.
Rev., 70, 91–106 (1963)

6. Atkinson, R. C., Bower, G. H.,
Crothers, E. J. An Introduction To
Mathematical Learning Theory
(Wiley, New York, 429 pp., 1965)

7. Atkinson, R. C., Carterette, E. C.,
Kinchla, R. A. The effect of information feedback upon psy-
cophysical judgments. Psychon.
Sci., 1, 83–84 (1964)

8. Atkinson, R. C., Kinchla, R. A. A
learning model for forced-choice
detection experiments. Brit. J.
Math. Stat. Psychol., 18, 183–206
(1965)

9. Baird, J. C., Biersdorf, W. R. Quantitative functions for size and distance judgments. Percept. Psychophys., 2, 161–66 (1967)

10. Beals, R., Krantz, D. H., Tversky, A.
Foundations of multidimensional
scaling. Psychol. Rev., 75, 127–42
(1968)

11. Bechtel, G. G. The analysis of variance and pairwise scaling. Psychometrika, 32, 46–65 (1967)

12. Bechtel, G. G. F tests for the absolute
invariance of dominance and composition scales. Ibid., 157–82

13. Beck, J., Shaw, W. A. Magnitude of
the standard, numerical value of
the standard and stimulus spacing
in the estimation of loudness. Percept. Mot. Skills, 21, 151–56 (1965)

14. Benzecri, J. P. Analyse factorielle des
proximités. Publ. Inst. Stat. Univ.
Paris, II, 14 (1965)

15. Bock, R. D., Jones, L. V. The Measurement and Prediction of Judgment and Choice (Holden-Day, San
Francisco, 370 pp., 1968)

16. Box, M. J. A comparison of several
current optimization methods, and
the use of transformations in constrained problems. Computer J., 9,
67–77 (1966)

17. Bradley, R. A. Another interpretation of a model for paired comparisons. Psychometrika, 30, 315–18
(1965)

18. Burke, C. J. Measurement scales and
statistical models. In Theories in
Contemporary Psychology, 147–59

(Marx, M. H., Ed., Macmillan,
New York, 628 pp., 1963)

19. Burke, C. J., Zinnes, J. L. A paired
comparison of pair comparisons.
J. Math. Psychol., 2, 53–76 (1965)

20. Bush, R. R., Luce, R. D., Rose, R. M.
Learning models for psychophysics.
In Studies in Mathematical Psy-
chology (Atkinson, R. C., Ed.,
Stanford Univ. Press, Stanford,
Calif., 414 pp., 1964)

21. Coombs, C. H. A Theory of Data
(Wiley, New York, 585 pp., 1964)

22. Cross, D. V. Metric properties of
multidimensional stimulus generalization. In Stimulus Generalization, 72–93 (Mostofsky, D. I., Ed.,
Stanford Univ. Press, Stanford,
Calif., 389 pp., 1965)

23. Dorfman, D. D., Alf, E., Jr. Maximum
likelihood estimation of parameters of signal detection theory—a
direct solution. Psychometrika, 33,
117–24 (1968)

24. Dorfman, D. D., Megling, R. Comparison of magnitude estimation of
loudness in children and adults.
Percept. Psychophys., 1, 239–41
(1966)

25. Eisler, H. A general differential equation in psychophysics: Derivation
and empirical test. Scand. J.
Psychol., 4, 265–72 (1963)

26. Eisler, H. A choice model for paired
comparison data based on imperfectly nested sets. Psychometrika,
29, 363–70 (1964)

27. Eisler, H. The connection between
magnitude and discrimination
scales and direct and indirect scaling methods. Ibid., 30, 271–89
(1965)

28. Eisler, H. On psychophysics in general
and the general psychophysical
differential equation in particular.
Scand. J. Psychol., 6, 85–102 (1965)

29. Ekman, G. Is the power law a special
case of Fechner's law? Percept.
Mot. Skills, 19, 730 (1964)

30. Ekman, G. Two methods for the
analysis of perceptual dimensionality. Ibid., 20, 557–72 (1965)

31. Ekman, G., Akesson, C. Saltness,
sweetness, and preference. Scand. J.
Psychol., 6, 241–53 (1965)

32. Ekman, G., Bratfisch, O. Subjective
distance and emotional involvement a psychological mechanism.
Acta Psychol., 24, 430–37 (1965)

33. Ekman, G., Hosman, B. Note on subjective scales of number. Percept.
Mot. Skills, 21, 101–2 (1965)

34. Ekman, G., Hosman, J., Lindstrom, B. Roughness, smoothness, and preference: A study of quantitative relations in individual subjects. *J. Exptl. Psychol.*, **70**, 17–26 (1965)

35. Ekman, G., Sjöberg, L. Scaling. *Ann. Rev. Psychol.*, **16**, 451–74 (1965)

36. Ellis, B. *Basic Concepts of Measurement* (Cambridge Univ. Press, London, 219 pp., 1966)

37. Fagot, R. F. Alternative power laws for ratio scaling. *Psychometrika*, **31**, 201–14 (1966)

38. Fagot, R. F., Stewart, M. R. An experimental comparison of stimulus and response translated power functions for brightness. *Percept. Psychophys.*, **3**, 297–305 (1968)

39. Fechner, G. (Adler, H. E., translator) *Elements of Psychophysics* (Holt, Rinehart & Winston, New York, 286 pp., 1966)

40. Frederiksen, N., Gulliksen, H. *Contributions to Mathematical Psychology* (Holt, Rinehart & Winston, New York, 189 pp., 1964)

41. Freeman, R. B., Jr. Absolute threshold for visual slant: The effect of stimulus size and retinal perspective. *J. Exptl. Psychol.*, **71**, 170–76 (1966)

42. Friedman, M. P., Carterette, E. C., Nakatani, L., Ahumada, A. Comparisons of some learning models for response bias in signal detection. *Percept. Psychophys.*, **3**, 5–10 (1968)

43. Galanter, E. *Textbook of Elementary Psychology* (Holden-Day, San Francisco, 419 pp., 1966)

44. Galanter, E., Holman, G. L. Some invariances of the isosensitivity function and their implications for the utility function of money. *J. Exptl. Psychol.*, **73**, 333–39 (1967)

45. Gioia, A. A. A note on Roskies' axioms for multiplicative representation. *J. Math. Psychol.*, **4**, 151–53 (1967)

46. Goude, G. *On Fundamental Measurement in Psychology* (Almqvist & Wiksell, Stockholm, 176 pp., 1962)

47. Gourevitch, V., Galanter, E. A significance test for one parameter isosensitivity functions. *Psychometrika*, **32**, 25–33 (1967)

48. Green, B. F., Jr. The computer revolution in psychometrics. *Psychometrika*, **31**, 437–45 (1966)

49. Green, D. M., Luce, R. D. Detection of auditory signals presented at random times. *Percept. Psychophys.*, **2**, 441–50 (1967)

50. Green, D. M., Swets, J. A. *Signal Detection Theory and Psychophysics* (Wiley, New York, 455 pp., 1966)

51. Greenberg, M. G. A method of successive cumulations for the scaling of pair-comparison preference judgments. *Psychometrika*, **30**, 441–48 (1965)

52. Greenberg, M. G. A modification of Thurstone's law of comparative judgment to accommodate a judgment category of "equal" or "no difference." *Psychol. Bull.*, **64**, 108–12 (1965)

53. Gregson, R. A. M. Representation of taste mixture cross-model matching in a Minkowski *r*-metric. *Austral. J. Psychol.*, **17**, 195–204 (1965)

54. Gregson, R. A. M. Theoretical and empirical multidimensional scalings of taste mixture matchings. *Brit. J. Math. Stat. Psychol.*, **19**, 59–75 (1966)

55. Gregson, R. A. M., Russell, P. N. Psychophysical power law exponent value for sucrose intensity. *Percept. Mot. Skills*, **20**, 294 (1965)

56. Handel, S. Classification and similarity of multidimensional stimuli. *Percept. Mot. Skills*, **24**, 1191–1203 (1967)

57. Harper, R., Stevens, S. S. Subjective hardness of compliant materials, *Quart. J. Exptl. Psychol.*, **16**, 204–15 (1964)

58. Hays, W. L. *Quantification in Psychology* (Brooks-Cole, Belmont, Calif., 87 pp., 1967)

59. Hodge, M. H. Some further tests of the constant-ratio rule. *Percept. Psychophys.*, **2**, 429–37 (1967)

60. Hohle, R. H. An empirical evaluation and comparison of two models for discriminability scales. *J. Math. Psychol.*, **3**, 174–83 (1966)

61. Imai, S., Garner, W. R. Structure in perceptual classification. *Psychon. Monogr., Suppl.* **2** (1968)

62. Indow, T., Stevens, S. S. Scaling of saturation and hue. *Percept. Psychophys.*, **1**, 253–72 (1966)

63. Jones, F. N., Woskow, M. J. Some effects of context on the slope in magnitude estimation. *J. Exptl. Psychol.*, **71**, 177–80 (1966)

64. Kinchla, R. A., Atkinson, R. C. The effect of false-information feedback upon psychophysical judgments. *Psychon. Sci.*, **1**, 317–18 (1964)

65. Kinchla, R. A., Townsend, J., Yellott, J. I., Jr., Atkinson, R. C. Influence of correlated visual cues on audi-

tory signal detection. *Percept. Psychophys.*, **1,** 67–73 (1966)

66. Krantz, D. H. Conjoint Measurement: The Luce-Tukey axiomatization and some extensions. *J. Math. Psychol.*, **1,** 248–77 (1964)

67. Krantz, D. H. Rational distance functions for multidimensional scaling. *Ibid.*, **4,** 226–45 (1967)

68. Kruskal, J. B. Multidimensional scaling by optimizing goodness of fit to a nonmetric hypothesis. *Psychometrika*, **29,** 1–27 (1964)

69. Kruskal, J. B. Nonmetric multidimensional scaling: a numerical method. *Ibid.*, 115–29

70. Künnapas, T. Visual perception of capital letters. *Scand. J. Psychol.*, **7,** 189–96 (1966)

71. Künnapas, T., Malhammar, G., Svenson, O. Multidimensional ratio scaling and multidimensional similarity of simple geometric figures. *Scand. J. Psychol.*, **5,** 249–56 (1964)

72. Künnapas, T., Sillén, M. Measurement of "political" preferences: A further study of direct and indirect scaling methods. *Scand. J. Psychol.*, **6,** 162–72 (1965)

73. Lazarsfeld, P. F., Henry, N. W. *Latent Structure Analysis* (Houghton Mifflin, New York, 294 pp., 1968)

74. Lehmann, E. L. The power of rank tests. *Ann. Math. Stat.*, **24,** 23–43 (1953)

75. Levelt, W. J. M., Van de Geer, J. P., Plonip, R. Triadic comparisons of muscial intervals. *Brit. J. Math. Stat. Psychol.*, **19,** 163–79 (1966)

76. Lingoes, J. C. An IBM 7090 program for Guttman-Lingoes smallest space analysis—I. *Behav. Sci.*, **10,** 183–84 (1965)

77. Lingoes, J. C. An IBM 7090 program for Guttman-Lingoes multidimensional scalogram analysis—II. *Ibid.*, **12,** 268 (1967)

78. Lord, F. M. On the statistical treatment of football numbers. *Am. Psychol.*, **8,** 750–51 (1953)

79. Lord, F. M., Novick, M. R., with contributions by Birnbaum, A. *Statistical Theories of Mental Test Scores* (Addison-Wesley, Reading, Mass., 568 pp., 1968)

80. Luce, R. D. On the possible psychophysical laws. *Psychol. Rev.*, **66,** 81–95 (1959)

81. Luce, R. D. *Individual Choice Behavior* (Wiley, New York, 153 pp., 1959)

82. Luce, R. D. A threshold theory for simple detection experiments. *Psychol. Rev.*, **70,** 61–79 (1963)

83. Luce, R. D. Detection and recognition. In *Handbook of Mathematical Psychology, Vol. I,* 103–89 (Luce, R. D., Bush, R. R., Galanter, E., Eds., Wiley, New York, 491 pp., 1963)

84. Luce, R. D. A generalization of a theorem of dimensional analysis. *J. Math. Psychol.*, **1,** 278–84 (1964)

85. Luce, R. D. Asymptotic learning in psychophysical theories. *Brit. J. Stat. Psychol.*, **17,** 1–14 (1964)

86. Luce, R. D. A "fundamental" axiomatization of multiplicative power relations among three variables. *Phil. Sci.*, **32,** 301–9 (1965)

87. Luce, R. D. A model for detection in temporally unstructured experiments with a Poisson distribution of signal presentations. *J. Math. Psychol.*, **3,** 48–64 (1966)

88. Luce, R. D. Two extensions of conjoint measurement. *Ibid.*, 348–71

89. Luce, R. D. Remarks on the theory of measurement and its relation to psychology. In *Les Modèles et la Formalization du Comportement,* 27–42 (Centre National de la Recherche Scientifique, Paris, France, 1967)

90. Luce, R. D., Mo, S. S. Magnitude estimation of heaviness and loudness by individual subjects: A test of a probabilistic response theory. *Brit. J. Math. Stat. Psychol.*, **18,** 159–74 (1965)

91. Luce, R. D., Suppes, P. Preference, utility, and subjective probability. In *Handbook of Mathematical Psychology, Vol. III,* 249–410 (Luce, R. D., Bush, R. R., Galanter, E., Eds., Wiley, New York, 537 pp., 1965)

92. Luce, R. D., Tukey, J. W. Simultaneous conjoint measurement: A new type of fundamental measurement. *J. Math. Psychol.*, **1,** 1–27 (1964)

93. Marks, L. E., Stevens, J. C. Individual brightness functions. *Percept. Psychophys.*, **1,** 17–24 (1966)

94. Marley, A. A. J. The relation between the discard and regularity conditions for choice probabilities. *J. Math. Psychol.*, **2,** 242–53 (1965)

95. Mashhour, M. On Eisler's psychophysical differential equation and his Fechnerian integration. *Scand. J. Psychol.*, **5,** 225–33 (1964)

96. Mashhour, M. *Psychophysical Re-*

lations in the Perception of Velocity (Stockholm, 176 pp., 1964)

97. Mashhour, M. Note on the validity of the power law. *Scand. J. Psychol.*, **6**, 220–24 (1965)

98. Mashhour, M., Hosman, J. On the "psychophysical law": A validation study. *Percept. Psychophys.*, **3**, 367–75 (1968)

99. McBurney, D. H. Magnitude estimation of the taste of sodium chloride after adaptation to sodium chloride. *J. Exptl. Psychol.*, **72**, 869–73 (1966)

100. McGee, V. Note on an "elastic" multidimensional scaling procedure. *Percep. Mot. Skills*, **21**, 81–82 (1965)

101. McGee, V. The multidimensional analysis of "elastic" distances. *Brit. J. Math. Stat. Psychol.*, **19**, 181–96 (1966)

102. McGuire, W. J. A multiprocess model for paired-associate learning. *J. Exptl. Psychol.*, **62**, 335–47 (1961)

103. Munsinger, H., Gummerman, K. Simultaneous visual detection and recognition. *Percept. Psychophys.*, **3**, 383–86 (1968)

104. Nunnally, J. C. *Psychometric Theory* (McGraw-Hill, New York, 640 pp., 1967)

105. Panek, D. W., Stevens, S. S. Saturation of red: A prothetic continuum. *Percept. Psychophys.*, **1**, 59–66 (1966)

106. Pendergrass, R. N., Bradley, R. A. Ranking in triple comparisons. In *Contributions to Probability and Statistics*, 331–51 (Olken, I. et al., Stanford Univ. Press, Stanford, Calif., 517 pp., 1960)

107. Pfanzagl, J., in cooperation with Baumann, V., Huber, H. *Theory of Measurement* (Wiley, New York, in press)

108. Pitz, G. F. Magnitude scales of line lengths. *Psychon. Sci.*, **2**, 213–14 (1956)

109. Poulton, E. C. Population norms of top sensory magnitudes and S. S. Stevens' exponents. *Percept. Psychophys.*, **2**, 312–16 (1967)

110. Poulton, E. C. The new psychophysics: Six models for magnitude estimation. *Psychol. Bull.*, **69**, 1–19 (1968)

111. Rachlin, H. C. Scaling subjective velocity, distance, and duration. *Percept. Psychophys.*, **1**, 77–82 (1966)

112. Robinson, R. E. Measurement and statistics: Towards a clarification of the theory of "permissible statistics." *Phil. Sci.*, **32**, 229–43 (1965)

113. Rosenberg, S., Cohen, B. D. Referential processes of speakers and listeners. *Psychol. Rev.*, **73**, 208–31 (1966)

114. Roskies, R. A measurement axiomatization for an essentially multiplicative representation of two factors. *J. Math. Pyschol.*, **2**, 266–76 (1965)

115. Rosner, B. S. Comment on note on numerical behavior. *Percept. Mot. Skills*, **21**, 120 (1965)

116. Ross, J. A remark on Tucker and Messick's "points of view" analysis. *Psychometrika*, **31**, 27–31 (1966)

117. Ross, J., DiLollo, V. A vector model for psychophysical judgment. *J. Exptl. Psychol. Monogr.* (In press)

118. Ross, S. *Logical Foundations of Psychological Measurement* (Munksgaard, Copenhagen, Denmark, 152 pp., 1964)

119. Rozeboom, W. Scaling theory and the nature of measurement. *Synthese*, **16**, 170–233 (1966)

120. Rule, S. J. Subject differences in exponents of psychophysical power functions. *Percept. Mot. Skills*, **23**, 1125–26 (1966)

121. Russell, P. N., Gregson, R. A. A comparison of intermodal and intramodal methods in the multidimensional scaling of three-component taste mixtures. *Austral. J. Psychol.*, **18**, 244–54 (1966)

122. Savage, I. R. Contribution to the theory of rank order statistics—the two sample case. *Ann. Math. Stat.*, **27**, 580–615 (1956)

123. Schoeffler, M. S. Theory for psychophysical learning. *J. Acoust. Soc. Am.*, **37**, 1124–33 (1965)

124. Scott, D. Measurement structures and linear inequalities. *J. Math. Psychol.*, **1**, 233–47 (1964)

125. Scott, D., Suppes, P. Foundational aspects of theories of measurement. *J. Symbolic Logic*, **23**, 113–28 (1958)

126. Shepard, R. N. Stimulus and response generalization: Tests of a model relating generalization to distance in psychological space. *J. Exptl. Psychol.*, **55**, 509–23 (1958)

127. Shepard, R. N. The analysis of proximities: multidimensional scaling with an unknown distance func-

tion. I. *Psychometrika*, **27**, 125–49 (1962)

128. Shepard, R. N. Attention and the metric structure of the stimulus. *J. Math. Psychol.*, **1**, 54–87 (1964)

129. Shepard, R. N. Metric structures in ordinal data. *Ibid.*, **3**, 287–316 (1966)

130. Shipley, E. F. Detection and recognition: Experiments and choice models. *J. Math. Psychol.*, **2**, 277–311 (1965)

131. Shipley, E. F., Luce, R. D. Discrimination among two- and three-element sets of weights. In *Studies in Mathematical Psychology* (See Ref. 20)

132. Stanley, G. Magnitude estimates of distance based on object-size. *Percept. Psychophys.*, **2**, 287–88 (1967)

133. Stenson, H. H. The psychophysical dimensions of similarity among random shapes. *Percept. Psychophys.*, **3**, 201–14 (1968)

134. Sternbach, R. A., Tursky, B. On the psychophysical power function in electric shock. *Psychon. Sci.*, **1**, 217–18 (1964)

135. Stevens, S. S. On the theory of scales of measurement. *Science*, **103**, 677–80 (1946)

136. Stevens, S. S. Concerning the psychophysical power law. *Quart. J. Exptl. Psychol.*, **15**, 383–85 (1964)

137. Stevens, S. S. Matching functions between loudness and ten other continua. *Percept. Psychophys.*, **1**, 5–8 (1966)

138. Stevens, S. S. Duration, luminance, and the brightness exponent. *Ibid.*, 96–100

139. Stevens, J. C., Hall, H. W. Brightness and loudness as functions of stimulus duration. *Percept. Psychophys.*, **1**, 319–27 (1966)

140. Stewart, M. R., Fagot, R. F., Eskildsen, P. R. Invariance tests for bisection and fractionation scaling. *Percept. Psychophys.*, **2**, 323–27 (1967)

141. Stouffer, S. A., et al. *Measurement and Prediction* (Wiley, New York, 756 pp., 1950)

142. Suppes, P. Measurement, empirical meaningfulness and three-valued logic. In *Measurement: Definition and Theories*, 129–43 (Churchman, C. W., Ratoosh, P., Eds., Wiley, New York, 274 pp., 1959)

143. Suppes, P., Winet, M. An axiomatization of utility based on the notion of utility differences. *Mgmt. Sci.*, **1**, 259–70 (1955)

144. Suppes, P., Zinnes, J. L. Basic measurement theory. In *Handbook of Mathematical Psychology*, 1–76 (See Ref. 83)

145. Sutcliffe, J. P. Some aspects of rank ordering and scaling with paired comparisons data. *Austral. J. Psychol.*, **16**, 137–49 (1964)

146. Thompson, W. A., Jr., Singh, J. The use of limit theorems in paired comparison model building. *Psychometrika*, **32**, 255–64 (1967)

147. Torgerson, W. S. Multidimensional scaling of similarity. *Psychometrika*, **30**, 379–93 (1965)

148. Treisman, M. Sensory scaling and the psychophysical law. *Quart. J. Exptl. Psychol.*, **16**, 11–22 (1964)

149. Treisman, M. What do sensory scales measure? *Ibid.*, 387–91

150. Treisman, M. A statistical decision model for sensory discrimination which predicts Weber's Law and other sensory laws: Some results of a computer simulation. *Percept. Psychophys.*, **1**, 203–30 (1966)

151. Tucker, L. R., Messick, S. An individual difference model for multidimensional scaling. *Psychometrika*, **28**, 333–67 (1963)

152. Tversky, A. A general theory of polynomial conjoint measurement. *J. Math. Psychol.*, **4**, 1–20 (1967)

153. Wickelgren, W. A. A test of Luce's two-state decision rule. *Psychon. Sci.*, **9**, 91–92 (1967)

154. Wickelgren, W. A. Testing two-state theories with operating characteristics and *a posteriori* probabilities. *Psychol. Bull.*, **69**, 126–31 (1968)

155. Yellott, J. I., Jr., Curnow, P. F. Second choices in a visual span of apprehension task. *Percept. Psychophys.*, **2**, 307–11 (1967)

156. Yilmaz, H. Perceptual invariance and the psychophysical law. *Percept. Psychophys.*, **2**, 533–38 (1967)

157. Zinnes, J. L. Review of S. Ross's *Logical Foundations of Psychological Measurement*. *Contemp. Psychol.*, **11**, 395–97 (1966)

158. Zinnes, J. L., Kurtz, R. Discrimination, matching and payoff. *J. Math. Psychol.* (In press)

AUTHOR INDEX

A

Aaron, R., 364
Aaronson, D., 165
Abel, S. M., 171
Abeles, R. P., 253-88
Abelson, R. P., 254, 260, 263, 274, 465
Abrahams, D., 220, 255, 276
Abrahams, N. M., 438
Abramov, I., 199, 200
Acker, S. R., 435
Adair, E. R., 63
Adam, J., 172
Adams, E. W., 455, 457, 458, 459, 460, 462, 469, 471
Adams, G., 5
Adams, J. A., 383, 388, 402, 403
Adelberg, K., 27, 37
Adelson, J., 217-52
Adler, L. L., 43
Adrignolo, A. J., 165
Affanni, J., 300
Agee, F. L., Jr., 169
Ager, J. W., 275
Agnew, N. M., 170
Agranoff, B. W., 89, 90
Ahonen, L., 162
Ahumada, A., 472
Aiba, T. S., 197
Aiken, E. G., 395
Ainsfeld, M., 15
Ainsworth, M. D. S., 7
Ajmone-Marsan, C., 331, 336
Akert, K., 294
Akesson, C., 468, 469
Akishige, Y., 159
Akita, M., 202
Albert, D. J., 97
Albert, R. D., 267
Alberts, W. W., 304
Albright, L. E., 435
Alcocer-Cuarón, C., 146
Aleksandrovskii, I. U. A., 327
Alexander, B. K., 147
Alexander, L. T., 173
Alf, E. F., Jr., 423, 437, 438, 473
Alfert, E., 235
Alker, H. A., 236
Allen, D., 352
Allen, E., 206
Allen, K. E., 27
Allen, S. A., 372,

398, 399
Allikmets, L. Kh., 293
Alluisi, E. A., 164, 361, 362
Alper, T. G., 230
Alpern, M., 160, 197, 202, 203
Alpert, R., 32, 37
Altner, H., 142
Altrocchi, J., 238
Amatsu, M., 145
Amoore, J. E., 129, 141, 144
Amster, H., 273, 384
Amsterdam, B., 8
Anastasi, A., 372
Anderson, B., 362
Anderson, C. C., 254, 272
Anderson, D. R., 432
Anderson, L., 20, 407
Anderson, L. R., 273
Anderson, N. H., 273
Anderson, R. A., 67
Anderson, R. C., 355, 356, 382, 384, 385, 392, 396, 397
Andersson, A. L., 162
Andersson, B., 294, 299
Andres, K. H., 131
Andrew, R. J., 297
Andrews, J. D., 229
Andrews, T. G., 361
Anger, J., 352
Ángyán, L., 297, 305
Antebi, R., 334
Antonelli, A. R., 146
Antrobus, J. S., 243
Appley, M. H., 235
Apsler, R., 256, 259, 260
Arden, G. B., 195, 197
Arias, L. P., 299, 300
Armington, J. C., 194, 197, 201
Armstrong, D. C., 274
Aronoff, J., 168
Aronson, E., 254, 255, 258, 263, 264, 265, 274, 278, 279
Aronson, V., 220, 276
Asanuma, H., 293
Ash, P., 422
Ashmore, R. D., 265, 266
Atkins, A. L., 257, 275, 279
Atkinson, J. W., 59
Atkinson, R. C., 383, 464, 472

Attneave, F., 169
Augustson, B., 167
Auld, H. D., 428
Averill, J. R., 235
Axelson, L. J., 372
Azrin, N. H., 76

B

Bach-y-Rita, P., 143
Back, K. W., 235
Badia, P., 239
Baenninger, R., 76
Baer, A., 290, 300
Baer, D. M., 27, 29
Baird, J. C., 169, 469
Bakan, D., 218, 219, 438
Bakan, P., 172
Baker, B. C., 367, 368
Baker, B. L., 435
Baker, H. D., 201
Baker, R. L., 399
Baker, W. J., 361, 363, 364, 365
Baker, W. M., 211
Baldwin, A. L., 43
Baldwin, M., 290
Baldwin, R. O., 173
Ball, G. H., 434
Ball, R. J., 204, 205, 209
Ball, T. S., 173
Balloun, J. L., 270
Balma, M. J., 440
Bamber, D., 165
Bandura, A., 29, 30, 232, 396
Bang, B. G., 129, 152
Bankes, J. L. K., 197
Banks, R., 173
Bannister, L. H., 131, 132
Bánréti-Fuchs, K. M., 175
Baratz, S. S., 234
Barber, V. C., 131
Barclay, A., 35, 244
Barker, R. G., 222
Barnwell, A., 400
Baron, R. M., 259
Barondes, S. H., 86, 88, 89
Barrett, G. V., 169, 432
Barrett, R. S., 437
Bartleson, C. J., 174
Bartlett, C. J., 349-80; 361, 372, 427
Bartley, S. H., 204, 205, 209
Bartoshuk, L. M., 133

479

Kelman, H. C., 220, 259, 276
Kemp, F. D., 397
Kendler, H. H., 22, 385, 405, 408
Kendler, T. S., 22, 385, 405, 408
Kennedy, D., 138, 292
Kennedy, R. S., 362
Kennedy, W. A., 27, 372
Keogh, R. P., 326, 340, 341
Keppel, G., 389, 401, 402, 403, 405
Kesner, R. P., 310, 311
Kessen, W., 391
Kety, S. S., 322, 343
Khaime, T. B., 333
Kidd, A. H., 160
Kiesler, C. A., 254, 263, 265, 266, 267
Kiess, H. O., 298, 388, 402
Kikuchi, Y., 110
Kimble, G. A., 233
Kimeldorf, D., 129, 149, 150, 151
Kimura, J., 137
Kinchla, R. A., 464, 472
King, D. J., 388
Kingdon, J. W., 264
Kingsley, R. C., 19, 407
Kinney, A., 169
Kinney, J. A. S., 204, 205, 208, 209
Kinslinger, H. J., 441
Kintz, B. L., 276
Kipnis, D., 225
Kirchner, W. K., 425
Kirk, R. E., 362
Kirkham, R., 166
Kirkpatrick, J. J., 421, 435
Kishto, B. N., 203
Kissinger, B., 421
Kitai, S. T., 307
Klausmeier, H. J., 360
Klee, M. R., 198
Kleemeier, R. W., 367
Klein, G. S., 165
Klein, J., 15
Klein, R. E., 9, 24
Klein, S. P., 434
Klemme, M. E., 167
Kliger, S. C., 430, 433
Klima, E. S., 15
Klineberg, O., 43
Klineberg, S. L., 41, 243
Klingaman, R. L., 172
Klinger, E., 230
Klinger, N. N., 24
Klinger, P. D., 89
Klumpp, R. G., 107
Knauss, T., 295
Knight, J., 193
Knight, J. M., 303, 304,

306, 307, 308
Knoblock, E. C., 362
Knott, P. D., 299
Knox, R. E., 264
Koella, W., 343
Koelling, R. A., 149, 150
Koenig, E. J., 88
Kofsky, E., 12, 21
Kogan, A. B., 309
Kogan, N., 234
Kogan, W. S., 436
Kohen-Raz, R., 4
Kohfeld, D. L., 357
Kohlberg, L., 36, 223
Kohlenberg, R., 100
Kohler, R., 271
Kohnstamm, G. A., 19
Kolb, D. A., 226
Kolstoc, R., 236
Konishi, J., 133
Konorski, J., 299, 300
Konrad, K. W., 11
Kopa, J., 290, 307
Kopp, R., 99, 100, 101
Korányi, L., 303, 304, 308
Korchinskaia, E. I., 324, 341, 342
Koresko, R. L., 328, 329, 341
Korman, A. K., 424, 440
Korn, J. H., 70, 76
Kornetsky, C., 323, 329, 336, 337, 341, 342, 344
Kosinar, V., 163
Koslin, B. L., 257, 258
Kostandov, E. A., 327
Kovač, D., 163
Koz, G., 364
Kozina, T. M., 173
Kraft, A. L., 170
Kragh, U., 162
Kramer, M. D., 327, 340
Krantz, D. H., 463, 466, 467
Krathwohl, D. R., 409
Krause, A. E., 326, 340, 341
Krauskopf, J., 201, 208
Krauss, R. M., 16
Kravitz, J. H., 171
Krebs, R., 223
Kriayev, V. Ya., 300
Krill, A. E., 209, 210
Kroeber, T., 236
Kropfl, W. J., 197
Krug, R. E., 372, 430, 432
Kruskal, J. B., 464
Kruskal, W. H., 278
Kuffler, S. W., 138, 197
Kugelmass, S., 34
Kulik, J. A., 225
Künnapas, T., 162, 466, 471
Kuraev, G. A., 310

Kurihara, K., 131, 145
Kurtz, R., 453
Kury, G., 333, 341
Kusyszyn, I., 392
Kutner, B., 254
Kutscher, C. L., 62, 73
Kuznesof, A. W., 65
Kyhl, R. L., 194

L

Lacey, J. I., 68
Ladd, C. E., 234, 349
Laffin, M., 208
Laffort, P., 129, 137
LaForce, R. C., 205
Lagutina, N. I., 294, 297, 303
Lakota, R., 233
Lamb, G. S., 396
Lambert, W. E., 43
Landauer, A. A., 169, 172
Landford, T. L., 119
Landis, D., 175
L'Angellier, A. B., 72, 73
Langs, R. J., 365
Lappin, J. S., 166
Larsen, R. H., 423
Larsen, R. M., 290, 291, 303, 304, 308
Larson, C., 76
Lashley, K. S., 310
Lát, J., 66
Latané, B., 279
Lathrop, R. G., 177
Latz, A., 337
Lauprecht, C. W., 294, 305
Laurence, C. L., 116, 120
Lavender, A. D., 172, 174
Law, A. W., 395
Lawler, E. E., III, 428
Lawrence, M., 160
Lawshe, C. H., 440
Layne, R. S., 330, 341
Lazarsfeld, P. F., 448
Lazarte, J. A., 334, 340, 341
Lazarus, R. S., 235
Leahy, W. R., 165
Leaman, R. L., 279
Lebovits, B. Z., 427
Lee, D., 335, 341, 342
Lee, F., 396
Lee, S. S., 389
Leebeek, H. J., 201
Leek, B. F., 132, 140, 146
Leete, C. G., 207
Lefcourt, H. M., 225
Legerski, A. T., 228
Legg, C. F., 173
Lehmann, D., 295

SUBJECT INDEX

A

Abilities, human, 349-80
 age and sex differences in, 367-69
 conclusion, 373-74
 creativity, 355
 cultural and ethnic differences in, 370-73
 definition of, 350
 drug effects on, 363-67
 environmental variables in, 361-62
 helicopter piloting, 360
 heredity of, 369-70
 information processing model of, 357
 and learning, 355-60
 mathematical methods in study of, 359
 measurement of special abilities, 353
 multivariate experimental psychology, 373
 organization of, 352-55
 perceptual-motor, 353, 357, 359-60
 physical fitness, 353
 project TALENT, 354
 role of transfer in, 358-59
 spatial, 354
 in stressful environments, 361
 task requirements and laboratory measurement, 360-61
 theoretical and conceptual issues, 350-52
  Cattell's theory of, 351
  Guilford's theory of, 350-51
  Piaget's theory of, 351-52
Acetoxycycloheximide
 and memory, 88-89
Acetylcholine
 on EEG, 327
Achievement
 developmental aspects of, 30-33, 229-30
 motivation for
  anatomy of, 31
  and behavior, 228-29
  dissonance theory of, 263
 parental factors in, 31-32
 and performance, 230-31

related to aggression, 242
Acquiescence
 and achievement, 229
Actinomycin-D
 on memory, 88-89
Activation
 neural model of, 68
Activity
 spontaneous, 64-68
Adolescents
 effects on early and late maturing, 41
 ethics among, 220
 field-dependence of, 244
 social processes and personality development in, 40-42
Adrenalectomy
 in schizophrenia, 322
Adrenalin
 on EEG, 327
 see also Epinephrine
Age
 and abilities, 367-69
 and EEG, 326
 perceptual changes as function of, 162, 167, 174
Aggression
 arousal and restraint, 239-40
 cathartic role of, 240
 in children
  peer validation of, 37
  developmental aspects of, 36-37
 and humor, 240-41
 measurement of, 241
 modeling, 240
 and over-control, 241
 related to achievement, 242
 role of olfaction in, 147
 stimuli for, 76, 239
Air Force Qualification Test
 see Tests and scales
Alcohol
 see Ethyl alcohol
Alcoholics
 attitudes in, 272
 test performance of, 336-37
Alligators
 stimulation of nervous system of, 293
Allport-Vernon-Lindzey Scales of Values
 see Tests and scales
Altruism

developmental aspects of, 37-38
Amblyopia
 defective color vision with, 210
Amnesia
 experimental production of, 85-99
 see also Memory
Amobarbital
 EEG effects of, 330
Amphetamine
 on EEG, 326
 on human abilities, 366
Amygdala
 electrical stimulation of, 290, 293-94, 300, 306
 and schizophrenia, 322, 334
Anality
 dissonance experiment on, 244
Anatomy
 of retina
  S-potential, 197
 of sense organs, 129-32
Anticholinesterase
 to produce amnesia, 93
Anxiety
 meaning of, 233-34
 measurement of, 220, 231-34
 in parachutists, 231-32
 and perception, 176
 and performance, 234-35
 reduction of, 232-33
  comparison of methods of, 238
 separated from defensiveness, 233-34
 and test performance, 425
Aplysia
 heterosynaptic facilitation of neurons of, 303
Army Alpha Scale
 see Tests and scales
Arousal
 different forms of, 68
 of fear
  and communication, 261-62
 hyper-
  in schizophrenia, 339
 and learning, 383
Ascending reticular activation system (ARAS)
 in schizophrenia, 322, 335,

266-67, 276
Rotter Incomplete Sentences
Blank
see Tests and scales

S

Salmon
olfaction in, 143
Scaling, 447-78
conjoint measurement, 461-
64
detection, 471-73
logic of measurement, 453-
61
definition of fundamental
and derived measurement,
453-55
permissible statistics, 457-
61
scale types, 455-57
multidimensional models of,
464-68
conditions generating a
metric, 467
empirical properties,
466
nonmetric, 464-65
separable and nonseparable
dimensions, 466
subject difference allow-
ance, 468
triads, 467-68
new books on, 448-49
overview of, 473
pair-comparison theories
and experiments, 449-
53
choice theory and Thurstone
model, 449-52
and magnitude estimation,
471
new pair-comparison mod-
els, 452-53
power vs. logarithmic functions, 468-71
magnitude estimation, 470-
71
nonlinearity, 469
semantical issues, 469
technical differences in definition of scale types,
457
theory of choice, 447
Thurstone bibliography,
448-49
use of correlation coefficient
as accuracy measure,
465
Schizophrenia
attitudes in, 272
brain changes in, 333-
34
in children
developmental and autistic
processes, 335-36
social learning among,

27, 29
coincidental with seizure,
333
EEG studies of, 324-31
compared to controls, 324-
25
difference between lower
occipital and frontal-
occipital voltages, 326
drug activation of EEG,
326-28
as index of central state
of patient, 327
normalization of, 327
quantitative EEG analysis,
325-26
sensory evoked responses,
329-31
sleep studies, 328-29
hyperarousal in, 339-42
inverted U models of test
performance in, 338
neuropsychological bases of,
321-48
classification, 339-44
conclusion, 339-44
history of, 321-22
introduction to, 321-
24
psychopharmacology and
psychophysiology, 336-
39
and organic brain disease,
331-35
CNS effects of schizophrenic serum, 334-35
direct current effects on
brain, 335
epilepsy, 331-32
pathological and neurosurgical studies, 332-34
types of, 325, 339-44
table of, 341
Scopolamine
on human abilities, 365
on memory, 91-92
SCORES
see Tests and scales
Secobarbital
on schizophrenic sleep,
329
Self-esteem
and effectiveness, 227-28
and job selection, 424
and persuasibility, 263
Self-stimulation
motivational effects of, 295-
99
Semantics
of persuasiveness, 260-61,
275
Senses
see Chemical senses
Sensitization
-repression
and defense style, 237-
39

Sensory system
in schizophrenia, 329-
31
Sex
and abilities, 354, 368-69
Sex drive
interaction with hunger and
thirst, 74
Sex role
and decision-making, 236
developmental aspects of,
35-36
and personal adjustment,
228
Sexual behavior
elicited by brain stimulation,
293-94
olfactory aspects of, 147
self-stimulation, 296-
98
Signal detection
personality aspects in, 243
Sinusoids
as noise masker, 125
Sleep
from brain stimulation,
295
deprivation and test results,
337
Rapid-Eye-Movement, 328-
29, 341, 343
requirements of
discrepancy in, 257
in schizophrenia
EEG studies of, 328-29,
341, 343
Smell
anatomy of
olfactory mucosae, 130-32,
136-38
true olfactory region of
nose, 137
coding problems in, 141-
45
comparison of human and
animal thresholds, 137
mechanical factors in, 146-
47
membrane puncturing theory
of, 145
odor similarities' statistics,
143
preferences and aversions
in, 147
role of killing, 76
spatiotemporal patterning of,
143-44
in X-ray detection, 150-
52
see also Chemical senses
Smoking and lung cancer
to study attitudes, 259, 261-
62, 266, 268, 270-71
Social attitudes
naturalistic methodology of
studying, 222
Social desirability

CUMULATIVE INDEXES

VOLUMES 16-20

INDEX OF CONTRIBUTING AUTHORS

513

INDEX OF CHAPTER TITLES

VOLUMES 16-20